The Media in the
Network Society
Browsing, News, Filters and Citizenship

Cardoso, Gustavo, *The Media in the Network Society: Browsing, News, Filters and Citizenship*, Lisboa, Portugal. CIES – Centre for Research and Studies in Sociology, 2006.

Cover Design | Interior Layout | Composition:
Jorge Urbano and Ana Abranches

CIES – Centre for Research and Studies in Sociology
Edifício ISCTE
Av. das Forças Armadas
1649-026 Lisboa (Portugal)
Tel. +351.217903077
Tel. +351.217941404
Fax +351.217940074
Email: cies@iscte.pt
http://www.cies.iscte.pt/en

ISBN 978-1-84753-792-8

The Media in the
Network Society
Browsing, News, Filters and Citizenship

Gustavo Cardoso
Preface by Manuel Castells

cies
iscte
centre
for research
and studies
in sociology

About the Author

Gustavo Cardoso is an associate researcher at CIES/ISCTE and Professor of Technology and Society at ISCTE in Lisbon. He also works with the Department of Communications and Performance Studies of the University of Milan and with the Portuguese Catholic University. His international cooperation in European research networks brought him to work with IN3 (Internet Interdisciplinary Institute) in Barcelona, WIP (World Internet Project) at USC Annenberg, COST A20 "The Impact of the Internet in Mass Media" and COST 298 "Broadband Society".

Between 1996 and 2006 he was adviser on Information Society and telecommunications policies to the Presidency of the Portuguese Republic.

He is co-editor, with Manuel Castells, of the book Network Society: from Knowledge to Policy.

For Mafalda and Guilherme, to whom the future belongs.

Contents

Index of Figures

Index of Tables

Preface

Communication is the key process of any social organization. The technological revolution that took shape in the 1970s, and then diffused around the world, is characterized by the transformation of the communication process by microelectronics-based digital networks. Internet and wireless communication are fundamentally modifying the way we communicate, and therefore behave, locally and globally. Yet, most public communication continues to be processed by the mass media, by television, by radio, by the print press. There is however a growing interaction between computer mediated communication and other media. But this interaction takes place within the specific logic of each medium. Internet does not eliminate television, it transforms it. And the persistence of television, radio, and the print media, contributes to an increasingly diversified media system, which is made of the interplay between the different forms of communication, each one with its own logic, its own traditions, and its own set of values and interests inscripted in their institutional organization.

Furthermore, the emergence of a new media system has different manifestations and consequences in various cultural, social, and institutional contexts. Even with the global diffusion of technology, and with the global networking of media business, what happens in California or Italy is different from what happens in Portugal or Brazil. Thus, both for analytical purposes and for policy design, it is essential to understand this process of transformation in its common features and in its cultural specificity. This is the value of the research of Gustavo Cardoso presented in this book.

Cardoso analyzes the technological and social transformation of the media, both in the world, and in the specific setting of his observation, in Portugal, by relating the evolution of the media both to technological change and to social change. He emphasizes the emergence of a network society, built on social and organizational networks powered by electronic communication technologies, as the industrial society relied for its development on energy distribution networks.

And he shows the key role of the media in this social evolution, while analyzing how society affects the media. He grounds his analysis on several, well crafted empirical studies, including the first statistically representative survey of the Portuguese population focused on the social uses of the Internet. And he studies a number of sources in Europe, and the United States, keeping a comparative perspective in his inquiry. He examines the relationships within the triangle formed by the network society, the media, and the Internet, and makes sense of his observation by referring to recent trends of social theory from diverse intellectual traditions. The result is a masterpiece of research that illustrates the coming of age of a new generation of researchers on communication technology and society, a generation that understands technology, society, and empirical research, and puts aside vague pseudo-theoretical jargon for the benefit of producing knowledge and understanding of the new paradigm in which we are already living. Thus, beyond futurology, and after postmodernism, social science research claims its rights to lighten the path of our choices.

The book you have in your hands will be widely used and read in universities and professional media organizations throughout the world, because it is one of the few, and best examples of understanding the relationship between the media and the Internet in the broader context of our transition to the network society. It exposes the logic that is currently shaping the communicative fabric of our lives.

Manuel Castells,
Wallis Annenberg Chair Professor of
Communication Technology and Society
Annenberg School of Communication, University
of Southern California, Los Angeles.

Acknowledgements

The work that I now submit to your analysis and criticism would not have been possible without the suggestions, critiques, support and access to bibliographic archives and empirical data provided by a group of colleagues, friends and family members.

First and foremost, I must extend my heartfelt gratitude to my wife, Cristina Cunha. A pharmacist by profession and also a researcher in the field of genetics, in my expeditions into the world of the information technologies, she has helped me to understand the revolution in progress in genetics, thus making my vision of the information era more complete. Her assistance in translating written works was also inestimable, as was her support throughout the years I have dedicated to compiling and writing the information contained on these pages. For the support and strength they gave me, I am also deeply indebted to Mafalda Jorge and Maria José Guerreiro Duarte, a historian of symbols and myths.

The real-time analysis of the process of social change brought about by the expansion of the Internet and other information and communication technologies harbours certain risks, particularly that of mistaking the enthusiasm of persons (and things) around us for effective interest as a valid object of research. In my personal case, this risk was considerably reduced by the cooperation and debate I have maintained over the years. This not only helped me to formulate my research, but also to bring it to the concrete form you will find on the following pages.

In the ten-year period from 1996 to 2006, I had the fortune to work and research together with a group of people who have provided valuable assistance in formulating the questions I seek to answer in this work on the role of the media in the network society and on how citizenship is closely linked to our capacity to understand and socially appropriate the media.

Thanks to the invaluable cooperation, support and friendship of José Manuel Paquete de Oliveira, it has been possible for me to contact with a group of international researchers through the Master's Degree course in "Communication, Culture and the Information Technologies" at the ISCTE Lisbon, where, for the last five years, I have held a chair entitled "Informational Society Theories". My contacts with researchers from Europe and the United States, such as Peppino Ortoleva (Italy), Roger Silverstone (United Kingdom), Brian Loader (United Kingdom), Mark Deuze (The Netherlands-US), Cees J. Hamelink (The Netherlands), David Lyon (Canada), Mark Poster (US) and Frank Webster (United Kingdom) have allowed me to build up a fruitful network for the exchange of ideas on the role of the information and communication technologies and social change that has influenced all my work.

Of fundamental importance for the connection between the research traditionally carried out on television and the new approaches suggested by the diffusion of the Internet were the cooperation, friendship and support given by Fausto Colombo of the Catholic University of Milan. I am indebted to him and his research team at the *Osservatorio della Comunicazione* for being able to accompany their research into generational relationships with television, their studies on the use of mobile phones and a new look at the cultural and communicational fruitions of the media audiences. The research work carried out in Milan helped me to focus my attention on the dimension of the interrelation between different media in the everyday life of the populations.

The intellectual challenge from my contacts with João Caraça (ISEG/ Calouste Gulbenkian Foundation) and António Firmino da Costa (CIES-ISCTE) provided not only a stimulus for my research but also resulted in effective support for my analysis of the Portuguese society and its transition to the network society. This cooperation took the concrete form of the "Network Society in Portugal" project.

I must also highlight the fruitful exchange I have had over the last few years with my colleagues, José Barreiros (ISCTE), Rita Espanha (ISLA-Lisbon) and Carmo Gomes (OberCom), and with my graduate and post-graduate students of the Journalism course. Much of the work produced and many of the questions raised by my students played a fundamental role in visualizing new approaches and achieving more in-depth knowledge of the reality of the media in Portugal, Europe and the US. Many of them are currently working (or have worked) on research projects, which, in the medium term, will constitute an important source for more in-depth knowledge of the network society.

The period from 2000 to 2005 was also one of intense investment in international contacts and gaining knowledge of the realities in European countries in terms of the appropriation of the Internet in politics and the mass media. The fact that I had the opportunity to coordinate the participation of Portuguese researchers and establish partnerships in the European research networks, COST A14 (Government and Democracy in the Information Age) and COST A20 (The Impact of the Internet in the Mass Media in Europe), was fundamental for the study of the questions I developed throughout this period. Amongst the many colleagues of diverse geographic origins with whom I have had the pleasure of discussing the matters analyzed herein and whose contribution I wish to acknowledge are: Jens Hoff (Denmark), Carlos Cunha (US); Thierry Vedel (France); Peter Filzmayer (Austria); Hans J. Kleisteuber (Germany); Ig Snellen (The Netherlands); Colin Smith and William Webster (United Kingdom); Wim van de Donk (The Netherlands); Lance Bennett (US); Colin Sparks (United Kingdom); Ramón Salavérria and Charo Sabadá (Spain); Piermarco Aroldi and Barbara Scifo (Italy); Robert Picard (US/Sweden); Pekka Himanen (Finland); Hernan Galperín (Argentina); Imma Tubella (Spain/Catalonia); Jonathan Taplin (US); Dale Jorgenson (US); Jorge Machado and Vicente Riccio (Brazil); Carolina Aguerre (Uruguay); Belén Amadeo (Argentina); Sérgio Godoy (Chile); and Lucy Kung (United Kingdom/Switzerland).

Also in the area of partnership in research networks, I would like to acknowledge the role of Bill Dutton of the Oxford Internet Institute and Jeff Cole through the "World Internet Project" (WIP) network (Annenberg, US), whose manifest interest in the Portuguese reality in terms of the use of information and communication technologies allowed for Portugal's adherence to the WIP (through CIES/ISCTE) and for my access to comparative data on the use of the Internet covering countries as different as China, Japan, Singapore, South Korea, Taiwan and the US.

The period from 1996 to 2006 was also, for me, one of discussion and learning in defining the policies in the area of telecommunications and the informational society. The contact with the political and economic reality also gave me better insight as to what the media represent in our society. For that reason, I would also like to mention those who were kind enough to listen to me and to debate with me (and, at times, challenge) my analyzes and formulations. Here, my particular thanks go to the former President of Portugal, Mr. Jorge Sampaio and to Erkki Lükanen (former European Commissioner for Information Society).

Finally, I must make a special mention to Manuel Castells, whose work on the information age and the network society has had a profound and constructive influence on the work here presented, thanks to the opportunities I have had to work with him in joint research projects.

Lisbon, Portugal, June 2006

The Media in the Network Society

Europe lies, resting upon her elbows:
From East to West she lies, gazing,
Romantic locks hang down across her eyes,
Greek, full of memories

The left elbow is tucked away;
The right stands at an angle in its place.
That one marks Italy in its repose;
This one says England where, gathered apart,
It holds the hand up to support the face.

She looks, with her sphinx-like, fatal gaze,
To the West, future of the past.

The face with which she stares is Portugal.

Fernando Pessoa, *The Message* (Own Translation)

The beginning of any analysis requires contextualization in space and time. As Fernando Pessoa's poem suggests, this is an analysis that seeks to look at the media in a global context, though from a European perspective. By European perspective I mean that my starting point are the affiliations that connect Europe to social, identity, economic, cultural and political networks and places as distant as South America, North America, Africa, Asia and Oceania.

In terms of time frame, the analysis focuses on the last ten years and the evolution, in that period, of the role of the media in the network society. In other words, how the *media system* [1] is organized and how the uses we make of it configure it.

In the network society, the organization and development of the media system depend to a large extent on how we socially appropriate the media.

It is through the way in which we attribute social roles – of information, entertainment, action and organization – to each of the media that we design the networks of interdependence between them.

However, although the media have accompanied us since we organized the communication codes in a systematized form (Eco, 1977), it is only in this moment of our history that we find a network-based media system organization. Why is this? Because, in an initial phase, the emergence of the Internet has allowed for the migration of the traditional mass media from analogue to digital technologies, thus building the necessary bridges between the old and the new media. In a second phase, the Internet (and, to a certain extent, mobile phones and SMS technology), enabled the establishment of a growing number of interconnections between all the media forms, be they digital or analogue.

The initial hypothesis for characterizing the media system in our current society is, contrary to what is often suggested (Ortoleva, 2001), not so much technological convergence, but the *networked organization* of the system. That organization takes place at various levels, from the technological dimension to the economic organization and the social appropriation. [2]

---

[1] *Media system*, as formulated by Peppino Ortoleva, refers to the set of interconnections between technologies and organizations that guide the diverse forms of communication. It is a category of an essentially institutional and economic origin that helps us to explain, on the one hand, the evolutive dynamics of the media and, on the other, how each society establishes, amongst the diverse media, a division of the function, which is born out of the complex socio-cultural processes but later finds its legitimation in the companies and legislative frameworks (Ortoleva, 2002).

[2] Using a suggestion by McLaughlin (Ortoleva, 2001), one can describe convergence as the overcoming of the technological, economic and institutional barriers, made possible by digital technology. These barriers divided the media into four main sectors: the editorial sector dominated by the private press

According to opinions frequently voiced by consultants and diverse opinion leaders in newspapers and magazines, be they specialized or general interest publications, in recent years we have witnessed a trend towards convergence in diverse dimensions of the media universe. However, I believe that in endeavouring to answer the question as to what extent that convergence has been effected one must maintain an open and critical mind.

Although the mergers of media giants such as AOL and Time Warner (Castells, 2004) have given rise to diverse mimetic processes the world over, in reality the management essentially continues to be based on the logic of differentiated management units (see Sony Records and their processes against the illegal exchange of music in the Internet and the simultaneous promotion of mp3 by the Sony hardware division).

Also in the technological dimension, the endeavours to incorporate different, already socially appropriated media technologies (such as television and the computer) in one single piece of equipment have met with differing levels of success (WebTV was a flop, but mp3 technology has transformed mobile phones into walkmen).

The argument put forward here is that the current media system seems to be organized not around the idea of convergence, made possible by digital technologies, but around *networking*.

Even in cases of success, such as mobile telephones, mp3 capability continues to depend on the establishment of a network connection with the PC or Mac for the downloads, which, if legitimate, places them in a network relationship with online stores such as iTunes. Another example of this networking is the so-called media servers (for example, the Sony Vaio), in which, despite there being a convergence of signal in the network over IP protocols (Taplin, 2005), the diffusion in the home is effected via wireless technology (Galperin, 2005), the destinations being the music player or mobile phone for mp3, the television for films or for broadcasting, voice over IP for the telephone and the Internet for the PC. There is no convergence, but rather the *networking* of media and their uses.

How is this networking structured? The hypothesis argued herein is that the media system is structured more and more around two main networks

---

and governed by copyright; the transmissions sector, i.e. the distribution networks, which include the postal and telecommunications sector and the Internet; the broadcasting sector, based on advertising; and the hardware sector based on the production and distribution of the communication equipment (video cameras, stereo systems, cassettes and periphericals).

that communicate between each other using various communication and information technologies. These two networks are based on the television and the Internet, establishing nodes using various communication and information technologies such as the telephone, the radio, the print press, etc.

Why two main networks? The answer is a complex one and it will be the object of in-depth analysis to be presented on the following pages. Nevertheless, one can put forward the hypothesis that this has to do with the dimensions of interactivity made technologically possible by each one and the way in which we socially value those different interactive dimensions. This is an interpretation that results from analysis of the fruition practices, for which the concept of media matrix is fundamental. [3]

According to Colombo (2002), one of the reasons why we self-limit our capacity for understanding the role of the media in society has to do with the theoretical analysis choices, which concentrate too much on an individualized idea of the media. In other words, what can the isolated study of radio, newspapers or the Internet tell us about the society in which we live? Probably not very much, for, as social beings, we do not use only one single medium as a source of communication, information, action and entertainment. Only an in-depth analysis of the media diets can reveal the complexity of our uses and representations of society *through* and *with* the media.

Looking at the role of the diverse media in the network society, as the product of our individual media matrixes, raises several questions.

The first has to do with the role of television in the network society. At the beginning of the 21st century (as we witness a reduction in television viewing times by Internet users), watching television continues to be the most frequent daily activity, followed by regular get-togethers with family members and friends (Cardoso et al., 2004, Castells et al., 2003). For this reason, the question as to whether television is still the central element in the media system (Ortoleva, 2001) and the dominant form of culture in our contemporary societies would seem to make very good sense. Following the same logic, one could likewise ask the question of whether or not we can attribute to the Internet an erosive effect on television's central role.

Throughout the following chapters, we will seek to discuss to what extent the *network society* (Castells, 2002) is a society in which the Internet

---

[3] A term originally used by Meyrovitz (1993) to underline that fact that we all subjectively tend to create a mental hierarchy for the different types of media and the importance of them in our lives. These hierarchies are strictly individual but also shared socially.

challenges the power of the traditional media (Cardoso, 2003) or if the forces at work are more subtle, creating a new *mediation* space, in which radio, television and the press link up with the Internet, taking on their own specific roles in the *mediation* process.

Another question on which we should focus our attention is whether we are really replacing the "old media" with the Internet. Answering this question means identifying the uses and finding out what the really new uses made possible by the Internet are.

In order to address the questions posed we will focus attention on two of the *autonomy* construction dimensions [4]: the communicative and socio-political autonomy projects. The choice of these two autonomy projects results from the fact that the institutional elements involved (such as formal and informal organizations and political institutions) and the complexity of their interaction influences the need for the combination of different media use strategies.

Hence, we have opted to analyze the practices of combined use of the Internet and other media, using as a starting point the study of a European society in transition to the network society – Portugal – and then to compare it to other European, American and Asian informational countries and nations. The proposed analysis is illustrated throughout using three dimensions: the media fruition practices; the relationship between the elected representatives and the electorate in relation to the political State institutions; and participation in social and citizenship movements.

But, before proceeding further in this introduction, we should take a somewhat more detailed look at the approach taken and the cases chosen and analyzed.

The construction of communicative autonomy has first to be contextualized in terms of the challenges made to the mass media themselves. The media sector in the period under analysis has been characterized by a context of sensationalism and obsession with scandal, increased focus on real life-based entertainment (both on television and in the tabloid newspapers) and the emergence of the Internet as a new technology presented as putting an end to the need for *mediation* professionals and heralding in the triumph of the *informed citizen* (Poster, 2001).

---

[4] Autonomy is here understood as the capacity of an individual to manage an individual or collective project he/she has defined. That project may have individual or collective assertion objectives, depending on its definition in terms of legitimizing, project or resistance identities. (Castells, 2003).

The repositioning of the mass media is thus taking place in a context of change with the driving force, i.e. the interest, looked at as being outside the media sector (although, as we shall see, we cannot ignore the media's instrumental role in the development of that context). This repositioning is essentially being carried out in terms of the type of contents produced (Ortoleva, 2001) and the new inter-relations between the diverse media system access networks, thus of particular interest to us is the analysis of the generalization of Internet access being carried out. Given this contextualization, we need to ask how the Internet has changed the mass media (and television, radio and the press in particular), with analysis of the online and offline presences of those media, and also how that change has affected our forms of appropriation of the media.

A second analysis dimension looks at how the mass media have attempted and are attempting to change the Internet. The diverse studies on the development of, and expansion in, the use of the Internet have shown us that the genesis of the culture in this space, in its diverse dimensions, promotes innovation and the much more rapid transformation of processes and tools by the users themselves (Castells, 2004). This has not prevented an attempt at greater control of the individual options in order to serve better the traditional economic paradigm of the mass media: control of accessible contents and reduced interactivity making advertising revenue possible. A control symbolized by the so-called *portals*, and which have been, to a certain extent, quite successful, and which are the product of a formula proposed by the telecommunications companies together with the mass media.

The economic alliances between the telecommunications sector and the content producers (a term attributed to the mass media by the former) have formalized a new constellation of functions and uses attributed to the Internet and, consequently, the development of products and tools to be offered to the users. Obviously, the users themselves tend to challenge continuously those functions and uses, but, nonetheless, the portals still very much incorporate the essence of what the Internet is for the general public.

The practices here analyzed in the context of the construction of communicative autonomy will thus focus on the use, by individuals, of the diverse television channels, be they general interest or specialized, national and local radio stations, reference and tabloid newspapers and the Internet in their different information and entertainment functions.

The analysis of the construction of socio-political autonomy projects constitutes the second autonomy dimension analyzed herein. To this end,

I have made use of the analysis of a group of case studies on the appropriation of the different media by citizens and political institutions, both national and supra-national.

The first group of case studies centres on the political system and the role of the Internet and the media in its functioning, based on an analysis of a group of European political systems with particular emphasis on countries such as The Netherlands, Denmark, Austria, Germany, Norway, Portugal and Scotland.

However, such an analysis would not be complete without a study of the appropriations of the media by the electorate and also of how the elected representatives themselves look at these media and use them in their communication with the citizens. Having that in mind, the second group of cases analyzed focus, in the construction of the socio-political projects in the Information Age, on the appropriation of the media by social and civic movements. Their selection was based on criteria of exemplariness, not only for the relationship between the different appropriated media, but also for the singularity of objectives, chronological amplitude and comparability with other national contexts.

The first movement analyzed is the public wave of protests at the closure of the Portuguese-language portal "Terràvista" (which included users from Brazil, Portugal, Angola, Mozambique, Cape Verde Islands, Guinea-Bissau and Macao). It was a portal managed by the Portuguese Ministry of Culture. The protagonists in the process were the newspapers that published a news story on the fact that images showing the *manga* hero Goku, from the Dragon Ball series, involved in pornographic acts were accessible on the site. This situation immediately led the Ministry of Culture to close the portal, giving rise to protests from some of its thousands of users. Although this was a protest that originated around the use of the Internet, it was through the conquest of attention in the press and television channels by the protesters that the movement sought to achieve its objectives, thus making it an interesting case study for protest strategies centred on the media against bodies of sovereignty.

The second case study focuses on the movement that was unleashed in May 2002 after the public announcement of the restructuring of Portuguese state television by the PSD-PP government. It was an announcement that exemplified many of the contemporary fears as to the relationship between politics and public television, which can also be seen in the recent Italian conflicts surrounding Berlusconi government's and RAI and in some Eastern European countries during their years of transition to new European Union Member States. Government-related anxiety that can be summed up in the following question: can a government govern today and make policy without being an active partner in the field of television, be it through public television, through tight regulatory bodies or through various connections of somewhat doubtful ethical nature with private TV stations?

The announcement led to a wave of protest led by the state television administration and journalists themselves and it had, in the Internet, a decisive element for publishing opinions of the viewers on what was transformed into a movement against the closure of RTP, the Portuguese state television and radio corporation itself. The representations aired by television itself, and those of Internet users and newspaper columnists on the same question provide an excellent starting point for characterizing the appropriation of the diverse discussion forums by different viewer groups and the way in which the Internet (from forums to blogs) changed the spheres of opinion dissemination.

The final social movement analyzed took place during the month of September 1999. The pro-East Timor movement involved, and attracted the attention of a significant part of the Portuguese and world population. For the duration of one month, through the combined use of the mass media and the Internet, it mobilized anonymous citizens, politicians, human rights associations and diplomats in a global action of protest and formal and informal diplomacy directed at Indonesia, the United Nations, Australia and the United States. For this reason, it can be considered the civic movement that mobilized the most persons and resources in Portugal since the years immediately following the revolution of 25th April 1974 and can be compared, in terms of its structure and geographic expansion, with the protests at the WTO summit in Seattle in the same year. The East Timor movement is thus an example of mobilization by the media and protest through the Internet.

Although the analysis of the cases listed above can reveal, through the media practices analyzed, the existence of *media matrixes* and different *media diets*, this is not in itself sufficient for directly answering the question: what different models of appropriation of the media in the network society are there? [5]

---

[5] The testing of the hypotheses formulated here was carried out using a set of qualitative and quantitative case studies as well as a national survey. The methodologies applied included participating observation, interviews, questionnaires and content analysis. A number of sources originating in national and foreign entities were also used and their quantitative analysis was adapted and interpreted in the light of the subject matter dealt with herein.

As Colombo (2002) suggests, the forms in which the media overlap reveal the existence of social uses that are transversal to the media themselves. We share common social functions in diversified media diets. Before deciding if we want to use this or that medium we decide what we want to do and only then do we decide which of the available media best serves our purpose. For this reason, the hypothesis put forward by Colombo and Aroldi (2003) is particularly indicated for the further development of this analysis. The way in which we interact with television is, to a large extent, the fruit of how we establish our "media profiles" (Colombo, 2003), i.e. the set of expectations, tastes, preferences and familiarities in terms of genres and texts, interpretation modes and functions attributed in the media consumption discourse. The establishment of these profiles results to a large extent from the process of socialization with the media in a given period of our lives: that of infancy to adolescence. Based on this proposal, the third guiding hypothesis in the analysis of the media in the network society, is that the media matrix (Meyrovitz quoted in Ortoleva, 2002) of each individual is different but that it is possible to individualize different appropriation logics depending on the shared social dimensions, such as the generation variable.

On the basis of these formulations one can expect that, just as the users of television have different representations and practices that influence their relationship with television itself, it is also possible to characterize the Internet users in a similar way. If this characterization enables us to identify differentiated media profiles will it be possible to reach a conclusion as to the networking or not of the media in current society? Is there an *Internet age* as opposed to a *TV age*? And how are these networks of social appropriation of the technologies linked to each other in the construction of the autonomy projects of the different individuals?

Contextualizing the Media in the Network Society

Understanding the media in the network is not possible if we limit our analysis to the physical space of one single country. Today, the national media systems are interconnected due to the fact that the respective institutions, companies and organizations belong to multiple relational and power networks, indeed just like the citizens themselves, thus sharing *space of flows* (Castells, 2003). Hence, the analysis carried out in the following chapters does not stop at the political and physical borders of the nation state. It extends beyond borders to include the European space and also other geographic regions such as Asia and North and South America, using a space of flows that is shared by thousands of people, who have common objectives and potentate them through use of the media.

In terms of time frame, the analysis carried out focuses essentially on the period from 1998 to 2004, a period characterized by rapid expansion of use of the Internet (at times with annual growth rates of more than 100%) and also by reorganization of the media[6] and telecommunications sectors at the global level.

In many places (Castells, 2003), the years 1998 to 2001 were likewise a period marked by the possibility of experimentation and innovation in the media sector, namely the ways in which television, radio and the press appropriated the Internet, thus demonstrating the network established between entrepreneurs, specialized professionals such as journalists, integrated financial systems and a culture built around the central role of information (Cardoso, 2003 and Castells, 2003).

In the analysis we wish to carry out on the way in which we understand the function and social role of the communication and information technologies, one must take into account that they are been appropriated in different forms in the discourses of journalists, politicians and academics. Although the term *Information Society* has established itself as legitimization of the central role of the information and communication technologies in our everyday life, it is nevertheless reductive, constituting only one example of many approaches.

We must ask ourselves whether the term *Information Society* is that which bests captures the essence of the social change brought about by the appropriation of the information and communication technologies. To this end, we enlist the help of authors such as Frank Webster (1995), who sought to establish the idea of the existence of a current of thought that could be termed Information Society Theories and other such as Peppino Ortoleva, Majid Tehranian, Fausto Colombo, Anthony Giddens, Umberto Eco, Mark Poster, Dominique Wolton and Manuel Castells, who have worked on how

---

[6] When we use the definition of media system, we are deliberately including technologies that we usually define as new and old media (something that will be discussed in the following chapters), telecommunications and their networking with information networks that provide contents and communication, such as the Internet.

the social appropriation of communication and information technologies seems to be linked to social change.

Of the authors cited above, Manuel Castells' analysis (2002) of the *network society* constitutes the central axis for the analysis proposed on the following pages. Castells' proposal is particularly useful as, contrary to others, it is more transversal in its social, economic and political approach to societies as well as conferring a global dimension upon the analysis, focusing on differences and similarities between populations and regions. Implicit in the idea of the network society is a logic of coexistence and not immediate substitution. In other words, the network societies coexist with the industrial societies, just as the latter coexisted (and, in some cases, still coexist) with elements of societies with predominantly agrarian characteristics.

As the media are an instrument of social appropriation, understanding the society in which they are incorporated is also of fundamental importance. We know that, although the predominant social organization models in a given moment in time have to be read in terms of their application in a certain social, political, economic and cultural context, it is also true that the Portuguese society shares with other countries and nations certain characteristics inherent in a given modernity (Costa, 1998 and Machado, 1998). If it is possible to understand the similarities between network societies in transition, such as the Catalan and Portuguese societies (Castells et al, 2003 and Cardoso et al, 2004), one could also expect there to be similarities between other social and geographic spaces that help us to better understand change. For this reason, in order to give this analysis a dimension of comparability with analyses of the social appropriation of the media carried out (and being carried out) elsewhere, it is important that we conduct an in-depth analysis of some of the examples of societies in transition to the network society. Examples that proceed from the analysis of a European society, Portugal [7], but also deal with other societies in transi-

---

[7] The study that served as the basis for this analysis is the fruit of the information collection work carried out by CIES/ISCTE/Gulbenkian Foundation in cooperation with the "Projecte Internet a Catalunya" of IN3 and Universitat Oberta Catalunya led by Manuel Castells. The data used come from a questionnaire given to a sample of 2450 individuals representative of the Portuguese population. Amongst other dimensions, the data allow one to identify the socio-demographic characteristics of the individuals, namely their autonomy and self-definition level; their Internet literacy; their use of the Internet in comparison to other media; the results they have achieved since they started using the Internet (career promotion; education; sociability alterations; strengthening or weakening of social values; socio-political involvement level; feeling of empowerment in specific dimensions of their social life; and offline living patterns in the various key dimensions of their lives).

tion, such as the societies of the southern European Union Member States of Spain, Italy and Greece and also the four largest new Member States, Poland, Czech Republic, Slovakia and Hungary) and the leading South American countries (Argentina, Brazil, Chile and Uruguay).

What the analysis of the data on societies in transition allows us to do, more easily than in societies that are more homogeneous in terms of use of the new technologies, is to identify the different population groups and what differences there are in terms of literacy for interacting with the different media.

The approach taken here has the objective of drawing a profile, establishing the similarities and differences between two typified populations in relation to the use, or non-use, of the latest media form to emerge amongst those that make up the media system: the Internet.

The Internet is analyzed here as a tool for the construction of individual projects developed from different dimension bases. Why can the Internet be analyzed as an individual project construction instrument? Because, in its constitution and appropriation, the Internet is flexible, interactive, omnipresent, global, accessible and is not dependant on past or existing powers (Castells, 2001).

However, one must take into consideration in our analysis that, as the Internet is an instrument, if it is only used as one more way of doing something that we already do, then its use will be limited and not necessarily competitive in relation to the other media.

Bearing this in mind, the proposed analysis of autonomy projects, media matrix and media diets has sought to begin with the identification of the projects of individuals and social groups and measure how the Internet furthers those projects, becomes an obstacle, or remains relatively neutral (as a mere facilitator without value added).

Even if the above-mentioned analysis of societies in transition to the network society could produce an interpretative framework for the trends at play at the different levels of our life, that analysis of the media system we have undertaken could only be really complete if we also place the cultural industries and their development trends in context.

If the study of the practices and representations of individuals gives us one half of the equation necessary for analyzing how the media system functions, the other half is provided by knowledge of the entities that supply and produce cultural assets. And because some of the traits of the change in progress in the field of the cultural industries must not be looked at only in the context of one country, but in a global perspective, it also becomes necessary to observe some logics of change in progress within the global cultural industries sector itself, namely the sector(s) that can currently represent a transition in progress: the creation of new meta-systems in the field of entertainment. This can be individualized for the entertainment segment around the multimedia games/cinema/television constellation and, for information, around the Internet/television constellation.

What kind of culture is, then, generated in the Information Age? In order to understand the amplitude of this question we first have to analyze socially shared definitions as to the role of technology in social change. In most cases, these derive from popular culture generated within the cultural industries themselves (in the form of books, films and games) and subsequently divulged by them. A popular culture based on works of science fiction and their visions of the future, now utopian now dystopian, and the role of technological change in that construction. This is a fundamental analysis, as it gives one a perspective as to what extent, many times, it induces an erroneous social construction of the real and the virtual – two fundamental concepts for understanding what culture is in the network society. Following the above-mentioned argumentation, I would suggest that the answer to the question asked at the beginning of this paragraph is that it is a *real virtuality culture* (Castells, 2002). [8]

The Information Age culture is a real virtuality culture because once more in the historic *continuum* it has given rise to a new system of symbolic communication directly associated with what is known as the *crystallization* of the relationships of production/consumption, experience and power in specific territories, originating, thus, *collective cultures and identities* (Castells 2002). [9]

---

[8] For Castells, we are living in a culture of real virtuality. It is virtual because it is mainly constructed through electronic virtual communication processes. It is real (and not imaginary) because it is our fundamental reality, the material basis on which we live, construct our representation systems, carry out our work, relate with others, obtain information, form opinions, act politically and nourish our dreams. That virtuality is our reality (Castells, 2004).

[9] The term *culture* is used here in the sense of the whole social network and that of one society in particular. It comes close to Stuart Hall's (1997) vision of culture as the expression of the identity of people, which also changes in accordance with the needs of the individual and the communities in expressing their identity. Stuart Hall defines culture as a set of shared meanings that allow individuals to understand each other and communicate. In his view, these meanings are not static, nor are they simply a collection of behaviours and values that characterize a social group. On the contrary, the cultural meaning is produced and exchanged; it is a process, a set of practices. Meaning is produced

It is a culture generated through the cultural industries and their production and innovation processes but with the difference, historically speaking, that it is characterized by greater power exercised by the cultural needs of the consumers over the cultural industries themselves. A power originating in the increase of its interaction capacities, namely through access to technologies such as the Internet, digital film cameras and mobile telephones, and to thus generating symbolic capital for exercising influence on the cultural industries and society in general.

For Castells (2003), it is mainly through virtuality that we process our creation of meaning, thus suggesting that the analysis of the creation of meaning in the Information Age has to take into account the combined analysis of the *communication* and *mediation* processes.

As Silverstone argues (2004), the growing centrality of the *media*, in the exercise of power and in conducting our daily life, places the study of mediation at the top of the agenda of social research:

> The analysis of mediation, as I have suggested, requires us to understand how the processes of mediated communication shape both society and culture, as well as the relationships that participants, both individual and institutional, have to their environment and to each other. (Silverstone, 2004)

The study of the mediation is not in itself a rejection of the different approaches to the role of communication. On the contrary, it is one more contribution. The proposals by academics such as Paquete de Oliveira (1995), amongst others, on the relationship between information and communication, Colombo (1995) on synthetic communication, Umberto Eco (2001) on the precedence of the media over content, Ignacio Ramonet (1999) on narrative systems and technologies, and even writers such as Kenzaburo Oe (1999) on language and communication, are of fundamental importance for providing a more in-depth knowledge of how, through our practices, we generate and experience a culture of real virtuality and how this influences, conditions and boosts our autonomy projects.

---

and exchanged in very diverse forms, including: group identity and group differences; personal and social interaction; mass media and global communications; everyday rituals and practices; narratives, stories and fantasies; rules, norms and conventions. These different aspects of culture are closely linked and interact in the construction and transmission of social meaning.

Media, Autonomy and Citizenship

The central argument that will accompany us throughout the following chapters is that we live in a society that is fundamentally different to society as we knew it up until the early 1970s (in some cases the society is in transition to that different state, such as those analyzed in greater detail herein).

That society is termed the *Network Society* by Manuel Castells (2003-2004). It is characterized by a change in its form of social organization made possible by the emergence of the information technologies in a period that coincides with a need for economic change (characterized by the globalization of the exchange and movement of money) and social change (characterized by the search to affirm new liberties and individual choice values that begun with the student protests of May 1968).

In this Network Society, the autonomy of decision is directly linked to our capacity of interaction with the media (which are here understood as the apparatuses of mediation and access to communication and information). Why?

Firstly, because, as the human species is characterized by communication, it is communication that sustains the social fabric we create and in which we live. Secondly, the complexity of our societies, as characterized by Giddens (1998), establishes the need for permanent interaction with, and between, spatially differentiated zones and different areas of social, professional and cultural relations. Thus, we communicate by means of the most diverse technologies in symbolic mediation spaces with our children, parents and family members who live nearby or further way, in the same town, in the same country or in other countries and continents. We work in companies that buy products from abroad, or in other zones, that require manuals translated from other languages, and that have to export and receive orders or simply have to access bank accounts online. We watch films, soap operas and stage plays produced in our own country or adapted from other cultures.

Our world is a world of communication mediated by technologies such as the pencil, paper, the telephone, television and the Internet. And it continues to be a world of face-to-face communication.

Our societies have a long history of social appropriation of the communication technologies (Winston, 1999), the changes they have made to daily life – and even to our living rooms (Silverstone, 1994) – and the anxieties they have originated (Eco, 1991). Anxieties because, for some of the researchers, it is not so much about what one has to gain in a society in which the *mediation* technologies have diversified, but what there is to lose. For example, Dominique Wolton (1999) argues that the more we deal with technologies that allow us to segment contents depending on our choice and interests, the more we tend to lose the social link that television, radio and press provided. For Wolton (1999), the multiplication of the media, even if it strengthens the autonomy of individual projects, corresponds to a loss of strength for collective society projects. Wolton's argumentation, in addition to being challengeable at the level of the relationship between the media and social reconstruction (Castells, 2003), is thus based on the idea that what we should be concerned with is the type of technology we interact with, reworking arguments frequently used on the apocalyptic dimension of a given type of communication (Eco, 1991).

There are, however, other possible approaches. One of these is central to the analysis proposed herein. Instead of merely attributing functions to the media and fearing their consequences, we should analyze what the reality of the appropriations and uses shows us. The question we really have to answer is to what point this increase in access possibilities, in daily exposure to, and interaction with the media boosts, or not, our autonomy and, in the final analysis, the exercise of citizenship in its multiple forms? [10]

Citizenship recognizes an individual's belonging to a form of political organization (the State or another form) of a secular nature and the development of universal rules for participation in a society. Citizenship and the degree of autonomy attributed by it are, thus, one of the dimensions of the legitimizing identities of the modernity project (Giddens, 1997) and also of new *project identities*, though not necessarily of *resistance identities* (Castells, 2003). [11]

Practically all who read these pages will be *de jure* and *de facto* citizens (although the same cannot be said of all those with whom we share this planet). We normally acquired that quality after our birth when we were

---

[10] According to Turner (1994), citizenship can be defined as a set of practices of individuals as competent members of a community, with their sphere of activity consisting of a vast field that ranges from the application of T. H. Marshall's (1964) proposals on the existence of legal, political and social rights to the discussion on the existence of cultural citizenship and, naturally, as Turner (1993) suggests, cultural rights including the right to communication (Hamelink, 2004) and information.

[11] Resistance identities can choose to be based on religious ties and communal belonging patterns in an act of resistance (because they cannot achieve that citizenship or because they reject it and desire an alternative to it).

registered at a registry office. However, in the course or our lives, we may decide to change our origin by marriage, or be obliged to do so due to a geo-political alteration we have nothing to do with (as in the case of the separation of Kosovo from the former Federal Yugoslav Republic when it was placed under United Nations management) or because, for reasons of need or ideology, we deliberately choose a transition between citizenships (from ex-Timorese citizen of a Portuguese overseas territory annexed by Indonesia, to Timorese citizen of East Timor). Belonging to a certain space constituted as a nation state, a federal state or a nation without a state but possessing autonomy, we are part of a society where the rules for living together are more or less structured. That space in which we share with others the limits to our individual actions, in other words, in which our rights and duties are known and recognized.

Obviously, knowing who guarantees that our rights can be exercised and to what point this occurs in liberty is as important as knowing what our common rights are.

Citizenship is, thus, the fruit of the degree of autonomy of action that is conferred upon us by the society in which we live, but it is also the fruit of the individual and collective projects of which we are a part. More than an individual and inalienable historic heritage, citizenship is a product of the choices we make and the societies we construct. For our autonomy also depends on the modes of production and development in which we live. Accordingly, citizenship in a capitalist production mode is different from that in a State-run mode (Castells, 2002). Just as citizenship in a traditional patriarchal society differs from citizenship in a society in which men, women and children have equal rights and duties. Citizenship also differs depending on whether the power exercise model is based more on identification with a democratic ideal (as in the European Union democracies) or on a mitigated model, as in the case of Russia (Rukavishnikov, 2002), or on totalitarian models, such as those rooted in religious fundamentalism, xenophobic nationalism or the dictatorships that the Iberian Peninsula and Latin America experienced for a number of decades in the 20th century.

How is citizenship exercised in the Network Society? The answer to this question depends on the hypotheses formulated above on the evolution of the media system and our relationship with the communication and information technologies in the form of the media matrix and media diets. It also depends on the questions formulated about our use of tools such as the Internet and television in the service of our autonomy projects.

Manuel Castells provides us at the outset with a partial answer, for the network society seems to be characterized by the formation of relational networks around individual and collective projects emerging from interests and values shared by the individuals. In other words, from a model of centralized communication and the shared minimalist definition of joint objectives, would follow a proliferation of new collective projects shared through the network. These projects can range from a joint interest in solving a neighbourhood problem, to national or even global political projects and to the mere defence of a television channel's programming that is appreciated because it is an affirmation of our identity.

Although the Internet furthers these networks created on the basis of spontaneous projects that emerge in society, constituting the technological platform that is most appropriate for their affirmation, it is also true that the exercise of autonomy not only depends on the Internet. Not only because the Internet, even though it links all the nodes of exercise of power in the network society, is still a minority technology in terms of access, but also because the identities in everyday life need to exist in the audiovisual space that the Internet doesn't offer.

Neither television nor the Internet alone can ensure and allow for the management of individual autonomy and social participation. That is, perhaps, what the citizens, and also institutions, have been discovering through individual experimentation over the last decade. *The social appropriation of the information and communication technologies in the Information Age is characterized by their being networked.*

The success of the exercise of citizenship in the network society depends on the networking of the diverse media, and also on the individual mastering of the literacies necessary for interacting with the *mediation* tools – those that provide access to the information and those that enable us to organize, participate in and influence events and choices.

That is the power of the media in the final analysis – the power conferred by *listening, speaking and being heard* (Silverstone, 1999). The power that the media confer by enabling the citizens, in their diverse roles, to access the symbolic space produced by the *mediation* technologies and, consequently, to make use of them in constructing their individual or collective autonomy: the power of mediation. For Silverstone (1999), that power is the power to create meanings, persuade, prescribe, and reinforce; to guide reflection and reflectivity; to focus and inform; to relate and articulate memories; to present, reveal, explain; to give access and participation;

to listen, speak and be heard. But it is also a limited power, for it depends on the context in which it is exercised. In other words, although the media have the power to influence (and change) political, economic and social processes and to change the balance of power, that power is also denied them by the State, by the market, by resistant or proactive audiences, by the citizens and by the consumers (Silverstone, 1999).

The exercise of the power of mediation occurs, as we have seen, within a certain context in a media system that is organized in accordance with the interdependencies between different mediation technologies with different historical origins and different appropriation logics (Livingstone 1999).

The communication and information technologies in the network society do not substitute each other. On the contrary, they interlink. Television communicates with the Internet, with SMS technology and with telephones. Just as the Internet offers connectivity with all the mass media, telephones and thousands of personal and institutional websites on the net.

This network of technologies is not the mere product of technological convergence, but the result of a form of social organization created by those who use the technologies.

The suggestion that we write and listen to music using the Internet but listen to life through the radio and see the world through television (Castells, 2001) is one example of our new personal networked relationship with the media. *And it is through the selection and networking of those different media, depending on our individual projects, that autonomy is generated and citizenship is exercised in the Information Age.*

If we accept the challenge of observing and analyzing the practices of the social and institutional actors in network in relation to the media, we likewise have to consider the hypothesis that the *mediation* technologies are appropriated in accordance with the users' needs. And, given that, in history, none of the mass media has substituted its predecessor (Eco 2003), one can imagine that 3G telephones (with all their voice, SMS and moving image functions), newspapers, radio, television and the Internet are attributed different social roles by the users and that, amongst the latter, there may be different representations as to the utility and functions of the different media.

Proceeding from the possibility of adding new sources and purposes to our communication, we have also created new networks interlinking different media, conferring upon the network society the characteristic that we are living more than ever *by and with the media* (Cardoso, 2004 and Castells, 2003).

1. The Multiple Dimensions of the Network Society

Researchers in the fields of the social sciences practically unanimously agree that we are currently witnessing a vulgarization of the term Information Society and the generalized acceptance, by the most diverse commentators, that it is an established fact that that we are living in an Information Society (Webster, 2004).

When one speaks of the Information Society, even when one recognizes the existence of a standardized official discourse, one is not always speaking of the same reality. There are those who value more the economic dimension of information, others who value the political dimension and others still who value the personal, cultural and educational enhancement as the strongest characterization elements of our society.

In analyzing the social role of information, when we look in greater depth into the qualitative and quantitative dimensions of it, we find significant differences in response to the question: what is the Information Society?

Although I would disagree with some of the premises presented by Webster (1995) in his work, he nevertheless has the merit of highlighting the relative impreciseness of the concept of the *information society* as seen by the social and economic sciences in the last four decades.

This situation is of fundamental importance to the analysis proposed in this chapter, in which I will argue that, *the concept of the information society is neither the most appropriate for portraying the complexity of the changes currently taking place in contemporary society nor for understanding how the different media configure themselves as facilitators of individual empowerment and, consequently, of communicative and sociopolitical autonomy.* [12]

Before continuing the above line of argument it is necessary to first of all clarify certain concepts. Firstly, what do we understand by *information*? Information can be seen from at least three complementary perspectives: as the collection, processing and analysis of data and the consequent production of information (the Information Sciences perspective); information associated with the content of the message and the communication that is established between two or more entities, whether that communication is technologically mediated or not (the Communication Sciences perspective); and, more recently, information as *life*, in a reference to the genetic dimension of DNA (the Life Sciences perspective).

However, the emergence of the information technologies and communication via networks (such as minitel, the Internet, intranets and other local networks, Wi-Fi or other), on the one hand, and the digitalization of contents in association with to the trends (albeit seldom concretized) towards technological convergence between computers, telecommunications and television, on the other, has brought the interests of the communication and information sciences closer together.

For a number of decades, through the proposals of Shannon (Mattelart, 1998) and his mathematical model of communication (which made explicit the relationship between sender and receiver through the channel in which the message circulates), the information sciences were characterized by a predominantly quantitative orientation, with analyses centring on the information technologies, whereas the communication sciences focused more on the qualitative study and explanation of the phenomena, diverting attention away from the information and communication technologies due

---

[12] By *individual* empowerment one means to what extent the use of the communication and information technologies (media) serves to increase the capacity of each individual to influence the holders of the means of information and the decision making processes in society. For example, the capacity to obtain information and communicate horizontally, autonomously (patients getting information and consequently being in a better position in relation to the health system; people informing themselves about their own lives and the *world* without exclusive dependency on the mass media; consumers being able to compare prices and products and make their decisions; people being capable of organizing themselves and debating questions, be this in social movements or other causes; citizens seeking new forms of involvement in and monitoring of the political process, etc.).

to the condition these were in for a great many years. In more simple terms, as long as computers were islands not communicating between each other they were not taken into account in the objectives of the communication sciences.

As Mattelart (1998) suggests, the evolution of technology and its social appropriation in the last twenty years has meant that cybernetics (as defined by Norbert Wiener, i.e. the science that analyzes communication and control) has dethroned the mathematical model of communication.

The concept of the network made up of individuals connected with one another through communication flow patterns proposed by Everett Rogers (Mattelart, 1998) thus took on new preponderance in the analysis of the role of information in our societies.

On the basis of the preceding argumentation I have chosen to use in my analysis the definition proposed by Manuel Castells and Daniel Bell, i.e. the operational definition of information proposed by Porat: "information refers to data that have been organized and communicated". [13]

From the point of view of the cultural construction that is the information society, as a summary of the debate so far, we can accept that when we speak of the Information Society we mean *a society in which the exchange of information is a central and predominant social activity.*

However, because that is an ideologically occupied concept, we can define the *information society as a process of social change based on information,* which itself is the expression of human knowledge. The information society is fruit of the technological process that enables us to process, store, select and communicate information in all forms available in it – oral, written and visual – without distance, time or volume-related restrictions – giving the human being new capacities and changing the way in which we live and work together (European Commission 1998, quoted in Karvonnen, 2001).

It is not my intention here to carry out an in-depth analysis of the work of the diverse authors who have studied the information society over the last twenty years, or to carry out an extensive analysis of the analytical division proposed by Webster. However, because theorizing consists in identifying the main trends and removing the accessory ones, an introduction

---

[13] Manuel Castells defends his choice on the basis of the fact that other definitions proposed by other renowned authors in the field, such as Machlup (who simply defines information as "the communication of knowledge"), are, as Bell also suggests, very general. (Castells, 1996).

to his thought would be pertinent with a view to sustaining a critique of the validity of the concept of the information society as the most appropriate one for theorizing on and explaining the social change in contemporary societies.

In his book, *Information Society Theories*, Webster argues that it would be more correct to see the explanations for the role of information in our societies from a point of view of historic continuity, as he considers it incorrect to speak of an information society. According to Webster, we can speak of the existence of certain types of information for defined purposes, for specific groups with particular types of interests that are developing but that is not sufficient to be able to speak of an *information society.*

For Webster (1995), what became known as the *information society theories* have in common the idea that a change is taking place in contemporary societies and that this change is due to the dominant role of information and communication. Webster argues that the opinions of researchers can be classified depending on the level and extent of the changes and their understanding of the concept of "information".

Webster's view is in some ways similar to the proposal of David Lyon, although it does consolidate the considerations of the latter. Indeed, for Lyon, the academic formulation of the concept of the information society has its origins in the 1960s with Daniel Bell, containing ideological and utopian presuppositions centred on the information workers, the political aspects of the globalization of information and, finally an information culture (Lyon, 1995). For Lyon, the theoretical discourse on the information society is characterized by two types of theses: one more descriptive in character (favouring the view that great changes are coming and seeing this as something positive) and another more problematizing, looking at the possible transformations in a more open and cautious approach.

In Webster's proposal there are likewise two thesis types: that of those authors who focus their analysis on a *radicalization* of the trends (either of a negative character or in a positive direction, but always accepting the radical change) or that of *integration* in the current context (in other words, acceptance of the change but relativizing it in terms of its real social impact). On the one hand, according to Webster, we have those who argue that we are experiencing radical change in paradigms in the most diverse sectors of society and that it is therefore possible to speak of the emerge of a new type of society – the information society as a new stage of social evolution. On the other, we have those who, similar to the first group, recognize the current importance of information and communication but have reservations as to the emergence of a new society, in this case one based on information. For this group, the transformations taking place are not ruptures with the existing forms of social organization, but rather are evolutions within a previously established context.

Given that the central question for this work resides in explaining the role played by the media in a society in which information is an anchor element, we have a lot to gain from asking the question whether *Information Society* is really the most correct term for understanding the dynamics involved. In other words, is the concept of *Information Society* that which most directly reflects the interdependencies that exist between the dimensions of information and communication and social change?

The Network Society

Today we are witnessing the emergence of signs of transformation in different areas of society that are not mere isolated changes but have a significant enough impact as to constitute substantial transformations and have an impact on the whole social fabric.

Webster's (1995) sectorial view of the different theories on the information society can best be countered from a perspective of intersectorial analysis that examines the role of information in culture, society and the economy, as suggested by Manuel Castells in his book *The Information Age* (1996-2004).

Castells is not alone in proposing an intersectorial analysis. For, as Anthony Giddens (1998) argues, we are experiencing changes in some of the axes that characterize modernity, particularly at the economic level, in what Castells terms the passing from an *industrial development mode* to an *informational development mode*.

This change that is taking place in the industrialism and capitalism axes of modernity – not forgetting the changes at the level of experience, the formation of identities and culture – automatically has an impact on the other axes.

In the view taken in this analysis, which I have developed in *Para uma Sociologia do Ciberespaço* (Cardoso, 1998) there are points of contact with Webster's proposal but, at the same time, I disagree with his view on the degree of changes that are taking place.

The view on which I have based the analysis presented herein is that of a growing radicalization that is in progress in some axes of modernity, the origins of which are to be found in the role that information and the communication and information diffusion networks play in our societies.

The radicalization of modernity I refer to allows us, without doubt, to speak of changes in the form of social organization and of an Information Age (Castells, 1996). Taking into account all of what has been said above in the context of theoretical analysis, the question must be asked: *does the information society exist or not?*

The most correct answer would be that the *Information Society* exists as a set of essentially political objectives developed within the context of European Union institutions and then appropriated by the individual Member States. It has since been incorporated into the discourse of many global and multilateral political and economic organizations.

It likewise exists as a discourse diffused – and, to a certain extent, internalized by the general public – through the many ideas vehicled by the media. Ideas originating in the economic and political spheres of society. However, that discourse is transformed and adapted on a daily basis, taking into account the experiences of the information and communication technologies by the users of the Internet, mobile phones and also by the interconnections with the mass media offered by these technologies.

The Information Society, as shown in the preceding chapter, exists as a cultural construction, which is not the same as affirming that it exists. Why? Because, as Anthony Giddens (1998) argues, and Manuel Castells also summarizes, the communication of knowledge has been critical in all societies, including the societies of mediaeval Europe, which were culturally structured and, to a certain point, unified by scholastic education, i.e. in general an intellectual infrastructure (Castells, 1996).

Contrary to Webster (1995), I do not think one can claim the existence of a theoretical set that could be unified around the idea of the information society. However, the analysis carried out by Webster (1995) includes a central contribution, which is that of showing the one-dimensionality of most of the approaches, which focus on only some of the dimensions of the social change, failing to explain the whole or the multidimensional relations that are established.

Despite the criticism of his work (Dijk, 1999), the concepts of the *informational development* and *informational society* modes and the *network society* defined by Manuel Castells are perhaps those that best respond to the need, on the one hand, to analyze the social change from multiple angles and in multiple dimensions and, on the other, to perceive that, although there are changes that are sufficiently *radical* to be worthy of our attention, those changes coexist at all times with other continuities, which can be corroborated by looking at the historic dimension of humanity (Braudel, 2000). [14]

Manuel Castells suggests a characterization of contemporary societies not as *information* societies but as *informational* societies, highlighting the central attribute of a new form of social organization in which the production of information and its processing and transmission become the main sources of productivity and power thanks to the new technological conditions emerging in the present period of history.

By using the adjective *informational*, Castells seeks to establish a parallel to the distinction between *industry* and *industrial*. Just as an industrial society is more than a society in which industry exists, but is a society in which the social and technological forms of industrial organization permeate all spheres of activity (Castells, 1996), it also necessary to establish an analytical distinction between *information society* and *informational society*. Hence, the informational society is a product of a specific historic context covering the last three decades of the 20th century.

In the formulation used by Castells, the analysis of the social change allowing us to conclude whether or we are witnessing the emergence of a new social structure that is sufficiently different to the previous structures is based on the detection of structural transformations in the production, power and experiences relations. According to Castells, it is these transformations that lead to a significant change in the social forms of space and time and to the emergence of a new culture.

The argumentation is powerful and is, perhaps, that which provides a starting point leading to the questions to be raised, identifying a model for explaining the changes in the different dimensions but without prejudging and anticipating the future that is being built. It gives us a certain degree of autonomy of analysis to endeavour to identify both the changes

---

[14] Van Dijk's critique of Castells is centred on what van Dijk considers a one-dimensional view of the network society. For, according to van Dijk, there is a technological determinism running through the whole analysis that has its roots in Castells theory and method. This results in a one-dimensional view of technology that leaves little space for the political choices. For van Dijk, the analysis of the network society ignores the possibility of resistance within the system and therefore assumes that all forms of resistance are external. (1999).

in progress – at the level of different societies (for not all societies are in the same stage of development, nor are they identical in their cultural, economic, political and social dimensions) – and to also investigate in greater depth some of the dimensions that have emerged out of it, such as the *role of the media.*

The informational society is, therefore, correlative to a restructuring of capitalism, of which the most obvious characteristics are globalization of the main economic activities, organizational flexibility and greater power on the part of the employers in labour relations. This restructuring is only possible in the dimensions given in the preceding paragraph, with the temporal coincidence with a new type of technology, the information technologies, which were appropriated by the economic fabric with the aim of stimulating flexibilization of the organizational and spatial relations on the global scale. Together with the restructuring of capitalism, during these three decades we have also witnessed the practical disappearance of statism – both the Soviet model and one based on exacerbated nationalism – as a form of structuring the production relations in the contemporary world.

However, the informational society does not consist of economic dimensions only. The last three decades of the 20th century, thanks to the emergence of the social movements at the end of the 1960s and their multiplication in the following decades, brought with them new forms of looking at experience and defining objectives for social claims.

As Manuel Castells (1996) points out, the aims of the young members of these activist movements included a multidimensional reaction to arbitrary authority, a revolt against injustices and the search for personal experimentation.

Although he recognizes that the changes championed by these movements were fundamentally cultural and independent of the economic and technological transformations, Castells emphasizes that they did have an impact on the economy and technology, as well as on the resulting restructuring processes. Examples of this influence can be found, according to Castells, in the influential libertarian spirit of the individualized and decentralized use of technology; in the distancing from traditional trade union policies, leading to a subsequent weakening of the trade union movement; in the cultural opening that stimulated the experimental manipulation of symbols, creating the current model of social appropriation of the media; in its cosmopolitanism and internationalism as a bridge to a global socialization space; and, finally, in its aversion to the State, which weakened the legitimacy of the democratic systems.

One of the main characteristics of the informational society that Castells proposes as the fruit of the technological and economic changes and the social movements over the last three decades is that it has a network logic as its basic structure.

Although the network, as an organizational form, has accompanied human societies throughout history, it was only with the development of the information technologies and their domestication (Silverstone, 1994) by the organizational structures of companies that the dissemination of a model that allies flexibility with effectiveness and efficiency has become possible.

Our societies are therefore informational for the fact that the production, processing and transmission of information have become the principal sources of productivity and power, but the are also network societies, just as the hierarchical organization of the industrial model permeated all of the industrial society, the decentralized and flexible model of the network permeates our contemporary societies.

A social structure based on networks is, therefore, a highly dynamic and open system, capable of innovation and containing low threats to its balance. Networks are the appropriate instruments for the economy, work, politics and social organization of our era.

In technological terms, the network society – although its genesis is rooted in the possibilities offered by the development in communications, software and hardware in the 1970s – had its moment of exponential diffusion outside the spheres of large corporations or the State with the diffusion of the Internet in households and in the business fabric in general during the second half of the 1990s.

Hence, after three decades of existence, the Internet is spreading at an unparalleled speed, when compared with all other means of communication (from radio to television), and is rapidly becoming a tool that is used for multiple applications. But why now? We can answer Castells' question by concentrating first on technological reasons: the diffusion of the personal computer (PC) and, later, a whole range of computing and communication devices; the World Wide Web's user friendliness; the growth of computer literacy, particularly amongst the younger generations and the promotion of the use of the Internet at home, in the workplace and in the education system (Lee, 1999).

However, part of the recent success of the Internet may have to do with a reality that has already been studied in the history of technology (Winston, 1999): it responds to a fundamental need of society, a need that is rooted in social evolution and finds in the Internet a privileged tool for its concretization. But at the same time, through its utilization, the people themselves change the technology and that is a characteristic made possible by the open technology model itself (a logic lacking in the preceding communication and information technologies such as television, telephone, radio, newspapers, etc.).

If functioning in a network constitutes a supervening social need (Winston, 1999), for what do we use it and with whom? To answer that question, we have to consider the process of social evolution in the so-called *Information Age* (Castells, 2003).

As Castells points out, the existence of this new world of informational development and the dominance of space of flows over space of places results in a growing globalization, and although that in itself is not a bad phenomenon – for it represents the idea that we can all communicate with each other, buy and sell globally and thus form a global community – in reality the globalization represents, for a large part of humanity, that political power is being taken from it and it is being given economic impoverishment (Castells, 1997).

These people, who live in the space of places and do not participate in the space of flows, do not have any type of control over the investments, do not have the necessary education and are, therefore, "overtaken" by the power of the global capital flows. They also cannot negotiate with their employers because the latter possess the means to change the locations of their operations, resort to outsourcing or bring in supplies or workers from other locations.

This duality, which Castells terms "condition of structural schizophrenia", introduces a general perturbation in the most diverse cultures at the global level, giving rise to identity crises in those geographically and historically defined spaces.

For Castells, the "incarnation" of the legitimizing identity of our contemporary societies, the Nation State, is currently experiencing a decline in power. He also points out, however, that although it is losing power, this is not directly reflected in its capacity of influence. The loss of power derives from its loss of sovereignty, the fruit of the globalization of strategic economic activities, the media, communications and also the globalization of crime and the military or paramilitary "policing".

The most obvious example of this loss of sovereignty can be found in the financial markets, which, in the 1980s, grew beyond the capacity of any central bank to exercise their control and led to the need to interlink the national currencies, which in turn implicated financial coordination that thus deprived the national governments of scope for formulating their economic policies independently.

Also according to Castells, living today in a turbulent world in which power can no longer be measured by the physical, human and material structures that a given entity has at its disposal, the political and economic centres see their factual power being questioned when they are sometimes forced to negotiate with other forces that may be of lesser dimension but operate in a network. Castells uses the example of the Zapatistas and the Mexican government, and this is also the case for ecological groups such as Greenpeace and the governments of the most developed countries.

Nevertheless, the Nation State continues to play a fundamental role, for it is the only entity with legitimacy under which the multilateral mechanisms can be created that enable us to deal with problems that are becoming increasingly global in character. One example, given by Anthony Giddens, is the fact that, sooner or later, governments will have to regulate the global financial markets to prevent the global economy from resembling more and more a "casino economy" (Giddens, 1997a).

The State in the *Information Age* is experiencing profound contradictions, for whereas, for decades, it was the inducer of the diffusion of technologies and financer of investigation into them, today it has become a victim of that process as its diminished power is the result of a shift in the exercise of power from the space of places to the space of flows.

We are also witnessing changes in the relationship between political power and the media. As Castells (2000b) writes on the role of the media, politics today are not defined by the media but within media space, which is occupied by the countless and ever more varied television stations and, increasingly, the Internet. Contrary to what it may look like at first sight, due to the emergence of alternative information networks, the media will be reporting more and more on what goes on in society. The end of the monopoly on information also represents the end of the government monopoly on action.

The Culture of the Informational Societies

If, as Castells argues, the changes in the production, power and experience relations also lead to a significant change in the social forms of space
and time and the emergence of a new culture through the alteration of the
communication model (or, if we prefer, the mediated symbolic exchanges)
then what kind of culture is generated in the *Information Age?*

I think that to understand the scope of the question we first have to analyze definitions that are socially shared in relation to the role of technology
in social change. In most cases, these definitions derive from a culture, the
synthesis of the time in which we live (Colombo, 2000) created in the cultural industries themselves – in the form of books, films and games.

A culture based on works of science fiction and its visions of the futures
– sometimes utopian, other times dystopian – and the role of technological
change in that construction. This is a fundamentally important analysis,
for in it we will find a particular vision of the relationship between *real*
and *virtual* (two fundamental concepts for understanding the culture of the
Information Age).

In an historic incursion into how the cultural actors represent the new
technologies we can find a recurrent use of the theme of the relationship
between the new technologies, the body and power.

One example of this relationship is the film version of Philip K. Dick's
book "Blade Runner" (1982) directed by Ridley Scott. It expresses the
anxiety felt in relation to the information and communication technologies,
which, when taken to the limit, might result in the creation of a humanoid
being in the joining of the body and the emotions through information
technologies.

Continuing this historical exploration of the representations in popular
culture of computers and body/machine interfaces, we can cite as paradigmatic examples three works with different conceptions of the human/
technology relationship (Irvine, 1999 and Chandler, 1998): Mary Shelley's
Frankenstein in its multiple screen adaptations; *Dr. Strangelove* by Stanley
Kubrick and the *Star Trek* series, which crossed over from television to the
cinema screen.

The myth recreated in Mary Shelley's book is that of a solitary individual – in the original story, a scientist (but it could just as well be a large
corporation or a government) – who, by means of technology, in this case
electricity (although one could name other works in which that technology

is replaced by atomic radiation, computers or computer networks), is given destructive powers that induce terror in the community in the form of an agent that becomes autonomous (the agent can be a monster, as in the case of Frankenstein, but it can also be a robot or a form of artificial intelligence in a computer or a network).

The *Strangelove* effect – named after the character of a Nazi scientist (played by Peter Sellers) living in the US of the 1960s who overcommits himself to the fight against Communism – combines computerized technology with corrupt or stupid leaders who have the power over weapons of mass destruction. This alliance portrays a conspiracy in which those involved themselves are cheated or are mad. The military and government members experiment new weapons linked to advanced computers, which threaten society and always lead to great destruction.

Finally, there is the *Star Trek* effect. Here, we are not dealing with the present or a dystopian near future (as is the case in "2001: A Space Odyssey", also a Stanley Kubrick film based on a novel by Arthur C. Clark), but, above all, with a distant future and the experience of a utopia through technology. In the series, in which Captain Kirk and Mr. Spock are the leading characters, we experience a utopia of useful machines and harmony between races (from earth) and species (members of the Federation) and in which war, be it with the *Klingons* or the *Romulans*, always ends with the signing of a peace treaty by which the Federation establishes classless government, in which the industrial production (and its environmental consequence) is invisible and there is no sign of a valid monetary economy and liberal and democratic social values and structures are shared by all.

This identification of effects associated with the technology-inspired cultural production is particularly useful for understanding the contemporary cultural contributions that have become known as "Cyberpunk". The keyword that defines this genre of science fiction is *hybridization*. "Cyberpunk" mixes high and "low" culture and state-of-the-art technology with trash visuals. In the literary style of a novel, central elements of social and political criticism are incorporated, sometimes reaching the point of endeavouring to create a philosophical dimension, always with the aim of imagining the unimaginable – the search for the limits of fiction. The origins of "Cyberpunk" are to be found in a number of counterculture and mass culture movements, in which, starting from traditional fiction models, an avant-garde writing style is added to the detective story model, seeking a scenario inspired by horror novels, whereby the action is always set in hyper-urbanized spaces in which rock and alternative music combine with a psychotropic drug culture and television and mass culture and in which the central element is the hacker culture and the use of computers, networks, cybernetics and artificial intelligence. [15]

As a form of social, political and economic criticism, "Cyberpunk" presupposes a *postmodern* world [16] with the omnipresence of multinational corporations and state-of-the-art technology and a *society of the spectacle* [17], in which the image superimposes itself on reality in a culture of hyper-consumerism (Kellner, 1995).

For a paradigmatic example of the "Cyberpunk" culture one can look at the film "The Matrix" by the Wachowski brothers, not only for the characteristics present in the screenplay but also for the success it achieved worldwide. Since it was released in March 1999, it has grossed more than 500 million US dollars at the box office, sparking off a trilogy, video games and comic books. "The Matrix" represents the paradigm of the relationship between the real and the virtual that cultural products (be they novels, comic books, TV series, computer games or films) have been constructing over the last two decades. Its storyline gives continuity to the relationship between fiction and the body, power and the machine mirroring contemporary fears in relation to the technologies so present in the different spheres of everyday life in our society – the information and communication technologies.

The film "The Matrix" can be seen as a re-combination of cultures (the code that begins the film made up of inverted Japanese characters and the

---

[15] For Pekka Himanen, hackers are defined by The Hackers Jargon File as "people who program enthusiastically" and believe "information sharing is a powerful positive good, and that it is an ethical duty of hackers to share their expertise by writing free software and facilitating access to information and to computing resources whenever possible" (Himanen, 2001a). The word hacker, in its original meaning, subsequently distorted by the mass media, refers to those who sought to innovate and advance their technological capacities.

[16] The post-modern concept presents various acceptions. Here its use refers to what Frederic Jameson (1991) terms late capitalism, i.e. transnational consumption economies based on post-industrial global capitalism, in which, culturally, one witnesses a hybridization of forms and genres that mixes styles from different periods and cultures and decontextualizes them.

[17] In coining the term "Society of the Spectacle", Guy Debord places us in a world where capitalism produces mass spectacles and where the desire created by these spectacles acts as a diversion from the political and economic realities. For Debord, the dominance of appearances is the characteristic of that capitalism and the political relations are perpetuated through the control of the representations, i.e. the view of reality mediated by images. (Debord, 1989).

action in an Anglo-Saxon urban context), epochs of history (from the Oracle of Delphi to the retro design of the furniture), state-of-the-art technology (Nokia mobile phones and landline phones from the 1950s and latest generation computers in casings that look like they are made of recycled materials), religions (from Buddhism in reincarnation to the Christian trinity and from the Greek gods to the Babylon of the Old Testament's Book of Daniel), other cultural products (such as comic books, authors such as Lewis Carroll with the icons in his "Alice in Wonderland", which includes episodes such as Alice going through the looking glass and meeting the white rabbit), but also academic output itself, as in the choice of the work of Baudrillard (1999) for creating the background for various dialogues and scenes.

One can, therefore, define "The Matrix" as a corollary of "Cyberpunk" culture itself and its discourse in relation to the role of the information and communication technologies. By featuring Baudrillard's book "Simulation and Simulacrum" so prominently and by introducing the concept of the "Desert of the Real" in the explanation Morpheus gives to Neo of the relations between the two universes (the matrix and outside the matrix), the film condenses all that Cyberpunk, as a cultural genre, understands as virtual and real and the relationship between these two dimensions.

The global acceptance of the film, which can be measured by success indexes such as the number of news stories generated in the traditional media (but also on a large scale on the Internet, both on sites and in chat rooms), the merchandising sales and the passage of significant aspects of the product into common language, translates to the socially accepted idea that a central characteristic of the new information technologies cultures is *virtual reality.*

However, given the choices made in constructing the script, if we wish to be more rigorous in our assessment of "The Matrix", the message that is transmitted is that of the association of the information technologies emerging from the *Age of the Simulacrum,* as suggested by Baudrillard when he argues that we are experiencing the end of an historic moment, the end of the Society of the Spectacle, and that we are now living in a simulational culture – hyperreality.

In the final analysis, what results from the success of the film is the association between "Virtual Reality" and "Simulacrum" and the existence of a simulational hyperreality culture as the central element of cultural characterization of the social networks and contemporary societies.

However, this association between "Virtual Reality" and "Simulacrum" is not the most correct one, for they denote different concepts, and it is also very questionable that we can regard being dominated by a simulational logic as one of the main characteristics of the "set of shared meanings that enable people to understand and communicate with one another and create identity" (Hall, 1995).

Pimentel and Teixeira propose the following definition for "Virtual Reality": generally speaking, the term Virtual Reality refers to an immersive and interactive experience that is generated by computer (Pimentel K., K. Teixeira, 1992). Immersive, but in a new dimension of involvement, following the long evolution in the sphere of art from painting in perspective to the creation of computerized three dimensional effects. Interactive because it enables modification of the surrounding environment, following a logic of placing the spectators on the stage and allowing them to be actively involved, too. The degree of interactivity depends on various factors, such as, the speed or assimilation of the input by the mediated environment, the reach, i.e. the number of possibilities available for an action in a given moment, and the mapping, i.e. the capacity of the control system to adapt the environment in a natural and predictable way.

There is a third element that characterizes "Virtual Reality", which is the control of the relationship between the sensors and the environment, i.e. to what point navigation is allowed through objects not accessible to humans in their physical form.

Even though we may sometimes use the term "virtual" to, by way of example, characterize the spaces of social interaction that take place on the Internet, if we consider the Pimentel and Teixeira definition, we cannot call those spaces virtual, given that what is taking place is written communication mediated by the computer and not the creation of a space with characteristics of immersion, mapping and control of the relationship of the sensors with the environment. [18]

"Virtual Reality", however, cannot be considered a form of communication as it does not implicate transforming ideas into language or symbols. Accordingly, we cannot speak of "Virtual Reality" culture as an element that characterizes our society, given that culture implies a set of shared

---

[18] Virtual community is the term used to designate the creation of meeting points designed to bring together, in one single Internet *space*, all those who share a specific set of interests but who, due to geographic distance or other restrictions, could not do so without the network in question.

meanings that enable people to understand and communicate with each other. Clearly, "Virtual Reality" cannot make that contribution, neither through its diffusion nor through its characteristics.

As outlined above, what distinguishes "virtual" from "simulation" is its transformational structure, if, when immersed, subjects and objects interacting give rise to new spaces and events.

In his analysis of the culture of contemporary societies, Baudrillard introduces the idea of hyperreality as fruit of the evolution of the relationship between representation, image and simulacrum. For Baudrillard, there are four successive phases of representation through the image: the image as reflection of reality (e.g., maps); the image that masks or perverts the basic reality (e.g., the Society of the Spectacle); the image that masks the lack of a basic reality (e.g., Simulation, like the Gulf War of 1991 transmitted on television); the images have no relation whatsoever with reality, so that they assume themselves as simulacra (e.g. the "Disneylandization" of experience, the construction of Euro Disney based on the model of Disneyland in the US). In his opinion, we are now experiencing the fourth phase, in which, in the extreme case, we live in a hyperreal universe, a world where the image is more powerful than the real reference, in which the substitute for reality produced by the world of electronic images is the rule. That is the context for the predominance of a simulational culture.

Obviously, we know that language, signs and images are mediations of reality; they are not transparent windows. We therefore live in a world of mediations and representations. And as Umberto Eco (1977) suggests, the universe of visual communication exists to remind us that even if we communicate via strong codes (e.g., language) and very strong codes (e.g., Morse code), most of the time we communicate using very fallible, imprecise and mutating codes. Images are, therefore, *texts* in which we can discern elements of articulation but are much more subject to imprecision than other types of communication. But it is an enormous step from this to the argument that our culture is dominated by the simulated image, without any reference to the real, as Baudrillard argues. The examples put forward by Baudrillard, such as the Gulf War and Euro Disney, are exceptions rather than the rule.

What the analysis of the *mediation* suggests is the coexistence of, on the one hand, the Global Village (McLuhan, 1997), in which the image dominates, and the re-emergence of the Gutenberg Galaxy, recreated by the Internet. For example, Ignacio Ramonet (1999) argues that thanks to the economic and technological changes, the rhetoric model is also in transformation. The visual has gained in predominance over the textual, whereby the only area in which text apparently still dominates is the Internet. Beyond this, what dominates is rhetoric based on the visual culture, a culture founded on simplicity, rapidity and emotion, in which, in the words of Ramonet, it is enough to see to be, to repeat to inform. But these characteristics are not the same as simulation.

The Internet, in turn, represents a form of vengeance of the written text against the image. Communication in the latter half of the 20th century was dominated by the image, by television. Through the concept of the "Global Village", analysts like Marshall McLuhan (1997) glorified the success of the image and the way in which, through the image, we were building a planet that was gradually becoming like a village, due to the proximity of events. If we can return to Umberto Eco (1996) once more, we could leaf through his text "From the Internet to Gutenberg", in which he depicts that the Internet will bring about the return of writing to the top of the communication pyramid. Eco argues that in the Middle Ages the images were sculpted in the cathedrals, which communicated knowledge to us. Gutenberg changed that situation with the printing press. Later, television and cinema dictated the success and omnipresence of the image in our everyday life and the Internet saw the return of writing as the central element of communication.

The image is there on the Internet, but mostly the still image, the photographic image and not the moving image.

It is obvious that, with the increase in transmission bandwidth capacity we may see the return of the moving image in a not-so-distant future.

However, that comeback will, perhaps, not take place in the same dimension as the information and entertainment organized by the traditional public and private entities that today already dominate the image (television channels, production companies, studios, communication companies). The written word will probably continue to be the basic element in the communication dimension of the Internet. Why? Firstly, because, although all people can produce and place information on the Internet, not all have the same resources at their disposal. Secondly, because the written word is a technology that induces greater privacy than the image and allows one to better manage the cultural difference and distance.

The question left unanswered by Ramonet and touched upon by Eco (1996) is that of knowing how the relationship between image and text will evolve when new media themselves seek joint technological supports and further interdependence – for example, through the use of chats and e-mail in televised talk shows – and when the television channel websites enable real-time viewing of their programmes (but that is an analysis that will be taken up in subsequent chapters).

The arguments put forward in relation to *simulation culture* can also be questioned on the basis of a more careful analysis of the profusion of television entertainment genres in which one promotes, not the perform-ance, but the *being oneself,* recreating one's *self* in front of the cameras and not simulating the *id,* even if this implies the rejection of reservation and privacy (Eco 2000a).

Perhaps more resounding in the critique of the logic of simulation, is the representation of the identity of the Internet itself, despite the fact that analysts like Sherry Turkle (1997) identify an association between the ex-istence of a simulation culture and the creation of virtual communities and, therefore, a space of knowledge of the *self* and the *other,* of simulation and approximation to the true identities that make up the social space. Empiri-cal analysis has shown that both the creation of personal websites (Cheung, 2000) and the communication mediated by the computer, via chats and e-mails essentially follow identity expression models based on personal information categories that range from the description of the individual's personality to his/her stance on personal, social, cultural and political ques-tions and to other websites considered interesting by that individual or con-sidered within the scope of his/her interests and views (Paquete de Oliveira et al., 2000). Also here, the information follows a pattern that is more in line with the expression of the multiple components of the different catego-ries of social and cultural belonging (following the emancipating logics of the medium that allow for a "more polished" and elaborate version of the *self* than a face to face meeting) and not a predominance of a simulational logic.

As stated in the introduction, Stuart Hall (1995) defines culture as a set of shared meanings that allow people to understand and communicate with each other. In his view, these meanings are not static nor do they simply constitute a collection of behaviours and values that characterize a social group. On the contrary, the cultural meaning is produced and exchanged – it is a process, a set of practices.

The meaning is produced and exchanged in much diversified ways, which include: group identity and group differences; personal and social interaction; mass media and global communications; everyday rituals and practices; narratives, stories and fantasies; rules, norms and conventions.

These different aspects of culture are intimately interlinked and interact in the construction and transmission of social meanings.

If we take Hall's proposal as a starting point, and if we accept Castells suggestion that, associated with the crystallization of a context of alteration in the production/consumption, experience and power in specific territories is the emergence of a *new system of symbolic communication*, thus giving rise to *collective cultures and identities* (Castells, 2002), then we have to ask ourselves which of the symbolic exchange dimensions identified by Hall (1995) are most impacted by the emergence of a new system of symbolic communication in the Information Age. The answer is, without doubt, the mass media and global communications.

During the last decade, along with the normal evolution of the non-mediated exchange dimensions, there were profound changes in the mass media and the global communications and in the electronically mediated exchange of symbols, sounds and images.

How, then, do we process our creation of meaning in the Information Age? The suggestion left here is that we continue to do it through the formation of group identity and group differences, personal/social interaction and everyday rituals/practices, understanding (and changing) of the rules, norms and conventions, access to the narratives, stories and fantasies, but that we do so accumulating the face-to-face interaction with a growing mediation possibility offered by the mass media and global communications and visible in the number of hours in which we interact with the different media and their presence in our daily life.

Continuing the guiding thread given in the preceding paragraph, I would suggest that the answer to the question on what kind of culture the Information Age is, is that is a *real virtuality culture*. As Castells states, "it is virtual because it is constructed mainly through virtual electronically based communication processes. It is real (and not imaginary) because it is our fundamental reality, the material basis with which we live our lives, construct our representation systems, do our work, relate with others, obtain information, form our opinions, act politically and nourish our dreams. This virtuality is our reality" (Castells 2004b). The culture of a society in which *mediation* has gained enough space that it is shoulder to shoulder, in terms of the importance we confer upon it, with communication.

Throughout this chapter, I have endeavoured to demonstrate the inadequacy of the use of the concept of information society for characterizing the social changes in course in contemporary society. I have further argued that the notion of *network society* (Castells 2002), as illustrative of a change in the organizational paradigm, would be more adequate for characterizing societies, which are not information, but clearly informational societies. In this context, the culture of the informational societies also differs from culture models of up to a few decades ago. Informational societies are culturally characterized by their taking on of real virtuality features. But if the technology is shared, just as the social organization model, the network and the cultural characteristics are also shared, this does not mean that we are dealing with one single informational society model. On the contrary, societies continue to be built on what they already are and choose to be in cultural, economic, political and social terms. Accordingly there are multiple network societies, some of which are in transition and others searching for the affirmation of different informational models. Models which also deal differently with the *mediation* spaces and the forms of autonomy that they encourage.

As Nordenstreng suggests (2001), taking the concept of the informational society as a starting point, both in historic and economic terms, in the definition of what information means in our societies (or of how they appropriate the information) constituted a particularly useful contribution, given that it allows for a contextualization for understanding the media system and the way in which we domesticate the technologies and their use in the symbolic *mediation* spaces (Silverstone, 1999; Ortoleva, 2004 and Colombo 2003). Accordingly, the first stage in understanding how *autonomy is managed and citizenship is exercised in the Information Age through the selection and articulation of different media* is necessarily an analysis of the different informational society models that we are developing in different countries and areas of our world.

2. Societies in Transition to the Network Society

Several analysts have put forward the idea that societies are currently experiencing significant change that can be characterized by two parallel trends that frame the social behaviour: individualism and communalism (Castells, 2003b).

Individualism, in this context, denotes the construction of meaning around the realization of individual projects. Communalism, in turn, can be defined as the construction of meaning around a set of values defined by a restricted collective group and internalized by the group's members.

Various observers have looked at these two trends as potential sources of disintegration of current societies, as the institutions on which they are based lose their integrating capacity, i.e. they become increasingly incapable to giving meaning to the citizens: the patriarchal family model, the civic associations, companies and, above all, representative democracy and the nation state. These institutions have been, to some extent, fundamental pillars of the relationship between society and the citizens throughout the 20th century (Castells, 2003 and 2004; Giddens, 2000).

However, another hypothesis is possible. Perhaps what we are witnessing is not the disintegration and fractioning of society, but the reconstruction of the social institutions and, indeed, of the structure of society itself, proceeding from autonomous projects carried out by society members.

This independence (i.e. independence from society's institutions and organizations) can be regarded as individual or collective, in the latter case in relation to a specific social group defined by its autonomous culture.

In this perspective, the autonomization of individuals and groups is followed by the attempt to reconstruct meaning in a new social structure on the basis their self-defined projects. By supplying the technological resources for the socialization of the projects of each individual in a network of similar subjects, the Internet, together with the mass media, becomes a powerful social reconstruction tool and not a cause of disintegration. This social (re)construction, will not have to follow the same values logic of the late industrial society, whence the new structure emerges.

However, as the Internet is a technology, its appropriation and domestication (Silverstone, 1994) may also take place in a conservative way and thus act merely to promote continuation of social life as it had already existed.

The examples are manifold. If we wish to expand our field of vision we can look at the Internet as, for example, an instrument for the maintenance of a patriarchal society rooted in a fundamentalist interpretation of Islam, when we see it being used for the recruitment of volunteers for Al-Qaeda, or as an instrument for the perpetuation of old public administration models, when the websites of the ministries offer nothing more than the telephone numbers of the various services, in what amounts to the mere substitution of the yellow pages, in hardcopy form, by hypertext in a closed institutional circuit. Or when we limit ourselves to constructing a personal page in which we centre content around our own personality and identity without any connection to any entities to which we belong or are affiliated, thus rejecting the logic of sharing in a network of interests.

In other words, the hypothesis for the analysis of social development and the role of the Internet in that development is that the Internet is a tool for the construction of projects. However, if it is merely used as one more means of doing something we already do, then its use is limited and is not necessarily different from that of the other media (for example, television, as far as entertainment and news information are concerned).

As one can verify by means of the study of the reality of two societies in transition – Catalonia and Portugal (Castells et al, 2003 and Cardoso et al, 2005) – the Internet is appropriated in different ways by different people and not all of them effect uses that distinguish the Internet from what the other media could offer. This is a reality that is, perhaps, more perceptible in societies where the Internet utilization levels are still quite low. However, different studies conducted in different societies (Cole, 2005) demonstrate that that is a reality that is not directly linked with the character of transition or affirmation as an informational society, but with variables such as the education and generation dimensions.

Nevertheless, there is something in societies in transition that accentuates the differences more. In other words, in societies in transition, the divisions between those who use and those who do not use technologies such as the Internet are greater and tend to make utilization of them more a question of the generation to which one belongs: the younger the generation the greater the use and the higher the education level the greater the use.

If it is a recognized fact that societies such as the United States, Finland and Singapore can be classified as "informational societies" (Himanen and Castells, 2001a), how can we define those societies in transition towards an informational society? In other words, societies in which the mark of networked social organization already asserts itself in broad segments of society?

In order to answer that question, we require a more in-depth analysis of a society whose characteristics, though profoundly European, also reveal similarities in terms of relations and values to countries of the American continent: Portugal.

The argument for the choice of Portugal as a typical example of a society in transition towards the network society is that Portugal is a country that shares, to varying degrees, development characteristics and historic-political values and conditioning factors with a group of other societies, for which the common denominator is the fact that they all experienced, in the last three decades, the democratization of their societies and, at the same time, have similar informational development rankings.

All of these societies are classified by different digitalization indexes (ITU 2003) in one and the same group: the high digital access countries. In the concrete case of the DAI (ITU 2003), the group is led by Spain, with Brazil bringing up the rear. It includes, amongst others, the countries we have chosen to study herein, i.e. those that were protagonists of waves of democratization in the last 30 years (Huntington, 1991 and Altman, 2002) in Europe and South America[19]: Spain, the Czech Republic, Greece, Portugal, Hungary, Poland, Slovakia, Chile, Uruguay, Argentina and Brazil.

---

[19] Huntington suggests that, during the 1970s and 1980s, there were transitions from non-democratic political systems to democratic systems and that those changes can be seen in the context of a greater

However, because it is necessary to compare this group of countries with a group of more informationally developed countries, we have also chosen to conduct a comparative analysis herein of Finland, the US and Singapore. Finally, we will also analyze the case of Italy in this transition context, for, although it is a member of the G7, Italy has a proto-information model (Castells, 2002) that is closer, on various levels, to a society in transition than a full informational society.

We will look at Portugal as a paradigmatic example of transition in progress, but at the same time we will seek to identify the characteristics that make societies that differ so much as Spain, Greece, the Czech Republic, Slovakia, Hungary and Poland, and also Argentina, Chile, Uruguay and Brazil, *societies in transition towards the network society.*

Societies in Transition in the Global Network

An analysis of the different informational society models can have as its starting point the individualization of four dimensions *(technology, economy, social well-being and values)*, through which one can better understand what each society's position is in relation to the global informational society panorama (Castells and Himanen, 2002). On this basis one can consider that *a society is an informational society if it possesses a solid information technology: infrastructure, production and knowledge* (Himanen and Castells, 2001a).

Finland, the United States and Singapore are advanced informational societies. They are also dynamic economies because they are internation-

---

trend towards transition to democracy. Without going into the various premises put forward by Huntington in more detail, I think that his contribution is of interest for the analysis of the societies in transition to the network society due to the fact that he establishes a link between different geographic zones and societies at the values level. In other words, all the societies studied herein have shared one common value in the last three decades – the search for democracy – and seek today integration in the global economy as informational societies, with most of the indicators placing them in a transition zone.

Almost all of the countries analysed here as being in transition to the network society are referred to by Huntington as common examples of transition to democracy. Huntington defines three types of transition, which include all the countries analysed here: 1) transformation (for example, Spain, Hungary and Brazil), where elites in power took on the leadership of the transition processes; 2) substitution (as in Portugal and Argentina), where opposition groups led the democratization process; 3) transplacements (as in Poland and Czechoslovakia), where democratization occurred from joint action by government and opposition groups.

ally competitive, have productive companies and are innovative. But because "(...) technology and the economy are merely a part of the story" (Himanen and Castells, 2001a: 31), one can say that a society is *open* if it is so politically, i.e., at the civil society level, and if it is receptive to global processes. Likewise, its social well-being can be assessed in terms of its income structure and the coverage offered to the citizens in terms of health and education.

When looked at in terms of the evolution of development models, Portugal is a country that is going through a transition process from the industrial society to the informational society. However, we are speaking of an industrial society, which, similar to the Italian and Spanish societies, is to a large extent made up of small and medium-sized enterprises and has never asserted itself as a large-scale industrial producer (Castells, 1996). In the second half of the 20th century, Portugal assumed what can be termed proto-industrialism and is now seeking to achieve proto-informationalism (Castells, 1996). As an example of a society in transition, the analysis of Portugal reveals that it is a country which, through its multiple affiliation networks (which range from membership of the European Union to the maintenance of good relations in terms of defence with the US and to the establishment of partnership networks with Brazil, the former African and Asian colonies and the autonomous regions of neighbouring Spain), seeks to adapt to the conditions of global economic change. And that is a pattern common to all societies in transition.

Nowadays, one can frequently read, in documents produced within the European Union institutions or within the framework of the OECD or even UNO, that the equation for the economic and social development of countries, cities and zones in the *Information Age* is the appropriation of the use of the technological tools and their introduction into the production and personal relational circuits, requiring for this that the whole of the country, city or zone in question realize their effective insertion both into the entrepreneurial fabric and at the State level (in the management of the republic/ kingdom, in education, in management and defence of the territory, etc.).

In the latter half of the 1990s, investment in information technologies as a source of GDP creation in countries such as the US, United Kingdom and Canada equalled in percentage terms the isolated contribution made by labour or the investment in capital not coming from the information technologies (Jorgenson, 2005). The trend towards the convergence of the investment contribution in information technologies with the contribution from other investments in capital or the labour contribution would seem to be a general one for all the more developed countries, albeit in varying degrees. Likewise, there is a trend in all countries towards an increase in the value added provided by the information technologies in the creation of value added in the services sector (OECD, 2004).

To clarify this a little, one should add that, contrary to general perceptions, the productive fabric in the information age does not consist merely of the technology companies (the so-called "dotcom" companies) but also that of companies that are able to incorporate the information technologies in their productive, organizational, distribution and promotion processes.

Hence, the new economy is not only the likes of *amazon.com, e-bay* or the telecommunications companies, although these are indeed part of that economy, but also companies like INDITEX (a Spanish group that owns ZARA and other clothing brands) that have been able to use the Internet to achieve their economic objectives (Castells, 2004b).

Indeed, the new economy includes many more companies from traditional sectors than purely technological companies or those with a direct vocation for *online* business. It is normal for the productive fabric today, as has always been the case down through the centuries, to be led by one driving force sector, as well as others that will make use of that dynamism to innovate.

In order to triumph in this game, any country or geographic zone also requires a workforce with the capacity to use the new technology to innovate, be it in the private sector or in the State. Workforces that carry out repetitive – or not creative – work but with the use of the technologies, a telecommunications structure, an innovative entrepreneurial fabric, a State that is able to create the appropriate vocational training conditions, conversion of organizational and management models and establishes legislation on regulation, frameworks and incentives.

The data contained in the following tables compare Portugal and the other countries in transition to three informational society models. These models that can be given the names of *Silicon Valley,* an open society model guided by the market; Singapore, the authoritarian information regime model; and, finally, the Finnish model of an information-welfare society (Himanen and Castells, 2001a).

If classification of a society as an informational society is based on a solid information technology at the infrastructure, production and knowledge levels, what position do these countries have in terms of these dimensions?

Most of the countries classified here in terms of the technological development index in 2001 (UNDP, 2001) were in what we can call the second division of countries – the so-called potential leaders – whereby this second division is led by Spain (19th place) and Italy (20th). Brazil closed the list of countries in transition to the network society in analysis here.

However, Brazil is worthy of special attention, for, as the IMD (2004) refers, if we consider the competitiveness dimension for the whole of Brazil, the country occupies 53rd place. If we consider only the state of Sao Paulo, where a number of high-potential technological centres are centred around the University of Campinas and the contribution to the GDP in 1998 amounted to roughly to one third of the Brazilian total, then the position of Sao Paulo at the global level places it in 47th place. However, this is by no means a peculiarity of Brazil, as, as far as societies in transition are concerned, there would seem to be geographic differences in terms of integration in the global economy.

Table 2.1 – Technological Achievement Index (2001)

Country	TAI Position	Group
Spain	19	Potential Leaders
Italy	20	Potential Leaders
Czech Republic	21	Potential Leaders
Hungary	22	Potential Leaders
Slovakia	25	Potential Leaders
Greece	26	Potential Leaders
Portugal	27	Potential Leaders
Poland	29	Potential Leaders
Argentina	34	Potential Leaders
Chile	37	Potential Leaders
Uruguay	38	Dynamic Adopters
Brazil	43	Dynamic Adopters

Source: UNDP, 2001.

The selective inclusion to which Castells (2003) refers when analyzing the space of flows is a perceptible reality in the case of the relation established between Catalonia and Spain or Lombardy and Italy (IMD 2004) or between the Greater Buenos Aires area and Argentina (Amadeo 2005).

The more populous countries apparently seem to be incapable of effecting, or prefer not to effect, this transition to informational and network societies for the whole of their territory and population, at least in this phase of history.

The similarity between the countries listed above is confirmed by other international indices such as that of the ITU (International Telecommunications Union), the DAI (2003). Namely, because the DAI (Digital Access Index) establishes identification categories, such as: infrastructure (relating to telephone lines, mobile phone and Internet subscriptions), cost (Internet access and use prices in comparison to the national income); knowledge (literacy and inclusion in the education system); quality (international bandwidth and broadband subscribers) and use of the Internet.

If we compare these categories in the leading countries (such as Finland, US and Singapore) and the societies defined as *transition societies*, we see that it is not only the low levels of technology use in the latter that makes the difference. Indeed, in recent years we have come to understand that studies carried out by those involved in the technological processes themselves, such as the telecommunications operators, are beginning to accept that the communication infrastructure is not the only element that can explain the differences between countries and that income and education also play a very important role (ITU, 2003). Only if we look at society in an integrated manner – taking into account the infrastructure, production and knowledge (Himanen and Castells, 2001a) – can we identify the transition processes in progress in contemporary societies.

The analysis of international comparisons in the technological domain reveals an apparently converging reality amongst the different societies analyzed here. They all present figures for machines connected to the Internet that are approximately one quarter of the average for the advanced economies and also one third of the high technology exports achieved by the advanced economies (with the exception of Poland, Uruguay and Argentina), presenting, finally, Internet using values of more than two-thirds of the average for the advanced economies (with the exception of Argentina and Brazil).

In general terms, the countries analyzed here always present better results and more balanced values in the technological "knowledge" dimension than in the "infrastructure" and "technology production" dimensions. However, the irregularity of the performance in these two latter categories would seem, in itself, to be a distinguishing mark of these societies and the fruit of the fact that, in the transition process, they have not yet been able to stabilize good results in all categories.

Examples of this irregularity in terms of results are the percentage values for Brazil (19) and Hungary (25) in relation to the average high technology export figures for the G7 (21) or the number of mobile phone contracts in Portugal, Spain, Italy, Greece and the Czech Republic, which are all above the G7 average, and also the growth rates for secure servers in Portugal, the Czech Republic, Slovakia, Hungary, Poland, Greece, Chile and Argentina, whose figures are close to, or above, those of the three information economies analyzed here (Finland, US and Singapore). However, we also have to take into account some peculiarities of the societies in transition, without which it would be difficult to explain some of their performances. By way of example, let us look at the question of secure server penetration. The fact that Portugal and Spain have higher ATMs per million inhabitants rates (CEB, 2003), with 1,047 and 1,230 machines compared to an EU average of 700, has allowed for the development of alternative systems to the use of credit cards and secure servers for online purchases. The fact that Portugal has a debit card system common to the whole banking system, the so-called "Multibanco" system, has made it possible to make online orders with payment through the ATM network, thus creating an alternative and more secure electronic channel for transactions. This is one example of many that help us to understand that, in addition to the common and individual traits, there are sometimes situations common to two or more countries that allow for the identification of some characteristic sub-groups in the context of the transition analyzed here.

Table 2.2 – International comparisons in the field of technology

	Finland	US	Singapore	Portugal	Spain	Italy	Czech Rep.	Advanced economies
Infrastructure								
Machines connected to the Internet (per 10,000 inh.) 1	1707.25(3)	3714.01(1)	478.18	239.28	133.24	117.28	209.78	819.15
Mobile phone contracts (per 1,000 inh.) 2	867	488	796	825	824	939	849	740
Production								
High technology exports as a percentage of the total exports 2	24	32	60	7	7	9	14	21
Electronic commerce secure servers per 100,000 inhabitants) 3	14.9	33.28 (1)	17.31	2.34	3.2	2.2	3.8	16.3
Growth rate for secure servers, 1998-2001 (%)	656	397	527	600	358	460	796	555
Ratio between hosts and secure servers (2001)	1144	1139	357	1054	423	527	541	692
Knowledge								
Internet users (%) (2001) 4	75.95	71.1	40.8	37.79	35.45	53.21	46.51	53
Ratio of participation of the highereducation student population in sciences (%) *	37	13,9	24,2	31	31	28	34	25,0
Scientist and engineers in R&D (per thousand persons) 2	7110	4099	4052	1754	1948	1128	1466	2778
PISA Test – mathematical literacy	544 (2)	483 (25)	-	466 (29)	485 (25)	466 (29)	516 (12)	504
PISA Test – scientific literacy	548 (1)	491 (20)	-	468 (31)	487 (22)	486 (22)	523 (5)	510

Source: 1 Values for all countries taken from World Indicators, ITU, http://www.itu.int/itunews/issue/2002/04/table4.html; 2 Values for all countries take from the UNDP Human Development Report 2004; 3 Values obtained by Netcraft in December 2001: http://www.atkearney.com/shared_res/pdf/Secure_servers_2002_S.pdf 3 Host values taken from World Indicators, ITU http://www.itu.int/itunews/issue/2002/04/table4.html ; 4 ESS Data 2003, WIP 2004 and http://www.internetworld-stats.com/stats2.htm ; 5 Adapted from Castells and Himanen, 2002, except for data for Portugal, taken from the UNDP Human Development Report

* UNESCO definition for the indicator in question: "gross enrolment in tertiary education – total enrolment in tertiary education regardless of age, expressed as a percentage of the population in the five-year age group following the secondary-school leaving age".

Table 2.2.a – International comparisons in the field of technology

	Slovakia	Hungary	Greece	Poland	Chile	Argentina	Uruguay	Brazil	Advanced economies
Infrastructure									
Machines connected to the Internet (per 10,000 inh.) 1	134.29	168.04	135.18	126.82	79.20	124.14	210.93	95.31	819,15
Mobile phone contracts (per 1,000 inh.) 2	544	676	845	363	428	178	193	201	740
Production									
High technology exports as a percentage of the total exports 2	3	25	10	3	3	7	3	19	21
Electronic commerce (secure servers per 100,000 inhabitants) 3	1,9	1,8	1,7	1,7	1,2	0,8	-	0,9	16,3
Growth rate for secure servers, 1998-2001 (%)	1040	936	765	1830	678	1000	-	429	555
Ratio between hosts and secure servers (2001)	697	941	813	743	645	1604	-	1303	692
Knowledge									
Internet users (%) (2001) 4	-	46,21	25,87	38,68	34,8	14,9	34,5	9,9	53
Ratio of participation of the higher education student population in sciences (%) *	43	32	-	-	43	30	24	23	25,0
Scientist and engineers in R&D (per thousand persons) 2	1774	1440	-	1473	419	684	276	323	2778
PISA Test – mathematical literacy	498 (19)	490 (22)	445 (32)	490 (22)	-	-	422 (34)	356 (38)	504
PISA Test – scientific literacy	495 (18)	503 (14)	481 (25)	498 (17)	-	-	438 (33)	390 (38)	510

Source: 1 Values for all countries taken from World Indicators, ITU, http://www.itu.int/itunews/issue/2002/04/table4.html; 2 Values for all countries take from the UNDP Human Development Report 2004; 3 Values obtained by Netcraft in December 2001: http://www.atkearney.com/shared_res/pdf/Secure_servers_2002_S.pdf 3 Host values taken from World Indicators, ITU http://www.itu.int/itunews/issue/2002/04/table4.html ; 4 ESS Data 2003, WIP 2004 and http://www.internetworld-stats.com/stats2.htm ; 5 Adapted from Castells and Himanen, 2002, except for data for Portugal, taken from the UNDP Human Development Report.

* UNESCO definition for the indicator in question: "gross enrolment in tertiary education – total enrolment in tertiary education regardless of age, expressed as a percentage of the population in the five-year age group following the secondary-school leaving age".

It is also in the knowledge dimension, in this case not merely technological knowledge, that the generational mark that seems to be common
to all these societies manifests itself most. The question of education is
fundamental for analyzing the transition to the network society with an
informational economic organization because, as we shall see, there is a
strong correlation in all the societies between the educational competences
given and the number of users of the basic network society technology: the
Internet.

The Internet use figures constitute once reference value for characterizing
the transition of a society to the network society because they reflect both
the dimension of use in the socialization context and the market potential.
Indeed, without a high number of users, there would also be no incentive
for increasing electronic commerce (be it at the inter-company level or with
private use).

Table 2.3 – Use of the Internet per country according to user's highest education level (%)

Country	Not completed primary education*	Primary or first stage of basic*	Lower secondary or second stage of basic*	Upper secondary*	Post secondary, non-tertiary*	First stage of tertiary*	Second stage of tertiary*
Portugal	21.10	18.86	37.24	48.87	-	48.61	50.00
Austria	16.66	-	33.88	51.45	77.09	-	76.62
Belgium	7.69	10.61	29.94	45.22	61.53	-	77.39
Switzerland	35.29	-	39.78	52.88	73.91	82.89	90.47
Czech Rep.	30.00	-	14.28	23.74	47.61	62.50	60.00
Germany	-	-	-	-	-	-	100
Denmark	-	20	46.07	61.08	73.46	84.50	100
Spain	0.91	1.69	16.63	31.68	44.64	61.79	68.42
Finland	25	15.18	55.55	63.94	-	79.20	100
France	6.08	8.93	25.10	24.16	49.57	67.06	77.04
R.U.	-	-	26.34	66.60	57.21	74.71	91.83
Greece	0.90	0.431	6.04	14.12	31.81	47.00	60
Hungary	1.51	16.58	6.63	23.49	-	40	58.69
Ireland	-	9.09	28.94	46.47	65.38	77.77	75.00
Israel	-	5.40	24.59	30.61	37.25	64.07	67.44
Italy	-	0.88	21.83	50.35	55.40	59.27	85.96
Luxembourg	-	20.00	50.00	61.53	-	100	100.00
Netherlands	-	21.875	38.57	66.02	71.79	79.40	80.00
Norway	-	-	25.49	60.75	77.77	80.51	90.00
Poland	-	3.70	5.63	12.40	18.79	42.95	43.64
Sweden	88.88	37.43	57.44	83.33	-	83.01	89.74
Slovenia	-	-	19.51	15	53.84	55.55	85.71

Source: European Social Survey 2002/2003. *Note: given the different names for education levels in the European context we opted to use the original ESS terms.

An analysis of the preceding table shows that the relation between access and use is dependant on a fundamental conditioning factor, the education level. Age is also a mobilizing factor, as it facilitates use via the group affiliation and practices amongst populations attending school (Table 3.5). However, different studies show that the stronger direct relationship is established between the education level and effective use of the Internet.

As far as the comparative analysis of the countries is concerned, the figures show that in the informational societies use of the Internet by persons who have completed secondary education is between 60% and 90% of the users with higher education, while in the societies in transition, these values are less than 50%. The exception here is Portugal, with values of around 90%, as the number of Portuguese citizens who have completed secondary education is relatively low and, consequently, is closer in percentage terms to the numbers who have concluded higher education.

Although the analysis has thus far practically made reference to European countries only, a more geographically comprehensive study, such as that proposed by the World Internet Project (2005), establishes the same relationship between Internet use and education.

Table 2.4 – Internet use rates in the population with secondary and higher education (%)

	Secondary	*University*
United Kingdom	64.4	88.1
Portugal	64.8	75.1
Germany	66.0	62.6
Hungary	14.6	45.5
Italy	53.5	77.3
Japan	45.7	70.1
Korea	44.9	77.7
Macao	49.5	76.7
Singapore	66.3	92.2
Spain	47.6	80.5
Sweden	76.4	83.8
Taiwan	18.2	54.9
US	61.0	87.1

Source: CIES, *Network Society in Portugal* Survey, 2003 for Portugal; for all other countries the WIP (World Internet Project).

In characterizing societies in transition, the similarities are crossed with the exceptions and the question of Internet access offers a new example for the affirmation of singularities. Although it is possible to establish similarities between the access rates in some of the countries studied here (Portugal, Poland, Spain), we also immediately find differences as to the effective use of that access. Indeed, if we establish a ratio between access and use, we see that Portugal is one of the countries that makes most use of the existing availability, putting it on a par with leading countries such as Norway, the Netherlands and Finland and ahead of other societies in transition such as the Czech Republic, which has high access figures but very low effective use by its populations.

What this use of the existing access availability ratio measures is the effective use of the technology, demonstrating that there must be other factors endogenous to each society that could explain why there are differences in the use of a technology even when the access is equally high to begin with.

Analysis of the values for Portugal and the other European countries shows that, in certain conditions, even when the access rate increases, that increase is not necessarily directly reflected in an increase in use, for there are dynamics peculiar to each country at play that can explain the different socialization rates for the technology.

Table 2.5 – Internet access/use of access ratio

Country	Has Internet access at home or at work* %	Uses the Internet** %	Access availability usage ratio
Portugal	37.79	29.72	0.79(4)
Austria	67.22	54.37	0.81(3)
Belgium	67.14	43.70	0.65
Switzerland	72.89	57.85 (3)	0.79(4)
Czech Republic	46.51	27.56	0.59
Germany	-	-	-
Denmark	76.61 (3)	62.39(2)	0.81(3)
Spain	35.45	22.20	0.63
Finland	75.95 (4)	56.19	0.74
France	50.00	37.28	0.75
United Kingdom	57.55	45.21	0.79 (4)
Greece	25.87	13.40	0.52
Hungary	46.21	19.63	0.42
Ireland	66.12	40.39	0.61
Israel	54.25	39.22	0.72
Italy	53.21	30.51	0.57
Luxembourg	68.57	51.43	0.75
Netherlands	73.05	55.88	0.76
Norway	75.29 (5)	62.07(4)	0.82(2)
Poland	38.68	23.88	0.62
Sweden	77.96 (2)	66.94(1)	0.86 (1)
Slovenia	78.92 (1)	36.14	0.46

Source: European Social Survey 2002/2003. *Note: the figures refer to the aggregated sum of all those who responded that they at least have access regardless of the degree of utilization. **Note: the figures refer to the aggregated sum of those who make effective personal use of the Internet (whereby personal use is defined as: private or recreational use that has nothing to do with the professional occupation of the user).

If the relationship between Internet use and education seems to be transversal to all countries, there is also a characteristic in the education dimension that seems to be common to almost all countries analyzed her: all of them, with the exception of the Czech Republic, reveal strong generational differences in terms of the completion of secondary education and tertiary education. The countries under analysis can be grouped into three distinct groups. The first group includes most of the countries: all those which present growth rates for completion of the education level ranging from 300% to 50% between the generations. This first group is also heterogeneous, for though countries such as Greece and Hungary present values in the younger generations that place them above 70% completion of secondary education, Portugal, Brazil and Uruguay are below 40%. Also in this group, in an intermediate position, are Spain, Poland, Argentina and Chile, which all have values close to 60% of the population with secondary education completed in the younger generations. This first group (with the exception of Greece) is also characterized by figures for the completion of higher education that are clearly below the average for the G7 countries.

Table 2.6 – Percentage of citizens per age group that have completed secondary and tertiary education in selected countries

	Finland	US	Portugal	Spain	Italy	Czech Rep.	Slovakia	Hungary	Greece	Poland	Chile	Argentina	Uruguay	Brazil	Advanced Economies
Secondary >55 years	52	84	8	18	24	80	68	48	28	37	28	28	23	15	60
Secondary 25-34	88	87	35	58	60	88	93	82	72	53	61	52	38	32	80
Growth rate	69.23%	3.57%	337.50%	222.22%	150.00%	10.00%	36.76%	70.83%	157.14%	43.24%	117.86%	85.71%	65,22%	113,33%	
Tertiary >55	23.4	33.2	4.6	10.5	6.7	10.6	8.6	12.6	10.2	10.5	6	9	7	6	18
Tertiary	39	39	15	37	12	12	12	15	24	16	12	15	9	14	27
Growth rate	66.67%	17.47%	226.09%	252.38%	79.10%	13.21%	39.53%	19.05%	135.29%	52.38%	100.00%	66.67%	28.57%	133.33%	

Sources: Secondary education figures: Education Outlook OECD 2004; tertiary education figures: Education Outlook OECD 2003

A second group of countries, made up of the Czech Republic and Slovakia, seems to be in a better position, presenting diminutive generational differences in terms of education, given that even in the older generations completion of secondary education was close to or above 70%.

Finally, we have a third group made up by Italy alone, a country characterized by high growth rates for the completion of secondary education in the younger generations and values very close to those of Finland as far as investment in tertiary education by the younger generations is concerned. Italy presents itself, once more, as a dual society: simultaneously an informational society and one in transition.

The generation analysis focusing on the question of education can also be observed when we look at the relationship between age and use of the Internet.

Table 2.7 – Use of the Internet by age interval per country (%)

Country	15-24	25-34	35-54	over 55
Austria	81.81	75.28	65.73	21.02
Belgium	75.60	63.35	48.18	12.69
Switzerland	88.00	76.82	71.48	29.14
Czech Republic	73.07	39.82	38.46	10.31
Denmark	91.66	81.33	72.95	33.33
Spain	50.15	35.98	28.81	3.78
Finland	91.93	82.53	63.94	22.29
France	62.67	53.90	45.00	13.28
UK	73.34	62.05	59.49	20.01
Greece	32.60	25.71	15.73	1.95
Hungary	63.55	27.55	15.24	4.15
Ireland	62.79	56.60	46.78	16.34
Israel	55.68	52.631	37.93	18.69
Italy	48.87	52.83	33.28	8.67
Luxembourg	85.71	80.00	54.54	18.18
Netherlands	87.09	76.26	67.30	29.97
Norway	85.71	80.00	74.28	30.70
Poland	53.32	34.25	18.81	3.43
Sweden	66.30	65.45	50.97	21.21
Slovenia	67.85	53.57	38.33	7.54
Average	68.91	57.56	46.56	16.61

Source: European Social Survey 2002/2003.

Another characteristic common to the societies in transition, in this case with bearing on our analysis of European societies, is the fact that there is a considerable difference between the use rates for the older and younger generations.

For all societies in transition for which there are comparative data (Portugal, Spain, Czech Republic, Greece, Hungary and Poland), one can verify that the older citizens using the Internet correspond to only 10% of the younger users. In the case of the other European informational societies, the figures are almost always somewhat above 20%.

Table 2.8 – International comparison of Internet use per age group (%)

	United Kingdom	Portugal	Germany	Hungary	Italy	Japan	Korea	Spain	US
16 to 24 yrs	80.1	58.8	59.6	45.1	66.4	80.6	95.1	70.2	90.8
35 to 44 yrs	72.8	30.4	55.6	13.7	37.4	63.0	49.5	31.7	74.5
55 to 64 yrs	38.7	5.4	31.6	4.3	9.0	22.2	11.5	11.7	67.3

Source: CIES, *Network Society in Portugal* Survey, 2003 for Portugal; for all other countries: WIP (World Internet Project)

The age dimension also can be used for comparison not only at the European level, for the European societies and the American and Asian societies all offer the possibility of comparative inter-generational analyzes. Italy figures as a country in an intermediate position between information societies such as Germany, the United Kingdom, Japan and the US and other societies in transition such as Portugal, Spain and Hungary.

The explanation for these differences between the generations in using the Internet seems, for the societies in transition, to lie mostly in the difference in the possession of basic forms of literacy, whereas in the more developed informational societies the differences probably have more to do with the availability of contents that adapt to the interests of all generations and, furthermore, the dimension of the sociability networks that the technology can offer to more senior citizens.

All the factors analyzed so far in the infrastructure, production and knowledge dimensions and also those relating to acquired skills, employment structure and predominance of low and medium technology areas in the economy, are also reflected in the economies' compared productivity levels and their GDP *per capita.*

On a competitiveness index of 0-100, where the average for the advanced economies is 74 points, the societies in transition under analysis here occupy very varied positions. Chile (26th), Spain (31st), Portugal (39th) and Slovakia (40th) are amongst the top forty countries or regions, while the remaining countries occupy positions between 42nd (Hungary) and 59th (Argentina).

Whereas the Portuguese GDP *per capita* represents 67% of the average for the advanced economies, placing it amongst the top thirty countries in an international comparison (together with Spain, Italy and Greece), the other countries (with the exception of the Czech Republic, Slovakia and Hungary) present values below 30% of the GDP *per capita* of the G7 economies.

Table 2.9 – International comparison of informational development indicators

	Finland	US	Singapore	Chile	Spain	Portugal	Slovakia	Hungary	Advanced Economies
Competitiveness (scale 0-100) 1	83 (8)	100 (1)	89 (2)	69 (26)	67 (31)	58 (39)	57 (40)	57 (42)	74
GDP per capita (US $) 2	26,190	35,750	24,040	9,820	21,460	18,280	12,840	13,400	27009
Stock market capitalization growth, 1996-2000 (%) 3	894	429	n.d.	70.7	70.4	35.1	7.9	20.2	71.44
Investment in R&D as a % of GDP (2001) 4	3.4(2)	2.8	2.1	0.5	1.0	0.8	0.6	0.9	2.0
Investment in knowledge as a % of GDP (2000)5	6.2	6.8	-	-	2.5	2.2	2.4	3.1	4.7
Revenue derived from intellectual property and licences (US $. per 1,000 inh.) 4	107.5 (5)	151.7 (4)	-	0.4	9.0	3.1	-	35.3	26

Source: 1 Figures obtained directly from the source cited in Castells and Himanen (2002), i.e. the IMD (2004); 2 Values for all countries taken from the UNDP Human Development Report 2004; 3 Adapted from Castells and Himanen 2002, except the data for Portugal, which were supplied by the Portuguese Securities Exchange Commission (CMVM) – http://www.cmvm.pt/consulta_de_dados_e_registos/indicadores/indicadores.asp – whereby the figures for Portugal refer to 1997-2000 (Shares – BVL 30); 4 Adapted from Castells and Himanen (2002) for Finland, US and Singapore; remaining data taken from the World Development Indicators Report of the World Bank 2002 (capitalization 1990-2000); [5] Investment in knowledge is defined as the sum of expenditure on R&D, higher education and software (OECD Factbook 2005). Note: (*) relative position.

Table 2.9.a – International comparison of informational development indicators

	Czech Rep.	Greece	Italy	Brazil	Poland	Argentina	Uruguay	Advanced Economies
Competitiveness (scale 0-100) 1	56 (43)	56 (44)	50 (51)	48 (53)	41 (57)	36 (59)	-	74
GDP per capita (US $) 2	15,780	18,720	20,528	7,770	10,560	10,880	7,830	27009
Stock market capitalization growth, 1996-2000 (%) 3	21.6	51.7	40.2	26.9	15.0	100.9	0.8	71.44
Investment in R&D as a % of GDP (2001) 4	1.3	0.7	1.1	1.1	0.7	0.4	0.2	2.0
Investment in knowledge as a % of GDP (2000)5	3.7	1.6	2.3	-	1.9	-	-	4.7
Revenue derived from intellectual property and licences (US $, per 1,000 inh.) 4	4.4	1.1	9.4	0.6	0.7	0.5	0.2	26

Source: 1 Figures obtained directly from the source cited in Castells and Himanen (2002), i.e. the IMD (2004); 2 Values for all countries taken from the UNDP Human Development Report 2004; 3 Adapted from Castells and Himanen 2002, except the data for Portugal, which were supplied by the Portuguese Securities Exchange Commission (CMVM) – http://www.cmvm.pt/consulta_de_dados_e_registos/indicadores/indicadores.asp – whereby the figures for Portugal refer to 1997-2000 (Shares – BVL 30); 4 Adapted from Castells and Himanen (2002) for Finland, US and Singapore; remaining data taken from the World Development Indicators Report of the World Bank 2002 (capitalization 1990-2000); 5 Investment in knowledge is defined as the sum of expenditure on R&D, higher education and software (OECD Factbook 2005). Note: (*) relative position.

A comparison of the societies in transition in terms of the informational development indicators reveals more differences than common traits. Nevertheless, as far as investment in R&D and knowledge are concerned, it is possible to present two different transition stages.

Thus, Italy, Brazil[20], Spain, Portugal, the Czech Republic, Hungary and Slovakia are representative of a stage in which the countries invest approximately 50% of the values of the advanced economies in R&D and knowledge. A second group of countries – led by Greece, Poland, Chile, Argentina and Uruguay – presents values below 0.7% of the GDP.

Table 2.10 – Position of the information economies under analysis

	Connectivity	Business environment	Consumer and business adoption	Legal and policy	Social and cultural environment	Supporting e-services	Overall score
Category weight	0.25	0.20	0.20	0.15	0.15	0.05	-
Finland	6.06	8.51	8.45	9.05	9.00	9.25	8.08 (5)
US	6.25	8.50	8.22	8.45	9.30	9.40	8.04 (6)
Singapore	6.70	8.44	8.14	8.31	9.00	8.75	8.02 (7)
Spain	5.18	7.96	7.49	8.58	7.50	8.00	7.20 (21)
Italy	5.40	7.29	6.80	8.49	8.00	8.25	7.05 (23)
Portugal	4.98	7.49	7.65	8.52	7.25	7.50	7.01 (24)
Greece	4.49	6.77	6.91	8.19	6.75	7.50	6.47 (27)
Czech Rep.	4.74	7.37	6.81	6.73	7.25	7.00	6.47 (27)
Chile	3.82	8.00	6.26	7.69	6.88	7.13	6.35 (29)
Hungary	4.08	7.18	6.49	6.87	7.25	7.00	6.22 (30)
Brazil	3.21	6.36	6.95	6.05	5.88	6.13	5.56 (35)
Poland	3.01	7.10	5.32	5.88	6.50	6.25	5.41 (36)
Argentina	3.32	5.91	5.95	5.54	6.88	6.38	5.38 (37)

Source: *The Economist* e-readiness report, 2004. Note: The countries leading the ranking are Denmark, United Kingdom, Norway and Sweden.[21]

---

[20] For Brazil, the analysis refers only to the R&D value.

[21] *Connectivity and information technologies*: measures the use of the basic telephone network, the mobile network, the Internet and the use of computers, as well as the cost, quality and reliability of services. *Business environment:* evaluate the general business climate in a country, including the strength of the economy, political stability, the regulatory environment, taxation, competition policy, the labour market, the quality of infrastructure and openness to trade and investment. *Consumer and business adoption:* assesses how prevalent e-business practices are in each country, i.e. how the Internet is used to automate traditional business processes and how companies are helped by the development of logistics and online payment systems and the availability of finance and state investment in information technologies. *Legal and policy environment:* assesses a country's legal

Still in the context of the international comparison of development we can also analyze the economies in transition according to two other classification levels: the readiness of economies for an informational development model and their growth and competitiveness rates.

In terms of the incorporation of technology into the society and economy, *The Economist's* e-readiness report for 2004 proposes an index that measures the readiness and receptiveness of economies for an informational development model, basing its ranking on six dimensions: connectivity and information technologies, business environment, business and consumer adoption, legal and policy environment, social and cultural environment and supporting e-services.

For example, Portugal achieves good results in the "business environment", "business and consumer adoption" and "legal and policy environment" dimensions, on the basis of which one can conclude that, in terms of business infrastructure and state actions, the conditions are given for the national economy developing in that informational context.

However, the informational model does not consist of these conditions alone. It needs technological infrastructure conditions, specialized support services, sufficient user numbers and also a technically qualified workforce.

The countries and regions that lead the first half of the e-readiness ranking, namely Scandinavia, the UK, the US and the Netherlands, achieve good results in all of the fields analyzed. The societies in transition essentially show bad performances in terms of the use of the basic telephone network, the mobile network, the Internet and the use of computers, as well as the cost, quality and reliability of service. [22] These data are corroborated

---

framework and the specific laws governing Internet use – how easy is it to register new businesses, how strong is protection of private property, and whether the governments support the creation of an Internet-conducive legal environment or are more concerned with censoring content and controlling access. *Social and cultural environment:* evaluates the literacy and basic education, which are preconditions for being able to use the new technologies, experience using the Internet and receptivity to it and the technical skills of the workforce. Finally, the existence of *supporting e-services:* the existence of consulting and IT services, the existence of back-office solutions and consistent industry-wide standards for platforms and programming languages.

[22] *Connectivity and information technologies*: measures the use of the basic telephone network, the mobile network, the Internet and the use of computers, as well as the cost, quality and reliability of services. *Business environment:* evaluate the general business climate in a country, including the strength of the economy, political stability, the regulatory environment, taxation, competition policy, the labour market, the quality of infrastructure

by other sources such as the OECD figures (Figure 2.1) or the World Economic Forum, whose ranking is analyzed below.

Figure 2.1 – Businesses using the Internet and businesses receiving orders over the Internet, percentage of businesses with ten or more employees, 2002 and 2003 or latest available year

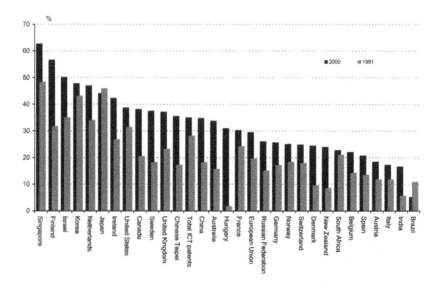

Continuing with the comparisons in terms of competitiveness, the Global Competitiveness Report (2004) produced by the World Economic Forum employs a ranking system based on three indexes: technology, quality

and openness to trade and investment. *Consumer and business adoption:* assesses how prevalent e-business practices are in each country, i.e. how the Internet is used to automate traditional business processes and how companies are helped by the development of logistics and online payment systems and the availability of finance and state investment in information technologies. *Legal and policy environment:* assesses a country's legal framework and the specific laws governing Internet use – how easy is it to register new businesses, how strong is protection of private property, and whether the governments support the creation of an Internet-conducive legal environment or are more concerned with censoring content and controlling access. *Social and cultural environment:* evaluates the literacy and basic education, which are preconditions for being able to use the new technologies, experience using the Internet and receptivity to it and the technical skills of the workforce. Finally, the existence of *supporting e-services:* the existence of consulting and IT services, the existence of back-office solutions and consistent industry-wide standards for platforms and programming languages.

of public institutions and macro-economic environment.[23] The GCI index reflects the balance between technological development and adoption and the reliability of the public institutions and macroeconomic environment.

In a table led by Finland and the US, Portugal occupied 24th place in 2004, having climbed one place in relation to 2003. Indeed, Portugal is accompanied in its leadership of the societies in transition by two other countries that have also climbed the table: Spain and Chile.

Despite presenting high figures at the technological level, the second group of countries analyzed here, consisting of Greece, Hungary, the Czech Republic, Slovakia and Italy, has lower scores in terms of their public institutions. The third group, which includes Uruguay, Brazil, Poland and Argentina, is penalized essentially by the negative scores for the macroeconomic index.

---

[23] The *technology index* is obtained using a set of data with differentiated weighting. The measured variables are Internet access in schools, whether the state of competition between ISPs is sufficient for guaranteeing high quality, low failure rates and low prices, whether the government programmes are successful or not in promoting the use of the information technologies and whether the legislation on e-commerce, digital signatures, consumer protection are developed and enforced. Furthermore, mobile phone penetration and the number Internet users, Internet hosts, telephone lines and personal computers are also measure; the *public institutions index* is measured on the independence of the judicial system in relation to political power, citizens and companies, whether the property rights, including movable goods, are well defined and protected by law, whether the state is impartial in awarding public contracts and whether or not organized crime constitutes a high cost to economic activity. Also measured are corruption dimensions, in particular to what extent bribery is common for achieving import and export authorizations, access to public assets and avoiding taxation; the *macro-economic environment index* is based the probability of the economy experiencing recession in the coming year and to what extent access to credit for companies is more or less difficult than the previous year. Also assessed are the state debts or surpluses in the preceding year, as well as the savings, inflation and exchange rates and the spread for loans and financial applications. Two further factors assessed are the country's rating in terms of international credit and to what extent the state supplies necessary goods and services not supplied by the market and distortive government subsidies.

Table 2.11 – Growth Competitiveness Index (GCI)

	Finland	US	Singapore	Chile	Spain	Portugal	Greece	Hungary
GCI Ranking (2004)	2	1	7	22	23	24	37	39
GCI Ranking (2003)	2	1	6	28	23	25	35	33
GCI Rating 2004	5.82	5.95	5.56	5.01	5.00	4.96	4.56	4.56
Technology index	6.24 (1)	5.92 (3)	5.11 (11)	4.55 (32)	4.86 (20)	4.78 (23)	4.42 (38)	4.66(29)
Quality of public institutions index	6.48 (3)	5.74 (21)	6.21 (11)	5.77 (20)	5.16 (34)	5.69 (23)	4.74 (44)	5.07 (37)
Macro-environment index	5.04 (15)	5.47 (3)	5.79 (1)	4.71 (27)	4.99 (16)	4.42 (34)	4.52 (31)	3.95 (55)

Source: The Global Competitiveness Report 2004, World Economic Forum.

Table 2.11.a – Growth Competitiveness Index (GCI)

	Czech Rep.	Slovakia	Italy	Uruguay	Brazil	Poland	Argentina
GCI Ranking (2004)	40	43	47	54	57	60	74
GCI Ranking (2003)	39	43	41	50	54	45	78
GCI Rating 2004	4.55	4.43	4.27	4.08	4.05	3.98	3.54
Technology index	4.88 (19)	4.67 (28)	4.08 (50)	3.92 (56)	4.24 (42)	4.19 (45)	3.87 (57)
Quality of public institutions index	4.56 (51)	4.64 (49)	4.64 (48)	5.23 (32)	4.62 (50)	3.70 (80)	3.77 (79)
Macro-environment index	4.22 (41)	3.98 (54)	4.27 (38)	3.10 (90)	3.28 (80)	4.05 (51)	2.96 (94)

Source: The Global Competitiveness Report 2004, World Economic Forum.

Societies in Transitions, Values and Social Well-Being

The informational societies are characterized not only by the appropriation of technology but also their internal openness and social well-being.

None of the countries in transition analyzed have an authoritarian regime and the dominating values in those societies today are those of an open society. The openness of a society can be measured by various dimensions, such as the ratio between the population in prison and the total population.

As one can see in the following table (Table 2.12, 2.12.a), whereas the Finnish model is characterized by a ratio twice as low as that for the US, Portugal registers figures that are twice those for Finland, with values that are very close to the average for the G7 societies. However, if we look at the total number of countries in transition in terms of their prison inmate figures, we find that, with the exception of Italy and Greece, all of the remaining countries have an inmate population above the average for the advanced economies.

In terms of gender equality, the majority of societies in transition are below the average for the advanced economies (661), representing societies that are still very unequal in terms of gender. Only Spain and Argentina achieve better gender equality scores, bringing them closer to the egalitarian model in terms of gender relations: *Finland* (820).

To add a further dimension, we can also compare the well-being of the populations of the societies in transition to the well-being models associated with the three information society models under analysis (*Finland, Singapore* and *Silicon Valley*), by looking at the income structures.

Hence, measured by the ratio of the 20% richest to the 20% poorest is concerned, the *Finnish* model of an information welfare society presents the greatest equality of income (3.8). At the other end, the market-governed information society model (*Silicon Valley*) and the authoritarian model (*Singapore*) show much greater unbalance in terms of income distribution, occupying third and second place in the ranking of the advanced economies with the worst ratios between the income of the richest and that of the poorest (8.4 and 9.7 respectively).

Table 2.12 – International comparison of citizenship indicators

	Finland	US	Singapore	Portugal	Spain	Italy	Czech Rep.	Slovakia	Advanced Economies
Freedom of the press (index 0-100; 0 = free) [1]	9 (free)	13 (free)	64 (not free)	14 (free)	19 (free)	33 (partially free)	23 (free)	21 (free)	17 (free)
Gender equality (0-1,000, 0 = unequal) [2]	820 (4)	769 (14)	648 (20)	644 (23)	716 (15)	583 (32)	586 (30)	607 (26)	661
Membership of at least one association (%) [3]	80	90	-	29	29	40	60.5	65	53
Social trust (%) [7]	56	35.5	-	12	35	31.5	24	15.5	31
Inmate population (per 100,000 inh.) [4]	71 (-157)	714 (-1)	392	128	140	98	184	165	126
Foreigners or persons born abroad (% of population) [5]	2.6	12.4	33.6	2.3	3.2	2.8	2.3	0.6	8.8
Environment: CO_2 emission (metric tons per capita) [2]	10.3	19.8 (-2)	14.7	5.9	5.3	6.6	11.6	6.6	10.4

Source: 1 Adapted from Castells and Himanen (2002), all data from the Press Freedom Survey 2004: http://www.freedomhouse.org/ ; 2 Adapted from Castells and Himanen (2002), except data for Portugal, which are taken from the UNDP Human Development Report 2001; 3 Adapted from Castells and Himanen (2002) and Norris, Pippa "Gender and Social Capital" 1999-2001 World Values Survey; 4 For all countries: International Centre for Prison Studies, King's College http://www.kcl.ac.uk/depsta/rel/icps/worldbrief/highest_to_lowest_rates.php; 5 Adapted from Castells and Himanen 2002, http://www.un.org/esa/population/publications/ittmig2002/WEB_migration_wallchart.xls [3] . Note: (*) relative position. Based on Norris, Pippa "Gender and Social Capital" 1999-2001 World Values Survey (% of the population that responded that it generally trust others).

Table 2.12.a – International comparison of citizenship indicators

	Hungary	Greece	Poland	Chile	Argentina	Uruguay	Brazil	Advanced Economies
Freedom of the press (index 0-100; 0 = free) [1]	20 (free)	28 (free)	19 (free)	23 (free)	35 (partially free)	26 (free)	36 (partially free)	94
Gender equality (0-1,000, 0 = unequal) [2]	529 (39)	523 (43)	606 (27)	460 (58)	645 (21)	511 (46)	-	83
Membership of at least one association (%) [3]	29	57	25	50	42.5	-	-	53
Social trust (%) [7]	22	21	18	22.5	15.5	-	-	32
Inmate population (per 100,000 inh.) [4]	165	82	209	204	148	209	183	126.
Foreigners or persons born abroad (% of population) [5]	3	5	5.4	1	3.8	2.7	0.3	8.8
Environment: CO_2 emission (metric tons per capita) [2]	5.4	8.5	7.8	3.9	3.9	1.6	1.8	10.6

Source: 1 Adapted from Castells and Himanen (2002), all data from the Press Freedom Survey 2003 : http://www.freedomhouse.org/; 2 Adapted from Castells and Himanen (2002), except data for Portugal, which are taken from the UNDP Human Development Report 2001; 3 Adapted from Castells and Himanen (2002), except data on Portugal, which are taken from Cardoso et Al., 2004, *The Network Society in Portugal (The Network Society in Portugal)*, CIES; 4 For all countries: International Centre for Prison Studies, King's College: http://www.kcl.ac.uk/depsta/rel/icps/worldbrief/highest_to_lowest_rates.php; 5 Adapted from Castells and Himanen 2002, except data for Portugal which were taken from the National Statistics Office's (INE) population report. Note: (*) relative position.

Table 2.13 – International comparison of social well-being indicators

	Finland	US	Singapore	Portugal	Spain	Italy	Czech Rep.	Slovakia	Advanced Economies
Combined rate of students of the first, second and third cycles [1]	106 (1)	92	87	93	92	82	78	74	94
Functional literacy (%) [2]	89.6 (2)	79.3	92.5	52	-	-	84.3	-	83
Life expectancy at birth (years) [1]	77.9	77.0	78.0	76.1	79.2	78.7	75.3	73.6	78
Health care coverage (%) [3]	100	82	-	100	100	100	-	-	n.d.
Number of working hours per annum per person [7]	1713	1792	-	1676	1800	1591	1972	1814	1636
Ratio of the 20% richest to the 20% poorest [4]	3.8 (3)	8.4	9.7	8.0	5.4	6.5	3.5	4.0	5.8
Percentage of population below the poverty line [5]	3.8 (4)	14.1	-	21	-	-	-	-	10.6
Gini coefficient [6]	26.9	40.8	42.5	38.5	32.5	36	25.4	25.8	28.57

Source: 1 Adapted from Castells and Himanen (2002), except data for Portugal, which were taken from the UNDP Human Development Report 2001; 2 Adapted from Castells and Himanen (2002), except data for Portugal, which were taken from the UNDP Human Development Report 2003, calculated on the basis of the "Lacking functional literacy skills" indicator, http://hdr.undp.org/reports/global/2003/pdf/hdr03_HDI.pdf; 3 Adapted from Castells and Himanen (2002), except data for Portugal. Given the existence of a universal National Health Service, one can presume total coverage of the Portuguese population; 4 Adapted from Castells and Himanen 2002, except data for Portugal, taken from http://www.worldbank.org/poverty/wdrpoverty/; 5 Adapted from Castells and Himanen 2002. The value for Portugal was taken from Capucha (2004), Desafios da Pobreza (The Challenges of Poverty), Lisbon, ISCTE, p.131 (Doctoral Thesis). Relative poverty measurement referenced to a threshold of 60% of the average of the income available to households; 6 Data for all countries based on UNDP 2004.

Table 2.13.a – International comparison of social well-being indicators

	Hungary	Greece	Poland	Chile	Argentina	Uruguay	Brazil	Advanced Economies
Combined rate of students of the first, second and third cycles[1]	86	86	90	79	94	85	92	94
Functional literacy (%)[2]	66.8	-	57.4	95.9	96.9	97.6	87.3	83
Life expectancy at birth (years)[1]	71.7	78.2	73.8	76.0	74.1	75.2	68.0	78
Health care coverage (%)[3]	-	-	-	-	-	-	-	-
Number of working hours per annum per person[7]	-	1938	1956	-	-	-	-	1636
Ratio of the 20% richest to the 20% poorest[4]	4.9	6.2	5.8	18.7	18.1	10.4	31.5	5.8
Percentage of population below the poverty line[5]	14.5	-	23.8	19.9	28.4	-	23.9	10.6
Gini coefficient[6]	24.4	35.4	31.6	57.1	52.2	44.6	59.1	28.57

Source: 1 Adapted from Castells and Himanen (2002), except data for Portugal, which were taken from the UNDP Human Development Report 2001; 2 Adapted from Castells and Himanen (2002), except data for Portugal, which were taken from the UNDP Human Development Report 2003, calculated on the basis of the "Lacking functional literacy skills" indicator, http://hdr.undp.org/reports/global/2003/pdf/hdr03_HDI.pdf; 3 Adapted from Castells and Himanen (2002), except data for Portugal. Given the existence of a universal National Health Service, one can presume total coverage of the Portuguese population; 4 Adapted from Castells and Himanen 2002, except data for Portugal, taken from http://www.worldbank.org/poverty/wdrpoverty/; 5 Adapted from Castells and Himanen 2002. The value for Portugal was taken from Capucha (2004), *Desafios da Pobreza (The Challenges of Poverty)*, Lisbon, ISCTE, p.131 (Doctoral Thesis). Relative poverty measurement referenced to a threshold of 60% of the average of the income available to households; 6 Data for all countries based on UNDP 2004.

All of the South American societies in transition (Brazil, Chile, Argentina and Uruguay) reveal extremely high inequality figures, sometimes three times as much as the US (Brazil) or twice as much (Chile and Argentina).

As for the European societies, there is a division into two large groups. The first is made up of Portugal, Italy, Greece and Poland, with inequality values close to the US informational society model. The second group includes the Czech Republic, Slovakia, Hungary and Spain, which are closer to the Finnish information society model.

Highlighting once more some of the specificities of each society under analysis, when we refer to the education level, it is also worthwhile stating that the openness of an information society does not depend only on the combined rate of students in the three education cycles, for if we neglect the school drop-out dimension (which the figures do not take into account) we would have a situation that would place Portugal and other societies in transition on a level with the US and Finland, which are countries with much lower drop-out rates. [24]

In the field of education, a comparison between the countries as far as functional literacy, i.e. the capacity to apply knowledge acquired in school in the society one lives in, shows that there are also great divides between the countries, even in the European context. Thus, Portugal, together with Poland, presents the worst results of the European countries studied – with a functional literacy rate of only 52% as compared to an average of 83% for the advanced economies and more than 80% for the US and Finland.

The openness of a society can also be measured on the social involvement of the citizens in everyday life. Together with Spain, Hungary and Poland, Portugal has the lowest rates of participation in associations, whereas Argentina and Italy present intermediate figures of around 40% for participation in associations. The Czech Republic, Slovakia, Chile and Greece are countries with over 50% of the population participating in associations.

The reasons for the low participation levels are varied, but it is possible to identify some guiding hypotheses if we focus on a specific reality such as the Portuguese one.

---

[24] The data show that the drop-out rates in the EU are relatively high, with an average of 22.5%. However, there are considerable differences between the Member States. The Northern European states achieve better results than the other members. Portugal (40.7 %), Italy (30.2 %), Spain (30.0 %) and the United Kingdom (31.4 %) present high rates, while Germany (13.2 %), Austria (11.5 %) and the Scandinavian countries (Sweden 9.6 % and Finland 8.5 %) present below-average values (European Union, 2000).

Of the reasons for this lack of civic engagement, we can list, first and foremost, the degree of public confidence in the politicians for Portugal. Although it can be considered a global phenomenon (Castells 2004), the development of the degree of trust of the citizens in politicians is not identical in all societies. Whereas Portugal is in 28th place in terms of public trust in the honesty of its politicians, sharing this level with a group of European countries – Belgium, France, Italy and Ireland – Finland, in 3rd place, is one of the countries with the highest degree of trust in the honesty of its politicians in the world.

The analysis of the civic engagement levels in the different countries must also take into account historic conditioning factors of both a global and local nature. What is known as *unconventional political participation* has increasingly become the most common form of civic engagement in our developed societies. Petitions, boycotts and other forms of direct action have become more common. For this reason, we should pay more attention to these forms of engagement than to membership in parties or trade unions and participation in demonstrations.

Table 2.14 – Civic engagement in European countries (%)

Country	Contacted politician or government member in the last 12 months	Worked in a political party or activist group in the last 12 months	Worked in another organization in the last 12 months	Signed a petition in the last 12 months	Boycotted certain products in the last 12 months	Bought a product for political/ethical environmental reasons in the last 12 months	Engagement ranking
Portugal	11.16	3.89	5.24	6.80	3.16	7.53	23rd (-1)
Austria	17.35	9.39	17.52	27.72	21.92	29.18	9th
Belgium	17.73	5.42	23.25	33.92	12.79	26.98	10th
Switzerland	16.91	7.61	16.74	40.40	33.66	46.93	2nd
Czech Rep.	21.42	3.87	13.98	15.07	11.05	22.10	15th
Germany	12.98	3.83	18.18	31.32	24.60	39.69	6th
Denmark	17.93	4.13	17.28	28.27	22.98	43.67	5th
Spain	11.66	5.79	14.60	22.25	7.72	11.48	16th
Finland	24.28	3.56	30.71	24.04	26.73	41.90	4th
France	16.83	4.52	17.03	33.75	25.84	27.46	8th
R.U.	18.33	3.16	9.30	39.45	26.19	32.78	7th
Greece	14.46	4.97	5.67	4.63	8.52	6.62	19th
Hungary	14.65	2.85	2.85	4.21	4.83	10.43	22nd
Ireland	22.36	4.63	13.71	27.24	13.33	24.41	13th
Israel	11.59	5.89	6.98	16.92	12.96	16.41	17th
Italy	12.13	3.25	8.16	18.49	7.90	6.34	18th
Luxembourg	17.14	2.85	16.66	27.77	14.28	28.57	12th
Netherlands	14.66	3.28	22.84	22.74	10.98	27.11	14th
Norway	23.85	9.48	28.16	37.17	20.11	36.59	3rd
Poland	9.55	2.89	6.03	7.15	3.84	10.50	21st
Sweden	16.43	4.96	24.55	40.75	32.45	55.12	1st
Slovenia	12.19	3.63	2.42	11.58	4.87	9.75	20th
Average	14.59	4.12	13.61	25.74	17.17	24.53	-

Source: European Social Survey 2002/2003.

However, in terms of civic engagement measured in these terms, Portugal has even lower scores. The engagement index measured on the basis of different forms of civic involvement and participation in organizations shows that Portugal occupies the last place in an international comparison of 22 European countries and Israel. Despite the cultural and geographic proximity to Portugal, countries such as Spain and Italy have much higher levels of civic engagement.

The historic context of each society can also help us to understand the participation levels a little more. For example, in his analysis of data gathered in more than 70 countries, referring to more than 80% of the world population, on participation in established democracies and new democracies, Inglehart (2001) has linked the scarce civic participation in some societies to the *post-honeymoon* effect. Periods of high civic participation levels are followed by decreases or stagnation in participation, but in the long term the trend is for growth in participation.

Table 2.15 – Participation over time in established and new democracies

	During and before change of regime	After change of regime	Change
Argentina	34	29	-5
Brazil	25	25	0
Chile	38	25	-13
Mexico	32	22	-7
Bulgaria	28	18	-10
Czech Republic	24	23	-1
East Germany	75	63	-12
Hungary	20	24	4
Poland	20	26	6
Slovenia	27	30	3
Slovakia	28	15	-13
	1981/1991	*1995/2001*	*Difference*
Portugal	25	27	2
Spain	31	34	3
Italy	52	62	10
US	68	79	11
Belgium	39	75	36
France	54	72	18
Denmark	55	68	13
Japan	49	55	6
West Germany	54	60	6
Switzerland	62	68	6
United Kingdom	71	80	9

Source: Adapted from Inglehart (2001) on the basis of 1981-2001 World Values Survey.

According to Inglehart (2001), the data show that in 21 countries studied between 1981 and 1990, although the people vote less regularly, they are not becoming more apathetic. On the contrary, they would seem to have become more interested in politics. This opinion is confirmed by the studies carried out by Castells (2003a) in Catalonia and Cardoso (2004) in Portugal.

As Table 2.15 shows, interest in politics increased in 16 countries and decreased in only 4. Portugal is in the group of countries where political participation is lowest and has stagnated, as is Spain. In both countries, a period of rapid increase in participation in the 1970s was followed by a process of democratic normalization.

Although Inglehart does not present data that allow one to compare the 1970s, the decade of revolution and transition to democracy in Spain and Portugal, one can observe this type of behaviour in the new democracies in Eastern Europe, which are characterized by periods of a rapid surge in participation followed by periods of less civic involvement. What the data do allow us to infer is the relative proximity of the participation levels between all the countries that have gone through transition to democracy in the last thirty years, regardless of whether they are in Europe or South America. The *post-honeymoon decline* is no doubt significant but the fact that these societies experienced authoritarian regimes, be they of the left or the right, for many years is also justification for the low levels of political participation.

A third factor one must take into account in analyzing participation is the relationship between participation and trust in others. The World Values Survey data (2001) furthermore shows that countries with geographical and cultural affinities with Portugal – such as Spain, France and Italy – present relatively homogeneous intermediate values for membership of associations.

Table 2.16 – Signed petition in the last 12 months, according to highest education level (%)

Country	*Not completed primary education	*Primary or first stage of basic	*Lower secondary or second stage of basic	*Upper secondary	*Post secondary, non-tertiary	*First stage of tertiary	*Second stage of tertiary
Portugal	0.91	4.63	2.11	15.26	-	19.44	50
Austria	9.09	-	20	25.85	32.57	-	43.58
Belgium	15.38	13.39	26.06	36.65	43.10	-	50.89
Switzerland	35.29	-	29.03	38.03	50.74	52	60
Czech Rep.	-	-	5.55	14.72	22.72	25.64	46.66
Germany	-	1.70	21.00	30.34	37.34	40.46	60.75
Denmark	-	16.66	24.50	23.26	36.73	42.25	33.33
Spain	3.40	15.90	24.09	28.99	34.54	40.00	38.88
Finland	-	8.86	22.22	27.89		31.68	33.33
France	15.72	20.24	31.71	39.34	33.33	44.731	53.58
R.U.	-	15.15	32.13	46.54	44.44	51.64	61.22
Greece	1.75	2.56	2.68	4.51	7.46	12.93	20
Hungary	-	3.01	3.52	4.37	-	9.83	11.11
Ireland	7.69	11.11	24	31.42	38	38.88	38.09
Israel	-	5.26	14.75	12.92	13.46	27.45	29.26
Italy	-	6.84	16.06	25.47	21.91	30.53	64.91
Luxembourg	-	18.18	25	33.33	-	-	40
Netherlands	10	10.07	17.26	22.80	30.76	34.44	20
Norway	-	-	26	36.02	33.33	43.42	52.63
Poland	-	2.48	4.94	9.90	7.46	20.80	12.37
Sweden	-	31.28	40.57	44.51	-	47.61	46.49
Slovenia	-	12.5	7.31	7.69	17.64	11.11	21.42

Source: European Social Survey 2002/2003. *Note: given the different names for education levels in the European context we opted to use the original ESS terms.

In Spain, the figures, for men and women respectively are 32% and 26%, for Italy 46% and 38% and for France 36% and43%. Where the differences are clearly greater is in the *trust in others,* for Spain (35%), Italy (32%) and France (20%) are clearly above the Portuguese values. This mistrust in relation to others is also obviously a factor to be taken into account in analyzing the low levels of civic participation.

Continuing the analysis of the possible factors that condition political participation in the context of the informational development models, one must including one more explanatory factor – education.

An analysis of the participation dimensions must also make reference to the Putnam analyzes (1993) on the relationship between reading newspapers and participation in civic associations. Putnam argues that there is a direct correlation between reading newspapers and membership of associations (other than religious associations) and that the regions with the highest readership levels are also those that, as a rule, have the strongest civic communities. If we test this hypothesis, we see that, at least in Europe, more than just influencing engagement, newspaper readership (and membership of associations) is directly correlated to the education level of the citizens. As we see (Table 2.18), education, much more than newspaper readership or watching TV news, is a central element in the civic engagement options made by the different citizens.

Table 2.17 – Contacted politicians/government members in the last year, by education level (%)

Country	*Not completed primary education	*Primary or first stage of basic	*Lower secondary or second stage of basic	*Upper secondary	*Post secondary, non-tertiary	*First stage of tertiary	*Second stage of tertiary
Portugal	3.66	10.62	8.45	17.42	-	20.83	-
Austria	9.09	-	10.61	18.04	18.18	-	30.76
Belgium	14.28	11.50	10.24	17.94	25.86	-	26.54
Switzerland	17.64	-	4.34	14.89	25.37	30.26	23.80
Czech Rep.	10.00	-	9.60	23.27	18.18	30	20
Germany	-	1.70	5.71	11.14	22.28	20.44	39.243
Denmark	-	20	12.74	15.84	22.44	26.76	33.33
Spain	2.782	9.66	10.37	13.40	15.90	22.62	61.11
Finland	12.5	13.92	18.51	23.97	-	37.62	66.66
France	7.49	16.66	14.21	14.34	16.66	18.07	26.28
UK	-	42.42	12.96	15.22	23.11	29.40	46.93
Greece	10.52	12.82	13.42	12.99	19.40	20.68	40.0
Hungary	5.97	7.53	16	15.30	-	25	31.11
Ireland	23.07	20	22.36	21.42	25.49	22.22	28.57
Israel	-	7.89	11.29	7.43	13.46	14.70	21.951
Italy	-	7.74	7.89	17.12	16.43	21.23	42.10
Luxembourg	-	9.09	25	16.66	0	0	25.00
Netherlands	-	5.38	10.28	13.18	11.53	27.66	20.00
Norway	-	-	14.00	22.04	25.00	31.16	42.10
Poland	0.89	3.41	7.08	11.20	13.33	18	23.10
Sweden	11.11	10.76	14.18	14.74	15.38	23.58	25
Slovenia		12.5	7.31	7.89	15.38	11.11	26.66

Source: European Social Survey 2002/2003. *Note: given the different names for education levels in the European context we opted to use the original ESS terms.

Table 2.18 – Relationship between watching TV news and reading newspapers, by education level/country (%)

Country		*Not completed primary education	*Primary or first stage of basic	*Lower secondary or 2nd stage of basic	*Upper secondary	*Post secondary, non-tertiary	*First stage of tertiary	*Second stage of tertiary
Portugal	Watches TV news	92.15	95.87	97.18	98.48	0	97.22	100
	Reads newspapers	9.25	48.38	63.88	70.67	-	82.19	50
Austria	Watches TV news	88.88	0	93.60	96.93	97.52	0	98.63
	Reads newspapers	58.33	-	83.51	86.53	87.21	-	88.60
Belgium	Watches TV news	71.42	93.75	90.18	93.06	96.49	0	96.22
	Reads newspapers	35.71	54.86	56.62	62.93	60.68	-	68.42
Switzerland	Watches TV news	93.33	-	92.13	95.40	96.82	95.38	100
	Reads newspapers	94.11	-	83.87	90.88	91.30	89.47	90.47
Czech Republic	Watches TV news	70	-	93.44	97.30	95.23	100	100
	Reads newspapers	44.44	-	69.84	82.75	86.36	92.5	93.75
Germany	Watches TV news	89.28	91.08	97.06	99.37	99.85	100	89.28
	Reads newspapers	57.26	71.41	84.72	84.93	90.76	93.67	57.26
Denmark	Watches TV news	100	100	93.87	98.5	100	98.59	100
	Reads newspapers	100	80	68.31	77.22	79.59	83.09	100
Spain	Watches TV news	82.35	92.46	88.88	92.07	91.78	96.07	100
	Reads newspapers	24.88	43.26	45.58	67.40	69.19	80.49	89.47
Finland	Watches TV news	100	96.10	98.70	98.60	-	98.98	100
	Reads newspapers	87.5	92.40	92.59	91.83	-	95.04	100
France	Watches TV news	90.66	91.15	92.77	97.43	96.24	96.65	96.14
	Reads newspapers	57.14	66.66	58.27	67.21	62.43	55.53	69.48
UK	Watches TV news	100	84.84	90.78	94.99	96.13	95.06	95.65
	Reads newspapers	-	21.21	74.53	78.58	78.53	77.80	71.42
Greece	Watches TV news	100	84.84	90.78	94.99	96.13	95.06	95.65

Table 2.18 – Relationship between watching TV news and reading newspapers, by education level/country (%)

Country		*Not completed primary education	*Primary or first stage of basic	*Lower secondary or 2nd stage of basic	*Upper secondary	*Post secondary, non-tertiary	*First stage of tertiary	*Second stage of tertiary
	Reads newspapers	6.14	22.97	38.00	42.69	52.23	62.93	80
Hungary	Watches TV news	100	84.84	90.78	94.99	96.13	95.06	95.65
	Reads newspapers	40.90	74.37	80.61	89.07		88.33	93.33
Ireland	Watches TV news	84.61	87.5	89.33	92.95	94.11	94.44	95.23
	Reads newspapers	76.92	85.45	84.21	88.88	82.69	94.44	90.00
Israel	Watches TV news	71.42	91.42	86.20	89.05	91.30	91.30	94.87
	Reads newspapers	22.22	47.36	64.51	72.29	75.00	72.81	80.95
Italy	Watches TV news	80.93	97.30	93.75	96.34	89.04	97.56	100
	Reads newspapers	16.20	51.61	68.28	82.64	94.52	92.79	100
Luxembourg	Watches TV news	90.90	100	91.66	100	100	100	90.90
	Reads newspapers	.	72.72	75.00	83.33	100	100	80.00
Netherlands	Watches TV news	90.90	94.48	96.82	97.75	98.70	99.65	100
	Reads newspapers	72.72	69.23	82.14	81.64	87.17	86.71	100
Norway	Watches TV news	-	-	98.03	97.82	100	100	95.00
	Reads newspapers	-	-	96.07	96.25	88.88	97.40	100
Poland	Watches TV news	89.47	94.34	95.49	97.40	97.69	100	99.64
	Reads newspapers	24.10	44.53	60.28	74.60	79.10	76	87.37
Sweden	Watches TV news	88.88	95.36	97.12	95.42	-	98.03	97.39
	Reads newspapers	88.88	90.30	93.57	89.10	-	88.67	93.96
Slovenia	Watches TV news	-	85.71	87.80	89.74	94	100	92.85
	Reads newspapers	44.44	73.17	79.48	88.23	88.88	92.85	44.44

Source: European Social Survey 2002/2003. *Note: given the different names for education levels in the European context we opted to use the original ESS terms.

Another of the indicators of an informational society is the relationship it has with its media, i.e. both the freedom of the media to report freely and give opinions and the relationship between the beneficiaries and producers of the information.

Of all the societies in transition under analysis here, only Italy, Argentina and Brazil are classified as partially free in terms of the freedom of the press.

In classifying the freedom of the press, factors such as the legal framework for journalism, political influence and economic pressures on the freedom of expression are taken into account. Between 2001 and 2003, Portugal improved its general score (going from 17 to 15), accompanying a trend similar to that of Finland, while the United Sates revealed an opposite trend (from 17 to 19) and Singapore continued to be classified as a country without freedom of the press. [25]

Positive development, such as in the case of Portugal, may conceal that the final value is due to a positive assessment of the evolution of the legislation and regulation that may influence the contents of the media. However, this is offset by an increase in the economic pressures on news content. To quote the *Press Freedom Survey,* 2003, "Most media outlets are independent of the government; however, print and broadcast ownership is concentrated in the hands of four main media companies." (Press Freedom Survey, 2003).

Table 2.19 – Average daily time spent on various activities, Internet users and non-Internet users (minutes)

	China		Portugal		Canada		US		Chile		Japan	Macao
	Users	Non Users	Users	Non Users	Users	Non Users	Users	Non Users	Users	Non Users	Users	Users
Television	135.0	182.4	135.3	175.7	99.2	125.1	99.4	138.85	100.8	146.9	202.4	150.0
Radio	27.6	30.0	147.5	155.4	117.4	95.14	66.8	69.4	66.4	106.0	21.1	36.0
Newspapers	45.6	54.6	34.5	33.1	36.8	44.5	24.0	40.8	15.0	15.5	25.0	42.0
Mob. phone	n/a	n/a	36.3	19.7	27.4	21.4	n/a	n/a	n/a	n/a	n/a	n/a
Telephone	n/a	n/a	29.9	17.6	35.1	40.2	n/a	n/a	n/a	n/a	n/a	n/a

Source: CIES, Network Society in Portugal Survey, 2003 for Portugal; all other countries: WIP (World Internet Project).

---

[25] Identical positions emerge when one looks at the online presence analysis. Finland, Portugal and the US are amongst the least restrictive of media freedoms and Singapore is included in the moderately free (*Press Freedom Survey, 2001*).

However, in the analysis of the media we also have to take into account that it is not only the ways in which the media system is organized that determine what the media are in a determined national space. As the table 2.19 demonstrates, the diffusion of the use of the Internet and the historic and affective relationship with the different media also produces such distinct realities such as the daily average of minutes listening to the radio (95 minutes in the US and 135 minutes in Portugal, or such similarities as the common trend towards reduction in television viewing that seems to be taking place in countries as distinct from each other as China, Portugal, Canada, Chile and Japan.

Other differences in relation to the media can also be found in the forms in which trust in the media is assumed in different national contexts. For example, although geographically close to each other, Portugal and Catalonia differ in terms of trust in the television they watch and the newspapers they read. Trust in the newspapers is generally higher in Catalonia and trust in television, by Internet users, is lower in Catalonia (Castells et al., 2003) than that shown by the Portuguese (Cardoso, 2005).

Where differences are we can also find points of similarity, as, for example, when we study the relation between the audiences of a particular country and the national and foreign media. Even in countries less open to democracy, such as China, there is an almost always overwhelming preference for the national media (Liang 2003) over the foreign media. In the field of online news, trust seems to know boundaries. The data compiled by Liang (2003) for China and those of Castells (2003) for Catalonia and Cardoso (2005) for Portugal seem to demonstrate that trust continues to be linked to the more traditional news brands and vehicles of technological information dissemination.

The comparison of models of social openness and citizenship carried out here, as well as the analysis of the social well-being, reveals much more clearly the differences than the data related infrastructure, knowledge and production, common to all the societies dealt with herein. However, this is to be expected, for although they share values such as democracy and the wish to adopt informational society models, each society has its individual history and own identity, as well as different well-being models.

Media and Social Change in the Network Societies

The characterization of the societies in transition that we have endeavoured to achieve in this chapter, reflects the transition of populations with lower education levels to a society in which the younger generations have already more consolidated educational competences. However, this analysis also reflects societies, which, though they have made great efforts in the area of knowledge, are still trying to assert themselves in the infrastructure and technology production dimensions.

This analysis also reflects a socio-political transition – first from dictatorships to a democratic institutional politicization and then to a routinization of democracy. In a process that combines growing scepticism in relation to the political parties and the government institutions and an increase in civic engagement, using autonomous and, at times, individualized forms of expression on the part of civil society.

It is in this context that one produces a fundamental transition in these societies: technological transition. A transition expressed through the diffusion of the Internet and the appearance of the *network society* in the social structure and practice.

After reading the above data and analyzes, there is one question still to be answered: is there a generation divide or nor in all the societies analyzed here? Though it is true that the data for the Portuguese society confirm the existence of that divide, it is not present in all the societies analyzed. Some of the exceptions are Eastern European countries such as the Czech Republic, Slovakia and Hungary.

The generational divide is not the result of an option; it is, rather, the fruit of a society in which the necessary cognitive resources are distributed unequally amongst the generations, so that societies in which formal learning and literacy are historically better established present transition processes that accentuate the generational differences to a lesser degree.

The society we live in is not a society in social division. It is a society based on an informational development model, in which some cognitive skills are more valued than others, namely: the highest education level, formal literacy and technological literacies. All these are acquired and not innate skills. As such, social division is not inevitable; there is, rather, a process of transition in which the protagonists are those who most easily master these skills.

At the same time as experiencing multiple transition processes, societies such as the Portuguese and Catalan societies preserve strong social cohesion via a dense network of social and territorial relations. They are societies that change and maintain their cohesion at the same time. They evolve at the global level, while maintaining local and personal control over that which gives meaning to life (Castells, 2004c). In the societies in transition that balance between change and social cohesion could be one of more common trait.

However, although they share global networks, each societal reality is unique and only a more in-depth analysis of each nation would show us the signs of future evolution in each of our societies. That is the challenge in understanding the transitions in progress in our societies as they become network societies.

What is then the role of media in bringing in societies from industrial ones to network or transition societies?

In societies where mediation has become increasingly central in the social and economic changes media plays a powerful role. A role that has been present during the 20th century through the mass communication model and that has on the network communication model of the 21st century a new player.

3. From Mass to Networked Communication: Communicational Models and the Informational Society

In the area of facts, mass media report what is happening now, but in the area of interpretation, they can only say what was already expected twenty years ago.

Umberto Eco,
University and Mass Media

Communicational Models and the Informational Society

Umberto Eco poses the question to what extent one can expect to understand reality from the explanations provided by the media only. His answer is that that is not possible. The evolution of interpretative knowledge developed in the universities is parallel to its appropriation by the media and not obligatorily confluent. In other words, the very ways in which the media are organized and function don't allow for their rapid interpretative updating. They might not shun common sense, but they do take refuge in the most known, and at times least updated, theories to try and explain phenomena.

Following a similar logic, in answering the question as to what characterizes communication in contemporary society, we cannot limit ourselves to simply saying that it is the use of the new media together with the use of television, radio, newspapers and the telephone.

For that is the automatic answer, the product of rapid observation repeated countless times in the discourse of the media themselves, and not the product of reflection. Although it is correct in its genesis, the answer does not allow for an interpretation of the reasons for, and modes how, these media articulate with one another, the needs of economic market strategies and the representations attributed to them by the users – the media matrixes – and also their uses, or if we prefer, the media diets.

The aim of this analysis is precisely to examine what characterizes the existing communicational model(s) and to endeavour to capture their essence and interpret it.

All of us deal with the media – from the written media to orality – in our daily lives and in our relationship with images. We are permanently interpreting and incorporating that information in the decisions we make, in a process Giddens (1998) terms reflexivity.

However, in the naturalness of our daily experiences with the media we tend to interiorize practices and representations in relation to them without questioning them in terms of their articulation, characteristics and functionalities.

If the culture of our society is a *real virtuality* culture (Castells, 2002) and if *mediation* is the key concept (Silverstone, 2004) for understanding the characteristics of the networked organizational model, how can we identify its communicational models?

How do the different media configure themselves as facilitators of individual empowerment and, consequently, of communicative autonomy? And what degree of autonomy do these relations configure?

In agreement with the analysis of Castells (2002) and Ortoleva (2004) as to the dominant role of networks, Fausto Colombo (1996) argues that to answer the question of what the communicational models are we first have to understand that the media, and the mediation processes, operate in the context of a technocultural system in which the media play both a transforming role and are themselves transformed. A *technocultural system* is, thus, fruit of the interaction of multiple dimensions – from the economic to the cultural[26], from

---

[26] Here one must clarify that we can identify four levels of culture in our analysis: *Culture of the Elite:* defined as "the best that has been thought and written" (1869, Matthew Arnold cited in Colombo), which always implies an updating for each era and is defined by mediators who have been given symbolic capital amongst the elite. *Average Culture:* the product of the education system as a political,

the technical-scientific to the socio-anthropological and from the political to the ethical[27].

Through analysis of the different dimensions it is, therefore, possible to identify key dimensions of possible opportunities and limitations in the media for the construction of communicative autonomy in our society.

A first characterization can be given by identifying that, in addition to the economic globalization processes, today we are also witnessing communicative globalization processes. And, as we shall see further below, that is a decisive factor in characterizing the communicational models.

Communicational Globalization in the 20th Century

The society in which we live today is itself the product of the historic confluence of developments that took place in diverse areas of human activity (Castells, 2003). But that moment of confluence is also an arrival point for a process that began in the 20th century.

The centrality of communication and information is a relatively recent phenomenon, for, up until the late 19th century, the idea of *communication* as an autonomous and independent entity within the more general concept of transport (just like the idea of media as something distinct from other instruments useful for exchange or travel) was not generally

---

economic and social emancipation movement expressed in the ideal of modern culture ("the times in which we live") through music, television, fashion and consumer and lifestyles. *Popular Culture:* the largest in numbers. Today, due to the gradual disappearance of the working class it is increasingly the subject to devaluation within its own ranks. *Particularist Cultures:* popular culture is giving way to cultures characterized by difference-based distinctions (e.g., women, regions, minorities), thus diminishing the "universal dimension" of popular culture (Colombo, 2000).

[27] The different characteristics given by Colombo encompass in the economic dimension the rules and norms that apply to culture and information acquisition and consumption behaviours and their relationships with the activities of production and distribution. The analysis of the cultural dimension seeks to identify the trends in society through identification of modalities and criteria of valuation of contents, language and knowledge, expressive styles and educational processes that confer interpretations of the world and society.

As for the technical-scientific dimension, this refers to the degree of development and the peculiarity of the technological potentials of a given society.

The socio-anthropological dimension has to do with the processes of adaptation and social self-organization and the political dimension in the relationship between the citizen and society under the cover of the explicit rules and the institutions delegated to guaranteeing it.

Finally, the ethical dimension comprises aspects of personal choice, the acceptance of responsibilities and logics of behaviour of the individuals as participants in social life (Colombo, 1996).

discussed (Ortoleva, 2004; Winston, 1999; Richeri, 1996). The births of the new means of communication – such as cinema and radio, the comic book and gramophone, the telephone line – were not seen, at the time, as unitary phenomena that could be grouped together in one single concept (Ortoleva, 2004).

However, as we have seen, the idea of communication and information not only imposed itself in its specificity and autonomy, but also asserted itself as a central idea of social life, before becoming, in the late 20th century, an objective in terms of development (Cardoso, 2004). Today we have an unprecedented variety of communications at our disposal and also an unprecedented choice between apparently equivalent media (Eco, 2001). For Ortoleva, these are the two bases for our life at the beginning of the 21st century in the developed world (2004).

Another fundamental contribution for the contextualization of this discussion is the fact that, in relation to other periods of the history of humanity, the century just passed is an exceptional moment (Ortoleva, 2004), for communication has traditionally been one of the most stable resources and the object of prudent and conservative management (as demonstrated by the whole history of writing from ancient China to the Egypt of the pharaohs and the Middle Ages).

What types of social demands and processes have resulted in the formulas and techniques of communication? And why were they privileged with large resources with a view to sustaining the intensity of development that was registered? One possible answer is given by various researchers when they refer to the discontinuity that took place from the 1970s onwards (Castells, 2003 and Ortoleva, 2004).

As we have already seen, contemporary societies have witnessed a change in the economic paradigm to a model based on information. Indeed, information seems to have replaced energy as the central element in economic life – first of all in the more developed countries – before expanding to all areas of the planet following market economy rules. But something more is changing.

When one speaks of the informational economy at the end of the 20th century, one understands not only an economy in which the free circulation of information is a pre-condition for the existence of a market but also an economy in which the sector that produces the communications and brings them into circulation also takes on a driving force role in relation to the industrial sector that traditionally dominated the markets: the manufacturing industries. In this analytical context, Giddens offers some important starting points. [28] When asked if the concept of *Information Society* could correctly be used to characterize the changes going on in our societies, Giddens responded: "Not really, no (…) Information Society does not give us much perception of what is happening" (1997). *Economic and communicational globalization*, and not information society, are, for Giddens, the most visible characteristics of a society in change as a result of the increasing fusion of information technologies, communication and computerization.

It is likewise on the basis of these two dimensions that Peppino Ortoleva (2004) sets out to explain the development of communication in the 20th century: using, on the one hand, the relation between communication and the complexification of the social system and, on the other, the role of communication in the market.

As our modern society gradually becomes more complex, thanks to specialization and symbolic guarantees (Giddens, 1998), and configures itself as a system, relying on organizations of the systemic type, the need arises for instruments that interconnect, as rapidly as possible, the different points of the system itself (Ortoleva, 2004). These processes may be visible in the development of the transport network systems, which had as a prerequisite the development of the telegraph and the timetable systems unified on a national and then global basis or, for example, the adoption of the naval telegraph by the navies only after the introduction of steamships visible from a great distance (Winston, 1999) or also in the relationship between the development of great productive and bureaucratic apparatuses and vertically and horizontally hierarchical communication (from paper to the first computerization) in contrast with the Internet and network communication (Castells, 2004) or, finally, the development of advertising made necessary and possible through the development of another system, that of large-scale distribution (Ortoleva, 2004).

The spatial and temporal complexity of the social organization is the starting point for the communication models in the informational societies, giving rise to communicative globalization.

---

[28] Although I agree with James Slevin (2000) on the lack of a direct analysis of the role of the media and the Internet in the published work of Anthony Giddens, one can, however, find in his interviews a series of arguments and formulations that qualify his analysis as being fundamental for the theoretical contextualization of the understanding of the role of the media in individual empowerment.

One of the dimensions of the spatial and temporal complexity that most contributed to this communicative globalization was the economic dimension and the evolution the markets. As Castells (2002) demonstrates, the need for a restructuring of capitalism provided the impulse for the adoption and diversification of the media and the development of the information technologies and their articulation in networks.

However, one must point out that the relationship between market and communication was a constant throughout the 20th century, taking on different characteristics depending on the moments in which the relationship manifested itself.

During a large part of the 20th century, it assumed different meanings than to that of the current configuration in networks – hierarchical concentration. Between the crash of 1929 and the oil crisis of 1973, a development of communication models took place that was characterized by radiophonic broadcasting and experimentation with television, simultaneously with an impulse towards an expanded and massified consumption (Ortoleva, 2004).

Our social reality in terms of communication models is, thus, a product of these historic movements that have taken place throughout the last century.

Our society today is one in which television and the Internet (in the access to the diversity of sources and instantaneousness of them) represent a factor of change in our lives, through the sharing of one and the same information environment by elected and electors and an increasingly greater role conferred upon reflexivity as an instrument of choice.

There is thus an alteration in our temporal and spatial dimensions, in the life of society. That alteration can be identified in the reduction in the time for the delivery of symbolic forms, from television to downloadable texts on the Internet, or in the fact that spatial distance does not imply a proportional temporal distance. The present era is the first in which we have the discovery of aspatial simultaneity (Thompson, 1995), i.e., the coordination and visualization of events taking place at the same time in different spaces (for example, the worldwide demonstrations against the war in Iraq in February 2003).

Bearing in mind the preceding definitions, one must point out that the media, due to their historical contextualization and the technological developments also evolve. For example, the media that were born with the technological innovation at the end of the 1970s facilitated new form of production organization, of access to knowledge, new forms of functioning of the economy and, consequently, new forms of culture. Similar to Thompson (1995), Castells (2004) argues that the media, in this particular case the Internet, bring a different form of managing the time and space of our relational networks with companies, between family members, between friends, between the State and citizens and between nations.

But this is also a society in which our sense of the past and the ways in which we perceive the present and the future depend more and more on a field of exposure of mediated symbolic forms or a real virtuality (Castells, 2002 and Thompson, 1995). The relation between media and society – the fruit, in particular, of the expanded social appropriation of the concepts of certain authors by the media themselves, as in the example of McLuhan and his *global village* – contributed largely to the current acceptance of very precise correspondences between the communication models and society models (Ortoleva, 2004).

If it is the case, as it indeed appears, that the communication and information technologies can facilitate the adoption of social organization models, is it possible to argue that there is correspondence between communication models and social models? The answer is yes. However, before justifying that answer, we must first clarify certain points.

The ties between the media and society have been diverse in nature throughout history. On the one hand, there are those who point out the deterministic cause/effect relationships, such as the idea that the mass media "create" the mass society. That is, for example, the idea of a group of analysts defined by Umberto Eco (1991) as "apocalyptic", which establishes almost direct connections between the information and entertainment model originated in the media and processes of social massification and cultural homogenization (Ortoleva 2004 and Colombo 2003). In accordance with the deterministic theories – for example, traditional Marxism – mass communication would be the expression of an authoritarianism produced by the reduced power of control over technical development. That same view, as we have analyzed above, re-emerges in the technocultural discourse in the context of the information society at the end of the last century, in particular in the opposition between interactive media and the passive media, or, if we prefer, the new media (such as the Internet) and the old media (such as television).

Another approach is taken by those who argue that the media express, both through their structure and in their contents, the very nature of the society in which they are generated (Ortoleva 2004). This is the case for analysts such as Poster (1999) and McLuhan (1997). According to Poster, there are three main phases in the *Mode of Information*, which coexist with each other for they are not consecutive. These are the symbolic exchanges mediated orally, in writing and electronically. In each of these stages, the relationship between language and society, the idea and the action, the *self* and the *other* is, therefore, different. Just as, in the 19th century, the print media played a fundamental role in forming the notion of the independent and rational subject by constituting a sphere of public debate – which, according to Habermas (1986), created the bases for the democracies of the 20th century – the new media, and in particular the Internet, are promoting, through their characteristics, a multiple, decentred and disseminated subject.

According to McLuhan (1997) one cannot speak of one single model of society corresponding to all the mass media, but of two distinct models. The first, the model of the press and, later, cinema and, to an extent, radio, which was based on a clear division of roles and a strongly hierarchical order. The second, which emerged with television and was reinforced in the ulterior forms of electronic communication (informatization and automation), was based on a system of horizontal and strongly interactive relations.

The central presuppositions of the analyses of Poster (1995) and McLuhan (1997) thus refer to the view of the non-neutrality of the media and to the idea that technologically different media are the fruit of the society in which they emerge and which promotes, through their use, differentiated socio-cultural realities.

A third approach, identified by Ortoleva (2004) as relation of complementarity, argues that a re-equation of the effective reach of the mass communications takes place, with its denominated "effects" (Wolf, 1992), and underlines that the users of the media find correspondence in a network of interpersonal relations that measure, condition and filter the reception of the messages. A complementary approach is taken by Pierre Levy (2000) in proposing for the relationship between technology and society the notion of influence, in opposition to impact. The action of any form of technology, such as the media, cannot be considered outside of culture and therefore it interacts with a culture, which hosts it and modifies it from its birth.

Considering the three dimensions depicted above, the position that prevails in my analysis is closest to that proposed by Mauro Wolf (1992).

Reflexivity, enabled by the information and communication technologies, is a fundamental element in individual decision making and life construction, but it, too, demonstrates that it is not only through technological development and scientific innovation that we can, in some form, control or define what the future will be. The future is opaque and problematic and we know that what we say also contributes to those scenarios. It follows that the future itself also has a very reflexive and problematic dimension (Giddens, 1997).

If we wish to typify the relational process between communication, information and society, then it is essentially a bi-univocal relationship. Bi-univocal in the sense that, on the one hand, communication facilitates different models of social organization (Castells, 2004) but, at the same time, there are supervening social needs (Winston, 1999) that also foster new forms of communication. In this sense, one can speak of correspondence between communicational and social models.

Mass Media and New Media: the Articulation of a New Communicational Model?

It is fundamental to the analysis herein that we define what we call *media* and what differentiates the individual media, for only thus can we discuss what characterizes the communicational models that have emerged over the last decade.

Although one can take different paths to achieve that, the process I have chosen here is that of endeavouring to desegregate the various media components on the basis of what they supposedly influence: from the organizations to the political processes and from global commerce to everyday life, etc.

Bearing in mind that the media are technological apparatuses and also that the technology is shaped by the uses thereof, the de-aggregation of components could serve to define what distinguishes television from the Internet or from mobile phones as mediation technologies.

One of the first questions could precisely be: why the aggregation of the different technologies alluded to in the preceding paragraph? All of these – from the telephone to television and to the Internet – can be termed media because they guarantee, in different forms (through sound, text and image) the coded transmission of symbols between sender and receiver within a predefined structure of signs. Amongst these are the multimedia media, which use sound, image and text in a combined and interlinked form (in hypertext or not). The valuation of the symbolic forms (i.e., how they are appreciated by the individuals) may or may not be accompanied by an economic valuation (the attribution of an economic value to the symbolic forms). In other words, not all the media come with a direct economic compensation (payment) for the communicational fruition (there is one for the telephone and for newspapers but not always one for the Internet or for television and practically never for radio).

If, in the case of telephone, and as far as the voice functionality is concerned, up until now, the opinion would seem to be unanimous that it is not a mass medium, there is less agreement as to the classification of the Internet.

Dominique Wolton (1999, 2000), for example, argues that the Internet is not a mass medium for that would require simultaneous generalized diffusion to a large audience, as is the case for a newspaper or a television station, which are based on a pre-conceived notion of the target audience. This is something that, in Wolton's opinion, the Internet does not have. Therefore, he argues that it is an *information system* and a *media system.*

Proceeding Thompson's (1995) concept of cultural transmission, James Slevin (2000), argues that the Internet, similar to other cultural transmission forms before it, has all the attributes for classification as a mass medium. Slevin (2000) recognizes in the Internet technical mediation attributes (such as the fixation of information, the reproduction of contents and participation of the users), an institutionalized apparatus of visible transmission in the selectivity of the diffusion channels and in the mechanisms of restricted implementation and, finally, a certain type of space and time distancing involved in the transmission.

For Thompson, mass medium is a definition applicable to newspapers, cinema and television and a term that cannot be applied to the majority of the media, present and past. A mass medium implies an image of a vast audience made up of thousands or even millions of individuals. However, mass communication is not given this attribute on the basis of a fixed and stipulated number of individuals making up its audience, but on the basis of whether or not the media in question are, in principle, available to a plurality of individuals in a process of public circulation of symbolic forms, whereby this constitutes another difference in relation to media such as the telephone, video, teleconferences, etc. As Thompson classifies, Dominique

Wolton proceeds from a false premise when he subjects the definition of mass media to the condition that the transmission has to be directed at the totality of a population and when he considers that the Internet did not have a representation of its target audience in its genesis and a relationship between an individual and a collective scale. None of the mass media in history is or was aimed at, in any phase, the totality of a given community of values, be it a country or a region, even if this is asserted in editorial terms.

The mass communication that takes place through the Internet can also be termed a mass medium. To not consider these technologies as mass media on the grounds that they are not aimed at a vast audience, is to make the error of regarding the Internet user, or television viewer, as a passive element in the communicative equation (something that Umberto Eco demystified in his analysis of the 1970s entitled "Does the audience have bad effects on television?" [1985]). The user, because he is not passive in relation to the Internet, just as he is also not passive in relation to television, shares with his social networks of acquaintances and friends and family similar tastes and the word of mouth effect means that the widespread attention of many millions of individuals, at different or coinciding times, seek out the same Internet addresses in search of the same information or entertainment.

Wolton's argumentation would imply that we not consider the existence of activities such as television zapping or Internet browsing and also that we accept that whoever seeks information and entertainment does so using the same interest patterns only. It would likewise mean that the interpersonal communication through recommendations coming from our relational networks would not lead us to the alteration of behaviours and attitudes or that criticisms of programmes or analyzes of websites and software in the Internet would not lead us to share information and entertainment, simultaneously, with thousands of other persons who visit the same page in the same second.

In reality, there are several Internets and not all can be classified as mass media. Given its dimension, discussing whether or not the Internet can be *something* is an ungrateful task due to the inherent bias. That is the conceptual error made by both Wolton and Slevin. The Internet with the characteristics that Slevin attributes to it – those of a mass medium – does exist but that doesn't portray the entirety of its universe. Wolton commits a double error in seeing the Internet merely as a space of information, disregarding other dimensions. In doing so, he also forgets that in a space of globalization in which a *lingua franca* (English) flows and in which globally shared values interact with personal identities and local values, a medium based solely on one community of localized language, values and references has ceased to be the sole medium model and become only one of the medium models – from CNN to SKY, in television, or from news.bbc.co.uk to slashdot.org – we find variants of this medium formula (Cardoso, 2004).

Whoever creates a web page on the World Wide Web knows their target audience and shares languages, values and references but they do so in different scales and in different forms. They are communicating through a mass medium and are not creating a mere information system.

Wolton is, however, correct where he argues that the Internet is not a mass medium, as only a part of the communication that takes place on it is developed on the basis of software that promotes the institutionalized production and generalized diffusion of symbolic goods, fixing and transmitting information and symbolic contents. The part of the Internet that can be classified as a mass medium is the part in which the communication in the World Wide Web takes place, for example. What are, in this order of ideas, the other dimensions of the Internet beyond that of a mass medium?

To answer that, we require the help of Pierre Bourdieu (Cardoso, 1998). By using the concept of the *field* to designate the delimitation of the analysis of an object, Bourdieu provides us with the theoretical tool for characterizing the different Internets. If we break the Internet down according to the type of communication established by means of the different types of software, we see that E-mail and real-time chat programmes are part of the interpersonal communication *field*, just like the telephone or conventional mail correspondence. And that the World Wide Web, file sharing programmes (P2P) and newsgroups make up another *field*: that of mass communication or mass media.

In addition to being a medium, the Internet is also a means of interpersonal communication and a mass medium.

It is important now that we analyze why we sometimes refer to the Internet as a new medium. We do so not only because it is new, technologically speaking – as it dates from the end of the 1970s – but also because its use does provide novelty.

As we know through the accelerated diffusion of one of the most celebrated information and communication technologies, the Internet, one of the novelty characteristics that allow us to classify something as a new medium is coexistence on the same technological support, in this case the TCP/IP protocols.

In the case of the Internet there is another new development: for the first time a technology presents one single standard for interpersonal communication and mass communication.

Hence, we can deduce that the novelty has its origins in the fact that the technology is new, but the novelty can also reside in the fact that the technologies promote new forms of communication and new social and economic organization models, create new audiences, have new forms of rhetoric and contents and also provide new forms of knowledge.

What we can say for certain is that when one speaks of the new media, one presupposes the existence of chronologically older media and points of differentiation in relation to them.

Fausto Colombo proposes the following definition of new media: all those means of communication, representation and knowledge (i.e. media), in which we find the digitalization of the signal and its content, that possess dimensions of multimediality and interactivity (Colombo, 1995). This definition, although technologically oriented, has the advantage of being comprehensive, inclusive of everything from the mobile phone to digital television and also embracing game consoles and the Internet. Roger Silverstone has also made a contribution to providing a definition for the new media by making the reservation that, when looked at in isolation, the majority of the supposed characteristics that distinguish the new media (digital convergence, many-to-many communication, interactivity, globalization and virtuality) are not distinctly new. What makes them new is their conjugation in one and the same technological support (Silverstone, 1999).

In order to better clarify the definition of the new media we can also make a distinction between those that are born digital and those originating in digital migration. Third generation mobile phones (3G/UMTS) and on-line newspapers and radio and television stations are examples of the new media arising from digital migrations, as they were previously available on other supports that then migrated to digital.

Examples of the new born-digital media are the computer game consoles (Playstation, X-Box, Sega, Nintendo), the interpersonal communication fields on the Internet in general (e-mail, chats, newsgroups) and the mass communication fields (World Wide Web and publications of individual persons and entities created especially for the WWW).

The new media may be termed thus because they are mediators of communication, because they introduce the novelty of incorporating new technological dimensions, because they combine interpersonal communication and mass media dimensions on one and the same platform, because they induce organizational change and new forms of time management and because they seek the synthesis of the textual and visual rhetoric, thus promoting new audiences and social reconstruction tools.

Bearing the preceding definitions in mind, how can we define the communication model that characterizes an informational society?

As a starting point, I should point out that what we have witnessed over the last 20 to 30 years is a consequence of the fusion of different technologies, i.e., the information technologies, communication technologies and computerization.

The economic and social appropriation results in an interesting relationship between the market and democracy.

Although the economic dimension of globalization is fundamental, it must not be seen as an economic phenomenon only but also a communicational one (Giddens, 1999). When we live in a world in which the news take on an almost instant character and in which the diversity of information contexts is the rule (see, for example, the differences in the satellite television coverage of the Iraqi insurrection of April 2004 by CNN and Arab television channels such as Al Jazeera), we have to accept that globalization also means a change in the communication systems. That change transforms the local lives of the people at the same time as it modifies the economic structure of life itself.

The ambivalence that characterizes the media in this historic context can also be found in their role of management of communicative autonomy and the possibility of individual empowerment they can provide.

The media in general have a double role to play in the modern world. On the one hand, they are instruments of democracy, as illustrated by the role of the television channels in the revolutions of 1989 in Eastern Europe, the Russian putsch against Gorbachev and Yeltsin's rise to power (Giddens, 1999) and also in the awareness given to the drama of the people of East Timor in 1999 (Cardoso, 2003). On the other hand, media such as television tend to subvert the spaces they open, pursuing a rhetoric of personalization and trivialities in a process of preoccupation with personalities and the trivial – something that often has a negative effect on the social dialogue.

As a result of that duality, the present time is the first time in history in which governments and citizens coexist in the same information environment, and this is taking place as a result of technological change, in addition to other developments. For the first time, governments have to change the way in which they treat their citizens. When governments and citizens live in the same information environment there are many things that the citizens cease to tolerate – they have much less toleration for corruption, negotiations in the wings, secret deals and the use of connections. The more the same environment is shared, the less all that seemed normal in politics up to a few years ago is accepted as normal (Giddens, 1999).

Although agreeing with Giddens' diagnosis of commercial television as seeking dichotomies (for example, by resorting to dramatization in providing information and distorting the narrative pattern, seeking to present the *good* and *just* in opposition to the *bad* and *unjust*), one must also call attention to the hypothesis of the so-called multiple effects associated with the media.

Communication may take place as a process of free and equal exchange of meaning, development of communities and advancement of social solidarity between nations and individuals or it can systematically distort perceptions and create fantasy enemies, fabricate consensus and consent for wars of aggression and target particular ethnic groups or nations into sub-human categories (Tehranian, 1999).

This possibility of multiple effects, already present in televised communication, has been added to the new media, but modern communications make dualistic explanations more difficult, or even unfeasible. An example of this is the criticism of the CCN coverage of the Iraq conflict by FAIR (*Fairness & Accuracy In Reporting Media analysis, critiques and activism*) divulged in a mailing list on the Internet. This is a practical example of how we cannot continue to think that the access to, and management of information are possible through one single technology only, in this case, television.

CNN to Al Jazeera: Why Report Civilian Deaths? April 15, 2004
As the casualties mount in the besieged Iraqi city of Fallujah, Qatar-based Al Jazeera has been one of the only news networks broadcasting from the inside, relaying images of destruction and civilian victims – including women and children. But when CNN anchor Daryn Kagan interviewed the network's editor-in-chief, Ahmed Al-Sheik, on Mon-

day (4/12/04) – a rare opportunity to get independent information about events in Fallujah – she used the occasion to badger Al-Sheik about whether the civilian deaths were really "the story" in Fallujah.
Al Jazeera has recently come under sharp criticism from U.S. officials, who claim the Iraqi casualties are 95 percent "military-age males" (AP,4/12/04). "We have reason to believe that several news organizations do not engage in truthful reporting," CPA spokesman Dan Senor said (Atlanta Journal-Constitution, 4/14/04). "In fact it is no reporting." Senior military spokesman Mark Kimmitt had a suggestion for Iraqis who saw civilian deaths on Al Jazeera (New York Times, 4/12/04): "Change the channel to a legitimate, authoritative, honest news station. The stations that are showing Americans intentionally killing women and children are not legitimate news sources. That is propaganda, and that is lies." (…). Source: http://www.fair.org

In the current context one must look at the media as a whole and think of them in terms of their agency functions and territorial reach, for it is through that double dimension that it is possible to understand how they articulate with each other.
One proposal for classifying the media is put forward by Tehranian (1999). He suggests classification as *micro-media, meso-media* or *macro-media,* with a view to identifying different media related to individual empowerment in the field of communicative and socio-political autonomy:

The *macro-media of communication* (television satellites and the Internet) seem to be acting as *agents of globalization.* Through global satellite and computer networks, trans-border data flows, scientific and professional electronic mailing and commercial advertising, the macro-media are supporting the globalization of the national markets, societies and cultures;

The *meso-media of communication* (print, cinema, and broadcasting) are primarily under the control of national governments or pressure groups and therefore function mostly as agents of *national integration and social mobilization;*

The micro-media of communication (telephone, copying machines, audio and videocassette recorders, musical tapes, and personal computers and the Internet) have primarily empowered the *centrifugal forces of dissent at the peripheries of power.*

Tehranian's proposal is a good starting point for an analysis of the mediation processes. Particularly because he introduces a global vision of the media and does not distinguish between them on the basis of technologies but on the basis of the objective of their appropriation.

Global communication is, for Tehranian, as it is for Castells (2003), a fundamental element for the creation of a global market. Global communication has enabled infrastructures for the communication of data, news and images and thus increased the desire for the ownership of products and access to services. But this process of association between communication and market has also given rise to a complementary effect: it has given power to the silent voices of those who claim self-determination and social justice and have responded to the consumerism through the assertion of identity.

Global communications (from the press to the Internet) have played a multiple role in these processes. The global media simultaneously promote the homogenization and differentiation of markets; they promote the centralization and, at the same time, dispersion of power; they implement cultural integration and pluralization.

If the *macro-media* have facilitated globalization, the *micro-media* have given empowerment to peripheral resistance and opposition. In contrast, the *meso-media* (opinion newspapers, scientific and professional journals) have brought communities of affinity close together in a global civil society that shares the flows of space (Castells, 2002).

One concrete example of these mediation processes is the impact of global communication in various areas of international relations (Tehranian, 1999). The global communications allow for new types of public, people and virtual diplomacy. Examples of the so-called *CNN effect,* in which one can ascertain that the public visibility attributed to a given type of event can have different effects, are, on the one hand, Somalia and Kurdistan and, on the other, the Gulf War, Chechnya, Bosnia, Kosovo and Iraq (Tehranian, 1999).

Whereas in the case of Somalia and Kurdistan the visible effect was the realization of humanitarian operations, in the cases of the Gulf War, Chechnya, Bosnia, Kosovo and Iraq a different effect seemed to manifest itself, i.e. a symbiosis between the discourse of the governments and the media in the coverage of international questions.

Another example of change made possible by the media is that which Tehranian (1999) calls *people diplomacy,* which opens up new arenas of intervention previously reserved for politicians only, namely in areas such as humanitarian solidarity, ecology or human right, leading to the subsequent desire to contact an organization. Also, the exercise of virtual diplomacy, through video and audio recordings of events not covered by the international and national media (such as the Iraqi resistance tapes or the Bin Laden message videos sent to international satellite channels), or also the protest against Indonesian suppression of the results of the self-determination referendum in East Timor in 1999 (where solidarity networks were created through e-mail and faxes that lead to an interruption in the E-mail and fax servers of the Security Council delegations and the various offices of the permanent members of the United Nations Council).

The media do not act in isolation but in conjunction. In other words, the practices of the social agents in the network society are practices that combine media in the endeavour to obtain results. They are not isolated uses of a specific medium. We should look at the media not as isolated technologies but as objects of social appropriation that are diversified and combined depending on the concrete objectives defined.

Contrary to the current discourse on the information society, in which one proposes a hierarchization of the media or subordination to the most recent one (as in the example of Web TV, which represents the subordination of the logic of television to the Internet), the media constitute a whole, a media system (Ortoleva, 2004), articulating with each other in networks depending on the dialectics of objectives between those who appropriate them and those who manage them. A whole that is appropriated on the basis of individual choices that are shared socially, thus constituting what we can call a media matrix (Meyrovitz, 1993).

The *media* are not isolated elements. We do not limit ourselves to listening to the radio only, or reading newspapers only or surfing the Internet only. The general practice is the combination of various media in everyday life at home, at work, at school or in getting from one place to another.

One example of this interdependence between media and individualized, but socially shared, appropriation can be found in an analysis of the communicative processes that took place in Spain between the attacks of 11 March 2004 in Madrid and the day of the Spanish general elections, 15 March 2004.

Before going onto an analysis of this tragic event, I would first like to recall a text called "Does the audience have bad effects on television?", which argued (contrary to the view then commonly held by intellectuals and elites that television was an instrument capable of controlling the minds of the target audience through its messages) that, although a message has the objective of producing certain effects, it can find itself confronted with local situations, other psychological dispositions, desires or fears and end up producing a boomerang effect (Eco, 1985 and Philo, 1999).

In an article published in March 2003, Umberto Eco argued that what we witnessed in Spain after the attacks of 11 march constituted precisely a situation to which his aforementioned line of argument applied. He writes that "the messages of the government were meant to say 'Believe us, the attacks were the work of ETA', but because the messages were so insistent and peremptory most of the users read "they are afraid to say that it was Al-Qaeda" (Eco, 2004).

The second phenomenon analyzed by Eco in the communicative logic that followed 11 March was what he termed the "Semiotic Guerrilla" (Eco, 1985). In other words, if one cannot have control over the sender of the communication – for example, a television network – then *one has to occupy the first rows in the rooms in which we watch television.* Semiotic guerrilla tactics consist in a series of interventions that do not act on the source of the message but on its target, inducing the users to discuss and criticize the message and not merely receive it passively (Eco, 2004).

In Spain, the 11 March attacks took place in an era that was no long of television or radio, but in an era in which the media included, through appropriation by a vast portion of the population, the mobile phone and the Internet.

The contemporary semiotic guerrilla tactic, contrary to the formulation by Eco, did not proceed from the action of elites but developed in a network process, a process of the creation of spontaneous nodes echoing the logic, coming from interpersonal communication – the rumour heard and passed on from person to person. This time, however, the mobile phone, mainly through the use of SMS, was used with the aim of spreading the message that the "government was lying and inviting people to gather at the headquarters of the party in government, the Partido Popular, or public buildings in protest" (Eco, 2004).

What we witnessed was the search for an alternative communication channel, using personal communication devices in a mass communication process with a view to establishing an alternative to the broadcast communication of the television stations. Personal communication can be transformed into a mass medium when it takes place in an electronic network (such as that of the mobile phone). Interpersonal communication thus took on a collective phenomenon dimension, in which the people watched television and read the newspapers but at the same time communicated with each other and asked whether or not what was being said was true and compared the news they read and heard on the national broadcasting channels with the information they were able to obtain on the Internet and through foreign newspapers and satellite television channels (Eco, 2004).

Other similar and likewise complex examples of networked appropriation of the media can be found in the protests in Seattle at the time of the WTO (World Trade Organization) "Millennium Round" in 1999. As highlighted by diverse analysts (Rodotà, 2000; Castells, 2004 and Wieviorka, 2003), the Seattle protests were organized via the Internet but they only gained visibility and power of mediation with the images divulged by television channels the world over. Here, the Internet took on the role traditionally played by personal structures in local networks, i.e. making it possible that people with similar interests, but dispersed geographically, could coordinate their actions.

In addition to this organizational role attributed to the Internet, the interest in analyzing this form of protest lies in the fact that it gives insight into the ideal of complementarity for the effectiveness of the mediation of the means. The participants in the protest actions understood very well that using the Internet only would not give them the legitimacy or the necessary force to achieve a stand off at the Millennium Round, hence the need to take to the streets in protest actions, which were organized via the Internet but divulged by television, the more widespread mass medium.

The main conclusion to be drawn from the analysis of Eco, Tehranian, Castells and Rodotà is the decisive role played by the articulation of the personal media, which, when networked, can become mass media and thus configure their flexibility and ambivalence. And that, consequently, any analysis of media-related individual empowerment has to take into account not only television, radio, newspapers and the World Wide Web but also the telephone, the mobile phone and Internet messaging (e-mail, newsgroups, chats, instant messaging, etc.).

One hypothesis we will come back to repeatedly in this analysis is that as a result of the relationship between the media's technological and services offer and the appropriations by the audiences, we are witnessing a networking between different mass media through interpersonal media, giving rise to the construction of a network rhetoric in which the divulged image can be countered through text and which is characterized by a media system that is also articulated in a network – from the economic dimension to the political, social and cultural dimensions.

Rhetoric, Accessibility of Information and Narratives

If the above is the context in which communication through the media is carried out, do we witness change in communicational paradigms or not? The answer must be yes, and that change is currently in progress in our societies.

Because technological development and the appropriation of the media place in coexistence, the interpersonal communication media and media that combine the two in their own genesis matrix, such as the Internet, the principle characteristic that pervades the whole sphere of communication must be that of ambivalence. That ambivalence, as we shall see, can be visualized in the communicational paradigms but also in other dimensions that contribute to defining a communicational model.

The current stage of economic development is characterized by the concentration of the possession of contents, transmission and access, with the economic groups incorporating possession of the provision of access to, and diffusion of information in their strategies. The era of the purely communicational group model is coming to an end (Ramonet, 1999). Large corporations are active in various economic sectors and, between them, they also hold mass media and telecommunications companies. For Ramonet, the three dimensions that traditionally make up the communication activity are undergoing transformation, whereby the informative and cultural dimension is gradually being given a minority role in relation to communication (which is the main attribute of public relations, advertising, political marketing, corporate image, companies etc. and agents), leading us to the question of whether or not there is a contradiction in the notion of freedom of the press when those who own the media are precisely the ones the news has to report on. This question cannot be answered with total clarity for it depends to a large extent on the particular situation each journalist finds himself in and also on the reading we ourselves have of how the definition of the news value takes place (Wolf, 2001).

Given that it is through the interdependence between technology, media economic models and rhetoric forms that one establishes a media system in a given moment in history and the communicational paradigms are shaped, if these elements are altered then the communication paradigms are also altered.

As a result of these economic and technological changes, the rhetoric model is undergoing transformation. The visual has gained in importance over the textual, with the Internet being the only field where the text still seems to dominate.

Outside the Internet, it is a rhetoric based on visual culture, a culture founded on simplicity, rapidity and emotion in which "to see is enough to be, to repeat to inform" (Ramonet, 1999). However, remaining in the sphere of rhetoric, there is one question left unanswered by Ramonet, though it is touched upon by Eco in "From Internet to Gutenberg" (1996): that of how the relationship between image and text will evolve when the new media themselves seek common technological supports and promote interdependence, for example through the use of chats, SMS and e-mailing in televised talk shows and when television channel websites enable real-time visualization of their programming.

Beyond the change in the rhetoric and the narrative formulas, the emergence of the new media also introduces the construction of new audiences through changes in the processes of social appropriation and diffusion of technologies.

According to Livingstone (1999), all technologies are accompanied by diffusion processes that result in complex interaction between the imagined and the actual uses, between the cultural representations and the individual concerns and between the emerging market form and the content developed for it. The diffusion process is always accompanied by a process of appropriation, i.e. the domestication of an unfamiliar object through its integration into the pre-existing social practices. With the new media, there also emerges new types of audiences (Roscoe, 1999). We are witnessing the multiplication of the personal media in the families, the diversification of forms and contents in an attempt to adapt them to the diverse lifestyles (themed channels, segmented information production, design), the convergence of technologies and the eradication of social barriers (home/work; entertainment/information; education/recreation; feminine/masculine) and, as a result of interactive communication, the construction of media by the users themselves and the assumption of new dimensions of identities instead of them being mere objects (for example, the case of desktop images or open source programming). Through the analysis of the audiences and their relations with the different media we can, therefore, identify possible differences in terms of communication models.

In characterizing what the current communicational model is we have also to take into account the accessibility of information dimension. In both the political discourse and certain dimensions of the academic discourse on the *information society*, there frequently emerge associations between technological change and greater availability of information and the association of this with greater creation of knowledge, which, in turn, will nourish the processes of economic and social innovation. But can we affirm that this is also a characteristic of the communicational model?

Although we can include the greater accessibility of information dimension as an attribute of the current communicational model in an informational society, it must also be looked at in terms of its real social reach. Because the availability of information depends on how the media system is organized, Eco (2000) believes that in order to analyze the relationship between availability of information and communicational models one must, first of all, understand the changes in the structure of the media and their rhetoric. Only then can one infer how the greater availability translates to real changes in the communication patterns.

The availability of information allows for a new cultural democracy, for in traditional societies the cultural world was divided into two parts: producers and consumers, people who write books and people who read them (Eco, 2000). The information technologies in general, and the Internet in particular, change this in a positive way, making it possible for everyone to write about everything. But, at the same time, that cultural democracy means that there is an exponential increase of information and, considering that there are limits, i.e. that too much information is the same as no information at all, that availability can have only very limited effects (Eco, 2000). During the Internet launch of the "Interactive Manual of Knowledge", Eco pointed out that the Internet can be seen as the virtual equivalent of the universe in which we live. Just as there are forests and cities and countries (from the US to Burkina Faso) in our universe, on the Internet we also find everything – from Nazi propaganda pages to those trying to sell something and pornography. The idea that only through information that is more conveniently accessible and more rapidly consultable can we find solutions to our individual and collective problems must therefore be something tempered by the very context of the society in which we live (Eco, 1996).

Up until the large-scale dissemination of the Internet amongst the citizens, the churches and scientific institutions, amongst others, had the function of filtering and reorganizing knowledge and information. By acting in this way, these intermediaries restricted our intellectual freedom but also guaranteed that the community had access to the essential. The Internet has done way with the institutional filters or, at least, obliges us to think about constructing new filters and developing individual filters (Eco, 1996). For this reason the discussion of access to information must also take into consideration that there is, indeed, too much news [29] and that the only way to guarantee access to useful information is to decimate it (i.e. apply positive and negative filtering criteria choosing one option out of every ten). The problem is that the filtering likewise implies knowledge of the mechanisms that produced the information, which brings us to the question of the necessary literacies.

Abundance of information is not in itself a guarantee of the social usefulness of that information. One must have the necessary skills so that one can act as an information filter, know how to distinguish and select, or the access to all the information available will be fruitless (Eco, 1999). "One cannot understand, in the most critical and comprehensive sense of the term, a film if one has no notion of the technique of filming and editing." (Eco, 1999)

Communicational autonomy does not depend on access only, just as the fruition of information may have little capacity of individual empowerment if the necessary literacy is not used, or is not present in the selection and filtering processes. As Paquete de Oliveira (1994) suggests, the problem of knowledge is today one of the main problems in democratic states. Although the world of today is inundated with information, the diffusion of knowledge (i.e., the capacity of manipulation and assimilation) is not accompanying the growth in information (Morin, 1994 cited in Oliveira, 1994).

---

[29] According to Denis McQuail, *news* can be defined as the most common form in which information on public events is transmitted by the most diverse media. There is a great diversity of types and formats as well as strong cultural differences between the diverse divulgation supports. The basic characteristics are generally defined as: actuality, relevance and reliability.

Just as accessibility is of itself insufficient for defining a new communicational model, "information" is not enough either. It is questionable whether we can adequately describe societies with only one comprehensive variable and, even if that were possible, one could question that information is a more precise category than other equally applicable ones such as entertainment, spectacle, vigilance or risk (Hamelink, 2001). It follows that, as a corollary of that criticism, "information" is not a category that can correctly define the identifiable trends in course, for it is not possible to establish a direct equivalence between, for example, information and power, just as it is by no means certain that just because the people are better informed about each other that they will better understand each other and be less inclined towards conflict. This because most of the presuppositions as to the role and effects of information and knowledge are based on cause-effect models, in which information and knowledge are conceived as key variables in the social processes, as if it were possible to guarantee that, due to the way in which they are processed, specific social effects will take place (Hamelink, 2001).

By focusing on the ethical dimension, Hamelink (2001) raises the question of whether a new communicational model in formation would be based on the right to information or the right to communicate. For the exchange of symbols between human beings now seems to be less and less subject to space and time restrictions. By enabling many-to-many communication, simultaneous reception, the alteration and the redistribution of cultural objects and by thus promoting instantaneous global contact and placing the *subject* in a network relationship, the new information and communication technologies are, in a certain way, making McLuhan's *global village* at least technologically possible (Poster, 1995). Hamelink highlights one of the characteristics of the new technologies in general, and the Internet in particular: the fact that we can all be producers of information. In other words, in addition to all of us being able to access information we also have the right to communicate the information we choose. Hamelink's line of thought, which follows similar proposals by Eco (2000) and Castells (2004), is that citizenship can only be complete when one possesses the literacy for the use of the new technologies, which in itself implies access to the cultural and educational domain and, consequently, exercise of the freedom of choice.

The greater availability of information is one of the elements that must be considered in analyzing the definition of a communicational model but it alone is not a decisive element of differentiation.

In characterizing a communicational model one must also bear in mind not only how the relations of appropriation of the media by the audience are established, or how economic management between media occurs (as in the case of television game shows and SMS) but also how that relationship is processed at the level of the definition of what news are and what entertainment models are or, if we prefer, the narrative dimension of the media information and entertainment.

Thanks to the needs for economic evolution of the traditional mass media, leading to the territorial expansion of their audiences (via satellite and cable television), and to the dissemination of the use of the Internet, we are witnessing the disappearance, or devaluation, of certain concepts that until now were socially and culturally valued. One of the first concepts that were questioned by the globalization of communication was the notion of boundary. The fall of communicational boundaries brought about by the new information and communication technologies has produced two conflicting phenomena. On the one hand, there is no longer a national community that can impede its citizens from knowing what happens in other countries – even in dictatorships it is increasingly difficult to rule this out. On the other hand, the globalization of communications has introduced modifications at the monitoring level. Until very recently exercised almost exclusively by the states, this function is now being shared by (and sometimes transferred to) other centres of power (Lyon, 1995; Poster, 2000 and Castells, 2003).

For Eco, the Orwellian *Big Brother* is not the television version, where millions of "voyeurs" watch one single exhibitionist. Today, the *Big Brother* watching us does not have a face and is not on his own: it is the totality of the global economy (Lyon, 1998 and Rodotà, 2000). And it is on the basis of this growing sharing of the monitoring role that one is producing a movement of cultural change in the perception of what we socially value in relation to *reserve* (Eco, 2000).

The cultural dimension of valuing privacy or, if we prefer, our reserve, is by no means an acquired fact. On the contrary, if we disregard the privacy activist groups in the Internet (Castells, 2004), there are few others who deal with these questions in the public context, i.e. beyond those who wish to maintain commercial transmissions secret, those who are against the violation of personal correspondence secrecy and secrecy of income and those who elaborate research data that they do not yet wish to publish, there are few for whom question of privacy on their agenda (Eco, 2000 and Castells, 2004).

Although technological evolution may interfere in the cultural perception of the concept of reserve, there are also reasons that are rooted in the evolution of the mass media economic models itself which may help to explain the devaluation. Over the last two decades there has been a clear evolution in the definition of what a news item is, which, to a certain extent, can be explained by reasons of the media's economic survival, but which also involves entertainment model criteria.

Eco (2000) argues that the first variation in the field of the definition of news emerged in the written press. Up until very recently, there were only specialized social gossip publications, traditionally referred to as the "pink press". The mostly wrote about famous people – actors, singers, monarchs in exile or playboys – who voluntarily exposed themselves to the observation of the photographers and chroniclers. The readers knew that many times the events featured in the news stories were themselves concocted by the journalists, but the readers were not turning to these publications for news or, if we prefer, the truth (Traquina, 2003). What they wanted was entertainment.

With the aim of competing with television and also given the need to fill a greater number of pages with stories, the generalist and reference press began to take a growing interest in social events, show business and gossip, thus altering its criteria on what constitutes a news story. Gossip became a reference information matter and even targeted those that were not its traditional targets – reigning monarchs, political and religious leaders, state presidents, scientists, etc. – giving rise to the idea that becoming the object of public gossip was equivalent to acquiring the same *social status* as a famous actor or politician.

This was an important development, for it introduced an alteration in social values and allowed for a further stage of evolution within the *media*, which emerged when television began to idealize programmes in which the protagonists were no longer those who gossiped about persons not present, but those who were the object of the gossip and who willingly presented themselves in public gossiping about their own lives and those of others. This second stage took place fundamentally in the entertainment dimension, which confers upon it a logic of association between the contestant and his actions as a universal model, for the logic is "if he exposes himself, anyone can do it" (Eco, 2000).

The contestant's exhibitionism convinces the public that no dimension of the reserve warrants privacy, not even the most intimate, and that the exhibition of all events is always rewarded (Cardoso, 2003). However, that dimension cannot only be attributed to television, given that on the Internet we also find many sites that follow exactly the same values of exhibitionism (Gauntlett, 2000). The profusion of web cameras, with or without a profit making purpose, uncovering the privacy of private or semi-private places, personal home pages revealing all under "who I am" and self-exhibition in photographs, even of such intimate details as the insides of one's own body (Eco, 2000), are examples of this relationship with the reserve.

This contribution by Umberto Eco to understanding the narrative dimension and the information and entertainment dimension is of twofold usefulness. On the one hand, it demonstrates the bidirectionality that is established in the influence relationships between the traditional media (television, press and radio) and the Internet and, on the other hand, it introduces the relationship between economy and media contents. A fundamental relationship for being able to question the emergence of the processes of communicative globalization and that of networking of the media and, consequently, the networked *mediation*, and above all the alteration of the news and entertainment models in a cultural context that corresponds to a real virtuality culture – the culture generated in an informational model of the networked society. But, is this sufficient to be able to confirm the existence of a *new media system?*

A media system, as formulated by Ortoleva (2002), refers to the framework of interconnections between technologies and organizations that guide the diverse forms of communication. This is a category of essentially institutional and economic origins that helps us to explain, on the one hand, the evolutive dynamics of the media and, on the other, how each society establishes a division of functions between the diverse media, which is born out of the complex socio-cultural processes but finds its legitimacy *a posteriori* in corporations and legislative frameworks (Ortoleva, 2002). Traditionally we can distinguish four orientations or, if we prefer, four ideological models that preside over how communication is regarded in the institutional and economic organization of a given media system (Williams, 1999 and Ortoleva, 2004). It is possible to characterize the current media system as the product of a search for balance between a commercial and a democratic communication model.

On the basis of a number of developments it is possible to argue that a new system has slowly been establishing itself over the last decade. During this period we have seen the simultaneous birth of hundreds of new press titles and the use of the most diverse technologies for divulging messages in a process that can be characterized as "the media preceding the message" (Eco, 2001).

In the 1970s McLuhan argued that the media were the message (McLuhan, 1997), meaning that any single medium induces behaviours, creates psychological connections and shapes the mentality of the receiver, regardless of the content vehicled in that medium.

Castells (2002), in turn, characterized the organizational relation of the current media as being based on the "message being the media", i.e. the media are shaped depending on the message one is trying to get across, seeking that which best serves the message and the audience at which it is aimed. And as that message automatically has an economic component produced by a regime of competition, the advertising supports are directed at whoever produces messages that appeal to a large number of persons, giving rise to a levelling of themes and programmes between the different channels. The channel or medium is no longer neutral with respect to what it vehicles (Eco, 2001).

Furthermore, the media precede the message when the technological acceleration produces multiple new channels that exist before there is content to be placed there, creating a new challenge of an economic character, thus rendering transmission feasible without having equated what is to be transmitted (as in the case of interactive and digital television or the interactive CD-ROM).

In addition to the economic challenge, this is also a cultural change that marks a new paradigm of communicative organization and it is also visible in the fact that the majority of the new communicational channels were presented to the general public in a process of active experimentation which Castells has defined as "learning by doing" (Castells, 2002).

According to Ortoleva (2004) this is not merely a conjunctural alteration in the mass media system. One sign of this transformation is the fact that the object of attention of those involved has shifted from the contents to embrace also the economic, technological and legal dimensions. This new media system, whose consolidation phase took place between 1990 and 2001 is characterized by a group of global trends that are mutually contradictory.

The so-called convergence is identified as one of the basic characteristics of the 1990s in the media system. Following the legislative/legal alterations, a number of barriers to the constitution of large groups – which had maintained the previous division of the media system into single units (publishing houses, telecommunications providers, broadcasters, and the communicative hardware and information access industry) – were broken down. But this endeavour to overcome the cultural, institutional and technological divisions with a view to enabling the formation of unitary industries and mixed communicative models, i.e. multimedia, did not take place. Although we have witnessed large-scale merger and acquisition processes and the collapse of legal barriers, the idea of the generalized hybridization of the media, although attractive on paper, proved to be impracticable more times (for example, television and the Internet) than it was successful (mobile phones and mp3 music). Only rarely did the mergers and acquisitions bring an effective unification of the production processes of diverse media types. There was a financial and not so much industrial logic governing the decisions and for that reason we have also seen many drawbacks, such as those in the internet portals and the financial losses associated with them, or the sale of assets in the television, radio and press sector after a precipitated acquisition by many telecommunications companies.

Another of the characteristics of this moment in the history of the media is the so-called "content adventure" (Ortoleva, 2004). There is no doubt that the circulation of one and the same content through various supports is an important possibility for the optimization of profits for the media industries, for example the cinema industry. But what ended up characterizing the media system in the 1990s, as far as content questions was concerned, was more the establishment of a battlefield for social and cultural conflicts than a huge increment in the source of revenue.

Finally, there emerged what Ortoleva defines as the central role attributed to software which constitutes, in the opinion of that author, the true segment in growth within the media sector: the programme or application that cannot be classified as a *support*, i.e. that which defines and profoundly conditions all the contents to be produced, but is not yet content because its function is preliminary to the elaboration of the information. Examples of this are, amongst other things, the television programmes and game shows sold to the diverse television stations around the globe (mainly factual programming, but also shows and serials).

A fifth characteristic that can be added to Ortoleva's proposals lies in the central role of the Internet. The Internet has emerged as a technology which, thanks to its capacities of adaptation to, and interaction with, other technologies has become the paradigm of the new media. The Internet is an example of the new media but it is a new medium which, as a result of its diffusion and social appropriation, constitutes itself as the technology with which all the rest seem to want to interact through the establishment of digital links (for example, E-mails being sent to radio stations) or analogical links (such as newspaper internet sites that publish surveys conducted online).

As the Internet is at the same time a mass medium and a medium of interpersonal communication, the two dynamics are present simultaneously. As a technological base, the Internet serves both those dimensions and for that reason the *Market* and the *State* have adopted it as the new central element in the media system.

Networked Communication

All societies are characterized by communication models and not only by information models (Wolton, 2000, Colombo, 1993). Before Internet usage became widespread, the interpretative hypothesis proposed by Colombo (1993) for characterizing the current communicational model focused on its synthetic dimension.

That formulation also constitutes the starting point for the characterization of the new communicational model I propose herein. A new model that can be added to the three preceding models, which can be ordered in terms of their social affirmation cycles (Ortoleva 2004). The first is what has been defined as interpersonal communication, which is characterized by the bidirectional exchange between two persons or several persons within a group. The second model, likewise deeply rooted in our societies, is one-to-many communication, in which one single individual sends one single message to a limited group of people. This is the typical public discourse situation, be it proffered in an election campaign rally, a theatre or on a soapbox at Hyde Park Corner in London, but it also traditionally characterizes education.

The third model, with which we have the least experience in terms of time, is that of *mass communication*, in which, thanks to the use of specific mediation technologies, one single message is directed to a "mass" of people, i.e. it is sent to an audience whose real dimension is unknown and, as such, not delimited in advance.

The term "synthetic", which helps characterize the fourth communication model, suggests diverse interpretation keys. On the one hand the essence and consequent rapidity associated with the binary logic of machine language – the basic communicational formula associated with the information technologies. On the other, one can suggest the idea of velocity as a value in the search for proximity with human interactivity. Thus we have witnessed a process of contraction, through the reduction of time in the communicative factors, and, at the same time, a process of dilation, due to the resistance existing in the non-communicative factors in our society (Colombo, 1993). The adjective "synthetic" also refers to the dimension of imitation. Synthetic communication is also a communication of active and passive simulation, as it seeks to imitate other communication models and transfer them to the space of the information and communication technologies (Colombo, 1993).

Fausto Colombo's proposal allows one to conceive the first element of identification of a new form of conceptualizing the communicational relations in our society, i.e., the genesis of a new communicational model allowing for participation and isolation, spatial and temporal compression and binary synthesis (Colombo, 1993).

However, there is another characteristic, a more central one, that is fundamental to understanding this new communicational paradigm, the *network*.

Networked communication results from the ways in which the different dimensions of a technocultural system interact with each other and the dominant technological paradigm. In this case, the information technologies that enable networked organization models and also networked communication. How does *networked communication* differ from the two defined types of mass communication, i.e. the press and circular diffusion (broadcasting based media)?

In the case of the written press, or newspapers, the objective of reaching many different people with the same message was based on reproduction through the copy. This implied a temporal hiatus between the moment of sending and moment of reception as well as an industrial-type production apparatus.

The possibility of direct to the masses communication was introduced for the first time with broadcasting, i.e. the possibility of creating, for a vast area, the simultaneously shared experience of accessing the same message. As Ortoleva (2004) points out, the mass media involved in broadcasting offered, for the first time, the possibility of reaching the domestic space without posterior filters and mediations (Meyrowitz, 1992 in Ortoleva, 2004). The third innovation introduced by broadcasting refers to its cultural dimension. Contrary to the press, it does not offer us a text or a succession of texts, instead we are offered programming. This is a flow (Williams, 1999), a form of organization of the discourse that has no beginning and no end; it is there and continues there, regardless of whether or not we are syntonized with the broadcast.

Networked communication presents itself as a new cultural form of linking audiences and senders for it functions in accordance with a hypertextual logic, in the sense that it promotes articulation between the classic concept of text, the concept of flow and interpersonal communication.

However, the hypertextual logic is different to affirming the concretization of a hypertextual technological support based on multimedia convergence (Castells, 2004). Let us try to clarify the preceding affirmation, using, for example, Umberto Eco (1997), who identifies three different possibilities of conceiving hypertext:

Hypertext as a system, which is visible in the encyclopaedia and allows us to establish new relations, i.e. knowing that two historic persons shared one and the same place or circle of friends, it is possible to imagine that they worked together, etc.;

Hypertext as the transfer of a text to hypertext through a story in which the narrative is open (something that Eco points out is not a literary novelty and can be found in the work of Joyce), in which the text does not configure as a linguistic or encyclopaedic system. A textual hypertext is finite and limited even though it is open to innumerable and original questions;

And *hypertext as a form of creation*, i.e. the notion of hypertext as unlimited and infinite, in which the classic notion of authorship disappears.

What all these definitions have in common is the existence of a textual dimension – mediated writing. But for the definition of *networked communication* what is more important is the use of a cultural definition of hypertext (Castells, 2004).

"Hypertext can transform each reader into an author" is one of the most repeated phrases that have been said about the Internet. However, it can be re-read in the light of the networked media, in the sense that one can affirm that the interconnection of diverse media through hypertext (or hypermedia), flows and texts allows for the fusion of interpersonal communication and mass communication, bringing us into a world of communication that allows us to be authors, senders or simply receivers.

It is our use decisions, in interaction with the possibilities given by the technologies, and the influence that we exercise on the production and offer of the media (be it in terms of hardware or software) that create not a technological hypertext (or hypermedium) but a functional networked articulation of the different forms of communication depending on our individual and collective objectives.

As we have seen, the characteristics of interdependence, ambivalence and synthesis in the universe of the media (from the cultural to the economic dimension) have allowed for the development of a networked media system based on the coexistence of broadcasting media (radio and television and newspapers) and the metamedia (Colombo, 2000), i.e. media which, like the Internet and, to a certain extent, the mobile phone (Eco, 2004) combine interpersonal communication and mass communication. Communication in the informational societies is thus characterized by five features: 1) communicational globalization processes; 2) alterations in the news and entertainment models; 3) the networking of the media; 4) and consequently, networked mediation; 5) a cultural framework that corresponds to a real virtuality culture – the culture generated in an informational society model that articulates its social processes in a networked communicational model.

Examples of this synthetic nature of the communication model can be found in the hypertextual technological articulation, and not technological convergence, of the different media through the use of technological interfaces (normally the Internet or SMS) in the search for a linguistic expression that combines written, visual and audio elements.

Although the interdependence between these communication circuits is indisputable, the interactions between them are complex and difficult to foresee.

It is on the basis of these, fruit of the relation between the offer of technology and services by the media and the appropriations by the audiences, that we are witnessing a networked articulation of different mass media through interpersonal media using, for example, text, and thus generating multiple processes of varying degrees of interactivity.

The communicational model generated in the informational societies, where the prevailing social organization model is the network, is that of networked communication – a communicational model that does not replace the previous models but articulates them, producing new forms of communication and also enabling new forms of facilitation of individual empowerment and, consequently, communicative autonomy. In the Network Society a new communicational model has been taking shape. A communicational model characterized by the fusion of interpersonal communication and mass communication, connecting audiences, broadcasters and publishers under a hypertextual matrix linking several media devices (from newspapers to videogames). This communicational model is hypertextual, in the sense that several devices, analogical or digital, connect to each other. It is hypertextual also because, due to our own appropriations and representations, we attribute to different media different linking combinations. This is a model that promotes articulation between the more classic concept of text, flow and interpersonal communication, in what we can call "Networked Communication".

Networked Communication is able to join the interpersonal and mass communications dimension into a new network communication strategy and agency. Networked communication refers to a media system where interactivity gives shape to its organizational model. A media system, that offers two central nodes, one centred on low interactivity, where television rules, and another where the centre is the Internet, offering high interactivity. Those different media nodes are connected mainly through interpersonal media (although they can beused as mass media): mobile phones; E-mail; iPods; etc.

Networked communication develops under a media system where, due to the economic options, technology availability and social domestication, the current meta-system of information is organized around television and the Internet, whereby the former is the central and the latter as the emerging player, and where the entertainment meta-system is still mainly populated by television and cinema but where multimedia games have arrived to stay.

The *Networked Communication* model is the informational society's communication model. A model that must be understood also in terms of the literacies it requires in order to have a broader choice on how to build our media diets, media matrix and Internet gatekeeping (Cardoso, 2003).

4. A Constellation of Networks:
Mass Media, Games, Internet and Telephones

As we have seen, communication is always the product of three conditions: 1) the economic organization of the *media system,* i.e. how the different media relate with each other in terms of transmission and production of
contents; 2) the different *media matrixes* that we use to classify the media
depending on our needs and objects, or, if we prefer, our representations
in relation to the media; 3) and our *media diets,* or practices involving the
media.

That conjugation of diverse dimensions has produced the communicational model that asserts itself in the informational societies, which is
characterized by its networked structuring and a synthesis of different dimensions already present in other communicational models, so that we can
call it *networked communication.*

If, as is suggested, there is a network-based structuring, how is this
articulation processed?

The hypothesis I propose herein is that the media system is articulated
more and more on the basis of two main networks, which, in turn, communicate with each other through various communication and information
technologies.

These networks are built, respectively, around the *television* and the
Internet, establishing nodes with different communication and information
technologies such as the telephone, radio, the press, etc.

On a second level, one also must ask why two main networks existence.

The explanatory hypothesis requires an understanding of how the interactivity dimensions made possible technologically occur, both in the Internet and in television, but also of how we socially value the different technologies depending on their different entertainment and information functions.

Proceeding from the analysis of the role of the diverse media in the network society, there are various questions raised by the concept of a media system. The first question has to do with the role of television in the informational society and network society.

At the beginning of the 21st century, watching television continues to be the most common daily activity, followed by regular socializing with family members and friends (Cardoso et al, 2003).

However, we are witnessing a reduction in television viewing time by Internet users (Cardoso, 2004 and Castells, 2003b), so the question whether or not television is still the central element both in the media system (Ortoleva, 2004) and in the dominant culture form in our contemporary societies – the real virtuality culture (Castells, 2002) – is a completely valid one. Accordingly, the question must be asked whether or not the Internet is having an erosive effect on the central role of television.

An Entertainment Meta-System in Transition: from Multimedia Games to Television

A great part of the uses made of multimedia in the context of the new system of *communication mediated by technology* (a result of the articulation between the subsystems of computer-mediated communication and globalization of choice at the level of the mass media) will depend on the options taken in the first phases of utilization.

If we base our analysis on the public and private sector investment in Europe and the US, what we are witnessing is a duality of commitments.

In other words, as far as new technologies such as the Internet and mobile phones are concerned, the public sector is essentially interested in furthering the infrastructure and access, proceeding from the idea that achieving the potential of the new communication and information technologies in areas such as education, health and the arts will bring better living conditions and opportunities for the citizens.

The private sector's strategy for the Internet and the new technologies, on the other hand, is to invest in the development of an entertainment structure, together with the more traditional technologies such as television or cinema. This structure has been the private sector's driving force and, as such, it represents the most profitable option.

The entertainment industry was the fastest growing industry in the mid-1990s in the United States with a turnover of more than 350 billion dollars per annum and more than 5 million workers (and an employment growth rate of approximately 12% per annum). These figures were only surpassed by the information technology industries in the closing years of that decade (Castells, 2002).

There are characteristics that seem to be transversal to the informational societies of the European Union and the United States and which, as such, merit reference in this analysis. These are, for example: the fact that the amount of time available for leisure seems to be decreasing even though this is accompanied by more diversified cultural practices (Cardoso et al, 2004); the fact that the family budgets are not accompanying the expansion rates offered by the technological possibilities; and, finally, the fact that the amount of contents available is not accompanying the transformation of the system (Eco, 2001), which, in turn, places the need for the acquisition of already existing contents exchanges and their adaptation to the new technological distribution resources.

Another fact that has been borne out by several studies (Castells et al, 2003 and Cardoso et al, 2004) indicate that it is not true that people, when using all the new technologies, merely desire more entertainment instead of using the multimedia for access to more information, community matters, political involvement and education. This observation would suggest that banking on mass and diversified production of entertainment might not be the obvious choice for multimedia users, though it is clear that that is the strategy of the business corporations operating in the field.

The interpretational hypothesis formulated herein is that after an initial phase of experimentation characterized by the transference to the Internet of business models and relations with the consumers that are characteristic of the mass media, this readjustment would result from the adaptation of the production world to the demands of *consumption*. The entrepreneurial concentration in the multimedia sector, the reliance on blockbuster productions in the cinema (accompanied by a reduction in the number of products and concentration of the revenue) and the vertical and horizontal consolidation in the context of the cultural industries can be seen as a response to the tensions listed above, thus endeavouring to potentiate easily sellable contents and banking on a management of scarce resources, such as the time and money available for consumption and entertainment to families. None of these developments is contradictory to the understanding of the media system in development in Europe, America and Asia put forward by Castells (2003). A pattern based on segmentation of messages and the consequent cultural and social differentiation of audiences, on the growing social stratification amongst users and on the integration of the messages in a common cognitive pattern.

However, that is a media system that differentiates between entertainment and information.

As far as information is concerned, there are multiple options, which can effectively turn the user into a producer and consumer of information when we think of, for example, the possibilities provided by the Internet. But it is that same system which, in the entertainment sphere, places the hurles to the entry of new producers too high (with the exception, perhaps, of the generalized availability of music through mp3) through the banking on high-cost productions and which, although the increase in the offer is indisputable, continues to function under a model of control of distribution and management of the offer capacity.

In the current media system, in terms of the entertainment offered by the new digital multimedia technologies, interactivity often goes no further than the increase of the pre-defined choice possibilities in option menus such as those that come with films on DVD. [30]

In the context of entertainment multimedia, the organization and production logics were inherited from the broadcasting system associated with the audiovisual mass media. [31] This is indeed hardly surprising when we understand that audiovisual services, despite the fact that multimedia games play an increasingly important role within the system, are still today to a large extent dominated by a revenue structure based on television. In other words, they depend on distribution via television for their profits.

---

[30] Entertainment is one of the central activities in media production and consumption. It covers a whole series of formats with the common features that are designed to attract and divert attention "to other spaces". The term *infotainment* is used to identify forms of entertainment that invade the sphere of reality – particularly, news, advertising, education and politics. (Hartley 2004).

[31] The sum of cinema, video, DVD, TV and radio broadcasting, music production and multimedia games.

Table 4.1 – International Trade Balance (US$ million)

	1995	1996	1997	1998	1999	2000	Average growth
US revenue in the EU market							
Cinema	1178	1392	1494	1734	1721	1750	
TV	2026	2645	2880	3187	3781	4384	
Video	2092	2224	2272	2392	2540	2898	
Growth		18%	6%	10%	10%	12%	11%
EU revenue in the US market							
United Kingdom (UK)	426	499	536	550	705	691	
Rest of EU	92	115	132	156	148	136	
UE/UK ratio	22%	23%	25%	28%	21%	20%	
Annual growth in revenue		17%	7%	3%	28%	-2%	11%

Source: European Audiovisual Observatory Yearbook 2002.

The two largest audiovisual markets in the world – the European Union and the US – were worth about 270 billion euro in 2000 and presented very similar revenue structure, in which television accounted for approximately 60% of the total, followed by radio and music with approximately 20% and then video (6.5% EU and 8.9% US) and multimedia games (7% EU and 4.5% US). [32]

Given that the average growth rates are identical for the two markets, i.e. 11%, the differences have to be understood in a cultural perspective of proximity between the different cultures. In other words, although it has greater receptiveness for other English language cultures, North American culture is not familiar with continental European productions. This is a situation that Europe does not have in relation to culture produced in the US.

---

[32] Speaking of multimedia games today means analyzing a concrete part of the Media System in which there is a trend towards convergence into an open space of interaction: the Internet. So far we have witnessed the need to separate the games depending on the necessary support hardware and the ease of finding markets for subsequent analysis of them. In the case of the SEGA, Sony or Nintendo consoles, the initial term adopted was *video games*, as one required a television to play them. When the personal computer (PC) came along, the name chosen was *computer games*. The question that arises is whether or not this division still makes sense at a time in which it seems certain that none of the markets is likely to replace the other and in which the games for PC are seeking new interaction spaces on the Internet and the latest generation consoles (128 Bits) are basing their marketing on the news possibilities of connecting to the Internet and playing online. For this reason one common term is becoming more and more common: multimedia games, but it is based more on the interaction possibilities and spaces than on mere technological choices.

If one compares the audiovisual markets in the EU and US, the greatest similarity can be found in the multimedia games level. In this dimension the European market corresponds to 80% of the US market, whereas for cinema it represents only 54.4% and for television only 51.2%.

Although there is some similarity in the revenue structure of the European and North American markets there are also particularities within the European Union itself that are worth highlighting.

Figure 4.1 – Comparison of audiovisual markets, US and EU – 15

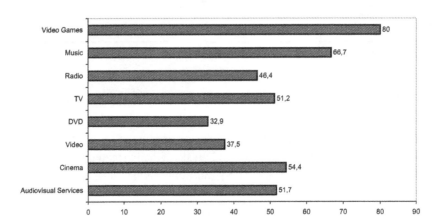

Source: Cinema, TV and radio in the EU Statistics on audiovisual services (Data 1980-2002) Luxembourg: Office for Official Publications of the European Communities, 2003.

For example, the Southern European Countries (France, Portugal, Italy and Spain) have a greater proportion in the cinema segment in the dimension of the box office sales than northern countries such as Germany and the United Kingdom.

In terms of the revenue structure for DVD and video, the United Kingdom is closer to the United States than to the other European countries included in the list.

Table 4.2 – Audiovisual services revenue 2000 (EUR millions)

	Cinema Box office	Video	DVD	TV	Radio	Music	Games	Total
US	8413	15916	4237	105403	20891	15231	8012	178103
EU-15	4577	5962	1392	53925	9649	9891	6408	91804
Germany	825	764	183	13335	3416	2630	1507	22660
United Kingdom	947	2107	469	15225	1676	3061	1765	25250
France	891	1186	380	8749	1383	1125	1059	14773
Portugal	66	44	4	416	109	154	64	857
Italy	545	545	73	4969	628	368	383	7511
Spain	536	352	70	4017	546	626	517	6664

Source: Cinema, TV and radio in the EU Statistics on audiovisual services (Data 1980-2002) Luxembourg: Office for Official Publications of the European Communities, 2003.

As for radio, the greatest contributions are registered for Germany and Portugal. This is a trend which, in the Portuguese case, is all the more extreme when one takes into account the dimension of music sales (Portugal contributed 18% of the revenue structure as opposed to only 4.9% from Italy). [33]

Table 4.3 – Use of audiovisual services 2001 (units per year)

	Cinema visits	Video purchase	Video rentals	DVD purchase	DVD rentals	CD purchase	Games purchase
US	5.2	4.4	33.5	11.9	21.6	9.2	-
EU-15	2.5	2.4	5.7	9.2	6.3	6.9	11
Germany	2.2	1.2	4.5	6	4.8	5.6	15
United Kingdom	2.6	5.5	9	13.8	8.3	10.9	10.6
France	3.1	2.9	3.3	9.1	3.3	5.6	10.3
Portugal	1.9	3.1	2.8	18	4	7.6	6
Italy	1.9	2.5	3.7	9.3	3.1	5.6	10.3
Spain	3.7	1.4	9.9	7.4	5.3	10.6	6

Source: Cinema, TV and radio in the EU Statistics on audiovisual services (Data 1980-2002) Luxembourg: Office for Official Publications of the European Communities, 2003.

Although we have so far focused essentially on revenue for insight into the specificities of the different markets, we must also include in this

---

[33] On the music markets and their transformation as a result of digitalization of concepts and the emergence of the Internet, see: Mansell (1998), McCourt (2003) and Richeri (2004).

analysis the consumption frequency dimensions for the populations. What the data would seem to indicate is that there are differentiated media diets depending on the national cultures. Also, in Europe, going to the cinema is a less common activity than is the cultural practice in the US.

In this introductory analysis of the media systems at the global level one must also take a brief look at the economic policy on piracy. The introduction of the P2P networks has led to a hardening of positions: on the one hand, Internet users have increased the free and non-legal downloading of films and music and, on the other, the phonographic associations and film producers are increasing the clampdown on this type of Internet use. This hardening of positions is, in turn, always an indicator that a change in the system is coming and, although one cannot predict how things will evolve exactly, it would seem to be clear today that the production and revenue model for the music and film industries will have to be altered. Signs of the times in the field of music are the aggregated success of Apple's iPod and iTunes for the sale of music and the alternatives sought by bands such as U2 in the relationship they established with iTunes. As U2 vocalist Bono Vox argues, in the current music business format the record companies are not potentiating their relations with the buying public (Assayas, 2005). Thus it is no surprise that today we see a hardening of positions amongst the public, which is increasing the number of illegal mp3 copies, and the record companies, which are applying legal pressure on their own current and future economic base – the younger music lovers.

As Bono Vox has pointed out, and is borne out by the analysis of the CD marketing structure (Richieri, 2005), the price of a CD was initially very high due to the production costs, which have since changed as the years went by. An analysis of the current music industry situation allows for the conclusion that the model that is being designed will not consist of one single model for the relations between artists, record companies and public but will be a combination of various models. On the one hand, there will be a policy of providing bonuses for the purchase of CDs, such as books or DVDs, and on the other, there will be greater investment in online music distribution, offering what is often the reason for the illegal use of mp3, i.e. live versions, acoustic versions, studio versions, etc. But the most striking feature would seem to be the alteration of the philosophy based on the product with a view to consolidating the relationship with the fan. In other words, it will be more and more necessary for musicians and groups to deal with their audiences in terms of a sharing of identity in order to guaran-

tee loyalty and a proximity between the both sides, for only empathy between the public and the artist(s) can guarantee the option to purchase and
not to illegally download. The implications of the alteration of the models
are far reaching in particular for the record companies, which will face
greater problems in terms of their catalogue management – in particular,
for musicians and groups whose commercial life is considered short and
may not warrant the investment. New artists will also resort to new forms
of affirming their identity through the Internet before tying themselves to
a record company. This relationship between artists and new distribution
channels is by no means a thing of the future; it is already exemplified
by the U2 commercial practices, e.g. polyphonic mobile phone ringtones,
soundtracks for games (and not just films) and the personalization of mp3
players (such as the U2 black iPod). Furthermore, music today is a much
more widespread phenomenon than it was 20 years ago, not only because
there are much more radios and music players in our homes but also because the apparatuse communicate with each other in networks. If there are
threats, there are also new opportunities, and creativity in business terms,
which was traditionally the reserve of the record companies, has, in part at
least, been passed on to the musicians themselves, for they themselves are
part of the same generation that uses mp3.

Another field undergoing change is that of cinema, for one also has to
take into consideration what is going on in terms of P2P networks in the
area of film. One of the major uses is the exchange of pornographic films
produced in the US and Europe by large production companies such as
Vivid, Digital Playground, as well as the compilations produced by ama-
teurs using excerpts with their favourite porn stars. This is, indeed, one of
the main uses but it does not directly affect the major production companies in US cinema. One must also take into account that part of the traffic
in the P2P networks is taken up by European cinematographic productions, which find in this exchange space an alternative, but unpaid, diffusion channel to the theatres that are reserved mostly for US produced films.
Finally, much of what circulates in the P2P networks are Spanish, Italian
and French dubbed versions of US films or Russian or Korean subtitled
versions. Another issue that must be addressed is again the several functions that the users ascribe to P2P films and TV series. Some people just
collect them without ever seeing them, others just download copies of what
they wouldn't pay to see at the cinema, and others again download things
that they have already bought.

Piracy or illegal downloading would seem, in certain cases, to be understood as being morally more justifiable when the musicians in question are not our favourites. In other words, they are those whose records we would normally not buy. The same goes for films produced far from us by large global corporations, at least for Internet users outside the US.

This observation helps us to understand that what we generically term piracy is, in fact, a very diverse phenomenon and that, apparently, the use of the Internet for "swapping films" has different functions. It may well be true that the same applies to the cinema industry as to software, i.e. as one cannot legally control all the global markets it is perhaps preferable to allow pirate copies of certain types of filmography to circulate, for one can thus create loyalty amongst future clients in markets evolving towards legality.

The question of piracy is complex and probably requires different approaches to understanding the different reasons why it is carried out and the indirect gains and direct losses associated with it. It also needs to be taken beyond a simplistic analysis of the defence of piracy as a weapon against the perceived monopolistic activities of the US cinema industry or its condemnation as an out and out criminal act.

Table 4.4 – Audiovisual revenue structure (%)

	Cinema Box office	Video	DVD	TV	Radio	Music	Games	Total
US	4.7%	8.9%	2.4%	59.2%	11.7%	8.6%	4.5%	100%
EU-15	5.0%	6.5%	1.5%	58.7%	10.5%	10.8%	7.0%	100%
Germany	3.6%	3.4%	0.8%	58.8%	15.1%	11.6%	6.7%	100%
United Kingdom	3.8%	8.3%	1.9%	60.3%	6.6%	12.1%	7.0%	100%
France	6.0%	8.0%	2.6%	59.2%	9.4%	7.6%	7.2%	100%
Portugal	7.7%	5.1%	0.5%	48.5%	12.7%	18.0%	7.5%	100%
Italy	7.3%	7.3%	1.0%	66.2%	8.4%	4.9%	5.1%	100%
Spain	8.0%	5.3%	1.1%	60.3%	8.2%	9.4%	7.8%	100%

Source: Cinema, TV and radio in the EU Statistics on audiovisual services (Data 1980-2002) Luxembourg: Office for Official Publications of the European Communities, 2003.

The relationship between rentals and purchases is another interesting phenomenon in the comparison of the European and North American media diets. It would seem that renting is much more common in the US than in Europe, while there is greater similarity between the two continentes in terms of purchase of video and DVD audiovisual services and music CDs (despite the particular differences between European countries). In terms of TV viewing, the US has values considerably higher than the European average of 204 minutes per day per person. The United Kingdom is the European country with the highest daily television viewing time (218 min.), followed by France (192 min.) and Germany (192 min.). [34]

The two most regular markets in terms of revenue structure in the group of selected countries are television and multimedia games. Given that, of all the audiovisual services analyzed here, the games are those that most deserve the term new media and also given the evolution of their market it is necessary to look in greater detail at their role within the media system in the entertainment dimension.

The New Entertainment Player: Multimedia Games

Between the years 2000 and 2003, the multimedia games market grew by approximately 40% in Europe and 50% in the US. For the first decade in the 21st century the average sustained growth rates are expected to be 10% in the EU and 24% in the US.

In its "Global Entertainment and Media Outlook: 2004-2008" report, the consultancy firm Price Waterhouse Coopers (2004) identified video games as the sector with the most rapid growth in the coming years, with a CARG forecast of 20.1 per cent – totalling US$ 55.6 billion in 2008. According to the same report, the computer games market will decline and the console game market, with the new generation of machines, will expand. The main distribution channels that will accompany the new generation of consoles will be online and wireless, incentivated by the growing penetration of broadband and the new mobile phones, which will be used as much for entertainment as for communication.

Even if it is clear in our analysis that the initial growth values referenced for the 2000 to 2003 period reflect the emergence of a new generation of consoles – the 128 bit console – with the value of the hardware consequent-

---

[34] Data relating to 1999 for OberCom and 2000 for CE/Eurostat (1) The OberCom data refer to five countries. (2) Taking an average session duration of 120 minutes, 0.50 represents 30 seconds; (3) The source for the date on EU-15 and US is the publication Statistics on Audiovisual Services, data 1980-2000, European Commission Eurostat, Theme 4, Industry, Trade and Services, EC, 2002 (supposes an average of 120 minutes per session). Source: Economia Pura, March 2004, no. 63, Lisbon, pp.28.

ly contributing to a large extent to the segment's growth, it is predictable that similar growth is repeated when the new generation of consoles comes on the marke, such as Playstation 3, Xbox 360 and Nintendo Revolution and mobile consoles such as PSP and mobile phones such as the NOKIA NGage. The estimates presented herein, and also my analysis, therefore take this into account. [35]

However, there is another factor influencing the growth of the multimedia games market [36] that has nothing to do with the simple increase in the offer or the development of the games in terms of quality or the emergence of new hardware products: it is an expanding market also in terms of the number of consumers. That is an indisputable conclusion when we look at the age structure and the market division by gender.

The users are no longer limited to adolescents of the male sex. The demographic structure of the users is gradually becoming similar to that of the universe of the population in general [37]. Hence, we are witnessing, on the one hand, a trend towards balance between the sexes in the use of multimedia games, both for console game and PC games, although the trend is more clearly pronounced for computer games. On the other hand, the age structure of the users also seems to be changing. ESA (Entertainment Software Association) data for the US indicate that approximately 50% of US citizens play multimedia games. Of these, 39% are women and the average age of the user of multimedia games is 29 years. The age structure also presents data that is of equal interest for understanding the use of games. The majority of frequent users are older than 18 years of age and 41% of PC multimedia game users and 22% of console users are 35 years of age and older.

Another analysis dimension for understanding the connections established between games and other technologies in a *networked communicational model* is the relationship with the Internet.

---

[35] At the global level, piracy cost software producers something like US$ 11 billion in 1998. One must, however, bear in mind that these figures are estimates and that the reality in piracy is very diversified, ranging from the use of CD writers in American and European universities to piracy on an industrial scale in developing countries. The reference to piracy here serves the purpose of providing a real idea of the dimension of the multimedia games market, i.e. the total constituted by the sum of the sales and piracy. This makes it clear what exactly this cultural industry represents today both in terms of revenue and target audience.

[36] The multimedia games include video consoles and the software.

[37] Worldwide Videogame Hardware and Software Forecast and Analysis, 2003-2007: Midlife Changes, IDC, November 26, 2003.

As far as multimedia gamers are concerned, the data available for Portugal indicated that those who use the Internet to play games make up 21% of the total Internet users, whereby the male-female ratio is 3 : 1.

In analyzing these figures, one must bear in mind that the emergence of the multimedia games introduced new realities into the media system, such as: the contribution of games to the audiovisual services revenue equalled the cinema box office revenue in the US in 2000 and was 2% higher than the box office takings in the European Union in the same year.

This is a trend that began to show in the European space from 1997 onwards, the first year in which the revenue from sales of interactive software in Europe surpassed the cinema box office revenue. The trend has been confirmed over the subsequent years by steady growth rates.

Table 4.5 – Global video games market (millions of euros)

	2003	2004	2005	2006
Europe	9068.4	8482	8736.2	11844.5
Japan	4416.7	4157.2	4978.7	7513.5
US	12055.4	11319.2	11077.5	14729

Source: IDATE (estimates for 2005 and 2006)

Having said that, one must also state that, whereas until recently the driving force behind the production of entertainment fiction was essentially cinema, a new form of organization seems to be emerging that is based on the sharing of dynamization and innovation procedures by the cinematographic industrial culture and the games industrial culture.

The sharing of processes between the film and multimedia games industries is not only taking place at the revenue level but also at the level of the very formulation of the market and its production structure. This is borne out by a more in-depth analysis of the games universe and its participation in the media system.

Due to the need for ever greater investments in production and for obtaining more widespread distribution in the world markets, with a view to amortizing costs rapidly, the companies in the multimedia game segment are witnessing a trend towards consolidation and mergers, thug giving rise to a small group of major operators. According to the opinions of those involved in the multimedia games system themselves, the concentration trend will see the constitution of five or six major companies, which, thanks to their capacity for raising financing and targeting large distribution markets, can guarantee that their involvement in the multimedia entertainment market is profitable. The production costs for games for the new generation consoles (128 bits) today compare to Hollywood film budgets. The average cost of a game is approximately 3 to 4 million euro (as opposed to 1.5 million in 1998). During the 1 to 2 years of product development, the financial risk is, therefore, too high for small independent studios (in 2002 alone, two French companies in the European Top 20, Kalisto and Cryo, declared bankruptcy).

We have also been witnessing a reduction in the possibilities in terms of the number of themes available for licensing and available in the market. The majority of brand names and characters are today registered to multimedia segment companies, as a result of the consolidation logic. This renders the use of contents previously available on other supports difficult. Although many games continue to be based on traditional theme development models, today we are witnessing a diversification that may include the use of new types of screenplay as yet unused in the world of games (e.g., horror novels such as *F13* by Stephen King and *Half Life* and also the simulation of familiar soap opera or reality show environments, e.g. with the *Sims*) or the exploitation of licences based on films, cartoons, books and television series.

After the decision to go into production, launching a game in the market can take up to 2 years. This need to find new screenplays in turn produces a certain bidirectionality in the exchange of ideas between the diverse segments of the entertainment industry. Multimedia games are thus no longer inspired by contents coming from the cinema, book and television segments and have themselves now become the inspiration for films based on game characters (Super Mario, Outcast, Lara Croft, etc.) and other forms of artistic expression. Cinema itself has exploited the role of games, be it in the construction of image-based narratives, as in *The Matrix*, or in the use of action scenes with a structure inherited from combat games such as *Tekken* or *Mortal Kombat*. Another example is the film *Existenz*, which has a screenplay based on the games industry itself and its evolution, whereby the central story line revolves around the complexification of games and the relationship between the real and the imaginary – but an imaginary that is experienced in the first person.

Another characteristic of this segment is the growing competition between new games. For example, in the first six months of 1999 alone, approximately 2,500 new titles were launched in the market, of which only a small number will have met with the preference of the consumers. The sales charts show that the 20 most popular games alone make up more than 50% of the revenue of the operators in the segment, which seems to confirm that a company, to be successful, has to develop a large number of games so as to minimize the possibility of financial losses. Capacity for promotion of the games is a precondition for success and here, too, there are barriers to the entry of new market competitors. Only companies with the dimension of Electronic Arts (EA) can aspire to being able to advertise their football games on prime time television in competition with other consumer products. Therefore companies like EA, Infogrames and Eidos, together with the traditional Japanese companies and the rising star Sony, will tend to dominate the market just like the corresponding Hollywood companies in the area of cinema have been able to do so through the institutionalization of a system that tolerates independent companies while ensuring their own world hegemony through huge budgets and the distribution chains.

The global top 20 ranking of multimedia game producers is today dominated by Sony and Nintendo, both Japanese, following by the American companies EA and Activision and then Konami and Sega, also Japanese. The first European company, Infogrames, in 8th place, is from France, as are most of the European companies with a global dimension. [38]

The approximation to cinema is also taking place at the production structure level, as can be exemplified by one of the first games to adopt a similarity of processes: *Half Life*. [39]

A game like *Half Life* requires an elaborate creation process in which the first step is the creation of a multidisciplinary work team including

---

[38] Source: Cinema, TV and radio in the EU Statistics on audiovisual services (Data 1980–2002) Luxembourg: Office for Official Publications of the European Communities, 2003.

[39] Half Life is a game produced by Vivendi Universal Games. Launched in 1998, it has won some 50 awards from different publications for the best game of the year and Part II was launched in 2004. Despite its age, which is considerable for the games market given the high degree of rotation of titles, it is still the object of new adaptations, as exemplified by the Team Fortress version (which can be played by multiplayer teams made up of players who assume characters with diverse skills) and the most recent version, Opposing Force (in which the player can become Adrian Sheppard, a Marine, whose task is to eliminate the leading character in Half Life, Gordon Freedman). Half Life deserved all its awards and established a new scale of values (or standards) in a genre that is as common as it is normally brainless – the First Person Shooter – giving it texture and depth. António Saraiva in *Exame Informática*, March 2000.

programmers, designers, screenplay writers and musicians. The team may have between 15 and 30 members. The quality and acceptance of a game will essentially depend on the team members' capacities to combine the different components into a final product that has appeal and is easy to play. The *Half Life* script was not the product of game-obsessed programmers or a graphic animator, but was written by the award-winning horror novelist, Marc Laidlaw. The game thus invests in a complex but nevertheless user-friendly story, combining the suspense of Stephen King novels with the creation of a main character, paying particular attention to his personality structure. There is more to the game than just shooting; it is equally important to analyze what the character can or cannot do and how to interact with the environment and the secondary characters. Also, the presentation of the game itself – with Freedman's course from the entrance to the mountain to his underground laboratory, accompanied by an ambient music that suits the situations experienced – refers us to a discourse construction that has a lot more to do with film production than the Symbolic Games Era (Bittanti 1999).

Finally, one must highlight the feature that introduces a new game dimension – the possibility of interacting with other online players via the Internet. This is a situation in which scenarios change and the teams play against each other (red team vs. blue team), but in many of the game situations the players have absolutely no prior knowledge of each other, and although they sometimes develop partnerships continued in daily online meetings to play, they finish many games without the slightest notion who their team companions and adversaries are. There are, however, also teams formed in advance that play each other in tournaments organized on the thousands of servers existing for playing the game.

The new development *Half Life* brought with it in the field of the Internet was the possibility of playing in an easy way and without additional payment, thus reducing the technical and cost barriers and furthering the development of new forms of interaction. The commitment by the entertainment industries to games via the Internet is an investment in the expansion of the market through an increase in the number of potential players thanks to the standardization of the game modes – stripping the games of their almost handcrafted aura created by groups of players, while at the same time introducing possibilities of the creation of scenarios through the provision of game motors that can be adapted by the players. The players are thus given the possibility of using a complex reality, that of the already produced game, combined with the possibility to create interaction spaces with their own characteristics (for example, using a game editor, any player can recreate the space of his workplace and play *Half Life* there) and the possibility of interacting, in the newly created universe, with other players, thus expanding social networks beyond the traditional time and space boundaries.

The current multimedia games are the fourth generation[40]. This new type of game must be looked at in multiple dimensions – through analysis of their production, distribution and consumption logics – and also at the level of the interaction processes. In terms of content (which, in the current phase, still shares the idea of the Romantic perspective argued by Mattoti, see Bittanti, 1999), there is a trend towards a differentiation from preceding models, so that we can call them *Complex Reality Games*. In other words, they are the product of investment in the construction of strong themes and scripts which look to cinematographic output for many of their characteristics and which are capable of attracting audiences through more than the mere application of more advanced technologies, while at the same time valuing the creation of a type of star system, using real or virtual characters with relatively elaborate personalities (such as Morgan Freedman, Lara Croft, Sonic, etc). We are thus witnessing a complexification of the games' narrative structure.

At the level of interactivity, the Internet also represents qualitative changes in the logic of social interaction provided by the multimedia games. Hence, the games industry is converging towards alteration of the interaction logic itself, both in space and in time. From the possibility of playing games within our own closed social networks, with school or neighbourhood friends, we have progressed to the Internet enabling us to interact with users identifiable only through their *aliases* in a likewise differentiated temporal dimension – real time.

---

[40] After the *Age of Symbolic Videogames* from 1971 to 1984, in which, according to Mattoti, the technological limits of the hardware prevailed over the suggestive elaboration of the neo-artists; the *Age of Classic Videogames* (1984-1993), in which there was a balance between technological capacity and suggestive elaboration; and the Age of Romantic Videogames (1993-...), a phase in which contrasting trends emerged – on the one hand, an exponential increase in the technological potentials and, on the other, a return to the past with the reworking of many topics – we are now witnessing the emergence of a new generation of multimedia games involving also the development of new analysis dimensions (Bittanti 1999).

But perhaps the most interesting observation is the fact that the narrative itself allows for the intervention of secondary factors – although most of the time they are not directly noticeable to the player, but present nevertheless – which can take the game in a certain direction, but only if the player goes along with that. This narrative structure enables the player to visualize what would have happened if they had managed to overcome a certain situation on their own. The game is thus a space of multiple possibilities. The player may or may not follow the narrative rules and may break them if they so wish but taking that option is also a sign that they are not skilled enough to master the situation created by the narrative.

This is the cultivation of a learning process based on trial and error, but one must bear in mind that playability always comes first in the attempt to construct a complex reality. A game must, in the final analysis, be easy to play, even if offers several difficulty levels to the player. Only thus will it be marketable and fulfill its function of economic object in addition to cultural object.

The current generation of games can be called *Complex Reality Games*, a term that conveys, on the one hand, the complexification of the production, interactivity and narrative relations and, on the other, highlights, or perhaps criticizes, the idea that the ultimate objective of the games is to create a narrative model that recreates reality through virtuality.

Hence, more than just wanting to reproduce realities through technology, using almost real images and advanced artificial intelligence, multimedia games are an attempt to create complex relations aimed at simulating the high number of hypothetical choices we are faced with in everyday life.

This simulation is different to recreating identical parts of our reality in a virtual reality format. Even the airplane, car or sports simulators are, in the multimedia context, instilled with an entertainment dimension.

Just as the cinema, as an entertainment industry, is instilled with a fantasy dimension (in opposition to documentary cinematography), as far as multimedia games are concerned, we must bear in mind that the objective is not to recreate reality but to recreate the complexification of the choices. That is the essence of interactivity in multimedia – the idea that, just like in everyday life, one cannot choose all the possible options (although they still constitute a reference framework in our social construction of reality). In the multimedia games, too, the objective is to make the choice hypotheses so extensive and their causal relations so dependent that one creates the illusion of the construction of a parallel reality. More than the simulation of reality, the complexification of the constructed reality is, thus, the central characteristic of the historic dimension that we are currently experiencing in multimedia games.

Another sign of the growing complexity is the fact that the game's narrative structure itself conceives, from the roots up, a whole panoply of tricks and passwords that are not readily available to the player but are supplied by the game-dedicated press and Internet sites, thus establishing communities for the exchange of experiences and interests and also fostering a parallel industry of magazines, Internet sites and television programmes created around the narrative universe of the games and the possibility of exploring their limits and thus creating new sources of income for the audiovisual services industry.

As McLuhan (1997) suggests, the games are extensions of our social *self* and, as such, mass media given that they are situations constructed to allow the simultaneous participation of a high number of persons in some significant dimension of their social lives.

Proceeding from the proposal of Fausto Colombo – that videogames are a central example of the evolution of the new media and manifest all the characteristics of the new media in terms of both structure and dynamics, it would seem possible to say that the multimedia games are acting as a synthesizing element in the transformation in progress in the contents industry and in the logics of networked interaction and can, therefore, in their current phase of development, constitute a fundamental part of the *Entertainment Meta-system*. [41]

As a result of the emergence of an interactive narrative, the role of the games would be that of feeding, together with cinema and television, the entertainment industries circuit and also receiving raw material from these, thus constituting, within the current media system, a central element in the *Entertainment Meta-system* created around the new media.

---

[41] By using the term *Entertainment Meta-system* one is putting forward the idea that, in addition to treating the multimedia games as a medium of communication, we should also be asking the question whether or not the current trends towards concentration and networking will, in the medium term, turn the multimedia game industry into the second entertainment pillar together with television, taking the place of cinema.

The Reaffirmation of TV as a Central Element of the Entertainment Meta-System

If it is true that, in this new media system, cinema continues to play a central role in the *Entertainment Meta-system* and the multimedia games have emerged as a new element to be taken into consideration in the strategies, what is the role of television in the entertainment sphere?

Although we often see television as a source of information, today, in terms of programming, it is essentially a source of entertainment (with the exception of the 24 hour news channels). However, that is not a starting point, but a point of arrival. For, as Colombo (2003) demonstrates, television was not always thought of in that way.

If we look at the history of television as consisting of three distinct chronological phases, we can identify an initial phase, which in most European countries corresponds to the two decades from 1950 to 1970 (whereby, in Portugal, broadcasting began in 1957 and the country had a dictatorial government model up until 1974 and Eastern Bloc countries experienced dictatorial regimes up to the 1990s). We can name this phase a monopoly phase, for the television medium was identified with public service, with the same applying to radio and the production and diffusion of contents. Television's cultural dimension was seen as educational, promoting complementary literacy of the population and the idea of culture as a repertoire defined by television programming itself, in which intellectuals played the role of divulgers of culture.

In this model, the role attributed to information was inspired on the monopolistic radiophonic and elitist model. It had a marked institutional dimension, in which two models of relations with the daily newspapers coexisted: competition and autonomy. The first model is one in which the objectives of television were to provide information and achieve a cultural objective of an educational nature.

The second phase of European television corresponds to the period between the latter half of the 1970s and the end of the 1980s, which saw the formation of a mixed system of public and private television, in which public service was defined on the basis of an informative role, identification with the national institutional culture and own television language models that distinguished it from the practices of private television stations. The central function of state television in that period was that of democratizing culture through the widening of access to culture and decentralization (from the cultural production centres to the peripheries). Culture was thus seen as the spontaneous circulation of ideas and not as a fixed defined repertoire, allowing for space for experimentation and cultural vanguards. In this second phase, information in state television came to represent the literal meaning of the word itself – all that is worthwhile being communicated, but in a specific context considered peculiar to a public service, leaving the private stations to adopt a more comprehensive definition of what information was. In this context, there was a shift in competition away from television vs. newspapers to private vs. public TV stations. [42]

The third phase, the *duopolies system*, is characterized by the identification of what public service has to do with the idea of quality of service, with the elaboration of transmedia contents (i.e. contents for radio, the Internet and satellite, cable and analogue television all within one complementary service model) and the definition of what is public being based on what is supplied by the public service itself in a self-legitimizing process. In the current model, culture is dealt with in a postmodern perspective, in which there is a plurality of the culture producing instances and in which culture itself is seen as a television genre and not as an objective in itself, conferring upon the intellectual elite a market role, that of experimenting new approaches which in the future may constitute new products that could be marketed even by the private sector. The role of information in this third phase of public television was that of a specific genre competing with multiple rivals, from the commercial television channels to the new offer via Internet.

The moment in which the cultural objective ceased to be of an educational nature and culture was understood as a genre in itself opened the door to the coexistence of different television models that, although they proposed different programming, placed a much greater emphasis on the entertainment dimension than on information.

That is an historic evolution in television (Smith 1998) already identified by Umberto Eco (1985) and Francesco Caseti (1990), who divided the history of television into two major periods: *paleo* and *neo*-television. [43]

---

[42] In the Portuguese case the second phase took place later. Television was democratized as a result of the Revolution of 25 April 1974, but the beginning of private broadcasting did not take place until 1992. Therefore the monopoly situation in Portugal continued until the early 1990s, whereas in the rest of Europe the erosion of the public monopoly began in the mid-1970s.

[43] As Ortoleva (2003) states, in relation to these two television production models, not only the television genres change but also the programming structure undergoes alteration, so that one can "(...) say that the viewers' expectations are redefined with neo-television (...) the narrative or cognoscive pleasure

The first phase, termed *paleo*-television, was dominated by the institutionalized logics of the State and pedagogic communication with the viewer. The second phase, *neo*-television, is characterized by a set of transformations that have brought about an increase in the number of operators, an expansion in the broadcasting hours and the nature and structure of the broadcasts and, above all, the alteration of the programme production models and consumption modalities. In short, the objective reformulation of televised communication. Essentially the creation of spaces of interaction and socialization was privileged with a view to entertainment becoming the primary function of television.

Table 4.6 – Television show formats as a percentage of broadcasting in Portugal, 2002

	RTP(%)	SIC(%)	TVI(%)
Religious and political party broadcasts	1.5	0.04	0.00
Non-daily information	2.2	0.95	0.00
Music and erudite	3.3	0.74	0.00
Children and youth	7.6	13.53	11.7
Documentaries and culture	8.2	4.51	1.9
Sports information	9.2	1.47	1.6
Broadcasting continuity, spots, promotion and others	11.7	24.78	26.4
Variety, light music and talk shows	16.3	18.72	14
Drama and fiction	19.9	26.12	31.8
Daily information	20.1	9.25	12.6

Source: Calculated on the basis of OberCom, *Anuário da Comunicação* 2002/2003. Note: given that each channel uses different classification categories, it is possible that different formation logics are used for the same categories.

In Portugal, generalist hertzian television broadcasting by two public channels (RTP 1 and 2) and two private channels (SIC and TVI) showed an average information / entertainment ratio of 24.51% to 54.57%. However, these values conceal greater differences between the commercial private stations and the public stations. Whereas, on the public channel RTP, the ratio of information to entertainment was 41.2% to 47.1%, in the commercial stations the figures were 16.22% to 59.11% (for SIC) and 16.1% to 57.5% (for TVI).

---

provided by one single programme has given way to an audiovisual stream that accompanies one uninterruptedly and occupies entire segments of time itself".

Although it is impossible to apply common methodologies, one can nevertheless draw up a comparative profile for European television programming using several sources on the European reality. Thus, in the years 2002-2003, half of programming of the generalist European television channels consisted of fiction and music/entertainment (24% and 26%, respectively) (Colombo, 2005), while the other half was divided up amongst culture (16%), information (12%), advertising (6%) and others (16%).

What characterizes the entertainment and information models in modern day television? And how do the viewers value the information and entertainment offered to them?

In analyzing this question using the most popular programmes in European television we must bear in mind that, despite all common trends, each country has its own particular specificities. Secondly, one must also understand that, although there are always new formats, there is nevertheless a dominant continuity of television genres.

Continuity does not necessarily mean maintenance of the same relations of importance between the different television genres over time. Those are the main characteristics of television programming. Hence, to understand the television entertainment model of the real virtuality culture (Castells 2004) one has to take seven dimensions into account: sport; film; game shows; reality shows; scripted fiction; factual programming; and interactivity.

Figure 4.2 – Number of sports events in the 20 programmes with the largest audiences in selected countries

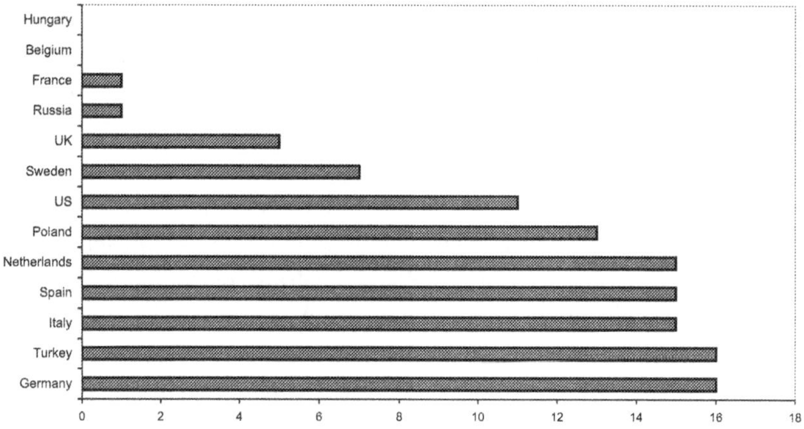

Source: IP Network GmbH, European TV Key Facts, January 2004

Television worldwide may follow similar contents and format patterns (Wolton 2000), but it continues to incorporate a strong national identity dimension. This has less to do with policies for the defence of national contents than with the media diet practices themselves in relation to television

Thus, Hungary, together with Poland and Italy, has the highest daily television consumption figures (more than 245 minutes), while Denmark, Austria, Sweden and Norway present the lowest figures (below 170 minutes per day).

Likewise, there are differences in the viewing patterns. In Southern Europe – i.e., Portugal, Spain and Italy – there are two daily prime time periods, between 1.00 p.m. and 4.00 p.m. and 8.00 p.m. and 10.00 p.m., while Germany, Sweden and Denmark have only one prime time period, from 6.00 p.m. to 11.00 p.m.

This differentiation is also visible in terms of content types. As the next figure shows, in many European countries sport is the most common television genre amongst the twenty programmes with the highest viewer ratings. There is a clear division between those countries in which sport accounts for 75% of the programmes with the highest ratings, clearly approaching the data from the US, and those in which sport makes up less than 30% of the most popular programmes. There are also differences in the most popular sports genres, which is perfectly understandable in geographic and cultural terms – for example, football (soccer) as a sport without frontiers vs. the winter sports that are more appreciated in Central and Northern Europe and Scandinavia.

A report produced by Kiefl (2003) for the Canadian Radio Television and Telecommunications Commission identifies a number of global and other clearly national trends, thus demonstrating that the television universe is a result of interaction between the global and the local. Despite McLuhan's (1998) suggestion, the village may be global in the information dimension it is without doubt less so at the entertainment level.

In the North American, European and Australian prime time, despite the growth in reality shows, drama/fiction has remained the most important category over the last five years. However, one must register certain differences, for, whereas in Europe and Australia television fiction has not seen much change in terms of weighting, in the US the situation is quite different. In America, a substantial percentage of comedy output has been replaced by reality or game shows (Kiefl, 2003). As we will see, European prime times have seen an increase in domestic fiction production, whereas in Australia home products have declined somewhat.

Figure 4.3 – Viewer ratings for programmes per sports event in 2002 in selected countries (adults)

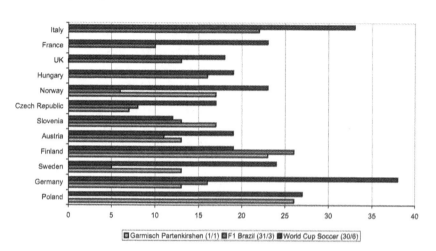

Source: IP Network GmbH, European TV Key Facts, January 2004.

There are also differences within the European space, where television differs in terms of the type of fiction formats preferred in each country. In 2001, fiction series was the prevalent format in the UK and Spain, while Italians preferred mini-series and in Germany and France made-for-TV films dominated the programming.

Another relationship that can be looked at is that between the decline in the importance of game shows and the success of the so-called reality shows. This would seem to be borne out by the data for diverse countries (such as the US, UK, Germany, France and The Netherlands). However, here one must also take other factors into account that have more to do with short-term programming management policies.

In this analysis one must also take into consideration that, while the European realities all differ from each other, there are also differences between the North American and Australian trends and the general European trends. Hence, in 2000 the top ten television programmes in the US featured more reality/game shows than any other market analyzed herein. *Big Brother*, *Survivor* and *Who Wants to Be a Millionaire* were amongst the ten shows with the highest viewer ratings on American television. However, these shows did not completely dethrone fiction and shows such as *E. R.*, *The Practice* and sitcoms such as *Friends* and *Frasier* and news magazines such as *60 Minutes* on CBS and events such as the Academy Awards and the Super Bowl (Kiefl 2005) also featured amongst the programmes with the highest ratings.

In Australia, the top ten included only one fiction series, *Friends*, and one TV film, *Seachange* 3rd series. It also featured three news programmes and two magazines along with the game show *Who Wants to Be a Millionaire* and the music reality show *Popstars*.

If we compare the two aforementioned countries to the same year in the UK, Italy and France, we see that most of the viewing choices in the latter countries focus on entertainment and films. In the UK three soap operas were in the top ten (*Coronation Street, Eastenders* and *Emmerdale*), along with two drama series (*Inspector Morse* and *Heartbeat*), one documentary, one televised event (National TV awards) and one entertainment programme and one football match. The only game show, *Who Wants To Be a Millionaire*, was in tenth place. The Italian reality was dominated by entertainment (3 programmes), films (3 in the top ten), news programmes, the San Remo Festival and football coverage. Italy also had only one reality show in the top ten – *Il Grande Fratello*, the Italian version of *Big Brother*. In France, films dominated the top ten ranking (4 films), followed by television series (3 in the top ten), televised events, news and football (Kiefl 2005). One characteristic common to all five countries mentioned here is the fact that national productions (even if they are adapted formats) were always in the majority.

If cinema was the driving force behind the entertainment industries in the 20th century, the emergence of television as a mass viewing medium has since wrestled that role from cinema[44].

In *L'Esprit du Temps* (1962), Edgar Morin, proposes the division of the contemporary history of mass culture into three periods: 1900 to 1930 was the popular urban period, with the triumph of cinema (silent in the initial phase and then ending with the first talking film experimentations), a period with a dominant vision of entertainment as a primordial element; from 1930 to 1955, talking movies produced a new mythology, that of individual

---

[44] In his analysis of cinema's role in society, Morin looks at mass culture as a sociological object and adopts a definition of culture inscribed in the anthropological tradition – culture as a complex body of norms, myths and images that penetrate the individual's intimacy, senses and emotions. This culture would constitute a specific system for the fact that is it produced in accordance with the rules of industrial production and disseminated by the media; it seeks to identify the dialectics that link the economic instance (production, creation, consumption) and the psychological instance (projection, identification, transfers).

happiness – the improvement in living standards after 1945 both in real life and in cinema fiction led to the cultivation of a happy end mythology; from 1955 onwards we have been witnessing the crisis of happiness, with the problematization of private life – cinema ceased to be the example of mass culture and was substituted by television.

Figure 4.4 – The five films with the highest TV audience ratings in selected countries (1993-2002) (%)

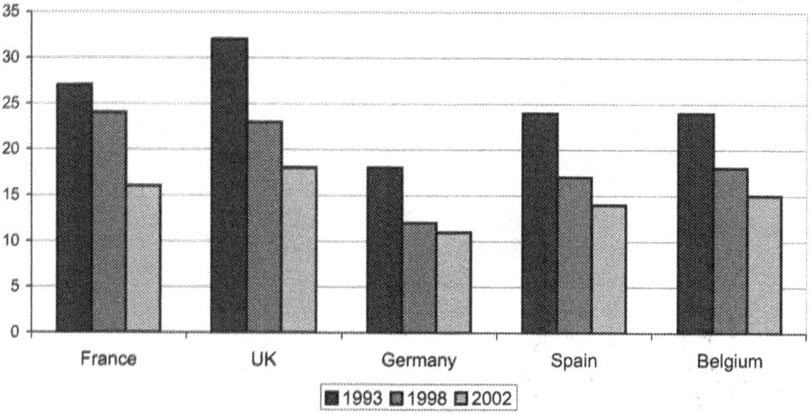

Source: IP Network GmbH, European TV Key Facts, January 2004.

However, although cinema has forfeited its leading role played to television, through the televised screenings of films it has won back its contact with the masses – in this case in the form of a wider public, at least numerically. This model, however, has since gone into decline, or at least the evolution of cinema in prime time television would lead one to that conclusion. This decline and the establishment of a new model, which, in the terminology of Morin (1976), favours a synthesis of the problematization of private life and entertainment, has been the result of the success of the DVD and the Premium cinema channels on cable and satellite television and also the evolution in the relationship between fiction and television.

Although we are witnessing the aforementioned changes, there is a constant that remains unchanged – the origin of the most popular films shown on television. In Europe, with the exception of the Czech Republic, in the year 2000 US cinema productions accounted for more than 50% of the films with the highest viewer ratings, with seven American films amongst the ten most popular films. Although the figures for national and European productions are very similar, in reality what we seem to be experiencing is a preference for domestic productions in the television channels of each country and not an inter-exchange of European productions.

Figure 4.5 – Countries of origin of the 10 films with highest viewer ratings on television, adult viewers in selected countries (2002)

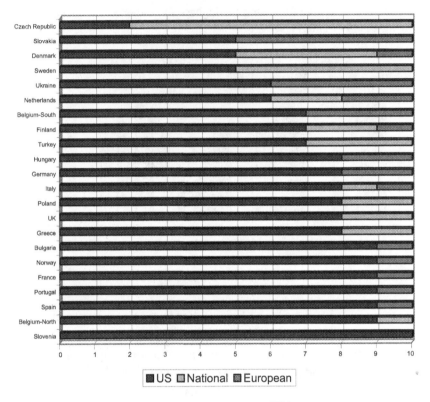

Source: IP Network GmbH, European TV Key Facts, January 2004.

In Europe, the preference for the screen of films on televisions would seem to be first American film productions, followed by domestic films and then productions from other European national cultures. One explanation for this phenomenon could reside in the economic questions related with the purchase of television distribution packages, as well as the programming option. But the phenomenon may also be rooted in the above described currently valid model for cinema.

Whereas American films seek a synthesis between problematization of private life and entertainment, European cinema very often seeks only to explore each dimension separately, thus limiting the amplitude of its cultural reach to the national as opposed to the global. That could be one of the reasons for the greater trans-frontier appeal and success European films beyond their national borders in Europe and even in the US when the synthesis of the model is applied (examples of this success are *Goodbye Lenin*; *Jet Lag*; *Amélie Poulain* and also the films of Pedro Almodovar).

In the area of entertainment there is another question, in this case relating to television game shows. After the major successes of the 1990s and first few years of the new millennium, they are currently losing ground in terms of audience. The television game show model would seem to follow two logics. On the one hand, the successfully established formats can aspire to quite a long television life, while, on the other, this does not mean that game shows do not have their own life cycles. In other words, although formats such as *The Weakest Link* and *Who Wants To Be A Millionaire* have been present in more than 20 markets each (since 2000) and in more than sixty countries (since 1998), there is a limit to the audience's interest.

Figure 4.6 – Television Game show audiences in selected countries (1999-2003)

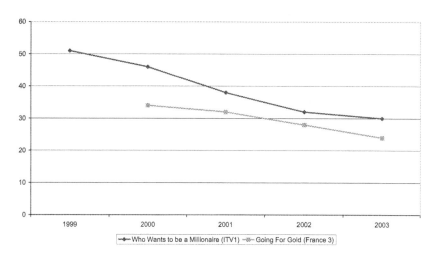

Source: IP Network GmbH, European TV Key Facts, January 2004.

Another relationship one can look at is that between the decline in the importance of game shows and the success of the so-called reality shows. This is a trend that the data from several countries (including the US, the

UK, Germany, France and The Netherlands) would seem to confirm. However, one must also take into account other relationship factors that have more to do with the short term programming management policies.

The question often asked in relation to the traditional fiction formats (drama series, films, situation comedies, movies made for TV, etc.) as to whether or not they are being replaced by reality shows such as *Big Brother* and quiz shows such as *Who Wants To Be a Millionaire* and *The Weakest Link* can and should be analyzed here.

The available figures confirm a decrease in game shows and a simultaneous increase in reality shows. However, if we examine the data more closely we see that other programme formats are also growing.

Figure 4.7 – Total of entertainment shows, by genre, for selected countries (1998-2002)

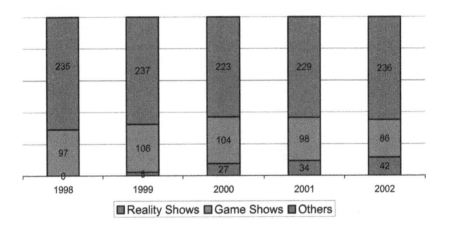

Source: IP Network GmbH, European TV Key Facts, January 2004.

Before we look at this other variable, it is worthwhile studying the field of reality shows in more depth. We can define three types of reality show genres: the so-called *reality games* (examples: *Survivor* from Sweden, first broadcast in 1997; *Big Brother* from The Netherlands, which first went on the air in 1999 and *The BAR*, also Swedish, which began in 2000); the *reality soaps* (which often centre around romantic involvements, such as in *Temptation Island,* first aired in the US in 2001; another example of a reality soap is *The Osbournes,* which also premiered in the US in 2001); and the *reality competitions* (such as *Operación Triunfo,* first broadcast in Spain in 2001; *Popstars*, originally from New Zealand, where it first aired in 1999; and *Star Academy* an originally French format, from 2001) [45].

All these formulas are not transmissions of unmediated reality but are fictioned realities. As Vanda de Sousa (2004) points out, even in the case of *Big Brother*, which was presented as a "real life soap opera" in Portugal, "of the 24 hours taped (multiplied by four image streams) only 35 minutes were broadcast per day, which, as they were the object of selection, will always be an interpretation of the real and not the real itself. The daily programme selected the images also on the basis of the classic rules of narrative. In other words, telling a story (…)".

Figure 4.8 – Advertising income as a percentage of the total income of media groups in selected countries

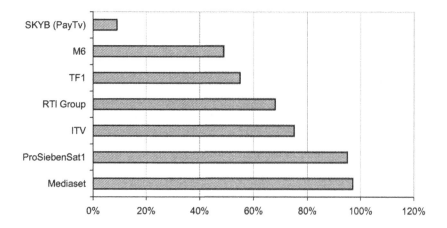

Source: La vie Financière, 20/02/2004

The hypothesis argued here is that game and reality shows are short-term tactical weapons often managed by the television stations as a way of replacing a programme that flops (be it a comedy programme or a soap opera).

---

[45] "Big Brother" was sold to more than 10 European countries and the USA using the same basic format. The concept is based on the observation of a group of ordinary people (although there is a version for celebrities) 24 hours a day. When it first went on air it generated fierce criticism in all countries but proved a success in terms of viewer ratings. "Survivor" represents a second take on the same format, in which the contestants work in teams and are given tasks to carry out until only one contestant remains. Programmes designed to create new pop music stars constitute a third version of the same format.

Nevertheless, there is a fundamental difference between game shows and reality shows. The latter are shorter lived. Although programmes such as *Big Brother* and *Survivor* achieved quite significant viewer ratings in diverse markets, today they are in decline in all those markets. Between series I and series VI of *Survivor,* there was a drop of 40% in viewer ratings in France and from the first to the third series, a drop of 18%. The same trend is even more pronounced for *Big Brother*: between the first and last series broadcast, the programme registered a drop in viewer ratings of 66% in The Netherlands, 43% in Spain, 36% in Switzerland and 30% in Denmark and also registered similar drops in France, Germany and Greece. Also, by way of example, of the 32 reality series in the American television market in 2002-2003, only 12 survived into the 2003-2004 season. [46]

For this reason, the economic exploitation of these programmes in sub-products (such as magazines, videos, CDs and spin-off programmes) also has to operate at a much higher speed and in accordance with a short-term profit strategy. The non-advertising sources of revenue derived, to a large extent, from viewer subscriptions on channels such as Sky and other channels distributed via cable or satellite. The emergence of the diverse models of so-called reality shows has allowed for a diversification of revenue, as has the re-exploitation of television series issued on DVD (for example: *X Files*; *Poirot*; *Sherlock Holmes* or *La Piovra/The Octopus*).

However, the reality shows enable a degree of diversification of alternative revenue sources that cannot be achieved with other genres. This diversification ranges from public relations actions by the contestants to official magazines, from the licensing of the programme itself (for the producer) to music CDs and videos/DVDs, from audiotel/SMS voting to official Internet sites, and from board games to, in some instances, multimedia games or live performances. [47]

Although they are presented as an irrefutable success model, reality shows constitute only one part of the television entertainment model and not a radical transforming influence on television broadcasting models,

---

[46] IP Network GmbH, European TV Key Facts, January 2004.

[47] Examples of this complementarity of revenues can be found in many television genres. The reality show Popstars on the German channel RTL II led to sales of 2 million CDs for the group Bro'sis and 3 million for another band, No Angels. Animation series are also fertile ground for the diversification of television channel income. For example, Dragon Ball Z sold 200,000 units of its soundtrack and 300,000 DVDs/VHS. The Digimon series produced sales of 130,000 comic book versions and the YuGioH series sold 2,600,000 packs of cards and 370,000 video games.

even though their emergence has since given rise to two new cycles centred around scripted reality.

Firstly, we have witnessed in recent years the crossing of celebrities with scripted reality in programmes such as *Big Brother*, *Survivor* or *Fear Factor*. This was followed by more and more *scripted hybrids*. In other words, programmes that combined fictive reality with a script. Examples of this are, in the US, the comedy of customs and drama series *Murder in a Small Town* and *Big Fat Obnoxious Fiancé,* both on Fox Television and, in Germany, various programmes on Sat1 or RTL in which real life police inspectors deal with crime cases especially constructed for the programmes.

Figure 4.9 – Origin of the 10 most popular fiction series in the European Union in 2002

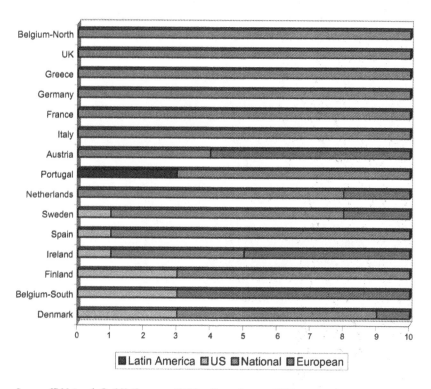

Source: IP Network GmbH, European TV Key Facts, January 2004.

Returning to the analysis of the evolution of TV entertainment genres in the 2000-2002 period, we see that the most consolidated growth was in the Others group (which increased 3% but continues to represent more than 65% of the totality of the entertainment genres), over the reality shows (which, although they grew more than 50%, continue to represent little more than 10%) and game shows (which, although they decreased more than 20%, continue to represent 24% of the total programming). [48]

Programmes that are not sports, films, reality shows or game shows hence continue to dominate the television screen.

What a comparison of the different television markets in Europe would seem to show is that as far as fiction series are concerned, be they drama or situation comedies, the prime time period is dominated by domestic productions, followed by productions from other European countries and then those from the US (whereby the latter are confined to specific markets such as Finland, Denmark or Francophone Belgium).

The odd man out in this analysis is Portugal, with its significant presence of fiction series from South America, in this particular case, Brazil. Due to its cultural affinity with Brazil, Portugal seems to not follow so closely the trend in other European markets, such as the 10 new European Union Member States (with the exception of Cyprus and Malta), where the percentage of soap operas amongst the series with the highest viewer ratings decreased by 70% between 1999 and 2000 and were replaced by national fiction series. [49]

These options can be explained on two interlinked dimensions: one cultural and the other economic.

Culturally speaking, of all the TV entertainment genres, the fiction series perhaps guarantees the greatest viewer loyalty. In economic terms, it is, at the same time, the genre that guarantees the greatest demographic amplitude, allows for repeats, and has the greatest export and ancillary revenue potential (for example, DVDs and merchandising) – although it also has the longest production processes involving the greatest risk. [50]

However, if there is a maintenance in terms of options on the part of the viewers and programmers in national fiction, the influence of the rise of reality shows can today be felt in another dimension, that of infotainment.

Infotainment or factual reality is a new television genre that fits into neither the traditional fiction models nor those of the reality shows or scripted hybrid programmes. Although they still account for only a small percentage of television programming, their growth in Europe has been

---

[48] Source: IP Network GmbH, European TV Key Facts, January 2004.

[49] Source: IP Network GmbH, European TV Key Facts, January 2004.

[50] In terms of export, American and German series dominate the European television markets. Source: IP Network GmbH, European TV Key Facts, January 2004.

quite considerable in countries such as France and Germany in the years 2002 and 2003 (22% in France with 81 prime time programmes on TF1, FRANCE2, FRANCE3, M6; and 88% in Germany on the channels ARD, ZDF, SAT1, RTL). [51]

Many of these programmes are imported by, or copied in, other countries. One of the most well-known infotainment programmes is *Changing Rooms*. The infotainment genre covers various models ranging from programmes focusing on crime to others oriented on family matters, changes in personal lifestyles, the property market (redecorating houses, purchasing property, etc.).

From Interactive Television to Networked Television

If, so far, we have looked at the television content dimension in terms of entertainment genres, we must also bear in mind that, in addition to the retention of certain genres and the emergence of others, interactivity is a fundamental factor for characterizing not only the current entertainment model but also the information model centred on television.

The death of television has been predicted practically since it began by an endless number of people, i.e. by those who, since the Hollywood golden era of the 1940s, have seen in the remote control the end of the television advertising model and have reasserted this with the fragmentation of the television market due to the rise of cable and satellite networks and now the DVR such as Tivo.

Television seems to be capable of innovating without forfeiting its identity, i.e. without losing that which makes it what it is: a low interactivity source of information and entertainment. Television's capacity for survival has been linked to its own dimension of social appropriation. If we examine the data obtained by the World Internet Project (2005) for the US and those presented for the same market by Lyra Research (2004) [52], we see two apparently contradictory trends. On the one hand, Internet users confirm that they generally watch less television and, on the other, those who have acquired DVR Satellite or Cable, Replay TV or Tivo say they watch more television. There are, therefore, other checks and balances be-

---

[51] Source: Freemantle Media, cited in Network GmbH, European TV Key Facts, January 2004.
[52] Lyra Research Inc. DTV View of Digital Video Recorder Users 2004

ing constructed, namely through the substitution of direct viewing by deferred viewing.

The truth is that the television we grew up with will never be the same as the television we will have when we die. Television, as a mirror of our societies, has evolved but its basic contents structure has remained, even if it does integrate new developments. For precisely that reason we can likewise ask what the effective change currently in progress in our television at the beginning of the 21st century is. To what extent does it differ from what it was ten years ago and what is different about it today that allows us to predict its change? If we look at the academic output on television published in the media and studied by futurologists, the immediate answer would be: interactivity.

Interactivity is today the foundations for most of the practices and strategic policies of companies involved in digital television. However, as Fausto Colombo and André Bellavita argue, digital television at present can be considered an "unpopular medium" as it has still not managed to penetrate the "social agenda of the viewers" (2002), with the exception of the United Kingdom (Born 2003). [53]

Digital television can be defined on the basis of two attributes: firstly, it follows a pattern of greater interaction with the viewer, which is why it is *interactive*. Secondly, it is linked with paid television, for the business model relies not so much on advertising but on the choice of the viewer and the *payment for the service* has to do with this possibility of choice.

In the last 20 years, the experiments in digital television (be it terrestrial, by cable or by satellite) have met with more failures than successes (Richeri, 2004). Up until the mid-1990s, digital TV was synonymous with Pay TV (which developed through cinema and sports [mainly football] channels) and was a success in countries such as the US, UK, France, Spain (Kleisteuber, 1998) and Portugal.

However, Pay TV has not been equally successful all over, for we do not yet have a standardized digital model at the world level. Thus, cable is predominant in the US and Portugal (30%), while DTH satellite television achieves penetrations in countries such as Germany and Austria close to 40%. In other countries again, the figures are well below one third of the

---

[53] For a contextualization of digital television in its political and economic dimensions see Papathanassopoulos (2002) and Galperin (2004).

population (Kiefl 2003): Italy (16%), US (15%), France (18%) and the UK (22%).

In the late 1990s Europe witnessed an expansion of Digital Terrestrial Television (DTT). This expansion was based on the decision of the majority of European countries to switch off their national analogical transmissions by 2010. Thus, the development of digital television in Europe is almost exclusively rooted in a political process coupled with economic imperatives (Papathanasopoulos, 2002), and not in the demand of the viewers suppressing a social need through technological innovation (Winston, 1999).

The introduction of digital TV is also a milestone in the development of European television, initiating what we can call the third phase. The first phase was dominated by the monopoly of the public television services, which was followed by a phase of coexistence of public and private stations. However, what will happen in this third phase is still uncertain, mainly because of an already existing trend towards greater segmentation of the public services and an increase in the available channels. So far, digital TV has not altered the television formats, both in terms of the accessible contents and the way in which the programmes are conducted by their presenters, journalists and others involved (Richieri, 2000). Both in talk show and reality show models, the introduction of interactivity continues to adhere to traditional models of distribution of power of control over broadcasting and contents. And these are the content models most exploited and seen as the paradigm of interactive content in the television of the new century. According to Kaitatzi-Whitlock, there are three types of agency (programme producers or hosts; guests and audience) and the interactivity is controlled in decreasing order by all these agents, with greater power of interactivity attributed to the producers and less to the audiences (Kaitatzi-Whitlock, 2004). The same takes place through the limitation of interactivity in fictioned reality programmes, where the interactivity is limited essentially to choices of candidates and to their continuity, placing, therefore, the decision of the type of choice in the production of the programme.

Given the similarity of results in different countries, our analysis of interactivity in television could benefit from a brief look at the realities of digital television in Europe. Our tour, so to speak, starts off in Scandinavia and ends in Portugal, which will be the object of more detailed study.

Currently, the number of homes in the *multichannel system*, i.e. those receiving TV other than through analogue terrestrial diffusion, is 51% in

EU-15, 53% in the 10 new EU Member States and 84% in the US. Curiously enough, the growth rates between 1995 and 2002 in Europe were more or less the same for the 25 EU Member States, approximately 45%, and 30% for the US. [54]

However, if we look at the market penetration of digital television at the end of 2002 in Europe we can identify three groups of countries. Most [55] of European countries have domestic digital television figures in the non-existent to 10% of the homes range. This group is followed by a one including Denmark, Germany, Switzerland, Spain and France that has coverage rates of between 10% and 20%. Finally, we have a third group including Ireland, Norway, Spain and the UK, which are all above 20%. [56]

Allan Brown's (2004) analysis of and explanation for the failure of the Swedish TDT project can be applied to diverse European countries in their diverse explanatory dimensions:

A major defect in the design of the Swedish DTTV project is that viewers are required to pay a subscription fee, even to receive programs that are available free of charge on analog, including those of SVT for which they already pay an annual licence fee. The extremely poor take-up of only 2.5 per cent after four years indicates that Swedish viewers consider the costs of subscribing to DTTV outweigh the benefits. Part of the difficulty in attracting viewers to pay for DTTV – in Sweden as in other countries – is that because multichannel television was available first on cable and satellite, these platforms have a significant 'first mover advantage' over terrestrial. This has enabled them to gain long-term access to 'strategic programming', especially movies and sport that are key to selling pay-TV subscriptions. Most viewers are likely to be more interested in the programming they can receive than in the form of transmission. (Brown 2004).

The case of the United Kingdom is an exception and, as such, an interesting example. In the UK in January 2004, the figures for households with digital television ranged from 45% to 50% (with a predominance of digital

---

[54] Source: IP Network GmbH, European TV Key Facts, January 2004.

[55] The set of countries with percentage lower than 10%: Austria, Portugal, Poland, Finland, Netherlands, Hungary, Estonia, Slovakia, Czech Republic, Latvia, Belgium, Lithuania, Greece, Romania, Slovenia, Croatia and Bulgaria.

[56] Source: IP Network GmbH, European TV Key Facts, January 2004.

satellite access, which accounted for more than half of the connections, followed by non-paid DTT and then paid digital cable television). [57]

The UK case differs from other approaches in that it includes strong commitment on the part of the government in building the information society. According to governmental directives, public television (BBC and Channel Four) also made investments in addition to the private station, Sky Television (Digital Satellite Service). Even though approximately 35% of the households had DTT in 2001, a large portion of the viewers were – and still are – reticent. Between 30% and 40% of the population says that it has no interest in migrating to digital (Born 2003).

In Spain, the digital terrestrial broadcaster Quiero TV stopped broadcasting in 2002, only two years after beginning operations. The merger of the two satellite digital television broadcasting platforms (the Canal Satellite Digital and Via Digital) was announced in May of the same year. These two decisions were based on the low market penetration of digital television, which continued even after the decision of Quiero TV to complement its offer with interactive services and Internet access (Fleishmer – Somalvico 2002).

In a universe of ten million potential viewers, generalist television in Portugal offers a total of four channels transmitted via hertzian waves, cable and satellite. Of these four channels, two are privately owned – SIC and TVI (belonging to business groups that also have interests in the written press and radio) – and two are public – RTP1 and the recently renamed "Dois" (formerly RTP2).

For a better understanding of the Portuguese television market, we must highlight another element – cable television. The cable platform currently has a penetration rate of approximately 30% of Portuguese households (although coverage does not yet include the total territory of continental Portugal and the Portuguese islands), offering subscribers more than 60 channels and the possibility of Internet access and interactive television.

Another of the particularities that come with the diffusion of the new technologies and is visible even in countries with very different Internet access figures, as is the case for Portugal (29%) and Canada (72%), is the fact that access to digital television (be it by cable or satellite) is a facilitating factor in the decision to use the Internet.

---

[57] Estimate of 50% for OFCOM and 45% for the measurement carried out by FIVE-BARB. Source: IP Network GmbH, European TV Key Facts, January 2004.

4.7 – Equipment and subscription of services in homes in Portugal and Canada (2003)

Equipment and service subscriptions	Internet users Portugal	Non-users Portugal	Internet users Canada	Non-users Canada
	%	%	%	%
Telephone	70.3	58.1	n/a	n/a
Mobile telephone for personal use	96.5	61.9	73.0	40.0
Television	99.8	99.4	n/a	n/a
Cable television	55.4	29.1	67.0	64.0
Free access to satellite television	11.7	4.0	26.0	24.0
Satellite television subscribers	4.3	2.3	n/a	n/a
Access to interactive television through cable	1.2	0.2	n/a	n/a
Computer	75.1	19.0	75.0	25.0
Internet connection	57.8	6.2	88.0	n/a
Game consoles: PS2, Dreamcast, Xbox, Sega	23.4	5.3	44.0	22.0
Mp3 player	n/a	n/a	22.0	3.0
Digital camera	n/a	n/a	43.0	13.0
Palm Pilot	n/a	n/a	21.0	4.0

Source: The Network Society in Portugal CIES-ISCTE, 2003 and WIP Canada, 2004.

Taking into account the analysis of the European digital experiences, as well as the failure of projects such as Qube in Columbus, Hi-OVIS in Higashi Ikoma, Orlando and Quebec, amongst others (Richieri, 2004 and Rodotà, 1997), we can venture a number of explanations based on the specificity of the interactive television projects in each country, namely in terms of the historical development of their television systems and the options of the business models.

Returning to the British case (Born, 2004), which has one of the highest digital television acceptance rates in Europe, we have seen that the general migration to digital cannot be controlled by the market only. On the one hand, the new developments in digital technology have always to compete with digital systems that at the moment already cover the social needs of the viewers and, on the other, only the reformulation of the idea of public service can overcome the reticence of a large section of the population in relation to the forecast shutdown of analogical signals in many countries. Both the UK, with Freeview, and Italy, with its subsidizing of set-top boxes, show that, without some type of state intervention, digital television technology will not reach a large proportion of the population.

However, the low social appropriation of the new technology raises other questions. One of the most common approaches to explaining this phenomenon references the technological limitations that do not allow the viewer full satisfaction in terms of interactivity. Nevertheless, experimentation in the field of interactivity has evolved, as has the relationship between the viewer and television. New technologies such as the Internet and mobile telephone have achieved good penetration rates, allowing the television viewer to interact with television. Furthermore, the importance of more traditional technologies such as Teletext is, in many countries, on the increase, particularly in combination with SMS services.

The television stations have understood the importance of combining these technologies for generating additional income to that obtained with advertising and, in the case of the State-owned channels, public funding. This requires the implementation of new business models and contents strategies that will allow for these new technologies to be incorporated into the programming.

An analysis of the generalist television stations, cable channels and media consumption practices in Portugal (Cardoso et al 2004) shows that recent years have seen evolution in the forms of social appropriation of television – which is visible particularly in terms of interactivity – despite the fact that the presence of a digital interactive television model is still weak, or residual.

Thus, one can reasonably argue that interactivity *in* and *with* television is not directly associated with the digital format only, and an understanding of the phenomenon must be sought in other dimensions, namely in what is termed *networked television*.

For a better understanding of this phenomenon we must first recognize that there are various possible forms of interactivity and that different types of interactivity are technologically associated with the different media and socially appropriated by the users of those technologies.

Before one can attempt to summarize the evolution of the general interactive television trends, one must first define and discuss the concept of *interactivity*.

Let us first look at the theoretical approaches to the concept and then we can consider its practical applications in two technologies: interactive television (iTV) and the online presence of the mass media in the Internet.

According to Kim and Sawney (2002), there are two theoretical approaches to interactive communication in the context of the new technologies applied to the media: the *communicational approach* and the *environmental approach* of the media. The communicational approach sees interactivity as the relationship between communicators and exchanged messages. In this sense, not only the electronic media, but also letters to the editor, telephone calls to television programmes and audience participation in the programmes are regarded as forms of interactivity. In this perspective, the interactive media are those that can simulate interpersonal exchanges through their communication channels. In the environmental approach, in contrast, interactivity is defined as "a technologically offered media experience in which the user can participate and modify the forms and contents of the media in real time" (Steur quoted in Kim/Shawney 2002). According to this definition, characteristics such as interaction in real time and immediate response are considered of vital importance for the creation of an interactive environment.

Another interesting proposal is the typology consisting of four cumulative dimensions of interactivity developed by van Dijk (Rafaeli 1988; van Dijk 1999, 2000). The first dimension is the *spatial dimension* of interactivity, which refers to *point-to-point* communication. The second dimension refers to *synchronic communication*; interactivity is affected by various forms of non-synchronic communication due to the excessive time lapse between action, reaction and reaction to the reaction. The third dimension is the *temporal dimension* of interactivity, i.e. the possibility of exchange between sender and receiver at any time and in any place, whereby both have identical control and contribute equally to the message. Finally, the *action and control dimension* corresponds to the possibility of contextualization and shared understanding – a dimension which, for the meantime, is only present in face-to-face communication.

If we focus on the relations of power within the communicative structure of different technologies we also have to recognize that interactivity takes many different forms or, in other words, different appropriations.

When we look at the different possibilities effectively offered by iTV, we see that there is a cultural contradiction between interactivity as a form of communication and the organizational model of television (Kim/Shawney 2002). Interactive television maintains the organizational structure of traditional television both in its programme formats and in the roles that the journalists and entertainment programme presenters take on as mediators and organizers of the interaction with the audiences. Thus, iTV is much more reactive than interactive.

Table 4.8 – Types of interactivity of interactive television applications

Type of activity	Application	Interactivity level
Choice of channels and programmes	Conditional access; EPG; video decoder	0 (digital TV)
Choice of menus/ transactions	VOD; personalization; more channels; e-commerce	1 -3 (interactive TV)
Production of information	Programme participation; reaction to programmes; contribution to programmes and channels (not directed by third parties); production of programmes and channels	3 (interactive TV)
Communication exchange	Communication on/simultaneous with TV programmes; viewer communities	4

Source: Adapted from Corcoran (2004) in Colombo, (ed), TV and Interactivity in Europe. My-thologies, theoretical perspectives, real experiences, Vita e Pensiero, Milan.

The freedom of action offered by interactivity can be found much more easily in the Internet and not in the models of interactivity proposed by interactive television. Characteristics such as one-to-many and many-to-one communication, flexibility of use and communication through voice, text and video, both between individuals and in groups, the use of the medium as a platform for the production and processing of information and the potential for the creation of own messages have much more do with a networked computer than with interactive television.

The experiments in iTV over the last two decades can, in almost all cases, be reduced to the creation of platforms incorporating various technologies allowing the users, through payment of a fixed rate or pay-as-you-go rates, to choose from different camera angles in a football game, vote in talk shows or similar programmes or choose their own film (Richieri 2000). The low innovation in terms of content is above all due to the incapacity to invest substantially in iTV so as to produce new contents capable of being interactive. As Richieri suggests, this is a period of strong barriers to change, due to the desire on the part of the television stations for rapid return on any investments made. This is, perhaps, a reality that is difficult to surpass, even if we consider the Internet on TV, i.e. the possibility described by Tadayoni (2002; 2004) of Out of Band (OOB) and In Band (IB), which are the transmission of the broadcast via the same diffusion channel as the television signal and the return via another parallel channel (usually the telephone) or the transmission together with other television broadcasting signals. Or also Television on the Internet, which is technologically more difficult due to the bandwidth necessary for enabling it (HDTV requires 20Mbit/s and SDTV 4 Mbit/s).

In the former case, experimentation has demonstrated that the Internet is essentially an activity centred on locations limited to intellectual work (i.e. the office at home or at work), while television is associated with the relaxation spaces at home. As far as the latter is concerned, the possibilities of integration could be more interesting, even taking the warnings of Aldo Grasso into consideration. Grasso suggests that the problem is not the technological invention nor one of contents but the need to invent a new audience: an audience in which the viewer who wishes to interact will need to have a lot of time on his/her hands, understand foreign languages and have money to spend if he/she wants to choose from a large spectrum of options. In other words, for Grasso (2004) it is necessary to overcome the *mental gap* and not just the *digital gap*.

Without wishing to devalue the merit of Grasso's approach, it is true that one can already identify the existence of an interactive audience today, even it does not constitute the majority of the population.

In order to carry out that analysis we must first consider that the uses of interactivity by the online mass media on the Internet are much higher than those experimented by iTV, even considering that a significant part of the possibilities of interactivity is not used by the former, as has been identified in diverse studies. (Bayè 2000; Seibel, 2000).[58]

Due to its organizational structures, the interactivity offered today by television is mostly based on the simulation of interpersonal exchanges, be they through the characteristics of the programme formats or through the role conferred upon the presenter or journalist. On the other hand, due to the characteristics already mentioned, interactivity on the Internet is closer to the concept of interactivity proposed by the media environment approach (Kim/Shawney, 2002).

Following the reasoning above on the interactivity models, an analysis of television and the interactivity dimension presents us immediately with a problem that requires clarification: should we analyze television on the basis of its interactivity possibilities or the concrete practices of interactivity?

---

[58] According to Mark Deuze, interactivity with the contents in an online environment provided by the Internet can be characterized by three aspects: *surfing*, referring to the tools made available on the pages; *functionality*, relating to the use of media for interacting with site contents and authors; and *adaptability*, i.e. the tools offered for the personalization of the site (Deuze 2004).

The interactivity we must take into account for understanding how television is organized, in both its entertainment and information sphere, and how it positions itself in a central role of the meta systems of entertainment and information, is the interactivity of the current practices (in a communicational logical) and not that of the imagined possibilities of digital interactive television, a single interface incorporating various technologies previously only available separately (in an environmental logic) through technological convergence.

As mentioned above, the end of the 20th century (and beginning of the 21st century) in the media has been characterized by enforcing convergence: economic, technological and market convergence. But we can also argue that, in the end, what measures the success of that convergence is whether or not it is successful in terms of social appropriation. The successes at the economic level are patent, particularly in terms of the acquisitions and mergers between broadcasters and content producers (even if, for example, Vivendi-Universal has run into problems and the Time Warner-AOL merger has proved to be a decision of doubtful effectiveness for Time Warner).

At the technological level, however, we have witnessed developments of considerably varying degrees of success: the online presence of newspapers; the possibility of listening to radio on the Internet; the connections between music, the cinema and the Internet (although many of these taking illegal forms); the multimedia telephone, etc.

However, the presence of television on the Internet clearly falls short of the expectations. As we have already seen, this situation is due, amongst other factors, to the lack of investment capacity of the television channels, the low availability of bandwidth and the incapacity of television to assert itself in the digital sector.

For this reason it is argued that the current phase is not characterized by the diffusion of interactive television and technological convergence but by the success of *networked television* in a process of divergence.

What is *networked television?* The answer to that question can be found through analysis of the viewer practices, the formulas of interaction with television and also in the formulas of organization of interactivity by the television programmers and the technological articulations that are designed in the current media system.

Digital television interactivity is today offered simultaneously in different technological supports, which range from the offer of TV (Tadayoni, 2004) to the television channel Internet portals, from Microsoft's commitment to interactive television to digital terrestrial television and from satellite and cable broadcasting to mobile telephone networks and, obviously, television combining the use of the Internet, SMS and telephones.

When asked what means they used to contact television and radio stations, both Portuguese Internet users and non-users stated that they prefer the telephone and text messages (SMS) over E-mail and normal mail correspondence (Cardoso et al., 2004).

If the media practices or, if we prefer, diets favour the SMS and the telephone call, because they are the technologies that are most widespread amongst the population and most easily share the same space in the home as the television, how is the media system organized in the channels it offers for viewer interactivity?

As one can see from the list of programmes presented in Table 4.9, there were would seem to be a common trend in the international sphere favouring the use of technologies where monetary revenue is more easily associable with interactivity, i.e. the predominance of SMS and telephone to the detriment of the Internet. There is also another reason for this preference for the SMS and telephone over the Internet. The management of revenue at television stations is currently dominated by a multicentric approach, i.e. it is no longer the advertising that guarantees a channel's operation. One example is the reality show *Loft Story 2* in the French channel M6, where, in addition to the 240,000 subscribers to the dedicated channel (€12.00/month) one can add the 200,000 magazines sold, 1.3 million CD singles sold and the 14 million votes from the viewers (35% by telephone and 65% by SMS). [59]

A survey of mobile phone users in Belgium, France, The Netherlands, Scandinavia, Spain and the United Kingdom revealed that 42% of respondents (and 70% of adolescents) are interested in the forms of interaction provided by SMS-TV (McKinsey 2004). According to the same study, the advertising revenue generated by SMS-TV currently accounts for 2% of the total advertising income (€22 billion) generated by the European open signal TV broadcasting market. [60]

---

[59] Source: EGTA 2003 cited in IP Network GmbH, European TV Key Facts, January 2004.

[60] However, this economic model also gives rise to some problems, for its success has resulted in diverse *negotiation difficulties* between the television broadcasters and the mobile network operators and in disagreement as to the distribution of the revenue. The main concern of the broadcasters is that it impossible to maintain a similar distribution of income between the fixed landline network operators and the mobile network operators.

Table 4.9 – Analysis of viewer participation forms in reality shows

	American Idol (US)	Operacion Triunfo (ES)	Survivor (US)	Big Brother (UK)	The Salon (UK)	I'm a Celeb. (UK)
Type of broadcast						
Open	X	X	X	X	X	X
Cable/Sat./Digital		X	X	X	X	X
Direct	X	X	X	X	X	X
Viewer participation						
Televoting	X	X		X	X	X
SMS with voting	X	X		X	X	X
SMS with survey	X			X	X	X
Internet – chat rooms	X	X	X	X	X	X

Source: FREMANTLE cited in IP Network GmbH, European TV Key Facts, January 2004.

Given that the Internet does not produce direct revenue through its use in interaction with the programme, the design of the interactivity in preparing the scripts for the programmes favours other technologies and attributes to the Internet a role that has more to do with promotion than generating revenue. For this reason, use of the Internet is not promoted to the extent that use of the telephone, or mobile phones, is.

In Europe, some programmes running on open-signal television channels that have adopted SMS-TV have increased their audiences by some twenty per cent. The justification for its acceptance in part has to do with the user-friendliness and also the low level of interactivity that adapts exceptionally well to the current TV models. For SMS-TV has an interactive character, it dynamizes the relationship between the TV and the target audience and reinforces the loyalty of the viewers.

Interactive participation through the voice recognition software of the landline networks attributes 80% of the amount charged to the end consumer to the TV broadcasters (a situation that is only possible because the fixed network operators have low fixed costs given the lack of competition). The mobile networks, however, have to deal with high competition levels and, accordingly, high fixed costs. In addition to bearing the cost of the SMS transmission, the mobile operators also have consider the costs for network maintenance and invoicing. For this reason, the network operators demand the greater part of the revenue generated by SMS-TV. According to Jacques R. Bughin, the TV broadcasters keep somewhere between 35 and 50% of the revenue generated by SMS-TV. However, the revenue generated by the messages themselves is little compared to the potential effects of SMS-TV in terms of Direct Marketing and increased audiences (McKinsey, 2004).

SMS has thus taken on such a central role in the relationship with interactivity that Espen Ytreberg (2004) has proposed a characterization of
television programmes supported by SMS in three categories, the typology
of which we can suggest can encompass the following designations: traditional, mixed and pure formats (Cardoso, 2004).

Table 4.10 – Television Formats with Use of SMS

TV format	Description
Traditional (debate; information and entertainment magazine; game show; music programme)	The SMS is read out loud by a presenter or shown graphically on the screen.
Mixed (SMS and video)	The graphic design of the programme incorporates a chat scroll with SMS texts.
Pure SMS	There is no reference to video in the basic design of the programme.

If we take as a starting point Ytreberg's (2004) affirmation that SMS-
TV presents not a promising future but interactivity in a mundane and socially already fully appropriated form in the daily practices of communication and mediation, we can better understand the success of this networking of television and mobile phone. In the different television realities in
Europe and the world we can identify certain specific and some global
SMS-TV models (as in the case of MTV Re:action). Whereas, in Portugal,
the programmes that make most use of SMS messages are the morning and
afternoon talk shows (for expressing opinions on the programme, sending
messages to the presenter(s) and guests, sending love messages to third
persons, to further meetings between age-old friends or re-encounters with
old friends), there are also other realities, similar as those in Northern Europe.

Interactivity in Portuguese television is essentially characterized by its
use in entertainment programmes, with the information dimension playing
a very minor role. In the current media system, as we shall see, informa-
tion-related interactivity is essentially a characteristic of the Internet and
not so much of television.

In countries that have taken the exploitation of SMS-TV formats further we also find three models (Ytreberg, 2005) in terms of the influence
the participants themselves have on the structuring of the programme. The

first model, "limited influence", can be found in MTV Europe programmes (such as MTV Access, Top Ten at Ten, Re:action) and also in programmes from the North of Europe and parts of Southern Europe. This model is based on the presentation of one message at a time and sometimes there is the possibility of voting for songs or persons/contestants, as in the case of the Big Brother reality show. The possibility of the viewers communicating with each other does not exist. The second model, "partial influence", allows those interacting to have some direct and formative input influencing the development of the television programme itself. In this model, the participants can chat with each other and with the presenter. Finally, in the third model, "dominant influence", the SMS becomes the central element of the programme, and the programme's whole interaction and content is dominated by the conversation that is generated between the participants and the presenter. In some cases this "dominant" model comes very close to Internet chat room models, turning the television screen into an IRC. There are numerous examples but the most well known are the Mikamika and 4deitti channels in Finland [61].

This analysis of interactivity in television shows that the majority of people who interact with television do so: (1) to express an opinion, be it on a particular topic or in a vote; (2) to communicate with other people, as is the case for messages sent to TV programmes so that they can be read by other persons – such as a boy/girlfriend or a missing family member – or to chat via SMS or other communication interfaces offered by TV on the Internet (such as forums). They do so fundamentally in a context of participation motivated in the context of entertainment or purposes of socialization with third persons, such as the search, using SMS, for relatives or colleagues participants have lost track of, in a model that makes them independent of E-mail or postal correspondence, which are more time consuming and require other types of literacy.

As Ytreberg points out (2005), SMS-TV involves a change in the conception of the television audience. This change implies that we no longer see the activity of watching television as a singular activity and instead conceive it as the fruit of multitasking involving various technologies working together in a network. For the television industry, SMS-based television also constitutes a change in terms of new forms of revenue.

---

[61] Ytreberg, Espen et al, Small talk makes a big difference: recent developments in interactive, SMS-based television, (forthcoming) Televison and New Media.

Given the relationship between digital technology and television contents and the exploration of the social appropriation of interactivity, one can argue that, although one can agree with the idea that television as we know it today is an evolution of *Neo-television* (Eco, 1985 and Caseti, 1990) with a greater opening to the audience (Vitadinni, Marturano and Villa, 1998), we are no longer in the period of experimentation of a necessary opening in order to legitimize television in an environment dominated by the arrival of the new media. On the contrary, what we have is the assertion of a new television model – *networked television.* [62]

Networked television is open to the audience in the sense that television continues to be the medium that is accessible to the greatest number of persons and does not have to acquire a new legitimacy (Vitadinni, Marturano and Villa, 1998). On the contrary, television assumes its role as part of a larger network of mediation technologies, interacting with the other technologies but not forfeiting its characteristic of success, which is based on the low level of interactivity with the television viewer (or, if we prefer, in its communicational interactivity model).

As Umberto Eco (2004) constantly reminds us, television will most likely not be replaced by the Internet or another technology in the medium term, nor does it seem to have undergone a radical change in technological terms, precisely because it continues to perform a social and economic role that is different to that of the Internet.

Television is an entertainment and information medium. It informs us about the world and our own part of it in the most diverse areas of life. Television today is still the main medium of cultural diffusion on the planet and it continues to be a fundamental support for the current global economic model by allowing for the passage from a market primary needs goods market to a totally multifaceted market (Kiefl, 2003).

By opening up to other technologies, television has been able to retain the centre of the social dimensions of the media – characterized by low interactivity in the relations with entertainment and information. A social function that is generally activated when we arrive home after a day's work

---

[62] The transformations brought about by neo-television are characterized by expansion of broadcasting hours, an increase in the number of channels. But neo-television is essentially characterized by the change in programme contents and forms of fruition. As Santiago suggests, "(....) more and more, television is coming into the viewers' homes providing moments of socialization and diversion, appealing to emotion and neglecting the role it used to perform in the field of informing and even educating the individual". (Santiago, 2003 pp. 36).

and that accompanies us at our daily meal, while competing with other technologies for our spare time, when we are not engaged in conversation with family members or friends.

Networked television also differs from interactive television in the sense that it is not carried out under the cover of technological convergence. On the contrary, it combines various communication technologies – analogue and digital – interacting in a network form with the aim of furthering interactivity with the viewers.

Thus, networked television is carried out in an environment of technological *divergence*. This is borned out by the data collected, which clearly show the use of various mediums, such as the telephone, SMS, E-mail and WWW, as ways in which the audience can interact with the programmes.

It is not only in the area of interactivity that one seeks to value a network dimension in television, also in cultural terms the area of design is used to emulate the network logic through an interface design that transcends the traditional media boundaries (Cooke, 2005) and brings television closer to other technologies such as the Internet or the world of mobile phones and SMS (Ytreberg, 2005).

On the other hand, the analysis shows that the other television interactivity models still have a residual importance, both in terms of their penetration in homes and the interaction between viewers and iTV. [63]

The implications of this analysis are not irrelevant. For some years now, the television stations have built their business strategies around two ideas: (1) that interactivity is carried out on the basis of a system of digital convergence; and (2) that the television viewers would be prepared to invest time and a part of the family budget in a higher participation level. [64]

If the social appropriation of the media is going in the direction of networked television and not digital iTV, it is possible that the television stations and software and hardware companies will be forced to rethink their strategies. This does not mean that we are not witnessing a development towards digital television – from the current low interactivity television

---

[63] For an in-depth analysis of the television interactivity models in Europe see Colombo, Fausto (ed.) 2004 and Born, Georgina (2004).

[64] More recently a third component has joined the strategic thinking of television stations: mobility, i.e. the idea that people will watch TV on their mobile phones or iPods. Although being too soon to assert the real effectiveness of such a strategy, history of the media in the near past requests moderation on the enthusiasm brought by mobile TV.

distributed via hertzian waves, cable or satellite to a consolidation of the interactivity dimensions and other technological models.

The development of the television stations and the viewers shows that television is adapting to a new media matrix (Meyrovitz cited in Ortoleva 2002) determined by the social use of the media. By thus adapting, television ends up redefining its position within the media system. And this is a development that is still in progress, for today we find many projects and proposals for the further development of television that will succeed and others that will not be appropriated by society.

However, the greatest change will, perhaps, be less technological in nature and have more to do with format. Due to the need to increase revenue, we may see the duration of series episodes changing from 30 – 40 minutes to 15 minutes so that they can be more easily downloaded from the Internet to laptops and mobile phones and to adapt them to the advertising time needs.

Another field of change and one that is characteristic of networked television will be that brought about by IPTV, but only for those with the necessary literacies for using the Internet and provided that the music and cinema industry gatekeepers become comfortable with the new revenue models that this model of access to television will generate. This list of possible changes will also have to include new nodes for the global interconnection network between television, the Internet, mobile phones, persons, music, films, series and news, i.e. the experimentation of old and new commercial, public or hybrid television models in new markets, such as the Chinese television market.

However, even this relationship will be one of complementarity between supports and not one of the replacement of the living room or bedroom by viewing on public transport or in the workplace. It will also be governed by the social interaction customs in each different society.

Networked television is the product of the social and economic appropriation of one of the dimensions of interactivity: low interactivity. Television is, at the same time, the central technology in terms of media practices, or diets, and media matrixes, or representations of the social agents, as far as information and entertainment are concerned. It also constitutes a driving force behind the entertainment meta-system on account of its economic dimensions. Its presence in the entertainment dimension is characterized by a hybrid system in which traditional and new television genres influenced by the emergence of reality shows live side by side.

As we will analyze in the following section, in the information and news meta-system, the Internet takes on the emerging role that the multimedia games have apparently assumed in the entertainment dimension – without, however, achieving the same revenue level (income levels are much higher in the games industry than in the maintenance of informational presence on the Internet, where direct or indirect free services still predominate).

At the same time, the Internet assumes the role of the central node in the second network of interactivity – that of high interactivity.

Television and the Internet today constitute the main mediation technologies, with each one disputing the centre of two different interactivity networks that are interconnected through links offered by different interpersonal communication technologies.

By means of differentiated social and economic appropriation processes, television and the Internet are today the *two central nodes in one and the same mediation network*. But before making that assertion, we must first contextualize the history of the evolution of the mass media, in which the Internet has begun to assert itself as a partner to take into account in every media strategy.

5. Has the Internet Really Changed the Mass Media?

Whereas, in the preceding chapter, I have endeavoured to characterize the main elements of the *entertainment meta-system*, in this chapter I will focus on the *information and news meta-system*.

As already stated, in addition to its role in the field of entertainment, television continues to play a central role in the provision of information and news in society.

This is not only a result of the economic investment in television but also has to do with the fact that it is the chosen medium for political and economic agents as the prime vehicle for public communication, given its high level of penetration in homes.

However, in the recent past television did not perform the task of transmitting information on its own, but shared it with radio and the newspapers. Today it shares it with the Internet, too.

The Internet is a new vehicle for the newspapers, radio and television providing new ways of reaching their audiences and creating new ones.

The Internet is also a space in which many collective or individual projects for the presentation of the most diverse opinions, news and information flourish – from fauna and flora to shopping, from social mobilization to sex and to formal education, to name only a few areas.

As we have seen, the Internet offers us mass communication and interpersonal communication and we, the users, attribute different functions to it: we socialize through chat or telephone over IP conversations, or the sending of cards or photos; we make bank transactions and purchase books and tickets, etc. online; we carry out forms of entertainment such as *online* games, exchanging music files and visiting pornographic sites[65]; we search for information so as to inform ourselves better on our shopping decisions; we seek specific information for work, study or personal purposes; and we also inform ourselves on news and sports news.

It is this last aspect, the news, that will be the centre of interest in this section. I will endeavour to understand how the Internet has changed, or has not changed, the news and the way news is made available by television and radio stations and newspapers online and offline or, if we prefer: what has changed in terms of the contents offered and the model of journalism practised?

From the End of Journalism to Its Reconstruction

The question "will the Internet lead to the disappearance of newspapers, radio and television?" was one frequently asked in the confabulations of many journalism professionals at the beginning of the second half of the 1990s. Strange as it may seem now, it was an apprehension shared by many when, in 1998-1999, the Internet began to expand to large sections of the population.

When I say that the question is somewhat "strange", it is because the development of the Internet has shown just how much that interpretation of the future was wrong.

But why was the question even raised? Technologically the Internet enables us all to both consume and produce information and entertainment. If we have the possibility of going directly to the sources, why would we need mediators such as newspapers, radio, television and their professionals?

However, experience has shown that that was not the path taken.

Today there are hardcopy and online publications, analogue and digital television stations[66], and although blogs have multiplied the possibilities

---

[65] According to the study carried out by CIES/ISCTE in Portugal in 2003 (Cardoso et al., 2004), even if the data indicate very low rates for viewing pornography on the Internet (10%), when asked in the context "There are studies and research that show that many people use the Internet to view adult pornography; on the basis of what you know or have heard do you agree or disagree with this statement?", more than 70% of the respondents, both male and female, agreed with the statement.

[66] Henten and Tadayoni (2002) clearly define the different concepts for television. Thus, Digital TV

of having one's own opinion column, journalism continues to be a profession that is very much present in our societies and the greater part of our news information still comes from journalistic editorial teams.

When radio first emerged, the playwright Bertolt Brecht (1932) focused his attention on the innovative potential and the response it could offer in terms of information and journalistic output. [67]

What a reading of Brecht's (1932) thoughts in the context of the early 21st century allows us to enunciate is the need to place the Internet in the wider context of the environment of the evolution of communication and the media (Winston, 1999). This is necessary so that we can understand the Internet not as a technological discontinuity generating ruptures in journalism, but as an innovation appropriated by the profession in the context of prior experience of appropriations of other media and supervening professional needs (Winston, 1999).

The Internet and its relationship with the mass media are one more episode in the history of the transformation of the media caused by the complex combined action of perceived needs, competitive and political pressures and technological innovations (Resende, 2002).

The history of the mass media shows that a new technology does not eliminate any preceding one, but constitutes an alternative (Eco, 2004 and Lutfi, 2002). In most cases a new technology is an extension of the preceding ones, and the production modes are considered to be in mutation and not the news substance produced (Lutfi, 2002). This being so, each new medium is the result of a metamorphosis, of a preceding medium evolving and adapting to a new reality instead of disappearing (Fiddler, cited in Keck, 2000).

Although we may have forgotten them, the 1970s and 1980s saw the development and use of two electronic means for sharing text and image –

---

refers to the technology distributed through standard DVB in Europe, also using an MPEG-2 compression system. IPTV is the distribution of television using IP protocol, for example via LAN. Finally, Internet TV refers to TV broadcasting and video services via the Internet.

[67] "Radio is one sided when it should be two. It is purely an apparatus for distribution, for mere sharing out. So here is a positive suggestion: change this apparatus over from distribution to communication. The radio would be the finest possible communication apparatus in public life, a vast network of pipes. That is to say, it would be if it knew how to receive as well as transmit, how to let the listener speak as well as hear, how to bring him into a relationship instead of isolating him. On this principle the radio should step out of the supply business and organize its listeners as suppliers." ["Der Rundfunk als Kommunikationsapparat" in *Blätter des Hessischen Landestheaters Darmstadt*, No. 16, July 1932] http://telematic.walkerart.org/telereal/bit_brecht.html

videotext and teletext – which sought to respond to information needs that were as yet unsatisfied in the emerging information society (Boczkowski, 2000). The investment in these two media followed two strategic orientations, namely the accompaniment of the computerization of production and distribution methods in progress and, given the increase in competition and production costs associated with this and the growing heterogeneization of the public's tastes (Bozkowski, 2000), the endeavour to replace paper as a platform.

Even though these media fulfilled the objectives set for them, they were not commercially appealing on account of certain logistic limitations, such as the relatively low speed of transmission and the strong similarity between its contents and those of the platforms that predated them (Boczkowski, 2000).

In the 1980s, the reproduction of contents made available by the news agencies or printed in the newspapers proved to be the most frequent practice for these two media and the creation of contents specifically conceived for them remained a mirage (Boczkowski, 2000).

Parallel to this there are registers of the use of videotext, essentially by private individuals but also by journalism professionals, for establishing communication channels between each other, as in the case of Minitel (Castells, 2003). In the professional field – in the editorial staff rooms – the use was more or less marginal, an unexpected and relatively unexploited sub-product (Boczkowski, 2002).

In the 1990s the massification of the personal computer, the development in telecommunications infrastructures and the emergence of the first browser resulting from the development of the Internet (Castells, 2003) gave rise to a new wave of activity in the use of electronic platforms for making news contents available (Boczkowski, 2002).

The introduction of the Internet, no matter how revolutionary it may have been, took place in a context in which the prior experimentation with other information technologies had been ongoing, albeit without the desired success – given the failure of these technologies to adapt to the practical needs of the journalism professionals and the need for differentiation and/or complementarity in relation to the already existing supports and the lack of critical mass in terms of the number of users amongst the public. The Internet presented itself as a technology that could be better moulded to suit the journalist's needs and could also aggregate a potential mass public. For these reasons, the Internet technology did not challenge any journalistic model or replace any of the other models of access to information, but it did help to transform, to a certain extent, the relationship between the producer and user of information and also relationships on other levels, such as sources (Colombo, 2000 and Regan, 2000).

Although we can understand why it is possible to establish a critique of the inevitability of the rupture of the existence of mediators and why journalism was ready to try the appropriation of a technology such as the Internet, there is one other point that must be examined.

The reason why the idea of the end of journalism found resonance cannot only be explained by the opposition between the old and the new, which, in this case, took the form of the opposition between the *classic mass media* (characterized by their vertical communication logic and mono-directionality) represented by television, radio and the print media on one side and the *new media* (interactive, participative and paritary) on the other side, emblematically represented by the Internet. It was a conflict essentially played out on a symbolic level, in which the former embodied a negative myth – the past, Orwell's Big Brother (2000) – and the latter represented a positive myth – the future, liberty (Scifo, 1998).

There are other historical factors, whose reference is fundamental for understanding the discourse produced in the mid-1990s on the end of journalism. These factors have to do with society's perception of journalists and also the economic organization model of the media in the latter half of the 1990s in the more developed countries.

The hypothesis raised here is that the possible replacement of the dominant journalism model and the reorganization of the mass media found fertile ground for germination because the expansion of the Internet amongst the normal population coincided with a phase of profound criticism of the way in which journalism functioned (Bourdieu, 1997) and a negative perception of the profession in Europe – with journalists being rated at the same level as businessmen and immediately after politicians (Eurobarometer 55, June 2001) – and also, though to a more limited extent in the United States of America – in the wake of the interpretation of the television coverage of the Gulf War in the early 1990s (Taylor, 1999).

Figure 5.1 – Regard for professions in the European Union
% higthest regard (EU 15)

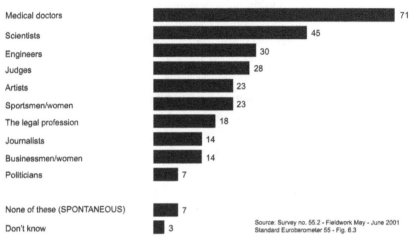

Source: Survey no. 55.2 - Fieldwork May - June 2001
Standard Eurobarometer 55 - Fig. 6.3

Source: Eurobarometer no.55.

Other figures available comparing the year 2001 to 1999 suggest that people believed less in the media, confirming a trend that already showed up in studies carried out in 1997 (Eurobarometer 55.2, 2001). [68]

This critical stance in relation to journalism, and television journalism in particular, reached its greatest level of public visibility, and visibility in the media, in Europe through Pierre Bourdieu's (1997) study on journalism in France. Because an analysis of Bourdieu's thoughts can give us a better understanding of how journalism functions, it is worthwhile looking at his analyses in the field of the media in greater detail, also taking into considerations the criticisms of his approach.

In Bourdieu we can identify three stages in his approach to the media (Decorate, 2000). In his first works, he developed a critique of the non-empirical analysis of the media, attacking, for example, the approaches of

---

[68] However, if one looks at the three mass media separately in the various European countries one can identify some other trends. Since 1999, confidence in the written press has increased only in Portugal (+10) and Luxembourg (+5). The levels of trust remained the same in Italy. In all other countries the trend is towards less trust in the written press. Trust in radio increased only in Portugal (+7) and there were not significant changes in Italy and Denmark. In all other countries, the public finds radio less trustworthy. Portugal is also the only country in which an increase for television was registered (+7), with the Danish trust level remaining more or less the same and the remaining countries registering decreases in the trust levels for television.

Edgar Morin (1962), which he considered too vague and homogenizing. In partnership with Patrick Champagne (1996; 2000) he then went to analyze the media as an instrument of reproduction and social domination – and never as a medium of emancipation and individual autonomy – through the production of an illusion: the existence of a public opinion as the mere added sum of individual opinions.

It was only in the final phase of his academic life that the media and journalism took on the role of central objects in the perversion of the public debate and the activities of reflection and creation.

For Bourdieu (1997), the media, through the journalistic practices, constitute a playing *field* for specific interests that are difficult to perceive for those outside, i.e. the television viewers.

As in all *fields*, there is a relationship of force between institutions and agents in the endeavour to monopolize characteristics that are specific to this profession.

There is generally a feeling of solidarity between competing institutions, as they have one objective in common: safeguarding the monopoly they collectively hold over all instruments of production and diffusion of information on a large scale. This is an area in which two legitimization principles face each other: consecration by journalist peers and consecration by the greatest number of persons (i.e. audiences, readers, circulation or print run).

Further according to Bourdieu (1997), the field of the media and journalism has a specific characteristic that distinguishes it from the remaining fields of cultural production: it harbours less resistance in relation to external forces and the commercial pole. This characteristic is emphasized by the fact that television has become the mass medium with the greatest presence among the population and, as such, its effects go beyond the practices in the professional field itself and extend into social, cultural and political affairs.

The greatest of these effects would be the establishment of a structural and invisible censorship that would be exercised by the journalists themselves through their choice of the news stories and their interpretation of them, thus, primarily, giving rise to a depoliticization – through the strengthening of logics that favour *soft* news, sports and certain types of moralism over ethical conceptions – and, secondly, uniformization, or in other words, a circular phenomenon of closure to the social world by the elites of journalism copying from one another.

The corollary of Bourdieu's analysis of the media and journalism is that, under the cover of the idea of pluralism, there would indeed be entrenchment and a closure of the democratic debate and under the cover of objectivity one would witness the production and diffusion of social "sprectres".

Bourdieu's critique was nothing new in the analytical discourse on the media. What was new was his focus on television and not the press.

In an article entitled *Sulla Stampa* (1999), Umberto Eco argued that, in the sphere of information, and in particular the written press, the 1960s and 1970s were essentially characterized by a debate on the *difference between news reporting and commentary* and, consequently, the question of objectivity and also the influence of the owners of the large economic groups and the political parties on the political orientation of the press (Rebelo, 1997) [69].

Although one must acknowledge the fact that Bourdieu's approach was not new, his contribution must nevertheless be seen as a useful critique for discussing the logics of functioning and change within the media system and journalism as a profession. However, it must not be taken as the only and definitive explanation of the complexity of the relationships in the context of journalism. The explanations must take into account not only the economic and professional dimensions but also the cultural and social dimensions that the media have as a centre and means of mediation (Heinonen, 1999).

Bourdieu's concern, and that of many other researchers in the field of the media, is centred on the fact that, since their emergence, the media constitute sources of information and formation of public opinion (Alger 1998).

---

[69] As Rebelo (1997) suggests, though his formulation does not coincide with that put forward by Bourdieu, objectivity takes on the character of a defence for journalists when they are accused of impartiality. More than a consistency, objectivity is a professional ideology. Journalists select facts and events that make the news (thus leading to the occultation of other events) on an ideological basis – whereby ideology is understood as a set of values and practices common to a given group. Objectivity finds its protection in the regulating principles of the profession (the journalistic criteria on which the selection and hierarchization of information are based). Objectivity is the fruit of a process determined by history and associated with the emergence of the mass communication model based on the massification of audiences. Objectivity is therefore linked to an information press model (Rebelo 1997) to the detriment of an opinion press model (Habermas 1986). For Rebelo, the idea of information free of subjectivity has to be contextualized bearing in mind that the social reality is simultaneously a reserve at the disposal of the producers of information and at the same time the effect of that same information, with the event being at the point of convergence between the occurrence and the respective perception thereof by the journalists, for the latter are agents of symbolic mediation.

In contemporary societies, the capacity of dissemination of representations of the social reality is even more centred on the media, so that the influence of the contents they divulge cannot be ignored (Miguel 1998).

To this recognition one can add the fact that the cognitive and interpretative categories that the individual has for assimilating the news contents are also the direct or indirect product of the action of the media through the individual moulding of the perception of reality (Silverstone, 1999).

This being so, the media and the communication systems contribute to an exchange and circulation of information that are of vital importance to modern democracies, given how they transform the perception of reality for the citizens.

In Bourdieu's line of argument, the political and, in particular, the economic influence dimension in the media is seen as a threat to the democratic balance in contemporary societies because the media perform their social role in a context of entrepreneurial concentration, in which the *"political and business interests, and not the public interest, can define the news reporting agenda"* (Lutfi, 2002:31).

In his critique of Bourdieu's analysis, Maffesoli (1997) points out precisely that the underlying message in Bourdieu's work is that the mechanisms of television and, as a consequence, the media in general, are subject to economic and political restrictions. Consequently, such operating conditions would impede individuals from developing a critical conscience. However, on the basis of the diversified research carried out in recent decades, Maffesoli (1997) criticizes Bourdieu's approach as far as the supposed passiveness of the public is concerned. As other authors analyzed herein have demonstrated (Eco, 1977 and Castells, 2003), the public must be seen as a group of active, critical and autonomous individuals in relation to the media. Consequently, these technologies are not passive but decidedly interactive, for the audience interpret the contents in accordance with their individual aspirations.

Although Bourdieu's view of the dangers of the concentration of economic power is real and shared by other authors, such as Correia, for whom the concentration of various media could constitute a serious threat to pluralism and the safeguarding of compliance with the role of defending democracy (Correia, 2000)[70], the fact is that Bourdieu relied on a too corset-

---

[70] The concentration of the media may effectively lead to private forms of censorship (Alger 2000), if we consider factors such as competition for viewers and the advertising or even the intra-medium

ed vision of the elements in action in the media field and failed to include the role of the phone and its reception of news in his research agenda.

Also, the idea of the thematic homogenization by the media suggested by Bourdieu is also worthy of criticism (Maffesoli, 1997 and Colombo, 2001), for despite the fact that they promote industrial competition models, the cultural industries, such as television, nevertheless produce innovation and novelty, even in the context of news. Proceeding from the idea of *margin or frontier* of the cultural industry proposed by Colombo (2001), one can offer a critique of the idea of cultural homogenization, as put forward by Bourdieu. To this end, one must look at the audience dimension, for the consumption of culture and of news always requires variety, diversity and originality.

Even if there is a rigid structure for the production of information and that structure also features uniformizing forces, one must also bear in mind the existence of a contrary force – the autonomy of the informative roles of journalists, an autonomy which, in democratic systems, is also nourished by the audiences.

The production of news is a compromise between the emerging forces of the social environment and the forces of censorship, sublimation and normalization coming from the economic and political power apparatus. It is thus the fruit of both the producer and the user (Paquete de Oliveira, 1988).

One must also make reference to Daniel Bougnoux's (1998) critique of Bourdieu's analysis of the media. Bougnoux argues that an analysis of the media may not be one-dimensional but must be based on a combination of three complementary approaches: the semiotic, the pragmatic and the *medialogic.* [71] Journalism must be understood as something that evolves in the context of the society of which it is a part. It has the capacity to transform – and often it does – but it is also restricted and altered by the socio-

---

hierarchical position as influencing the definition of information contents. (Correia, 2000: p: 2)

[71] Whereby semiotics focuses on the analysis of the relationship between image and text, analyzing both for the images and the sounds their characteristic and how it connects to reality. And pragmatics relates to the enunciative polyphony of audiovisual messages, i.e. who speaks through the media, the text, the image, the presenter, the newsroom staff, the direction, the broadcaster. Although it cannot throw total light onto the reception, given that each receiver is unique, it would allow for more in-depth analysis of that dimension. The medialogic approach, which takes into consideration the type of supports and formats that produce a grammar for the messages, focuses on the construction of meaning stating that the space-time of the various media is different to that of the school, political institutions, judiciary institutions, etc.

cultural dimensions [72] associated with the audiences, economic powers [73] and the regulatory, professional and technological dimensions (Heinonen, 1999 and Silverstone, 1999).

By way of summarizing the critique of Pierre Bourdieu's approach, we can suggest that the *field* and *structure effect* analysis proposed by him can only characterize part of the media reality. By leaving out two key dimensions pertaining to the audiences – passion and interactivity – Bourdieu's proposals are condemned to portraying only one of the dimensions – the offer – and even then they do so only partially as they do not take into account the dimensions of change involved in the practice of the profession of journalism (Maffesoli, 1998; Bougnoux, 1998; Heinonen, 1999).

Given the technological innovation – the Internet – and the existence of a period of particularly harsh criticism on the evolution of journalism and the organization of the media system (Ramonet, 1999), the conditions were created for the existence of two scenarios on the effect of the Internet on the practice and evolution of journalism – one termed the *revolutionary* and the other the *evolutionary* scenario (Heinonen, 1999).

The main characteristic of the revolutionary interpretation is that the Internet, and that which it represents (digital communication, interactivity in horizontal and vertical communication, global accessibility, etc.), marks a moment of change in the history of journalism.

The evolutionary interpretation sees the Internet as introducing changes in journalism as an economic and social institution, as a profession and

---

[72] Heinonen gives an example of the change in journalism in the socio-cultural dimension mentioning the fact that the audiences have also been transformation over time. The growth in literacy has placed new audiences at the reach of journalism and the changes in lifestyle and living conditions (urban development, working parents, single-parent families, ageing populations, unemployment, etc.) affect the ways in which the public consumes, or in which it is possible for it to consume, journalistic products. (Heinonen 1999, p. 21).

[73] Economically there are three different traditions as far as economic influence on changes in journalism is concerned. The first can be termed *Business-Economy* and has its origins in the view that journalism is a means of production of a product, a news item, meaning that the public is seen as the consumer and the media in general as an industry. The change here is seen as originating in purely economic criteria associated with balancing the books. A second tradition is that of political economics, which centres the analysis of the change on the incompatibility of interests between journalism and business-related interests. Finally, one should also not the more political dimension, which is present, for example, in several authors (Philo 1995, Schiller 1996, Chomsky 1988), and in which, in the context of a capitalist economy, the role of the media is the defence of the political, economic and social agenda of the privileged groups of a specific society (Heinonen 1999, p. 23).

also changes in the role of the journalist, but, in essence, journalism will continue to be carried out in relatively conventional forms.

As far as publication is concerned, the revolutionary interpretation considers the technological platform as being so advanced and having so many communication possibilities with the audience that, in practice, the thought centres on the idea that journalism should proceed from the principle that when an article is written, its primary form of publication would be online and then, following that, publication through the remaining technological supports.

From the evolutionary viewpoint, the hertzian wave radio platforms (analogue or digital), digital and analogue television (by satellite, cable or hertzian wave) produced for reception on the television set – and not on the computer – and hard copy continue to be the basic platforms for journalism. The Internet is seen as one more form of reaching the audiences, provided that it does not cannibalize the main products.

These two different viewpoints also find expression in terms of the empowerment of the journalist. Thus, Heinonen distinguishes the more revolutionary view that sees the Internet just like the telephone, in other words one more indispensable tool in the work of the journalist, while the evolutionary view proposes a more cautious use of the Internet, emphasizing the need to understand its true impact on the practice of the profession. Just as the telephone enables direct contact while substituting personal contact with the sources, the information technologies also bring about changes, for example in terms of access to archives and the records produced on a certain topic. If technology can make procedures easier it can also change practices, which may bring unexpected changes in the medium term (Colombo, 2000). For this reason, from the evolutionary viewpoint, it is necessary to at least understand what changes to be able to question the effects in the ethic dimension of journalism.

Perhaps the greatest difference between the two perspectives has to do with the professional role of the journalist. Whereas, for the *revolutionaries*, the idea prevails that the role of the mediators will diminish, meaning that the journalist will be made more accountable to the audiences and to the logic of cooperation, thus brining the audiences and the journalists closer together, the *evolutionary* outlook emphasizes the role of the journalists as mediators. This vision does not disregard interaction with the audiences but also does not consider it a priority objective. As information increases, there will be more and more need for mediators to particularize all the information available.

Although theoretically, given the idea of technological development, the revolutionary approach may make sense, the practice in recent years has also revealed its many analytical weaknesses.

The reasons why the revolutionary model did not assert itself can be divided into two groups. The first group has to do with one of the basic characteristics of the media in democratic states: credibility. What the print media, radio and television offer is credibility, or, if we prefer, *the truth*. Someone has to verify and guarantee that a certain piece of information is correct. In most cases, the user does not have the literacy necessary for doing that alone in the World Wide Web and requires someone to validate the information for him.

Just like journalists, the mediators continue to play a fundamental role in guaranteeing a process of credibilization of news reports and other types of information. For this reason, the role of the journalist continues to be a central one that cannot easily be replaced.

Therefore, instead of the replacement of the journalist, what we have witnessed over the last decade has been the complementarity of access, by the audiences, to products coming from the practice of the profession of journalism, i.e. the news, and their complementarity with information accessed directly from primary sources, news agencies or simply archives, or opinions mixed with news, as is the case in blogs.

The second group has to with the financial and economic dimension. The newspapers, television and radio understood that they *had* to join the Internet. They did so for different reasons: fear of missing out on the revolution in progress, because the Internet is a work tool for the journalist; because they saw new business opportunities; as a survival strategy [74] by means of transformation of the Internet itself; or as a means of repositioning themselves in relation to the other media.

But if not everyone can effectively assume the role of journalist – be it because they do not have the technical/professional capacities or because, although everyone can theoretically produce information, the monetary and human resources at their disposal are so different that it would be difficult for an individual or a group – outside a specialized context such as a blog – to aspire to compete with the information services of newspapers or radio

---

[74] The need for a survival strategy emerges because, on the offer side, new rivals outside the Internet to the already existing newspapers and radio and television stations could emerge. On the demand side, the user could look to satisfy his needs in a vaster universe.

or television stations. It is also true that, given the above criticism of the way in which the media function, one could have expected the emergence of a new type of journalistic practice different to the models currently in place in television, radio and offline newspapers.

As Deuze (2001) suggests, to a certain extent that was what happened with the emergence of new models of approaching news reporting made possible by the Internet and with the emergence of journalism projects that did not originate in economic investments by newspapers, radio or television stations or telecommunications companies.

In the Internet, the role of the journalist was redefined on the basis of new ethical questioning (commercial pressure, the use of links, sources, privacy, regulation and news collection methods) and, for this reason, it would make sense to speak of a new type of journalism (Deuze, 2001). This ethical question emerged from the basic features that the Internet places at the disposal of whomever wishes to produce contents within that medium, such as hypertextuality, interactivity, multimediality, networking and usability (Deuze, 2001 and Heinonen, 1999).

Online journalism in the editorial newsrooms – that which Deuze (2001) terms Computer Assisted Reporting (CAR) – did not emerge as a result of a linear process of the introduction of the technology. On the contrary, it is the result of non-organized incursions in the newsrooms by journalists, resulting from business opinions taken by the newspaper management or from an editorial intuition as to the need to innovate. Through experimentation and innovation – including, at times, partnerships with freelance technological teams not belonging to the staff – editorial teams created their own type of news reporting: *online journalism* (Deuze, 2001).

However, the introduction of the Internet into editorial staff rooms not only gave rise to the online presence of the traditional mass media. It was also dominated by the access of journalists to researchable archives, databases and sources. This kind of use brought with it benefits for the profession, in the form of access to more information and sources – in most cases free of charge. But it also brought less pacific challenges and questions, such as the use of materials, in diverse supports, without added financial retribution or even the editing of the same news item according to different criteria in different supports. Another challenge brought about by the introduction of the Internet was that the journalists – just like the users – had to learn how to use computer mediated communication in an environment in which validation of information is extremely difficult.

So, how does *online journalism* differ from other types of journalism, such as radio, press or television journalism?

First of all, because of the technology involved – the Internet. In the context of multimediality, the journalist makes decisions as to the most appropriate format for a given topic – should it be the written format with sound, whether or images are to be used and whether or not those images should be animated. If he uses interactivity the journalist has to manage the possibilities and spaces for the audience to write and interact. If he uses hypertextuality, he has to consider the forms of linking his article to others, in the form of archives or other contributions via links.

Online journalism is, hence, not just one type of journalism, but four different types of using the possibilities offered by the Internet managed in accordance with the content, the communication level and the participation of the users.

On the basis of this relationship, Deuze (2001) identifies four types of online journalism: news sites; index and category sites; commentary sites and meta-sites; and share and discussion sites.

The most widespread form of online journalism is the news site, which offers editorial content and a moderate and minimal form of participative communication – examples of this are the online presences of the television stations CNN, BBC, RTP and SIC; newspapers such as "The Guardian" and "Público"; and radio stations such as TSF, RR and BBC.

The second type of online journalism, index and category sites, generally applies to the editorial logic on search engine sites and portals – such as Altavista, Yahoo!, Sapo, Google News and Clix. These offer links – sometimes categorized and annoted by editorial teams based on other news sites in the World Wide Web. Portals and search engines, generally speaking, do not offer much editorial content of their own, but do sometimes offer areas for chat and the exchange of news stories.

Another dimension of online journalism, the commentary sites, has given rise to the blogs, which are pages of contents, sometimes of a personal nature, produced by a person who in most cases is not a journalist, relating stories on online experiences or other matters of opinion and links with commentaries to contents on the World Wide Web. [75]

This third category also includes the news meta-sites, where people write about the news and the media in general. They are sites in which the

---

[75] For a detailed discussion on information blogs, see Matheson (2002).

way the media work is analyzed and criticized – for example, in the cases of Mediachannel and FAIR – or extensive sites of news categories on the media – such as the European Journalism Centre Medianews or Europe-media. This "journalism on journalism" or meta-journalism flourishes in particular online.

The final category of online journalism is made up of the share and discussion sites. These use the potential of the Internet to promote platforms for the exchange of opinions and articles, which often focus on a specific theme, such as anti-globalization activism – as in the case of the Indymedia platform (Platon, 2003) – or news on the information technologies, of which Slashdot is an example. All these models introduce alterations to the practice of journalism, whereby those that offer *public journalism* are those that have introduced a greater level of interactivity and alteration of the paradigms of the offline journalism model. [76]

The migration to the Internet by mass media print titles, channels and stations and their introduction to news sites and index and category sites was the object of an intense amount of experimentation and the allocation of financial and human resources – resources, which, in addition to the success or failure of the editorial products in question, also led to changes in the overall panorama of the media and news online.

Regardless of how it has been appropriated, the Internet has changed the way in which the mass media supply information because it presented them with a set of possibilities for change to which they were forced to respond.

Sparks (2002) identifies these possibilities in his analysis of the migration to digital by newspapers and radio and television stations. He defines nine dimensions of questioning and possible change that confronted the mass media: one single delivery technology; reduction of distribution costs; consumption patterns; erosion of traditional location advantages; removal of time-related advantages; greater competition for the revenue channels; editorial and advertising desegregation; direct relationship between advertisers and consumers; and a reduction of the boundaries between editorial, advertising and business transaction material.

---

[76] According to Deuze (2003), public journalism does not take away the journalist's control over the news, nor is there anything in this type of journalism that one could say diminishes the power of the news companies or journalists that work in them. The notion of differentiation between "us and them", between the journalist and the citizens, still exists.

The offline media have clear and distinct delivery technologies – in terms of material, time, function and *place*. The television broadcasters operate in the radio-electric spectrum and the newspapers use paper. They have their own temporal logics, for a newspaper may be daily or weekly and the main television news is broadcast in the evening. They also have a well defined function: one can listen to radio while driving or studying and watching television is a common form of winding down. Place also has a lot to do with the function: one normally reads the newspaper outside the home – except at the weekend – and one normally watches television at home. The Internet has only one delivery technology – TCP/IP-based digital delivery – which can take place at any time and, theoretically, in any place. This introduces a second difference, which is the reduction of distribution costs – although it may increase overhead costs and personnel costs.

The material that carries the symbolic representations in the offline media is quite costly to distribute – newspapers have to be printed and shipped and radio and television have to operate or pay the rental fees for the signal distribution networks and for renting the spectrum. The online mass media do not require these mechanisms and the distribution costs are transferred to the public, which has to buy the computers, Wi-Fi, routers and printers and pay for the Internet connection – and every time we print things out we have the additional costs of paper and printing.

The online mass media do not yet have clearly defined consumption patterns. They are normally consumed in front of a computer screen and are available any time of the day. This lack of definition results in the search, by the media themselves, for models that allow them to find their role in the public's work and recreation spaces. In an era in which the marketing of goods and services is based to a large extent on the distinction between work and leisure, understanding the phenomenon of the use of online services and their target publics is of fundamental importance for mass media strategies.

Therefore, what is of interest is whether the Internet will represent, for the mass media, a logic similar to that of television – a family and leisure time activity – or if, like radio, it will essentially be an ambience in which activities can be carried out simultaneously.

Another of the changes the traditional mass media are confronted with in their migration to digital is the erosion of time and space. They are traditionally bound to places – and that logic is often reflected in their names, such as Rádio Televisão Portuguesa, Washington Post, etc. Newspapers are bound by the available distribution network and the radio and television broadcasters by the configuration of their networks. However, the mass media operating on the Internet do so on a global scale that is not determined by distance or geo-political factors. They are no longer limited, or protected, by the location – although language is obviously a barrier. Here, though, the examples of BBC Online and CNN, with their services in several languages, are food for thought on the limits of the language barrier.

The erosion of the temporal advantages must also be mentioned. The online media are accessible 24 hours a day and their contents, contrary to that of print newspapers and television, can be updated regularly.

What we can consider as a *non-change* is the fact that almost all of the media, even the public service ones, are today managed as enterprises (Sparks, 2002) and this is also true of the Internet. However, with the arrival of the Internet, new problems emerged for a market in which the *intra and inter-media* competition was already considerable: companies from other sectors entered the news reporting scene, seduced by the exploitation of less costly modes of production and distribution and new sources of revenue and also by the creation of new target audiences with the subsequent overlapping of those pertaining to the print media, thus altering the economic geography of the sector (Heinonen, 1999; Kamerer, 1998; Chyi, 2002). In an entrepreneurial journalistic setting, economic profitability, and not technological availability, is the factor that determines the options taken (Sparks, 2002). The question of the survival of online news initiatives has less to do with the quality of the journalism practised than with the entrepreneurial context they are a part of (Sauter 2000), whereby the adaptation of content production routines to the consumption types is generally determined by the cost (Maynard, 2000). Nevertheless, there are few newspapers that actually generate a profit from their online presence. There have been many unsuccessful online journalism initiatives (Lutfi, 2002) or projects that proved to be of little profitability (Heinonen, 1998 and OberCom, 2001).

The business model for each online medium will depend on its characteristics and the market it is aimed at. For this reason, there is not just one model, but several (Sparks, 2002). The offline media traditionally have three main sources of revenue: subsidies, fees, transfers from the State budget; subscription – particularly in the case of the press; and advertising and classified ads. The online media present a number of challenges to that traditional model.

The financing models designed for the online press comprise five types. The first is subscription, which is not very attractive for Internet users already accustomed to free contents and only works for specialized publications.[77] Although it has not been studied much, given the decrease in the public media sector in the European context, there is another form of compulsory subscription used online – that of the audiovisual fee. However, this is a limited model that has generated some controversy, in particular in a period of economic recession in which the public mass media compete online for the attention of the private media; examples are the BBC and RTP. The second model is that of charging for individualized contents, which is not always feasible on account of certain technological limitations and its compatibilization with the privacy of the choices. A third format is the exploitation of advertising revenue, which is the most frequent form. However, the actual revenue, on the basis of the real accounting of the number of contacts, is difficult to typify, and for that reason it is generating an ever-decreasing return. The fourth format is based on classified ads, which appeal to the local/regional base of readers and constitute one of the income sources that newspapers do not wish to forego and which are well adapted to the logic of the Internet, so that they can well compete with the traditional sources of revenue of the offline media. Finally, the fifth model comprises a set of experiences in course in an endeavour to structure possible new models and includes, for example, commission on online commerce (Kamerer, 1998 and Poole, 2001), or trans-media advertising within the same group with a view, for example, to turning radio audiences into readers, or readers into television viewers (Poole, 2001).

Given that the Internet has already reached a significantly high number of users in most developed countries, one can expect the financing model for newspapers to be increasingly similar to that experienced by companies such as Google or Skype, that is, either low-budget advertising or licensing of the newspaper brand on other products. Other forms of revenue include the marketing of access to archives, the sale of Internet access[78] or the creation and hosting of sites (Mensing, 1998) and the selling of contents

---

[77] Subscription is relatively non-existent – despite the frequently mentioned case of the Financial Times, a very special example that reflects its audience and the business subscriptions, or the case of the Expresso newspaper in Portugal, the success of which depends on its target public and the substitution of purchases of the printed version by the online version.

[78] Portugal, curiously enough – or perhaps not – seems to have been somewhat innovative in the area of procuring revenue, one example being IOL. Portugal has a vertical integration model for the Internet – content provider companies holding telecommunications companies or vice-versa – so that the access to certain contents can be limited to those connected through a certain ISP. Although this model cannot be extrapolated to other locations, in the specific case of Portugal it represents a new opportunity for generating revenue without threatening the offline media.

to other media (Regan, 2000). This latter form represents, indeed, another possible future for the financing of online newspapers. Online news reporting initiatives will see themselves more and more as suppliers of contents and less and less as simple newspapers (Regan, 2000). What is not strange to his scenario is the fact that the news themselves do not directly generate the income, but the profitable exploitation of the audience (Weir, 2000). In this context, the news contents are increasingly drawn up and presented as consumer goods with the maximization of their appeal in mind (Poole, 2001). Site visit counters and the consequent management of the profitability of certain articles can lead to the excessive marketing of the news content, making it more and more like an entertainment product (Rainie 2000).

Another change dimension listed by Sparks (2001) has to do with the relationship between the editorial material and the advertisements. The greater part of the offline media administers advertising and editorial material together – examples of this are commercials in the intervals in films or print advertisements alongside articles in newspapers. If one wants to see one, one has to see the other. The indexation and research possibilities offered by the Internet have questioned that logic. Audiences can sidestep the advertising and go directly to the content – there are programmes that prevent advertising from appearing on the screen or the search for an article can take us directly to the article without passing though HTML pages containing advertising. On the other hand, audiences can seek out the advertising without passing through the media – here we just have to think of car and clothes brands with online presence without the use of the mass media. As we have already analyzed in the first part of this chapter, the direct relationship between suppliers and consumers is a characteristic feature of the Internet. Whereas, outside the Internet, the mass media are necessary for establishing that relationship, on the Internet the audience can do directly to the sources and the advertisers can directly contact the consumers. Having the possibility does not automatically mean realization, but the mass media have had to take this kind of advertising into account in positioning themselves online and were forced to alter their traditional operational model.

Finally, let us focus on a question related with the journalistic logic itself – the erosion of the borderlines between editorial material, advertising and business transactions. The offline media have a set of conventions enabling them to separate advertising material from news reporting material. When these borders are crossed, the result is usually disastrous for the mass media, as their credibility is questioned. Such conventions do not exist yet for the online media and, in the opinion of Sparks, they may turn out to be weaker due to the importance of business transaction material for the survival of the mass media. Imagine you are reading a news article on a holiday destination in online newspapers and, in the portal hosting the newspaper, there is also a link to a travel agency's site. If a holiday trip booked by a reader does not go well, the newspaper could lose credibility for something it has nothing to do with and cannot control – the service provision by the travel agency.

Altogether, Colin Sparks' proposals for the analysis of the change in the mass media represent a set of challenges for the offline media, for they challenge their own identity, their market niches and their revenue sources. However, this process challenge is by no means one way. The online media are also facing challenges deriving from their Internet presence. They do not have an innate credibility. For example, the success of several newspapers online has a lot to do with the credibility of the newspaper in its printed version and is not merely due to its being a reference online presence. The online media do not have a success story in commercial terms – in other words, they do not have a readership that makes purchases depending on the advertising carried by the newspaper – and, consequently, they have difficulty making money.

In one of the as yet rare comparative studies on the patterns of change in journalistic practice, Quinn (2002) analyzed twenty-four online news services, which either migrated to digital or were born digital, in France, Denmark, the United Kingdom and Ireland. Taking as points of departure four dimensions taken largely from the theoretical approaches to the change in news reporting paradigms [79], the study sought to identify the current trends in online media practice. The conclusion was that there is little evidence of a "new paradigm" emerging on the sites studied. In other words, there is little evidence of disappearing boundaries between producer and user or of the merging of professional journalism with other non-professional activities (Quinn, 2002). This essentially means that the journalism based on what was criticized by Bourdieu (1997) and contextualized by Maffesloi,

---

[79] Namely, the new forms of interaction between producers and users; new forms of telling stores; news forms of production based on the collection and sharing of information amongst non-professional users; and the change in the role of the journalist in society (Quinn 2002).

Colombo and Bougnoux, has migrated to the Internet in the form of online television and radio stations and newspapers.

The adoption of practices of interactivity with the users is limited and uneven, although it would seem to be more visible in theme-specific news sites, which are normally net-native and less frequently derived from migration to digital. A comparison of the analysis carried out by Quinn (2002) and that coordinated by Aquino (2002) on convergence in editorial teams and the online presence of television stations and newspapers in four countries would seem to confirm this idea. [80]

However, what the different studies make quite clear is that the impulse for change in journalistic practice is much more due to third factors than purely to the introduction of technological innovation into newsroom.

The innovation essentially seems to depend on the culture involved in the online initiative – in other words, its editorial dependence on or independence from an already existing editorial staff and the target audience. It is these characteristics that allow the public and producer to come closer together and, consequently, allow for greater freedom of experimentation oriented towards common points of interest.

The Information Meta-System and Its Network Organization

So far we have seen a number of questions that the Internet presence or, if we prefer, the migration to the Net, has raised for newspapers and radio and television stations and the journalism they practise.

However, the *information meta-system* [81] also includes the offline media, so that we have to ask ourselves how television, radio and the newspa-

---

[80] The study conducted in the United Kingdom included the BBC, ITN, The Times, The Guardian, The Financial Times, The Daily Mail; in Sweden it included SVT, TV4, Dagens Nyheter, Aftonbladet; in Spain it included Antena 3 TV, Televisio de Catalunya, VilaWeb, El Pais, El Mundo, Marca, El Periódico; in France it included TF1, France 2, I>TV, Libération, Le Monde, Le Telegramme, Le Parisien, Ouest-France.

[81] At the beginning of this analysis of the Media in the Network Society a definition of information as an economic element was given using the acception established by Daniel Bell (cited in Karvonnen, 2000) and subsequently re-used by Manuel Castells (2003), i.e., in the broad sense of the word, information is the content of all forms of intelligible communication. However, in a narrower sense of the word relating to the field of the mass media, information refers to the verifiable and thus trustworthy facts on the "real world", including both opinions and reports on world facts. In an even more restricted interpretation applied to the Internet and its role of facilitator of information practices, information can

pers have changed their contents, forms of journalism and economic strategies since the arrival of the Internet.

Such a study would obviously have to include analysis of the news contents in an effort to understand how the mediation on the Internet, and outside the Internet, is processed. But an in-depth study will also have to take the practices of the audiences into consideration, for, as Silverstone argues (1999), we also study the media with a view to characterizing the *experience*, whereby *experience* is understood as our movement in space in time and the inter-relations.

Studying the media is studying their contribution to the general texture of experience, for our distinctions and decisions are also based on the media. The media measure the dialectic that is established between the classification that forms the experience and the experience that gives colour to the classification (Silverstone, 1999). Hence it is necessary to understand the technology and the new forms of administering and communicating information. How do the desires, the influencing and pleasing interact with each other? And what are the new ways of making them, transmitting them and giving them meaning?

On the basis of the analysis presented herein so far, what stands out is that if, on the one hand, the mass media – television, radio and the newspapers – seek to maintain, in the information dimension, their traditional communication supports (such as analogue diffusion through hertzian waves and paper), they have simultaneously set out to conquer new spaces of contact with their audiences, altering the transmission technologies, i.e. migrating to digital, and subsequently seeking multiple channels of interactivity – ranging from SMS or Internet voting and the publishing of results in print versions of newspapers to the online presences of radio stations and the reception of television on third-generation mobile phones already equipped for multimedia reception.

Furthermore, the most diverse editorial commitments at the online information level have emerged – some assuming logics similar to the strategies adopted by the mass media in their migration to the Internet and others opting for innovation. Some achieved success and many others were left behind, like the ghost towns in old Wild West films – the abandoned remains of sites.

---

taken as meaning "communicated" data, which, by providing insight into a certain domain of reality, reduce the uncertainty of the receiver.

Table 5.1 – Activities carried out using the Internet or E-mail in Portugal

Activities using the Internet or E-mail	Yes		No		Total	
	n	%	n	%	n	%
Surfing the Internet without a precisely defined purpose	454	64.9	246	35.1	699	100.0
Consulting libraries, encyclopaedias, dictionaries, atlases, etc.	335	47.9	365	52.1	699	100.0
Participating in chats or newsgroups	278	39.8	421	60.2	699	100.0
Reading news in the general press	275	39.3	425	60.7	699	100.0
Downloading music	238	34.1	461	65.9	699	100.0
Researching information on scheduled shows/concerts	215	30.7	485	69.3	699	100.0
Downloading software	201	28.8	498	71.2	699	100.0
Reading sports news	199	28.5	500	71.5	699	100.0
Researching travel information	199	28.4	501	71.6	699	100.0
Researching information on public services	197	28.2	502	71.8	699	100.0
Researching information on one's city	196	28.0	504	72.0	699	100.0
Researching information on education/training	173	24.7	527	75.3	699	100.0
Carrying out banking operations	170	24.3	529	75.7	699	100.0
Contacting friends when down/bored	164	23.5	535	76.5	699	100.0
Arranging dates with friends	163	23.3	536	76.7	699	100.0
Playing videogames on the Internet	148	21.2	551	78.8	699	100.0

Source: The Network Society in Portugal CIES-ISCTE, 2003.

As the figures show, of the sixteen most frequent activities carried out on the Internet in Portugal, the news is only one of the multiple information dimensions. What the table reveals is that, when an Internet user has a pre-defined objective in mind when logging on, the use of the Internet is characterized by the search for information.

If we wish to classify the Internet in Portugal in terms of its uses, it is primarily a space for the search for information (35.9%). In second place, it is a space for socialization (28.8%) and acquiring software (28.8%). The search for entertainment (27.6%) and electronic commerce (24.3%) take third and fourth place respectively. [82]

Amongst the searches for information, educational purposes are the most frequent (47.9%), followed by general press (39.3%) and sports press (28.5%) news and the search for information on services and purchase decisions (with an average use rate of 28%). [83]

Figure 5.2 – Importance of the Internet as a source of entertainment, selected countries (%)

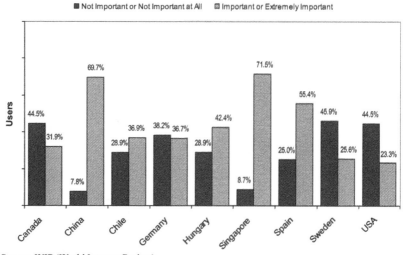

Source: WIP (World Internet Project).

The Portuguese data are comparable to those for countries such as Canada, China, Germany, Chile, Spain, Hungary, Singapore, Sweden and the US (Figures 5.2. and 5.3). The data illustrate, with the exception of China, that using the Internet is always considered to be more important for the information sphere than for the entertainment sphere.

---

[82] Note: the entertainment values are calculated on the basis of the average of the music download and online game playing values; for the average socialization values, the factors used were participation in chats and contacting and talking to friends; the information values were based on the averages for the different types of information, news and library and other archives researches; electronic commerce corresponds to the category listed in the table as "Carrying out banking operations" and other purchases.

[83] Note: the research on services and purchase decision category includes researching information on scheduled shows/concerts, travel, public services, one's city and education/training courses.

If, as far as Internet use is concerned, there seems to be no doubt as to the importance of its role as an information technology and, as such, an *emerging node* in the new information and news meta-system, what is the role of television? Will it have the role of the *central node*, just like in the *entertainment meta-system*?

Bearing in mind the data analyzed above, in the year 2002 Portuguese hertzian television presented an average information / entertainment ratio of 24.51% to 54.57%. Entertainment was clearly more important. Although the relationship is more balanced for the public television channels[84], the figures nevertheless raise some doubts as to the role of television in the field of information.

Figure 5.3 – Importance of the Internet as a source of information, selected countries (%)

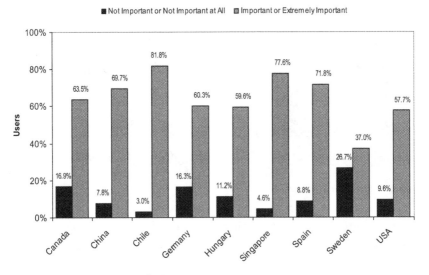

Source: WIP (World Internet Project).

These doubts must be clarified using an analysis of the use of television in Portugal and comparing the data with the European universe.

On the basis of the data on the communication practices of the Portuguese (Cardoso et al., 2004), television's role of central *node* in the information organization network would seem to be much clear.

---

[84] The figures for the relationship between information and entertainment in public television are more balanced: 41.2% vs. 47.1%.

It suffices to determine that when we compare the relationship between news audiences and the three most common media for accessing news (television, radio and newspapers), television news programmes are regularly seen by 97.4% of the population, while only 67.2% state that they had read any newspaper in the last week. And whereas 86.9% normally hear radio, only 33.6% of these are radio listeners for whom the information dimension is important (Cardoso et al., 2004). According to the data in the same study, television plays a leading role both in terms of the choice of means of information on a local/national incident and on international affairs. When asked "When there is a local/national incident, what is the main medium you use to get information?", the responses are always over 85% for television, except in the case of major international news, where, the values for the Internet as a source of information reach 11.5% for Internet users.

Table 5.2 – Television programmes and viewer ratings/popularity in Portugal, by format (%)

Television programmes (by genre)	The normally most watched programmes		Programmes you most enjoyed seeing in your life	
	n	%	n	%
News	1189	48.5	530	21.6
Soap operas	354	14.5	350	14.3
Game shows	160	6.5	265	10.8
Other information programmes	146	6	134	5.5
Morning talk shows	84	3.4	80	3.3
Celebrity talk shows	63	2.6	68	2.8
Real life talk shows	64	2.6	101	4.1
Documentaries	58	2.4	113	4.6
Comedy	57	2.3	86	3.5
Music programmes	54	2.2	89	3.6
Films	55	2.2	76	3.1
Sport	28	1.1	26	1.1
Series and cult series	28	1.4	68	2.7
Entertainment and variety	18	0.8	61	2.5
Theatre, opera and dance	16	0.3	15	0.6
Reality Show (private life and music)	7	0.2	62	2.5
Cartoons	3	0.1	15	0.6
Others	19	0.8	17	0.7
Don't watch TV	14	0.8	35	1.4
No response	41	1.7	258	10.5
Total	2450	100	2450	100

Source: The Network Society in Portugal CIES-ISCTE, 2003.

Another argumentation factor in relation to the centrality of the information dimension of television is the relationship between the use of television for entertainment and information. If the entertainment/information ratio is clearly favourable for the former in terms of the general TV stations' programming, the opposite is true when we look at the reason for using television. Information and news programmes make up almost 50% of the responses to the question "what programme do you most regularly watch" and more than 25% of the choices for the programme the viewers "most enjoyed seeing" in their life. [85]

The numbers presented for the preferences in terms of information in Portugal are even more interesting when we compare them with the daily airing time that each of them occupies (Table 5.2). We see, for example, that the news programmes, which account for an average of 12% of broadcasting time are regularly seen by 48.5% of viewers.

As far as entertainment programmes such as soap operas are concerned, the relationship between time on the air and viewing figures is a similar one – on the two Portuguese channels that most rely on the genre (SIC and TVI) they have broadcast time figures of 13% and 14.5% for the programmes normally most watched by the audiences.

The data for Portugal are to some extent corroborated by other studies, namely that carried in 2002 on the participation of European in cultural activities (Eurobarometer 56, 2002). According to this study, the four types of programmes most watched by Europeans are the television news and information programmes (88.9%), followed by films (84.3%), documentaries (61.6%) and sport (50.3%). [86]

---

[85] Given the daily regularity of news programmes, the values relating to information in the medium/long-term memory are rather significant. Even though entertainment accounts for almost 80% of the choices there are still more than 20% who are of the opinion that the news was the programme they most liked in their life.

[86] There are, however, also national specificities, given that Denmark has the highest number of people watching the television news (97.7%), as well as documentaries. Films have the highest viewer ratings in France (89.6%) and Germany (89.4%). Sport programmes are most popular in Sweden (62.9%) and Finland (62.8%).

Table 5.3 – Relationship between use of media and news fruition, selected countries (2002-2003) (%)

Country	Daily television viewership	Daily newspaper readerhip	Daily radio listenership	Daily news viewership on television	Daily readership of news on politics and current affairs*	Daily news listenership on the radio*
Portugal	98.7 (2)	54.5 (-3)	70.7 (-3)	96.2	89.2	81.5
Austria	94.3	86.7	89.0	95.9	91.7	93.8 (1)
Belgium	97.2	60.6	83.5	93.0	79.5	81.6
Switzerland	92.5	89.9	83.6	94.4	91.3	88.2
Czech Republic	98.9 (1)	83.3	85.3	96.6	88.8	75.0
Germany	97.9	84.1	87.8	96.7	93.7	91.8 (2)
Denmark	98.5 (3)	76.3	88.4	97.5 (3)	92.5	90.1 (4)
Spain	97.6	53.5 (-2)	66.6 (-2)	90.4	84.9	71.9
Finland	97.0	92.6	84.5	98.2 (2)	91.7	74.2
France	95.7	61.7 (-4)	81.1	94.1	83.8	76.2
United Kingdom	97.9	76.1	81.2	92.6	78.5 (-4)	76.4
Greece	97.2	36.5 (-1)	60.2 (-1)	85.7	80.8	47.4
Hungary	96.5	79.2	80.6	94.5	82.1	89.7
Ireland	98.2	87.1	92.4	90.9	83.3	82.7
Israel	91.3	70.9	81.8	88.7	75.6 (-3)	81.6
Italy	98.4 (-4)	69.3	66.6 (-2)	95.1	67.0	58.1
Luxembourg	96.4	77.8	84.3	92.8	75.0	88.1
Netherlands	98.3	82.9	83.1	97.2 (4)	90.5	82.6
Norway	98.7 (2)	96.4	87.8	98.5 (1)	92.4	90.8 (3)
Poland	96.1	62.5	77.6 (-4)	96.1	75.0 (-2)	87.9
Sweden	98.2	90.9	79.6	96.5	88.6	83.3
Slovenia	95.4	81.1	88.2	91.5	67.9 (-1)	79.9
Average	96.85	75.18	81.78	94.23	83.81	80.58

Source: European Social Survey 2002/2003. Note: the figures presented in each column are the aggregated sum of all answers that indicate the conduction of that activity regardless of the duration and weekly regularity. *These values refer to the listening of programmes on politics and current affairs (defined as: government and public policy matters and the persons involved in them).

Completing the analysis of Portugal and the specificities of the fruition of television, the preceding table (Table 5.3) presents a comparison between television, newspapers and radio for twenty-two European countries.

As the table shows, in most countries fruition of the media follows the general order TRN (television, radio, newspaper). Only in Switzerland, Finland, Italy, Norway and Sweden is reading the newspapers more important than listening to the radio.

As for the news fruition dimension in comparison to the entertainment dimension, although we cannot extrapolate the contents offered in the diverse media in the different countries, the pattern seems to be one of dominance of information via television, followed by the newspapers and radio (the TNR rule), with the only exceptions being Hungary, Israel, Luxembourg, Poland and Slovenia, which are countries in which radio seems to be a medium devoted less to entertainment (i.e. to music and phone-in and talk show programmes).

The conclusion we can draw from analysis of these data is that, for Europe as a whole, the *Internet emerges as the emerging node and television as the central node*. Together they constitute the two networked poles of the information and news meta-system.

Television: the New Online Functions

Portugal offers its ten million inhabitants four general interest television channels that generally broadcast via hertzian waves and cable, whereby the cable companies often combine cable with satellite broadcasting for less populated zones in which the laying of cables is less profitable. As we have seen, two of these four channels are private enterprises belonging to media groups with interests both in the written press and in radio. The two remaining channels are public and are part of a holding that also includes the public radio stations RDP1, RDP2 and Antena 3.

Table 5.4 – Weekly broadcasting time occupation strategies per television channel in Portugal

RTP1	RTP2	SIC	TVI
Other information programmes (1)	Other information programmes (1)	Cartoons (1)	Films (1)
Films (2)	Cartoons (2)	Soap operas(2)	Soap operas (2)
Entertainment talk shows (3)	Documentaries (3)	Television news (3)	Television news (3)
Television news (4)	Television news (4)	Morning talk shows (4)	Reality shows (4)
Morning talk shows (5)	Films (5)	Entertainment talk shows (5)	Morning talk shows (5)
Game shows (6)	Sport (6)	Films (6)	Cartoons (6)

Note: the order is based on the data in Table 5.2, with the genres presented in decreasing order of weekly broadcasting time.

As table 5.4 illustrates, in terms of occupation of their typical broadcasting time, the four channels share, in most cases, the same television programme genres.

Hence, the greatest difference between them is the attention given to "other information programmes" in the public channels, while the private channels opt for giving prominence to soap operas – of Brazilian and Portuguese origin on SIC and Portuguese on TVI – and the "reality shows", in the case of TVI.

Beyond these differences, what stands out are essentially the similarities between the options in terms of genres, although the contents thereof may be very different amongst themselves.

Although the television universe is relatively small, in their online presence the Portuguese channels have also taken different approaches.

Given this initial contextualization of television in Portugal, how can we go on to give a general account of how the generalist television stations established their online presences?

In attempting to answer that, we must first analyze the types of contents and services made available online by the generalist television stations, as well as the profitability models and how the identity of the sites seems to be constructed vis-à-vis the television channels' broadcasting. [87]

Is it possible to say that all news is identical? And that the identity created outside the Internet by television to some extent influences its online presence? Over the following pages, we shall attempt to position ourselves in a global context by comparing the situation in Portugal with that of television from countries in five continents: Portugal, Germany, Australia, Chile, China, India, Israel, Jordan, Russia, South Africa and the US (Shoemaker, 2005; Cardoso and Silveira, 2005). [88]

---

[87] The data analyzed here result from a reformulation of the analysis of data obtained in two studies carried out in Portugal in 2002 and 2003. In 2002, the news programmes of the four Portuguese channels were taped for six weeks with a view to analyzing the criteria for the choice of the news stories. This study was carried out by Cardoso and Telo for the AACS (High Authority for the Media). In 2003, as part of the COST A20 network, a comparative analysis of television channels and sites (Cardoso and Santos) was carried out in three phases. The first phase was the descriptive analysis of the generalist television sites (RTP, SIC and TVI).The second phase was an online/offline comparison in terms of information provided. The material was gathered from the prime time news programmes of the three television stations: Telejornal on RTP1, Jornal 2 on RTP2, Jornal da Noite on SIC, Jornal Nacional on TVI and Jornal das Nove on SIC Notícias, on 11, 12 and 15 March, i.e. two weekdays and one weekend day. Likewise, the news stories on each site on the same days were also gathered. In the third phase those in charge of each site were interviewed with a view to establishing bridges between our analysis and the real work of each online project.

[88] All these countries are different in the way in which their systems of national media interlink. Whereas Germany is representative of a market in which public channels are still dominant, with more than 40%

First we shall look at the news in its dimension as television flow in the search for an identification of different journalistic identities before coming back to an analysis of online news.

Traditionally, the provision of TV news is organized in the format of television news programmes, which can be differentiated according to their contents and also their enunciative and performative dimension. Therefore, the analysis of the main Portuguese general interest channels and also the news channel with the largest audience on cable TV (SIC Notícias) carried out in 2003 (Cardoso and Santos, 2003) allows us to identify, following the model proposed by Giorgio Simonelli (2001), how the enunciative models influence the identity of television news in different national contexts. [89]

---

of market share in 2001, the Portuguese situation is that of a market with 3 general interest channels and an almost equal division of the market among the three. In the case of the US and Australia, private and not public service channels dominate. The US example is worth special examination because it is a market in which there is also a high level of fragmentation, i.e., the three major networks (ABC, NBC, CBS) each have a prime-time share of around 12-13%, while Fox, which is regarded as the fourth major network, today has an almost identical share (Kiefl 2003).

[89] In a study conducted by Giorgio Simonelli on Italian television news, the author identified two enunciative models: the generalist-objective model and the interpretative-explanatory model.

The generalist model focuses on information, i.e., on the journalistic piece, the journalist having a secondary role. The anchor's role is to order and establish connections between the various items presented. According to Simonelli, "In this model of television news, the viewer has the impression that s/he is directly watching events, while the discourse on the events is made via their very presentation" (Simonelli, 2001:21). Journalistic pieces are not presented as a discourse on reality, but as a direct vision of the event. The reporter has a secondary role and in most cases does not appear on screen, recounting the facts in a voice over.

The interpretative-explanatory model – This model of television news favours live news and the anchor as key pieces in the broadcasting of information. While the former model is defined as objective by the primacy given to the journalistic object, the event in itself, this is characterized as interpretive for its focus on the informer-subject and for the importance given to the space and the time of information production. Besides presenting the news, the television newsreader also interprets it, and his discourse can assume various possible registers, from a paternalistic to a colloquial tone, from a familiar discourse to the use of proverbs and clichés, to a more erudite style. While in the generalist-objective model the first block of news is the most important, in the interpretive-explanatory model more stress is placed on lighter themes (curiosities and human interest stories) and the rhythm is maintained in a circular fashion, with the last news item very often a return to the opening item. In the generalist-objective model, the journalistic pieces are presented as individual and separate, while in the interpretive-explanatory model the different items are linked together, in a relationship of dependence and reciprocal integration, like the pieces of a puzzle which when all joined together give an explanation of the problems faced. The distinctive trademark of television news' interpretive-explanatory model can be summed up as "not only representing the process of transforming events into news, the interpretation of reality and the informer-subjects responsible for this operation, as also bringing to the scene their efforts to make events comprehensible and intelligible" (Simonelli, 2001:27).

Based on the observation of television news programmes broadcast in prime-time by the four Portuguese general interest channels (SIC Notícias, as a dedicated news channel, is a case apart and will be looked at separately), we can conclude that a variety of news presentation models are employed.

TVI's *Jornal Nacional* is the one that most closely adheres to the *interpretative-explanatory model*, both in the way the presenter conducts the programmes and in the news line-up and use of live reports. The programme's distinguishing feature is the journalist Manuela Moura Guedes, who is also head of the channel's news department.

The way she conducts the programme is characterized by the addition of comments at the beginning and end of each news item. These comments abound with so-called "platitudes" and proverbs, delivered in what is very often an indignant tone with regard to the topics presented and suffused with adjectives. An alternative way of interpreting the news presented is to use commentators, in the aim of establishing interpretive frameworks for events at the national and international level.

The programme's news line-up presents a circular approach to the news via the topics looked at, with no clear distinction evident between items of greater or lesser importance. The opening news item is just as likely to appear in the middle or end of the programme as at the beginning, the viewer's attention held by the use of "headlines" referring to the same news item throughout the programme.

Jornal on the public channel 2 (formerly RTP2) is also closer to the interpretive-explanatory model in the sense that there is greater concern, in the programme's format, with explaining the issues looked at. The extended daily slots (in some cases up to ten to fifteen minutes) dedicated to interviewing experts or figures from the topic in question contribute greatly to this. On the other hand, this news programme organizes the news in a way that is more akin to the *generalist-objective model*, beginning with the most important items first and finishing invariably with the weather forecast and a curiosity or lighter item. It can therefore be considered the closest example to a hybrid, product of the balance between the two models proposed by Simonelli (2001).

As regards SIC's *Jornal da Noite* and RTP1's *Telejornal*, both programmes are similar in their approaches to presenting the news. Both favour images and the journalistic object, relegating interpretation to a secondary plane and are closer to the *generalist-objective model*.

Jornal das Nove on SIC Notícias, as a cable news channel programme, has a split personality. The first half of the programme, approximately the first half an hour, is more like the *generalist-objective model*, with reports and short up-to-date news stories in which the presenter plays a secondary role. The second half, dedicated to the discussing of a major current affairs issue by two commentators, has more in common with the *interpretive-explanatory model*, in which the presenter becomes the moderator and takes responsibility for guiding the debate.

Characterizing the various channels, therefore, reveals that in the world of Portuguese TV news broadcasting, there is as much room for *hybrid models* (*Telejornal* on 2 and *Jornal das Nove* on SIC Notícias) as there is for a *generalist-objective model* (practised by *Jornal da Noite* on SIC and *Telejornal* on RTP1) and an *interpretive-explanatory model*, which is the trademark of TVI's *Telejornal*.

Irrespective of the enunciative model adopted, television news is still entertainment, a performative space, in the sense in which by the association of a word, *and increasingly text*, with an image, information is transformed into theatre. As Giuseppe Mazzei suggests, "nothing in TV news is immune from the element of show business" (Mazzei, 2002). "The way of sitting, dressing, gesticulating, speaking, the framework chosen by the journalists for their 'routine' or links with the outside, the organisation of space in the studio, the way the presenter interprets his or her role, and the news line-up, it is all show business combined with news and images" (Mazzei, 2002: 54-5).

This show business element is not objectively negative, as it is therein that television's great advantage lies. When we watch the news on TV, we expect to see, as we have grown used to since childhood, a combination of text, sound and images that no other medium prior to the emergence of the Internet can provide.

The first aim of the TV news programme is to be seen, therefore it has to grab its viewer's attention from the moment it goes on air. The first attempt to grab the audience's attention (and it continues throughout the broadcast) is the studio set. The set is regarded as the programme's image, the personality that it emits to its audience.

Telejornal on RTP1, Portugal's public broadcasting service's main channel, is easily associated with the idea of "a window on the world". An information access site, like a mediator that makes what is news in Portugal and around the world and is important to know intelligible to the viewer. On both channels, there is an association between sets and the channel's colours: RTP1's is blue and 2's is green. In contrast to channel 2's news programme, RTP1's *Telejornal* defines itself by the importance given to new technology.

Figure 5.4 – RTP1 *Telejornal* (Evening News) Logotype and RTP1 *Telejornal* studio design

Source: Official website of Rádio Difusão Portuguesa (RDP) and Rádio e Televisão de Portugal (RTP).

The set is the programme's editorial team, in which the table at which the presenter sits is prominent in the foreground. This table has a screen incorporated into it on which are shown fixed images related to the news being read by the anchor and the image that links to the report. The editorial team's large number of computers and screens stand out.

A constant presence is the scrolling news at the foot of the screen (absent on channel 2), which is only interrupted when news reports are shown, and which correspond to the titles of the news articles available on RTP's website.

These titles on the one hand publicize and link the programme to its website and on the other provide viewers with fast access to the day's main news.

The distinctive feature of *Jornal Nacional* broadcast by the Portuguese private channel TVI is the attempt to be an "open microphone", in the sense that it is associated with the opening of the media to new protagonists who are rarely classified as news, and fresh topics, exemplified by the importance given to local social problems. The set is based on tones of red, yellow and blue (the channel's colours). The presenter's table is placed in front of the editorial team, giving a broad view of the work of TVI's journalists. Besides various computers arranged around the studio, several TVs can be seen both on the wall and on the table behind the presenter.

During the broadcast of the news, text constantly scrolls across the foot of the screen. In contrast to that on RTP1's *Telejornal*, this is not the same information that appears on TVI's website, but items to be developed during the programme.

Information about the website also appears in the scrolling information. At different moments, three virtual "windows" emerge on the right of the presenter in which appear the central image from the previous news item, that currently being broadcast and that coming up (an idea already explored by the business channel Bloomberg).

As far as camera angles are concerned on TVI, these are not just limited to the more common framings of news broadcasts – the "half figure" plan – diversifying the type of positions, which allows the viewer a general view of the editorial staff.

The *Jornal da Noite* on SIC, which is also a private channel, is based on an image that combines technological innovation, for which the studio set is greatly responsible, with the idea of journalistic "independence". The station's colours, yellow and red, entirely clothe the set. This has, at its centre, the presenter's table flanked by two tables for potential guests and a bank of TV screens behind, allowing brief glimpses of the journalists working behind. Like the news on RTP1 and TVI, news scrolls across the foot of the screen including the habitual publicity for the programme's website.

As once perceives from the description of the sets and the *enunciative models* used, the news presenter is the mediator par excellence between the viewer and the news.

The anchor is responsible for performing four functions simultaneously: that of *guide* – s/he is the one who conveys the news; the *moderator function*, it is s/he who directs the interviewees and what they have to say; the *emphatic function*, in commenting on the items and the interviews; and, lastly, the *delegate function*, in assuming the role of viewer when directing interviews (Simonelli, 2001).

To these four functions must also be added a fifth, that of *news selection*, as the news presenter also has some responsibility for the choice of the news presented and for the moment when it will be presented – the *news line-up*. [90]

---

[90] "In the organisational scheme of Portuguese editorial teams, and RTP in particular, the role of the anchor is extremely influential. He does not decide everything that is to be done, but very often influences the decisions... he influences 5%, 10% of what is done, of the topics that are touched on every day; but he influences much more than that, perhaps 40% or 50% of the way some topics are dealt with... certain decisions, whether this or that topic justifies an interview, or whether it justifies a live report ... And then afterwards he influences above all how the information is perceived by the

The absence of an anchor or, if you prefer, presenter and the absence of the functions identified by Simonelli (2001), with the exception of *news selection*, constitutes the first big difference between the two genres of TV: broadcasting and online TV news.

And as it is on the basis of this absence that the formulation of the identity of the presence of television on the Internet is structured, the absence of this distinguishing feature impels, from the very beginning, the news production of a television channel's official website – irrespective of the use of audio or video or not – to resemble closely the online presence of the newspapers. This, as we shall see, is one of the issues raised by television journalism on the Internet.

The online presence is therefore characterized from the very beginning, in the majority of TV websites, by the provision of news, by means of articles unmediated by an anchor.

But what differentiates the television channels in terms of news material also includes the content made available, or better still the line-up of the news programme and the opening item chosen. Therefore, the comprehension of what online television identity is also involves understanding how, in the broadcasting of TV news, television channels differentiate themselves from each other and also to what point there is a shared content identity between the two worlds of information: television and the Internet.

One of the daily tasks of a television news programme's editorial team is the choice of news, as out of the hundreds of items of daily news twenty or thirty have to be chosen for the line-up. This involves an exercise which is both subjective and objective. Objective because an extensive analysis of the news can reveal a thread that links the topics. Subjective because the choice also has to do with the quality and type of people working on the editorial team every day and, consequently, with all the contingency factors that journalism faces.

Although very often remarked on, this difference in themes ("topics") between different channels can only be discussed based on a comparative and extensive empirical analysis.

The table below (Table 5.5) is a comparative analysis of categories of topics on general interest channels in eleven countries (Shoemaker, 2005

---

audience... through what leads are used for each story."(José Alberto Carvalho, quoted in Cardoso and Santos, 2003).

and Cardoso et al., 2005), allowing us a better idea of the origins of the national identity of TV channels based on their choice of topics.

Analyzing the spread of topics on the different television news programmes looked at, we can conclude that in most cases, except for Germany, Australia and China, over half of all the news broadcast falls into four categories (i.e., internal politics, sport, internal order and international politics). Irrespective of the qualitative aspects of their presentation and the differences between cultures, there appears to be overall agreement about which topics are seen as central for the public's information and for successfully capturing audiences or for providing a public service, depending on which applies.

Table 5.5 – Distribution of television news topics in selected countries (%)

	Portugal	Australia	Chile	China	Germany	India	Israel	Jordan	Russia	South Africa	US	Total
Domestic politics	14.0	5.1	27.5	29.8	14.5	33.0	6.6	17.3	20.1	19.0	10.8	17.9
Sport	14.9	26.0	7.5	.6	5.6	8.4	18.0	9.2	3.9	14.6	29.1	13.8
Internal order	12.8	11.1	10.2	3.8	14.1	17.6	10.4	2.7	13.0	13.1	10.8	10.4
International politics	11.5	4.5	5.4	9.5	1.2	13.2	4.7	39.1	17.5	14.6	.7	10.2
Business/commerce/industry	2.3	4.3	3.6	12.1	8.8	6.6	1.4	3.1	2.6	7.3	5.2	5.6
Cultural events	3.1	1.8	4.2	7.6	11.6	.7	19.9	.0	3.9	1.5	1.8	4.6
Human interest stories	6.4	11.1	2.1	1.9	4.4	.4	8.1	3.4	1.3	2.9	6.3	4.5
Weather	2.0	7.1	.3	.6	5.6	5.1	.0	6.1	3.2	.7	9.6	4.3
Disasters/accidents/epidemics	6.1	9.8	2.7	.6	7.6	2.9	2.8	.3	3.2	6.6	2.2	4.0
Health/welfare/social services	5.4	3.3	5.1	7.0	3.2	1.5	1.4	3.7	2.6	2.2	4.5	3.7
Transportation	1.7	5.8	3.6	6.0	3.2	.0	.9	.3	.6	3.6	4.7	3.3
Ceremonies	2.9	1.8	5.7	2.5	2.0	1.5	2.8	3.4	5.8	1.5	1.6	2.7
Economy	3.15	.5	3.3	6.0	2.0	.4	2.4	2.7	3.9	2.9	2.2	2.5
Education	1.9	.8	3.9	1.0	2.0	.0	3.8	4.1	.6	2.9	2.9	2.2
Labour relations/trade unions	3.8	1.0	6.0	.3	.4	.7	.9	.0	.6	3.6	.9	1.5
Environment	0.4	1.3	1.2	2.5	.8	1.1	4.3	.0	.0	1.5	1.3	1.4

Table 5.5 – Distribution of television news topics in selected countries (%)

	Portugal	Australia	Chile	China	Germany	India	Israel	Jordan	Russia	South Africa	US	Total
Social relations	1.5	.3	2.4	.3	3.2	1.1	2.8	1.7	.6	.0	.4	1.2
Housing	1.0	.0	1.5	1.3	5.2	.4	2.4	.0	1.3	.0	.4	1.1
Military and defence	.9	1.0	.6	.6	.4	.7	.5	.7	9.1	.0	.4	1.0
Communications	1.4	1.0	1.5	1.0	1.6	.7	1.4	.7	.6	.0	.9	1.0
Science/technology	.5	.5	.9	3.5	.4	.0	.5	.0	3.2	.0	1.6	1.0
Energy	.0	.0	.3	1.3	1.6	2.9	.0	.7	.6	.0	1.1	.8
Entertainment	.0	1.8	.6	.0	.0	.0	.0	.7	.0	1.5	.0	.5
Fashion/beauty	.4	.3	.0	.0	.0	.4	3.8	.0	.0	.0	.0	.3
Population	.6	.0	.0	.0	.4	.7	.0	.0	1.3	.0	.4	.2
Total*		100.0	100.0	100.0	100.0	100.0	100.0	100.0	100.0	100.0	100.0	100.0
(N)		(396)	(334)	(315)	(249)	(273)	(211)	(294)	(154)	(274)	(446)	(2946)

Source: Shoemaker, Pamela J. (2005), News Around the World: Content, Practitioners, and the Public, Routledge, London. For Portugal, Comparative Study on the Analysis of Television News Content, commissioned by the AACS, directed by Joel Silveira (2003). *Note: the high percentages evident for the 'sport' category are due to the participation of the Portuguese national football team at the 2002 World Cup. *Total N may not actually be 100.0 due to rounding.

Nevertheless, within this commonality of topics it is possible to group some countries and also identify situations that are the product of the national identity of each country and their own historical and political context.

Like Portugal, therefore, the US, Australia and Israel seem to place particular emphasis on what are known as human interest stories, while this category only figures to a small extent in the remaining countries. Internal politics, in turn, is essentially a central attribute in countries such as Chile, China, India, Russia and South Africa, where it accounts for between 20% and 30% of all topics examined. In the longer established and unmitigated democracies, there appears to be less attention dedicated to politics on the news.

Also as regards international politics, statistics reveal that more attention is also paid to this topic in countries within geographical proximity of conflict zones, as in the case of Jordan and Russia. Israel is an exception, given that its model of news scheduling puts more stress on the topic of internal order than international politics, the result of its policy towards the Palestinian territories.

Still in the area of shared peculiarities, we can see that sport is king in the US and Australia, reflecting similar TV news models in both countries. The same can be said of the emphasis given to the weather in these two same countries. Lastly, we can verify the occurrence of choices that seem to be characteristic of only one country, as in the case of Russia, with its concentration on military matters, education in Jordan, disasters, epidemics and accidents both in Australia and Germany, health in China and trade unions in Chile.

In Portugal, the three most recurring categories are *internal order*, *internal politics* and *international politics*.[91] However, if we extend our analysis to a greater number of sub-categories, we can see that some singular features occur at the channel level. Namely, in Portugal, TVI has two thematic categories: "Health, well-being and social services" (whose occurrence in its news broadcasting equates in percentage terms to the emphasis on "national politics") and "human interest stories" (which is the third most common category in the private channel's news broadcasting).

---

[91] With the exception of the "Sport" category, due to the effect of the 2002 Football World Cup on the sample in question.

What the statistics seem to bear out is that, just like in many other countries (Dahlgreen, 2002), there is room for a popularization of journalism via a resort to not only sensationalism, scandal, personification and excessive dramatization, but also for a *broadening of the concept of news* (Eco, 2000) to include daily life, the antithesis of the event, thus attempting to establish ties with people's normal lives.

This explains the decision by some channels to increase the length of their news programmes to respond to an editorial need to give, besides traditional news categories, equal treatment to *new* categories promoted to the level of newsworthiness – such as some sub-categories within the categories of "health, well-being and social services" and "human interest stories".

What we can conclude from this study of topics on TV is the search for models that differentiate different news programmes, thereby attempting to respond to the increase in information available and the increase in competition for viewer's attention (Eco, 1995 and Dahlgreen, 2002). Thus, in Portugal, TVI is an example of a news identity model that can be termed *popularization of journalism* (Dahlgreen, 2002), while the remaining three channels can be described as having *similar news value models* (Traquina, 2002), approaching the concept of public service journalism (Raboy, 2001).

However, before we take this similarity of *news value models* as read, we must take into consideration two further aspects, namely verify the type of news dealt with in the most significant categories of the programme line-ups. This is because, as Raboy (2001) has noted, public service channels have also traditionally attempted to distance themselves from their private competition in terms of news reporting. However, the same author, in his report on the state of public service broadcasting in Europe also mentions that it is undergoing a period of identity crisis, in Portugal and other countries, and very often starting to adopt practices from its most direct competitors (Raboy, 2001).

Among the themes that can be considered to make up a concept that is more faithful to the notion of a *public interest service*, we can identify the environment, culture, education, science and technology and health. In Portugal, we can see in the analyzes carried out (Cardoso and Telo, 2003) that the only category that comes close to the top news stories on all channels is health. However, a more in-depth analysis allows us to identify in health a similar logic to that employed in the personalization of politicians

(Castells, 2004), only that in the case of health this does not promote the individual to a state of permanent stardom, but rather momentary fame (Eco, 2000). In most cases, the logic is that of the reality show applied to news, or, if you like, the infotainment model (Dahlgreen, 2002).

The discussion about the variation in television news models is also imbued with cultural and historical conditioning factors, in the sense that whereas in Europe this debate seems to centre on the contrast between public and private television, in the US it appears to focus on the cable *vs.* network broadcast axis (State of the News Media, 2005).

According to the Project for Excellence in Journalism, the relationship between network broadcast and cable news in the US is characterized by a higher number of reports on the former than on the latter and also greater correspondence between the images and the report. News stories on cable follow the interpretive-explanatory model more closely and there tends to be less balance in the phatic function between different angles of the same story (State of the News Media, 2005).

In an analysis carried out of content on three cable channels (Fox, MSNBC e CNN), it was shown that on any one day the percentage of news either partially or totally repeated from 7am – 11pm reached around 70% of all news stories broadcast. This model results in the US in fewer numbers of topics covered than on network evening newscasts, not to mention the Internet or the press, where there is even greater diversity.

Table 5.6 – Topics on cable and network news US, percent of all time (%)

	Cable	Network Evening	Network Morning
Government	17	29	25
Defence/Military	7	1	0
Foreign Affairs	9	14	8
Elections	14	11	8
Domestic Affairs	11	20	15
Business	1	4	1
Crime	3	1	5
Science/Technology	1	4	3
Celebrity	14	2	4
Lifestyle	9	4	7
Accidents/Disasters	2	4	3
Other	12	6	21

Totals may not equal 100 due to rounding.

Source: State of the News Media 2005.

As we can see in the table above, news on cable TV expends much less time on covering material related to the workings of government and around half the time dedicated by network newscasts on covering issues such as the environment, transportation, health, social security, education, the economy, and science and technology, etc. However, lifestyle, entertainment and celebrity topics, which normally feature less on the evening news or in the benchmark newspapers, constitute the largest group on cable news.

As we know, quantitative analyzes also have their limitations with regard to establishing differences and similarities. While their contribution is essential, they cannot answer all of our questions, particularly when we know that the enunciative dimension plays a fundamental role in characterizing television news models (Simmoneli, 1999).

Based on precisely that premise, below are the results of the analysis of three days of newscasts on Portuguese television on the 11, 12 and 15 March 2003 (Cardoso and Santos, 2003).

On these three days, each of the fifteen opening news stories analyzed was exceptional. For example: the assassination of the Serbian prime-minister; the crashing of a military helicopter in the United States; the Lajes summit between Bush, Blair, Aznar and Durão Barroso; diplomatic relations on the eve of the military conflict in Iraq; the Casa Pia paedophile trial in Lisbon; and the contamination of poultry with nitrofurans in Portugal.

Table 5.7 – Opening news item for the television news programmes by topic in Portugal, 11, 12 and 15 March 2003)

	Opening news stories by topic				
	RTP1	*2*	*SIC*	*SIC Notícias*	*TVI*
11th March	Nitrofurans (National)	Disaster (International)	Casa Pia paedophile (National)	Diplomacy (International)	Nitrofurans (National
12th March	Casa Pia paedophile (National)	Serbia (International)	Casa Pia paedophile (National)	Serbia (International)	Casa Pia paedophile (National)
15th March	Lajes summit (National)	Lajes summit (National)	Casa Pia paedophile (National)	Casa Pia paedophile (National)	Casa Pia paedophile (National)

Source: Cardoso and Santos, 2003. Comparative analysis of Portuguese television channels – 11, 12 and 15 March 2003.

Let us take the opening news item on 11th March 2003 as an example. On at least two channels, the opening news item had to do with food safety, a topic which since the so-called 'mad cow' crisis has become front page news (Philo, 1999). The time dedicated to news related to nitrofurans in poultry differed depending on the television channel. TVI's *Jornal Nacional* and RTP1's *Telejornal* chose it as their opening news, while on SIC's *Jornal da Noite* the subject was relegated to a later slot halfway through the newscast and on RTP2's *Jornal 2* related news was broadcast at the end of the programme. [92]

TVI's *Jornal Nacional* was the one that gave the story most coverage, with 14 minutes of consecutive broadcast, including five reports, one of which live, one item about a related subject in the Netherlands and studio-based commentary. The story about poultry infected with nitrofurans was presented with extreme seriousness, stressing the Portuguese government's incompetence, in this case the Ministry of Agriculture, in dealing with the issue; on the contrary, in the item relating to a similar problem in the Netherlands, the swiftness with which the Dutch government resolved the issue ("but the government in The Hague reacted im*media*tely...") was highlighted.

The texts prior to the showing of the report and those accompanying it were read with an alarmist tone, resorting to platitudes and generalisations: "Nitrofurans have been banned for nine years, but in Portugal this ban has never been implemented ... the conclusion is that for nine years the Portuguese have been eating chicken containing banned nitrofurans ... and while things remained the same all well and good, but now that nobody is eating chicken, something is finally being done."

RTP1's *Telejornal* dedicated five news stories to the subject, including the opening item. The items consisted of four reports on chicken farmers, on the closed egg farms, on combined egg and chicken farmers and a story that attempted to show the life of a bird on a poultry farm. In contrast with TVI, the emphasis was not placed on the government's incompetence, but rather on technical and logistical inabilities and farmers' lack of understanding of the problem: "Tens of thousands of chickens were sold because farmers had no idea they were harmful."

---

[92] According to Felisbela Lopes, the opening news item "reflects the unusualness of a reality regarded as anodyne; it is part of a whole of which one expects a certain consistency and is regarded as the most important item of the news: it is the first." (Lopes, 1999: 119).

SIC's *Jornal da Noite* presented three reports and one news item, approximately halfway through the newscast. The reports consisted of two press conferences, one with chicken farmers and the other with combined chicken and egg farmers. These two press conferences were also mentioned on RTP1 and channel 2, but only the latter was referred to on TVI. The second report was about the closed farms and the topic of the story was the closure of a rabbit farm and a pig farm, the story accompanied by archive pictures.

In the case of RTP and SIC, more importance was given to the press conferences, while TVI preferred a more direct approach with reports on the closed farms. Curiously, the live report showed only the journalist speaking about an interview he failed to obtain with the manager of one of the farms, thereby calling into question the real need for a live report.

As Susana Santos (Cardoso and Santos, 2003) suggests, comparatively speaking the news services of RTP and SIC are the most similar, TVI's *Jornal Nacional* thereby being the most different in the way it deals with the news.

Analysis of this opening news item therefore confirms the different positions mentioned above, between a model that popularizes journalism and a model that aims more towards a public information service.

Remaining with the issue of how much influence television news models have on creating the identity of TV news (Simonelli, 2001), we also need to understand to what extent the relationship between studio news and live news can differentiate a news model.

Live news is the television genre par excellence in the sense that, "by transforming current time into presence, proximity into simultaneity and periodicity into sequentiality" (Sanabria, 1994:69), television differentiates itself from all other media.

In the live news report, the reporter legitimizes the event, speaking directly to the viewer without recourse to the mediation of an anchor or editorial team, conveying the sensation of an immediacy and improvisation that is not always real, as, like other news services, it is also rehearsed. According to Felisbela Lopes, "The live report is assumed to be an original narrative, in which four moments coincide: the event, the narrative, the broadcast and the reception" (Lopes, 1999:80).

However, as can been seen in Tables 5.8 and 5.9, even on cable television the role of live news can vary in its use as a differentiating factor vis-à-vis the rest of television (in the case of the US, it can exceed 50% of the time of the entire news broadcast), as in some countries like Portugal, where it can achieve figures lower than those for network newscast.

Table 5.8 – Story origination on cable news US (% of all time)

	Packages
Staff Package	24
Staff Live	52
Anchor Voice Over/Tell Story	17
Live Events	6
Banter	1
External Outlets	1
Totals may not equal 100 due to rounding.	

Source: State of the News Media 2005.

This differentiation between channels also occurs with regard to the diversity of opinions. While it is true for the US, as Table 5.9 attests, those non-cable news broadcasts tend in general to be more diversified in their opinions than cable, it is also possible to find differences between channels. For example, in the treatment of a theme such as the War in Iraq, we can clearly identify differences between cable channels.

Table 5.9 – Range of viewpoints, cable versus network news US (% of all applicable stories)

	Cable Daytime	Cable Newscast	Cable Talk Shows	Network Evening
Mix of Opinions	18%	39%	26%	72%
Mostly One Opinion	24	28	13	8
All One Opinion	59	33	61	20
Totals may not equal 100 due to rounding.				

Source: State of the News Media 2005.

While in 98% of news stories about the Iraq War covered by CNN and 71% covered by MSNBC no view was given by the journalists, in the case of Fox in 73% of items the journalist gave an opinion (State of the News Media 2005).

Table 5.10 – Live reports in television news programmes in Portugal, 11, 13 and 15 March 2003

	Yes	Mixed (Studio+Live)	No	Total
RTP1	18	7	62	87
2	8	4	56	68
SIC	18	1	82	101
SIC Notícias (Cable)	6	3	52	61
TVI	14	2	109	125
TOTAL	64	17	362	442

Source: Cardoso and Santos, 2003. Comparative analysis of Portuguese television channels – 11, 12 and 15 March 2003.

In the sample selected for Portugal, 64 items were broadcast live (14.4% of the total) and 17 in mixed format (with the newscasts of SIC Notícias and RTP2 being those which least used this genre). The use of live reports also contributes fundamentally to the identity of different television stations. In the same market segment, some stations make more use of studio-based news.

It could be argued that, by comparing two countries like the US and Portugal, what we see more than opposition between cable and network is the simultaneous coexistence of two models of TV journalism that each has its origins in the development out of two traditional styles that exhibit the emphatic function of television (either interpretive-explanatory or generalist-objective) and the broadening of the thematic concept of news.

This conclusion can also be supported by the fact that, in the US, while there is a tendency for the models used by cable and network newscast to differ, there are also differences in their use between different channels.

After analyzing the performative and enunciative dimensions of television news production, what conclusions can be drawn to characterize TV's online presence?

Though both use different technology, the newscast on Internet and television have certain things in common, and not only in terms of the multimedia aspect of the language.

One of these is the logic associated with the mediation and closeness that is established between the person broadcasting and the person receiving the news. If we bear this in mind, then live television is similar to the concept of online breaking news.

Besides the potential parallels between these two forms of transmitting the news, there also exist methods of contamination between the two media.

An example can be found in TV news in the scrolling text during broadcasts. This serves two purposes. On the one hand, it is an attempt to emulate the logic of Internet-style "breaking" news, creating a television substitute. On the other, it establishes the written *communication networks* necessary to create interaction with the Internet and mobile phones.

The "contamination" between technologies is also visible in the influence that the Internet can have at the level of the models of organisation of television. Namely the emergence of sequences of images based on the hypertext concept provides new ways of showing them in newscast line-ups.

As José Alberto Carvalho (quoted in Cardoso and Santos, 2003), refers who organizes a newscast and is suddenly faced with dozens of subjects which he has to put in order, has mentioned, he also has to find a logical sequence in his head so that it all makes sense.

What José Alberto Carvalho is actually suggesting is that there exists another level at which new technologies have an influence, in short, a demonstration of how the logic of the Internet can also modify our way of mentally organizing and presenting information even in media whose functioning is not technologically dependent on hypertext.

From there it is possible to argue that the Internet, even if only indirectly, is contaminating television discourse. Sometimes more obviously, other times more subtly. [93]

One of the dimensions of this contamination is newsworthiness, as these criteria also find themselves imbued with hypertext logic in the aim of grab-

---

[93] With the rise of the Internet, for the first time the way we organize information on a daily basis is faced with a media whose memory we find has the same way of functioning as our own brain, in short, the non-sequential linking of information between neurons. In some way, technological hypertext recreates the model of biological organisation of our brain, perhaps this also constitutes one of the many reasons for the success of the Internet technology. José Alberto Carvalho, an RTP journalist and newsreader of *Telejornal*, argues similarly that "(...) there is a sequence to things in a book; it has a beginning, a middle and an end and you cannot reverse that order. On the Internet, the order is the impulse. The narrative structure of the Internet is completely different because of that possibility, of that which exists and which we were accustomed to in books and which we continue to teach our kids even though the reality around us continues to say otherwise. We continue to teach children to read sequentially and to understand sequences of facts and chronological tables. I realize that that helps to structure knowledge. But I do not think that it is the one and only way to present and organize things (...)" (quoted in Cardoso and Santos 2003).

bing the viewer's attention. Given its technological characteristics, television has to gamble much more with hypertext logic than, say, a newspaper.

For the reader of a newspaper, interactivity is much greater in terms of the management of information. S/he can turn the pages, skip articles, manage his or her time much more according to his or her own personal taste. In the case of TV, the hypertextuality has to be managed by the news line-up itself, as the logic of the inverted pyramid (Deuze, 2004 and Traquina, 2002) cannot apply to the line-up at the risk of losing the viewer's attention.

In the case of television news, the aim is to inform and consequently the aim of the journalist who works there is to get the viewer's attention from the opening item to the last piece of news. Just as the editor of a newspaper aims to grab his readers and increase his readership, by establishing loyalty or giving the reader information about all kinds of topics from the front to last page, so in TV the same holds true. This logic transposed to TV cannot be achieved by means of applying the logic of the inverted pyramid, in which the most important issues are the first and the least important the last, because if that approach was applied it would mean that people would all focus on the start of the newscast and, gradually, as the programme progressed, change channel.

That explains why only the recourse to a certain hypertextuality, with announcements of news coming up in the line-up, on the interlinking of subjects in it and also the actions of the anchor become fundamental characteristics of a television newscast. However, the hypertextuality in television news, which is also the product of a contamination of the logic underlying the Internet, also coexists with a more traditional model inherited from the print newspapers in which the topics in the line-up are ordered according to "national" and then "international" news, followed by "sport" and "miscellaneous" and from most important to least important, general to particular.

If we want to delve further into this idea of the presence of television hypertextuality, we will have to agree that it is much more evident in the area of TV entertainment, particularly at the level of stations such as MTV (Frith, 1993), which also combine entertainment and news dimensions and present an alternative model of information management in a television context that deliberately seeks a hypertextual construction of programmes and news line-ups. [94]

---

[94] "... MTV was the first interesting contribution to the deconstruction of this type of utterly compartmentalized view of things. MTV won over millions of viewers, young viewers, by using techniques

If the set of characteristics referred to up to now have allowed us to identify the different models of television news, if it is possible to establish what connections occur between the TV screen and the computer screen and if the performative dimension allows us to identify points of contact between the two technologies, does there also exist any relationship between the news presented on the TV and that written on the websites of different channels? A joint study undertaken on television news and official websites of Portuguese TV channels (Cardoso and Santos, 2003) appears to infer that the answer is yes.

In a comparison of the news carried by the various channels online and offline, the online media provided, as would be expected given the fewer limitations in the relationship between space and time, a higher number of news stories (574 items out of a total of the 1016 studied). Of the three sites looked at, that of RTP was the one with the most news (340 stories), followed by SIC (156) and then TVI, which had the least (78).

Table 5.11 – Source of news articles, comparison of television *vs.* online presence in Portugal (%).

	News Agencies	Press Releases	Journalists	News Agencies and Journalists	Unspecified	Total
RTP	4.6%	-	82.2%	1.1%	11.5%	100%
RTP *Online*	67.9%	-	2.9%	28.8%	0.3%	100%
SIC	-	1%	94.1%	-	5%	100%
SIC *Online*	3.2%	-	44.2%	6.4%	46.2%	100%
TVI	2.4%	-	86.4%	2.4%	8.8%	100%
TVI *Online*	46.2%	-	41.0%	12.8%	-	100%

Source: Cardoso and Santos, 2003. Comparative analysis of Portuguese TV channels – 11, 12 and 15 March 2003.

As far as the origin of news is concerned, most presented on the television news services is written by journalists (more than 80% on average). In the online editions, this figure decreases considerably, although differences exist between the three websites.

---

that the manuals until then had said should not be used, that they were anti-TV, such as the average length of a plane, such as frames, such as colours, and a host of other things." (José Alberto Carvalho quoted in Cardoso and Santos, 2003).

The model of journalism employed on Portuguese TV websites is clearly different from that used in television. Not only because of the absence of the anchor mediator and the replacement of moving images with writing, but also because it gives a greater role to news agencies, which send text in digital format to editorial teams which then reformulate them and put them online.

The pattern, common to all three channels, seems to be that of a clear complementarity between online and television.

Table 5.12 – The topic areas most referred to on television channels *vs.* online presence in Portugal (%)

	International Politics	Internal Politics	Internal Order	Sport	Culture	Economy	Health, Well-being and Social Services
RTP	18.4%	17.2%	17.2%	13.8%	-	-	-
RTP *Online*	-	19.1%	-	24.1%	11.2%	12.1%	-
SIC	22.5%	12.4%	26.4%	-	-	7%	7%
SIC *Online*	14.1%	-	16%	19.2%	9%	-	-
TVI	9.6%	-	33.6%	-	-	4.8%	20%
TVI *Online*	35.9%	6.4%	14.1%	-	-	-	11.5%

Source: Cardoso and Santos, 2003. Comparative analysis of Portuguese TV channels – 11, 12 and 15 March 2003.

The online topics explore different dimensions from those given greatest prominence in the television news broadcasts. But at the same time they also look at some of the topics in more depth. Their aim seems to be not to lose the identity of the topics between the news on both media, but, equally, to explore fresh areas of news interest as well.

What relationship models between the Internet and television can we identify then? Obviously, most of the data presented here on the presence of TV on the Internet characterizes the present situation of the online editorial teams of Portuguese television channels, in a dated record that is also subject to change. However, the analysis of diverse studies on the state of TV in Europe – Aquino and Bierhoff (2002) or Shahin (2002) and Punie (2002) – would seem to conclude that it is possible to typify the online presence of television channels (Tettamanzi, 2000).

The starting point for this characterisation is the theory that alongside successes such as that of the BBC (Kung, 2000), in which, despite a promotional dimension to the programmes (via the homepage http://www. bbc.co.uk/), the central focus is the news production of BBC News (via the homepage http://news.bbc.co.uk/), there also exist other television-Internet models.

Figure 5.5 – BBC and BBC News web pages, United Kingdom

While BBC News represents one of the paradigms of the appropriation of the Internet by a television channel (emphasizing the textual character of information and complementing it occasionally with video and sound), there also exist other models by which television appropriates the Internet. The model employed by the BBC, which we shall term *news* (in a paradigm that returns public service broadcasting to the written press, only now in digital format), is also the model adopted by private channels such as CNN. In both cases, the channels' online presence competes with all other media, from newspapers to online radio and even with their own television editorial teams, to capture an audience in search of news.

Figure 5.6 – CNN.com web page, US

This is a state of affairs that is only possible when the individual TV editorial staff (and also those of online newspapers and radio) have a strong identity in which prefixes are added to the original brand that identify a distinct journalistic culture, as in the case of "BBC News" and "CNN.com", and therefore can be designated the *Internet News Model.*

The second variant of the informative model can be exemplified by the case of the private Portuguese TV channel SIC and the public channel France 2, in which the model's essential purpose is to complement the news provided on television. This second variant of online information can therefore be termed the *In-Depth News Model.* [95]

Figure 5.7 – TF1 (France) and Canale 5 (Italy) web pages

At the opposite end from the informative model, exist cases such as the Internet presence of private channels like TF1 in France and Italy's Canale 5, owned by Mediaset, in which the main aim is to promote their own entertainment programmes and to attract those surfing on the Internet to watch their TV programmes, developing the topic pages of the website around the same programmes and thereby attempting to explore a *cult* dimension, with information playing a very small role in the page's overall purpose. This model can be designated *Enhanced EPG.*

---

[95] Mendes (2003) suggests that in online media, television has an advantage over its competitors as channels can promote their websites via their large audiences. This promotion can work reciprocally, feeding viewers to the website and Internet users to TV. The best results are achieved when this occurs during newscasts, chiefly when mention is made of the existence of additional details about a story broadcast by antenna (Murrie 2003). In this relationship of additional details, the chance of using infographs figures as one of the elements of the complementarity of information. Complementarity is achieved not only with recourse to more information on a topic, but also by use of the tools that bring the web page closest to the television broadcast, i.e., the multimedia infograph.

Figure 5.8 – TVE (Spain) and RAI (Italy) web pages

In the case of sites like those of the Spanish (TVE) and Italian (RAI) public television channels, they appear to share, even if in different ways, the logic of the *television portal model*. In short, their pages serve to show everything connected to the channels and that has been produced for the Internet. There is no affirmation of a Web culture or attribution of a specific function, except that of content, leaving the user the choice of deciding what best suits his interests.

Figure 5.9 – Globo (Brazil) web page

Where TVE's portal is essentially institutional in character, enhancing institutional links to the media group and therefore essentially establishing a link to what is broadcast on the TV channels, in the case of RAI the attraction is consultation of the material that has been produced specifically for the Internet. RAI typifies the broad content choice model, in which, for instance, under information you can choose between news from the three national TV channels, radio or RAINews24. For that reason, this variant, like the online resource of Brazil's Globo, can be designated the *content* portal variant and the model personified by TVE as the *institutional portal model*.

Table 5.13 – Online presence models for television channels

Model	Dominant characteristics	Examples
Internet News	Predominantly informative function; online editorial teams with strong identities; competing to achieve the same status online as that enjoyed by TV news.	BBC News (UK) CNN.com (US)
In-Depth News	Complements information provided by TV; Develops topics dealt with in the information blocks and introduces fresh areas.	SIC (Portugal) France 2 (France)
Enhanced EPG	Promotes its entertainment programmes; Attracts Internet users to its entertainment programmes on television.	TF1 (France) Canale 5 (Italy)
Content portal	Permits users to choose what best suits their needs from the available content; Attraction to consult what has been specifically produced for the Internet.	RAI (Italy) e Globo (Brazil)
Institutional portal	Essentially institutional portal; Institutional information about programmes on its channels.	TVE (Spain)
Networked interactivity	Creates interactivity with its own TV programmes during regular broadcasting; Interactivity includes news, chat and entertainment; Combination of different technologies (e.g.: SMS; Internet; chat; scrolling text and television).	RTP (Portugal), TVI (Portugal) Televisio de Catalunya (Catalonia, Spain)

Lastly, there is the television online presence model that can be termed *network interactivity*. Although all the models mentioned above contain an interactive dimension (email, chat and SMS), this dimension is just one among many being offered, thus not assuming a central role.

In the case of the online presence of the Portuguese channels RTP and TVI and that of Televisio de Catalunya, its principal function is to establish interactivity, not with the online editorial staff or with the site managers of a specific programme, but with the television programmes themselves as they are being regularly transmitted. In short, the Internet presence serves to promote the use of SMS, teletext and at times voice via telephone and mobile phone.

The use of email is in turn subordinated. In the case of RTP, it is only available when searching for information about a given programme on the EPG. SMS are sent (as already seen) almost entirely to entertainment programmes, such as quiz and talk shows.

Figure 5.10 – Catalonian Television web page

As regards teletext, this is essentially a means to promote interaction via the chat channels. In this model, it is the news aspect that makes the most use of the Internet. Television news programmes (in this case those of TVI and RTP[96]) establish a link to the news on their website via the scrolling news text. Thus, viewers of the news on TV can visit the web page in search of extra information, whether more in-depth, or on other themes, or simply more up-to-date. This *network interactivity model* is, therefore, the model that best mirrors the idea of *networked television*. This is also a model that can only be implemented in societies in which mobile, Internet

---

[96] Available data on the habits of Internet user's vis-à-vis the online presence is somewhat limited. The web pages are consulted solely by those who watch television, i.e., the online presence does not generate more television viewing. Those who consult them do so because they watch the channel and wish in some way to deepen their interaction, whether via more news information or by interacting with the programmes. The Internet is arrived at via television and not vice versa.

and teletext technologies are widely distributed as they form the basis on which it is structured.

What then has changed in TV since the arrival of the Internet? Any attempt at an answer is based on the idea that the change depends on the traditional TV model, i.e., on a television identity built around a given relationship between entertainment and information. But, seeing as the original purpose for the Internet presence of television channels has almost always been to offer news, any change is also dependent, up to a point, on the news model employed by the editorial team of the television news of each TV station.

Television's online presence, just like those of the newspapers and radio, is a product of the interaction between the two foremost means of communication: information published offline (which is its point of origin) and the online environment of the Internet, or better still its culture, which represents its point of arrival (Castells, 2004 and Scifo, 1998).

As with offline media, the ultimate aim of online media is to be recognized and valued by society. This recognition derives from who produces and projects it and also from the multi-dimensional aspect of the Internet's communicative environment (Scifo, 1998) and the relationship established with its offline identity from the start.

In the final assessment, the degree of change that the Internet has introduced into television depends on the choices that the TV company decides to take and allows to be implemented (Kung, 1999). The change introduced by the Internet into television occurs in two phases. The first corresponds to TV's move online. The second phase, depending on the technological capacity, strategy and original identity model, presents the chance to develop, or not, towards new models of television that take into consideration the network logic between different media. A presence on the Internet can, if maximized, contribute to the emergence of a *networked television* interacting with diverse other *media*, personal or mass, and diversified content or, in a dimension of less change, establish only fragile bridges between two media without any real interaction between them: *television to be merely seen and the Internet to be navigated.*

The impact of the Internet on television, in Europe, is essentially visible in terms of consumption and not in terms of production or distribution. The models of entertainment and news programmes have been changed very little in content and form by the emergence of the Internet. Also in terms of distribution the impact is more visible in the digitalization of the signal using technologies such as cable, satellite or terrestrial digital broadcasting than by the few experiences of broadcasting over IP via Internet (Colombo et al., 2004). Where the difference is most noticeable is in the decline in the number of hours that Internet users now spend watching TV (Cardoso et al., 2004; WIP, 2004).

In that sense then, should we not be looking at the online presence of TV channels from the perspective of whether they are using the Internet to try and reduce their loss of audience? In the case of television channels that have adopted the online model of network interactivity, they have available a function to forward Internet users to the screens of their TVs, making use of the interactivity provided by different technologies to achieve that end.

From Radio Interactivity to Newspaper Time Management: the Media Network

Umberto Eco (1997b) suggests that, in the context of current society and the organisation of its media, there exist various possible courses that newspapers can take in order to prevent themselves from becoming slaves to the television information model. In Eco's opinion, newspapers that have for years been dailies can become "weeklies", increasing the number of pages while broadening their definition of news beyond the more traditional notion, putting more stress on sport, fashion, the ephemeral world of celebrity news and also the new personalities in the public eye, like, for instance, participants on Big Brother.

Although with different degrees of intensity, the television agenda interacts with the newspaper agenda and vice-versa, but for Eco what we are witnessing is not merely the use of journalistic *tricks* from other media, but rather the emulation of a distinct news model.

Umberto Eco in his analysis of the relationship between television and the press (and therefore in an attempt to find an organisational logic for the information framework), concluded on the subject of the Italian press that "there is no press anywhere in the world where television news appears on the first page, unless Clinton or Mitterrand had spoken to the small screen the night before or the chief executive of a national (information) network had been sacked" (Eco, 1997b:69). Also according to Eco, following the emergence of television from the 1970s onwards, the latter became the primary source of news dissemination and the daily newspaper, in reply, increasingly began to resemble the weekly, which in turn had also to change, dealing with the same news as the dailies but in greater depth and providing at the same time a broader range of useful information, ranging from shows to travel and real estate (Eco, 1997).

As a culmination of this whole process of adaptation, what is considered news, first in the newspapers and then on television, also tends to have its standards of definition altered, becoming broader, in the fear that it will lose its interest if it is not given at this precise moment in time (hard news), in the sense of a growing legitimacy of a timeless type of news (soft news). [97]

If we take Eco's premises as valid, what state of affairs do we find in the relationship between the news presented by the two largest news sources to the Portuguese public, i.e., television and the leading daily and weekly newspapers? And is the situation in Portugal comparable to that of other geographical zones, such as, for instance, North America?

By analyzing a sample of newspapers and television news programmes in the months of March and July 2003, it was hoped to obtain a diverse range of topics dealt with, both in light of the newspapers and channels chosen and also the type of events (stories that monopolize the media agenda, as in this case with the start of the war in Iraq and other diverse current affairs topics). [98]

---

[97] According to Rebelo (2002), all the facts that correspond to something more than normality is, from the perspective of commonsense, event. In event theory (Neveu 2002), this expression corresponds to a happening of absolute, singular, unrepeatable and unforeseeable nature. The issue of what constitutes 'news' has been controversial for a long time, despite the fact that we deal with it naturally every day. McQuail (2000) notes that "there appears to be a stable perception on the part of news decision-makers about what is of interest to an audience within the same socio-cultural parameters". As such, the definition of what constitutes *news* may be different from society to society. For Shoemaker (1996), the definition of news is that of "a special type of communication", "a new piece of information about a subject that is of public interest and which is seen as such by a substantial part of the public". How information that interests the public turns into news is a question which we do not intend to answer here, but if we believe Eco's analysis and the empirical data from comparative studies conducted internationally by Shoemaker (2001) and also the analysis of Portuguese television production (Cardoso and Telo, 2003 in Silveira, Joel, 'Study for the AACS', unpublished), there would seem to exist if not qualitative differences in the topics chosen for the news to be presented to the different audiences then at least quantitative ones. But there exists a common tendency to broaden the definition of news in the sense of resorting to a timeless type of news (soft news).

[98] Although the number of newspapers on sale was greater than those included in the table, the aim was to select those which, both in the studies of the market and in the analysis of their communicative practices (Cardoso et al., 2003), were the most widely read by the Portuguese public.

Studying the information contained both in this analysis and the following tables seems to suggest that Eco's theories can also be applied to other national environments.

Between 20% and 30% of the news on the prime-time newscasts of Portuguese television channels also appeared on the front page of that day's morning newspaper. In equal measure, the following morning's newspapers almost always include the same news stories featured in the line-ups of television news, so long as they did not break after the newspaper had gone to print that day.

But there are some differences between the television channels' most common choice of newspaper and the type of press news selected for inclusion in their line-up.

Thus, all four television news programmes, with the exception of the TVI channel, align their choice of news not according to the newspapers with the highest circulation or popularity, but rather in accordance with those that are considered to be the benchmark,[99] or reference newspapers, in other words, the *Diário de Notícias* and the *Público*.

Some synergies also exist based on media ownership. Both the SIC channel and the weekly *Expresso* newspaper belong to the same group, therefore it is no surprise that the TV channel makes above average use, compared with other channels, of the paper's news.

---

[99] Both the *Diário de Notícias* and the *Público* are generally considered, and consider themselves to be, benchmark newspapers. A benchmark newspaper demonstrates greater interest in topics of a political nature and maintains a greater distance from and seriousness with regard to its analysis of topics dealt with in other newspapers. Rocha (2003) suggests that benchmark newspapers are aimed chiefly at a managerial audience (associated with political, economic and cultural decision-making), while the target audience of popular newspapers is more generalized. When using this definition however the criticisms of Bourdieu (1979: p. 518) should be taken into consideration, who suggested that an overly Manichean split between "sensation" and "information" type newspapers should be avoided on the basis that very often this is an ideal model that does not exist in the field of analysis. Benchmark newspapers for McLuhan are the continuity of a model of the press that lies in the extension of the "book" media, while the tabloid model represents the variety and irregularity of daily life and the influence of new ways of communicating (Mesquita, 1998). Following this line of reasoning, we can say that the *Diário de Notícias* and *Público* satisfy the functions designated as features of a benchmark newspaper, namely being used by other newspapers, being a platform for society's leaders to express themselves and also being used abroad as indicators of the real state of affairs in the country.

Table 5.14 – Average coincidence between items on TV news and in selected newspapers in Portugal (%)

	Expresso*	Correio da Manhã	Jornal de Notícias	Público	Diário de Notícias	Average coincidence
RTP1	14.3%	25.1%	17.3%	28.3%	34.3%	24%
2	14.3%	18.3%	14.2%	29.8%	32.3%	22%
SIC	29.4%	26.0%	14.6%	31.2%	39.3%	28%
TVI	23.8%	30.5%	10.6%	29.8%	28.3%	25%

Note: the news stories analyzed refer to the line-ups of prime-time television news on the four channels and to the articles on the front pages of the five newspapers on 11, 12, 18, 19 and 22 March 2003 and 21-26 July 2003. *This is a weekly newspaper. [100]

At the level of the type of news, in particular of the genre – hard or soft – and topics, there is a clear difference as regards the use made of news in the newspaper. The TVI channel gives priority in its news line-up to stories about petty crime and accidents reported by newspapers that also give greater emphasis to these topics, which, in our sample, are represented by the *Correio da Manhã* and *Jornal de Notícias*.

Another analysis possible on the link between different media in the information meta-system is a comparative study of the opening items on the television news and front page news. What is interesting about this comparison is the fact that for both media, television and newspapers, these news stories are the ones that normally decide the theme chosen for the news for that day. As the newspapers are published in the morning and go to print first thing and television news programmes are broadcast at the end of the same day, normally between 8pm and 10pm, the fact that TV resorts to opening news that is shared by the newspapers can give us another insight into how the relationships between both media are organized and to what extent the premises delineated by Umberto Eco in the latter half of

---

[100]The Portugal Global group, created on 24 February 2000, is a holding company that lumps together Portugal's public television channels (RTP), radio channels (RDP-Rádio Difusão Portuguesa) and the LUSA news agency.

SIC belongs to the Impresa group, which besides the TV station also includes various newspapers and magazines, foremost among which is the weekly broadsheet *Expresso*, with which the SIC website has a very close relationship, as well as interests in portals, cable TV, film and telecommunications. The Media Capital group, headed by Miguel Paes do Amaral, owns TVI. Like the Impresa group, Media Capital has a wide range of business interests in various companies in the communications sector, from telecommunications to radio stations, newspapers and magazines, by way of publicity companies and a share in a Portuguese first division football club.

the 1990s (Eco 1997b) may or may not also characterize other countries Portuguese press and audiovisual panorama.

Table 5.15 – Coincidence of opening items on TV news with the front page of newspapers in Portugal

	RTP1	2	SIC	TVI
11-03-2003	With all	No	No	With all
12-03-2003	No	No	No	No
18-03-2003	With all	With all	With all	With all
19-03-2003	With all	With all	With all	With all
22-03-2003	With all	With all	With all	With all
21-07-2003	Correio da Manhã	Correio da Manhã	Correio da Manhã	Correio da Manhã
22-07-2003	No	No	No	No
23-07-2003	Yes	Yes	No	No
24-07-2003	Yes	Yes	Yes	No
25-07-2003	Yes	No	Yes	Yes
26-07-2003	Yes	Yes	No	No

If we look at the table above, we can see that only when the subject of a news item is so all-encompassing that it is seen as an event that disturbs normality do we find total agreement between the front pages of the newspapers and the opening items of TV news programmes. This is the case with the item "War Imminent", that cemented the almost immediate threat of attack that the president of the US, George Bush, issued to Saddam Hussein at the time – 18 – 22 March 2003.

The time difference between the newspapers (morning) and TV (between 8pm and 10pm) also influences the opening items on television news.

Thus, on 22nd July 2003, the death of Saddam Hussein's sons occurred after the newspapers had gone to print, with the result that the opening items on TV news on all four channels reflected the event, as on 12 March, when the opening item occurred after the newspapers had been distributed, and also on 21 July, when the opening news on television was dictated more by the developing forest fires – though the topic was the same in the *Correio da Manhã* newspaper, which had chosen to focus on the fires, but those from the day before.

As a means for TV stations to differentiate between themselves, when it is realized that the source of the news in the preceding days was the same, what can happen, as on 26 July 2003, is that while two channels – RTP1 and 2 – choose an item already in the morning edition of a newspaper for their opening item, the others opt for a different strategy. In short, on that day, the SIC channel opted to maintain the same topic on the agenda, in this case returning to the issue of paedophilia and the Casa Pia home for minors. And the TVI channel chose to open with a breaking news item on another topic.

From this analysis we can conclude that if on the one hand the view of Umberto Eco (1997b) about the methods of linkage between television and newspapers continues to hold good, we must also bear in mind the existence of situations, though less frequent, in which topics totally coincide, whether they be international (the War in Iraq or the 1999 massacre in post-referendum East Timor), or national (such as the collapse of the bridge at Entre-os-Rios or the Casa Pia paedophile case in Lisbon). [101]

If we focus on the situation in North America, even though we do not have comparative statistics for opening news on TV and in the newspapers, the following table allows us to reach the conclusion that there is a tendency for the most important themes in the newspapers to also be the most important, in terms of topics, on cable, network newscast and online.

Table 5.16 –Topics in newspapers A1 versus other media, US (% of all stories)

	A1 All Nwsps	A1 Large Nwsps	Comm. Evening	Comm. Morning	Cable	Online
Government	35	30	27	20	14	32
Foreign Affairs	14	17	14	7	9	16
Military	2	2	1	0	6	1
Domestic	14	15	21	16	13	19
Election	9	13	9	7	12	8
Entertainment/Celebrities	1	1	2	6	13	3
Lifestyle	10*	7*	5	5	10	5
Crime	4	3	2	4	4	2
Business/Commerce	4	5	8	2	3	3
Science	3	3	3	3	1	1
Accidents/Disaster	3	1	4	5	3	6
Other	2	2	4	25	11	3

Totals may not equal 100 because of rounding.
*Includes 3% sports coverage for both "all newspapers" and "large papers."

Source: State of the News Media 2005.

---

[101] As analysed by Daniela Santiago (2003) in the case of the tragedy of the sinking of a bus and cars during the collapse of the bridge at Entre-os-Rios.

The interest in Eco's contribution, irrespective of his premises being connected to a specific national context like Italy's, stems from the fact that his analysis demonstrates the link between *media* and how both the newspapers and radio try to reposition themselves in the face of the medium that they consider to be the leader in the field of information, i.e., television.

The second important contribution resides in the fact that Eco (1997b) identifies the Internet as part of one of the possible strategies for newspapers to respond to television, that which he describes as the "homemade newspaper". This strategy is combined with the 'Fijian' model of a newspaper containing only the essential, or to the "broadened attention" model, in which all news of 'soft' events is discarded to concentrate on the news and its events, contextualization and possible developments.

If the Internet can be an answer to the needs of radio and the newspapers vis-à-vis television, then what is the instrumental role of the Internet for newspapers and the radio? And is this trend the same in all cultures?

The answer, naturally, can be looked at from two angles. On the one hand, via a look at how the newspapers and radio have used the Internet in the type of society that is in transition to a network society (such as Portugal) and other informational societies, and, on the other, by the fundamental examination of how the practices vis-à-vis these two media seem to have evolved in the last few years.

In Europe, according to a survey conducted on people's participation in cultural activities, around one in every two Europeans (46%) read newspapers 5-7 times a week, with the highest levels recorded in Finland (77.8%), Sweden (77.7%), Germany (65.5%) and Luxembourg (62,7%). The lowest were in Greece, Spain and Portugal (20.3%, 24.8% and 25.1%, respectively).

In the case of radio, around 60% of EU citizens listen every day. The figure is over 70% in Ireland, Sweden, Austria, Denmark and Luxembourg.

As regards the type of radio programme listened to, the favourites are music programmes (86.3%) followed by news and current affairs (52.9%) and then sport (17.4%).

Radio listeners in Luxembourg and Denmark are the ones who are proportionally more inclined to listen to the news. As for music, the type listened to is essentially 'rock/pop' (55.1%) followed by 'lounge' (32.1%), 'folk' (29.9%) and 'classical' (28%) (Eurobarometer 56, 2002). [102]

---

[102]The type of music listened to varies greatly from country to country. 'Lounge', for instance, accounts

The study of the current situation in Portugal in terms of the online versions of newspapers and radio demonstrate that only 3.3% of Internet users that read newspapers online do not also read the print version. In the case of radio on the Internet, 3.6% stated that they consult online radio but that they do not listen to it.

In either of the cases, contrary to certain analyzes, the Internet seems to be used in a more complementary sense rather than as a substitute. People read the newspaper online, but also read it in print; they listen to radio over the airwaves, but also via the Internet. [103]

Table 5.17 – The most read newspapers and most popular radio stations, online and offline in Portugal (%)

	Most listened to radio stations	Most visited radio stations (Web)	Most read print newspapers	Most visited newspapers (Web)
1st	Rádio Renascença (23.7%)	Rádio Comercial (24.6%)	Jornal de Notícias (31.9%)	Público (18.7%)
2nd	RFM (20.2%)	Antena 3 (14.2%)	Correio da Manhã (23.8%)	O Expresso (14.8%)
3rd	Rádio Comercial (9.6%)	TSF (12.1%)	Diário de Notícias (11.2%)	A Bola (14.3%)
4th	Rádio Cidade (6.9%)	RFM (11.4%)	A Bola (7.0%)	O Record (10%)
5th	TSF (6.2%)	MEGA FM (7.5%)	Público (6.8%)	Jornal de Notícias (9.5%)

Source: Cardoso and Firmino da Costa, 'The Network Society in Portugal', CIES-ISCTE, 2004.

As regards the newspapers and radio stations most read and listened to offline and online in Portugal, it is necessary to highlight several structural points. The first refers to the fact that of the five radio stations and newspapers listed, not one of the media outlets maintained its relative position.

---

for 70.5% of listeners in Finland, while in Greece, Austria and Portugal 'folk music' is the genre most listened to (62.5%, 44.8% and 65.1%, respectively). Classical music is most listened to in Luxembourg (45.8%), Sweden (41.3%) and the United Kingdom (40.9%).

[103] Studies like that published by NETsonda and publicized in the *Público* on 29-01-2004 and in the *Diário Económico* on 28-01-2004 indicated that people tended to read the print version less regularly (in 49% of those asked) once they started to use the Internet. However, other analyses (Cardoso et. al 2004) reveal that a comfortable majority did not change its behaviour (87%), which when combined with the statistics for those who exclusively read the online version (3.3%) would seem to indicate a different scenario.

In the case of newspapers, the reason for this disparity is two-fold. On the one hand, much of what a reader looks for in the print version either the online version does not provide or adds little to what is already provided on paper. On the other hand, there is the question of the quantity of users versus quantity of readers.

As Internet users are fewer in number than newspaper readers or radio listeners, and as they constitute a younger and more highly-educated audience, this difference is reflected in the choice of online radio stations aimed at younger audiences and the higher number of benchmark newspapers with an online presence.

A second structural dimension is the characterisation of the state of the radio and press industries.

In Portugal, entertainment and music stations predominate. Only one news channel (TSF) and two general interest channels (Antena 1 and Rádio Renascença), on which news is accepted as a main editorial feature, exist. [104]

In the field of newspapers, sports papers are preferred by around 12.5% of readers, and, in one case, have a larger readership than a benchmark newspaper (Cardoso et al., 2004).

Having arrived at this stage in our analysis, it is possible to answer how newspapers attempt to use the Internet?

Analyzing newspapers and their relationship with the Internet presents a series of challenges, namely because the written form of communication

---

[104]Radio broadcasting in Portugal is organized on the basis of four large economic groups. TSF, a news focused radio station that broadcasts nationally, belongs to Global Notícias group. RFM, along with Rádio Renascença (a Catholic faith-based radio) and Mega FM, is part of Grupo Renascença and is a general interest station for listeners that are aged between 25 and 35. Mega FM is a general interest station that defines itself as the group's younger audience offering, with listeners mostly aged under 25.

As regards public radio, Antena 1 is the general interest public station and devotes a large part of its broadcasting to information. Antena 2 is the public radio channel whose aim is cultural broadcasting, with special emphasis on classical music. Its site, like the channel, is equally oriented towards dissemination and information.

Antena 3 began broadcasting in 1994. It is RDP's third channel and is defined as public radio aimed at a younger audience. One of the channel's concerns, seen as fundamental, is to play Portuguese music.

The fourth group of channels is constituted by Rádio Cidade. Founded in 1989 as a small local radio station in the Amadora district, it is currently part (with Rádio Comercial) of the Media Capital group. Rádio Cidade is specifically intended for listeners between 18 and 25 (but also the segment between 26 and 35) and social classes A, B C1 and C2. Rádio Comercial regards itself as a general interest channel aimed at a 25-35 year old audience and directly at the same listeners as RFM.

that they practise is so well adapted to the technological medium provided by the Internet and also because, of all the mass media (television, radio and newspapers), it was the newspapers where the profession of journalism first established and consolidated itself and they constitute the most lasting example of journalistic activity, despite the successive challenges they have been confronted with by more recent forms of mass media.

Printed newspapers constitute one of the oldest and most crystallized media. Despite transformations at the content and format level, the *print* platform has remained the same over time, implying specific constraints on journalistic activity (Boczkowski, 2002). Foremost among the features of traditional journalism are the character of the front page – where the titles of the day's main stories are to be found – the development of each of the stories on later pages, organized by theme, the concise writing of the articles resulting from the limitation of space inherent to the use of paper (Keck, 2000), and the association with each news item of values such as objectivity, novelty, and contextualization (McNair, 1998).

Online newspapers, however, rarely exist as independent entities. The print edition usually acts as a supplier of varying degrees of content for the online edition. Despite constituting taking little advantage of the potential of the Internet, the advantages of reproducing the contents of the print edition online is the fact that it makes establishing the newspaper on a virtual medium easier and less of a burden, while the transfer of the identity and credibility of the print edition onto the new medium makes it more appealing to the reader (Keck, 2000). This taking little advantage is also a product of the process of establishing online news services, characterized, for example, by the fact that the established media in the traditional medium are the principal operators online, given their financial resources – namely investment capacity – and news resources – existing archives and contact networks.

In order for us to move forward in our analysis, we also have to attempt to establish to what extent newspapers published on and off the Internet are similar, irrespective of their countries of origin.

The statistics presented below (Tables 5.19 and 5.20) try to give an answer to this. The comparison between four European countries (Ireland, Italy, the Netherlands and Portugal) demonstrates how, even in the print editions, there exists a diversity of journalistic and graphic utilisation between different national contexts (Cardoso and Neto – PT; O'Sullivan – IRL; Fortunatti – ITL; van der Wurff – HOL, 2003). For example, in their print editions, Italian newspapers give greater importance on their first pages to full articles, while the Irish and Dutch papers have a greater number of references to news inside the newspaper. In terms of publicity, Portuguese newspapers are the ones that promote themselves the most, via products sold separately with the newspaper, such as books and CDs, and references to other media belonging to the same group.

The Portuguese model is also the one that resorts most often in all formats to an almost similar split between local, national, national-international and international, while in the other countries studied, attention is mostly directed at national occurrences in the print formats and split between national and international in the online format.

Table 5.18 – Relative size of first page contents per type, in selected countries (% of total size)

Medium	Printed newspaper					Online edition of printed newspaper					Purely on-line newspaper				
Country	IRL	IT	NL	POR	SL	IRL	IT	NL	POR	SL	IRL	IT	NL	POR	SL
News	71%	82%	71%	76%		46%	47%	57%	44%		70%	38%	66%	47%	
Advertising	18%	10%	13%	10%		12%	7%	8%	7%		18%	16%	10%	32%	
Self-promotion	0%	3%	5%	8%		17%	6%	3%	10%		0%	0%	4%	1%	
News indicators	11%	5%	11%	6%		25%	31%	28%	31%		8%	46%	15%	17%	
Non-news indicators	0%	0%	0%	0%		0%	9%	3%	8%		3%	0%	5%	4%	
Communication	0%	0%	0%	0%		0%	1%	1%	0%		0%	0%	0%	0%	
Number of first pages analyzed	3	4	4	8		3	8	8	14		1	1	2	4	

Table 5.19 – Relative number of news stories, selected countries (% of all items)

Medium	Printed newspaper					Online edition of printed newspaper					Purely on-line newspaper				
Country	IRL	IT	NL	POR	SL	IRL	IT	NL	POR	SL	IRL	IT	NL	POR	SL
Type															
Teasers	66%	21%	36%	100%		93%	88%	93%	87%		91%	100%	100%	80%	
Shorts	0%	33%	11%	0%		0%	1%	5%	0%		0%	0%	0%	0%	
News with photo	0%	9%	6%	0%		7%	2%	2%	0%		9%	0%	0%	0%	
News text	34%	16%	28%	0%		0%	4%	0%	6%		0%	0%	0%	20%	
Analysis	0%	5%	2%	0%		0%	0%	0%	0%		0%	0%	0%	0%	
Other	0%	16%	17%	0%		0%	4%	0%	6%		0%	0%	0%	0%	
Items with illustrations	22%	32%	30%	59%		52%	22%	49%	27%		9%	0%	100%	100%	
Geographical reach of news item															
Local	6%	0%	6%	25%		0%	2%	2%	17%		0%	0%	7%	0%	
National	63%	65%	60%	28%		66%	53%	50%	41%		64%	80%	43%	25%	
National -international	13%	11%	4%	25%		14%	8%	5%	13%		0%	0%	0%	30%	
International	16%	19%	28%	22%		21%	27%	30%	26%		36%	0%	43%	45%	
Other	3%	5%	2%	0%		0%	10%	13%	3%		0%	20%	7%	0%	

Regarding the number of news stories on the first page, we can see that, among the different newspapers, the Portuguese model differs from that of other countries for the print edition. While in Portugal the first page normally only has titles or teasers, in the Netherlands and Ireland it contains around 30% of full articles and in Italy uses a model in which over half of the occurrences are titles and short news stories.

However, there is much more uniformity in the online version, which in almost all countries is based on the use of titles and teasers.

Online news in North America, characterized by the Project for Excellence in Journalism (PEJ), differs in some points from that analyzed here for European countries. In the analysis undertaken by the PEJ (2005), the online presence of television channels, newspapers and Internet portals is compared, as the presence of online television in North America, in terms of news provision is significant, whereas in the case of Portugal, as we shall see, makes only a small contribution to information provision and is being replaced by online radio.

However, common points emerge from the analyzes in the two continents. For instance, we can identify similar trends in the big variation between newspapers in the way they profit from the use of the Web, even between the most popular publications on and offline. Nevertheless, the online presence of newspapers seems to be continuing to develop positively.

The constituent elements of an online newspaper can be summarized via the relationship between navigation space and functions attributed to that space. Thus, the main functions of an online newspaper can be broken down into information space, memory space, commercial space and communication space (Scifo, 1998).

Information space is the space dedicated to selecting, exhibiting and organizing news, in short, that which equates to the traditional function of the mass media. Memory space is information archive space. Commercial space is visible in the adverts and also in the market logic, via the promotion of different types of commercial transaction. Lastly, communication space refers to interaction, of communicative exchange, which is expressed in three different forms of communication: news comment, conversation with news interlocutors (journalists, editors, etc. – all those whose email address is accessible) and, lastly, forums and chat between users of the newspaper's website.

Analysis of the written press between the end of the 1990s and the period used as a sample for this study fits into a historic moment characterized by a significant editorial vitality seen at the level of publications of a popular or thematic nature, a contraction in the consumption of the general interest press, a shrinking of investment in online publishing initiatives, the relative rise of info-entertainment and criteria of profitability in contrast to the criteria of news objectivity with consequent pressure on the journalist, an increase in the horizontal and vertical concentration of means of information and the internationalisation of its capital (Correia, 2000). [105]

---

[105] Seven Portuguese newspapers were analysed – the dailies *Correio da Manhã, Diário de Notícias, Jornal de Notícias, Público* and *Diário Económico* and the weekly *Expresso* – in particular their print editions from 18th and 19th March 2003 (with the exception of the *Expresso*, for which the print edition from 22nd March was analysed) and respective online editions as found at 9am and 8pm on the same days. For an in-depth comparison, the exclusively online editions of *Diário Digital* from the same days and times were also analysed. The material under analysis, therefore, included eleven print editions, twenty-two online editions of printed newspapers and four editions of exclusively online newspapers (Cardoso and Neto 2003).

The Portuguese publishing panorama is dominated by five large groups: Global Notícias, Impresa, Media Capital, Cofina and Portugal Global. Global Notícias, has a radio station (TSF), three general interest daily newspapers (*Diário de Notícias, Jornal de Notícias* – the 3rd and 1st most popular Portuguese dailies by average number of copies sold – and *24 Horas*), a weekly (*Tal & Qual*), various specialized national publications and three regional newspapers (*Jornal do Fundão, Açoreano Oriental* and *DN Funchal*), in a total of 20 publications. It also has a stake in the press distributor VASP and a share of around 18 per cent in the LUSA news agency; Sports Newspaper *O Jogo* and the TV rights for the transmission of the Portuguese Football League; *Impresa* – the group headed by the former prime minister Francisco Pinto Balsemão owns the free-to-air TV channel SIC – one of the channels with the largest audience in Portugal – as well as various channels on the cable service (SIC Notícias, SIC Radical, SIC Gold and SIC Mulher), and has an agreement with TV Cabo that gives it priority over the creation of Portuguese language channels for cable. In the press, it owns the weekly *Expresso*, the daily *A Capital*, the magazine *Visão* (also weekly), various specialized publications (*Executive Digest, Caras, TV Mais* and *Telenovelas*) and also the freely distributed *Jornal da Região*, in a total of 32 titles. It also has a 33.3 per cent share of VASP and owns 25% of the LUSA agency, a company mostly made up of public capital; *Media Capital* – the group constructed by Miguel Paes do Amaral controls TVI – another of the market leading channels – and the main producer of NBP soap operas. In radio, it owns an important group of stations, among which are Rádio Comercial and Rádio Cidade (which are among the most listened to), as well as Best Rock FM and Rádio Clube Português. In the press, it has a series of specialized publications: the magazines *Fortuna* and *Expansão*, the *Diário Económico* and *Semanário Económico*, revealing a significant presence in this specific market niche of the economic press. It is also owner of the online newspapers *Portugal Diário* and the business site *agenciafinanceira.com*", as well as the portal IOL; *Cofina* – is the group belonging to Paulo Fernandes which controls the daily newspapers *Correio da Manhã, Jornal de Negócios* and *Record*, besides its share in the magazine *Máxima* and in around a dozen other specialized publications, in a total of 19 publications. It also has shares in the distributors VASP and Deltapress, which control more than 90 per cent of the distribution market in Portugal; *Portugal Global* – is a state-owned holding company that controls the RTP television channels and RDP radio station and also controls the Lusa news agency by means of a 51 per cent share.

We know that alongside these tendencies, the newspapers' online presence was seen as a possibility to increase the diversity of news, both in terms of themes and geographical dimensions, as well as a possibility to develop and update news coverage. Between these possibilities and their realisation, how has the online written press fared over the last few years? Looking at an informational society, the US, and a society in transition, Portugal, both have more in common than they do differences.

In Portugal, the content of the news published with regard to geography maintains the same pattern in the online version as in the print version of the *Correio da Manhã*, *Jornal de Notícias* and *Diário Económico*, which focus above all on regional and national issues.

The reverse is the case with the *Público*, whose first page of its print edition contains above all articles of a regional/national character, its online edition dealing more with European or even world issues, an area that the *Diário Digital* also, and mainly, dedicates itself to.

Table 5.20 – Segmentation by country of business news stories in Portuguese newspapers (%)

	Europe %	US %	Asia %	Other %	All %	US-Europe %
Agência Financeira	80.0	14.0	1.0	1.0	2.0	2.0
Canal de Negócios	82.0	10.0	5.0	1.0	1.0	1.0
Diário Económico *Online*	77.0	7.0	7.0	5.0	1.0	2.0
Diário Económico última hora (Web)	79.0	13.0	3.0	1.0	2.0	2.0
Diário Económico Papel	79.0	8.0	6.0	4.0	2.0	2.0
Total	79.0	10.0	5.0	3.0	2.0	2.0

Source: Resende, I.: 'Business Journalism: Digital Format *vs.* Traditional Format', post-graduate thesis in journalism, ESCS/ISCTE.

Developing this analysis per country, it is notable that, although there exists more available space online, it does not translate into the abandonment of a *Eurocentric* or *UScentric* news model. This analysis can be corroborated by the extensive study conducted by Resende (2001) on the relationship between Portugal's online and offline financial press.

As regards the types of topic addressed in the articles, it would appear that the emphasis is also on maintaining the same topics in the migration to the online edition, without detriment to increasing the number of articles. The only exception to this scenario in Portugal is the *Correio da Manhã*, whose online edition is more general interest, including more articles of a cultural character, without ever abdicating the strong national and domestic component of its content.

Table 5.21 – Percentage of news stories that are repeated on the other Portuguese business sites and newspapers (%)

	No. of news stories repeated	Percentage
Agência Financeira	161	58.5%
Canal de Negócios	141	62.7%
Diário económico Ultima hora	148	57,8%

Source: Resende, I.: 'Business Journalism: Digital Format *vs.* Traditional Format', post-graduate thesis in journalism, ESCS/ISCTE.

Although in the analysis of the different newspapers it has not been possible to realize a comparison for Portugal regarding the diversity of news, i.e., the number of news stories whose theme is repeated in different newspapers, Resende (2001) has conducted an analysis of this sort on the business press and verified that the topics are the same and dealt with in a very similar manner.

If we were attempting to understand to what extent there is a *convergence of content* in journalism, it could be concluded that even though new information exists (produced exclusively for that format) there is also a high degree of repetition between the different websites. The competition generated by the Internet, instead of being a catalyst for originality and diversity, seems to tend to favour uniformity also.

Continuing our analysis, Resende (2001) also concludes that, in the case of the specialized press, such as business (Cocoa, 1990), when online sites are created, there is a tendency for even greater topic segmentation to occur.

As we can see in the following tables, on the sites of *Agência Financeira, Canal de Negócios* and *Diário Económico última hora*, the percentage of economic news is far higher. On the contrary, where a print version already exists, the diversity of themes covered tends to be retained online, as in the case of *Diário Económico Online*.

Table 5.22 – Segmentation by topic of news stories in Portuguese business newspapers (%)

	Business	Politics	Culture	Society	*Media*	Sport	Bus+Pol
Agência Financeira	93.8	1.5	1.1	0.7	1.5	0.0	1.5
Canal de Negócios	96.0	0.4	0.0	0.4	2.7	0.4	0.0
Diário Económico *Online*	48.1	25.6	8.2	5.9	7.1	4.9	0.2
Diário Económico última hora	93.8	2.7	0.0	0.0	1.2	0.4	2.0
Diário Económico Papel	48.9	24.3	9.6	6.3	6.3	4.4	0.1

Source: Resende, I.: 'Business Journalism: Digital Format *vs.* Traditional Format', post-graduate thesis in journalism, ESCS/ISCTE.

In both analyzes (Resende, 2001; Cardoso and Neto, 2003), we can see that there is no change between the journalistic genre produced by the written press for the online version and that traditionally practised in the print editions.

Despite the increase in available space, the number of opinion columns does not increase in the online editions, with an even higher ratio of news to other journalistic genres, such as interviews, opinion columns, editorials and other. Also with regard to the contextualization of the news, i.e., the possibility that the online version might bring links to other sites, to a more contextualizing writing that attempts to bring more in-depth explanations and points of view to the story, there are no significant differences between the online and print editions.

The same occurs with regard to the authorship or origin of the articles observed on the first pages of the newspapers, where traces of editorial continuity between print and online editions can be seen again. With the exception of the *Diário Económico*, all the newspapers with print editions carry articles whose authorship is mostly attributed to one journalist, who is mentioned by name in both the traditional and virtual edition. In the case of the *Diário Económico*, a majority of signed articles in the print edition corresponds, in the online edition, to a majority of articles whose origins refer to third parties or press releases. Of note is the fact that there are countless unsigned articles in all the publications and that these constitute the most frequent type of article in the online editions of the *DE* and *Diário Digital*. This tendency in Portugal also seems to be common in the US.

Table 5.23 – Story origination, US (% of all stories)

Origin	Total	AOL	ABC	CNN	Dallas	Fox	Bloom.	MSNBC	WPost	Yahoo
Staff	32	1	25	54	12	14	96	13	83	1
Wire & Staff	9	0	1	15	14	24	1	24	2	0
Wire	58	98	74	30	73	62	4	63	15	99
Other Org.	1	2	0	1	0	0	0	0	0	0

Totals may not equal 100 because of rounding.

Source: State of the News Media 2005.

In the comparison in the table above, it is precisely the sites of newspapers that place most emphasis on originality. Almost the whole of Bloomington's online edition, *www.pantagraph.com*, is original content, suggesting a decision to emphasize coverage of local events, and 83% of the lead stories of the *Washingtonpost.com* site were also original. The broadcast-based sites have much lower levels of original content, and in the case of online portals their news is almost entirely sourced from news agencies.

In the North American case, just like in Portugal and the other European countries analyzed, there is a tendency to focus on fresh news and not updates of news that has already been given.

Table 5.24 – Story freshness, US (% of all stories)

Freshness	All Stories	
	2003	2004
Exact Repeat	21%	26%
Repeat: No New Substance	14	2
Repeat: New Angle	2	*
Repeat: New Substance	14	11
New Story	49	60

Totals may not equal 100 because of rounding.

Source: State of the News Media 2005.

Relative to *reader-content* interactivity, in the Portuguese case and in the majority of analyzed European newspapers, the most common dimension is that of the possibility of readers forwarding articles or content to third parties. It was observed that forwarding is possible for all of the articles on the first pages looked at of the newspapers analyzed.

Also as regards the interactive dimension, there are no polls relating to the articles published. Where polls are available, they are more related to an editorial topic than to a published news item.

Table 5.25 – Interactivity of online news US (%)

Origin	Total	AOL	ABC	CNN	Dallas	Fox	Bloom.	MSNBC	WPost	Yahoo
Communication	25%	85%	1%	14%	10%	3%	0	23%	12%	100%
Manipulation	24%	6%	1%	90%	21%	32%	0	42%	9%	13%

Source: State of the News Media 2005.

The North American situation is not much different from the European here either, with most sites (whether those of newspapers or TV) allowing communication with the journalist and, except for the case of CNN, with very few functions for customizing content. However, portals like Yahoo! and AOL permit some of the highest levels of communication.

Figure 5.11 – Online versions of the American newspapers *Washington Post* and *Pantagraph.com*

However, as Castanheira (2004) suggests, allowing readers to comment online neither implies recognition of its journalistic interest nor even its credibility as a source of opinion.

Figure 5.12 – Online versions of the Portuguese newspapers *Público* and *Expresso*

In analyzing the comments made by readers of articles in the *Expresso* during 2000, Castanheira (2004) discovered the topic that surpassed all others that year in terms of the number of comments (730): the creation of the Jorge Álvares Foundation by the last Portuguese governor of the Chinese territory of Macao, General Rocha Vieira. [106]

His conclusion focuses on the fact that what most characterizes the comments in the newspapers are their anonymity. In total, only 46 comments about the Jorge Álvares Foundation were wholly identified – 6.3% of the total of 730 comments.

And how do the journalists deal with this possibility of interactivity with their readers? Although only a case study, the analysis conducted by Castanheira (2004) constitutes an interesting example for characterizing the functioning of the newspapers and the way in which the Internet has or has not altered journalistic practice in this area.

Having questioned the twelve journalists and contributors to the *Expresso* responsible for writing the articles commented on about the Fundação Jorge Álvares on the frequency with which they accessed the electronic version of the newspaper and read their readers' comments, 41.6% replied they did, while the majority said that they never did or did so only infrequently. Another statistic obtained from this inquiry was the responses to whether they had ever replied to their readers' electronic com-

---

[106] Among the topics most commented on by readers of the *Expresso* in 2000, foremost were the relations between the former Portuguese President, Mário Soares, and the government led by António Guterres, the beatification of the witnesses to the Fátima apparitions and the crisis at the Portuguese air carrier TAP, alongside Angola, urban violence and the Internet itself. (Castanheira 2004).

ments. None of the twelve writers had ever replied to the online comments to their articles.

Only in the event that e-mails were sent to the personal e-mail of each of the writers did two of the journalists mention that they would customarily reply. However, four of the writers said that they usually replied to traditional mail but not to e-mail. Among the reasons given for not replying to readers' comments published online, the main one was the difficulty of verifying identification, followed by the insulting and provocatory tone of many of the messages and even practical impossibility, given the number of comments.

The main conclusion that can be drawn from this analysis on the interactivity between journalists and readers in online newspapers is that, on the whole, readers do not want to assume responsibility for their remarks, merely hoping to make them public and adding to the spiral of comments, and that normally the comments do not have any objective except that of expressing an opinion. Readers feel that there is no need to verify the veracity of their conjecture, while journalists do not feel that this type of opinion has any validity. Therefore, very often, interactivity in chats or published comments in the media has a function of pure social escape. In the same way that views are given about public figures among friends at the café, these opinions are written down. In this social function, the only difference about the interactivity of newspapers is the number of people that can be reached.

Castanheira (2004) questions whether this interactivity could be put in question due to the low value attached to the Internet as a vehicle of interactivity, seeing as it is neither used by readers or journalists in a constructive manner. However, perhaps online interactivity has merely introduced a new dimension into the relationship between readers and journalists. On the one hand, it has maintained the traditional relationship between reader and journalist in the exchange of letters about any given news item, but on the other, it has introduced a new function that does not directly promote the two-directional traffic that is the free expression of opinion, even if unfounded.

The question that is raised is whether the newspapers can accept co-existence in the same space (or even under the same electronic address) of two forms of writing and totally different communication objectives.

From what we have seen in this analysis about newspapers, we can identify two models of online presence: the *development* and the *brand*.

The digital migration of newspapers can be effectively put down, as considered by Scifo (1998),[107] to the question of competition via-a-vis other newspapers or the attempt at a repositioning vis-à-vis TV. Clearly, it is the latter of the two that leads to the development of the strategy of an online *brand*. As Poole (2001) suggests, the main assets of a publication are its content and the credibility of its brand. Therefore, maintaining the reputation of a brand is essential in the first few years of establishing an online newspaper (Keshvani, 2000). A reputation is created online by producing reliable content and trying to ensure that readers return to a news site (Dube, cited in Resende, 2001).

Table 5.26 – Newspaper online presence strategies

	Development	Online Brand
Diversification of news by theme	No	Yes
Topic development	In some cases	Yes
Multi-user interactivity	No	Yes
Reference to news from other media	No	Yes
Information topic areas	Yes	Yes
Breaking news	No	Yes
Network method in print edition (SMS and Internet)	No	Yes
Identical content to the print edition	Yes	Yes
News occupation rate on the first page	Lesser	Greater

Basing itself on the identity formed by the 'mother' paper in its print edition, the *online newspaper brand* attempts to achieve a new benchmark position vis-à-vis other media. In short, in the same way that there exist benchmark print newspapers, benchmark radio stations and more credible television information services than others, so the online newspaper attempts to be the foremost node for online information. By assuming that role, it also hopes to give the print edition a new impetus by providing it with rapid news publication and the creation of new daily points of contact

---

[107]The motivation stemming from the competition between newspapers, which are pushing editors to focus on establishing an online presence, are essentially three. The first consists of entering the online market as a necessity for managing the paper's image policy, i.e., the idea of being young at heart. The second has to do with the expectation of a radical alteration in the models of distribution and commercialisation of information and the need to stay in the running. And, finally, the idea of expanding the paper's readership. (Scifo 1998).

with readers at home and at work, thereby emulating some of the traditional characteristics of radio and TV, but also introducing its own logic to helps it chart its own unique course, by, for instance, creating connections via SMS and Internet (with poll and their simultaneous publication in print and online) with the print edition, promoting the new aspects presented in it, but evolving towards an editorial line that is consistent with that in the print version but exploring new areas. [108]

The *online brand* strategy therefore attempts to establish a different editorial line, but one that maintains parameters of association with the printed 'mother' brand.

As far as the *complementary* strategy is concerned, it is based on the digital reproduction of the print edition, limiting itself in most cases to transposing news and focusing on the development of some other areas and containing news produced but not published on the print format due to lack of space.

However, the typification of these two models does not mean that the newspapers' online presence can be considered mature yet, because as Salaverría (2002) argues the newspapers in their online incarnation are still an immature *medium*.

By analyzing the news coverage of online newspapers of the events of 11th September 2001, Salaverría (2002) identified a series of weaknesses that should be mentioned. First is the technical inability to deal with abnormal inflows to news sites. On 11th September 2001, there was a drastic reduction in accessibility to publications all around the world caused by the public's abnormal thirst for news. Newspapers like *Le Monde*, *NYTimes.com*, *DieWelt*, *Clarín*, and *ElMundo* witnessed double the normal traffic on their web pages and were left unable to provide an adequate news service. A second issue focuses on the lack of certainty with regard to sources. For instance, the newspaper *El Mundo* announced online that part of the Pentagon had been destroyed and that a car bomb had exploded at the State Department in Washington. Both reports were later proved to be false. The newspaper attributed them to news agencies, but it never identified them.

---

[108]The case of the *Público* newspaper is a good example. In the print version, an opinion poll about a current issue is published everyday and readers are invited to vote via the newspaper's online edition or by SMS. The results are published in print and also on the paper's website.

At their heart, online newspapers live a paradox with regard to their identity. As extensions of their print editions, they have to focus to the same extent on the analytical and interpretive functions that news tradition-ally assumes within the framework of newspapers, but, at the same time, it is required to provide immediate and concise information. And this is a two-fold demand that is not easy to resolve.

Radio constitutes the third element of the group of mass media broad-casting. Whereas the newspapers attempt as their ultimate goal to repo-sition themselves vis-a-vis television via the Internet, radio has already chosen a different route. It attempts by means of the Internet to explore some of its basic characteristics, namely to strengthen the intimacy with the listener, who online is also a reader.

Radio is a non-visual medium that functions based on auditory codes, as traditionally neither images nor text existed. Contact is essentially non-visual and until the emergence of the Internet its listeners could not see their broadcaster. Radio's symbolic codes are almost always auditory, con-sisting of discourse, music, sounds and silence (Crisell, 1994). Radio is an intimate medium, in the sense that every message broadcast is decoded by each individual in a different way, creating a unique "mental photograph" (Taborda, 1999 and Losito, 2002).

Another of the characteristics of radio is its immediacy in divulging news and information, which permitted it, until the emergence of the Inter-net, to be regarded as a form of mass media that reacted more quickly to managing news than newspapers or TV.

Another of radio's properties is *flexibility* (Crisell, 1994). Radio, like other musical dimensions, such as video and channels like MTV and VH1, for instance, is compatible with the simultaneous carrying out of other ac-tivities and permits the management of different levels of greatly varying attention.

However, the flexibility of radio does not always represent one of its central characteristics. According to Eco, the hypnotic function of radio, a characteristic of the 1930s, 40s and 50s, has begun to disappear (Eco, 2000). When McLuhan (2001) introduced the distinction between cold and hot media, i.e., between those that occupy various senses and those that only use one, he clearly classified radio as a hot medium. A hot medium, by making use of only one sense, does not give us any room to interact and thus possesses a hypnotic force. A cold medium occupies various different senses, does it in a fragmented way and asks us to collaborate in filling, connecting and elaborating what we receive. For McLuhan (2001), a conference or a film, which we follow seduced and passively, is hot, while a debate or an evening's discussion about television is cold. A photograph is hot and a comic strip cold, which represents reality by using schematic lines.

The characterisation of radio as a flexible medium is the product of a change in the system of medium, as radio over the past decades had to reposition itself, abandoning the living room and the evening. As Menezes (2003) affirms, TV did not kill off radio, it segmented it, confining it to certain times, places and specialized products.

Radio stations fight between themselves for their audiences, but also with other means of information, such as TV and the Internet, and with the choice constantly growing, with cultural and leisure activities. This multiplication of factors has led to a gradual segmentation with programming aimed at a target audience that is increasingly specific.

But the history of mass media demonstrates that the power of prediction is extremely limited. We therefore also have to ask if technological innovation might not place radio again at the centre of our most memorable and warmest experiences, experiences which we may not even have lived yet. (Eco, 2000c).

Radio has increasingly become a source of background noise. Comedy is watched on TV and music is listened to in grand measure on a walkman or CD or via the Internet, on a computer or on a portable MP3 player. As the Excellence for Journalism Report (2005) states, listening to the radio is to a certain extent a background phenomenon. The study, conducted in the US on the time people spent listening to radio, concludes that 83% of the sample listened to radio, but only 72% were aware of it.

Despite the above, radio today is not a traditional device, marginalized by a TV model based on little affection for the more highbrow, cultured and of a utility, in some way, less directly evident. Radio continues to be an important business partner, characterized by a distinct and high-level of pluralism of which no traces can be found in the current TV models. It is also a platform for non-profitable, voluntary, cultural and also prayer activities. It is a place of technological innovation, as in the case of digital radio. It is a clear example of the relationship between public and private. And it has global reach, revived by the Internet (Menduni, 2002).

Could it be in this way that the Internet makes us reformulate the analysis proposed by Mendelsohn (cited in Ruggiero, 2000) on the functions of radio? Could there be other functions for radio besides those of accompanying and structuring daily rhythms, mainly in the morning, in the role of "company" (helping to fill empty moments created either by loneliness or by routine and the execution of more monotonous tasks) or even that of adapting different content to the moods and psychological states of its listeners and also of its function of providing the listener with information and news?

To understand the possible new functions of radio and the way in which it has appropriated the use of the Internet, it is necessary to put the current state of radio broadcasting into context.

The segmentation of radio today has become so linked to its image that we forget that historically it was much more of a general interest medium. Segmentation is still, in some countries like Portugal for instance, a relatively recent process. However, it is a trend that has become manifest globally since the emergence of television.

Segmentation has led to the appearance of the concept of *format radio*, which began in the US and emerged as a response to the rapid rise of TV in the 1950s. The "format" designation refers, on the one hand, to a certain standardisation in terms of programming, and, on the other, to a structure that can be adapted to a specific audience.

In radio, a format tends to serve the entire programming and not only one programme, as in the case of TV. In fact, radio has gradually lost the concept of programme and oriented its programming towards a pre-defined target audience.

Today's format radio has become a medium which, a product of the management of programming according to pre-defined target audiences, reflects the lifestyles of society itself. In short, it takes into consideration the expectations of its listeners and emulates their tastes, values and cultural standards (Nordberg, 1996).

The great plurality of radio experiences makes it very difficult to undertake an exhaustive definition of radio formats. The formats constitute the identity of the radio network and represent the organisation of the flow structure of radio textuality (Colombo 2005). The two big macro-formats refer to talk radio and music radio. For talk radio, the prevalent formats are: all news, talk, news&talk, sport, children, political, comedy/drama/art, and ethnic/religious. As for music stations, these mark their identity around: contemporary hit radio, adult contemporary, easy listening, country, album oriented rock, classical and vintage.

Figure 5.13 – What Radio formats people listen to in the US (2003)

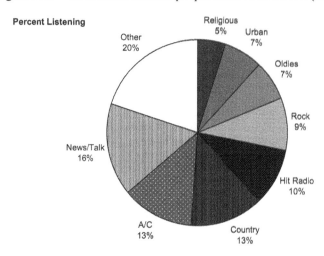

Source: Percent of the population 12 and older, 1998 to 2003 Arbitron "Radio Today" annual report.

The diversity of formats in the field of radio is also a product of its cost structure, as in Europe one hour of TV costs on average twenty times more than one hour of radio. In the US, in comparison with 3,500 TV broadcasters, there are 11,000 radio broadcasters (Colombo, 2005). However, the cost of radio is very low when compared to TV.

For example, among the different formats, we can identify the success of TOP 40 radio, which is based on the sales charts and listeners' requests. Its success is market success (Bastos, 2002). Very often these stations, products of the idea of inter-generational sharing and strategies for aiding communication between parents and children, include older listeners among their audiences

Formatted radio stations thus manage to build up listener loyalty quite quickly, though their share levels tend to be lower than those managed in situations where only stations with general interest programming exist. [109]

On the other hand, there also exist local radio stations, which are faced with a dilemma (Reis, 2002). Although specialized in a given geographic

---

[109] Audiences are a quantitative measure of analysis as a commercial indicator (Sorlin 1997). Audiences do not tell us if they like something or not, if they would prefer something else, or if there are aspects that they would like to see improved, etc. They do not establish the quality or the type of programme (Cintra Torres 1998).

locality, their audience is very varied and so have to opt for general interest programming. This dual aspect gives them various problems, particularly as regards consolidating audiences in areas where national radio stations have a firm hold.

Another radio format is that practised by AC (adult contemporary) stations, which are focused on a target audience of young people and adults (aged from 22-40). These stations mix recently released music with pop classics from previous decades. As regards new releases, these stations usually prefer first to wait and see whether they achieve chart success, what other stations are playing and what listeners are requesting (and for that reason the Internet is also a new and favoured medium of information).

Figure 5.14 – Online pages of the Portuguese radio stations RFM and TSF

The only stations that can be sure that its audience approves are the so-called 'oldies' (Nordberg, 1996), as these do not play recent music. Nostalgia is the emotional bridge to their listeners (Bastos, 2002). Also on the issue of formats, there also exist stations such as TSF, which is information-based and in which music is seen as a complement and as such secondary (Catolfi, 2002).

Within the framework of the formats that characterize radio, how does the Internet currently help to revive or not the relationship between stations and their listeners? One of the issues on which we need to reflect is to what extent the introduction of the Internet signifies a break with, or rather a continued development of, the characteristics of radio. We shall see, even though from one merely analytical point of view, the great differences that the appearance of the Internet on the scene might signify for the current fortunes and characteristics of radio.

In truth, on some fundamental issues, radio, of the three traditional media (television, newspapers and radio), is the one that reveals least differences in relation to the basic characteristics of the new information technologies: the issues of *time, immediacy* and *absence of time and distribution costs* are the main points of convergence.

If, for example, in relation to the newspapers, one of the big characteristics to bear in mind when we speak of the impacts of the Internet is precisely the fact there no longer exist significant time intervals between the production and distribution of information, this is not a significant fact for radio.

Figure 5.15 – The online pages of Radios Eldorado (Brazil) and Fox News Radio (US)

Also from the point of view of financing, traditional radio and online radio are financed in exactly the same way: almost entirely by profits from radio advertising.

For the radio stations, one of the major advantages of using the new technologies is the form and quality of broadcasting. Indeed, the possibility of using the Internet allows not only for unification of the signal diffusion system, but also means the end of dependence on the satellite and radio wave diffusion systems for broadcasting. A radio station broadcasting on the Internet from Lisbon can be heard in Teheran, Seattle, Santiago de Chile, Canberra, Paris or Beijing.

The influence the Internet has on radio can be measured essentially on two distinct levels. The first level has directly to do with the listener, the way he uses radio and the new potentials provided by the Internet; the second has to do with the station's news staff and the way in which the Internet transforms the daily work of journalists and presenters. It is this double sense (from the listener/user perspective and the perspective of the radio station itself and its journalists) that we will be looking at the impact of the Internet on radio.

Radio is not seeking to reposition itself in relation to television through the Internet, for speed of response is already one of its inherent attributes. Whereas it is true that, for the newspapers, the arrival of the Internet reduced a pre-existing limitation, in the case of radio the relationship with the time variable is a different one, given that radio has immediacy in common with Internet (i.e., unlike for the press and even television, there is no need to take into account the production times). Also, another possible transformation that online radio would have made possible, that of *sound memory* in a researchable format, has not been confirmed in most cases of appropriation of the Internet by the radio stations.

The major contribution of the Internet to radio derives from the interactivity provided by online radio in the seeking to intensify the relationship between the radio station and the listener.

As far as the interactivity strategies that materialize in chats, forums, e-mails and comments on favourite pop songs or on a certain news item are concerned, we can observe a very different type of use for the radio stations analyzed, which can be divided into two levels.

A first level, where we have radio stations with as yet tentative forms of promoting interactivity. In the case of news stations, this is achieved through commentaries on the news, while in the case of the entertainment stations it can be achieved through simple discussion forums or sending an E-mail. On the second level of interactivity, the radio stations mobilize the various forms of promoting interactivity with and between the listeners (E-mail, commentaries, forums and chats), which we can associate with stations for young listeners that clearly rely on these instruments as a form of pushing the idea of a listener community. The latter model also exploits the use of SMS in a logic of the establishment of networks with a dimension of proximity and intimacy between listeners and broadcaster.

As far as personalization strategies are concerned we can highlight the register and newsletters as fundamental forms of personalization. However, although these are considered one of the great advantages of the Internet, it is a strategy seldom used by radio stations.

Whereas the information radio stations invest in commentaries on news stories by their listeners, the entertainment stations opt for music on demand, characterized by personalized music choices of the individual users. One example could be the online radio stations segmenting for purely online broadcasting purposes – different stations with different music and information and entertainment formats. Another could be the radio stations with programming based on the choices of the listeners on their online sites.

Another question frequently referred to by authors who have studied the impact of the Internet on the traditional media (Deuze, 2004; Sparks, 2002; Castells, 2004) is the use of hypertextuality and the way in which it allows for the consolidation of information and the relationship between news stories on one site and between the sites and other sites on the Internet.

Focusing our attention on the study of the Portuguese reality, this is, indeed, one of the potentials of the Internet. However, here too, most domestic radio stations reveal very low exploitation of this opportunity. The links to other texts or news stories merely appear at the end of each text as "related news" and never in the body of the text as a way of getting more in-depth knowledge on a subject matter. The radio stations hardly ever establish links to outside their site or promote the reading of other articles on other pages on the same topic, not even on pages within the same group.

If we analyze the online presence of radio stations on the basis of a division into two groups of stations – one group that places the priority on the news function of their websites and another that uses their sites essentially for entertainment purposes – it is easier for us to typify their online presence strategies.

One of the characteristics in the field of information is the complementarity between the radio broadcasting and the online site. One clear example of this relationship is Rádio Renascença, which assumes a much stronger informative role on its site than in its daily broadcasting. This relationship is most likely due to the fact that, within the Portuguese Catholic Church's media group, we do not find a strong television, print media or news radio presence, so that the site filled in that gap and assumed the role of a part of the media group strategy.

A similar observation can be made in relation to the TSF radio station owned by the Global Notícias Group. Here, the investment in the Internet has included the greater promotion of the radio station to the detriment of the group's own print media (Diário de Notícias and Jornal de Notícias).

In the entertainment dimension we essentially find strategies whose objective is increasing the listener loyalty through the reading of the sites. The sites are promoted on the radio stations themselves and the ultimate purpose of the site is to get people to listen to the radio more both through the Web interface and the traditional radio interface. The strategies are normally centred on the games/competitions in interactivity with the site and the building of listener communities through the exchange of experiences that are sent in by E-mail.

The conclusion we can draw from the analysis of the online presences and the interaction between radio broadcasting (sound) and online pages (text), both in the fields of information and entertainment, is the exploitation of the proximity-intimacy function using the resources made available by the two technologies.

The use of the Internet follows practices such as that of the radio disc jockey speaking to the listeners or the television presenter who specifically addresses each viewer watching at home. In any of the three media forms, the aim is to develop a "distance intimacy" (Abercrombie, 1996; Horton and Wohl, 1956), i.e. to act informally, even intimately, with each member of the audience. The fundamental difference between genuine social interaction and this para-social interaction is, respectively, the presence and lack of reciprocity (Abercrombie, 1996; Horton e Wohl, 1956).

The objective of the appropriation of the Internet by radio would correspond to extending to a new medium the interaction practices that combine the mediated interaction between the participants (listener/moderator; guest/moderator) with the mediated quasi-interaction between them and the listeners that listen to the programme without intervening, which are characteristic of open channel programmes (Taborda, 2000)[110]. Programmes that traditionally generate a greater sense of proximity and intimacy between listeners, presenters and journalists. As Franquet, Vitadini and Fondelli (2002) affirm, this is a trend that is common to a number of countries.

---

[110]Thompson (1995) defines three types of interaction: *face-to-face interaction, mediated interaction* and *mediated quasi-interaction*. The first occurs in co-presence and in a shared system of space and time references. It thus has a dialogical character, as does mediated interaction, which differs from the former in that it separates contexts and uses technological interfaces that enable the inter-exchange of symbolic contents. Like mediated interaction, quasi-interaction takes place in technologically mediated environments. However, it has a monological character, given that it is directed at a non-definable universe of potential users from whom communicative reciprocity is not expected.

Crisell (1994) distinguishes three types of programme: *exhibitionist, confessional* and *expressive* programmes. In the exhibitionist model, the presenter encourages the listener to talk about himself and his interests. In the confessional model, the presenter performs the role of counsellor, to whom the listeners tells his personal problems in the hope that from the other end of the line will come an analysis that will prove to be a contribution to his personal situation. Finally, in the expressive model, the listener is asked to express his opinions on public issues.

In Spain, the national Spanish radio broadcaster, RNE, and the radio stations of the autonomous communities have their own websites. Catalunya Radio was the first to broadcast, in Catalan, via the Internet in April 1996. Currently, the majority of the independent radio stations broadcast a part of their programming via the Internet and are interested in developing that relationship of proximity and community with their listeners (Franquet, 2002). In Italy, the online presence of the radio stations is characterized more and more by the offer of community creating instruments. In addition to the traditional instruments (through the DJs and presenters; through the broadcast and through special events and local information) a considerable offer of forums and chat rooms has emerged that contribute to the consolidation of the user community (Vitadini, 2002).

With the emergence of the Internet, radio has maintained its segmentation logics, but has entered into competition with the online presence of the print media. Due to the economic and multimedia strategies of the media groups, a radio station can even be the leading element in a group's online presence, as is the case for the Portuguese TSF, or it may fill a gap, as in the case of Radio Renascença, for that which the Internet gives to the print media (rapidity of update) is a genetic characteristic of radio.

In both the information and entertainment fields, radio makes use of the Internet to consolidate its community logic, not only by open broadcasting, but also using a panoply of interpersonal communication and mass media technologies (such as E-mail, SMS and WWW), thus allowing it to increase the proximity with the listener and combat the logic of radio as a mere ambience medium. At the same time, it can reassume in part its attribute of hot medium (i.e. no longer using passive but active seduction, using E-mail as a means of expressing opinions, choosing music, participating in competitions, etc.).

Has the Internet really changed the mass media? A reading of this chapter would lead one to the conclusion that it has.

However, the change that has taken place can be seen as only partial, when one looks at each medium individually or when one looks from a transversal perspective. The transversal change is the change in the news reporting model itself. The panorama of the mass media is today much more diverse than it was ten years ago. Today, different journalism models coexist. The traditional model of verification and endeavouring to substantiate facts is, today, only one model amongst several. It coexists with a dimension of the popularization of information that is more assertive in character and, in societies such as that of the United States, is experiencing wide-reaching expansion both in talk radio and on cable. Furthermore, the blogosphere is introducing new voices to the field of information and also promotes a model of assertive culture, i.e. one publishes what one wants, in particular points of view (Project Excellence for Journalism 2005), and the investigation and verification can be carried out later by other members of the blogger community. Another hybrid example could be the Current TV project that Al Gore has promoted: a television channel that accepts journalistic reports produced by citizens equipped with cameras, which are also divulged via the Internet. That is a model that differs greatly from the model of prior verification of facts we have come to expect over recent decades.

The mass media are also producing new hybrid models of news reporting, such as the case of the Ohmynews service in South Korea, which presents some 38,000 "citizen reporters" and receives more than 2 million hits per day on its website. This is also a form of journalism that has generational characteristics, for its public is largely made up of young South Koreans. However, there are also negative aspects. In particular, the quality is very fluctuating and there is a trend towards a lack of objectivity. This citizen reporter system also features payment for the work produced, as each user can attribute a maximum of US$10.00 to each article they like, so that the best articles and reporters can be awarded prizes.

Journalism and the mass media, in their co-existence with the Internet, have been transformed and, in this new landscape, they perhaps have to modify their role somewhat. They perhaps have to change their central axis from gatekeeping to authentication. It will no longer be enough for the mass media to just have good professionals with privileged access to the circles of power, both political and economic. It will also be necessary to monitor other information sources, for that will be the best form of aiding the citizens and helping them to know what to believe in and what not to believe in.

6. The Massification of the Internet Experience

As we have seen in the previous chapter, the print, television and radio media have appropriated the Internet in different ways.

Concomitant to the action of the media, we have also witnessed the adoption of a logic of transformation of the Internet itself, with the aim of maximizing the economic dimensions of a technology that is highly mouldable through its use (Castells, 2004).

Putting the statement above on the strategy of transformation of the Internet into a better perspective, we can venture the hypothesis that such a strategy begins to a large extent as a result of acquisitions and mergers, such as those we witnessed in the mass media and telecommunications sectors from the latter half of the 1990s to the stock market crash of 2001. [111]

This strategy has included the fact that the print media and radio and television stations fear that, on the offer side, new rivals may appear and

---

[111] Economic theory distinguishes three categories of merger and acquisition operations: horizontal, i.e. between companies that offer similar products and belong to the same sector; vertical, i.e. between companies that produce different goods or services for the same end product; and conglomerations, i.e. between companies that belong to the same sector but operate in different markets (market extension), between companies that belong to different sectors but sectors that are related in terms of production or distribution (product extension), or between companies that belong to different, unrelated sectors (Perreti 2000).

because they understood, as far as the demand side is concerned, that the Internet user could seek satisfaction of their information objectives through new information sources in a vaster media universe. In the preceding chapter we analyzed to what extent these conceptions were justified or not. We will now go on to analyze the results of those strategies for the delineation of what the Internet is today and how the transformation of it can have an influence on the management of the communicative autonomy of the citizens.

In recent years we have seen mergers between communications corporations (such as Time Warner) and Internet companies (such as AOL). We have also witnessed strategic agreements and acquisitions of contents companies.

These economic partnerships were forged at the global level, often uniting companies that operate on different continents (as in the case of the Spanish Telefónica and Portugal Telecom entering the Brazilian mobile phone market with VIVO) and for this reason they represent an essential phenomenon for understanding what the Internet is today.

The multimedia groups are the result of these vertical integration and product extension processes. The vertical integration processes were particularly attractive for the video branch (i.e., the merging of companies that produce and distribute films – from video and DVD to television) and the product extension processes were of interest to all branches, whereby one can distinguish between the content extension processes (i.e. mergers between companies that produce cultural or entertainment value products) and the extension processes in the information branch (mergers between information producing companies).

The media sector is normally characterized by very high production costs in comparison to the reproduction costs (Perreti, 2000). In the sectors that have this particular situation, the retail price for the products has no correlation with the production cost, but with the value that each consumer is will to pay for the consumption. The strategy associated with this cost structure is based on the diversification of products and methods, so that profit is produced when the sum cover the investment in production. For this reason, this logic favours vertical integration (Perreti, 2000).

But this integration takes place in different forms between cultural content branches and information/news branches. The processes for contents branches are influenced by the possibility of one and the same product being transformed for diverse markets.

The typical example is that of the book, which can give rise to a film screenplay, a soundtrack or even a video game, an Internet site and diverse merchandizing.

The integration processes in the information branch can be analyzed in the light of economies of scale and variety in the field of the sale of advertising space. The print media, radio and television are the main fields of advertising activity and their integration allows for the reduction of the transaction costs associated with the joint management of the spaces.

In a multimedia corporation, integration between contents and information/news branches also allows for the gains inherent in the interest of the whole group and not only of the company in question. Hence, in the case of the online presence of media and telecommunications groups, both sides have to gain by allying the presence of trusted brands such as newspapers and television and radio stations to other contents and new services. Hence, at the same time as the provision of access, the traditional revenue source of telecommunications, is made profitable, the same thing happens with the contents, given that advertising depends on the number of accesses or visits. In other words, as we have already seen, the media companies live to a large extent off the purchases by their readers and/or the advertising (let us leave out the public communication sector for the moment).

The telecommunications companies live from the subscriptions and the Internet connections through their telephone networks. Both have profit as their objective and that profit, in the opinion of many social and economic agents, can only increase (and, in the case of some media companies, be maintained) when we have generalized use of the Internet if they work together with the common aim of hybridizing the Internet's network logic in the direction of a more traditional diffusion logic. [112]

To this end, it was necessary to create points of entry to the Internet that fix the user or, at least, make them return to those points with the highest frequency possible. The profitabilization of these spaces would come from advertising and in the future it could be guaranteed by paid contents. This concept of entry points has given rise to the so-called portals, to which the user is normally directed when they open their World Wide Web browser programme and where they can find, amongst other things,

---

[112] For a more detailed look at these opinions expressed by opinion leaders, see Chapters 1 and 2.

news, entertainment, organized information, search engines, commercial offers and chat rooms. [113]

The hypothesis analyzed here is that the Internet is no longer the same space of information research with the image that we have built up of a space of unlimited information available to all citizens that we knew until roughly the mid-1990s. And it is no longer so not because of a surveillance programme (such as the FBI's *Carnivore* or *Echelon*, a programme operated by various English speaking countries together), but because, for reasons for economic survival of the Internet access operators and of the traditional news information entities, it has come to be moulded for a more organized and limited use of the information available. That was the fundamental motivation for the connection between these two economic dimensions and the development of Internet presence instruments.

When we refer to the change from the network logic (many to many) to a certain return to the diffusion model (the traditional one-to-many model), we do not mean to say that the Internet as a whole is changing, for its technological structure furthers the existence of a multiple diversified and interconnected network. However, the telecommunications and media companies, acting in their own interest and seeking to satisfy the users' needs of organization and validation of information, have endeavoured to (and to a certain extent succeeded in) introduce a new logic to the Internet.

In other words, users do not have to browse on their own, for it is easier for them to browse as previously defined by the portal, whenever possible. This logic was developed with the aim of maximizing profits generated by advertising and contents that are exclusively accessible for clients of the telecommunications operator.

However, as we know, it is not only the will to offer that determines the success of a product or service. A large part of the success of the institutionalization of portals as predominant elements in the Internet landscape

---

[113] According to Microsoft Magazine, the term *portal* refers to a wide variety of websites, from internal sites for personnel (intranet) to external sites for consumers and partners (intranet and extranet). Generally speaking, a portal is a website that unites, in a contextual form, information, applications and relevant services.

A portal filters the complexity and variety of the information and services available to the user through one single interface that is aimed at the needs and interests of the user. The portals offer a direct response to the great variety and complexity of the online world (pp.19-20, issue 49, October-December 2004).

can be attributed to the real needs felt by the users of the technology. A need rooted in the extension of the Internet itself.

The New Frontiers and Their Entry Portals

The scope of a space is delimited by its frontiers, and the limits of the Internet are, at times, not very clear. In an interview in 1996, William Gibson (1996) stated that cyberspace is the space we have been living in since the end of World War II. It is the space where we talk on the phone, where financial transactions are carried out, where the information flows. Basically, it is the space where communication takes place on a digital format. From the point of view of the planet Earth, its frontiers are as far as the distances that our communications satellites can reach in space. The Internet is not the same thing as cyberspace. Its frontiers are, therefore, not the same. The Internet is contained within cyberspace; it is one of the latter's components.

When we speak of the dimension of the Internet, we are speaking in terms of its contents. In particular, the pages or measurement units of digitalized information, such as the bit or byte, that make it up.

Measuring is only possible on the basis of the information made public (Sherman 2001) or that which one at least knows to exist. For this reason, the data refer largely to the World Wide Web. Although it is possible to measure the E-mail traffic, E-mail is non-public communication between a sender and recipient and for that reason will not be analyzed herein.

To answer the question put forward above, there is, at the outset, a problem in delimiting the universe under analysis. Most countries do not yet have a systematic archive system, be it extensive or selective, for WWW pages or any other form of publicized information on the Internet. The closest thing we have to his is the development of search and indexation technologies on the Internet – the so-called *search engines* – by a number of Internet service providers.

There is, however, at least an alternative formula for calculating the Internet's dimensions. Steve Lawrence and Lee Giles (1999) have published a study on the dimension of the information available on the Internet and the thematic distribution of the available contents. The study estimated the size of the indexable, i.e. public, part of the Internet as at February 1999 as consisting of some 800 million pages distributed by approximately 2.8

million web servers. These web servers, in turn, each made available an average of 289 HTLM pages, the contents of which were dominated by commercial information, with 83% of the total contents, followed by educational information (6%), health information (3%), personal pages (2.5%), pornography (1.5%) and governmental information (1%).

The data presented by Lawrence and Giles and the study conducted by Internet Systems Consortium, Inc. (ISC) on the development of Internet hosts between 1999 and 2001, allow us to estimate the size of the Internet in 2001 at around 2 billion HTML pages.

Although the idea of a repository, or archives, of the global knowledge of humanity accumulated over hundreds or even thousands of years is a *wish* that seems to have been with us ever since writing was invented, the realisation of that dream was always accompanied by the need for maps identifying the location of the information or by authorized mediators in the search of information – the librarians. [114]

The Internet has often been described as a new Alexandria Library. A digital library functioning on a global scale, where, with the aid of a new technology – networked computers – and an ancient technology – writing – one can archive knowledge and make it available to all those interested. This library would operate 24 hours a day, covering all the time zones of the plant simultaneously. It would be added to and grow with the individual contributions of each of its users.

The Internet is not a library – at least not a library like the successors of the Alexandria Library, those we know today as school libraries or public libraries *Our* Internet is, perhaps, much closer to the Library of Babel imagined by the Argentine writer Jorge Luís Borges (2000) than to the mythical Library at Alexandria.

Although it is a collection of many different types of information, the Internet, as a whole, is not an indexable and catalogable universe. We can guess its size but we cannot index it (although, technologically, we can idealize it), for, financially speaking, that is not a viable project. The variables, particularly the whims of the users who create and delete information on the Internet in a constant and never-ending process, as still too complex to be able to implement a global system with a high degree of reliability.

---

[114] A desire that was finally realized when the alphabet first emerged in Greece around the year 700 B.C. The famous library at Alexandria in Egypt, which was initiated around 284 B.C. and was destroyed in 642 A.D., was one such attempt to gather all the knowledge existing at the time in one place.

Also, the Internet does not have librarians – be they human or a product of artificial intelligence and database management. At most, it has mediators of bits of information (such as the portals) and providers of clues/tracks (such as the search engines) for a given item of information or page – and even they are sometimes hard to find.

In contrast to public libraries, the Internet is a space in which being able to read is not enough for accessing the information.

On the Internet, researching information pre-requires having learnt to use computers and the software necessary for surfing and also a certain degree of analytical and relational capacity compatible with the culture in which the information is formed and made available. In other words, the Internet also requires literacy for the new media that is not only instrumental (the use of the machine and the software), but also cultural.

The Internet also has another characteristics that limits its use as a library. Public libraries were idealized as democratizing spaces for the access to culture and information. Although the Internet follows the same principles, it is, at least for now, much more restrictive in terms of its target population. [115]

Finally, access to the information available on the Internet, namely through search engines (such as *google.com* or *yahoo.com*) or Internet access portals does not adhere to public interest criteria the way libraries do, but is subject to the commercial interests of the companies that manage them.

Now that we have disproved the myth of the Internet as a library open to all, we have to introduce a question related with the way in which we access that enormous diversity of information that is the World Wide Web. As the following table illustrates (Table 6.1 and 6.2), despite the millions of pages available in the universe of the Internet, there is a significant concentration on the use of portals. Hence, approximately 40.2% of the last sites visited in Portugal were portals, while at the portals were also identified as the favourite websites on the browser by 34.2% of Internet users. This trend in Internet use is accompanied by the repute attributed to the different online presences. According to data provided by the *Observatório da*

---

[115] For examples of the costs of these entry barriers we do not have to refer to the analysis of the United Nations Secretary-General, Kofi Annan, before the International Telecommunications Union, where he calls attention to the fact there are more Internet users in New York than in the whole of Africa. We only have to remember a small news article in 2000 in the Portuguese weekly *Expresso* stating that the cost of Internet access in São Tomé and Príncipe was equivalent to almost four month's wages.

Comunicação (Communications Observatory) and Marktest, the popularity figures for Portuguese sites in the 2000-2002 period were led by portals in the top three places.

Table 6.1 – The importance of portals in the choices of Internet users in Portugal (%)

1st site mentioned as one of the last sites visited	*%*	*1st site mentioned as one of those listed in favourites*	*%*
SAPO – Portal	16.2	SAPO – Portal	15.1
CLIX – Portal	4.1	CLIX – Portal	3.9
Google – Search engine	4.0	IOL – Portal	3.2
IOL – Portal	3.8	Hotmail/MSN	3.0
Hotmail/MSN	3.7	Google – Search engine	2.9

Source: The Network Society in Portugal, CIES-ISCTE (Cardoso, G. et al., 2004).

The trends identified above for Portugal are also valid for other countries. Since 2000 the portals have been gaining ground and attention in other countries, such as Germany and France (NUA, 2000). In 2000, the French portal, Wanadoo, which is managed by France Telecom, received more than half of the French Internet traffic, with yahoo.fr being the second most visited site. In Germany, Deutsche Telekom's T-Online portal managed to attract more than two-thirds of German Internet users in the same year. In 2004, the use of the Internet in the United Kingdom, Australia and the US likewise featured a number of portals amongst the most visited sites, including those of Microsoft, Yahoo, Time Warner and the BBC. Also in China (Liang, 2003), the four most popular websites amongst Chinese users are portals (www.sina.com.cn; www.sohu.com.cn; www.163.com and www.yahoo.com.cn).

Table 6.2 – Internet use in the United Kingdom, Australia and US in 2004 (%)

Name	UK	Name	Australia	Name	US home	Name	US work
Microsoft	73.40%	Microsoft	76.51%	Microsoft	65.78%	Microsoft	87.76%
Google	52.38%	Google	54.91%	Yahoo!	57.18%	Yahoo!	73.72%
Yahoo!	45.45%	Yahoo!	41.23%	Time Warner	56.39%	Time Warner	69.80%
eBay	34.79%	Telstra	35.30%	Google	35.59%	Google	60.79%
BBC	33.34%	eBay	30.02%	eBay	26.79%	U.S.Government	51.22%
Time Warner	30.25%	Australian Gov.	25.66%	U.S.Government	20.23%	EBay	42.12%
Wanadoo	24.88%	Time Warner	21.76%	Ask Jeeves	16.80%	InterActiveCorp	33.98%
Amazon	22.76%	NewsCorp.	21.14%	Amazon	16.75%	Amazon	32.75%
Askleeves	21.96%	Fairfax Digital	19.41%	InterActiveCorp	16.42%	Landmark Com	29.79%
BT	20.37%	Commonwealth	15.78%	RealNetworks	15.97%	Walt Disney	28.35%

Source: Nielsen//NetRatings, 2004.

However, although the abovementioned sites all have in common the name of portal, one can establish, on the basis of the site classification model suggested by Ivan Montis (2001), that three different types of portals exist on the Internet. In other words, there are three different portal organization logics: portals with a greater emphasis on information; those that base their strategy on building a community (whereby the community is defined more by the communication and interaction models than by the socio-cultural or geographic origins of its members); and, finally, commercial portals, i.e. those with an emphasis on electronic commerce transactions.

The history of portals began with Yahoo!, a search engine created by two American university students, Jerry Yang and David Filo, in April 1994. In Portugal, the emergence of the portals with information and entertainment contents dates from the late 1990s. Early 2000 saw the multiplication of portal projects, some of them created large media groups. In this war of concepts, strategies and audiences, in addition to the so-called "horizontal" portals (i.e. more comprehensive), one witnessed the emergence of "vertical" portals (i.e. more specialized ones). However, the Portuguese market, which was too limited and small for so many brand names, determined the end of some of these projects and only a few survived.

Of those that survived the initial experimentation phase, the great majority were born out of a search engine, around which other information services and channels were created – which were divided into areas such as business, news, sports, health, leisure, technology and others. In May 2000 there were 10 major Portuguese portals (including horizontal and vertical ones). Five years on, only three large horizontal portals have survived. This is typical of the general trend for portals in recent years, confirming Picard's (2003) analysis of the Yahoo.com portal.

At the beginning Yahoo! was a access portal for Internet users, but over the years it expanded its activities, so much so that it describes itself today as a leader in the provision of online products and services to consumers and corporate clients. For Picard (2003), this change resulted from the risks associated with a business model focused on advertising, causing the company to modify its business model through the diversification of activities.

Both in Portugal and in the case of Yahoo! (Picard, 2003), as the portals' business model gradually changed, the contents they made available to their users also changed, leading to exponential growth in the commercial contents (Picard, 2003).

If we look at the functional logic that governs the organisation of the portals, we see that today they present themselves with an above-all commercial logic that is no longer based only on paid access via an ISP and they constitute a space of information and access to information (where one can highlight two fundamental aspects: news and information research) and also as a space of communication and interaction.

With regard to their informational dimension, and returning to the proposal of Montis (2001), one can say that all portals have an area of divulgation of the topics on which one can obtain information. The services that are common to Portuguese portals are horoscopes and weather and traffic news. The information model also allows for an area of interaction with the portal's creators and/or managers.

Figure 6.1 – SMS and Horoscope Service Pages of SAPO.pt

As far as the provision of news services is concerned, all portals do so through a diversity of alliances – normally within their own publishing group, if they are part of a group, or using the services of a news agency.

By combining the commercial logic with the information and communication logics, the aim is to achieve the same objective through different ways. If the users favour the commercial model they will purchase products and services, thus establishing a relation-ship of consumption with the portal. If they opt for the access to information they will be dealing with information from newspapers and magazines that mainly belong to the same business group. If, in turn, they opt for communication (participation in chats, forums, surveys, etc.) they will see that the majority of the topics suggested also those that are of most interest to the business groups in question. For example, there is a clear association between the topics of consumer surveys and competitions and the interests of the group in question or the products it wants to promote.

Figure 6.2 – Yahoo.com and yahoo.com.br portal pages

A portal is an infomediary (Mandelli, 1999), i.e., an aggregator of information on the World Wide Web that offers surfing services to the users, making research for them easier. Having initially developed out of the search engines, the portals gradually added other types of information aggregation services (channels, breaking news) and personalized services (E-mail, personal agendas, etc.)

Their business model is essentially based on advertising and also on commercial transactions, whereby the portal, for commercial reasons, has also evolved towards logics of upstream vertical integration, namely with specific browsers (Netscape and AOL) and ISPs (Portugal Telecom and Sapo).

The portals have made a decisive contribution to reconfiguring the offer and provision of information. With the opening of the World Wide Web to the general public, corporations and public administration bodies, the offer and provision of information is to a large extent being carried out through institutionalized sources.

The information in the information-communication flows in the Internet has created the need for spaces essentially dedicated to the organization, selection and updating of contents and the knowledge the individuals have of the medium. The organization, selection and transmission of information in the Internet space has thus become a strategically oriented activity.

The new gatekeepers of the network, which are attentive to the characteristics and profile of the medium itself, are based on specific representations of reception in the configuration of the information offer they develop. Together with the search engine, the portal is the vehicle *par excellence* for the users to structure many of their uses, consumptions and representations of the Internet as a medium. [116]

Figure 6.3 – Definition of online content dimensions according to Kung (2002)

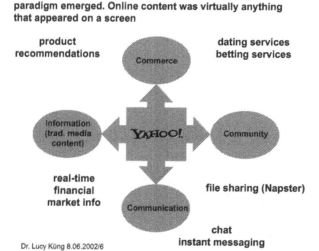

As the Internet sector established itself, a new content paradigm emerged. Online content was virtually anything that appeared on a screen

product recommendations

dating services betting services

Commerce

Information (trad. media content)

YAHOO!

Community

real-time financial market info

file sharing (Napster)

Communication

chat instant messaging

Dr. Lucy Küng 8.06.2002/6

Source: Adapted from Lucy Kung (2002).

The fact that the joining of interests common to both media and tele-communications companies, giving rise to the portals, took place precisely in this moment in history when the two had traversed much of the 20th century separated from each other (Ortoleva, 2004) also has to do with the cultural change that the emergence of the Internet sparked off with regard to the traditional definitions of information, as news, introducing the model of information as commercial content.

---

[116] A term that refers to the fundamental persons involved in the news production decision-making processes. Originally, the role was understood as being somewhere between those who gathered the news (the journalists) and the public. The editors guarded the gate, deciding if the information was newsworthy. Later, the field was extended to include media managers as well as the news agencies and the channel owners (Hartley 2004).

As Kung (2002) suggests, as the Internet became more widespread and the business culture came to mould the essence of the space (Castells, 2004), we have witnessed the emergence of a new content paradigm.

As the following table (Table 6.3) illustrates, one can say that the on-line contents are virtually everything that shows up on an Internet browser screen.

Table 6.3 – Differences between the *journalistic model* and the *portal model* in producing information

Characteristic	Journalistic model	Portal model
Proposal to the consumer	Information, education, entertainment	Synthesis of information, communication and services
Basic communication paradigm	One to many, mass	Bidirectional, personalized, interactive, on-demand, but commanded by a one-to-many model
Relationship between contents and technology	The message and not the medium	The message *and* the medium
What is quality?	Quality of content fulfils objects shared by society and has intellectual and artistic merit	Quality of content is what keeps users on the site; it is constantly updated
Who produces the content?	Specialists. The creation of content depends on artistic capacity and analytical minds	The client decides what, when and in which format. End of the logic that the journalist knows best. To a certain extent, the content can be generated by the users
Relationship with commercial elements	Content and commerce are clearly separated and labelled	Content and commerce are directly interlinked
Structure	Linear, pre-selected or presented narrative on a fixed timetable	Oriented around a hierarchical hypertextual matrix, but likewise pre-selected
Creativity focus	Artistic and intellectual elements	Information engineering

Source: based on Lucy Kung (2002).

In the opinion of the incumbent companies that devised these online presence strategies, the main characteristics of this new paradigm of the use of information included the implementation of a hybrid genre that brought together on one support information communication and services, seeking to realize their offer in an interactive way 24 hours a day, democratizing contents depending on the interests of the consumers, seeking to offer research possibilities and the creation of interactive communities and access to breaking news (Kung, 2002).

This range of characteristics clearly represented a model different to that practised by journalists, which is based on concern with the editorial integrity of the information provided. As Kung (2002) suggests, the Internet has produced a dichotomy between the "traditional" and "new" assumptions as to the significance of what information content is.

On the one hand we have the traditional view that content is the product of a profession whose main characteristics are creative and analytical capacities in relation to information, i.e. the profession of journalism. On the other, the more recent view that see content as being anything and not having to be the product of a specialist.

For this latter approach, that which prevails in portals, the access to consumers and the brand names are as important as the content.

In the preceding chapter we discussed the existence of new forms of journalism, but when we analyze the Internet and its relations with the traditional media, in their different forms of interconnection in networks, *we are also forced to take into consideration that there are new forms of communicating information that cannot be described as journalism, for they are based on new communicational paradigms, whereby the portals are their field of action par excellence.*

As we have seen, the conjugated and economically-oriented intervention of the mass media and telecommunications companies in the Internet has not only led to the institutionalization of an instrument, the portal (although it was previously experimented with due to the need for orientation in the Internet, but now structured according to a commercial approach), but has also given to a new conception of the information production model.

Media, Memory and Filters

And I enter the fields and roomy chambers of memory, where are the treasures of countless images, imported into it from all manner of things by the senses. There is treasured up whatsoever likewise we think, either by enlarging or diminishing, or by varying in any way whatever those things which the sense hath arrived at; yea, and whatever else hath been entrusted to it and stored up, which oblivion hath not yet en-

gulfed and buried. (...) And who can tell how these images are formed,
notwithstanding that it is evident by which of the senses each has been
fetched in and treasured up?

Saint Augustine, *Of the Nature and the Amazing*
Power of Memory, Confessions, Book X.

In the preceding discussion of the accessibility of information we made reference to the illusion of comparing the Internet to a library. However, the metaphor of the library carries with it another *illusion.*

For a library is a space that registers the memory of humanity – memory in the sense of history. The Internet, in contrast, is a space of choice for non-historic memory: the memory of events, persons, ideas, and social memory. This is because, as publication is much easier on the Internet than in the traditional publishing processes, the views of events/incidents are also much more diverse. [117]

The Internet is above all a space of first-hand publication, although, to a certain extent, we also find the analytical and organized processing of facts on it.

The whole logic inherent in the historic process, i.e., the strict definition of historic facts as being of significance, whereby significance is understood as a matter of value and not of truth that accompanies the selection of what is academically or editorially acceptable and, consequently, publishable in a book, is not part of the publication rules for the Internet.

What type of memory is produced by the media in general and what are the peculiarities of the memory created by the Internet?

The answer to this question is important, for the communicative autonomy of the social subjects is not constructed solely around information and news on the current situation or on a prospective specific development.

---

[117] Heilidhe (2000) argues, the key characteristics of the Internet are the decentralization of power and the subsequent empowerment of the individual, namely through the possibility of self-publication and the individual expression of opinions. Traditionally, the cultural industry developed a set of rules to be followed by authors before their work could be published. Although the Internet enables publication of and by anyone, the exponential growth in documents on the Web also means that not everything that is published will be read by someone. For once published, the information has to be found. The Internet depends on the search engines for structuring the thousands of documents placed online daily (Heilidhe, 2000). Given the complexity of the Internet, the common citizen values help in selecting information and given that, in many cases, the search engines produce thousands of hits to a user's query, there emerges a need to find hierarchization processes for the information they provide.

Communicative autonomy is also constructed on the basis of the access to news and information on the very recent past (such as the previous week) and the historic past (from millennia ago to our present century).

For Umberto Eco there are three types of memory. The first type is organic, i.e. made of flesh and bone and managed by our brain. The second type is mineral, and humanity has known two examples of this type of memory: a few millennia ago, memory was represented by plaques of clay and stone obelisks, but the memory of computers is also mineral, as it is made of silica. We also have a third type of memory, vegetal memory, represented by the first papyruses and books made of paper. Herein we will be looking at the mineral memory provided by the Internet.

But what is memory? And why do we insist on this dimension for characterizing the formation of communicative autonomy? For Roger Silverstone (1999), memory is what is achieved through collection, be it calmly or not, and through oral testimony and shared discourse. Memory is when the private connections of the past are united to give rise to a public reading, offering an alternative vision of the reality present in the official academic records or in historic archives.

For most of the time we are not even conscious of using memory. All of our habits, knowledge and information, thought schemes, values, representations and languages are part of our memory (Horta, 2001).

Individual memory is that which we build on a certain event, whereby that construction is susceptible to direct and experienced knowledge of the event or knowledge through mediation. The same is true for the construction of social memory.

According to Fentress and Wickham (1994), social memory consists of the memories we share with others because they are relevant for us and them. This may occur in a social group context of a certain type or in informal and temporary situations.

Memory is something complex and can include everything from a highly private and spontaneous sensation, that is possibly silent and without public repercussion, to a solemn public ceremony. Memory can be both action as well as representation, for, as Connerton (1993) points out, all hints contain an element of remembrance.

Memory is at the same time both medium and message. It is social because it is acquired in a specific context, takes place in interaction and through shared practices, experiences and symbolic codes, is structured by languages and is part of the process of social reproduction (Sobral, 1999).

However, the media are traditionally removed from the definitions of social memory. For Gonçalves (1992), social memory results from the interaction between historic memory, collective memory and individual memory. [118]

That definition obscures the role of the media, which can be better understood if we introduce the concept of cultural memory. In other words, shared memory outside the formal historic context, whereby the sharing is carried out through cultural products and is impregnated with cultural significance (Sturken, 1997).

Studying the social make-up of memory is studying the acts of transfer that render possible joint memory, which, according to Horta (2001), implies considering that language and communication are indissociable from memory. [119]

Going somewhat further, we could argue, with Luhmann (1992), that only with the context can we understand the meaning of what others are trying to say to us, that our context is our memory. And in a network society characterized by a real virtuality culture (Castells 2003) and in which there is a profusion of symbolic communication spaces, the media are the context and, consequently, also our memory.

In our society, in which mediation occupies a central position in our culture, it is the media that effectively enable the sharing of events that mark the memory and confer upon the present an appearance of immediate presence and historic authority (Nora, 1990).

The media discourses, therefore, constitute mythological letters to a community (Fentress and Wickam, 1994), whereby that community can be national or international.

However, mediatized memory, as marketing managers have shown, can also be commercialized, encouraging the passive consumption of the past (Abramson, 2001). Memory has, thus, also become an object of the consumer society that sells well (Le Goff, 1992).

Memory is important because it is *that* which *we* have to fit into space and, particularly, time, both in private and in public (Silverstone, 2000).

---

[118]Historic memory refers to a process of temporal, chronological differentiation; collective memory is understood as a process of identification between social groups; and individual memory is understood as the capacity to recall events in which one was involved (Horta 2001).

[119]As Horta (2001) suggests, Bourdieu's definition (Cardoso, 1999) of *Habitus* can also be considered a type of memory socially shared by a group of individuals that share a field of action.

Ever since oral register ceased to be central in our lives, media such as the book, together with science, entered the scene to register and fix social and individual memory. However, the emergence of radio, cinema and television – and, later, the Internet – opened the doors to a space with finer borderlines as to the multiple possibilities of what is understood as being worthy of coverage by the media – in other words, the public construction of the past.

One only has to think of the historical reconstructions on television channels such as the History Channel to understand how memory is created, and also the televized coverage of war such as those in Kosovo or Afghanistan, post September 11, or even films from the US dealing with the catharsis over the Vietnam war.

The difference between the Internet and television in representing the past, or the memory, is that television airs and divulges a certain news item or programme and whoever sees it can construct their own understanding of a given event. When the broadcast is over, the register, disregarding the occasional video recording made at home, is kept in the channel's archives and is accessible only by means a bureaucratic consultation process. On the Internet, a page is created and coexists in time. A version of the events by one side of those involved coexists with that of the other side and perhaps, although less likely, also with a version with the historical and journalistic analysis of the same events.

The war in Yugoslavia in 1999, between NATO and that country, is a very interesting example (as is how sites on the World Wide Web reported on the conflict in Chechnya between Chechenians and Russians) of how or social memory of events can differ according to the medium used.

At the time of the conflict in Yugoslavia, there were countless pages on the Internet with individual pro-Yugoslavia positions, individual pro-NATO positions, the positions of the Milosevic's Yugoslav Federation government, those of Milosevic's internal opponents, those of the Yugoslav free media (Radio B92, for example), those of the pro-Milosevic media, those of the international press, those of the NATO governments and those of NATO itself (Horvath, 1999 and Pantic, 1998).

Depending on the order of the hits for a search on a search engine page or portal, one is presented with varying visions of the conflict.

Obviously one can argue that if a person is really interested, they can look for the other side's perspective and not limit themselves to reading one side only. This is true. But precisely herein lies the difference between the Internet and other media. Not only do the users have the possibility of searching for information themselves, but the pages they choose to consult to form their vision of the past also depend on their own individual assessment.

That is fundamentally different to how television works. Television constructs a public view and divulges that view. We can debate it, but it is what is available.

On the Internet there exist various possible constructions of memory, or at least there is material available for a greater number of visions of the present and the past.

Through a combination of luck (in finding a certain page), the criteria of the search engine used, whether or not a page is still on the net and the personal assessment of the events, users construct *their* vision of *public memory* of past events.

The question we cannot answer is, over time, which pages will continue to be available and, consequently, what the possible combinations are for the diverse perspectives made available.

As we have seen in the preceding paragraph, there is, however, one characteristic the Internet and libraries and archives have in common: in the Internet it is also not possible to speak of memory without speaking of forgetting.

As Fausto Colombo (2000) points out, the information technologies are not the solution for overcoming loss of memory. Just like their predecessors – from the book to television – the new technologies are neither lasting nor stable. The Internet is a space made up of an archive dimension, but where, at the same time, the forgetting, deleting and disappearance of information also coexist. And just as the works in the Alexandria Library did not survive to be handed down to us, a lot of what we produce and visualize on the Internet will be lost. The information technologies are, therefore, both technologies of memory and of memory loss.

The perennity of information supports has always been a constant in the history of humanity, from the book to the computer disk. What the Internet has led to is that once again we have questions about forgetting and memory, but now these questions are raised in the light of a technology, about which we often build a false idea of infallibility.

The Internet has given many the possibility of reaching audiences identical – in both numbers and interest – to those offered by publishers operating in the global market, but, in doing so, it has not solved the question of how to make the communication last in time.

As the result of a decision by the author, the site administrator or a mishap on the part of a designer without "backup copies", what exists today on a website may not be available tomorrow. Servers and pages are deleted, changed and new versions posted.

If the memory of statuary, cities, oral cultures has gradually been integrated by us into other supports such as the book, film and even CDs, the truth is that, in addition to the fallibility and limited extension of the information indexed in the search engines, there is no systematization of the contents on the Internet to this day.

But would it be possible to determine the number of pages a user can expect to have access to?

Lawrence and Giles (1999) also analyzed the coverage of the various search engines and concluded that not only was the coverage limited (at most, 1/3 of the total information publicly available on the Internet), but also that there was a trend towards a decrease in the coverage the larger the Internet got.

Updating this analysis, using data presented by the online service, Showdown (2001), we can conclude that the trends seem to have remained the same. The best coverage of the World Wide Web is provided by the Google search engine, which represents slightly less than 1/3 of the total dimension calculate for the World Wide Web. The same ratio of coverage for HTML pages can be found in the .pt domain.

The dimension of the World Wide Web in the .pt domain that was directly consultable in 2002 was approximately 1,500,000 HTML pages, or 27% of what in reality existed.

As mentioned above, one of the dimensions of characterization of what memory on the Internet is made up of the type of information made available. Not all the information is of interest to everyone. The reasons for, and criteria applied to searching for information on the Internet are as varied as those for the publication of the information.

If the diversity of contents on the Internet is a given fact and if it is also true that whoever looks for information using the most common and functional tool available – the search engines – has their choice limited to a part of the available universe, can we then speak of new gatekeepers on the Internet?

Before answering this question we must first define what, traditionally, the concept of gatekeeping is. In his work Mass Communication Theories (2001), Mauro Wolf analyzes the news construction processes, of which gatekeeping is a part.

According to Wolf, filtering information in the mass media is controlled either by objective rules systems or by gatekeepers or guardians. The latter are individuals or groups that have the power to decide whether or not a given piece of information can be published or divulged or not.

The merit of the first studies on gatekeeping, particularly that by White (Wolf, 2001) is that they made it possible to identify where the point was, within the news production apparatus, where filtering was carried out institutionally and explicitly. The second wave of studies on gatekeeping focused on the idea of selection, in the context of a hierarchical process and in connection with a complex feedback network.

Gatekeeping in the mass media encompasses, thus, all forms of control of information that could determine the decision to codify messages, select a message, formation of the message, divulge, programme or totally or partially exclude a message (Wolf, 2001).

A third phase of communication studies in the area of gatekeeping has centred on the undesired distortion in the production of news, namely through social interaction in the context of bureaucratic and economic organizations.

As Wolf (2001) puts it, in the organizational context the mass media are governed by values that tend to have a conditioning effect on the editorial activity, namely: institutional authority and sanctions; the feeling of obligation and esteem in relation to superiors; aspirations of professional mobility; the existence of fidelity between groups; the pleasant nature of the work and the fact that the news item in itself has become a value (Wolf, 2001: 182).

We can thus define gatekeeping as the function of selection and editing that the news report undergoes until it achieve the final status of news report within the news organizations. The distributors of information have to decide what events to accept through the "gates" of the media based on their level of newsworthiness and other criteria. Central questions are the criteria and the logics systematically applied by journalists and publishers in performing the role of gatekeeper (Wolf, 2000; McQuail, 2000).

Taking the above definition as a starting point, to what extent can it be reformulated in the light of a new medium such as the Internet? A medium, as we have seen, where information is produced not only by journalists, where access to the information involves new filtering logics, such as those offered by the portals, and with the possible development of new competences validation of information and its reception by the end users.

For Williams and Carpini (1999), the traditional dimension of gatekeeping is part of what is known as the social theory of responsibility, to which it introduced, or reaffirmed, three significant conceptual distinctions. The first is the separation between news media and entertainment media. The second is based on the distinction between fact and opinion and the third on the separation between public and mediatizable and political elites.

As Williams and Carpini (1999) point out, the theory of social responsibility conceives the inevitability of a private centralized media system and a public system that is not very developed in terms of civic participation, thus transferring the civic responsibility to a new information elite created around the news construction process.

However, the Clinton/Lewinsky case was not reported on first hand by any of the major newspapers or television stations. It emerged in a World Wide Web page managed by Matt Drudge. Examples of how the mediatization of the Clinton/Lewinsky case and the non-editorial management of the information could indicate the failure of the gatekeeping model with the appearance of a medium such as the Internet. Thanks to its technological characteristics and the appropriation of it by the users, the Internet is evolving towards a system in which there are no gates for access to the information, thus short-circuiting the logic of the traditional construction of news itself. The conclusion was obvious to Williams and Carpini (1999) – if there are no gates there are no gatekeepers.

However, that may only be a half truth, for the gatekeeping procedures may not be undergoing an erosive process at all.

On the contrary, gatekeeping may be on the rise again, adapting to the characteristics of the Internet as a medium, which also promote new communication modalities.

Internet gatekeeping will perhaps challenge the social responsibility theory model only in the sense that, in addition to the traditional gatekeeping system in the offline media, a parallel system is developed for the Internet.

The Internet as a socio-cultural system (Colombo, 2000) introduces new information producers, new mediation processes such as the portals and their search systems, and new necessities for the public and producers of information in terms of information validation. This point of view is seconded, for example, by Hartley (2004), when he argues that the search engines can be understood as digital gatekeepers. The search engines have the function of deciding what information is relevant to the search query

entered by the user. The search engines may not be linked to personal ideologies but they are the product of the structural and organizational procedures of those providing them. Also, they may be subject to legislation that
stipulates filtering of information, meaning that they perform the role of
gatekeeper on behalf of the State (Hartley, 2004).

The Internet gatekeeping situation becomes a more sensitive analysis
element when we recognize that, for reasons of its technical quality and
market options, one search engine, Google.com, now has practically a monopoly on personalized online searches.

An historical analysis of the development of the search engines shows
that the once leading search engine, AltaVista, made the decision to become a portal and thus did not invest in the improvement of its Internet
search algorithms (Brandt, 2002). AltaVista offered its users many forms
of narrowing in the results of searches, most notably the possibility of
combining Boolean logic operators (such as AND, OR, NOT, etc.). Nevertheless, the users normally focus on the first twenty hits and not on
the many thousands of others that a search may produce (Brandt, 2002).
Google realized this and launched a search engine project based on the
Pagerank algorithm. [120]

There is a clear notion of the different types of objective criteria that
characterize the way in which search engines function. Normally, the criteria can be three types: popularity of the link (present in Google, amongst
others); page characteristics [121] and content analysis [122] (Brandt, 2002).
Each method has its own *raison d'être* and there are search engines that
use only one criterion or a combination of several.

---

[120]Pagerank is based on the decentralized structure of the Internet and on the existence of hypertextuality
for forming a value indicator associated with a given page. Thus, Google interprets a link from page
A to page B as a positive vote on the value of the latter. But Google looks for more than the number
of votes or links that a page receives from other pages. Its ranking is also depends on the page that
originated that "vote". The "votes" of pages that already, in themselves, have a high ranking produce
a more important vote for the definition of the final ranking. The Google research and indexation are
carried out on a monthly basis, whereby the sites with a higher Pageranking rating are the first to be
examined and are also those analyzed in most detail, in terms of their internal hierarchical structure,
and also the most rapidly.

[121]The page characteristics used in the classification include the font size, title, headings, anchored text,
word frequency, word proximity, file name, folder name and domain name.

[122]The content analysis generally takes the form of the creation of classification clusters associated with
a specific page in two or more categories. This allows for a search in data with a prior classification.

So, what is *Internet gatekeeping* and how has it influenced the communicative autonomy of the subjects?

To answer that question we must look at three dimensions: 1) gathering information; 2) news production; 3) and information validation.

These three dimensions, in the field of the Internet, are subject to restrictions introduced by three factors: the information available online; the quantity of information accessible; and the quality of that information.

The information quality and quantity aspects and the way to deal with them are, likewise, fundamental for reminding one that not everything can be centred on the need to give access to the new information and communication technologies. In addition to computer skills, critical and deductive thinking are basis tools for the diverse dimensions of social interaction in the network society.

At the beginning of the new century and millennium, one of the central questions is that of the quantity of information available. How do we look for information on the Internet and how should we orient ourselves, faced with the wide range of options?

Here we have to look at an analysis of the historic evolution of the Internet itself: from a non-regulated space to the regulation imposed by the need to render e-commerce viable and sustain the new economy.

If an perspective of mutual help presided over the emergence of the first search and classification services on the Internet, the commercial approach soon took hold of most of those services, as exemplified by the cases of directories such as Yahoo! and SAPO in Portugal. Initially created in the university environment, they later became central elements in what came to be known as the new economy, with stock market acquisitions or gains of considerable dimension.

What drove the commercial interest in the search engine services was the same reason that led to their creation: the value attributed to orientation on the Internet.

Perception of the value of orientation on the Internet, led, by means of a commercial strategy of consolidation of the presence in the new economy market and the need to bind consumers in their access to the Internet, to the emergence of the portals.

When they emerged, the portals were not mere search engines or information directories. They have commercial value due to the fact that they attract a large number of users, meaning that commerce was added to the initial functionalities of news services and news. But it is not enough to understand the central role of the portals in the management of information, one also has to bear in mind that the portals also act as gatekeepers, as filters – both positive and negative. A search carried out through a portal is done so on the basis of valuation or devaluation of hits.

And when the search uses only one engine worldwide, a result of commercial agreements between portals and search engines, the question of gatekeeping gains a more central dimension in Internet analyses.

Although they often do not know it, the users are confronted with a limited space and with a strong correlation between World Wide Web pages with references to one another. The greater the number of links to a certain page, the greater the probability is of that page being returned as a hit on a search engine. Finally, one must also say that many of the search engines themselves readjust the hits hierarchically depending on options made in previous searches. The use of popularity rankings for the purpose of choosing hits returned in searches tends towards making already popular pages even more popular and the less popular pages even less visible. Users also are often not aware of the temporal limitation of information (Wouters et al., 2004).

All search engines delete their oldest documents and replace them with documents that have a date stamp closer to the present. This leads to a loss of information in an historical dimension, meaning that the search engines essentially reflect the present and not the past. They thus become unreliable instruments for collecting information with the aim of reconstructing a certain moment or event in history. And, in a temporal analysis, they are also limited to the use of pages that have a concrete indication of when they were published, such as an issue of a newspaper.

This loss of information is not the result of a technical instability but an indexation option. As each search engines operates according to a different time clock, i.e. the collection and indexation of information is carried out at different times, the probability of the existence of time black holes that are not covered by any engine, is high (Wouters et al., 2004).

A third dimension, and one that also goes unnoticed to the user, is the commercial self-censorship or that imposed by the State on the search engines. There are, therefore, other limitations to the indexation other than purely technical ones.

In a study of the Google.com search engine and its national sites Google.fr and Google.de (in France and German, respectively), Zittrain and Edlman (2002) found that hundreds of thousands of sites that can be searched in the US cannot be searched by users in France and Germany.

The majority of these sites are racist in nature or deny that the Holocaust took place. The reason for these differences is that Google wishes to avoid possible legal action against itself as the search engine owner.

Being available on the Internet is not the same thing as being accessible to the user, for even if the readers know what they are looking for, they are dependent on the choices of the information producers, the search engine creators and the marketing teams of the search engines themselves, which specify the criteria for presenting hits.

Of the three conditioning factors that are responsible for the way information is gathered, news is produced and information is validated on the Internet, two have already been analyzed herein: the information available online and the quantity of information accessible.

The third conditioning factor is the quality of information, which, as it is a product of value judgement, to the user or the mediator, introduces a notion of high arbitrariness in any analysis.

However, it is possible to characterize the mechanisms that determine quality. On the Internet, the reasons for publishing something can be very diverse. That is the reason (together with the cost related with the task and the interests of whomever is looking for the information) why most of the portals do not effect a prior assessment of the information they make available.

The portals merely follow the traditional criteria of validation for the news articles they publish, for they are produced by journalists or taken from news agencies. Beyond this, the information they contain, even that existing in organized lists on subjects, is not validated by specialists: healthcare pages, pages on nutrition/diets, on building bombs, literary criticism or news originating from purely online publications.

Even when a user provides an URL for registration in a directory or search engine, in most cases the only form of validation is theme-based and is not concerned with the veracity, reasonableness or backing for the information.

Some services do, however, evaluate topics. They do not aspire to identifying all html pages on the World Wide Web on a specific topic, but only those considered the most important. They are the so-called Thematic Portals. They are less in number and, normally, not as well known to the general public. These types of services that cover specific topics or groups of topics rely on human intervention in the information organization process and endeavour to guarantee maximum quality of the results.

In most cases, the normal Internet user or the professional user, only has themselves to rely on for the evaluation of the information available on a site.

Although the reception theories on information on the Internet are not yet consolidated, we can rely on studies on other media and the information validation and compare them to the Internet reality. We can also use the experiences from studies on television as starting points for the study of the validation of information on the Internet. Despite the fact that it is interactive and includes an information production/consumption dimension, the Internet has essentially taken on many of the characteristics elaborated upon in the works published on reception theories by the members of the Glasgow *Media* Group. For example, Greg Philo (1999) points out the role of direct experience, the use of logic, individual/group value systems and source credibility as dimensions influencing acceptance or not of the message issued. [123]

Any one of these dimensions can help us to understand the factors that can influence the users' filtering of the information with which they contact on the Internet.

However, there is still one question left unanswered: the fact that the reception theories are dedicated to a certain type of information: that of the traditional media that tends to present a generalist character, aimed at a user used to interacting with a small number of alternatives.

The Internet, because of its inherent features, presents more segmented and less generalist information at the same time as not having the quality of its information guaranteed by any entity in particular. It is also characterized by an extremely sensitive regulation system.

These characteristics mean that some of the responsibility for validation of the information is transferred to the user. In the traditional mass media this role was performed by the State or bodies with public responsibility.

---

[123]The role of *experience* refers to the greater or lesser direct experience with the reality to which the received message relates. When there is direct contact with the even, the information is, as a rule, questioned more often than when there is no direct knowledge. The use of *logic* refers to the perception of a previous message considered to have little credibility or a contradiction that may result in rejection of the message.

The *group/individual value systems* play their part in the event of a message being removed from their convictions. In such a situation it can be easily rejected by the recipient.

Finally, the *source credibility* refers to the fact that the users assumes their role as credibilizers through the trust in the information sources they have built up in their relations with them and through the communication that they establish with their social networks.

In the traditional mass media, credibility precedes or accompanies, step by step, the information or entertainment event with which the user contacts. When we think of BBC, TVI, CNN, RTP or RAI, we attribute to them a certain degree of credibility. In the case of the Internet, the process is somewhat different.

The credibility and acceptance of information is constructed by the users as they interact with the information. If we wanted to hierarchize the reception dimensions proposed by Philo (1999), we could suggest that the role of direct experience and the individual/group value systems is, perhaps, the one that could be most easily transported to the Internet reality, whereas the use of the logic and source credibility have less influence, for the possibility of constructing, over time, a causal relationship between facts becomes less plausible. The search for information is not carried out based on the same sources and the construction of its credibility on the Internet involves social networks inherent in the Internet or prior evaluation by another entity that is external to the Internet.

We have described what the collection and validation of information on the Internet is and how these are influenced by technology, economic options and the users themselves. We have partly answered the question what Internet gakekeeping is – I say partly, because we still have to analyze the relationship established between the mass media and the Internet in constructing memory.

As an example of the aforementioned, the question that arises is that of knowing, when we are looking for information on a certain topic, whether what we find is an *opinion* or *news*?

If we take into account probabilities – because there are more HTML pages of other types than pages containing news – a person who is looking for information on a specific topic on the Internet is likely to find less news on the pages of newspapers and radio and television stations and more information, characterized as opinion, coming from organizations and individual. Could this deduction be correct?

On the basis of an analysis carried out by Cardoso and Morgado (2002) on the functioning of the search engines attached to the larger Portuguese generalist portals (SAPO, Clix and IOL) and a study of the representativeness of the media in the hits returned by the portals (Cardoso, 2003), we can identify the starting point necessary for the analysis of the contribution of the Internet, through information obtained from search engines, to the construction of social memory.

The conclusion one can draw is that memory of a certain event on the Internet is, above all, supplied by organizations and the media. In other words, the information a user has access to when carrying out a search on a search engine is essentially supplied by organizations and the media and not by individual persons.

The analysis of the results of searches on eleven news affairs topics on the search engines in three Portuguese portals (all of which use Google for international searches in English and Portuguese) showed that 60% of the hits were produced by organizations, approximately 30% by the mass media migrated online and only 10% by individual sites or blogs. On a conceptual plane, the Internet offers all, both private persons and organizations, the possibility of expressing opinions on certain topics, but in reality the high presence of hits originating from newspapers and radio and television stations offered by the search engines is not in proportion to the number of media entities present online. Hits for these entities are proportionately much higher in comparison to other producers of information.

An experimental analysis conducted in 2001 on an international topic, the Zapatista movement (Cardoso, 2003), had endeavoured to understand the importance of the media in search engine hits.[124] The findings were that the majority of the search engines had more hits related with media bodies, i.e. news (9 out of 15) than links to personal pages or opinion pages (4 out of 15). Of the 15 news references selected, 6 were also used in the hits of other search engines.

A comparative analysis of the search engines in Portuguese ISPs, in terms of international searches, likewise identified certain peculiarities. The number of repetitions was much higher, with the first hit being identical in 5 of the 6 portals. Nevertheless, the hits did feature a greater number of pages from organizations and private persons than from the media.

Although this analysis was just a small exemplary test of the role of filtering in search engines, it did raise fundamental questions, such as access to diversity of information and the positions of the diverse persons/sides involved and balance between the information produced by individuals and that presented by the online media.

---

[124] The EZLN (Ejército Zapatista de Libertación Nacional) of Sub-Commander Marcos that is active in Chiapas (México) and, since 1994, has been running a high media profile campaign promoting its actions via the Internet (Castells, 2004).

Despite the fact that there were in 2002, 4,923 newspapers, 4,090 magazines, 2,158 radio stations and 1,428 televisions stations with an online presence (Sparks, 2002), their incidence in the hits returned on search engines for certain topics was much higher than their per cent representation on the Internet.

Since 2001, the search engine panorama has changed substantially in Portugal and the world, due to a concentration of the offer. This situation has led to the existence of almost one single choice for portals for national and global searches – Google.

The choice of topics for this new analysis was based on a number of topics, both national and international, that made the news in 2002. The results for that period were compared to those for the period between 1997 and 2001 and one particular defining event in the Portuguese reality of the 1960s/70s, the colonial wars.

The group of topics chosen for the analysis is shown in the table below (Table 6.4). It includes subjects as diverse as the Nobel Prize for Literature for José Saramago, September 11, the alleged corruption scandal at the Universidade Moderna in Lisbon and President Lula da Silva's victory in the Brazilian elections.

The pattern for the presentation of information on the Internet seems to always follow a hierarchical logic, favouring, in first place, organizations, then the media and, finally, web pages or blogs written by individual persons – a hit presentation model that can be termed OMP, for the initial of each group of hits (Table 6.5)

This is a hierarchy that is structured around the presentation, first, of a greater number of hits from organizations with a direct interest in the search topic, be they non-profit organizations (NGOs), private companies or the State, followed by the media in second place and then individual persons expressing their own opinions on current affairs.

Table 6.4 – Table summarizing the topics researched in search engines (2002)

Search theme	Geographic dimension	Thematic dimension	Time dimension
"September 11"	International	Terrorism and war	Recent past (2001)
"War in Kosovo"	International	Terrorism and war	Recent past (1999)
"Sinking of Prestige, Galicia"	Portugal and International	Environmental catastrophe	Present (as at 2002)
"Death of Princess Diana"	International	Social and cultural	Recent past (1997)
"Pope's visit to Cuba"	International	Political	Recent past (1998)
"Lula's victory in Brazil"	International	Political	Present (as at 2002)
"Independence of East Timor"	Portugal and International	Political	Present (as at 2002)
"Nobel Prize for Saramago"	Portugal and International	Social and cultural	Recent past (1998)
"Universidade Moderna case"	Portugal	Political	Present (as at 2002)
"Casa Pia scandal"	Portugal	Political	Present (as at 2002)
"Port. Africa/colonial wars"	Portugal	Terrorism and war	Past (1960s/70s)

Despite the fact that the values relating to the media are lower than those in the analysis on the Zapatista movement, their online representativeness is, in percentage terms, much higher than the number of mass media presences on the Internet, so that one can conclude that there is a certain bias in the provision of online information that tends to favour media-sourced hits in searches on topics dealt with by them offline.

The reason for this number of hits in part has to do with the search engines' algorithms. It also the influence of the choices of those search engines by the users, given that people obviously continue to want information verified, evaluate and published by professionals.

Despite the diversity of information available on the Internet, many of the more popular addresses are those that edit, organize and manage information on behalf of the consumers. These are normally associated with the media, such as newspapers and television stations (Hartley, 2004). In other words, there are topics in the news, for which, even when one turns to the Internet for complementary information on them, the search hit results continue to be quantitatively dominated by information produced by the media and made available online by them.

This tendency is even greater when the topics are international ones and the searches are carried out with the aim of finding hits in Portuguese, for the probability of opinion pages existing in Portuguese is normally inferior to the occurrence of news pages.

Table 6.5 – Classification of the entities found in the first 25 hits, by online search carried out

Search topic	Organizations	Personal	*Media*	Date
September 11	57.50%	3.33%	39.17%	Recent past (2001)
War in Kosovo	72.82%	3.88%	23.30%	Recent past (1999)
Port. Africa/colonial wars	87.00%	8.00%	5.00%	Past (1960s/70s)
Nobel Prize for Saramago	58.65%	21.15%	20.19%	Recent past (1998)
Death of Princess Diana	47.52%	25.74%	26.73%	Recent past (1997)
Pope's visit to Cuba	83.33%	7.14%	9.52%	Recent past (1998)
Lula's victory in Brazil	44.66%	0.00%	55.34%	Present (as at 2002)
Universidade Moderna case	44.83%	20.69%	34.48%	Present (as at 2002)
Casa Pia scandal	29.03%	9.68%	61.29%	Present (as at 2002)
Sinking of the Prestige	80.00%	3.33%	16.67%	Present (as at 2002)
Independence of East Timor	85.00%	10.00%	5.00%	Present (as at 2002)

Another trend in the area of search engine hits related to the media is that the older the time of occurrence of an event, the less reference there will be to it in media pages.

However, this time dimension is also affected by other variables, such as the topic in question. Thus, topics that further civic involvement and participation by ecological organizations, human rights movement and the like (two examples are the sinking of the Prestige oil tanker off Galicia and the independence of East Timor) have a greater probability of the proportion of media news stories being less than the information published by organizations.

As far as blog pages or pages produced by individuals are concerned, the probability of greater presence for them in the search engine hits seems to be related to the personalization logic. Mediatized topics whose exposition is based on a celebrity dimensions, such as the Death of Princess Diana, the award of the Nobel Prize for Literature to José Saramago or the alleged corruption scandal involving the Portuguese Minister of Defence, Paulo Portas in the Universidade Moderna case, result in a greater proportion of hits for the Web on the basis of individuals not identified as belonging to organizations. [125]

---

[125]For Hartley (2004) *celebrity* is the semiotics of identity. It is only found in societies where identity is

While it is clear that it is the media (the media with a simultaneous online and offline presence) that produce the most hits obtained on search engines, the situation is less clear as far as organizations and individual persons are concerned. Who are they? Can we identify any analysis pattern in the hits?

Table 6.6 – Organisations and persons identified in the hits obtained in searches with search engines

Search topic	Identification
September 11	Support funds; education institutions analyzing the events
War in Kosovo	Anti-war activism
Port. Africa/colonial wars	Education institutions analyzing the events; veterans
Nobel Prize for Saramago	Persons who relate to his work
Death of Princess Diana	Admirers
Pope's visit to Cuba	Catholic organizations (pro), official organizations in Cuba (pro), exile organizations (against)
Lula's victory in Brazil	Parties and companies
Universidade Moderna case	Parties and trade unions; bloggers taking sides
Casa Pia scandal	NGOs of international activists
Sinking of the Prestige	NGOs (ecology)
Independence of East Timor	NGOs (supporting East Timor cause)

The preceding table (Table 6.6) is organized according to the topic dimension of searches carried out. As one can see, the diversity is substantial.

The factor common to all organizations is their direct involvement in the events – from the Catholic organizations and exile groups in the question of the Pope's visit to Cuba to the various NGOs involved in denouncing the sinking of the Prestige and to the criticism of the issue of paedophilia in the Casa Pia scandal.

---

an important socio-cultural and political question. Celebrities are individuals who gain notoriety for their identity in the media. Generally speaking, they may come from any field – music, sport, fashion, crime, cinema, television, radio and reality television participants.

As a descriptive category, *celebrity* would not normally include, for example, politicians in power or members of royal families. The concept of *celebrity* differs from that of *star* as the latter is considered the product of a specific environment, the film industry. The construction of celebrities is based on matters considered to be everyday or common (Hartley, 2004).

In addition to the differences already exposed with regard to the celebrity topic dimension, the greatest differences in the field of organizations are given in relation to the topic "War and terrorism", for which many hits are related to education institutions analyzing the events.

It would seem that, in this topic field, time differences do have such an influence on the hits relating to education institutions, as can be concluded from the comparison of the results for the September 11 attacks and the Portuguese colonial wars.

Given that the language the pages are written in is a factor to be taken into consideration in our analyses, it is interesting to note that worldwide searches offer the user more hits than national searches even when the topic is a domestic one.

Table 6.7 – Total hits for each search topic in 2004 (using Google)

Search topic 2004	In Portuguese	Worldwide
September 11	307,000	24,600,000
War in Kosovo	27,900	2,110,000
Port. Africa/colonial wars	56,300	147,000
Nobel Prize for Saramago	9,550	56,100
Death of Princess Diana	4,780	441,000
Pope's visit to Cuba	58,400	218,000
Lula's victory in Brazil	164,000	51,900
Universidade Moderna case	133,000	533,000
Casa Pia	29,400	38,800
Sinking of the Prestige	3,010	11,300
Independence of East Timor	18,500	515,000

Other important data on the role of language are the number of users who mother tongue is Portuguese, the number of sites in Portuguese and the distribution of the Internet in Portuguese-speaking countries.

According to GlobalReach (2002), there were approximately 25.7 million Brazilian, Portuguese and Portuguese-American Internet users in 2003 – approximately 29% for a population of some 10 million in Portugal, and 7.8% for a population of 184 million in Brazil (Cardoso et al., 2004; Nielsen NetRatings, 2002).

Furthermore, the number of public sites in English in 2002 accounted for 73% of the total information available on the Internet, as opposed to a percentage of users speaking English as their mother tongue of 37%. As for sites in Portuguese, they represent only 1% of the information available on the Internet, while the number of Portuguese speakers with Internet access makes up 3.1% of the total users. The sites/users proportion index for Portuguese i s 0.2, while for English it is 1.9 (OCLC and GlobalReach, cited in Castells 2003).

Table 6.8 – Internet users per 1,000 inhabitants in Portuguese speaking territories (%)

Country	Source	Internet users per 1,000 inhabitants
Portugal	UNDP	193.5
Macao	ITU	225.0
Brazil	UNDP	82.2
São Tomé and Príncipe	UNDP	72.8
Cape Verde	UNDP	36.4
Mozambique	UNDP	2.7
Angola	UNDP	2.9

Source: UNDP, Human Development Report 2002 and ITU 2002. Note: According to data provided by Timor Telecom, the number of East Timorese users is 1,000 in a population of approximately 900,000.

Considering the set of cases presented here, all of which were well consolidated by the traditional mass media, the hypothesis one can raise on the searching for information online is that the number of pages presented by a search engine is greater when there is civic participation prior to the event in itself.

One example of this is the fact that the sinking of the Prestige produces more search engine hits than a case of political corruption, such as the Universidade Modern case, or a paedophilia case, such as Casa Pia. For there is a longer tradition of organized activism in environmental issues than in the combat against political corruption or the sexual abuse of children and minors in Portugal.

Similar to the portals, the central role of the search engines in managing the social memory one has of a certain event, is its function of filter based on options of valuation and devaluation of occurrence and connection universes.

So, what is Internet gatekeeping? Internet gatekeeping is the relationship between the presence of search engines and the way in which information is provided and evaluated by the Internet user. If we take this to be true, then how can we detect the influences of these changes in the information practices of the citizens?

On the one hand, in the way the relationship with the Internet's information dimension is altered, for the portals produce a new reality as to what the Internet is. With the portals, the Internet has ceased to be an anarchic space of information and, through the *prior classification of experience,* it provides the information available that should inform that classification of the experience (Silverstone, 1999), a process that results from the emulation of the logics of the traditional mass media, such as the press and television. On the other hand, through associations and promotion of the use of search engines, the way in which *the Internet helps to construct the social memory* is also altered. These are the two ways in which the mass media and the telecommunications companies have sought to change, and, to a certain extent, have changed the Internet.

Internet gatekeeping is, thus, a product of the rise of the portals and the search engines and the way we appropriate them.

This is a fundamental concept for understanding how the memory dimension of communicative autonomy is built today.

In the last few chapters we have analyzed how the media system is organized in the network society. We have also sought to define entertainment and information meta-systems and what the role of the Internet is in them.

Following that line of argument, we have sought to define how the Internet and mass media establish their networks of interdependence and how the telecommunications companies have played a central role in the development of the portals, what we define as Internet gatekeeping and also its influence on the communicative autonomy of the subjects.

However, we have analyzed the uses of the mass media and the Internet as if the media diets and matrixes were identical for all subjects. That is not the case. And that differentiation is manifested in the way in which different generations deal with the media, resulting in differentiated conditions for the creation of communicative autonomy. The analysis and understanding of the phenomenon of generational differentiation and its relationship with the establishment of communicative autonomy and citizenship management is the subject of the next chapter.

7. Media and Citizenship in the Network Society

As Roger Silverstone (2004) and Manuel Castells (2002) argue, *reality* in the discourse of the last three decades of the 20th century has been transformed, and not only by the countless events experienced by those who participated in them in the first person – from the Cuba crisis to the fall of the Berlin wall and from Tiananmen to Seattle.

Our *reality* has also been transformed because a new form of perceiving it took form under the cover of a *culture of real virtuality* (Castells, 2002).

The culture of our everyday life is today a mixture of the physical and the virtual (Silverstone, 2004) or, as Thompson (1995) describes it, everyday life is now a complex of mediations, from the face to face to the quasi face to face.

Our experience of the world is framed by electronic *mediation*, so that our everyday life is a product of the experienced and the represented (Silverstone, 2004).

At the beginning of the 21st century, the media provide us with the symbolic space that is fundamental for the development of democracy. But it is a space with rules established, on the one hand, by the States' regulation instruments and, on the other, by the joint profit making and non-profit making interests (Cardoso, 2003, Castells, 2004).

It is a space whose functioning requires information on the facts, i.e. news, provided by the media, and information on the "state of opinion", provided by surveys that "construct a permanent representation of the public opinion" (Wolton, 1995).

It is a symbolic space in permanent mutation, brought about by the way the new technologies that emerge are domesticated, i.e. how the media matrixes (Ortoleva, 2002) of the citizens are formed, together with how the media diets (Colombo, 2004) mark the fruition of the different technological components and contents involved.

This mutation is visible in the way that the Internet and SMS messages, together with television, the print media and radio, have given rise to new forms of fruition of information and entertainment, but also the way that they enabled the emergence of new forms of individualized opinion and mass protest making use of interpersonal communication technologies (such as the mobile phone) and the way that the Internet allows for the organization of street protest and criticism of politicians and entrepreneurs (Castells, 2004).

The question that we must look at is that of understanding to what extent the media– through the form in which they offer us the basic conditions for us to mould the symbolic space of participation and, consequently, the construction of our communicative autonomy – influence the way in which our citizenship is carried out through our daily mediated civic practices.

We know that, to a large extent, civic participation levels have to do with factors such as the education level of the populations and the trust in others. But to what extent can different ways of assimilating, domesticating, making use of and observing the media mean different appropriations in their use in the exercise of citizenship?

In other words, to what point does generational sharing of ways of understanding the world through the media and our understanding or, if one prefers, literacy of the functionalities associated with the media (Mansell, 2001), influence how we position ourselves in the symbolic space to exercise active citizenship?

Mediation of Citizenship and Informational Literacy

The media are our connection between the lived and the represented. They are part of our daily life and one of the forms – together with others such as the experience of proximity with our families, our colleagues, in school or at work – that frame our experience and our identity, and help us to give meaning to life (Castells, 2004 and Silverstone, 2004).

However, accepting this role of the media in our connection with the world and in our capacity to lead our daily lives has a price: accepting this role of the media as part of the representation of daily life means that it is difficult for us to live without the media (Silverstone, 2004). In other words, the exercise of citizenship is more and more a combination of the mediated and the face to face.

In all its complexity of direct and mediated interactions, this exercise of citizenship, depends on the development of an adequate critical nature so that, when necessary in everyday life, we can place outside those structures (Silverstone, 2004), given that not always do the images, sounds and writing transmit a mediation of the reality free of noise, biased presumptions or interpretations based on some kind of common sense.

As Silverstone (2004) points out, we can abandon the field, turn our backs to the media images, sounds and texts but we cannot, without great effort and difficulty, go against them.

Furthermore, citizenship in the network society also depends on command of the instruments that enable us to deal with the media as one more natural language, or on the development of a literacy that goes beyond its more traditional definition.

Traditionally, literacy has been taken as meaning the real skills of reading, writing and arithmetic (Benavente et al., 1996; Gomes et al., 2001, 2003), i.e. the capacities of processing written information in everyday situations. [126]

However, this is not a definition that fits in with a society in which written mediation is only one of the many forms of mediation in the representation of everyday life.

According to the American Library Association (ALA, 2004), literacy should be understood in a more generic sense. Proceeding from its definition, we can suggest that *informational literacy* be defined as a set of capacities required of individuals with a view to recognizing when a piece of

---

[126]Literacy is not, and never was, a personal attribute or an ideologically inert skill that can only be acquired by individual person. Nor is it a mere technology, although it does require a means of production – both physical (pen and paper, computer and network) and social (a recognizes system of symbols or alphabet and a form of transmitting the knowledge necessary to manipulate it). (Hartley 2004).

information is necessary and them having the capacity to locate, evaluate and use the information efficiently.

In short, a literate person should be able to determine what type of information is necessary and useful, access it effectively and efficiently, evaluate the information and its sources critically, incorporate it into their knowledge base, use it to achieve specific objects and understand the economic, legal, social and ethical dimensions that condition its use. Although the ALA does not affirm it expressly, that is a concept of literacy that goes beyond writing and can apply even to media that function in flux (Williams, 1999), such as television. For, as Basili (2003) points out, there is a growing proliferation of information sources and multiple means of accessing them. [127]

In this, the *Information Age,* in which we witness the development of multidimensional processes of social and technological transformation, marking the emergence of a new social paradigm – the network society – in which the gathering, processing and sharing of information constitute the main forms of generating wealth (Castells, 2002), both the full exercise of citizenship and economic success are equally dependent on the informational literacy of the individuals. For, both for decodifying and acting in the political field and for perceiving the needs of clients and understanding the weak signs of change in the markets (Mendonça et al., 2004) it is necessary to analyze the information, understand how it is managed and master the information and communication management instruments.

Given this context, in which the informational strategies adopted by the diverse social agents constitute one of the most determinant forms of exercising power in modern times (Castells, 2001 and Silverstone, 2002), it makes sense to look at the media, in the broadest sense of the term, as an element whose analysis is extremely important for understanding citizenship (Webster, 2001 and Tarrow, 1998).

First and foremost, the development of a public opinion informed by the media plays a decisive role in the definition of political rights, of pluralism and in the creation of a public sphere (Pakulski, 1995: 73) – a *sine*

---

[127]Literacy came to be associated with writing and normally it does not apply to the deciphering of audiovisual media such as television. One of the reasons for this was the fact that, for the majority of people, such literacy was reduced to the capacity to read television and not produce it. However, with film cameras becoming cheaper and cheaper and the diffusion of software and Internet access, media literacy and info-literacy, as amply disseminated forms of bilateral communication, are already with us (Hartley 2004).

qua non condition for the survival of the media themselves and an essential link between the political instances and the citizens (Melucci, 1995). The fact that the mass media constitute the medium through which the majority of citizens establish contact with the public sphere contributes to that scenario. The very awareness of certain social problems is often the result of the assimilation and interpretation, by the media, of specific situations (Neveu, 1996), giving them visibility and incorporating them into the political agenda, thus altering the political field (Crook, 1992 and Gibbins, 1999). We can also find references to the media in an instrumental perspective associated with their role of mechanism of change in the context of citizenship, i.e. the way citizenship is exercised and also the type of rights involved in that exercise.

For example, for Giddens, the media are a key element in modern day life and in the exercise of citizenship through their role of agents of reflexivity (Nettleton and Burrows, 1998).

Because people are faced with a greater number of choices on which they have to make decisions (Giddens, 1991: 146) they also have to base those decisions on informed choices. To do so, they base themselves on and interpret information provided by "experts" (Loader et al., 2004), whereby the media are one of the "experts" to which they turn.

But the media not only have a reflexive function, they also contributed, throughout the 20th century, to the expansion of the dimensions of citizenship. They have acted, and continue to act as the guarantors of citizenship and also as a practical instrument of the individual and collective exercise of citizenship (Murdock, 1992, 1993). [128]

In analyzing their contribution to reflexivity, Murdock (1992, 1993) identifies three forms in which the media contribute to the *exercise of citizenship*. The first is the offer of information and counselling as to the citizens' own rights. Secondly, the media provide access to a vast body of information, viewpoints and debates on political matters and public issues. Thirdly, the media provide the means so that the citizens can express criticism and suggest alternative solutions to those presented to

---

[128]Murdock (1992) includes the modern means of communication amongst the mechanisms of decontextualization of social relations. He argues that the mediators of information and entertainment have expanded their field of action through the increase in potential audiences, which, in turn, has enabled temporally non-sequential management of messages for the latter. In other words, the information contained in the messages can be used in the contexts and at the times that are most useful to the audiences. Murdock, 1993.

them. Furthermore, in the experience dimension, the media constitute a reference framework for representations that can either be assimilate or rejected.

The media can likewise operate as *citizenship extension instruments* (Murdock, 1992, 1993). This occurs because the emergence of the media enabled the reconfiguration of the social and power relations. For example, through the possibility of communicating with someone close to us who is in another city or country via telephone or E-mail, etc., the media produce phenomena such as the extension of citizenship (Murdock, 1992, 1993), giving rise to an alteration in our concepts of distance and space (Castells 2003).

Media such as radio and television (Murdock, 1992, 1993), but also the Internet, have made *new forms of socializing* possible, from friends getting together at home or in a café to watch a football game on television to the computer-mediated interaction between adolescents in chat rooms and in My Space and to the way in which we use the media in our daily routines – listening to the radio while driving, watching the news in the evening while dining with the family, etc.

Murdock (1992; 1993) also confers upon the media a role of *guarantor of citizenship*, in the sense that is not enough to simply have rights.

If the citizens do not have the basic conditions for exercising those rights it is equally important that there are symbolic resources that allow for the denunciation of such situations.

One can perhaps say that Murdock's (1992;1993) most far reaching contribution towards understanding the interaction between the media and citizenship is that the media, by enabling the establishment of social relations with persons we have never met or with whom we have never spoken face to face, have introduced a new form of exercising citizenship. It is that characteristic that allows for the organization of individuals with common objectives even though they do not share the same geographic spaces. The media have thus enable the emergence of new forms of space without these having to correspond to specific physical locations.

As Scannell suggests (1996), the media have led to a change in public life through radio and television. Radio and television took the meeting point and the point where we share space, such as the café or stadium, to a space of diffusion that can be shared by entire populations. The Internet has taken this concept even further, introducing interactive dimensions with regard to information and activity organization (Cardoso, 2003).

By means of this process of expansion of the communicative universe, the media are responsible for the diffusion of the idea of communicative rights (Scannell, 1996), i.e. the idea that everyone has the right to be heard and to make themselves heard in addition to their voting rights. [129]

Likewise of interest for understanding the role of the media in the exercise of citizenship is the analysis by Livingstone and Lunt (1994) of television programmes with viewer participation. The daily television *talk shows*, as well as other open line programmes and some Internet forums (particularly on newspaper sites) can be seen as more than entertainment, for they also function as channels for expressing opinions and positions to the government and, to a certain extent, the expert elites, thus transmitting opinion, experiences, information and criticism to the elites.

Similarly, the media also allow the public to directly question and make accountable politicians and experts, providing a space for communication between the public and the legitimization of the opinions (Livingstone et al., 1994). [130]

There is, however, another contribution of importance in the analysis of Livingstone and Lunt (1994), although less reference is made to it. In recognizing new roles for the media, they introduced the idea that, although we can deal with the same technologies for long periods of time, as in the case of television, they may always be the object of different forms of domestication (Silverstone, 1995). In other words, new and old technologies can be appropriated for the exercise of citizenships in different ways and, above all, interactions between different networked technologies can take place – sometimes through a common technological interface, as is the case for networks established between Internet, SMS and television, and other times emulating genres from other technologies, as is the case of radio programmes with listener participation and the recreation of that format for television.

---

[129]The classic theory of citizenship, based on the work of T. H. Marshall (1964) recognizes three historic phases of citizenship: that of civic liberties (individual rights), that of political liberties (electoral rights) and that of social liberties (right to social welfare and employment). The recognition of the role of the media in contemporary society has led to the emergence of what has been termed *cultural citizenship* (Hartley 1999), meaning the achievement of cultural liberties or, if we prefer, rights of identity.

[130]Even though they highlight the positive dimension associated with the new forms of media contents, Livingstone and Lundt (1994) nevertheless the interaction model that characterizes them.

When speaking of the media and citizenship, one must also bear in mind that the media are not analysis objects free of controversy (Eco, 1991). If, to some, the media are seen as promoters and instruments of the exercise of citizenship, there is also ground for criticism as to the media acting essentially as reducers or emulators of citizenship.

One example of this view is the term *infotainment* used to denote radio and television programmes that favour emotion over reason (Hartley, 2004). Many of these programmes combine the presence of specialists with an audience that finds in their own personal experiences the argumentative basis required for the confrontation situations the programme sets out to create. Examples of this favouring emotion over reason can be found in tabloid-type current affairs programmes and in educational and lifestyle formats such as cooking, gardening and decorating programmes. And it is precisely the opposition between the rational or scientific and the emotive or common sense that is criticized, for example, by analysts such as those belonging to the so-called Frankfurt School (Adorno, Horkheim and, later, Jürgen Habermas), characterizing the media in general by a spectacularization of the political debate and by a lack of critically founded economic, social and political information (Kellner, 1989).

In the field of the media, this criticism inherited from the Frankfurt School can be exemplified by Poster (1995), when he states that the contemporary social relations seem to lack a basic level of interactive practices, which, in the past, were the matrix of democratic politics in the Greek *agora*, in the local church, in the café, in the public square, in a park, in a factory or on a street corner, placing the public sphere, as a central issue, in the reconceptualization of democracy. [131]

As television is today the most widespread mediation technology on our planet, it also the object of the majority of analyzes on citizenship and mediation.

In a similarly critical stance on the role of the media, one of the renowned and respected authors in the field of political communication,

---

[131] Although the concept of the public sphere has been defined by various authors in the 20th century, including Walter Lippman (1921), the notion is generally used in accordance with the conceptual framework formulated by Habermas, which refers to the relations between the media, communication and democracy. In his analysis, Habermas describes how "public" opinion was socially formed by the European bourgeoisie of the late 18th century and early 19th century: a group of people, mostly of the male sex, who discussed political issues in the context of meeting places such as clubs and cafés, their basis being the reading of newspapers, books, opinion publications, etc.

Robert D. Putnam (2000), is of the opinion that one of the things responsible for the erosion of the social capital, i.e. of the civic involvement of the citizens since the end of World War II is television, whereas the written press is an element that furthers civic participation. According to Putnam, television firstly constitutes the main leisure activity that inhibits involvement outside the domestic space, particularly social encounters or informal conversations. Secondly, televisions influences a more negative view of the world and of people, giving rise to a greater degree of distrust of the *other*.

The perspective of colonization of the political field and the public sphere by the media is also reflected in the contemporary perspectives of analysts such as Meyer and Hinchman (2002). According to the latter, we are currently in a "media democracy", as new political regime. In their opinion, the current political process is characterized by two crucial elements: on the one hand, the way in which the media represent the political field in accordance with their own rules, and, on the other, the way in which politics is transformed as a result of submission to those rules. Hence, the central question emerges: to what extent are the democratic processes in danger when the rules of the political system are replaced by the media's rules (Meyer and Hinchman, 2002)?

However, these analyzes have also been the object of criticism for being too simplistic in the conception of the control of politics and the public opinion by the media.

Several authors argue that the relations between the media and politics are more complex and can oscillate between mutual support and conflict. In other words, the description of "mediacracy" (Meyer and Hinchman, 2002) also has a plural and competitive nature and, as such, does not cease to be a democracy (Castells, 2004).

In essence, the rules are the same; it is the actors that assume new configurations in their public presence.

As a basic presupposition, for Castells (2004), the media are at all times integrated in a certain social context with a certain degree of indefinition regarding the interaction they have with the political system due to the variability of the strategies of the public agents and the specific interactions between diverse social, cultural and political fields. Given that the current democratic models strongly anchors the separation between the media and the State, leaving to the latter, in most cases, only an indirect control over the public radio and television services, at least in Europe or a indirect regulation policy in the US. The State is losing control over the media and communication, meaning that the control of information and entertainment and, consequently, of images and opinions, ceases to be a domain controlled to large extent by it. This loss of control is emphasized even more as a result of the expansion and diversification of satellite communication, the privatization of the majority of communication channels, television, radio and the print media and the growing globalization of capital, technology and authorship.

The political independence of the media as a crucial factor for their credibility (although they are subject to pressure from financial groups and advertising as its main source of revenue) hence comes its principal attribute. The broadcasting flux media and the print media become untouchable for democratic political regimes, which thus witness their capacity for directly controlling the information being restricted (Castells, 2004).

According to Carpini and Williams (2001), this evolution of the media has without doubt contributed to the erosion of the distinction between public, or political, matters and entertainment.

The division of the media organizations into distinct news, entertainment and sports sections has become more fluid and imprecise, and journalists, executives, politicians and entertainers are freer to move from one media type and genre to another. Furthermore, within the business groups the news production areas (be it in television, radio or the print media), which were previously regarded as a public service, have also come to be seen as potential income sources as part of the centralized management of the diverse content industries, which include films, music, cable and television, in world conglomerations.

In the last thirty years of the 20th century, television, radio and the press operated essentially according to two fundamental principles. The first of these was the struggle for higher audience ratings in a situation of intense competition between channels. The second was the investment in entertainment as a means of achieving market leadership, while at the same time distancing themselves from the political field as a form of asserting their credibility in relation to politics (Eco, 1997).

This combination of factors has, in many countries and in certain channels and newspapers, led to the news becoming more like entertainment, with the inclusion dramatic elements of suspense, conflict, rivalry and greed thus undermining the value of the content of the diverse agents' political messages (Carpini e Williams, 2001: 163).

In this context there is a tendency towards extreme simplification of the political news, with a growing personalization of events featuring the politicians and not the policies as the main protagonists and a negative association on the practice of political propaganda, transforming the model of political adversaries into a permanent scrutiny in the search for "winners" and losers" (Castells, 2004).

The main resource of the political actors for accessing the "media theatre" is, thus, the theatralization of their actions, as they resort to performance mechanisms such as the dramatization of events, personification of issues, verbal "duels", symbolic figurations, etc. (Meyer and Hinchman, 2002). And political life is based to a large extent on condensation symbols, i.e. symbols that have not intrinsic meaning but result from the beliefs of the people – condensed hopes, fears and emotions (Chadwick, 2001).

The symbolic scenarios of politics are never neutral, but they organize and structure the possible types of action for the citizens, whereby they are generally staged and artificial with a "heroic quality" of majesty and formality, thus functioning as extraordinary and dramatic theatre productions, even if they are at times without substantive content. [132]

Although these analyses alert us to the changes in progress in the field of *mediation*, particularly by television, we must bear in mind that the public or, if we prefer, the citizens do not limit themselves to receiving the information that is transmitted to them without criticism.

They interpret the information, on the basis of their own formulations and others acquired in society, showing high levels of rationality in their political analysis despite the fact that they "(…) are bombarded with strategic political and often emotional messages" (Bennett and Entman, 2001: 7).

---

[132] Although often considered a negative example of the closed nature of the field of politics, the organization of political events with the media in mind in particular (for example, the organization of rallies or press conferences to coincide with the evening news programmes, so as to guarantee live coverage) is nothing more than the sharing of common rules accepted by both parties involved. In itself this does not limit political freedom, for the political content and the existence of trust between elected representatives and voters are much more important than the form of communication. But this does not mean that there are no problems for the political communication, for, as we have seen, these do exist. What is important for the analysis of the informational politics model is understanding whether or not, for example, in a given context, there are diverse information models on television – some that are more in line with news reporting models, and others more akin to hybrid models, a cross between entertainment and news – in other words, verifying the existence of diversity of contents but also of forms of communicating them, for normally the audiences are different too (Cardoso, 2004).

This new environment not only escapes direct control by the states, it also constitutes a direct challenge to the authority of the elites (journalists, politicians, academics, etc.), as it gives more space to the public, as a more active agent in the construction of the social and political meaning, and to new and hitherto traditionally marginalized groups. Parallel to this process of change, the emergence of new media such as the Internet has also transfigured the media more as a space of political communication.

The transformation of politics and the democratic and civil participation processes is a result not only of the conditions of fragility of the nation states in the context of globalization and less formal political participation due to the breach of confidence between electors and the elected, but also of the influence of the changes in the area of the information and communications technologies.

The political practices and, consequently, the strategies of attaining power, have also had to change to respond to the changes in the mediation ambience and the social, economic and political environment.

There thus arose the need for an informational policy (Castells, 2004) that takes into account the functioning of the media and their communicational models, both on the part of the political parties and on the part of the social movements or those of citizens that pursue individualized objectives.

However, *informational politics* does not correspond to one single model of political practice.

The problem in the exercise of citizenship are not the media. It is not television or the Internet. The problem is the political system itself, for it is society that models the media. Focusing on the case of the Internet, Castells (2004) points out that were there is social mobilization the Internet becomes a dynamic instrument of social exchange; where there is political bureaucratization and strictly mediatic politics of representation of the citizens, the Internet is merely an advertising board.

The electronic media (radio, television and the Internet) and the print media together constitute the preferred space for politics, participation and the exercise of citizenship. A symbolic space in which the greater part of political communication and information produced in democracies circulates.

All the media can be extraordinary instruments of participation and citizenship, instruments of information from the political class, governments and parties to the citizens and instruments of interactive relations.

However, when they are mere one-way information channels for capturing opinions or simply converting the citizens into potential voters (so that the parties can obtain information for them to be able to adjust their campaigning) they forfeit their mobilizing and social participation role and their role of bringing electors and the elected closer together (Castells, 2004).

Hence, *informational politics* can be used both as a dynamic instrument of social mobilization and participation and as a purely mediatic instrument of role representation.

It is *informational* because it is carried out in a context in which the *mediation* plays a fundamental role. It is carried out in societies that favour models of informational development and is based on networked organization, but it does not insist on one single model of political communication.

The current media are both the most important source of information for the majority of the population, the basis on which they form their political opinions, and are an instrument of organization of and participation in civic participation protests or movements.

Consequently, the diverse parties and political agents and social and citizen movements use the media for divulging and mutually influencing and convincin each other of their political, cultural and social options, programmes and objectives (Bennett, 2001).

If a degree of autonomy of the media in relation to the political and economic power is guaranteed, the political actors subject themselves, at least in part, to the way they function, particularly that of television, radio and the newspapers. However, when that autonomy is seen to be reduced, the political actors seek alternatives, such as those offered by the Internet through, for example, the writing of blogs or adherence to the Indymedia movement (Cammaerts, 2003).

It is true that one of the predominant models of informational politics is based – in the European, Asian and North and South American democracies – on a tripartite relationship between top level political actors with media charisma, the media and permanent polls, thus creating a rhythm of interaction where political deliberation and participation lose in importance. But *informational politics* is also a way of combining diverse forms of technological mediation, from the Internet to television, and not all divulged descriptions of what politics is apply today to all forms of *mediation* in the service of citizenship.

The domain of the media has undergone considerable changes in the last 15 years as a result of the proliferation of videos, television remote controls, cable and satellite television, the growth of the Internet, the horizontal and vertical integration of the media, etc. These changes have drastically increased the quantity of information available, the speed of access to that information, the opportunities of interactive mass communication and the convergence of media types and genres.

These changes allow us to understand that Robert Dahl's (1989) proposed definition of democracy applies very clearly to our world of today. For Dahl, democracy is defined as an ideal of government implemented through the equal distribution of power. The majority of societies generally recognized as democracies have differing levels of capacitation and deliberation by the citizens. [133]

Thus, Dahl proposes the use of a polyarchy *continuum* – government of the many – to distinguish between different levels of popular sovereignty.

In one pole of the *continuum* there are the minimum conditions of polyarchy defined by equal voting rights and the existence of free and just elections. The symmetric pole, in turn, comprises the ideal of democratic governance as equality of the citizens in the defining, understanding and deciding the political agenda.

Indeed, only those systems that combine mass communication and individual communication media allow for an approximation to models that offer alternative and transparent information to the citizens, ensuring that the information comes from different sources. Our society is spatially and temporally characterized by the appropriation of the new electronic media by the citizens, by a part of the political elites, by ephemeral organizations and by other more lasting ones, thus opening up a space of participation and exercise of citizenship. However, that does not mean that the temptations for politics to exercise control over information disappear, even in democracies. Because today, information means even more *power* than in earlier contexts. The same dialectic forces are still in play in the *mediation* arena.

Which means that the opposition between centripetic and centrifugal forces, i.e. between those that further greater control and greater freedom (Colombo, 1999), continues to characterize the *mediation* and civic participation arena.

---

[133] Even in a case in which a section of the citizens does not participate in certain decisions, no citizen in a developed democracy is excluded on the basis of a discriminatory policy or obstacles that prevent him from obtaining information and expressing his choices.

Although they also offer new possibilities to the to parliamentary politics, the new media present in the mediation space seem to facilitate the conduction of extra-parliamentary politics (Dahlgren, 2001; Sparks, 2001; Sassi, 2000), given that, in most cases, parliamentary politics accepts the rules of the game as played by the informational politics practised by television, radio and newspapers, even when the autonomy of these media is perceived as a problem.

Because it rejects the rules of this informational politics model (or because those rules marginalize it), the extra-parliamentary politics of the social movements and citizens with individual political agendas finds in its access to the new media formulas for reaching the populations or recreating new connections with the traditional symbolic spaces of mediation of citizenship

The new media thus allow for: new and vast communication spaces for travelling, visiting and participating; the possibility of generating new spaces, such as sites, newsgroups, chat rooms, networks, action groups, etc.; the hypertextual structure according to an extensive "interspatiality"; the capacity of freedom of movement between different communicative spaces; personalization of information from countless sources; the development of channels of interactivity with the formal political system and its contacts with parties and representatives; and the online organization of groups and movements.

However, despite the discourses in praise of the potential of the new information and communication technologies' communicative action, they are also open to criticism. In particular because there are some differences between their potential and the realization of that potential. For example, according to Dahlgren (2001), the problems of the majority of public spheres in the form of newsgroups or chat rooms are evident in aspects such as their separation, their becoming spaces for individuals who share the same ideas, and the lack of space for diverging views; their unincorporated character in online communication; the lack of geographic references that suggest limits to the inter-subjectivity necessary in a public sphere, thus limiting the sense of common purpose and mutual understanding the individuals have. Nevertheless, these criticisms have rarely taken into account the need to look at the media as a networked whole – a network of different technologies and different forms of *mediation*. In reality, as there are different media there is also the probability of different uses and different representations of them in the context of a *network communication* model.

There are clear links between the different media specificities, allowing that the symbolic space of exercise of citizenship be appropriated by different forms depending on their outlined objectives (Bennett, 2004 and Castells, 2004), but also depending on the media matrixes of their users (Ortoleva, 2002).

For example, one can note a very close connection between the Internet as a public sphere and the public sphere of the mass media (Sassi, 2002). On the one hand, the public micro-spheres depend on the traditional media (such as television, radio and the print media) for making them known and politically more effective. On the other, the information available on the Internet, although previously devalued by the media, has become widely accepted, thus boosting the Internet's functioning as a mass medium and deactivating an alteration of the dominant discourses of the other media (contra-information or new topics).

Through an analysis of the contents available online it is also possible to characterize the different media specificities.   In their study of Usenet pages and chat groups, Hill and Hughes (1998) ascertained that politics does is not one of the central uses of the Internet when compared to other areas such as sex, television, films, religion, etc. Nevertheless, the Internet brings something new to the field of participation and exercise of citizenship, for of those sites with political content 20% are outside the traditional field of politics reflected by the more traditional media, namely the press, radio and television (Hill and Hughes, 1998). In other words, for the users, the Internet an expand the political margins of the public sphere. On the Internet, the users also favour certain specialized providers of information, as is the case in the mass media. These suppliers are sought out with the aim of procuring more in-depth knowledge on news stories seen in the traditional media.

What this introductory analysis of the media and citizenship in the network society shows us is that it is not enough to have rights because the mediation field is diversified and contains different technologies and because these technologies establish networked interactions between themselves. The exercise of citizenship in a real virtuality culture, where experience is formed and takes place to a large extent in the symbolic space provided by mediation, depends on having the necessary informational literacy. But what factors influence the choice of one medium over another?

We have already given one such factor. Even in a democracy, the degree of independence we attribute to a medium in relation to third-party interests is a determinant factor in its choice, as are the geographic and temporal reach we require (Tehranian, 1999).

In a culture in which our context of experience is to a large extent the product of mediation through television, the Internet, radio, the press and telephones, a free and diversified communications system is, indeed, a fundamental instrument for the exercise of citizenship by the populations.

However, we can venture the hypothesis that there could be other dimensions, coming from our own life experiences, that orient, condition and influence the choice of one medium over another or that cause us to have different representations of their functions (Colombo and Aroldi, 2003).

The Different Media Ages

Bearing in mind the articulation between different media, the differentiation of contents and also the specialization of the media in different mediation functions, is it possible to suggest that different generations of citizens have different representations of the media? And if that is demonstrable, is that differentiation of representations of the media reflected in different mediated participation practices?

If we take as the basis of analysis a situation that is common to various developed societies – the arrival of informatization in a shared historic moment – we can perhaps find results similar to those presented for Portugal in the following table (Table 7.1).

What one ascertains is that, when asked about the interests they associate with different information and communication technologies, the different generations share certain points but also give differentiated responses that allow one to identify unique identitary representations in relation to the media.

Although television is the preferred medium for all the generations presented in the table, one must note that the generations that became acquainted with the Internet in their childhood and adolescence have much lower figures for their interest in television than those generations that only became acquainted with informatization in later phases of adult life (41.2% vs. 80.4%).

As far as the second choice interest is concerned, one can divide the generations into two groups: those who came into contact with personal computers in their childhood, who consider the Internet to be the second most interesting technology, and those who responded reading newspapers, as they had not had that contact with personal computer technology. We can therefore constitute two clearly distinct groups – those aged 15 to 37 and those aged 38 to over 50 (as at 2003).

An equally differentiating factor is the way in which different generations deal with sound technologies such as radios and CD. There would seem to be a generational division based on the valuation of individual music choices. Thus, whereas the generation of 26 to 37 year olds are in a borderline position, as they value radio and the personalized music choice offered by CDs equally, the 15 to 25 year old generation has a clear preference for musical individualization and attaches greater value to listening to music on CDs and via music-themed television channels and the P2P for exchanging and listening to mp3.

Table 7.1 – Activity considered the most interesting by generation, 1st choice, in Portugal (%)

	15-25	26-37	38-50	>50
Playing video games	6.7%	0.7%	0.6%	0.1%
Talking on the mobile phone	6.7%	4.3%	1.9%	1.0%
Listening to music CDs	15.3% (3)	9.5% (3)	4.9%	1.6%
Listening to radio	9.3%	9.5% (3)	9.3% (3)	7.1% (3)
Watching television	41.2% (1ª)	54.9% (1)	66.0% (1)	80.4% (1)
Reading newspapers	3.9%	8.3%	11.3% (2)	8.3% (2)
Using the Internet	16.7% (2)	12.8% (2)	5.8%	0.7%
Don't know/No response	0.4%	0.0%	0.2%	0.7%
Total	100%	100%	100%	100%

Source: Cardoso et al., 2004, The Network Society in Portugal, CIES/ISCTE. Note: Definition of *interesting*: adj. causing curiosity; holding the attention. Concise Oxford Dictionary, Oxford University Press.

The older generations view radio, with its predefined music programming, as a clearly defined technology, as a choice of interest, although not very distant from reading newspapers.

The 15 to 25 year old generation is also the one that attaches most importance to music, attributing a total of approximately 25% of their interest to listening to music CDs and radio. They are also the only generation that places video games and mobile phones on the same interest level and only in the generation of the 26 to 37 year olds do we find similar values for interest in the mobile phone.

In our attempt to establish generational difference in terms of the appropriation of the media and the construction of communicative autonomy and practices of citizenship we chose to carry out for a more in-depth analysis of the fruitions of television and the Internet.

The choice of these two technologies is due to the fact that both assume the role of main *nodes* of the current media system, in particular in the field of information, whereby the former is the technology that continues to be the most widespread medium and the latter is the emerging technology that is registering the highest growth figures amongst the population.

Another reason for the choice was the fact that, chronologically, the last three widespread information and communication technologies to be domesticated were television, the Internet and the mobile phone. For this reason it makes sense, in this analysis, to chose the two that are mass communication technologies from the beginning (although, as we have seen, the interpersonal communication technologies, such as the Internet and the mobile phone, can also be used as mass communication technologies).

As we have already stated, the media are the first connection between the experienced and the represented. It is also through them that experience is constructed. Proceeding from that context, what is the role of the generational view of things in the construction of experience?

According to Colombo and Aroldi (2003), childhood and adolescence are the essential stages for the creation of a media profile in an audience through the definition of expectations, tastes, preferences, familiarity with genres and texts, interpretation patterns, etc. In other words, all the dimensions that characterize us as audiences.

Thus, during these stages, a certain matrix is created, a media literacy, an approach that defines consumption patterns and the future habits of that audience. One must, however, take into account that the generations are not watertight elements, for there are inter-generational exchanges and processes of contamination between the generations. This influencing can take place in vertical relationships (parents – children) and can lead to one generation influencing the other (Colombo and Aroldi, 2003).

Another factor to be borne in mind is the intra-generational dimension of creation of those matrixes. In other words, certain needs that manifest themselves are directly linked to the biological age of the individuals and related with characteristic objectives of a certain group and, in different periods of time, these needs can be satisfied by different types of media.

Fundamental concepts for this generational analysis are those of the *media biography* and the *media memory*. The objective is to understand to what point individuals of the same age group share the same media memories, the same consumption histories and, consequently, similar consumption patterns, which can also be observed in the media-related habits of the individuals in their daily lives (Colombo and Aroldi, 2003).

The historic experiences one witnesses during one's youth and the cultural products (books, cinema, television, music, comics, etc.) one uses during the same period are also considered to be decisive both in the formation of sensitivity and the tastes of each individual and in cementing the experience that integrates the individual in a certain generation. [134]

As Umberto Eco shows in his novel "La Misteriosa Fiamma della Regina Loana" (2004), the media also constitute, by means of their cultural production and the uses we make of them, a common memory and the reflection of spirit of a generation.

The fact that they were part of one and the same generation, and have shared a number of historic and consumption experiences means that individuals, even if they are separated by many other variables (such as gender, place of residence, education level, etc.), share certain values and a particular mentality (Gnasso, 2003). The process of the sharing of certain values and a generational mentality is therefore very closely linked to the media domestication processes. When applied to the information and communication technologies, the term domestication refers to the process whereby people adopt these technologies in their everyday lives, particularly in their homes or in structures such as organizations (Ward, 2003). Domestication focuses on the individual use of the media and the socio-cultural situation in which that use takes place. The concept of domestication suggests that the adoption of a technology into everyday life should be understood as a form

---

[134] Every generation is defined first and foremost as an age group in relation to a given historical period. According to Mannheim (cited in Hartmann 2003), a generation can only evolve in two ways, by becoming a lost or *an sich* generation, i.e. it makes no significant experiences of a historic or social character based on time and space, or it makes these experiences and becomes a real or *für sich* generation. Only the latter has a collection consciousness and, consequently, a significant impact on society. Other equally important aspects for the formation of a generation are innovative access to cultural resources and the creation of an own generational style (Winkels, 1997 cited in Hartmann 2003).

of integration in a given lifestyle or course. The artefact is incorporated into pre-existing patterns of everyday life and the use of technologies and social patterns. This is not a harmonious or conflict-free process. Dynamism is one of its characteristics, given that there is no permanent fixation with regard to the relationship with the object (Silverstone, 1994; Sorensen, 1994 cited in Ward, 2003). Skills and practices have to be learned throughout the process, while meanings are constructed in the same process. [135]

Domestication in the broader sense, i.e. the incorporation of new technologies into the life of each person, and into everyday life (using them, abusing them, misusing them, ignoring them) is a process experienced permanently by us all.

The domestication of a technology takes place when we cease to look at them as technologies to the extent that they take on different meaning. Two examples of this are the mobile phone (Ward, 2003) and the Internet, which for many have become an extension of us, in the sense that we are permanently contactable for those we value, such as friends and family, etc. It is through this total incorporation in our lives, the domestication of a medium, and the different ways in which different groups of people deal with it, that we are able to establish the importance of the generational dimension for understanding the phenomenon of the construction of experience through the media.

In their study of the generational dimension in the field of the media, Colombo and Aroldi (2003) start from two initial presuppositions, which also served as the basis for this analysis. The first presupposition is that of treating the individuals as being responsible for the construction of different and complex media consumption diets. The second is the relevance of the generation as a variable in the construction of a socio-cultural identity shared by a set of individuals, also clarifying that age becomes a central variable when treated as a common denominator of a group that shares, during one and the same period in history, the same cultural environment,

---

[135] S Silverstone identifies the process of domestication, outlining six steps in the integration of a technology: commodification, idealization, appropriation, objectification, incorporation and conversion. Commodification refers to the initial process of production of the artefact in industrial and commercial terms. Idealization is the entry of the technology into the consciousness of the possible user. Appropriation is the consumer acquiring the object and taking it into his home. Objectification refers to the object finding a physical place in the home. Incorporation refers to matters of time, the use of the technology as foreseen or in new forms. Conversion has to do with the home and the exterior world, both in material and symbolic form, and the public perception of the possession and use of the technology.

thus accessing the same media system and the same media (Colombo and Aroldi, 2003).

The first example suggested by Colombo and Aroldi (2003) is television in Italy, which was completely different in the periods from 1950 to 1970 and from 1970 to the present day.

An initial phase termed *Paleo-TV*, in which television was seen as a public institution with broadcasting times broken up into specific areas and with a general pedagogic outlook, was followed by a second phase, known as *Neo-TV*. Neo-TV was characterized by a commercial aspect oriented in a flux logic, event though it was through one and the same medium, which brought to the audience a totally diverse experience, this time based on entertainment, and gave rise to a radically different media system (Colombo and Aroldi, 2003). [136]

That difference also influenced the existence of four generations of Italian television viewers, which are characterized by the four periods in the life of the country and of Europe in general. The four Italian generations can be divided into the following two groups: the *Nostalgics*, those born between 1945 and 1952 (i.e. those who experienced the economic boom and Paleo-television from the late 1950s to the end of the 1960s) and also those born between 1953 and 1965 (i.e. those who experienced the youth protests of the late 1960s and Red Brigades terrorism e during the 1970s, the reform of Paleo-TV and the Paleo-informatics, from the late 1960s to the early 1980s), who share the same childhood approach to television, Paleo-TV (1954-1978). These are the people in Italy who are between 37 and 57 years of age. They were roughly 30 to 50 years old when the Internet began to become a widespread technology around 1994. The generational group characterized as the *Disenchanted*, which comprises those born between 1978 and 1988 (i.e. those who experienced the 1980s with the emergence of Neo-TV and initial computerization, experienced the second Italian Republic and the duopoly Neo-TV and became acquainted with the Internet first hand), are those who are now 14 to 24 years old and accessed the Internet for the fist time at the age of 6 to 16 years (between childhood and adolescence).

---

[136]The transformations that characterize *neo-television* are reflected in various areas: increase in the number of operators; expansion of broadcasting hours; the nature and structure of the broadcasts; and, above all, the changes in the programme production models and consumption modalities. In short, the reformulation of the purpose (the "ultimate goal") of television communication.

Bearing in mind this characterization of the relationship between television and its viewers in Italy, is it possible to establish a parallel between the qualitative analysis carried out by Aroldi and Colombo (2003) and the Portuguese and other national contexts?

The hypothesis presented herein, in terms of the choice of the decisive dates for the analysis of the generational relations between television and the viewing public in Portugal, also followed the identification of the historic imperatives of the then valid television models and the sharing of common moments in the country's history and in world history.

Hence one can argue that, in Portugal, we have only two clearly differentiated generations. The first is that which we will term the *Beginner Generation*, i.e. those who lived their childhood (at least from the age of seven to late adolescence) with Paleo-TV, though still under the authoritarian regime (1957 – 1973). [137]

The *beginner generation* was born between 1950 and 1966. This was a period characterized by the *Estado Novo* (New State) dictatorship, in which television and State blended for propagandistic and, at the same time, educational purposes (*Paleo-TV*). [138]

They are those citizens who socialized with television between their birth and the end of the Estado Novo regime (1957-1973) and who, in international terms, lived through the post-World War II period, the Cold War and the Portuguese colonial wars, as well as the periods of student protest and the end of European colonization in Africa and Asia. This group corresponds to all those who, in 2003, were between 38 and 54 years of age. [139]

---

[137]The age of 7 years was chosen as the youngest age in this analysis, given that it is the age at which socialization outside the home – thanks to the child beginning school, joining organizations such as the scouts and other children's activities – is added to family life and interaction with television. It is also more or less at this age that the media's function of socialization in the family context begins to interact with other mediated socialization contexts such as watching television with friends and schoolmates, thus extending the role of television beyond the home.

[138]In the programming model characteristic of Paleo-TV (Ortoleva 2004), in addition to films and other fiction genres, one also finds imports from the radiophonic "universe", such as game shows and soaps. The Paleo-TV model on both sides of the Atlantic alternates theatre, variety entertainment, chat shows with celebrities from culture and politics, football matches, cartoons and television movies, i.e. an episode-based narration constructed to occupy a precise period of time in the course of the programming. For an historical analysis of the public television service see: Scannell, P. (1997).

[139]In Portugal (following similar developments a few years earlier elsewhere in Europe), the first contract for the operation of a public television service was signed between the Portuguese government and RTP in 1956. The document established three classic principles – to inform, educate and entertain.

I have given the second generation with a clearly differentiated identity the name *Multimedia Generation,* as it is also the first generation to be dealing with a duality of screens – the television screen and the computer screen – since their birth, whereby the television screen is also often a portal for games, DVD films or the fruition of music.

This generation is those born after 1985, a period that coincides, in Portugal, with the launch of the new private television channels and, in political terms, corresponds to the longest period of government stability, with the second majority of Prime Minister Cavaco Silva and the emergence of Socialist alternative with António Guterres. This is also the generation that, internationally, was faced with a world that was already a post-Cold War space and where the war on terrorism and the construction of the European Union seem to characterize the media agendas.

This is the generation that became acquainted with television in the 1990s, the decade that marked the end of the public television channel's monopoly and the emergence of private operators from 1992 onwards. We can characterize this period as the moment in which the phenomenon of Neo-TV emerged in Portugal it its full strength, nourished by the programming dynamics meanwhile introduced by the private stations. A programming with a strong impact on the style and strategies of the television news programmes and the entertainment proposals. Whereas in Italy the period 1976-1991 represents the years of great transformation of television communication, in Portugal the *Neo-television revolution* (Eco, 1985; Caseti and Odin, 1990) took place closer to the beginning of broadcasting by the private operators in the early 1990s.

The multimedia generation is the generation that did not become acquainted with television until 1992, the Neo-TV phase, in a consolidated democracy and was less than 20 years old in 2004. [140]

As Lopes (1999) points out, the genesis of RTP cannot be dissociated from its role as the voice of the State and it was in this mixture of fear and fascination on the part of the dictatorship that television gradually established itself in the public space – as the voice of the nation, programmed in accordance with what the State considered to be the public interest. For the two decades up to 1974, television in Portugal accompanied important current affairs events: the colonial wars in Africa in the 60s and 70s; the landing on the moon in 1969 and the death of the dictator Oliveira Salazar in 1970. (Teves 1998).

[140] A television model, in which, according to Ortoleva (2004), one went from programming based on weekly programmes to essentially daily ones and in which morning and late night programmes took on more importance and the importance of talk programmes grew in relation to the more "classic" programmes (e.g. series, films and documentaries). In the field of fiction production, lengthy, episode-

Between these two generations in Portugal we find a third generation with characteristics of a *Transition Generation* – that which experienced adolescence between the revolution and the democratic normalization in the late 1980s.

The members of this generation are those who witnessed the experimentation of Paleo-TV in democracy and its gradual development towards Neo-TV. They have some things in common with the *beginner generation* as far as television fruition practices are concerned, particularly in terms of contents, but they are also very close to the multimedia generation in many fields.

The *transition generation* was born between 1967 and 1984, a period that comprises, more or less, the democratic revolution of 25 April 1974, democratic stabilization and the birth of public television as a democratic entity. This generation spent their childhood and a large part of their adolescence, with a Paleo-TV model, but also witnessed the changes in programming and style that marked the transition to the situation of free competition in the television market and the experimenting with Neo-TV models that were in the implementation phase elsewhere in Europe (1974-1991). In international terms, this is the generation that grew up in the 1980s, the years of the passing from a period of social contestation and economic growth to a globalization model of liberalizing character. The transition generation is made up of those who became acquainted with television in their childhood and adolescence between 1974 and 1991 and were aged 31 to in 2003.

The differences between the three generations can be identified both on the basis of their sharing of certain values as well as their memories and biographies in relation to television and in relation to the media in general.

---

based series, which were previously confined to relatively marginal spaces directed at less educated segments of the public, took on a dominant role and completely new genres such as music videos established themselves.

Table 7.2 – Analysis of generational representations and practices in relation to television in Portugal (%)

	Beginner generation 1957/1973	Transition generation 1974/1991	Multimedia generation 1992-(...)
Television enables us to enrich our knowledge of the world and the things that surround us (Agree)	38.1%	38.7%	37%
Watching TV is essentially something done in the company of the family (Agree)	25.0%	22.7%	19.3%
TV brings the family together, discussing the same topics and programmes (Agree)	18.6%	21.4%	22.3%
TV is a medium for maintaining the traditions and history of a community and its cultural heritage (Agree)	21.9%	21.1%	18.8%
Watching TV is essentially a form of relaxation and entertainment (Agree)	39.6%	42%	36.2%
Comparing the TV of today with that of your childhood/adolescence, would you say it is better, the same or worse? (Better)	46.2%	32.9%	25.6%
When you watch the TV news, at the bottom of the screen other news stories and information accessible on Internet sites is given. Do you normally consult these sites? (Yes)	22.6%	34.3%	32.8%
When you see something on TV that catches your interest, do you normally consult Internet pages or seek information online on that topic? (Yes)	34.7%	47.4%	40.5%
When you're watching TV do you tend to change channels? (Yes)	49.7%	59.0%	59.5%

Source: Cardoso et al., 2004, The Network Society in Portugal, CIES/ISCTE.

However, not all the values expressed allow for an individualization of the *difference*, for television also creates values transversally shared by the majority of viewers. For example, when asked if television allows us to enrich our knowledge of the world and the things that surround us, the response (Table 7.2) reveal a strong positive value associated with television as a source of knowledge. This is an inter-generational trend, to which one can also add a high degree of trust in the information one receives through television. On average, more than 75% trust or trust a lot the information they receive through television.

In comparing the television of today to that of their childhood/adolescence, the viewers almost always consider the former better. The *begin-*

ner's generation, which experienced *Paleo-TV* under an authoritarian political regime is the generation that which considers the television of today clearly better. The *multimedia generation*, in contrast, is the one that notes the least improvements. This assessment has to do with the fact that they are, age wise, closest to youth, as they are all young adults, but it also indicates that televisions changes its basic structures more slowly than we seem to accept, for often we think we see profound changes in the alterations in programming and formats when they are nothing more than fleeting or occasional phenomena.

The *transition generation*, which grew up with the paradigm changes, feels comfortable with the current model and also considers it positive. Watching television is, to a large extent, something done together with the family. For the older generations, the television has more of a connotation as an instrument of family social life than for the younger generations. For the *beginner generation* television is that the centre of the media diet and the family is the central element in this relation with the media.

However, the ritual dimension of watching television is valued more by the younger generations in the bringing the family together brought about by discussion of the same topics and programmes. In other words, the family togetherness produced by television seems to have more to do with allowing the younger viewers to be closer to the older viewers and to have something in common with them than with giving the later the symbolic codes necessary for coming closer to the younger viewers. The malleability of the television diets of the *multimedia* and *transition generations* is, thus, apparently greater, allowing them to use television as a means of feeling greater proximity with older generations.

As to the role of television as an instrument in keeping the traditions, history and cultural heritage of a community alive, this is a value shared equally by the *beginner generation* and the *transition generation* and clearly less valued by the *multimedia generation.* The memory and identity construction dimension of television thus seems to be a prerogative for the older generations. The *multimedia generation* seems to seek its identity construction in not one, but several different media.

In a more functional analysis of the role of the media we also find inter-generational differences. For the *transition generation* television is essentially a form of relaxation and entertainment. For the older generations, television also has a strong connotation of a primary source of information, but in the entertainment dimension it is seen as an escape, a flight into better worlds through the stories told (Colombo and Aroldi, 2003). Whereas the younger generations also value other media, such as multimedia games, mobile phones, pre-recorded music, etc., as a source of entertainment,

This multiplicity of relations with the media is something that also calls our attention to the fact that the media must be seen as part of an overall media system, with effects of return and reciprocal interaction in the social definition of the media themselves (Colombo and Aroldi, 2003). How, then is the relationship between two different but complementary media, such as television and the Internet, particularly in the field of information, established?

The attention given in news programmes to the scroll at the bottom of the screen announcing news articles and files accessible on the Internet or the searching the Internet for things not shown on television present a generational panorama where, in multimedia terms, it is the two younger generations that establish more connections between the Internet and television, both in the new dimension and in the general information and entertainment dimensions.

However, it is the *transition generation* that most integrates this relationship between the Internet and television into its daily practices. This is no doubt due to the fact that this generation, due to its integration into working life, has more diversified uses for the Internet through the combination of the professional, educational, new and entertainment fields

Also in the field of the practical appropriation of television, the *transition* and *multimedia generations*, in contrast to the older generation, are characterized by much more frequent switching of channels, or zapping. They therefore manifest much less loyalty to channels or to the beginning or end of a programme. Their television is that of flows and not that of predetermined viewing times and is closer to textual organization models. [141]

From these different behaviours in relation to television one can also conclude that there is an *emotional perception of the media* that differs from medium to medium (Colombo and Aroldi, 2003). Whereas the *begin-*

---

[141] As Ortoleva (2003) writes on Raymond Williams' definition of television flow: "For Williams, the flow is a different organization model from communication, discourse. The text, which is closed and based on internal rules, is followed by another form of communication, which is open and based above all on permanent negotiation between sender and receiver. It is not about choosing between one and the other because, according to Williams and despite its strong specificities, the flow is, in other aspects, the continuation and development of processes that have existed for two centuries: of that profound change in the "structure of listening" that was born out of the industrial revolution".

ner generation shares an idealized interest built around the television of the early broadcasting years, and they remember film titles and the names of series, the *transition* and *multimedia generations*, although they still firmly place television in the centre of their media diets, present a less static diet that is more open to other comparisons with the different media.

The younger generations also more easily effect new recompositions between media and, as they are more aware of the diversity of television genres and formats, they become less involved with that medium. In the most evident case, that mirrored by the multimedia generation, the emotional involvement is directed more at video games, mobile phones and music than at television.

The analysis of the television viewing practices in terms of contents and memory also gives us some interesting insight as to how the different generations seem to appropriate television in different ways.

The analysis shows similarities between the practices, but also clear differentiation logics that cannot be attributed to different generational needs. These differences must, therefore, be interpreted as products of different representations as to what the media and television are for different generations, which also grew up with different forms of television. Whereas the *beginners* and *transition generations* have the five programmes the watch most regularly in common, and four of those are news programmes (while the fifth is soap opera), as far as the way in which their memory registers television there are more substantial differences.[142] As far as television memory is concerned, only the hierarchy between the two first references is common to all – information and soap operas.

The *transition generation* introduces series as a television format valued in terms of memory, as well as comedy programmes. In the memory dimension, the *transition generation* values humour and entertainment more than the *beginner generation*.

---

[142]It is worthwhile introducing an interesting side note here. One of the most interesting facts in this study is how television memory, when this is asked about directly, centres almost exclusively on the present. For all the generations studied in all 15 responses taken into account (Table 7.3), there was only one reference to a programme that was more than one year old – the game show "1, 2, 3". In the younger generations, the memory of most liked programmes that are less than one year old is practically non-existent – except in the case of cult series such as X Files.

Table 7.3 – Analysis of generational television viewing practices, 1st choice, in Portugal (%)

Beginner generation (Paleo-TV under authoritarian regime) 1957 – 1973 [54 – 38 years]		Transition generation (from the revolution [1974] and democratic stabilization to Paleo-TV evolving towards Neo-TV) 1974 – 1991 [37-21 years]		Multimedia generation (Neo-TV in consolidated democracy) 1992 – (...) [...- 20 years]	
Programme most regularly watched	Programme you most liked or were most interest in	Programme most regularly watched	Programme you most liked or were most interest in	Programme most regularly watched	Programme you most liked or were most interest in
News programmes (25.6%)	General information (17.8%)	News programmes (19.9%)	General information (12.2%)	Other soap operas (10.2%)	Other series (8.8%) *
News programmes SIC (10.0%)	Other soap operas (6.8%)	News programmes SIC (8.3%)	Other soap operas (4.6%)	Comedy Levanta-te e Ri (7.3%)	Comedy Levanta-te e Ri (7.7%)
News programmes TVI (9.6%)	News programmes SIC (3.8%)	News programmes TVI (7.4%)	Music Reality Show Operação triunfo (3.4%)	News programmes (6.8%)	Other soap operas (6.0%)
News programmes RTP1 (7.3%)	Football (3.5%)	News programmes RTP1 (5.4%)	Films (3.2%)	Soap opera New Wave (5.6%)	Films (4.4%)
Other soap operas (5.0%)	Films (3.3%)	Other soap operas (4.6%)	Game show 1,2,3 (3.2%)	Films (5.6%)	Sports programmes (4.4%)
Soap opera Saber Amar (2.9%)	Game show 1,2,3 (3.2%)	Comedy Herman Sic (3.7%)	Other series (3.1%)	Sports programmes (5.6%)	Reality Show Big Brother (3.8%)

Table 7.3 – Analysis of generational television viewing practices, 1st choice, in Portugal (%)

Beginner generation (Paleo-TV under authoritarian regime) 1957 – 1973 [54 – 38 years]		Transition generation (from the revolution [1974] and democratic stabilization to Paleo-TV evolving towards Neo-TV) 1974 – 1991 [37-21 years]		Multimedia generation (Neo-TV in consolidated democracy) 1992 – (…) [...- 20 years]	
Football (2.9%)	Music Reality Show *OperaçãoTriunfo* (3.0%)	SIC Notícias (news) (3.0%)	Football (3.0%)	Football (4.5%)	General information (3.3%)
Information *Prós e Contras* (2.7%)	Documentaries – wildlife (2.6%)	Films (2.9%)	Comedy *Herman Sic* (2.9%)	Comedy *Herman Sic* (4,5%)	Football (2.7%)
Soap opera *A casa das 7 Mulheres* (2.0%)	Sports programmes (2.6%)	Football (2.9%)	Reality Show *Big Brother* (2.7%)	Soap opera *Saber Amar* (4.0%)	News programmes SIC (2.7%)
SIC Notícias (news) (2.1%)	Reality Show *Big Brother* (2.6%)	Soap opera *Saber Amar* (2.8%)	News programmes TVI (2.6%)	Comedy, *Os Malucos do Riso* (4.0%)	Comedy *Herman Sic* (2.7%)
-	Soap opera *Esperança* (2.4%)	Information *Prós e Contras* (2.0%)	Comedy *Levanta-te e Ri* (2.4%)	Other series (4.0%)	Soap opera *New Wave* (2.7%)
-	Information *Prós e Contras* (2.3%)	Sports *Domingo Desportivo* (2.0%)	Entertainment programmes (2.4%)	Music *Top + e MTV* (3.4%)	Music Reality Show *OperaçãoTriunfo* (2.7%)

Table 7.3 – Analysis of generational television viewing practices, 1st choice, in Portugal (%)

Beginner generation (Paleo-TV under authoritarian regime) 1957 – 1973 [54 – 38 years]		Transition generation (from the revolution [1974] and democratic stabilization to Paleo-TV evolving towards Neo-TV) 1974 – 1991 [37-21 years]		Multimedia generation (Neo-TV in consolidated democracy) 1992 – (...) [...- 20 years]	
-	Other Documentaries (2.3%)	Music Reality Show *Operação Triunfo* (1.9%)	Sports programmes (2.1%)	Entertainment programmes (3.4%)	Cartoons/Manga (2.2%)
-	Entertainment programmes (2.1%)	-	-	Music Reality Show *Operação Triunfo* (2.8%)	Soap opera *Saber Amar* (2.2%)
-	News programmes TVI (2.0%)	-	-	News programmes SIC (2.8%)	-

Source: Cardoso et al., 2004, The Network Society in Portugal, CIES/ISCTE. Note: all response categories are registered in the table that received more than 2% of the total answers of the respondents. * Only case in which a particular series is mentioned individually (X Files, 1.1%).

Another possible analysis of the data presented in the preceding table (Table 7.3) is to identify what is unique in terms of references for each generation.

As far as the *beginner generation* is concerned we can observe that what is unique about it, and only in the memory dimension, is the reference to documentaries.

If we disregard the *manga* dimension, the multimedia generation introduces the uniqueness of music programmes and cult series, i.e. those that refer to other media formats – from books to Internet sites, and to films, animated films, card games and computer games, etc.

Only the *transition generation* does not present unique and singular characteristics. Their television contents fruition practices are the product of a transition, basing themselves on the practices of the preceding generation and opening up the possibility of affirmation of a new model , that of the *multimedia generation.* An equally important point is that resulting from an analysis of the diversity. The generation that reveals the greatest number of references and the most diversity in terms of practices and memory is the *multimedia generation.* At the other end of the scale is the *beginner generation.* For the latter, television seems to have few valued genres and formats, probably because of the model of television they got to know in their first interactions with the medium.

If we now focus on the two television genres that are present in all the generations' responses, the *reality shows* and *soap operas,* we can likewise detect different valuation formulas. Hence, whereas the *beginner generation* seems to favour, in its television biography, Portuguese soap operas over those coming from Brazil, the *multimedia generation* seems to prefer the contrary. However, in terms of memory, both generations seem to favour the Brazilian soaps. The transition generation also seems to prefer Portuguese productions.

In the field of the *reality shows* one can also register singularities. In the case of those who mentioned the music contest *Operação Triunfo* as part of their television biography, the viewers seem to grow in numbers the younger the generation. In other words, it is chosen most by the *multimedia generation* and is absent from the choices of the oldest group, the *beginner generation.* The same is valid for the *Big Brother* programme: the younger the generation the greater the interest is in the show.

Both the preceding conclusions on reality shows seem to be in agreement with Colombo and Aroldi's (2003) analysis of the narratives, which suggests that the relationships between the younger generations and factual programmes (in other words, programmes in which reality, social interaction and identity manipulation are simulated) are more easily established. In this type of programme, the narrative is based on actions. Each participant is unique because what he/she does is different to what the others do. That is the most valued element in such programmes, to the detriment of the values that the participants may have or represent. In contrast, the older viewers seem to prefer a soap opera style, which proposes an imagined environment with a storyline derived from traditional genres in books, films and television programmes and in which the narrative construction is based on values and not skills (Colombo and Aroldi, 2003).

Now that we have characterized the generational differences and similarities in terms of domestication, practices and values in relation to television in Portugal, we can go on to focus the generational relationship with the appropriation of the Internet.

Traditionally, one has associated with the emergence of the Internet the idea of a new generation created on the basis of use of the technology. This idea can be characterized as the *web generation* and is defined by Hartmann (2003) and proceeding from the presupposition that there is a generational culture defined by means of the information technologies and based on the younger generations, which, connected to the world through networks, adopt the new technologies in a pioneering way and use them easily in any given moment and place (Tapscott, 1998; Kellner, 2003).

Heibecker (2001, quoted in Hartmann) also defines a generation on the basis of its relationship with the technologies but emphasizes that there are different subcultures involved. His argument is that it is not so much the number of users that defines a culture, but it is how some use the technologies and how they are seen to do so that creates a common place, although this is not sufficient to give rise to a generational denomination. [143]

The analysis developed herein in puts forward the idea that although each generation shares different subcultures, there are common traits in their relations with different technologies that allow one to individualize a generational sharing of practices and values in relation to the media as a

---

[143] Amongst the different subcultures suggested by the author are: the *Otaku*, for whom technology is a fetish; the cyberpunk, for whom technology is a lifestyle; the hacker, who is part of an organized, hierarchical subculture; and the cyberflaneur, who is distinguished by aesthetics and extroversion.

whole and, hence, the existence of generations without using the typification of subcultures.

Instead of one *web generation* (Hartmann, 2003), with the characteristics listed above, one can argue the existence of two *informational generations* with two distinct forms of dealing with the Internet and establishing relations with other media.

Two generations that characterized by the different relations with the Internet, but, contrary to the relation with television, are still minority generations in may societies in relation to those who do not yet use the technology.

Using the typology put forward by Colombo and Aroldi (2003) as a starting point, one can construct a new typology comprising two informational generations and two non-informational generations.

The *non-computerized generation* consists of those who, in their childhood and adolescence, had no direct contact with computers or with the practical results of their use by society's institutions and by companies. They are those born between 1943 and 1952 who were between 52 and 61 years of ages in 2004.

The *paleo-informational generation* is the generation, which, only in certain situations, experienced mainframes and indirectly lived their adolescence in a society in which the public policies and business life were influenced by the use of computers. Direct contact with the computer normally occurred in active professional life as a specialist or superior employee capacity. The members of the *paleo-informational generation* were born between 1953 and 1965 and were aged 39 to 51 in 2004.

The *first informational generation* is that which became acquainted with computers as personal arcade game machines (the Ataris and Zx Spectrums) and came into contact with first personal computers (PCs) in their late adolescence. In 2004 they were aged 27 to 38, having been born between 1966 and 1977.

Finally, the *second informational generation* is that which grew up, from their childhood and right through adolescence, with networked PCs and with massification of Internet access. This generation was born between 1978 and 1988 and was aged 16 to 26 in 2004.

Table 7.4 – Internet usage frequency by informational generation in Portugal (%)

	16-26 2nd informational generation (Internet)	27-38 1st informational generation (PCs)	39-51 Paleo-informational generation (mainframes)	>51 Non-computerized generation
Frequency of use at work	15.4%	47.8%	69.4%	56.4%
Frequency of use at home	50.2%	56.4%	68.3%	75.7%
Frequency of use at school/university	47.7%	4.4%	5.0%	0.0%

Source: Cardoso et al., 2004, The Network Society in Portugal, CIES/ISCTE. Note: the values represent the percentage of Internet users who make use of the net at least once per month in one of the place options.

In Portugal, the preferred place for using the Internet is the home. However, there are obviously generational differences. Thus, the *2nd informational generation*, the most recent to go through the education system, has the home and the school/university as almost equal and complementary points of access (Table 7.4).

In contrast, the generation closest to retirement, the *non-computerized generation* (non-computerized in their adolescence) is that which most chooses the home as access point. We can conjecture that less use at work also has to do with being in workplaces where computerization took place at a late stage or which still have not been penetrated by computers. Furthermore, the home offers this generation a space for experimentation free of the judgement of others with respect to difficulties experienced in learning processes and to surfing strategies and amount of time spent online.

Table 7.5 – Instrumental skills for using the Internet, by generation in Portugal (%)

	16-26 2nd informational generation (Internet)	27-38 1st informational generation (PCs)	39-51 Paleo-informational generation (mainframes)	>51 Non-computerized generation
Do you know how to receive and send E-mail messages with attachments?	74.5%	79.8%	70.2%	67.6%
Do you know how to use a search engine or find what you need by searching the Internet?	86.5%	91.9%	89.2%	100%
Do you know how to download things from the Internet onto your computer?	73.0%	73.6%	66.1%	63.2%
Do you know how to make a website?	35.7%	33.0%	30.8%	32.4%

Source: Cardoso et al., 2004, The Network Society in Portugal, CIES/ISCTE.

Whereas the *1st informational generation* is characterized by an interme-diate situation of the substitution of Internet access practices at school with the search for access times and logics at work, maintaining, or increasing, access at home, the generation that has the most balance combination of Internet use at home and at work is the *paleo-informational generation.*

One of the questions that accompanies the analysis of differences in use between the age groups is that of to what extent the possession or lack of skills conditions the use of the Internet. The analysis of the data presented in the preceding table (Table 7.5) reveals that, contrary to what one would suppose from the public discourse, Internet users have more or less similar skills regardless of their age.

Of the four skills analyzed, there is only a clear difference between the two older generations and the two younger ones in one of them: the ability to execute downloads.

Another almost transversally common trait to all four generations can be seen in two representations of the Internet, namely the ideas that the Internet "is a place with a lot of useful information for me" and "allows me to keep up to date".

However, if we analyze the responses given in the following table (Ta-ble 7.6) in conjunction with whether or not the respondents turn to the

Internet first to seek information they need, we see that the generations consisting of those aged 27 to 51 are those that most appreciate the Internet as an updated information dimension.

In other words, the *1st informational* and the *paleo-informational* generations are those whose representations are closest to the description of the Internet as a priority information space in relation to the other media.

Table 7.6 – Representations of the Internet by informational generation in Portugal (% of agreement)

	16-26 2nd informational generation (Internet)	27-38 1st informational generation (PCs)	39-51 Paleo-informational generation (mainframes)	>51 Non-computerized generation
When I need information I turn to the Internet first.	19.6%	23.0%	14.9%	21.1%
I agree completely that the Internet is a place where I can find lots of information useful to me.	54.8%	58.0%	56.6%	47.5%
I agree completely that the Internet enables me to be up to date.	54.5%	62.0%	60.2%	55.0%
Internet use makes it easier for me to communicate with people from other generations.	62.7%	53.9%	56.1%	64.2%
Surfing the web is a way to spend one's time, keep boredom at bay and is an alternative to other media.	65.5%	63.9%	45.4%	45.0%
I seek music in mp3 format on the Internet to exchange with friends and listen to on my mobile phone.	20.7%	12.9%	8.3%	0.0%
I frequently use the Internet while watching TV or listening to radio at the same time.	13.6%	13.9%	5.0%	7.9%

Source: Cardoso et al., 2004, The Network Society in Portugal, CIES/ISCTE.

In terms of the inter-generational approximation role that the Internet may play, the data in the preceding table also produce some interested conclusions: the youngest generation and the oldest generation are those that most value the role of inter-generational approximation, although perhaps for different reasons. Thus, for the *2nd informational generation,* the Internet confers a symbolic power by inverting the power relations within the family. The younger family members teach the older members how to use the new technologies, thus reversing the traditional parent (educator)/child (learner) roles. This functionality results in a new channel of approximation between progenitors and offspring in the context of the family.

For the *non-computerized generation* the reasons are different. For the older generations, the Internet is an instrument, the mastering of which enables them to conquer a place in the presence, in the modernity experienced by the younger generations.

One more conclusion one can draw from the analysis of the representations of the Internet in generational terms is that (when confronted with the idea that the Internet had a dimension of entertainment and occupation of spare time for them, i.e. that, in the entertainment domain, it was an alternative to other media, such as television, that already perform the same function in our everyday life) there is a clear generational division into two large groups. Hence, the two informational generations, which came into contact with the new technologies in their personal computer dimension during their childhood and adolescence, also see the Internet as away of passing the time and not merely as an instrument for the objective procurement of information.

The older generations, however, adhere to a much lesser degree to this ideal and seem to attribute to the Internet a very specific identity that cannot substitute the other media. Thus, these generations reveal greater user loyalty to the preceding technologies such as television and radio.

For the older generations, the new technologies respond to new needs and do not replace the response already given by the older technologies. In this sense, the younger generations are much more multimedia in that they are able to appropriate different media for different functions, ignoring the traditional representations as to the functions of a given technology. Multimediality as a practice, but seemingly also as a way of life, seems to be essentially present in the *2nd informational generation,* although there are also significant traces of this form of using the technologies identifiable in the *1st informational generation.*

The *2nd informational generation* is the generation that grew up with the Internet, that downloads pop songs online and swaps them with friends in a process of social valuation of music as a form of constructing a communal identity, while at the same time establishing network relationships between different technologies, such as the Internet and the mobile phone. It is also the generation that best exemplifies the multitasking logic, i.e. the capability of computer systems to carry out various tasks at the same time. Multitasking in the media-related terms refers to the simultaneous use of different technologies, for example using the Internet while watching TV and/or listening to the radio.

In their study on the Internet access reality in Japan, Mikhami (2004) and Ishii (2004) consolidated the reality of multitasking. Although the findings do not allow for identification of protagonists in generational terms they do reveal how this action is part of our daily routines. The five activities, in Japanese society, that allow for the greatest degree of multitasking are: the use of the Internet for consulting BBS; the use of message programmes such as Microsoft's MSN Messenger; listening to music on the PC; the use of chat programmes; surfing the Internet using mobile phones and playing games on mobile phones.

Table 7.7 – Rate (%) of major multitasking information usage patterns in Japan

	Watching TV	Listening to CD's/MD	Chatting with friends and family	Talking over landline phones	Talking over Mobile Phones
Talking over mobile phones	11,8	1,1	7,8	7,3	-
E-mail using mobile phones	22,9	4,5	16,4	0,9	4,2
Information site browsing with mobile phones	20,3	12,4	14,7	1,1	1,1
Games using mobile phones	22,0	13,2	5,5	0.0	0.0
Internet e-mail	11.4	1.7	7.3	8.1	2.1
Messenger using Internet	24.2	1.8	8.4	0.0	2.9
Chat using Internet	12.4	0.0	10.1	0.0	0.6
BBS on Internet	7.9	0.7	7.4	19.1	0.7
Website browsing using Internet	12.4	0.8	7.0	6.1	1.6
File transfer using Internet	7.4	0.0	0.0	2.8	3.9
Online games on Internet	3.1	0.0	9.0	0.9	0.0
Word processing, etc. with PCs	2.8	0.5	1.4	8.3	3.8
Watching TV with PCs	17.7	0.0	20.6	0.0	0.0
Watching TV recorded on PCs	3.7	0.0	0.0	0.0	0.0
Watching DVD using PCs	0.0	0.0	0.0	3.7	0.0
Listening music on PCs	2.5	10.0	11.3	0.0	0.0
Games on PCs	14.0	5.4	3.6	0.0	0.4

Source: Mikhami (2004) and Ishii (2004).

From the data presented in the preceding table on the Japanese reality one can conclude that of the five activities listed (watching TV, listing to music, chatting and talking on the phone and on the mobile phone) that which most facilitates multitasking is watching television. However, that form of multitasking is essentially achieved by the use of mobile phones for functions other than talking on the phone (for example, sending E-mails, surfing and games) or by surfing the Internet using a PC. Listening to music would seem to primarily facilitate chatting to friends and family and not so much other technological mediations.

Another generational analysis dimension for a technology domestication is the way the *mediation* is used in defining specific objectives.

Table 7.8 – Internet usage objectives by informational generation in Portugal (%)

	16-26 2nd informational generation (Internet)	27-38 1st informational generation (PCs)	39-51 Paleo-informational generation (mainframes)	>51 Non-computerized generation
Sending or receiving E-mail messages	72.9%	76.6%	69.4%	71.1%
Surfing the Internet without a specific purpose	68.2%	65.4%	54.5%	65.8%
Consulting libraries, encyclopaedias, dictionaries	51.2% (1)	45.0% (2)	43.3% (2)	48.6% (2)
Participating in chats or newsgroups	47.9% (2)	37.3% (5)	29.8% (4)	15.8% (-)
Downloading music	42.9% (3)	31.1% (10)	20.7% (-)	15.8%
Reading news in the general press	35.2% (4)	46.4% (1)	33.9% (3)	52.6% (1)
Reading sports news	31.5% (5)	32.5% (9)	16.7% (-)	15.8% (-)
Downloading software from the net	30.7% (6)	32.7% (8)	20.0% (10)	18.4% (10)
Getting information on shows/concerts	30.1% (7)	37.3% (5)	22.3% (8)	26.3% (7)
Arranging dates or nights out with friends	28.6% (8)	25.8% (-)	7.5% (-)	13.2% (-)
Playing video games on the Internet	27.9% (9)	15.4% (-)	15.0% (-)	10.8% (-)
Contacting friends when down	26.7% (10)	27.3% (-)	12.5% (-)	7.9% (-)
Researching travel information	19.3% (-)	39.9% (4)	29.2% (5)	42.1% (4)
Researching information on one's city	23.7% (-)	34.4% (7)	26.4% (7)	36.8% (5)
Researching information on one's own health and that of people close to one	13.5% (-)	23.4% (-)	20.8% (9)	23.7% (8)
Researching information on public services	13.0% (-)	40.9% (3)	45.8% (1)	35.1% (6)
Buying other things*	8.1% (-)	9.6% (-)	7.4% (-)	21.1% (9)
Carrying out banking operations	13.9% (-)	35.1% (6)	28.3% (6)	43.2% (3)

Source: Cardoso et al., 2004, The Network Society in Portugal, CIES/ISCTE. Note: * Things other than food and cleaning products, books or CDs, computer products and show/concert tickets.

If we compare the existing date for the globality of the populations using the Internet in countries/regions such as Portugal (Cardoso, 2005), Catalonia (Castells, 2003), US (Cole, 2005), Japan (Mikhami, 2004), Canada (Zamaria, 2004), Spain (Marina, 2003) and Chile (Godoy, 2004), they all indicate the prevalence of preferences for more generalist uses of the Internet such as E-mail and surfing the Net without a totally defined goal, in other words, browsing.

Although there are similarities between the practices of the different generations in relation to the Internet, one can also identify differences, for even when the practices are similar, their hierarchization is different.

The *non-computerized generation*, i.e. the over fifty year olds, is that which most corresponds to the stereotype of the Internet as an *information technology* (Cardoso, 1998). Their practices favour, first and foremost, the news, consulting information archives and specific information components (such as travel, the city one lives in, the public services, shows and concerts and one's own health and that of those close to one). This is also the generation that most values the *mediation* via the Internet with their bank and also most values the *mediation* in their purchases. Downloading software is, for this generation and the subsequent one, of residual importance, as it is the tenth most frequent activity carried out.

The *paleo-informational generation* has almost the same characteristics as the over fifty-one generation. However, while participation in chats or newsgroups features amongst the ten most frequent practices, the valuation of the uses by this generation is hierarchically different.

The fact that these two generations reveal practices that are essentially dedicated to obtaining information must be seen in the context of their media education being dominated by an information technology such as television, in the context of Paleo-TV, in which a social construction of the medium television as a distributor of information and instrument of education prevailed.

As for the two informational generations, the panorama is somewhat different. The *2nd informational generation* is that which most clearly reveals diversification of the representations it confers on, and practices it carries out with, the Internet. For this generation, as for the *1st informational generation*, the use of the Internet as an archive of information and library is a priority. However, there is a clear presence of an idea of the Internet as a *social technology* (Cardoso, 1999).

The second most frequent activity is participating in chats and news-groups. Although one can argue that socializing and the construction of friendship networks is essentially a characteristic of this age group (and hence its over-valuation), there are other factors to be taken into account. In a clear demonstration of the incorporation of the Internet as a social tech-nology, the 1st informational generation, also places chats and newsgroups as the fifth most frequent use of the Internet, as well as "using the Internet for arranging nights out with friends" and "contacting friends when down" (although these are in 11th and 12th place, thus well below the 8th and 10th place given to these by the youngest generation).

The valuation given by the two *informational generations* to playing games in network with friends can be subjected to an identical analysis. This use is one example of how the Internet, in particular for the 2nd genera-tion, is a social entertainment space.

Continuing the analysis of the two *informational generations*, one must mention the presence of music in their Internet-mediated activities. For the *2nd generation,* music is the third most frequent activity in the use of the Internet (and the tenth most frequent for the 1st informational generation). The generational dimension of the activities of chatting and listening to music is not an eminently Portuguese characteristic, for, as Liang's (2003) studies on China corroborate, approximately 60% of Chi-nese users between the ages of 17 and 24 download music from the Inter-net, while only 18% of the users aged 45 to 60 do so. The same trend is also valid for chatting (Liang, 2005). The importance of music in online practices can be illustrated by the data from different countries, which present similar values in terms user preferences: Catalonia with 37.4% of the users (Castells, 2003), Portugal with 34.1% (Cardoso, 2005), Japan with 23,2% (Mikhami, 2004), Chile with values approaching 40% (Go-doy, 2004) or Canada with average weekly hours listening to music on the Internet of 3.5 hours and 2.7 hours for downloading music (Zamaria, 2004) and the US, where the younger users spend 4.3% of their time on-line downloading music and the more experienced users spend 2.7% of their time online (Cole, 2005).

Hence, for both *informational generations,* the Internet, in addition to be an *informational technology* is also a *social technology* in three differ-ent dimensions: as a space of social network management; as social en-tertainment space and as an identity management space – through music, amongst other instruments.

The *1st informational generation,* the pioneer generation in the use of PCs and the Internet, discovered and domesticated the Internet in its own image, creating, in part, the Internet we all know today. It sees the Internet as a frontier to be explored. It realizes a strong identitary and emotional investment in fruition of the Internet, which is at the same time focused and productive. It ritualizes the time spent online and invests in learning new techniques for keeping up with the younger generations and not losing its lead.

The *2nd informational generation,* which became acquainted with the Internet at home or school, has a colder relationship with the Internet, while its emotive universe is greater in relation to video games, music and the mobile phone, the Internet only takes on an emotive dimension when it is used as a social network management space. In general, the Internet is seen as just another medium that is part of everyday life. It advances net-worked fruition with other media (on as an alternative to other media) and is characterized by usage marked by efficiency and multitasking (rapidity, high surfing speed and multiple windows).

Another characteristic associated with the greater degree of skills using the medium, and one that provides justification for the weak penetration of e-commerce in the informational generations is the fact that the better one knows the medium, the more one can assess the security limitations, thus creating new barriers to its use.

In the informational generations there would also seem to be a trend to-wards substituting some more media by others (namely television), but the time of exposure and the use of *mediation* tends to increase. Another trend seems to be that of creating networks between media, i.e. listening to radio online and using the Internet to check on programmes in other media.

However, in the field of the written press, there is a tendency amongst the younger generations to give more attention to sports new than the older generations. As far as the general interest press is concerned, there are con-tradictory signs in realities as diverse as the US, Portugal and China. In Portugal, it is in the older generations that we find online reading at over 50% of the users, while in China the values for all age intervals are always higher than the 50.8% for users ages 17 to 24 years old. For the US, the reality seems to be closer to that witnessed in Portugal, for, according to the Pew Research Centre (2004), approximately 36% of young adults aged 18 to 29 years old regularly consult online news. This age group is also that mostly likely to make use of news via the Internet and to make more use of sites such as Yahoo! or AOL News than those of the national newspapers (The Project for Excellence in Journalism, 2005).

These analyzes of the generational practices in relation to online news allows us to draw two conclusions. On the one hand, in online news there are cultural differences that can explain, in some cases, the greater adherence to reading newspapers online, as is the case for China, and, in others, the lesser adherence, for example in the US and Portugal. On the other hand, the tradition of a greater or lesser culture of reading the printed versions of newspapers in a given national context does not seem to have a direct impact on the reading of online newspapers or the propensity of younger users to seek the news in online newspapers. Taking as a basis the reality in the US, one can argue that it is not a case of the younger generations not being interested in news but one of in which format they are more interested in obtaining news?

The answer may be that the online newspapers do not obligatorily have to be the goal of the search for news by the younger generations but, as the Project for Excellence in Journalism report (2005) confirms, that there may be a change taking place, with the younger generations turning to resources that offer them news with less, or even no, editing, such as the portals. One can thus suggest that, as some studies seem to indicate (Cole, 2005 and Cardoso, 2005), Internet usage does not further cannibalization between the online and offline supports of one and the same medium but an accumulation of the Internet to the sources already used. However, we must bear in mind that the Internet does not turn non-consumers of news into consumers, as the studies seem to indicate that the largest consumers of online news are also the largest consumers of print newspapers and magazines and those who traditionally dedicate most time to televized information (Cole 2005). Similarly, if the younger generations consume less media, such as the newspapers, it is not likely that the online media will change that behaviour.

Nevertheless, there are some questions left unanswered, given that new relational forms and routines with the news are created and may also influence the generational practices. For example, consulting the news online does not overlap upon the traditional news consumption times (morning, lunchtime and evening) but has created a socially accept routine of permanent consumption throughout the day (Project for Excellence in Journalism, 2005). The social dimension that characterizes the informational generation is also fruit of a greater degree of domestication in relation to the new information and communication technologies and their networking, for what we have analyzed here in relation to the Internet could also be said about the mobile phone, for example. Personalization is more evident in mobile phones than in computers. In other words, the users choose ring tones but, for example, do not choose what type of news they wish to receive. The mobile phone is a personal medium but the computer is an individual medium (Hartmann, 2003).

The informational generations are also those that make most use of mobile phones. On average, in the two informational generations only 10% does not use the mobile phone for personal use, while the values for the *paleo-informational generation* are twice that figure and for the *non-computerized generation* reach more than 57% of those over 50 years of age.[144]

This analysis leads to the conclusion that the specific needs of a generation in the use of technologies such as the Internet – such as health problems in the older generations or the creation of social networks and the search for partners in the younger generations – manifest themselves in the specific *mediation* practices of each generation.

Table 7.9 – Number of hours per day spent watching television, by informational generation in Portugal (%)

		16-26 2nd informational generation (Internet)	27-38 1st informational generation (PCs)	39-51 Paleo-informational generation (mainframes)	>51 Non-computerized generation
Internet users	Up to 2 hours	59.7	70.3	71.6	67.5
	> 2 hours	40.3	29.7	28.4	32.5
Non-Internet users	Up to 2 hours	53.5	52.9	59.4	34.9
	> 2 hours	45.6	47.1	40.6	65.2

Source: Cardoso et al., 2004, The Network Society in Portugal, CIES/ISCTE.

However, because these specificities do not make up the whole spectrum of practices, one can confirm the existence of other decisive factors for the structuring of the media representations and practices of a specific

---

[144]In Portugal, 61.6% of households have a landline telephone at home and 71.9% of citizens over the age of 15 have a mobile phone for personal use. Source: Cardoso et al. (2004), The Network Society in Portugal, CIES/ISCTE.

generation in relation to a specific information and communication technology.

In a quantitative perspective, if we consider the time spent watching television and using the Internet, we see how unbalanced the media system is in relation to the practices. The older generations spend much more time in front of the television, while in the younger groups television viewing times are on the decrease.

Nevertheless, of those who use the Internet, the *2nd informational generation* is the one that has least reduced its daily television viewing time, most likely due to its capacity for multitasking and to the use of television as a sound and image backdrop. In other words, the TV is on, but is it not the object of permanent attention.

The younger generations would seem to be much more productive with their time, given that they approach the television medium in a multitasking perspective, whereas the older viewers do one thing at a time. Thus, in this sense, television would seem to be more oriented towards the older generations, while the Internet is directed more at the younger generations (Colombo and Aroldi 2003).

The hypothesis is, thus, that effectively the sharing of joint historic moments and specific media consumptions (Colombo and Aroldi, 2003) in some way moulds the future representations in relation to the media and the uses we make of them.

Different Media Ages, Different Forms of Citizenship?

Can one infer from the preceding analysis that the way we see the media also moulds our media matrixes and diets when our objective is to exercise participation, be it in a context of parliamentary participation between the elector and elected representative or citizen and public administration or even an extra-parliamentary context of campaigns protesting against or supporting a particular thing or body/person?

By way of contextualizing the practices of citizenship in Portugal, it is worthwhile bearing in mind that only 20.9% of the Portuguese belong to an association, club, NGO, trade union, political body or similar associative body. Those who belong to a form of association are, on average, members of 1.33 associations. The value is slightly higher amongst Internet users (1.41) in comparison to non-users (1.27).

In terms of active participation of the Portuguese in the associations they are members of, the average value is 0.95, whereby the difference between Internet users and non-users is somewhat greater (1.04 versus 0.88).

In terms of the use of the Internet in relations with the associations of which they are members, the mean value decreases to 0.33. The following table (Table 7.10) presents these distributions, taking into account the total number of associations.

Despite the very frequent complaints on the way the Portuguese public administration functions in terms of relations with the citizens, a large majority of 89.6% of Portuguese citizens have never taken part in or developed any kind of letter writing initiative to the official bodies (Cardoso et al., 2004).

Table 7.10 – Membership of and participation in associations, in relation to which the Internet is used, in Portugal (%)

Number of associations you belong to, in which you participate and in relation to which you use the Internet		Users	Non-users	Total
Total no. of associations you belong to	1 association	69.8	76.6	73.8
	2 associations	19.6	19.9	19.8
	3 associations or more	10.6	3.5	6.4
	Total	100.0	100.0	100.0
Total no. of associations you participate in	None	18.9	26.6	23.4
	1 association	57.9	59.0	58.5
	2 associations or more	23.2	14.4	18.0
	Total	100.0	100.0	100.0
Total no. of associations in relation to which you use the Internet	None	73.2	100.0	89.0
	1 association	20.5	0.0	8.4
	2 associations or more	6.3	0.0	2.6
	Total	100.0	100.0	100.0

Source: Source: Cardoso et al., 2004, The Network Society in Portugal, CIES/ISCTE. Note: these values refer to respondents belonging to at least one association (p<0.01).

In the general population, only 3.1% of respondents state that they have ever written a letter to manifest their opinion to the editor of a publication. This figure rises to 14% for contacts with the organs of local power – town/city councils or parish councils.

The two intermediate generations, i.e. the *1st informational* and the *paleo-informational* generations, are those that interact most with the public administration and their elected representatives.

However, the *1st informational generation* invests more in the use of E-mail and the Internet as a means of contact, perhaps because it has a more positive representation as to the effectiveness of that instrument and because it is the generation that most uses the Internet for contacts in the school/education context and therefore more readily incorporates this usage in their active lives and in civic participation.

In line with the trend described above for the *non-computerized* and *paleo-informational* generations, i.e. the valuation of the press as one of the most interesting media, it is also these two generations that write most to publications. However, the younger generations make most use of E-mail for this communication. Although they prefer E-mail, if available, the younger generations seem to value paper and E-mail on a similar level. As if to say the means is less important than the message.

Table 7.11 – Mediated forms of participation, by informational generation in Portugal (%)

	16-26 2nd informational generation (Internet)	27-38 1st informational generation (PCs)	39-51 Paleo- informational generation (mainframes)	>51 Non- computerized generation
Have you ever signed a petition or written a letter of protest to a state body or the public administration?	9.7%	13.5%	13.2%	6.4%
(...) and have you ever used E-mail or the Internet for that purpose?	25.0%	31.9%	21.4%	30%
Have you ever contacted your town/city council or parish council for information on something that affects the place you live in?	8.5%	16.7%	17.7%	13.8%
(...) and have you ever used E-mail or the Internet for that purpose?	5.7%	19.3%	10.5%	12.5%
Have you ever written to the editor of a publication to express your opinion?	2.6%	3.3%	3.9%	2.9%
(...) and have you ever used E-mail or the Internet for that purpose?	53.8%	43.8%	23.1%	33.3%

Source: Cardoso et al., 2004, The Network Society in Portugal, CIES/ISCTE.

As far as active participation in protests and causes is concerned, only 15.1% of Portuguese citizens state that they have ever taken part in civic or social campaigns for matters such as human rights, ecology, gender equality, poverty, the protection of children and other similar issues.

The fact that the figures for participation are low does not mean that the individual belief in the capacity to influence events is not high, should the respondents mobilize, particularly at the international level and amongst the younger generations and those that use the Internet (Table 7.11).

The Internet is used in matters related with these types of campaign by only 23.1% of Internet users (i.e. approximately 2% of the Portuguese population).

Of those who frequently support or participate in campaigns or actions for human rights, ecological matters, gender equality, poverty, the protection of children and similar issues, approximately one half (49.4%) also belong to an association. Of those who support or participate occasionally, the majority does not belong to any association (61.3%). One can thus establish a connection between association membership and participation. In other words, those who actively participate are likewise willing to belong to a body and those who participate irregularly prefer to be not affiliated in organizations, thus guaranteeing greater liberty of assessment, in each given case, as to their participation or not. From this one can infer that, in addition to the membership of associations, it is equally important, for achieving an understanding of participation in our societies, to learn in what forms occasional participation associated with different causes and taking place for relatively short periods of time takes place.

Table 7.12 – Capacity for influencing international and national political events in Portugal, by generation (%)

	16-26 2nd informational generation (Internet)	27-38 1st informational generation (PCs)	39-51 Paleo- informational generation (mainframes)	>51 Non- computerized generation
I agree with people being able to influence world events with political and social campaigns [Internet users]	70.2	74.2	67.5	70.0
I agree with people being able to influence world events with political and social campaigns [Non-Internet users]	61.6	54.4	56.4	48.2
I agree that it is impossible to influence political decisions [Internet users]	60.7	59.9	55.7	87.5
I agree that it is impossible to influence political decisions [Non-Internet users]	73.7	70.6	74.3	66.1

Source: Cardoso et al., 2004, The Network Society in Portugal, CIES/ISCTE.

As the preceding table (Table 7.12) illustrates, the intermediate genera-tions – the *1st informational generation* and the *paleo-informational gen-eration* – are those with the most association membership and also the most participatory.

Although its support for campaigns is close to the national average, incorporating the Internet in campaigns and focusing their interest in the reception of information and communication with others, the *2nd informa-tional generation* is not that which best integrates the use of the Internet in the context of participation.

It is the *1st informational generation* that uses the Internet in a more instrumental way, giving it, at the same time, a realization of objectives function. The *non-computerized generation,* in turn, uses the Internet for receiving information only. In other words, the 1st informational generation does not use the Internet only to receive information or exchange experi-ences with others. It incorporates it as an instrument of direct action in the resolution of problems or protest actions.

One way of achieving a better and more in-depth understanding of the way the media are domesticated in the context of participation is the analy-sis of a concrete case of mobilization and participation. I have thus endeavoured to analyze a case of widespread participation of the population – the post-referendum crisis of 1999 in East Timor – and the way in which that situation was experienced in Portugal.

Table 7.13 – Have you participated in or supported campaigns for actions for human rights, the environment, gender equality, against poverty, protection of children and similar causes? (In Portugal, %)

	16-26 2nd informational generation (Internet)	27-38 1st informational generation (PCs)	39-51 Paleo- informational generation (mainframes)	>51 Non- computerized generation
Are you a member of an association?	19.2%	24.7%	25.0%	17.4%
Do you support or participate in campaigns of this kind?	15.0%	19.6%	16.4%	11.2%
Do you use the Internet in these campaigns?	21.2%	26.6%	20.6%	15.4%
To receive information	85.7%	80.9%	42.8%	100.0%
To communicate with other, like-minded people	57.1%	38.1%	57.1%	0.0%
To act directly (individually or as a group)	14.2%	33.3%	14.2%	0.0%

Source: Cardoso et al., 2004, The Network Society in Portugal, CIES/ISCTE.

In the universe of the Portuguese population surveyed, 14.4% responded that they had taken part in a protest or solidarity action for the people of Timor. However, bearing in mind the participation levels of the Portuguese population, as cited above, that figure is rather high, thus offering a good starting point for the analysis we wish to carry out of the media diets related to participation.

Of the Internet users, 22.2% participated, in September 1999, in a protest or solidarity action for the Timorese people, while in the segment of those who did not use the Internet against the policies of the Indonesian governments or the Indonesian paramilitary organizations only 11.2% stated that they had carried out any type of action.

As to the forms of demonstration/participation, those that were most prominent were the country stopping for 3 minutes (78.3%), the white clothes day or hanging of white flags/sheets from windows (33.3%) and the placing of a disk on one's car in support of East Timor (10.9%).

Table 7.14 – Forms of pro-East Timor participation and protest in Portugal, 1999, by generation (%)

In 1999…	16-26 2nd informational generation (Internet)	27-38 1st informational generation (PCs)	39-51 Paleo-informational generation (mainframes)	>51 Non-computerized generation	Promoting entity
Did you take part in any protest or solidarity action for the people of East Timor?	13.5%	19.1%	16.9%	10.4%	-
Sent fax or E-mail to the UN	3.9%	14.6%	5.7%	3.5%	Radio TSF jingle and its website
Sent fax or E-mail to the UN Sec. Council	5.2%	6.8%	1.2%	2.4%	Radio TSF website
Sent fax or E-mail to the Indonesian president	1.3%	2.9%	0.0%	1.2%	Radio TSF website
Internet voting on CNN and BBC sites in support of UN military intervention	3.9%	4.9%	0.0%	0.0%	Word of mouth via E-mail
Petitions on websites	6.5%	3.9%	5.7%	0.0%	Word of mouth via E-mail

Table 7.14 – Forms of pro-East Timor participation and protest in Portugal, 1999, by generation (%)

In 1999…	16-26 2nd informational generation (Internet)	27-38 1st informational generation (PCs)	39-51 Paleo-informational generation (mainframes)	>51 Non-computerized generation	Promoting entity
Car disk supporting East Timor	6.5%	18.6%	6.9%	9.3%	Unknown
Wearing white for East Timor (9-9-1999)	37.7%	38.8%	33.3%	23.3%	Newspapers DN and JN; Radio TSF; TV: RTP, SIC and TVI
Throwing flowers into the river	6.5%	7.8%	0.0%	1.2%	Advertisement TSF
Stopping the country for 3 minutes (8/9/1999)	76.6%	76.7%	80.2%	80.2%	Trade Unions and the media
Demonstration outside the US embassy in Lisbon	5.2%	7.8%	4.7%	2.3%	Civil society and the media
Demonstration outside the Indonesian embassy in Madrid (12/9/1999)	1.3%	0.0%	0.0%	0.0%	Civil society; Radio Antena 3 and RDP

Source: Cardoso et al., 2004, The Network Society in Portugal, CIES/ISCTE.

The *paleo-informational* and *non-computerized* generations are those that almost always opted for forms of participation that required less personal involvement and were easier to perform (e.g., "stopping the country for 3 minutes"). Where the personal involvement was greater, the younger generations were the protagonists in protest actions (e.g.: "wearing white", "demonstration outside the US embassy in Lisbon" and "demonstration outside the Indonesian embassy in Madrid").

As far as the mobilizing role of the media is concerned, the survey shows that the actions with the highest levels of participation were those with greater involvement of the media and, in particular, those involving the greatest diversification of media. In other words, the actions promoted in joint actions by radio stations, newspapers and television were also those with the most participants (e.g., "stopping the country for 3 minutes" and "wearing white").

The *1st informational generation* was clearly more involved in participation in the protests. It was even prepared to publicly display its involvement through the use of private property for demonstrating support – as was the case of their cars.

An isolated analysis of the role of the different media in the mobilization shows that, as far as the involvement of the radio station TSF in the protests is concerned, whenever radio jingles were added to the publicity on the radio station's website, the older generations also adhered to the sending of E-mails and faxes to the UN. When the campaign was promoted exclusively via the TSF Internet site (sending fax and E-mails to the UN Security Council, sending fax E-mails to the Indonesian President), without being broadcast on the radio, the participation reached above all the younger generations. The data would thus seem to corroborate the above analyses on the association of interest in the radio and the *paleo-informational and non-computerized generations.*

When the mobilization was not mediated by radio, the newspapers or television and, involved different, geographically dispersed online media, such as the petitions or opinion polls, the latter were chosen more by the 2nd informational generation, whereas the remaining generations focused on the petitions.

This is an important analysis point because of the 14 international online polls available, only three (Time, CNN and BBC) were by international media of reference, while the 47 petitions available on the Internet were all of Portuguese origin. This option for the online polls (and, in particular, those of the television stations) illustrates greater digital literacy on the part of the *1ˢᵗ informational generation,* as well as recognition of the international media as being or more use for making one's voice heard in a way that could influence the course of events.

In the same way that different generations construct different media matrixes and diets and have different media biographies and memories, the appropriation of the mediated symbolic space, for the purpose of mobilizing and protesting, occurs differently in the different generations.

The conclusions that can be drawn from the analyzes presented here are, for example, that the 1ˢᵗ informational generation is that which best combines traditional media literacy, Internet-based action and organization strategies and traditional forms of activism, such as public demonstrations.

The *non-computerized generation* seems to participate more when organization by traditional social movements, such as the trade unions, teams up with mobilization through television, radio and the newspapers. It therefore almost exclusively commits to media happenings and less to actions such as demonstrations.

The practices of the youngest generation, the *2ⁿᵈ informational generation*, are very similar to those of the *1ˢᵗ informational generation*. However, the management thereof is still experimental and lest articulated. Furthermore, its literacy in relation to the traditional media (television, radio and newspapers) is different to that of the *1ˢᵗ informational generation,* so that the combination of these media and the Internet is accordingly less.

In one and the same social and cultural context, and sharing the same objectives of citizenship, the same media are used different in different generational contexts. As the analysis of the generational practices demonstrated, there are, therefore, different representations and different media networking practices and logics. These differences are also mirrored in the way the symbolic field of *mediation* is appropriated by the different generations. Taking these data as a point of departure, are we able to characterize the citizenship that the network society provides us? How can the communicative autonomy constructed in the context of a media system, with the characteristics described in this chapter and preceding ones, help us to manage or citizenship practices?

The next two chapters will help he answer these questions, using the analysis of a number of case studies on participation, mobilization and protest in the context of parliamentary political mediation, i.e. institutionalized mediation between citizens and organs of sovereignty, and also in the context of extra-parliamentary, or non-institutionalized political mediation involving different citizens' and social movements.

8. Mediated Politics: Citizens and Political Parties in Continuous Democracy

But do you believe in electronic democracy?
As much as I believe in democracy. We all know that we live in an im-
perfect democracy and that, as Churchill said, it is a terrible system,
but all other systems are worse. In short, it's a direction.

> Umberto Eco, Interview,
> *The nomenclature and electronic democracy*

Informational politics, as we have seen, can take place both in the institutional space of the organs of sovereignty, centred on the relationship
between elector and elected representative in a parliamentary context, and
outside that space.

We have also seen that the new media present in the *mediation* space
have been the object of interest and study by diverse researchers, while, at
the same time, their use has been exploited by political elites and citizens
in the context of what can be termed an ideal of *continuous democracy*
(Rodotà, 1997).

When Stefano Rodotà chooses the concept *continuous democracy* as
paradigmatic for our position in relation to contemporary democracy, he
does so in reference to the instruments that differ from those we are normally refer to as representative, i.e. the vote.

They are instruments that are appropriated without referring to the existence of a mediator, i.e. a party or an elected representative, as it is preferable to elect new *mediation* spaces. However, the concept must not be confused with that of direct democracy, given that the latter refers only to the final moment of a decision or to the presence of a certain decision making process (Rodotà, 1997).

The emphasis in the concept of continuous democracy is placed on the end of the intermittence of the political process as far as the presence of the citizen is concerned and on the fact that the new continuity proceeds above all from the interested parties themselves (Rodotà, 1997). But there are considerable differences between this ideal of the almost permanent presence of democratic practice and the real appropriation of the different media – and, in particular, the Internet – by citizens and also by the political elites.

Rodotà's definition has the merit that it enables us to escape the electronic definitions of democracy centred on technological appropriation formulas (Norris 2004) so that we focus on what makes the practices of *informational politics* different to preceding models (Castells, 2004). However, it also has its limitations, particularly in that it proceeds from the principle that the new *mediation* spaces provided by the Internet and mobile phones would superimpose themselves on the preceding *mediation* spaces in which television, radio and the print media were the protagonists – ignoring that, for the communication to take place, it is necessary that both sides have an equal interest in promoting the new channels. Moreover, Rodotà seems to discount the fact that in informational politics there are more than just two sides, citizen and elected representative. There are also the traditional media themselves (television, radio and newspapers) that are not willing to give up their role of central mediator of informational politics.

The idea of *continuous democracy* comprises two fundamental dimensions of informational politics: *continuity,* as opposed to intermittence, and *valuation of the mediation spaces*, to the detriment of the moment of election. However, it does not sufficiently value, on the one hand, the power of the process of domestication of the traditional media by the political elites and, on the other, the fact that the real change in the political paradigm can only take place if the will for change is really there on the part of the political elites – not only in their representations but also in their practices. Something that is dependent on the gains and losses perceived in the change bringing advantages, for, if they don't, the tendency will be keep the current *mediation* channels instead of changing them.

The *continuous democracy* process continues to be related with the new mediation spaces. However, it must not only be seen as a bottom-up process. It is also dependent on the will of the elected representatives and on the way that the mediators, journalists and traditional media perceive it, or not, as a threat to the exercise of their symbolic power (Bourdieu, 1989).

Understanding this relationship between *mediation* spaces and political elites is one of the objectives of this chapter. We will analyze the way in which citizens and politicians in the Portuguese institutional context (parliament, political parties, government and presidency) relate with each other in the scope of these continuous practices and multiple *mediation* spaces and compare it to other European parliamentary contexts, seeking, at the same time, to understand the informational politics these relationships seem to be generating. In other words, what continuous democracy does the current informational politics offer when practised in the parliamentary framework of a European democracy such as Portugal?

An Institutional and Parliamentary Framework for Continuous Democracy

Where exactly are we in understanding the relations between technological uses and democratic practices in the parliamentary contexts of our democracies?

To begin answering that question it is necessary to point out that, over the last three decades, the information and communication technologies have been presented mostly as a form of reducing the distrust on the part of the electors in relation to the democracy in which they live. What are the origins of this distrust?

It is the result of a more wide-reaching transformation of the economy, culture and society which has gradually taken place over the last few decades and which can be characterized in a global context as the emergence of the Information Age, powered by the information and communication technologies. It is also characterized by the incapacities of the current processes, institutions and political agents in responding to the citizen's anxieties (Castells, 2003).

Faced with these transformations, democratic societies find themselves in a phase of reassessment of their political practices, with signs of a crisis of legitimacy of the Nation State, democracy and the participation of the individual and collective actors in a general scenario of alteration of the political system itself. The political system has also undergone an expansion of its competences and spheres of influence, leading some authors to speak of a *political system in a networked model* that encompasses the global relations between governments and institutions, the government (at the local, regional and national levels), other regulating bodies, civil society organization, corporations and individual citizens (Dijk, 2000 and Castells, 2003).

The late 20th century and early 21st century is a period of cohabitation of contradictory phenomena (Giddens, 2000 and Castells, 2003). To give examples of this notion, Giddens (2000) shows how the development of communications at the global level has favoured the development of democracy in political regimes in Europe, Latin America, Africa and Asia while at the same time contributing to limiting the scope of influence of those very same democratic structures. In a globalization context, the world's capitalist economy, itself based on this logic of communication in global networks, introduces processes of the shifting of the centres, or nodes, of power hitherto managed by the multiple political centres, the Nation States (Lyon, 1992).

Consequently, the states forfeit part of their power of control over monetary and budgetary policies, resulting, in turn, in less power of organization of their production and exchanges and of the attribution and management of social benefits.

Together with this loss of economic power, there are also other types of limitations of the sovereignty of the states, to a large extent due to the sharing of sovereignty in the management of global economic, ecological and security matters that require global responses and solutions. This process has led Castells (2003) to speak of the emergence of a *networked global state.*

The political order thus constitutes itself as a plurality of institutions and organizations that interconnect the different states (regarded as strategic actors) through numerous agreement, conventions and relationships of exchange that shift certain decisions and fields of action away from individual countries that were previously their exclusive responsibility.

This process of sharing of sovereignty in certain matters (such as security, economy and the environment) results in both gains for, and the system erosion of, the power of states. This is so because, as Castells argues (2004), the continuous process of conflict, alliance and negotiation also wears down the credibility of the international institutions and the creation of global or regional bureaucracies often has a collateral effect: the paralyzation of the states' capacity to act, be it individually or multilaterally.

This networking process also takes place at the internal level in the different Nation States, through the decentralization of the politics of the Nation State (with its governmental institutions and public administration) to other actors within and outside the political system. This dispersion is described by various authors. In Beck's analyzes it is termed "displacement of politics" (Beck, 1992) and is referred to as "plurality of the sources of power" by Held (1987; 2000).

In a polycentric system, the centres of power are interconnected through the information and communication relations based on complex networks of capital, production, communication, crime, international institutions, supranational military organizations, non-governmental organizations, transnational religious structures and public opinion movements (Castells, 2004). Although the trend towards decentralization of the Nation State is one of the forms of dealing with the power management tensions created by the need for action on different levels, from the local to the global, it is *not the only one.*

Hence, we also find a leaning towards policies in the opposite direction, namely the concentration of politics in the State. This is a process that takes place in accordance with two main dimensions (Dijk, 1999). The first is the *modernization of bureaucracy* through the application of the information technologies, seeking to create a network that combines an increase in central control and a decentralization of the executive tasks, thus heralding a more transparent and efficient state with possible benefits for the citizens.

The second form of concentration consists of a greater merging of the State and institutional politics, giving rise, through political practice, to a new relationship between *State* and *party.* In other words, when they are running for election, the political parties prefer to be in the government or the public administration than to serve as the citizens' representatives in parliament. To achieve these objectives the political parties transform themselves into election campaign organizations, thus altering their traditional functions as programmatic associations for the political organization and mobilization of citizens.

In this search for new balances on the part of the State, be it with other individual states or at the global or local level, one certainty does emerge. Despite its debilities, the State still presents itself as a strong candidate for permanence as a central institution in our societies in the Information Age.

The states continue to be the most important actors in the field of political relations (Dijk, 1999; Giddens, 2000) due to the fact that they control a specific territory (national labour, production and service regulation policies), their monopoly on the means of force and their status as entities with the legitimacy for creating global and multilateral mechanisms.

There would also not seem to be an inevitable path towards a given, single model of change for the State. Precisely because the sovereignty of states has not diminished in a progressive, linear way. Due to the dialectic character of globalization and the influence of unequal development processes – in certain cases as the result of alliances, wars or political and economic changes – one can identify, in some cases, increases in sovereignty and in others a real decrease. Rejecting the argument of the end of the State as a political entity is not the same as saying that it is resistant to profound changes, which does not necessarily have to come from direct economic effects. In a world of cultural and transnational global networks, and given the phenomena of the growing valuation of identity-based dimensions in our societies, one must bear in mind that our own notion of State as Nation State can also undergo substantial changes through different forms of fundamentalism (Castells, 2004).

This crisis of legitimacy on the part of the Nation States – due to aforementioned factors related with the dynamics of the wealth, information and trans-organizational power networks – is very closely linked to the crisis of credibility of the political system, i.e. to the a persistent feeling of disillusion and distrust in relation to politicians and politics in general on the part of the citizens.

Conditioned to a large extent by the media, dependent on political marketing strategies of technological manipulation, and guided by a policy of personalization and emptying of the political discussion in the media, the party system has lost a lot of its legitimacy in the eyes of the public (Castells, 2004). As the following table shows (Table 8.1), in the European context this loss is a characteristic that traverses the public opinion of most countries, with the exception of a few Scandinavian states.

As suggested by Vedel (2002), the way in which democracies, in their parliamentary and institutional context, have seen the new communication and information technologies – from television to the Internet – has been largely governed by question "how can we use these technologies to improve governance and political participation?" In other words, how best to manage the legitimacy of democracy. Throughout history there has been a strong notion of a connection between information and communication technologies, social change and the political management of that change.

Table 8.1 – Trust in institutions in Europe (%)

		Political parties	Government	Parliament	European Union	United Nations
Portugal	+	17	39	46	61	59
	-	78	55	46	25	25
Belgium	+	22	38	40	45	43
	-	72	54	52	47	48
Denmark	+	39	53	68	40	74
	-	48	39	24	47	16
Germany	+	12	24	31	35	41
	-	80	65	56	42	39
Greece	+	20	47	54	65	36
	-	77	50	43	30	59
Spain	+	23	42	41	57	55
	-	69	50	46	30	31
France	+	12	30	33	37	40
	-	82	64	55	49	45
Ireland	+	22	31	34	53	62
	-	67	59	55	27	19
Italy	+	11	27	33	57	50
	-	78	62	53	25	33
Luxembourg	+	26	60	53	52	51
	-	60	31	33	38	35
Netherlands	+	26	37	41	38	51
	-	65	57	51	45	37
Austria	+	19	40	43	36	50
	-	72	51	45	52	36
Finland	+	19	49	52	33	62
	-	70	41	40	53	24
Sweden	+	18	42	53	28	73
	-	71	49	38	61	18
United Kingdom	+	12	24	27	20	51
	-	79	68	62	58	31

Source: Eurobarometer 60, Public Opinion in the European Union, October/November 2003.

In the 20th century the discourse on the advantages of electronic democracy did not begin with the Internet. Strange as it may seem, Hagen (1997; 2000) reminds us that the oldest concept of electronic democracy has to do with television. The introduction of cable in the early 1970s in the United States led many to consider that, in the 1980s, through diversified contents and localized information, television could bring about a revitalization of democracy.

According to Zittel (2001), the visions of political change emerged in the 1970s with the beginning of computer networks, interactive cable TV and other digital telecommunications mechanisms, boosting ideas of electronic democracy and objectives of making democracy more participative through these new technologies. In particular with the introduction of cable TV in the US in the early 1970s, activists, political scientists and sociologists argued in favour of the potentials (Barber, 1984; 1996; 1999, Dahl 1991; 1986; 1998). [145] The users could respond to questions raised in the cable programmes, using a system connected to a box with five buttons. Futurologists such as Alvin Toffler (1980) saw this as an example of the direct democracy possibilities the future would bring (Dahlberg 2001; 2002).

However, in the late 1970s and in the 1980s, numerous authors (Arterton, 1987; Laudon, 1977; Abrahamson et al., 1988) were already criticizing the technological determinism conceptions associated with the development of new communication media and their influence on political processes.

There thus emerged a feeling of disillusion due to the incapacity of cable TV to improve the forms of direct democracy and political participation of the citizens. The central criticism of the system was, and is, that the viewers cannot make an informed decision based only on what is being diffused on television. This criticism was one of the reasons for the abandonment off such television-related electronic democracy projects. [146]

In the 1990s, the theories on democracy and technology were given a new impulse thanks to the use, in election campaigns in the US, of encounters between candidates and the electors recorded for television and also thanks to new media technological advances (multiplication of channels, new television formats and the growth of computer networks).

Basing himself on four analytical concepts (technology, forms of democracy, political participation dimensions and political agenda) Martin

---

[145]One of the most elaborate projects for this concept was Qube in Ohio.

[146]Ironically, their failure for democracy was turned into a commercial success for the private and public television stations that reworked them for commercial purposes. The television stations in Portugal seem to have rediscovered the possibilities of interactivity with the viewers, with a view to achieving alternative income to advertising through added value numbers displayed during news and other programmes.

Hagen identifies three types of relations between democracy and technology: *Teledemocracy, Cyberdemocracy* and *Electronic Democratization* (Hagen, 1997, 2000). Although all three democracy types are based on the use of computer networks, each one has a different set of objectives and readings of the current way in which democracies function.

The case for *teledemocracy* is that computer mediated communication (CMC) can finally enable forms of political participation that were considered impracticable on account of spatial or temporal restrictions. The traditional forms of representative democracy can no longer manage the complexity of the Information Age, so that local forms of democracy and the strengthening of the individual are required, allowing CMC to execute this, given the need to promote the democratic uses of the media as a form of creating a balance check against the abuses of the commercial media. The forms of political participation promoted by teledemocracy are the provision of information and the possibility of discussing issues and voting on them through CMC. It is, therefore, a model based on the use of computer networks like the Internet, whose ultimate objective is to strengthen democracy through a form of direct democracy.

What Hagen terms *cyberdemocracy* has different points of departure and preferred forms of political participation, although it promotes the same direct democracy ideal. This model considers that the creation of virtual communities and, through these, new forms of physical communities, is of central importance for the construction of a 21st century democracy. In its perspective, information has become a central economic good, so that businesses and individuals should promote the use of CMC, the technology that can ensure their success as entrepreneurs and citizens. CMC promotes decentralized and self-manageable forms of government, providing concrete protection against abuse of authority on the part of the State in relation to privacy or content censorship.

The central forms of political participation for cyberdemocracy do not include voting, but rather discussion and the promotion of political activity.

For the apologists of cyberdemocracy, CMC supplies the tools for a direct democracy, but their aim is not the substitution of representative democracy. They promote CMC to a level on a par with that of the democratic representative institutions, making it possible, through the creation of virtual communities and the revitalization of physical communities, to create new forms of management of the citizens' needs.

At the same time as this new democratic management system is being implemented, the citizens can also further their individual liberty, for CMC gives them the necessary tools for their privacy and for management of access to information, sidestepping the action of the State.

Finally, Hagen analyzes a system that does not seek the creation of direct democracy but rather the improvement of the institutions of representative democracy. The arguments of the defenders of *electronic democratization* are based on the fact that political systems based on CMC allow for more and better access to crucial information on governments. Creating and managing electronic encounters between citizens and their representatives, using CMC, can contribute to political decision-making being based on the opinion of the citizens and to giving a new sense of belonging to the electorate. This is a model which, while recognizing the problems of contemporary representative democracy, sees CMC as a means for resolving the problems of apathy and participation. Because CMC allows for a reduction in the costs of communication and organization, it is seen as way of giving more power to civil society in its relations with the State. This is a model that values the use of CMC as a form of furthering discussion and access to information.

Seeking a balance between the different proposals as to the definition of the relationship between democracy and technology, I think that that which provides the best starting point to an analysis of informational politics is that put forward by Trechsel and Kies (2004), which defines *electronic democracy* as *consisting of all the electronic communication media that enable or provide empowerment to the citizen in his efforts for achieving public accountability on the part of politicians/governants for their actions.*

Depending on the particular aspects of democracy promoted, electronic democracy can use different techniques: increasing the transparency of the political process; increasing the direct involvement and participation of the citizens; and, finally, improving the quality of opinion forming through the opening of new information spaces (Trechsel et al., 2004). To this definition one can add that this can translate to the evolution of a participative democracy model on the maintenance of the logics currently present in liberal democracy models. [147]

---

[147] According to Hague and Loader (1999), the debate on the use of ICTs in politics is centred on a *continuum* between a participative democracy model (the closest to direct democracy) and a conception

As we have seen there are diverse definitions on the use of the Internet in the democratic process. Similarly, in the vast bibliography published on this theme, we can also find descriptions of the effects of the Internet on democracy that range from little influence on democracy to visions of a revolutionary role. So what is the reality in terms of appropriation of the Internet in the democratic process? Pippa Norris's work (2001) on Internet theories and democracy offers a relative concise answer. Norris (2001) proposes a theory classification based on the vision the authors have of the role of the Internet. The *cyber-optimists* argue that the new information and communication technologies have the capacity to *save* us from our more apathetic civic tendencies. It is hoped that the information available on the Internet has the potential to allow the public to become more and more knowledgeable of political affairs, more organized in expressing their points of view through E-mail, online discussion boards and chats and also more active in terms of rallying to causes in their communities.

As a new bidirectional communication channel, the Internet can help to strengthen and enrich the connections between citizens and intermediation organizations such as the parties, social movements and interest groups, the media and local, national and global entities.

Thanks to its erosion of barriers to political participation – for example with the possibility of accumulating information from diverse sources on a certain matter, mobilizing networks, connecting diverse global coalitions around political issues or contacting elected representatives – the Internet can have the potential for expanding the horizon of participation in public life.

In contrast, for the *cyber-pessimists* the Internet will only reinforce, but not radically alter, the existing patterns of political communication and democratic participation. From their point of view, the Internet may deepen

---

of representative democracy. Participative democracy tends to see the individual as part of a political community and seeks to involve the individual as much as possible in the political process; moreover, this model sees the representatives as delegates of their constituents and advocates a constant communication flow between the elected representatives and electors, with a view to the representatives getting to know the expectations of their constituents, and an open and transparent process designed to ensure accountability of the elected representatives. The liberal democracy model, on the other hand, regards the individual as autonomous and independent of the political community, acknowledging basic antagonism between the individual and the community. The individual is thus considered as a consumer who shows no interest in political involvement and develops interests outside the political community and frequently in conflict with that community.

the divide between the already active participants and the more apathetic inside the participation process.

For Pippa Norris (2001), representatives of the so-called cyber-optimists are: Howard Rheingold (2000), for his vision of virtual communities as a new public sphere for the exchange of ideas, debate and mobilization of opinions; Brian Loader (1999), who argues that the Internet has the potential for bringing about greater accountability on the part of the government in relation to the public and for creating a more informed citizenship, facilitating participation in decision processes; Roza Tsagaroussianou (1998), who argues the case for the use of the Internet as a source of revitalization of the civic networks in urban zones and neighbourhoods; and Budge (1996), who believes that the Internet will allow for direct democracy in the form of daily online referendums. The cyber-pessimist thought is concretized through analyzes of authors such as Margolis and Resnick (2000), who argue that the use of the Internet for promoting citizenship has failed because the established interests, large parties and traditional media have done everything in their powers to main the political status quo. Bimber (1998) argues that what the Internet has changed in the transmission for and not the contents, which are the same as those already in the traditional media. Abramson and Arterton (1988) also argue that plebiscitary democracy through electronic voting is the equivalent of head counting without the opportunity of deliberative debate.

Despite its conceptual usefulness, perhaps this division fails by centring too much on the measurement of positive or negative impacts attributed to the Internet and does not conceptually develop on the contributions to the currently applicable democracy model. Endeavouring to flee these positive and negative restrictions of the technological impact, Gibson and Ward (2000) outline three scenarios of the institutional and organizational impact of the information and communication technologies in general, and the Internet in particular.

The first scenario reflects a perspective of *revolution*, erosion and direct democracy, in which the representative role of the political organizations is to be replaced by the direct intervention of the citizens in their self-governance. This vision also has its supporters in the political sphere, particularly amongst anti-system parties or candidate. The most famous example is probably the document *Cyberspace and the American Dream: A Magna Carta for the Knowledge Age*, launched in 1994 by Newt Gingrich's *Progress and Freedom Foundation*.

The second scenario is that of *reform*, in which the political organizations, in order to survive, have to adapt to the new technologies and seek greater transparency and responsibility in the relations with the citizens. Thus, the government will attentively seek to take on board and balance the demands of the citizens instead of offering reformulation plans for society and democracy.

In this scenario, the parliaments and parties have to adapt to more direct forms of participation that will diminish their representative function. They will, however, continue to provide useful political leadership, mediating and aggregating the political agents.

The third scenario comprises a "politics as usual" vision of low impact of the information and communication technologies on the political practices and conceptions.

Given that preceding technologies – such as the telegraph, radio and television – also ushered in great alterations in the political processes, the traditional political forces can control and neutralize new pluralist tendencies of the new media through domestication processes and thanks to their economic and regulatory powers and their symbolic influence.

Furthermore, in this scenario the political actors use the information technologies to replicate their previous practices, using these technologies more to disseminate propaganda and political marketing and less as real mechanisms of interactivity with the citizens, focusing their attention primarily on the more politically active citizens. This latter scenario is based on the continuity of an already experimented model of *informational politics* based on television, in which the new technologies are predominantly used for information and marketing management, thus rejecting their radical potential (Dijk, 2000: 41).

In this model of continuity, the information technologies are used above all for election and information campaigns, in which, through television and the interactive media as the direct channels chosen for reaching a selected audience, the voters are the targets of the campaigns. The interested public can also access information through more advanced and more comprehensive public information systems, while at the same time new systems for registration in the government and the public administration are developed. Other means of consultation and conversation, such as online surveys and interactive meetings, are only used for the benefit of the political leadership and its popularity.

Bearing in mind the different characterizations of the history and possibilities of use of the information and communication technologies in the exercise of democracy and their possible impacts, what answer can we give to the question of what the role of the Internet is today in institutional and parliamentary informational politics?

An analysis of the Internet's role in the reformulation, or not, of the informational politics comings from a *mediation* space dominated by the traditional media (television, radio and print media) depends on three analytical dimensions.

The first dimension is the *availability of technological elected representative/citizen interfaces.* In other words, to what extent, and in what way, the parties, parliaments and other legislative and executive bodies position themselves in term of their online presence through the provision of sites and electronic mail accounts.

The second dimension refers to the *analysis of the practices and representations of the elected representatives* and parties in interacting with the citizens in the symbolic *mediation* field. In other words, understanding how this interaction functions and what forces mould it.

Finally, the third dimension is the real *interest and predisposition of the citizens for participating,* making use of the technological tools.

A fourth dimension, which is contextual in character and runs through the whole analysis, is the understanding of how television, radio and the newspapers position themselves as promoters of, or a barrier to the use of the mediation modalities between the citizens and their representatives.

In their study of European parliaments and political parties, Trechsel and Kies (2004) reached a number of important conclusions as to the first dimension, the *availability of technological elected representative/citizen interfaces* in the promotion of democracy in Europe by the political elites. The study consisted in the analysis of the online presence of political parties and parliament in 25 European countries during the year 2003. The study suggests the existence of different technologies in the online presences of parliaments and parties and also in the dimensions each technology tends to value in terms of democracy.

The technologies aimed at increasing transparency can be grouped under the definition *e-access,* i.e. the use of the Internet to improve electronic access to official documents and political information.

E-access is the most common technology used in the parliament and party websites. Although they are normally characterized by party-biased information models, there are, nevertheless, some examples of pluralistic information, such as the case of the Italian Radical Party (Trechsel and Kies et al., 2004). The experiments of Dutch and Finnish parties with tools that make it possible for the visitor to define their affinity with the policies of a certain party, through questions asked to the visitor, constitute another example of e-access.

The technologies aimed at increasing participation can be of three types: *e-consultation, e-petition* and *e-voting* (Trechsel and Kies et al., 2004).

E-consultation refers to the use of the Internet for disseminating information to a wider public, experts and interest groups and asking for their answers to questions dealt with on the site. The end objective is to achieve public participation in the decision processes. *E-consultation* may take different technological forms (forums, an invitation to send E-mails, a chat with political leaders) and may focus on many different topics. Examples are "Today I decide" in Estonia and the town council debates in Issy-les-Moulineaux, France (Trechsel and Kies et al., 2004).

Table 8.2 – Relationship between e-technologies and aspects of democracy facilitated

| | | ASPECT OF DEMOCRACY FACILITATED | | |
		Increase in transparency	Increase in participation	Increase in deliberation
	e-access	X		
e-technology	*e-consultation*		X	
	e-petition		X	
	e-voting		X	
	e-forum			X

Source: Trechsel and Kies et al. (2004), "Evaluation of the use of new technologies in order to facilitate democracy in Europe. E-democratizing the parliaments and parties of Europe." European University Institute.

A second technology is the *e-petition*. This tool enables citizens to start a petition on any public material. In the United Kingdom it is possible to send an e-petition directly to the Prime Minister. His site accepts and responds to online petitions. At the time of the study, in 2003, the website had

14 petitions on a diverse range of topics from the closure of a school, with 360 signatures, to a petition against the war in Iraq, with 14,479 signatures (Trechsel and Kies et al., 2004).

The United Kingdom approach is, thus, of the top-down type, as it promotes the reception of signatures on the site. But there are also examples of electronic petitions with a bottom-up approach, as in the Portuguese GUIA/PASIG case, in which a petition advocating the access of persons with disabilities to the Internet was launched and realized totally via the Internet. It was the first case of the acceptance of an e-petition by the Portuguese parliament.

E-voting is the last of the participation increase technologies analyzed by Trechsel and Kies (2004) in their study. They identify two models, whereby the first is simply the *substitution of the ballot paper vote* by a *computer mediated vote*. The second model offers the possibility of voting from a terminal or computer in any given place. One example is the Portuguese e-voting pilot project "Electronic Vote for a Modern Portugal".

Table 8.3 – Assessment of the Electronic Vote pilot project in Portugal, 2004 (%)

	Yes	No
Your assessment of the presential electronic vote experiment. Did you like it?	98.6%	1.4%
Would you be willing to vote electronically?	97.2%	2.8%
Your assessment of the electronic voting system?		
Easy	96.4%	3.1%
Swift	95.6%	4.0%
Secure*	86.1%	3.4%
Voter abstention would decrease	56.8%	39.7%

Source: UMIC, 2004, Evaluation of the Pilot Project e-Vote in Portugal, 2004. *Note: in the security dimension, the voters stated that they did not feel secure in terms of anonymity of the vote (48.1%) and its inalterability (40.1%).

Electronic voting in elections normally receives positive responses from the users and that is the case in both Portugal (2004) and Latin America (Dies, 2004). [148] It is essentially a different way of doing something that

---

[148] Assessment of the usefulness of change in the voting process depends on the advantages perceived by the voters. For example, the electronic vote in Brazil ensures a more rapid vote count and is seen as providing greater trustworthiness for results than the model involving the transport of ballot boxes

has both positive and negative points (see Table 8.3) and is not a techno-logical appropriation with the objective of developing a more participative democracy (Loader, 2002 and Oliveira et al., 2004).

Depending on the type of result to be achieved we can divide e-vot-ing into two categories: the e-*referendum*, in which the result may or not have a conditioning effect on the policies or may be merely informative in character and be begun by citizens or governments – one example is the e-*referendum* carried out in January 2003 in the commune of Angers (Can-ton of Geneva, Switzerland), in which one half of the 65% of voters voted via the Internet (Trechsel and Kies et al., 2004); and the e-election, which refers to the use of the Internet for voting, for example in the primaries for the election of party leaders.

As for the e-*technologies* for increasing deliberations spaces, the most common model is that of the development of e-*forums* with the objective of giving the citizens tools that allow them to exchange ideas and share their respective opinions. The space for the forums seems to be situated outside the parliament and party sites and is positioned in the media. One of the largest Polish newspapers, *Rzeczpospolita,* and the Portuguese daily, *Público,* both have moderated online forums where discussions take place, although their frequency and intensity are not very extensive. [149]

In addition to characterizing the formulas for appropriation of the In-ternet by parties and parliaments, Trechsel and Kies (2004) also present clear conclusions on the similarities and differences between European countries.

There is considerable variation in the use of the information and com-munication technologies, both at the national and supra-national level, and by both parliaments and parties.

---

from voting to counting site. In other countries, where trust in the democratic system is high, for example in Uruguay (45% according to the Latin Barometer 2004), the voters see no advantage in electronic voting (Diez 2004). But one must also take into account that the data presented for Portugal were the result of an experiment without a prior debate on the security having taken place, as in the case of the presidential elections in the US in 2004. The data show that the issue of anonymity is crucial in democracies where trust in the electoral system is high. The analysis of the data on distance voting technologies in Portugal (UMIC 2004) shows that the greater the direct connection to the home and to a technology perceived as personal the less the agreement is in using it – telephone vote (54.1%); SMS (49.0%); ATM (57.4%); Internet (59.0%). For background information on Latin America see also: GOMEZ, Ricardo (2000) and Altman, David (2002).

[149]http://www.rzeczpospolita.pl

That diversity is not directly related to the levels of wealth and development of the countries, given that these factors do not directly guarantee better online presences, be it by parliaments or parties. Also, the nature of the party system – i.e. its fragmentation, ideological orientation, voting levels in elections and the distribution between large and small parties – does not seem to have a significant effect on the diversity of contents and features of parliamentary and party sites.

For example, in the last European Parliament election in Portugal in 2004, the party with the best online presence in the campaign was the PND, which was running for the first time and receive approximately 1% of the votes.

However, outside the campaign context, the most developed sites in terms of e-technologies are those of the PSD (Social Democrats, centre-right), managed by a software company, and the PCP (Communists), managed by party members. The former was the party with the most votes in 2002 and the later is a small/medium-sized part with parliamentary representation.

Table 8.4 – E-Legislature Index (e-LIS) by component and European country

Information	Bilateral interactivity	Multilateral interactivity	Ease of use		e-LIS
United Kingdom	89.9 European Union	100.0 Germany	72.7 France	81.3	68.0
Italy	89.4 Greece	100.0 Denmark	45.5 European Union	62.5	67.0
Germany	89.1 Belgium	85.7 European Union*	27.3 Greece	62.5	65.0
Denmark	81.6 Republic Czech	85.7 France	27.3 United Kingdom	62.5	57.8
Greece	79.3 Finland	85.7 Poland	27.3 Finland	56.3	56.5
Poland	78.7 Germany	85.7 Finland	18.2 Italy	56.3	53.3
European Union*	78.3 Italy	85.7 Greece	18.2 Sweden	56.3	58.5
France	77.8 Lithuania	85.7 Lithuania	18.2 Denmark	50.0	62.1
Sweden	73.7 Sweden	85.7 Malta	18.2 Estonia	50.0	40.3
Lithuania	72.4 United Kingdom	85.7 Sweden	18.2 Portugal	50.0	46.3
Spain	71.5 Denmark	71.4 Czech Rep.	9.1 Czech Rep.	43.8	51.0
Czech Rep.	70.9 France	71.4 Italy	9.1 Germany	43.8	58.0
Hungary	69.5 Hungary	71.4 Luxembourg	9.1 Belgium	37.5	49.8
Belgium	69.3 Latvia	71.4 Netherlands	9.1 Latvia	37.5	39.2
Slovenia	67.7 Netherlands	71.4 Slovakia	9.1 Lithuania	37.5	53.5
Finland	66.0 Poland	71.4 Slovenia	9.1 Malta	37.5	34.3
Portugal	63.7 Portugal	71.4 United Kingdom	9.1 Poland	37.5	46.0
Netherlands	58.4 Austria	57.1 Austria	0.0 Slovenia	37.5	38.9
Austria	56.5 Estonia	57.1 Belgium	0.0 Austria	31.3	36.2
Ireland	54.7 Ireland	57.1 Cyprus	0.0 Cyprus	31.3	27.6
Luxembourg	54.0 Slovenia	57.1 Estonia	0.0 Ireland	31.3	35.8

Table 8.4 – E-Legislature Index (e-LIS) by component and European country

Information		Bilateral interactivity		Multilateral interactivity		Ease of use		e-LIS
Estonia	31.3	Luxembourg	54.0	Hungary	42.9	Slovakia	0.0	34.2
Slovakia	31.3	Slovakia	53.6	Ireland	42.9	Spain	0.0	45.9
Malta	25.0	Spain	53.0	Latvia	42.9	Luxembourg	0.0	32.7
Cyprus	12.5	Cyprus	50.4	Portugal	28.6	Hungary	0.0	38.3
Latvia	12.5	Malta	47.9	Spain	28.6	Netherlands	0.0	42.8
Average	42.5	Average	68.1	Average	69.2	Average	13.6	

Source: Trechsel e Kies e al. (2004), "Evaluation of the use of new technologies in order to facilitate democracy in Europe. E-democratizing the parliaments and parties of Europe." European University Institute [150]. Note: * 15 countries.

[150] The study coordinated by Trechsel and Kies et al. (2004) and carried out in Portugal by Cardoso and Sousa (2003) defined for distinct functionalities in parliamentary websites that allow for their characterization. These were: information provision, bilateral interactivity, multilateral interactivity and user friendliness. Bilateral and multilateral interactivity build on a distinction put forward by Andrea Römmele with regard to potential linkages using ICT between political parties and their members: "These linkages can take a bilateral form, such as email between the party and voter or member, or be multilateral, involving many actors in online chat rooms, bulletin boards or special question-and-answer sessions".

The Trechsel and Kies et al. study (2004) also concludes that one can only find significant difference in a comparative analysis between the EU-15 Member States and the 10 new members of the European Union. The parties and parliaments of the EU-15 states seem to have more elaborate online presences than the new EU Member States. There is also a propensity for the larger countries with larger populations and, consequently, larger parliaments to have better quality parliamentary online presences.

Hence, the option for the development of Internet presences and their valuation in the context of the political system does not seem to originate in factors external to the functioning of the parties, be they the parliamentary model or the country's development level.

Another possibility would be that the online presence was somehow dependent on the politicians' perception of the dimension of Internet usage in their countries. However, the Trechsel and Kies study (2004) demonstrated that there was no relation between these two dimensions.

The level of the presence of the information and communication technologies and access of the population to them does not have a corresponding impact on the parliaments and parties in terms of development of their online presence. In other words, countries with such different Internet usage figures as Portugal, Finland, Netherlands and Denmark may present similar qualities in the offer of information, interactivity and ease of use (see Table 8.4).

In this analysis, Portugal presents average scores in terms of the provision of information and good scores in terms of bilateral interactivity and ease of use of the online presence. However, it also gets a zero score as far as multilateral interactivity is concerned.

As for the party index in terms of use of the Internet, Portugal is in sixth last place in the table, revealing a weak exploitation of the functionalities offered by the Internet in the democratic context. Hence Portugal presents very low figures for the provision of information by the parties (42.2, second last place in the index) and values of roughly one third of the highest index rates (34.4 and 21.4) for the bilateral and multilateral interactivity dimensions led by countries such as Austria, Malta and Germany.

In the analysis of the online presence of the parties one must also taken into account two new dimensions, which are the *network* node dimension, referring to the possibility of creating points of contact between the members, and parties' mobilization capacity by means of the Internet.

Most parties from all countries present quite low mobilization values that are higher only than the low ease of use of the sites themselves. This would lead one to conclude that the mobilization online presences tend to occur in accordance with a highly intermittent model that is probably based on the election calendar, meaning that the sites are reborn during the campaigns to offer new functionalities to the users.

Table 8.5 – *E-Party Index* by European country

Country	E-party	Standard deviation	N
Germany	62.3	5.4	5
Spain	52.8	6.8	3
Austria	52.4	12.5	4
Sweden	52.3	6.9	7
Czech Rep.	50.5	3.6	5
Italy	49.9	11.6	6
United Kingdom	49.6	7.8	3
Greece	48.1	7.5	4
Poland	47.6	6.1	6
Netherlands	47.0	13.5	7
Belgium	46.0	8.7	10
Malta	45.9	3.9	2
Finland	45.9	7.8	7
Luxembourg	41.4	10.5	5
UE	40.7	21.4	6
France	39.9	4.1	3
Denmark	39.8	7.4	6
Hungary	35.8	14.5	4
Lithuania	34.9	7.1	5
Latvia	31.9	10.0	9
Portugal	30.6	20.4	4
Ireland	30.3	9.9	6
Slovakia	30.1	7.5	8
Estonia	28.6	15.0	6
Slovenia	27.5	13.8	8
Cyprus	13.0	5.1	5
EU-15	45.8	12.1	80
AC-10	33.3	13.6	58
Average/Total	41.3	9.6	144

Source: Trechsel e Kies et al. (2004), "Evaluation of the use of new technologies in order to facilitate democracy in Europe. E-democratizing the parliaments and parties of Europe." European University Institute.

However, using once more the Portuguese case and the European elections of 2004, from an analytical comparison of the party's sites and the online presence of the Portuguese parties during the European election campaign 2004 one can conclude that even during the election campaign periods, the use of the sites for mobilization purposes is reduced to the possibility of downloading images and logotypes in addition to the daily campaign programme (Cardoso and Sousa, 2004).

Although one cannot extrapolate the Portuguese case to the rest of Europe, an analysis the US presidential elections in 2004 shows how the Internet can be used by parties in election periods with demonstrated success in the field of mobilization. Hence, once again one can venture the idea that the reasons for the effective use, or not, of the Internet by the parties depend not on external factors but essentially on their own perspectives as to the usefulness of the Internet and on their own representations as to the comparison between the Internet and other media for political *mediation* purposes.

The clear conclusion of the "Evaluation of the use of new technologies in order to facilitate democracy in Europe" study lies precisely in the fact that one can verify the introduction of new technologies without the existence of clear objectives on the part of the political elites. In other words, the absence of positive representations that enable them to develop good use practices is unlikely to translate to radical changes in the nature of liberal democracy (Trechsel and Kies et al., 2004).

Figure 8.1 – Four relational clusters between *e-legislature* and *e-government* in Europe

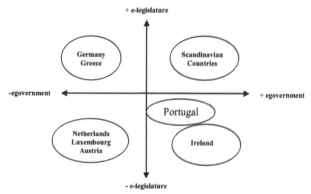

Source: Adapted from Trechsel and Kies et al. (2004), "Evaluation of the use of new technologies in order to facilitate democracy in Europe. E-democratizing the parliaments and parties of Europe." European University Institute.

The same conclusion can be illustrated by different means – the relations between e-government and e-democracy. [151] In other words, as various analyzes of the OECD (2003) have shown, the priority of the governments in terms of the definition of objectives in the use of the information and communication technologies very frequently incorporates e-government. One can, therefore, raise the hypothesis that high investments and interest in e-government would also reflect in the level of the incentives for electronic democracy (Trechsel and Kies, 2004). What the preceding figure (Figure 8.1) shows is that, although there are cases in which this happens, it is not always the case. The data suggest, once again, that if the parties and parliaments do not share the interest and incentivate good practices of use of electronic democracy, it will not prosper in terms of top-down initiatives.

Table 8.6 – Indexes of participation and e-government, selected countries

	Portugal	Finland	Singapore	US
e-government readiness index	0.646 (26)	0.761 (10)	0.746 (12)	0.927 (1)
Web measure	0.507	0.603	0.703	1.000
Telecom Index	0.409	0.691	0.666	0.801
Human Cap Index	0.94	0.99	0.870	0.98
e-participation index	0.448 (14)	0.448 (14)	0.466 (13)	0.966 (2)
e-information	11	9	11	16
e-consultation	12	9	10	25
e-decision making	3	8	6	15

Source: United Nations, UN Global e-government Readiness Report, 2003. Note: (*) indicates the position in the world ranking. [152]

---

[151] E-government, or electronic government, means the use of the ICTs for making government(s) operate more efficiently. (Trechsel and Kies et al. 2004).

[152] The creation of the indexes takes into account three components for the e-government readiness index. These are: the Web Measure Index, which measures the level of maturity and sophistication of e-government presence online; the Telecommunications Infrastructure Index, which is a composite of the number of PCs per thousand inhabitants, the Internet users per thousand inhabitants, mobile phones per thousand inhabitants, telephone lines per thousand inhabitants, online population per thousand inhabitants and the number of TVs per thousand inhabitants; the third e-government readiness index component is the Human Capital Index, which is a composite of the adult literacy rate and the combined primary, secondary and tertiary gross enrolment ratio, with two thirds of the weight given to adult literacy and one third to the gross enrolment ratio. The e-participation index is made up of the following: e-information (government websites offering information on policies, budgets, laws and regulations); e-consultation (government websites offer a choice of public policy topics online for discussion and encourage citizens to participate in discussions); and e-decision making (governments

Table 8.6 shows, through another perspective, the relations one can establish between the encouragement for citizen participation on the part of the governments and the preparation for the countries for exercising e-government. A reading of the indexes shows that it is not the type or political system established – which is less democratic in Singapore and more democratic in Finland – that conditions the type of participation, for the values for the three participation dimensions are very similar for an authoritarian informational society such as Singapore and the democratic, welfare model, Finland. As the Portuguese case shows, there may be an incentive for the search for information and discussion but this may take place without the mechanisms of concrete influence on the part of the citizens being provided.

Although so far we have based the analysis to a large extent on the Trechsel and Kies study (2004), it is also true that it does have some limitations. Given that it focuses almost exclusively on the offer of functionalities and services and devotes little attention to either the vertical communication dimension (between elected representatives and voters) or the horizontal communication (between parliamentary groups and within parties), there is an extensive field on which one cannot make any inferences.

As the analysis of the online presence of European political parties and parliaments shows, it does not suffice to measure the presence in terms of pages and their content. It is also necessary to understand to what extent the practices and representations of the elected representatives and those responsible in the parties for the Internet also mould the way in which the Internet is made available to the citizens.

As already mentioned, the second analysis dimension on the contribution of the Internet to reformulating the practices of informational politics in the institutional context leads us to the *analysis of the practices and representations of the members of parliament* and parties. [153]

---

indicate that they will take citizen input into account in decision making and provides actual feedback on the outcome of specific issues).

[153] The comparative analysis of the data of the partner countries in the research project "Parliamentary Elites and Information Technologies" as part of the European Action on Government and Democracy in the Information Age (GaDIA), COST A14, covered seven countries, which were: Portugal (PT): Austria (AU), Norway (NR), Netherlands (NL), Denmark (DK), Scotland (S) and Germany (G). The comparison was based on a common questionnaire-based survey conducted in these countries (each research team was free to add questions to or strike some from the questionnaire or to alter the response categories). The response rates were as follows: Portugal 34.8% (80 out of 230 MPs); Austria 43.7% (80 out of 183); Norway 41.8% (69 out of 165); Netherlands 40% (89 out of 225);

The analysis of the representations of European members of parliament reveals largely positive responses as to the relationship between democracy and the Internet. When the members of parliament were asked whether the Internet encouraged new forms of democracy and participation, whether it improved the dialogue between citizens and elected representatives and if it provided for a broadening of political subjects, their responses were always positive.

Denmark 49.7% (89 out of 174); Scotland 39.5% (51 out of 129) and Germany 10% (60 out 603). In all countries the application of the questionnaires was prepared through contacts with the different party leaders or spokespersons and/or the parliamentary groups or administrations. However, one must bear in mind that, in universes as small as parliaments, there is a strong probability that the responses in the countries with lower information technology penetration, such as Portugal, could represent more the MPs that use the technologies than the entirety of the population in the study. In other words, non-users automatically excluded themselves from responding. The data must therefore be analyzed with the awareness that what is of interest is understanding the similarities and difference between those that use the Internet in the different national parliaments more than understanding the difference in the usage rates between the countries. For a more in-depth analysis see: Cardoso, Gustavo et. al. (2006) Elites Parlamentares e Tecnologias de Informação, Oeiras, Celta Editores; Hoff, Coleman, Fitzmaier and Cardoso, Use of ICTs by Members of Parliament, Information Polity, Special Issue, Volume 9, Numbers 1,2, 2004, The Netherlands, IOS Press. For a comparison with the Swiss reality see: GALLAND, Blaise, CHAPPELET, Jean-Loup (2001) *"E-Parlement – L'appropriation de l'Internet par les parlementaires fédéraux"*, Cahier de l'Institute de Hautes Études en Administration Publique (IDHEAP). For background information on the parties in Portugal see FRAIN, Maritheresa (1997) "The Right in Portugal: the PSD and CDS/PP" *in* BRUNEAU, Thomas (ed.) (1997) *Political Parties and Democracy in Portugal: Organizations, Elections and Public Opinion.* Boulder, CO: Westview Press, pp. 77-111. On parliamentary recruitment and the electoral system see FREIRE, André (2001; 2002), Léonard, Y. (1998), Sablosky (1997) and Magone, M. (1997).

Table 8.7 – Opinion of parliament members on the impact of the ICT on the development of their country, selected countries (%)

	PT	AU	NR	NL	DK	S	G
Encourages new forms of democracy	60 (1)	55 (4)	70.5 (2)	68.3 (1)	50.5 (3)	78.5 (2)	61.8(3)
Encourages political participation by the citizens	40 (4)	86.3 (1)	50.8 (4)	40 (3)	50.5 (3)	80 (1)	73.5(1)
Improves the dialogue within the political system and between elected representatives and citizens	55 (2)	75 (3)	78 (1)	45.9 (2)	79.8 (1)	-	63.3(2)
Broadening of addressed political subjects	53.8 (3)	77.5 (2)	60.3 (3)	40 (3)	57.3 (2)	68.6 (3)	48.5(4)
No influence on politics and politicians	11.3	16.5	37.9	27.7	21.3	12.9	29.4

Source: Comparative analysis of European members of parliament, (2003) COST-A14, Cardoso, Gustavo (PT); Hoff, Jens (DK); Kleisteuber Hans (G); Snellen, Ignace (NL); Smith, Colin (Sc); Elvebaek, Beate (NR); Filzmaier, Peter (A).

Note: the figures refer to responses of "agree" and "totally agree" with the statements (the percentage figures do no make up 100% because the reading of the table is restricted to each one of the categories in the column in relation to the options in line.

Nevertheless, if we order the responses in terms of greater agreement with the statements we find that it is precisely the countries in which there is a higher level of trust between the voters and their representatives, such as Denmark (Eurobarometer 2003) that rank the hypothesis that the Internet can improve the dialogue between elected representatives and citizens in first place.

It would seem that those countries where voters trust in their representatives to a lesser degree (e.g., Austria, Germany, Portugal and The Netherlands), the members of parliament tend to value the role of the Internet more as a way of encouraging participation and new forms of democracy. In other words, they are aware that the Internet alone will not guarantee an improvement in the dialogue, as it is necessary to resolve the causes of the situation that cannot be overcome simply with recourse to a new technology. Notwithstanding, their representations are mostly optimistic.

If we wish to establish a trend that is common to all countries (Hoff, 2003) we can find it in the personal self-skills demonstrated and in the level of use of the technologies. The members of parliament with greater personal skills in using the Internet are generally less concerned about the possible negative effects of the technologies in the political field.

The data analyzed also show that there are differences, though slight, in terms of possession of the technologies by the members of parliament. Possession of a personal computer by members of parliament does not differ significantly between the countries in the analysis, with Germany and Norway presenting the highest values (100% and 98.6% respectively). As for the possession of laptops, the German members of parliament once again lead the ranking (89.7%), followed by the Austrians. Here, the Portuguese (19%) and Norwegians (23.3%) are the lowest in the ranking. As far as the possession of a mobile phone is concerned, the Portuguese members present the highest penetration rate (59.5%). These data confirm the penetration of this technology in general in Portugal itself (ITU, 2003). [154]

The domestication (Silverstone, 1994) of E-mail as a communication tool (more than 90%) can above all be seen amongst Norwegian, Dutch, Danish and Scottish members of parliament, in contrast to the Austrians and Portuguese (whereby the latter present the lowest figure of 56.4%). The trend is similar for the use of newsgroups, with the Portuguese members of parliaments being those who least use this means of communication, together with their Austrian and German counterparts.

The Scottish members of parliament are those that make most use of newsgroups (25.4%). They lead the field in this area perhaps due to the recent creation of their parliament, which enabled the intensive introduction of the ICTs into parliamentary work and the consequent integration of the technologies in the communication with other agents, from the decision to reactivate the parliament to its opening.

If we look at means of access to information, the German (89.7%) and Danish (77.5%) members of parliament are those that most access the World Wide Web (WWW), in direct contrast to the Portuguese members of parliament, as those who least access it (only 46.2%).

---

[154]Countries with a mobile phone penetration of more than 80 persons for 100 inhabitants: Taiwan (110.84); Hong Kong (105.75); Luxembourg (106.05); Italy (101.76); Iceland (96.56); Czech Rep. (96.46); Israel (95.45); Spain (91.61); Norway (90.89); Portugal (90.38); Finland (90.06); Sweden (88.89); Denmark (88.72); Slovenia (87.09); Switzerland (84.34); Ireland (84.47); United Kingdom (84.07); Austria (87.88); Macao (81.51). Note: these figures represent the total number of mobile phones attributed and therefore do not reflect the real numb number of persons using mobile phones in a given country, although they are still a good yardstick for comparison between countries.

Table 8.8 – Frequent/permanent use of the Internet in parliamentary work, selected countries (%)

	PT	AU	NR	NL	DK	S	G
E-mail	56,4	81,3	94,2	95	92,2	94,3	89,7
Newsgroups	2,6	3,8	10,4	10,8	11,2	25,7	4,4
Chat	1,3	1,3	0	0	2,2	-	2,9
Personal page	5,1	17,5	15,4	26,8	40,4	28,6	63,2
World Wide Web (WWW)	46,2	68,8	65,7	70,8	77,5	71,4	89,7
Intranet	30,8	53,8	54,4	44,4	41,6	90	88,2

Source: Comparative analysis of European members of parliament, (2003) COST-A14, Cardoso, Gustavo (PT); Hoff, Jens (DK); Kleisteuber Hans (G); Snellen, Ignace (NL); Smith, Colin (Sc); Elvebaek, Beate (NR); Filzmaier, Peter (A). Note: the percentage figures do no make up 100% because the reading of the table is restricted to each one of the categories in the column in relation to the options in line.

Regardless of the level of use of E-mail and the World Wide Web by the members of parliaments, the data allow us to infer that, in general, the parliamentary representatives see the Internet more as an interpersonal communication tool than as an information tool. The hypothesis raised there is that this is the case because there are other *mediation* tools that are more valued for fulfilling the information function.

Table 8.9 – Areas of use of ICT by members of parliament, selected countries (scale of 1 to 7)

	PT	AU	NR	NL	DK	Sc	G
Search for general information	5.3 (1)	3.2	4.5 (1)	5	5.2	5.5 (2)	3.4
Search for specific information	4.6 (2)	2.9 (2)	4.7 (2)	5.3	5.1	5.8 (1)	2.4 (1)
Internal communication	3.4	2.5 (1)	4.7(2)	6.5 (1)	5.9 (1)	5.5 (2)	2.9 (2)
External communication with constituents	3.4	3.5	5	5.5 (2)	5.3 (2)	5.2	3.4
External communication with others	2.8	3.5	5	5.1	5.1	4.7	4
Political campaign	2.2	5.5	5.5	0.7	3.9	4	5
Others	1.4	6.9	5.7	-	1.5	-	5.9

Source: Comparative analysis of European members of parliament, (2003) COST-A14, Cardoso, Gustavo (PT); Hoff, Jens (DK); Kleisteuber Hans (G); Snellen, Ignace (NL); Smith, Colin (Sc); Elvebaek, Beate (NR); Filzmaier, Peter (A). Note: the percentage values do not make up 100% because the "no response" and "don't know/no response" categories were not included. Note: the scales used in Austria, Norway and Germany should be read as 1 = [more] and 7 = [less], while in the remaining countries 7 = [more] and 1 = [less]. The values in (*) reflect the position in the column.

However, when we look at their practices we see that the preferred areas for using the Internet would seem to contradict that outlook: searching for information is almost always mentioned more than communication.

We believe that this apparent contradiction is rooted in the fact that the Internet is also a tool used for personal purposes and not only for work (Cardoso et al., 2004 and Castells, 2003). Hence, when asked about the areas in which they use the Internet, the members of parliament respond not only in the context of the parliamentary work but are referring to their more general use.

In confirmation of data already mentioned above, in relation to political campaigning the parliamentary representatives in general, with the exception of the Danish and Scottish members, rarely use the Internet for their campaigns. Another indicator of importance for forming and opinion and assessment of a technology is whether there is a direct relationship with that technology or recourse to "specialized proxies".

In the course of their parliamentary work, the Portuguese members of parliament are those that most use the Internet personally (52.5%), followed by their Norwegian (47.8%) and Scottish (45.7%) colleagues. The German parliamentary representatives are those that most rely on third persons (only 5.9% personally use the Internet, while 51.5% delegate tasks). [155]

Table 8.10 – Origin of E-mails received by members of parliament, selected countries (%)

	PT	AU	NR	NL	DK	Sc	G
Voters/citizens	21.3 (1)	13.6 (3)	13.7	20.6 (2)	21 (1)	18.8 (2)	20.1 (1)
Personal staff	17.9 (2)	21.6 (2)	19.5 (2)	14	14.4 (3)	13.4	16
Party colleagues	15.4 (3)	9.7	15.5	22.3 (1)	16.7 (2)	-	11.5
Interest groups	14.6	12.1	20.2 (1)	16.8 (3)	9.6	20.3 (1)	13.4 (2)
Party organization	11.5	21.9 (2)	18.6 (3)	10.3	12.8	10.8	10.7
Bureaucracy/government	10.9	8.9	5.8	4.5	8.9	15.7 (3)	13.3 (3)
Press/journalists	8.4	-	4.8	4.2	11.3	13.6	-
Members of parliament	-	-	-	-	-	7.4	-

Source: Comparative analysis of European members of parliament, (2003) COST-A14, Cardoso, Gustavo (PT); Hoff, Jens (DK); Kleisteuber Hans (G); Snellen, Ignace (NL); Smith, Colin (Sc); Elvebaek, Beate (NR); Filzmaier, Peter (A).

[155]One should point out that personal use of the Internet is also to some extent the result of the lack of parliamentary support staff that would normally perform part of the tasks involving communication and provision of information via the Internet.

Given the low rates of possession and use of personal web pages (with the exception of the Danish and German members of parliament), it is worthwhile exploring a little more the communicative dimension of the uses of the Internet, in terms of practices with E-mail, with the aim of testing the hypothesis that, despite the possibilities offered by the Internet in interpersonal communication, the members of parliament are in general not very proactive when it comes to developing top-down initiatives in relation to their constituents.

When we look at the origins of the E-mails received by the members of parliament, bearing in mind that citizens can contact their representatives both individually (voters/citizens) and in an organized form (interest groups), we see that, on average, the figure is approximately 30% for E-mails from the citizens, whereby the Scottish members of parliament (39.1%) are those that receive the most E-mails from citizens and their Austrian counterparts those that receive the least (25.7%). If we take into account the E-mails sent by journalists, only in the Scottish case do more than half of the E-mails originate from senders other than personal staff, the party or the government.

Bearing in mind that the contents in the E-mails focus on national political matters (and only in the cases of The Netherlands and Scotland do local affairs or specialized areas have a greater preponderance), can one say that the usefulness conferred upon them and the stimulus taken from them are considered positive things by the members of parliament?

If they have a high degree of usefulness it is possible to infer that, even in small quantities, the contribution of the citizens is valued and one could argue that this could be a sign of alternative forms of increasing deliberation. Also, if they provide a strong stimulus to parliamentary work one could find in them the beginnings of new opportunities for increasing participation, if the citizens receive the corresponding feedback from their elected representatives.

Table 8.11 – Contents of e-mails received by members of parliament, selected countries (scale of 1 to 11)

	PT	AU	NR	NL	DK	Sc	G
General national political matters	6.9 (1)	2.7 (1)	2.7 (1)	8.2 (2)	8.7 (1)	7.6 (2)	2.4 (1)
Party affairs	5.9 (2)	3.5 (3)	2.4 (2)	7.8 (3)	8.4 (2)	6.3 (3)	4.6 (3)
National political matters relating to their area of specialization	5.5 (3)	3.1 (2)	1.8 (3)	8.7 (1)	-	-	-
Questions/feedback/ criticism from citizens	4.6	5.3	1.2	7.9	7.2 (3)	6	4.2 (2)
Local/regional affairs relating to their constituency	4.4	4.6	1.2	6.8	6	8.5 (1)	4.8
Media contacts	3.8	5.6	0.9	5.9	6.5	5	6.7
Requests for information/ material	3.5	8	0.6	5.7	4.1	-	7.4
Lobbying	3.3	5.4	1.5	7	6.4	8	4.5
Advertising	2.6	7.7	0.6	3.8	3.3	3.6	7.6
Insults	1.7	9.8	-	2.9	3.2	2.6	8.5
Others	2.2	10.3	-	2.8	-	5.2	5.8

Source: Comparative analysis of European members of parliament, (2003) COST-A14, Cardoso, Gustavo (PT); Hoff, Jens (DK); Kleisteuber Hans (G); Snellen, Ignace (NL); Smith, Colin (Sc); Elvebaek, Beate (NR); Filzmaier, Peter (A). Note: the scales used in Austria, Norway and Germany should be read as 1 = [more] and 11 = [less], while in the remaining countries 11 = [more] and 1 = [less]. The values in (*) reflect the position in the column.

In the analysis of the responses as to the utility of the E-mails received, the most negative positions come from the German members of parliament, while the most positive ones come from their Scottish and Norwegian counterparts.

Portugal, Austria and The Netherlands reveal a somewhat cautious position, highlighting the irregularity of the contributions from citizens. Given the geographic variation in the responses, one can conclude that the increase in forms of deliberation made possible by the Internet's interpersonal communication dimension, will probably depend more on cultural factors and on the representations the elected representatives have of the voters than on the possibilities offered by the technology alone.

Table 8.12 – Utility of E-mails received by members of parliament, selected countries (%)

	PT	AU	NR	NL	DK	Sc	G
Frequently	7.5	16.3	41.5 (2)	0	-	81.4 (1)	1.5
Often	16.3(2)	37.5 (2)	53.8 (1)	27.1 (2)	-	11.4 (2)	32.4 (2)
Sometimes	62.5 (1)	41.3 (1)	3.1	62.4 (1)	-	4.3	42.6 (1)
Rarely/never	12.6	2.5	1.5	10.6	-	1.4	22.1

Source: Comparative analysis of European members of parliament, (2003) COST-A14, Cardoso, Gustavo (PT); Hoff, Jens (DK); Kleisteuber Hans (G); Snellen, Ignace (NL); Smith, Colin (Sc); Elvebaek, Beate (NR); Filzmaier, Peter (A). Note: the percentage values do not make up 100% because the "no response" and "don't know/no response" categories were not included.

As far as the stimulus for parliamentary work given by the E-mails received, the trends already detected for utility are confirmed again. The stimulus seems to be less than the utility attributed for the Scottish members of parliament only.

Table 8.13 – Stimulus from e-mails received by members of parliament, selected countries (%)

	PT	AU	NR	NL	DK	S	G
Frequently	6.3	13.8	32.8 (2)	2.4	19.1	37.1 (2)	0
Often	28.8 (2)	26.3 (2)	54.7 (1)	32.1 (2)	33.7 (2)	52.2 (1)	14.7
Sometimes	55 (1)	50 (1)	9.4	57.1 (1)	37.1 (1)	5.8	61.8 (1)
Rarely/never	10.3	7.6	3.1	8.3	6.7	4.3	22 (2)

Source: Comparative analysis of European members of parliament, (2003) COST-A14, Cardoso, Gustavo (PT); Hoff, Jens (DK); Kleisteuber Hans (G); Snellen, Ignace (NL); Smith, Colin (Sc); Elvebaek, Beate (NR); Filzmaier, Peter (A). Note: the percentage values do not make up 100% because the "no response" and "don't know/no response" categories were not included.

However, the analysis of the stimulus associated with the reception of E-mails does not in itself refute the fact that use of E-mail could bring about new opportunities for increasing participation. It is important also that one verify whether or not the citizens receive feedback from their elected representative.

Table 8.14 – Response to e-mails by members of parliament, selected countries (%)

	PT	AU	NR	NL	DK	Sc	G
Yes	27.5	36.3	23.9	-	42.7	22.9	-
Only in cases of concrete questions, requests for information/material, etc.	58.8	58.8	55.2	-	43.8	-	-
No, only E-mails from my constituency or special topics	11.3	3.8	3	-	9	-	-

Source: Comparative analysis of European members of parliament, (2003) COST-A14, Cardoso, Gustavo (PT); Hoff, Jens (DK); Kleisteuber Hans (G); Snellen, Ignace (NL); Smith, Colin (Sc); Elvebaek, Beate (NR); Filzmaier, Peter (A). Note: the percentage values do not make up 100% because the "no response" and "don't know/no response" categories were not included.

The Danish and Norwegian members of parliament are those that respond to all E-mails received the most (42.7% and 36.3% respectively), irrespective of where they come from and the content matter. Accordingly, the majority of respondents only answers E-mails when they contain concrete questions.

Trechsel and Kies (2004) also analyzed the elected representatives' rates of response, using the sending of E-mails with a concrete question on the individual position of the members of parliament on e-voting. The following table (Table 8.15) presents the results of that study at the European level. The response figures never surpassed the 45% value for The Netherlands, with the average for the parliaments of the 15 EU Member States being 5% in 2003. In the specific case of Portugal (Cardoso and Sousa 2003), of 230 members of parliament contacted, only 54 responded. The majority of these responses (92%) came from the two parties with the largest representation in the Portuguese parliament (PS and PSD).

Members of parliament in countries such as Portugal and Austria that state that they respond mostly to concrete questions asked in E-mails present low rates of response to the question formulated in the Trechsel and Kies (2004) study. One can thus register an apparent contradiction between the statements made and the practical demonstration of those statements.

Although one cannot generalize, there are indications in the data analyzed that the value the members of parliament attach to Internet-based communication with their voters is low. Is that really the case? And if it is the case, what could be the response to this limited valuation given to the appropriation of the Internet by the voters in the context of the European democracies?

Although we cannot look at all the context of the different countries in detail, it is worthwhile carrying out a more in-depth analysis of the Portuguese reality, for, if we have found certain similarities in other areas of analysis, it is natural that some of the interpretations made herein for Portugal may likewise be transposed to other European democracies.

First and foremost one must understand how the citizens use the *technological tools to participate and how their parliamentary representatives encourage, or not, the symbolic mediation offered by the Internet to civic participation.*

Table 8.15 – Results of the interactive test with European members of parliament

Country	Rate of response	n	% of MPs with E-mail address	n	No. of MPs
Estonia	44.6	45	100.0	101	101
Denmark	42.3	71	93.9	168	179
Slovenia	42.2	38	100.0	90	90
Finland	40.0	80	100.0	200	200
Netherlands	30.2	13	57.3	43	75
Luxembourg	28.6	8	46.7	28	60
United Kingdom	27.7	133	73.0	481	659
Slovakia	26.7	40	100.0	150	150
Austria	26.6	42	86.3	158	183
Portugal	23.5	54	100.0	230	230
Lithuania	22.6	31	100.0	137	137
Latvia	16.0	13	81.0	81	100
Germany	14.4	87	100.0	603	603
France	11.9	67	97.9	565	577
Sweden	9.7	34	100.0	349	349
Spain	9.7	22	64.6	226	350
Greece	9.6	16	55.3	166	300
Hungary	9.3	36	100.0	386	386
Italy	7.1	45	100.0	630	630
UE	5.1	21	65.4	409	625
Poland	2.0	9	100.0	460	460
Average	21.4	43.1	86.7	267	307

Source: Trechsel and Kies et al. (2004), "Evaluation of the use of new technologies in order to facilitate democracy in Europe. E-democratizing the parliaments and parties of Europe." European University Institute.

Only 10.2% of the Portuguese citizens state that they have ever signed a petition or letter of protest or complaint to a State or public administration body. Internet users are the most active: 18.7% of them stated they had already carried out one of these actions, while only 6.7% of non-users confirmed they had.

Of those that have undertaken such an initiative, 27.1% indicate that they did so using E-mail. When carried out by Internet users, the actions were directed mainly at ministers or other government members/bodies (41% of these cases), followed by members of the Portuguese parliament (16%) and the President of the Republic (13%).

Non-Internet users directed their initiatives essentially at town/city councils (mayors or aldermen – 28%) and also ministers (20%) and MPs (19%). One should also point out that schools and parish councils are the institutions this type of initiative is least directed at.

Table 8.16 – Signing of petitions or letters of protest or complaint to State and public administration bodies in Portugal (%)

Signing of petitions or letters of protest or complaint to State and public administration bodies	Users	Non-users	Total
Yes	18.7	6.7	10.2
No	81.0	93.1	89.6
Don't know/no response	0.2	0.3	0.2
Total	100.0 (n=711)	100.0 (n=1739)	100.0 (n=2450)

Source: CIES, Survey, *The Network Society in Portugal*, 2003 (p<0.01).

According to a survey of those responsible for the management of the electronic communication of the Portuguese Government, Parliament and the Presidency of the Portuguese Republic (DN, 5 February 2004), the E-mail communication between citizens and their elected representatives is used for multiple purposes – from expressing criticism, to sending felicitations and asking requests, which may range from employment to housing or, quite simply, money. On average, E-mail accounts for 10 to 30% of the communications received, the rest being correspondence on paper. Another question of interest for our analysis is whether or not there are substantial differences in the socio-demographic characterization of those who use the conventional letter and those who use E-mail to write to Portuguese MPs.

Similar to the characterization of the Internet users, who are more educated and younger, the data in the following table (Table 8.17) confirm that those with less schooling and the older prefer the conventional letter on paper. Also, if we look at their distribution in socio-professional categories, we find that there is a larger concentration of those who use E-mail in their communication with the Portuguese MPs in intermediate and upper professional levels.

The population that opts for E-mail is thus more educated and in higher professional positions than those who don't. They are almost always employed in the private sector.

Petitions are another form of using the information technologies in relations with the MPs. [156] When, in April 2002, the IX Legislative Period commenced in Portugal, 103 petitions, largely collectively signed, were pendent in the parliament and a further 62 new ones were added to that number in the course of 2003 (Público, 25 January 2004).

Table 8.17 – Characterisation of citizens that communicate with members of the Portuguese Parliament via conventional mail and e-mail (%)

		E-mail	Conventional mail
Sex	Male	60.0%	54.5%
	Female	40.0%	45.5%
Age	[15-24]	30.0%	36.4%
	[25-39]	50.0%	36.4%
	[>40]	20.0%	27.3%
Education level	Basic education	30.0%	36.4%
	Secondary education	30.0%	18.2%
	Higher education	40.0%	45.5%
	Middle management or specialist	42.9%	**
*Socio-professional category**	Skilled administrative, commercial or services employee	28.6%	20%
	Upper management or specialist; entrepreneur	28.6%	40.0%

Source: Source: CIES, Survey, *The Network Society in Portugal*, 2003.*Note: larger categories that make up the sample relating to the use of conventional mail or E-mail in communication. ** There is an equal distribution (10%) in the categories "Worker"; "Unskilled worker"; "Middle management or specialist" and "Entrepreneur".

---

[156] By petition one generally understands the submittal of a request or proposal to an organ of sovereignty or a public authority, but not a court, with a view to having specific measures taken, adopted or proposed. The right of petition can be exercised individually or collectively. Petitions can deal with any matter provided that their objective is not illegal and does not involve court decisions.

However, we have to go back to 1998 to find a petition submitted to the Portuguese Parliament that originated electronically. The Portuguese Petition for Access to the Internet aimed at facilitating Internet access for Portuguese citizens with special needs, such as persons with disabilities and the old age, through the creation of a number of basic rules to be applied when information and services for the Internet are conceived.

The petition was the first for which the signatures were gathered exclusively through the Internet and to be submitted electronically. It received a favourable opinion for the Portuguese Parliament and approved in the form of a Cabinet resolution in 1999. The petition had some 9,000 supporters and was promoted by GUIA (Portuguese Group for Accessibility Initiatives). Although the number of participants was smaller then that for other petition initiatives (for example, the request for a new referendum on abortion, which was signed by 75,000 people), the fact that it was a success was a clear indication of the potential of using the Internet for carrying out petitions and submitting them to the organs of sovereignty.

However, there is no institutional memory of that event, neither within the parliament nor amongst the population in general. In other words, besides GUIA's own site one can find very few references to the event, even if one carries out thorough online research using the search engines (Hock, 2001).

The fact that there is no collective memory of the effectiveness of online petitions in Portugal is also a result of the MPs not promoting examples of good practice.

This is the case partly because, given that they do not have individual support functionaries, as a Portuguese MP argues: *"(...) an MP who places himself in direct contact with the universe of voters via the Internet, well, risks being inundated with a number of communications (...)"* (Cardoso et al., 2005).

Generating frustration on the part of the citizens in view of the MPs' incapacity to respond to all is a danger of which parliamentarians are all too aware. Nevertheless, on the basis of a number of interviews with Portuguese MPs (Cardoso et al., 2005), one can also identify that, in addition to the lack of means argument, there are types of reasons for the limited valuation of the use of the Internet for vertical communication and resulting little incentivation by elected representatives for the increased use of the instrument.

In the MPs' discourse we can identify a position that recognizes that parliamentarians should generally play a more proactive role, but that also considers that the Internet constitutes an instrument that can be applied in incentivation to participation.

In the discourse of the MPs, if the Internet can help resolve the problem of participation, one should nevertheless seek to first combat the general causes of the alienation between citizens and representatives before valuing means of participation that only reach part of the population, such as the Internet. Their argument is that the Internet is not a principal medium of information and communication for the citizens (an argument that is, to a certain extent, refutable, if we bear in mind the studies of the uses of the different media by the citizens in different countries and the functions they attribute to those media) and whoever uses the Internet is already participating actively (another supposition that can be refuted by the data available on Portugal and other European contexts). A second line of argument put forward by the MPs as justification for the low-level vertical relations between voters and elected representatives carries complaints as to the not very reflective character of the participations by citizens on the Internet, while at the same time perpetuating considerably negative images of the voters in general. For example, an aide to the PCP (left wing), who, although he considers that E-mail offers positive dimensions as one more communication vehicle for Internet users, nevertheless argues that the majority of E-mail messages received almost always contained comments that were not very well elaborated and thus did not constitute information value added (Cardoso et al., 2005).

In the same register, and in an even more incisive form, a PSD (centre-right) MP suggested, as a reason for the lack of interest MPs have in the Internet as a mean of vertical communication, the weak political and civic participation by the citizens, who are neither sensitized nor sufficiently informed on the political issues in society to make the normal use of the Internet into a form of communication with the MPs (Cardoso et al., 2005).

Regardless of the reasons put forward, the visible result is a non-declared resistance on the part of politicians and political institutions to the influence of new political forms of information and communication for vertical communication originating amongst the citizens. In other words, the opening of new *mediation* channels with those in political offices, in which interactivity is favoured over unidirectional communication (even when the communication takes place and is a success, as in the case of electronic petitions) does not meet with a favourable response from the political representatives. Why?

In the analysis of the MPs' responses we must also take into account that they are aware of the highly negative representations the voters have of their elected representatives. Furthermore, the politicians themselves (at least in the Portuguese case) seem to have negative representations as to the capacity of the voters to play an active role that would be of use to the democratic process. In the final analysis, this situation leads to the inexistence of greater incentives, on the part of the parliamentary representatives, for greater participation through the Internet.

Hence, although the representations the MPs have of the Internet (as a democracy-boosting instrument) may be generally positive, they must nevertheless be contextualized in the mutual distrust that characterizes the elected representative/elector relationship.

The parliamentary representatives see the Internet as an effective formula for increasing democratic relations only when the trust between the parties is already on a high level. If level of trust is low, the Internet is seen only as a hope for the future renovations of the democratic practices, functioning more as a positive desire for something that is to take place in the future than as an element of change the current informational politics models.

The Internet as Hostage of Institutional Informational Politics?

Throughout the preceding arguments we have been analyzing the possible contribution of the Internet to changing the informational politics models, focusing on its role as an interpersonal communication tool, between voter and elected representative.

We have thus analyzed the availability and types of technological interfaces between elected representatives and citizens, the practices and representation of the representatives in relation to the Internet as a vehicle for participation and the *interest and predisposition of the citizens in participating,* making use of these technological tools.

We have deliberately left out we have identified as a fourth dimension, i.e. the understanding of how television, radio and the print media position themselves as promoters of, or barriers to, the new modalities of mediation between citizens and elected representatives offered by the Internet. This will now be the guiding element in our analysis.

As we have seen throughout this thesis, the Internet, when used proactively, through E-mail, can perform similar roles to those attributed to television and radio stations and newspapers, i.e. it can become a mass communication technology (Eco, 2004).

As suggested by Filzmaier, Hoff and Cardoso (2004), the use of the Internet in the parliamentary institutional context is not only a product of the skills and representations of those who deal with the technology in the context of the organs of sovereignty.

The use of the Net is also dependent on many internal factors, such as the legal and administrative structure of the parliament, the relationship between voters and elected representatives (result of the electoral system), the parties' work and organization methods, the political culture, the way in which the parliamentary representatives see themselves and the social origins of the MPs themselves. External factors are also as important as, if not more important than, internal matters and they may include the structure of the government and the relationship with it, general political culture aspects, the socio-demography of Internet usage and the *way in which the media system functions.*

The hypothesis put forward here is that, *to a certain extent, media such as television, radio and the newspapers also contribute, as instruments of inertia, to the changes in the political communication models on the part of the parliamentary representatives.*

This takes place because, on the one hand, the MPs see in the media (in particular television and the print media) mediation spaces that function well (although not always with rules to their liking) as far as vertical communication is concerned.

Moreover, the fact that the relationship between the media and politicians is normally a proactive one from the media point of view (they contact the MPs for news) and a reactive one from the politicians' point of view (although politicians have been known to exploit the media's need for news) is likewise a barrier to the development of an alternative informational politics model in which the parliamentarians and parties develop a much more proactive posture in the field of *mediation.*

Obviously, given the power attributed to them as unique *mediation* spaces, one must also take into consideration the interest media themselves (television, radio and the print media) have in retaining their role of central mediators. [157]

---

[157] I have deliberately decided not to include here the whole discussion on the replacement of the traditional media by the new media already dealt with in chapters 8 and 9, given that I have already made my view clear on the complementarity and networking model.

In the majority of the parliament's studies, the respective MPs primarily value the newspapers (Austria, Denmark and Germany) or television (Portugal and Norway) as the main political communication instrument.

Table 8.18 – The media considered important/very important for political communication by parliament members, selected countries (%)

	PT	AU	NR	NL	DK	Sc	G
Television	82.3 (1)	90 (2)	97.1 (1)	-	96.6(2)	-	91.1 (2)
Daily newspapers	65.4 (2)	100 (1)	95.6 (2)	-	97.8 (1)	-	97.1 (1)
Weekly newspapers	62.8 (3)	100 (1)	95.6 (3)	-	97.8 (1)	-	-
Radio	-	90 (2)	94.1 (4)	-	92.1(3)	-	70.6 (5)
Magazines	34.6 (4)	86.3 (3)	39.6 (6)	-	40.5 (5)	-	73.6 (4)
Internet	31.2 (5)	70 (4)	41.3 (5)	-	50.5 (4)	-	79.4 (3)

Source: Comparative analysis of European members of parliament, (2003) COST-A14, Cardoso, Gustavo (PT); Hoff, Jens (DK); Kleisteuber Hans (G); Snellen, Ignace (NL); Smith, Colin (Sc); Elvebaek, Beate (NR); Filzmaier, Peter (A). Note: the percentage values do not make up 100% because the reading of the table is limited to each of the each one of the categories in the column in relation to the options d in line.

However, when it comes to the role attributed to the Internet there are clearly two models: one in which the Internet is valued almost as much as the other media (Austria and Germany), reflecting greater appropriation of its use for mass communication; and a second model, where the dominant role, regardless of the possible different reasons, continues to be given to television, the newspapers and radio, with the attribution to the Internet of a role similar to that attributed to magazines, i.e. a mass, but specialized, political communication medium for specific audiences interested in particular issues.

In this second model, the Internet is given mainly the role of a complementary medium or added value, particularly during election campaigns. [158]

Also, the fact that there is no direct correlation between the number of Internet users and the representations of the MPs as to the importance of the Internet in mass political communication would seem to support our initial hypothesis.

---

[158]For more information on how the media, for example the public service media, cover election campaigns on their Internet sites see: Paulussen, Steve and Coppens, Tomas (2003).

The argument that the valuation of the use of the Internet in mass political communication is linked to the number of users in a specific countries is often used in the Portuguese context when, for example, one argues that *"(...) in comparison to other states"* in the EU and the US, there is a low number of users and as the politicians are aware of this *"do not want to run the risk"* and television has *"a much larger effective audience"* than the Internet (Cardoso et al., 2005).

As another Portuguese MP, also responsible in the government for the area of the information society, sum it up: in a *"mediatized society such as ours"*, television continues to play a central role in political communication *"(...) because it is seen more, has a certain shine, and because commercial brands and personal identities are created on television – they are not created in the newspapers or on the Internet or on radio. People become really well known through television and ideas have an impact through television"* (Cardoso et al., in the press). [159]

It would, therefore, seem clear that greater or lesser appreciation of the Internet as an instrument of political communicated is to a large extent linked to the way in which the media system is organized – whether it is more proactive or more reactive in its relations with the MPs. It does not have so much to do with the real numbers of newspaper readers, viewers of a TV news programme or Internet users. This is also confirmed by the fact that, throughout the 20th century, new communication technologies did not "kill off" or substitute those that preceded them (Eco, 2003). On the contrary, they essentially gave rise to processes of adaptation and complementarity.

---

[159] Similar analyses can be found in other MP discourses. For example, an MP for the CDS-PP stated that, considering that the politicians wish to reach the largest possible number of people, they will obviously favour television, followed by the newspapers, magazines and radio (the transmission vehicles with the largest audiences) and only then the Internet. The larger audience argument is also emphasized by a new CDS-PP member, according to whom the *"(...) importance of television has to do with the effectiveness of the message transmission. In other words, half a minute on a TV news programme is worth any number of permanent pages on the Internet as far as effectiveness in getting the message across is concerned".* To sum up, the question of the audiences of the political means of communication is essential for the Portuguese MPs interviewed. *"No matter how good they (the debates) are at the parliamentary level, if we don't get the message across in the media and, above all, the media with the largest impact (television stations and large circulation newspapers), no matter how good a policy is in terms of content and fundamental issues, it cannot get its message across and it will have an effect in terms of the electorate. And this is extremely important for us politicians."* (MP for CDS-PP).

Although the parliamentary and party political actors do not seem to favour this *relation of network complementarity* that the Internet has introduced to the media system, the citizens are aware of the possibilities and obviously make use of them, as illustrated by the analysis of the vertical communication established with organs of sovereignty, such as the Presidency of the Portuguese Republic [160].

Similar to the characterization of the citizens who contact their parliamentary representatives, those who contact the Portuguese President via E-mail are in the younger ages groups (the 25 to 39 years group accounts for 60% of all contacts). However, there are less differences in terms of education between the citizens who contact the President.

In terms of distribution in socio-professional categories, there is a greater concentration of contacts in the upper and middle management and entrepreneur segments (81.9%). The population that opts for E-mail in communications with the Portuguese President are in highly qualified professional categories.

Compared to the contacts with members of parliament, the number of civil servants contacting the President, be it through E-mail or conventional mail, reaches 30% of the contacts. [161] Communication with the Portuguese President can take place via a web form available on the presidency website

---

[160] Created in 1998, the official website of the Presidency of the Portuguese Republic – www.presidenciarepublica.pt – has as its objectives, in the light of the issue of the Information Society and the importance that access to information has, to contribute to the consolidation of the Portuguese democratic system through the establishment and solidification of a relationship of proximity and transparency between the citizens and political power, which require commitment to the use of the available tools and means of access to information. With a view to achieving these objectives, and as a way of promoting more and better knowledge of the President's institutional activities, in their contemporary dimension and in their historic context, the website provides information such as the biography and constitutional status of the President of the Republic and information on his/her daily activity, "(...) as well as on the promulgation and signing of laws, decree-laws, executory decisions and other decrees of the Portuguese Republic and on the ratification and signing of international treaties and agreements (...)" to which Portugal is party. In terms of services provided by the Presidency via the website, there is "(...) information on the nature and composition of the personal, technical, asset managerial, administrative and financial support services (...)" of this organ of sovereignty, as well as a virtual library including "(...) written, audio and audiovisual documents on the intervention of the President of the Portuguese Republic in various areas of his/her sphere of competence (...)".

[161] If we compare the data on the citizens that communicate with the President of the Republic via postal correspondence and E-mail with the profile of those communicating with the Portuguese MPs, one finds no significant differences in essence. This would make it possible, though taking into account the institutional differences between the organs, to extrapolate the practices of complementarity between media also in relation to the Portuguese parliament.

or, to a lesser degree, though the E-mail address. The majority of the visits to the site are made from Portugal, followed by countries in North America (US) and South America (Brazil) and then, at a distance, in Europe.

The figure below (Figure 8.2) shows how the use of the Presidency of the Portuguese Republic website takes place. We can register the number of messages sent from the website, the number of hits and the number of visits (visits counted per unique Internet server used by the person accessing the site). The latter two values provide an approximate idea of the frequency of access to the site. For Neto (2002) the analysis of the graph reveals two phenomena. Firstly, the hits and the visits have very similar frequency curves, offering a clear perspective on the evolution of interest in consulting the information on the website.

Figure 8.2 – Daily use of e-mail service and consultation of information on the website of the Presidency of the Portuguese Republic

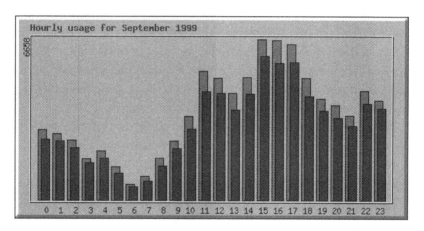

Source: Webalizer, Internet Server of the Presidency of the Portuguese Republic.

Secondly, the analysis shows that, while the site consultations do not increase as a direct result of the increase of broadcast time or coverage by newspapers on a given number of topical news, the messages received seem to vary depending on the types of subjects addressed. In other words, whenever an occurrence gains the status of incident/event (Rebelo 2000), and there is a phenomenal modification of the state of the world (unbalancing, felt by the citizens), this produces a relevance effect which, in turn, has an influence on the propensity for communicating with the organs of sovereignty, but such propensity tend to vary according to the type of news.

Another element in the characterization of message communication is provided by analysis of the daily site access routines. The hours of usage of the website and of electronic mail, both in a typical month and in an atypical one such as September 1999 (East Timor crisis), are similar. The site use peaks are between 3.00 p.m. and 6.00 p.m., while there is an increasing trend between 9.00 a.m. and 12.00 noon, with a decreasing trend after 6.00 p.m. In other words, the participation times via the Internet correspond to the normal working hours and there is little participation in after-work hours.

The analysis of the site use periods also allows us to establish a relationship between the sending of E-mails and the information routines of other media. When an event of importance, be it national or international, occupies the media agenda, the reading of the newspapers in the morning and the listening to the radio, as well as the consultation these media online, are the most influential references for the sending of E-mail message between 10.00 a.m. and 1.00 p.m. The communication figures between 2.00 p.m. and 6.00 p.m. are influenced by access to the lunchtime television news and by online information provided by the newspapers and radio. The habitual custom of watching the dinner-time TV news, between 8.00 p.m. and 9.00 p.m. is also an element to be take into account, given the increase in the number of visits to the site from 10.00 p.m. onwards.

Neto (2002) also offers a brief characterization of the messages sent, allowing us to contextualize, in terms of content, the use of E-mail as a participation instrument. As far as the language used in the communications is concerned, the overwhelming majority are in Portuguese (approximately 85.7%), followed by English, which is used in 12.1% of cases.

As for the country of origin of the messages sent, one can, on the one hand, highlight the fact that messages from Portugal account for 71.5% of the total. On the other, the figures show that in South America and Africa the number of messages from countries with stronger historic and linguistic ties with Portugal is higher than the total number of messages sent from the other countries on the same continent. Equally noteworthy is the fact that the number of messages sent from Europe (excluding Portugal) is almost identical to the number sent from North America.

As far as the contents are concerned, focusing on the dichotomy of *presidential competences vs. the competences of other organs of sovereignty*, 18.7% of the messages deal with the exercise of the office of Portuguese President, while 31.3% makes reference to the functions of other organs, a fact that would seem to indicate an emphasis, placed by the citizens, on the competences of analysis and monitoring of the actions of the government and other instances on the part of the President (Neto 2004).

Table 8.19 – Development in the number of letters and E-mails received by the Presidency of the Portuguese Republic (1998-2004)

Period	Letters	E-mail	% E-mail	Total	E-mail growth rate	Letter growth rate
1998**	12278	256	2.04%	12534	-	-
1999	13768	821	5.63%	14589	220.70%	12.14%
2000	13857	2250	13.97%	16107	174.06%	0.65%
2001	12638	1462	10.37%	14100	-35.02%	-8.80%
2002	15619	7069	31.16%	22688	383.52%	23.59%
2003	11719	2935	20.03%	14654	-58.48%	-24.97%
2004*	1814	414	18.58%	2228	-	-

Source: adapted from information provided by the Documentation Centre of the General Secretary of the Presidency of the Portuguese Republic. *Values refer only to the 1st quarter of 2004. ** Values refer only to the second half of 1998.

As far as the communication between the citizens and the Portuguese Republic are concerned, the table above (Table 8.19) registers the development in the number of letters and E-mails received by the office of the President between 1998 and 2004 and provides a number of interesting pointers for understanding the appropriation of E-mail by the citizens as an instrument of civic participation.

The first thing we can ascertain from the analysis of the data is that, since the creation of the official website in 1998, the number of communications with the Presidency of the Republic has increased overall. One can therefore conclude that either there are more people communicating with the organs of sovereignty since they have provided their online presence or the same people are communicating more.

Given that the increase in the E-mail messages is not accompanied by a decrease in the conventional mail, one can only conclude that there are new communication opportunities and, consequently, more people writing.

Comparing the variations in the E-mail messages and letters received by Portuguese Presidency, one establishes that both illustrate the same trends. In other words, when the number of messages received increases or decreases the same occurs in both *mediation* forms.

What these values reflect is the greater immediacy of E-mail, i.e. when the number of E-mails received increases it is because a given event is in progress or has just taken place. When that event is on the media agenda on television, radio or in the written press, there is a very sudden and intensive increase in E-mails. This happens because the writers hope that their writing to the President takes place in productive time, i.e. while the event still has media value. Given that, at times, the media life of an event is short, the E-mail, thanks to its technical characteristics of immediacy of sending and reception, seems to be particularly well adapted to accompanying the media that report in flux, such as radio and television. Although the conventional letter also seems to be boosted as a means of communication by the media-worthy dimension of an event, it seems to be used more for questions that are less in the eye of the media and more of the personal or institutional sphere (Neto 2002).

Table 8.20 – E-mails received by the Presidency of the Portuguese Republic, 1998-2002, by topic area (%)

	1998	1999	2000	2001	2002*	Total
Environment	4.08%	6.12%	57.14%	32.65%	0.00%	100.00%
Sciences	9.23%	13.85%	49.23%	18.46%	9.23%	100.00%
Media	3.03%	15.15%	21.21%	51.52%	9.09%	100.00%
Portuguese communities abroad	2.09%	13.61%	28.27%	40.84%	15.18%	100.00%
Culture	6.67%	25.83%	33.33%	22.50%	11.67%	100.00%
Economics/social matters	4.79%	14.16%	28.77%	38.81%	13.47%	100.00%
Legal	2.86%	20.71%	30.71%	41.43%	4.29%	100.00%
Youth	10.00%	5.00%	60.00%	25.00%	0.00%	100.00%
Education	6.75%	20.25%	36.81%	26.38%	9.82%	100.00%
Appreciation	15.44%	21.32%	31.25%	27.57%	4.41%	100.00%
Personal (insults)	22.22%	22.22%	44.44%	11.11%	0.00%	100.00%
Political/parliamentary	6.04%	6.79%	31.32%	44.53%	11.32%	100.00%
Regional and local	11.36%	5.68%	30.68%	37.50%	14.77%	100.00%
International relations	2.73%	19.13%	35.52%	38.80%	3.83%	100.00%
Administrative matters	7.67%	12.88%	19.94%	45.40%	14.11%	100.00%
Others	25.10%	22.39%	27.03%	21.62%	3.86%	100.00%

Source: adapted from information provided by the Documentation Centre of the General Secretary of the Presidency of the Portuguese Republic. *Values refer only to the 1st quarter of 2002.

The preceding table (Table 8.20) shows the trends in the matters chosen by the citizens to submit to the opinion of the Portuguese President, demonstrating a variation in the interests preferred over the period under in the analysis. They are explained on the basis of the generalized sending of messages on a given topic in a short space of time. The cases messages linked temporally to media coverage of certain topic on television, radio or in the newspapers are more frequent than organized strategies by groups of individuals or organizations seeing to call the President's attention to a given question or issue. In other word, mediatization normally precedes the mass sending of E-mails on a certain topic.

Another conclusion from the analysis is the fact that there is no direct correlation between the length of time devoted to an event on television and the intensity of the communication via the Internet on the same matter. Also, the fact that an issue has all the necessary spice for achieving larger television audiences, such as the case of the collapse of the bridge at Entre-os-Rios in Portugal – which combined "(...) a tragic accident, lost lives, families practically wiped out (...) and add to this, a veritable soap opera involving ministerial resignations, reshuffling of the Cabinet and in renowned public institutions, all of this followed step by step live" (Santiago 2003) – does not guarantee the necessary connection between the contact with the media reality and the effective use of the Internet in a context of participation.

As the data in the following table show (Table 8.21), the communicative relationship seems to be much more closely linked to the subject matter and the existence of a pre-formed opinion on the matter, or previous militancy in the question, than to the way in which television, radio or the newspapers deal with the matter or the broadcast time attributed to it. Two examples can justify this conclusion: in 2002 the issues that were most frequently the subject matters of E-mails received by the Presidency of the Republic were the question of the killing of bulls in bullfights in Portugal and the possible closure of the public television channel RTP2. A total of 4,628 documents were received expressing opinions against the depenalization of the death of the bull in Portugal and also tens of E-mails contained thousands of signatures and petitions in favour of maintaining the public television channel.

However, if we look at the media coverage of these questions we see that, although the two cases were strong presences in the television agenda at the time, they were not those with the most television broadcasting time.

According to the e-telenews report (2002), neither of the two topics was given in-depth coverage in the four national channels (RTP 1 and 2, SIC and TVI). In 2002 the three top stories, in terms of broadcast time, were: the Casa Pia paedophilia scandal with 676 news reports (making up 30 hours and 49 minutes of broadcast time); the sinking of the *Prestige* off the coast of Galicia, which was the subject of 770 news reports on television (or 30 hours of broadcast time); and the case of alleged political corruption and the misuse of monies at the private Universidade Moderna university, known as the Universidade Moderna scandal, which accounted for 466 news reports (equalling 17 hours and 5 minutes of broadcast time).

Following the same line of thought, one can register that two of the topics that were most in the news in 2003, the *War in Iraq* and *Casa Pia,* were given different receptions by the citizens. A topic such as the *War in Iraq*, which was subject to recurrent news reporting and for which there was a high degree of involvement and clearly predefined opinions on the role of the US in its relations with the world and with Europe, was the subject matter of 229 E-mails.

Table 8.21 – Number of e-mails received by the Presidency of the Portuguese Republic relating to organized campaigns or received coincidentally in time, 1998-2003 (no.)

	1998	1999	2000	2001	2002*	2003	total
Death of bull in bullfights (animal rights)	5	39	109	19	0	-	172
Promotion of sergeants (military)	-	-		14	-	-	14
Health Polytechnics (education)	-	-	22	-	-	-	22
Instituto Piaget (education)	-	-	-	-	31	-	31
Instituto Pupilos do Exército (education)	-	-	-	1	4	-	5
Legislation on teachers (education)	2	3	5	19	8	-	37
Depenalization of drug consumption (national politics)	-	-	64	3	1	-	68
Entre-os-Rios disaster (catastrophe)	-	-	-	14	-	-	14
Military programming law (military)				15			15
Reduction in the legal blood-alcohol rate (national politics)				4			4
Cancellation of visit to Austria (international politics)				15			15
September 11 (catastrophe)				17	1		18
Kosovo/Balkan crisis (war)		77	1				78
Situation in Cuba (human rights)	13			2			15
Handing over Macao to PR China (decolonization)		5	16	1			22
Timor Crisis (human rights/ decolonization)	1	203	15	8			227
War in Iraq (war)*						360	360
Casa Pia case (paedophilia)*						36	36

Source: adapted from information provided by the Documentation Centre of the General Secretary of the Presidency of the Portuguese Republic. *Values refer only to the 1st quarter of 2003.

Another topic, of national interest, the Casa Pia scandal, which configured much more what Santiago (2003) defines as attractive ingredients for direct and ongoing news coverage, totalled only 67 E-mail messages received during 2003.

Although one cannot extrapolate the findings presented here to other spheres of the use of computer mediated communication (for example, communication with the media and the forums created by online newspapers), the conclusions presented are, nevertheless, exemplary for the way in which the citizens interconnect different media in networks, i.e. how they create their mental hypertext between different media (Castells, 2004) in their communication with the organs of sovereignty, be they parliaments, the government or the Presidency of the Republic.

What conclusions can one make on the institutional informational politics between citizens and the organs of sovereignty and between political and party agents (the parliamentary representatives) and the same citizens in a context of continuous democracy?

The first conclusion is that informational politics, as described by Castells (2004), Dijk (2000) and Gibson and Ward (2003), i.e. the predominance of television and, to a lesser degree, the print media as instruments of political communication, is maintaining the current status quo because, even though the parties, parliaments and governments have invested in and made available *technological interfaces on the Internet between the elected representatives and the citizens,* the use made of them by the political elites is mostly reactive in nature. With the exception of election campaign periods, the use of the interfaces in a top-down approach (contact initiative taken by the organs of sovereignty) is limited. E-mail and websites are provided for whomever wishes to communicate with the organs of sovereignty but a strong political will to encourage this participation does not exist.

This under-use of the Internet's potentials derives, to a large extent, from the *representations of the elected representatives,* who, on the basis of their own experience or prejudices, do not believe that the contribution that civic participation makes to their work is a significant value added.

There are also signs in some countries that Internet usage in the institutional context does not necessarily have to be as described above. The cases of European countries such as Germany and Austria show that the use of the Internet can be valued in the context of the creation of alternative mass communication channels. However, it's a long way to go from intention to putting things into practice, particularly because the use of the more traditional media in mass communication continues to be seen as preferable, as per the study results presented (Kleisteuber et al. 2004, Fitzmeier et al. 2004). Also, because the television stations and newspapers, with their traditional diffusion models, have an interest in maintaining the current model that has applied for the last 20 years of political communication, the Internet is, to a certain extent, a *hostage of institutional informational politics.* It is in the interest of neither the media system nor the institutional political agents to concede spaces for the growth of Internet usage in mass political communication.

The Internet is seen more as a technology that replaces the sending of letter and retains the character of postal communication than as a technology for the diffusion of information and multilateral communication.

The current *informational politics* model favours political marketing strategies based on personalization and emptying of the political discussion in the media. Of course, the domestication of the use of the Internet by the political elites and the media, as far as politics is concerned, also followed that logic closely.

Hence, after approximately ten years of coexistence between politics and the Internet, of the different scenarios put forward by Gibson and Ward (2003), that which most realistically can be applied to the current situation is *"politics as usual"*. A scenario of limited impact of the information and communication technologies on the political practices and conceptions in the institution context of the relationship between the citizens and the organs of sovereignty.

In this scenario, the political actors use the information technologies to replicate their former practices, thus using the technologies more for the dissemination of propaganda and political marketing than for mechanisms of interactivity with the citizens, whereby their focus is on the more politically active citizens.

The informational politics we know today, irrespective of the emergence of the Internet, is still based on a "demo-elitist" conception (Hoff et al., 2000) of democracy and less so on a model more oriented towards civic participation, the "neo-republican model" (Hoff et al., 2000). [162]

The demo-elitist model is one that recommends various reforms in the agenda of contemporary governments, advocating proposals for promoting the democratic quality of the electoral policy and reinforcing the representative component. Examples can be found in the proposals for making party manifestos and the voting records and stances/positions of politicians available on the Internet as well as electronic conversations between the citizens and elected representatives, etc.

Meanwhile, parallel to the framework of practices of the political elites described above, *bottom-up* processes demonstrate that links are established between different communication technologies through the uses carried out by the citizens.

---

[162] As a communicational theory, this model puts forward a virtual public sphere mediated by electronic networks as the promoter of active citizens in the political process. Its defenders can be found both in the new social movement and in the new communitarism of the networked civic movement and their collective electronic meetings and virtual gatherings. The majority of these strive wish to see access to the information technologies as a fundamental social right that should be guaranteed to all citizens in the information society.

This does not mean that the pattern of current institutionalized informational politics is changing. It merely indicates that changes that do take place are not exclusively the will of the political elites and in the interest of the current media system.

The change is probably more visible in the context of the organized communication of social movements and the way they appropriate the information and communication technologies than in the institutional context of communication between citizens and the organs of sovereignty. That is the analysis to be carried out in the next chapter.

9. Media, Mobilization and Protests

As Bennett (2004) argues, the public spheres created by the Internet and the Web are more than parallel information universes that coexist independently of the traditional mass media.

The objective of this chapter is to examine how the relationship between the Internet and mass media (television and newspapers) is established in moments of mobilization and protest in causes protagonized by citizen movements and new social movements.

The three case studies around which our analysis is organized are all very particular cases that are difficult to integrate into the traditional characterization typologies for Internet usage in protest and mobilization actions. They were therefore chosen as paradigmatic study examples.

The first case to be studied, "Terràvista", was a protest organized in 1998 by Internet users of the portal financed by the Portuguese government for the diffusion of Portuguese-language contents. It is a clear example of how protests in the network society, even those seeking a solution to problems directly related the Internet usage (such as content censorship) cannot take place without gaining certain fame in the more traditional media, like newspapers and TV.

The Terràvista case illustrates how a small group of activists, which was not very representative of those harmed by the censorship measure of the then Ministry of Culture and in a context of the Internet that was of little interest in the public opinion, was able to makes it positions valid through the conquest of news and opinion space in the newspapers and television.

In the second case study we will look at the protest around the, at the time, forecast closure of the public television channel RTP2, protagonized by the then Minister of the Presidency, the public television workforce and the viewers.

During the month of May 2002, after the announcement by the government of a restructuring plan for RTP, there emerged a heated debate amongst opinion leaders, citizens and political parties on the future of television.

Given the economic interests involved, i.e. the RTP advertising revenue and the likelihood of it passing to the private channels and the fact that the majority of the newspapers belong to the same business groups that had an interest in the sale of RTP, the public opinion was confronted with a moment in which the media could not be impartial or objective. In particular when they themselves are the news.

During the month of May 2002 two information spaces on RTP were configured: one protagonized by the media themselves, through the news articles and opinion columns; and the other protagonized by the citizens in the public television station's own site.

An analysis of the body of newspapers, television broadcasts and posts to the RTP online forums gives us a better understanding of the role that each medium assumes and how the citizens deal with the media when they are seen as judges in their own cause.

Finally, we will look at the protest movement in support of East Timor, which, in September 1999, through various media from the Internet to television and from radio to the newspapers, sought to call the attention of Portuguese and worldwide public opinion (after the referendum that voted "yes" for independence from Portugal and the illegal occupation by Indonesia) to the humanitarian tragedy in East Timor and to the need to send a UN peacekeeping force to the territory to the north of Australia.

The atypical dimension resides in the central role of the media in mobilizing popular opinion. In contrast to the "White Marches" against paedophilia in Belgium (Walgrave et al., 2000), here the media actively cooperated with formal and informal social mobilization structures, clearly assuming their partiality in favour of East Timor and against the Indonesian regime.

The analysis of the pro-East Timor movement allows us to understand not only the functional division of tasks in a global-scale protest amongst the citizens, organized movements and the media, but also how some of the mediation instruments deal with a situation of mobilization and protest, thus showing how a mailing list functions during a mobilization for action phase, and how one and the same issue – in this case, the "situation in East Timor" – is seen by the different media in Portugal, Europe, US, Oceania and the Far East. In other words, the different lenses of journalistic objectivity in action.

All three examples listed above are exemplary of the complementarity and networking that are characteristic of the media and those that appropriate them with the aim of using the symbolic mediation space they provide to achieve clearly defined objectives.

One example of the relationship between different mediation spaces is the micro-mass media relationship that is the exchange of E-mails between NIKE and John Peretti that appeared on the Slashdot internet site before ending upon the online magazine Salon and, later, the US Today and Wall Street Journal newspapers, thus with each step coming closer to a news item instead of what it started out as – simply the exchange of messages between an activist and a business corporation (Bennett, 2004).

Although in a somewhat different register, we can find similar networking logics between mediation spaces in the process of the divulgation of the images of the torture of prisoners of war at Abu Ghraib prison by American soldiers. The photos that circulated on the Internet ended up making the opening news stories in news programmes and on newspaper front pages around the world. Also, when we look at the Al Qaeda communication strategies, which use web pages to videos of Bin Laden's communiqués or the execution of hostages and their subsequent use in global television networks such as Al Jazeera and CNN.

Another example of appropriation by movements or persons pursuing individual agendas can be found in the new models of rumours, i.e. the passing on of word, that often take the form of PowerPoint documents containing a narrative in text and images. They are distributed via E-mail and show the *other* side to the news – one that is different to that generally shown by the international agencies. Examples of these *multimedia rumours* can be found in the cases of the Israeli intervention in Nablus and Jenin in April 2000, or the civil unrest in Argentina during the crisis there in 2001.

If this logic of the networking of different mediation spaces constitutes a novelty, the same can be said for the changes in progress in the nature of civic participation, which has changed considerably over the last few decades.

For example, affiliation in associations/groups is no longer an adequate parameter for measuring the degree of participation in a given civil society or organization. Today, involvement is much less measured in terms of ideologies and formal political processes (Cammaerts et al. 2003). Furthermore, the great structural and emancipating causes are no longer the only reasons for getting involved. Hence, matters closer to home (location) or directed towards specific issues (animal rights, ecology, child abuse, etc.) and also matters related with what Giddens terms Life-Politics (1997) are on the increase as far as involvement of the populations is concerned (Cammaerts et al., 2003).

In terms of strategies there are also new developments in the panorama of participation. For example, whereas some social organizations and movements explicitly seek to influence politics through lobbying, i.e. entering into direct relations with the political parties, many others distance themselves from direct relations with formal representative politics and prefer to make politics through direct action, the change of values, alternative lifestyles or the development of counter-hegemonies (Cammaerts et al., 2003).

In this context of change in the media system and in the form of civic participation what is the attraction of the Internet for it to be appropriated by civic organizations and social movements?

Scott and Street (2001) list four reasons why the Internet is attractive to the social movements. The first is the fact that the Internet allows for meso-mobilization. In other words, the strategic alliance, online and offline, between movements, allowing a networked connection across borders without the need for a transnational hierarchical formula. The second reason is the fact that the Internet allows for a high impact without requiring a lot of resources. The third reason has to do with the fact that the Internet allows the organizations to maintain editorial control over contents and external communications. Finally, the Internet also allows them to sidestep State control and communicate in a secure system.

In addition to the four reasons above, we can also argue that the Internet offers a strengthening of the public sphere through the *mediation* of the political debate and the expansion of the political sphere (Dahlgren, 2002 and Sparks, 2002).

However, this does not mean that the Internet is exclusively a space of strong participation for those who chose it for the purposes of civic participation. As with the traditional protest spaces, participation online can be more active or more passive.

Strong, active offline participation can take the form of participation in protests or any other form of direct action, volunteer work, participation in meetings or becoming actively involved in an organization.

Passive offline involvement can, for example, mean being merely a member of an organization or participating in meetings, though not in an active way.

Online civic participation can also be more passive or more active. Posting messages or participating in direct online actions are seen as more active attitudes than merely receiving newsletters, visiting forums or subscribing to a mailing list without adding any message to it (Cammaerts et al., 2003).

If we want to typify the appropriations of the Internet for civic participation purposes in somewhat more detail, we can characterize the uses on the basis of the proposed objectives. There are various types of organizations that have been described as "virtual organizations". One can identify four ideal types of the organization within that definition (Cammaerts et al., 2003).

The first is that of the *umbrella organization,* which carries out certain tasks on behalf of its autonomous members, facilitating their work through the offer of resources and experts in diverse areas (not a very common type in the global universe of organizations but it can be found, for example, in APC.org).

The second type is the *portal organization,* which functions as a showcase and guides the users to information, sites and organizations through links. The portal organization does not provide information itself, although it does have functions of selection and editing. The information may be the product of individual organizations or networks of organizations (one example is LabourStart.org on trade unions and labour-related questions).

The *platform organization* offers a virtual platform for interaction, organization and communication. Ideally, the interaction is not moderated, nor is the information edited or censored, thus promoting a platform for the development of alternative discourses with the aim of influencing public opinion and advancing certain policies (one example is attac.org, analyzed by Le Guinou, 2004)

Last, but not least, we have the *web organization,* which refers to the use of more interactive web tools such as the forums, discussion boards and virtual communities (Cammaerts et al., 2003). The interaction is often carried out between individuals such as citizens or professionals. The objective is mobilization and the offer of alternative information sources (a typical case is that offered by the media structure at indymedia.org).

In most of the cases analyzed by Cammaerts (2003) and two cases studied in this chapter (East Timor and RTP), E-mail and mailing lists played a central role.

This is due to the fact that forums and mailing lists can have a great resonance in terms of participation and, as such, are a tested instrument of success.

However, they also have their limitations. For example, organizations with local bases are normally more inclined to develop offline strategies due to the high number of persons who are not online. For this reason, the use of the Internet tools is more common when the causes are national or global, except in societies where Internet penetration is already very high.

As far as the use of mailing lists is concerned, at times there is also a homogeneity of thought due to the low number of persons actively participating, giving rise to demotivation and monochordic discourses (Cardoso, 1998). On the other hand, unmoderated participation by a large number of persons can give rise to problems such as name calling and insults or the abrupt termination of conversations, etc. In either of the two situations – low or high participation – it is often not perceivable where the discussion will take the participants, as no conclusions emerge.

Although it is obvious that different organizations adopt different strategies to achieve their political objectives, both offline and online, appearance on the Internet has played an important role in gathering support, organizing protests and demonstrations and obtaining independent information from the public. It therefore represents a change in the panorama of mobilization and protest. However, if it is true that the Internet is an important instrument of recognized merit for achieving protest objectives, it is also nonetheless true that something more is required to guarantee that an action is successful, for the action and the objective have to reach both the public and the political agenda.

The role of the press, radio and televisions in amplifying the actions and objectives is fundamental in this aspect. Also, winning over the sympathy and support of the populations directly involved – either geographically or by having suffered direct impacts of the problem in question – continues to play an important role, without which the success of a given action often would not be possible. Success in appropriation of the symbolic *mediation* spaces is, thus, the product of the combination of various factors.

The following case studies are the product of atypical limit situation that are, perhaps, difficult to repeat in other national or global contexts.

However, it is precisely their atypicalness that makes them interesting. For by understanding how the practices of the different agents – i.e. the citizens, media and governments – unfold, we can draw up a conceptual framework that identifies the central elements in the processes in question and, thus, contribute to an understanding of other mobilization and protest processes that are less complete than those analyzed herein.

Goku vs. the Ministry of Culture: Terràvista, Television and Newspapers

Terràvista was presented in 1997, the year it was launched by the Portuguese Ministry of Culture as a public project offering free space for the hosting of non-commercial information in the Portuguese language on the World Wide Web.

The objective was to stimulate the growth of the Portuguese-speaking virtual community and to help make its voice heard. As there are some 200 million speakers of Portuguese, one of the aims was to boost the use of the Internet in education and as a form of connection to the Portuguese communities abroad, for example in Canada, but also to function as a link with Brazil, where most of the Portuguese speaking Internet users are to be found. Hence, agreements were signed between the Ministries of Culture of Brazil and Portugal for the creation of a Terràvista portal in Sao Paulo.

An example of the dimension of the Portuguese speaking world was the choice of names of beaches in Portugal, Brazil, Angola, Mozambique and Cape Verde for the personal pages of the users – names such as Água D'alto, Baía das Gatas, Bilene, Copacabana, Enseada, Fernando de Noronha, Guincho, Ilha do Mel, Meco, Meia Praia, Mussulo, Nazaré, Porto Santo and Vila Praia de Âncora.

As far as the user population is concerned, the Sociographic Data on the Terràvista Space show that its population was predominantly male (89%) and made up largely of Portuguese and Brazilian users.

The most represented age groups were those between the ages 11 and 35, which accounted for 85.7% of the population (40.2% of the creators of pages were in the 19 to 25 age group). As for the contents produced in Terràvista, they most common topics were general interest , computers, nightlife and sports.

The Terràvista case began on 29 July 1998 after a telephone call from the tabloid newspaper "24Horas" informed the ministry of improper contents – i.e. pornographic manga drawings based on the Dragon Ball series. In response to the news, the Minister of Culture, Prof. Dr. Manuel Maria Carrilho, decided to close down the Terràvista service, leaving more than 26,000 pages inaccessible. On the same day he announced that the service would reopen on 9 August. [163]

The central question in the whole process of the closure of Terràvista can be reduced to a political decision, by the Ministry, to close the service with a view to minimizing the negative impact of a news report in the media (i.e. pornography subsidized by the Ministry of Culture) and the interpretation of the closure by the users as censorship of the pages of all those users of the service who had nothing to do with the censorable contents.

Freedom of expression is an important issue in democratic societies and a recurrent theme in the media. If the first case of restriction of the freedom

---

[163]The Terràvista project was originally part of the Mosaico initiative of the Ministry of Culture that aimed at providing the free web hosting of contents to thousands of citizens and the creation of a vast Portuguese speaking virtual community, thus furthering "national production" on the Internet. Launched in March 1997, that same year and in the following year the existence of pornographic pages on the server was noted, but these were successively eliminated from the portal. However, in July 1998, following a news report on the hosting of more pornographic pages, the then Minister of Culture, Manuel Maria Carrilho, decided to close the portal down. A solution for the Ministry of Culture freeing itself of responsibility for the contents hosted on "Terràvista" – which is how the name was spelt at the time – was found on 7 August 1998, with the setting up of the non-profit making Associação Terràvista to manage the project. The service continued to expand until February 2000, when the Association, faced with high maintenance costs, decided to sell Terràvista to Jazztel Internet Factory, part of the Jazztel telecommunications group. Now integrated in Ya.com, the operator's Internet division, the project began to change identity, becoming a portal with its own contents, but still maintaining the cybernaut communities and the free hosting service. Meanwhile, the pages hosted on Terràvista now carried advertising banners, a change that was not to the liking of the clients, who were only notified of this change in policy two days in advance. On 4 September 2000 the Terràvista portal once again changed hands, with Jazztel announcing the sale of Ya.com Internet Factory, which included the Portuguese portal Terràvista and the Spanish Ya.com, for EUR 414.3 million to T-Online, an Internet provider in the Deutsche Telekom group. From this moment on the project and site became known as Terravista, without the accent on the first "a". The new administration later decided not to maintain a mass non-identified traffic generator product as it was no longer economically viable.

of expression on the Internet was the Terràvista affair in 1997, then, more recently, the case of the "Muito Mentiroso" blog highlighted how questions of censorship and freedom of expression can be raised despite the fact that the Internet has already been part of our media system in a more general form for a decade now. The aforementioned blog published uncorroborated information on the Casa Pia affair, before disappearing from the Internet (Público newspaper, Computers supplement, 15 November 2004). However, while the blog was still accessible many questions were raised – from the defamation that it possibly contained to the matter of whether or not the newspapers should make use of the anonymous information available them.

Figure 9.1 – Terràvista protest image

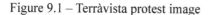

In a historical perspective, Peppino Ortoleva (1991) analyzes the development of the regulation and use of censorship in European and North American democracies, outlining the evolution from the prevalence of the idea of the "moral scandal" (i.e. "that which is considered corrupting for being seen or read alone") to the establishment of an ever greater consensus as to what is considered licit contents.

Ortoleva's contribution (1991) is fundamental for our understanding of two constant trends in the evolution of the media system. One trend is that every time there is technological innovation it is accompanied by resistance and the resistance always tends towards assuming the worst fears in terms of the possibly corrupting trends of the new media. The second trend has to do with the childhood sphere. In addition to the diffusion of the idea that the State has no right to interfere in the moral choices of adult individuals, there likewise emerged the idea that children of pre-puberty age are in a condition of particular need of protection in moral and psychological terms.

The condition of *childhood* has, therefore, since the 19th century become the motivation for campaigns against the way in which the media system functions. As Ortoleva argues: "we have the case of each generation defending the media system it was born and grew up with against that which emerges at a given stage" (1991).

This set of recurrent trends in the media system has given rise to a compromise solution in democratic countries, according to which just the most fundamentalist, religious or political tendencies are in favour of pure censorship of contents.

This compromise is based more on the market structure than on the sharing of ethics. Hence, contents considered scandalous by a considerable part of the population are prohibited for minors and channelled towards a parallel market, a more segmented market, where the motto is "each to his own (real or presumed) vice" (Ortoleva, 1991).

This contextualization of censorship and regulation finds in Slevin (2002) an interesting contribution for the contextualization of the question of why the assumption, on the part of the State, of a continuous interest in the regulation of the media system and the way in which the Internet is seen, is the heir of these visions. According to Slevin, the use of the modern information technologies has always been seen by the Nation States as a priority for their own interests and for that reason they require a certain regulation, for, to the Nation State, the technologies that can be used to transmit any type of message to relatively large audiences are of profound importance as a factor influencing the values and moral standards of modern societies (Slevin, 2002).

However, the Internet also represents a challenge for the Nation States, for it continues to constitute a certain uncertainty as to how best to regulate it as a medium and how to reconcile regulation and the citizens' interests.

As Slevin (2002) points out, in the endeavours to give the Internet a regulatory system that at the same time protects the interests of the State and the citizens, we have witnessed a debate between two models over the last decade. The governments tend to favour an approach to the Internet as a technology that facilitates the public diffusion of material and is thus akin to a broadcasting system – an activity for which content regulation systems have been developed over the last few decades. Civil society individuals and organizations have, in contrast, argued for an approach to the Internet as a technology derived from the telephone system – which has always been characterized by a very tenuous content regulation system. Both models seek to establish analogies between different media (already existing and new) and the regulation systems already in place. As in the Terràvista case, the debates on the regulation and/or censorship of the Internet have unfolded on the basis of the detection of the existence of problem, which is then given widespread media coverage, which, in turn, implicates the involvement of the public bodies, which announce the initiation of a regulatory process for the system. The debate that normally follows tends to take place either between specialists, who debate arguments in the traditional media, or between parliamentary groups, with the debate at times spreading to associations representing civil society when the constitutional rights, liberties or guarantees of the citizens may be at risk. This was also the case in the Terràvista affair.

However, in this particular case, the lack of an organized structure, widespread participation of the victims or an interest amongst the public in the defence of rights, liberties and guarantees gave rise to a somewhat atypical protest that thrived on the possibility of the interlinking of different mediation spheres to achieve its objectives.

When we analyze the media's role of political mediation in a context of democracy and the initial diffusion of a technology, there is normally a conditioning factor to be taken into account: that *the mediation process can only take place when all those involved confer upon the medium or media in question the same symbolic power.*

The Terràvista project case in the summer of 1998 is an example of the parties involved – the Ministry of Culture and the protest organizers – not sharing the symbolic power attributed to a given medium, in this case the Internet. This influenced the mediation processes. In this case, the need for a public reaction by the Ministry of Culture only took on form when the criticisms, which had been circulating for days on the Internet, were echoed in the traditional media.

By attributing greater importance to the visibility of the criticism in the newspapers and television, in comparison to the criticism expressed on the Internet, the Ministry of Culture was merely demonstrating that the attributions of symbolic power in a mediation process may differ from interested party to interested party. Situations may, therefore, be created in which the mediation does not take place – not because of lack of access to a medium but because of the non-sharing of the symbolic power attributed to it.

A chronological analysis of the Terràvista protest more clearly explains this line of argument. On 30 July an "Open Letter to the Minister of Culture with respect to Terràvista" was drawn up and distributed in the Portuguese newsgroups: pt.geral, pt.Internet and pt.Internet.www and forwarded via E-mail to the Minister of Culture. Parallel to this, all the media – radio, newspapers and television – prominently featured the closure of the service, not so much for the importance of the act itself, given that it was an Internet story involving a limited number of users, but because the story involved a Minister with a high media profile, Manuel Maria Carrilho.

Having understood this, the organizers of the protest, which included a number of journalists and hackers, decided that gaining media visibility on television and in the newspapers was of fundamental importance to their cause and not so much carrying out or attempting to organize protests through the Internet.

The whole strategy of sending E-mails to organs of sovereignty, such as the President of the Republic and the Government, followed that logic, i.e. the production of facts for exploitation by the mass media and not the use of a single mediation space, the Internet, to try and force the Minister to change this position. The space for the battle between the protesters and the minister was the traditional media.

Following the Portuguese strategy, Brazilian users fed the story to the newspapers in Brazil, once more seeking media coverage for the incident. The "O Globo" newspaper published an article entitled "Portugal censors site because of Japanese cartoon", criticizing the Minister's decision and referring to the wave on online protests.

This thus created a situation in which there were almost more news reports on the incident than signatories of the petition against the Minister's attitude and the event ceased to be a mere national affair and had all the makings of an international media affair.

After three days of this media strategy in place, on 4 August the Minister of Culture was obliged to respond to the 149 petitioners by giving an interview on television – on the "Journal da Noite" evening news programme, SIC channel – in which he was questioned on the closure of Terràvista and he confirmed that it would reopen on 9 August.

This was followed by a second phase. On 5 August (with the protest now counting 317 supporters, from more than 26,000 user pages) new international contacts were made, through the launch of the English-language version of the protest pages, and the protest also took off in various newsgroups (including the Brazilian newsgroups br.noticias and br.bras-net). In a mixture of tradional and online media, in which the newspapers and television channels were the main targets, amongst those that received the press communiqué on the protest were: Reuters agency, Time Magazine, MSNBC, Wired magazine, the site Disinformation, the newspaper US Today, the site Yahoo, Newsday, Universo *Online*, the newspapers Globo and Folha de São Paulo, the Brazilian magazines Veja and SuperInteressante. net, Computer World, Network World, PC World, AP-Associated Press, Bloomberg.com, Sky News, BBC, US Newswire, CNN, Agence France-Press, The Washington Post, The Independent, UPI – United Press International, Fox News and DrudgeReport. The Electronic Frontier Foundation (F. F. E. – created as a aggregating element for those involved in the protest) protagonized another media event, seeking a lawyer to take court action against the Ministry of Culture, regardless of the reactivation of the Terràvista service, and announcing this intention publicly. This was also the day that, for the first time, one of the mass media made a reference to the online protest movement. It was from the moment that the international press (such as "O Dia" newspaper in Sao Paulo, Brazil) began to feature the protest that SIC television in Portugal first began to divulge the online protest movement in its evening news programme. Regardless of the fact that the news programme anchorman had signed the petition, the event only became newsworthy for the television station's editorial line when other media, in other countries picked up on the events and placed them on the media agenda.

From that moment on, the story became mainstream news and was repeated, extended upon and looked into in greater detail by all the major national newspapers in Portugal (JN, 24 horas, Independente, DN, Público and Expresso, which also had one of its journalists as a supporter of the protest).

On 9 August (now with a total of 604 supporters, many of whom were led to participate by the news stories on television and in the newspapers), the site was reopened. However, the protest continued because the participants wanted more guarantees that the situation would not be repeated. Hence, they stepped up the campaign of divulgation of the case in the international media.

Press releases were sent to countless figures and institution of the European Commission in Brussels, calling attention to the form of construction of the Information Society in Portugal and to respect for the community directives in the Green Paper on Information Society, published by the European Union. The protest was thus no longer directed against one minister's attitude and was turned into one against the government's policy in the field of the information society.

Table 9.1 – Participants in the Terràvista protest, by country (%)

Country	Participants in the Terràvista protest
Portugal	73.04%
Netherlands	9.93%
Others, Europe*	3.03%
Brazil	8.67%
Macao	0.42%
Cape Verde	0.21%
Mozambique	0.10%
Australia	0.10%
United States	3.34%
Canada	0.63%
Georgia	0.10%
Uzbekistan	0.10%
Japan	0.10%
Mexico	0.10%
South Africa	0.10%
Total no.	957

*Note: Includes United Kingdom, Norway, Belgium, Denmark, Italy, Spain, Switzerland, Austria, Germany, Poland and Israel.

On the same day, the Minister of Culture, who, five days earlier, had appeared on television for the first time to speak of his reasons for closing Terràvista down, was obliged to address the matter once more.

On 12 August the protest was ended, after the final petition containing the signatures of 957 protesters in 27 countries was delivered to the Minister of Culture two days earlier. As the letter posted online marking the end of the protest states, the objectives were achieved.

Although Terràvista had well over 20,000 users, only over 900 of them signed the petition sent to the minister. However, from the moment onwards in which active journalists who were also Terràvista users got involved in the protest, it was possible to outline a strategy for spreading the online incident through the media. By first making use of the characteristics of informational politics, which favour the media treatment of political personalities, the minister was placed under the fire of the national and international media, obliging him to take to the public arena he had initially wanted to shun. The effect was that of boosting the low number of participants for a more widespread coverage. This step was achieved by reaching the Brazilian media and, in turn, to win over the interest of the Portuguese media.

As the organizers themselves have stated, "this online protest, the largest carried out so far in Portugal, was a success at all levels! Thanks to the efforts of all, we managed to achieve: (…) extensive news coverage on television channels and national newspapers for a period of more than 10 days! (…) to make a vast international offensive for the divulgation of the protest in organizations and the media (...) in Brazilian newspapers and on important American news sites (…)". [164]

What the analysis of the events demonstrates is that Internet protests can only function in a uni-medial approach, i.e. using only the Internet as a medium, when the two sides have attributed equal symbolic value to the medium. In the Terràvista case, the fact that the Minister of Culture did not attribute the same value to the Internet as a medium as the protesters led the latter to alter their strategy. The case was one of the use of the Internet for feeding the story to the newspapers and television and not of the Internet itself as a protest instrument.

Given the weak mobilization of the users, the protest could only have had success with a spreading of the protest. This was possible because those involved in coordinating the protest themselves possessed literacy in relation to the traditional media, for they were journalists, and literacy in relation to the Internet, for they were also hackers and original users of the site already immersed in the Internet culture (Castells, 2004). That combination allowed them to effect an example of networking between television, newspapers and the Internet in a *mediation guerrilla* logic. In other words, just Eco's term semiotic guerrilla (1991) referred to explaining what one saw and how to interpret it, the figure of *mediation guerrilla* underlines how the mastering of media literacies, in certain conditions, boosts the protests of a few individuals or protests on marginal issues for a society.

The Closure of RTP2: Television Seen from the Internet

An analysis of the news programmes broadcast by the three Portuguese channels (RTP, SIC and TVI) in the period between 10 and 21 May 2002 shows us an exemplary case study on what can happen when the most em-

---

[164]For more information, see http://come.to/protesto.

blematic of the media, the one with greatest penetration in society – television – becomes a news item itself.

The context in which the protest under analysis here unfolded was that of a European media system in which the public service television stations normally account for 30% to 40% of the market share, contrary to the situation in the US or Brazil. The exceptions are the UK, Denmark, Spain and Austria, with market shares of almost or above 50%. The values for the public channels in the ten new European Union Member States tend to be lower, ranging between 15% and an average of 20% to 30% (Kiefl 2005).

In the course of those 11 days in May 2002, a climate of conflict was generated between the public television and the government as a result of statements made by the Minister of the Presidency, Morais Sarmento, which indicated clear conviction on the part of the government as to the need to close down the second public TV channel as a first step in the financial recovery of the public service broadcaster (RTP).

Given the news of the end of RTP2 on the news programmes of the public station itself, what initially appeared to be the coverage of one more event on the media agenda amongst many others was transformed into a struggle for survival by the public service channel in relation to the other TV stations, mobilizing citizens in favour of RTP (in other words, against the closure of RTP2) and citizens in favour of the government (i.e. in favour of the closure), with all of them manifesting themselves on the Internet forum specifically created on the RTP website to discuss the question.

At the same time, the petitions signed by E-mail and directed at the President of the Republic, the Ombudsman and Members of Parliament multiplied.

Parallel to this, opinion leaders were discussing the same issues as the Internet forums, but on the pages of the national newspapers, while the minister and RTP employees began a mediation guerrilla warfare that ended up involving the news services of the private channel, SIC, and the approval, in record time, of the law extinguishing the RTP Opinion Board, which had rejected the new administration appointed by the government for RTP.

The starting point for characterizing what took place during these eleven days can be found in the partiality of the news reports issued by the three different stations. That partiality can be found both in the quantitative and qualitative dimension when one analyzes the news output during that period in May 2002.

Hence, RTP, the object of the crisis and the protest initiated by public figures and anonymous citizens, produced 108 journalistic reports on the topic of the "End of RTP", while SIC limited itself to 31 reports and TVI to 47.

With a view to providing more background on the social and economic context of the situation, one should mention that the RTP crisis also had other very particular traits.

For example, there was the Expresso newspaper, owned by the same company, IMPRESA, that is the majority shareholder in SIC, which, before and during the crisis, launched an open campaign for the end of RTP. And also the fact that both private channels were to be the potential beneficiaries of the transfer of advertising gains, due to the hypothetical sale or closure of the Portuguese public channels.

Completing the potential for the televized narrative dramatization (Santiago 2003) of this topic, one must also bear in mind that the RTP administration had, only a few months beforehand, hired the former SIC director, who had brought with him to the public channel a number of journalists and television presenters, thus creating a climate of emotional and commercial tension between the two stations.

In a situation like this, which was seen by the public as leading to the loss of impartiality by the mass media, how was the Internet appropriated for the discussion of the matter and how did it serve as a channel for protest? And in what way were the discourses produced on the Internet differ, if at all, from those in the media which traditionally give public visibility to the opinion column writers, i.e. the newspapers?

The protest movement against the closure of RTP show that, when the public television service is seriously threatened, there is a strong counter-reaction from the citizens. It also allows us to understand how, in the media arena, the forces in action identified by Tracy (1998), Raboy (2001) and Bustamante (2002) confront each other.

Returning to the initial questions as to how the Internet and television were appropriated during the protest over the *End of RTP,* from the following table (Figure 9.2) we can conclude that, given that the television news programmes with the highest viewer ratings are normally aired between 8.00 p.m. and 9.00 p.m., the protesters first watched the news on RTP, SIC or TVI before using the computer and the Internet connection to participate in the protest, as confirmed by the highest traffic of messages coming in the after-dinner period.

Figure 9.2 – E-mails on the topic of RTP2 sent to RTP, average per hour (24 hours)

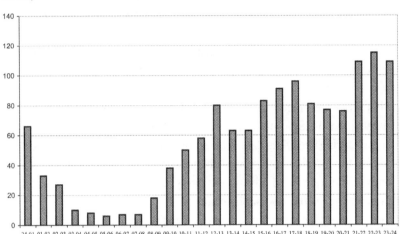

If we go on to analyze the general positioning of the television broadcasts of the three channels in their different news programmes – morning, lunch time and evening – one can say that the most impartial of the three in the analysis was TVI. As for SIC, after an initial strategy of confrontation based on responses and counter-responses to news reports on the RTP news programmes, it opted to focus less on the subject matter in an attempt to ward off criticism that it was being a "judge in its own cause" and putting journalistic objectivity at risk.

Altogether, SIC and RTP produced at least three episodes of direct news confrontation, which transmitted to the public the extent to which television itself can become a hostage of the news it produces and broadcasts.

The "RTP affair" began when RTP's late night news programme reported for the first time on the government's plans for guaranteeing public service television, which provided for only one channel and not the then existing two. The story only made the news in the other channels on the following morning of 10 May.

Generally speaking, the opening news stories, both on RTP and the other channels, were presented in an impartial manner, allowing for different opinions and emphasizing the notion that the issue was not closing down RTP altogether but merely one of its channels and also mentioning the argument of the high cost of a company with the structure RTP had at the time.

However, RTP, voicing the opinions of its worker's committee then started circulating the idea that the greatest beneficiaries of the alteration to the public service would be the private channels, SIC and TVI. This story was accompanied by an analytical report on how the political decision had led to an increase in value of the IMPRESA (majority shareholder in SIC) shares.

In the course of 10 May, other reports were produced by RTP and SIC that led to an exchange of accusations and the interpretation of the same data in different ways by the two television stations.

Thus, on RTP's lunchtime news programme on that day, an anchor-woman made a direct appeal for all those who did not want "RTP to be finished" to get together in public demonstrations. For the first time outside the political debate, the idea was pushed that the alterations to the current model were not merely conjunctural changes but rather a commitment to ending public service television in Portugal. From the beginning that was the vision that dominated the protests, while the Minister of the Presidency, Morais Sarmento, continued to argue that what was planned was a restructuring and not the end of RTP. Nevertheless, the public discussions from this moment onwards were to be dominated by the "End of RTP".

SIC also contributed to the climate of confrontation in the symbolic mediation field by airing a report in its evening news programme on the debts RTP had accrued and its bad financial situation, focusing its analysis on bad management of public funds.

RTP responded to the SIC report on the same day, doing so as if SIC had represented the mere transmission of the government's argument model and producing a report on the situation of the company that refuted those arguments. In its report entitled "The government announced the decisions arguing that the financial situation of RTP is unsustainable", RTP responded directly to the public affirmations made by the Minister of the Presidency and other commentators on the situation.

The public channel went on to explain that approximately half of the public monies never reach RTP. According to the report, RTP never received half of the public funding it was entititled to, in addition to the fact that is had lost revenue when the television tax was abolished and it sold its own transmission network. The conclusions of the report were clear: of the approximately EUR 970,000,000 it was supposed to receive in a nine year period, only approximately EUR 495,000,000 had entered the RTP coffers. The government's arguments were, therefore, false.

RTP was thus implicitly informing its viewers that the then government, and those before it, had never fulfilled their obligations and that the reasons for the planned restructuring can only lie elsewhere, namely economic or political interests. The confrontation Public Television versus Government and SIC was launched.

Meanwhile, RTP starting voicing the opinions of the citizens in their critical stance to the "End of RTP", bringing new arguments such as the public association between RTP and the social memory of the country and presenting RTP as the link between the Portuguese emigrant communities around the world.

At the same time, it incited viewers to protest and public demonstration by showing the demonstrations of workers, citizens and public figures in Lisbon, Porto and other cities in the country and asking to the views "not to switch off" for RTP was the TV station of the Portuguese people for the Portuguese people.

In the whole discourse produced by those involved in the demonstrations the suggestion of the government's attempt to control information as the central reason for the situation almost always came to the surface.

The second paradigmatic episode of this collapse of impartiality took place on 14 May, with the questioning of Minister Morais Sarmento on the state of the public television station in the Portuguese Parliament.

All three channels covered the event in their evening news programmes – Telejornal on RTP, Jornal da Noite on SIC and Jornal Nacional on TVI. Particular attention was given to the polemic between Morais Sarmento and the person responsible for RTP in the previous Socialist government, Arons de Carvalho.

Each channels had a different take on the controversy. Whereas RTP reported that "the debate on RTP heated up as a result of a claim by Nuno Morais Sarmento that Arons de Carvalho, former PS minister, had issued a comfort letter for a bank loan without the knowledge of the Ministry of Finance", SIC focused on the fact that "in the parliamentary debate, the position of the Member for the PS, Arons de Carvalho, on a bank loan to RTP catered for a heated moment in the discussion, with Morais Sarmento affirming that he had not been given all the documentation".

In other words, while RTP centred on the statement of the minister and the response by Arons de Carvalho, in which he stated that had proof of bad faith on the part of Morais Sarmento and suggested that the latter read a document he was refusing to read, SIC covered the events without focusing on the minister's refusal and concluding that there was satisfactory closure on the matter for both parties.

The third episode of clear confrontation of information between television channels came about as a result of the "Maya the Tarologist" case on 14 May.

In a context of criticism of the costs of RTP, SIC aired a report in its lunchtime news programme that the public channel had hired the astrologist Maya to contribute to its morning programmes for a fee of EUR 10,000 per month.

The story was developed upon in a report in the evening news, which stated that "RTP had invited the card reader Maya to present a programme, for which she was to receive EUR 10,000 per month, in accordance with a verbal agreement. Today, however, the RTP administration undid the decision and rejected the hiring".

RTP replied at the end of its late night news programme by reading a communiqué issued by the News Director, refuting the SIC story. In its first news programme on the following day, SIC featured the story as the second news item, reporting that "the RTP has tried to deny a SIC news report". In its evening news it reported that "RTP has denied having hired the tarologist Maya, as reported yesterday by SIC. SIC stands by its report based on declarations by the producer of the SIC 10 Horas programme".

The television audience was thus confronted with a situation in which those they were supposed to be able to trust for the truth – journalists and television news – were caught up in a web of contradictions and half truths as a result of the fact that they themselves had become news stories, turning the act of news reporting into a weapon in the fight to assert the greater truth of each channel's news reporting.

When the news on a given matter come close to the expression of personal opinions by journalists, with the journalists losing their function of filters of events, what happens to the *mediation* space? The answer is that the narrative factuality of the events is replaced by dialectic of opinion.

In a situation such as that described above, television (and, as we shall see, the newspapers, too) transforms itself into a discussion list, where the contributors in non-moderated channels are the journalists. Hence, the mass media, as far as their communicative characteristics are concerned, become extremely similar to the interpersonal communication in chats, in the case of television using not only text but also image.

In such a situation, journalists, politicians, opinion leaders and citizens occupy the symbolic *mediation* sphere that is offered us by the media in a form of equality of opportunity for making one's voice heard.

Here it is important to understand how the three nodes in the information metasystem – television, newspapers and the Internet – differ from one another.

Television and the way it functions has already been described herein. So that the opportunity we have now is to try and understand, through an analysis of the use of newspapers and the Internet, how opinion is constructed and communicated in the network society.

What is the difference between the communication of opinion in these two spaces, when, fortuitously, the conditions are created for the participation and protest of more persons than the habitual opinion leaders with the weekly columns in the newspapers and when, at the same time, the topic under analysis is the medium with the greatest presence in our lives – television?

In the newspapers the majority of articles published were opinion articles, which reflects how much this was more a matter of opinion and definition of concepts of the idea of public service television, which is its *raison d'être*. The reference newspapers were those that published the most articles.

Table 9.2 – Type of articles published in newspapers on the RTP2 question between 10 and 21 May 2002 (%)

Publication	Opinion article	News
24 Horas	-	100.00%
O Primeiro de Janeiro	-	100.00%
A Capital	-	100.00%
Euronotícias	25.00%	75.00%
Diário de Notícias	69,73%	30,26%
Diário Económico	59,25%	40,74%
Independente	75.00%	25.00%
Jornal de Notíicas	45,16%	54,83%
Público	61,538%	38,46%
Semanário	66,66%	33,33%
Correio da Manhã	33,33%	66,66%
Expresso	73,07%	26,92%
Visão	58,33%	41,66%

Note: Of a total of 299 articles published, 171 (57.2%) were opinion articles and 128 (42.8%) news articles.

If television did not manage to be impartial in its analysis, to what extent did the opinion articles in the newspapers reflect that lack of impartiality or not?

Using only those opinion articles in which the author expresses clear positions on the questions at hand, we can identify certain trends.

Overall there was a slight tendency towards expressing oneself the closure of RTP2 (52.8%). However, there were newspapers, which, if we are to base ourselves on the published opinions only, were clearly either in favour of or against the closure.

Público (SONAE) and the magazine Visão (owned by IMPRESA) were generally against the closure of RTP2, while Expresso (IMPRESA) and Diário Económico (*MEDIA* Capital, TVI) were in favour. The newspapers that sought greater balance were those belonging, at the time, to the Luso-mundo/Portugal Telecom Group, such as Jornal de Notícias and Diário de Noticias, which had not direct interest in obtaining the television advertising from RTP.

Table 9.3 – Relationship between the opinions expressed in opinion columns in publications on the topic of RTP2 (%)

Publication	In favour of closure of RTP2	Against closure of RTP2
Euronotícias	100.00%	-
Diário de Notícias	50.00%	50.00%
Diário Económico	60.00%	40.00%
Independente	100.00%	-
Jornal de Noticias	50.00%	50.00%
Público	18.80%	81.30%
Semanário	50.00%	50.00%
Correio da Manhã	100.00%	-
Expresso	66.7%	33.3%
Visão	-	100.00%

Source: Analysis of list of selected newspapers published between 10 and 22 May 2002.

An analysis of the comparative figure on the evolution of opinion articles in newspapers and E-mails shows, first and foremost, that the E-mail peaks reflect much more closely the developments in the actual case as it was reported on television. In other words, when the television news reports generated controversy the number of posts expressing an opinion increased and when the number of television news reports dropped the number of posts also decreased.

Figure 9.3 – Evolution of opinion articles on RTP2 published in newspapers and E-mail (10 to 22 May, 2002)

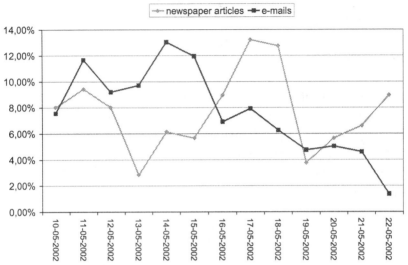

Source: Analysis of the list of posts on the RTP site and selected newspapers published between 10 and 22 May 2002.

In the case of the newspapers, there is a greater time lapse between the development of the events and the publication of opinion articles, which has to do with the way in which the publication of opinion articles is managed by the newspapers – either by free submittal by the authors or the existence of pre-defined columns.

One of the interesting findings for our characterization is the fact that, despite the great gender imbalance in all of the dimensions studied, equality of gender seems to be greater in the expression of opinion through the new media such as the Internet than through the newspapers, which traditionally constitute a more male-dominated opinion space.

Table 9.4 – Authorship of opinion articles in newspapers and online posts on the issue of RTP2, by gender

	Opinion in newspapers	Opinion online*
Male	91.90%	74.40%
Female	8.10%	19.50%

Source: Analysis of the list of posts on the RTP site published between 10 and 22 May 2002.

Of the participants in the RTP on line forum, 85.8% resided in Portugal, while 10.2% resided abroad (it was not possible to establish the origins of the remaining 4%). In most cases (97.6%) the posts were not aimed at responding directly to another forum participant.

As far as the relationship between opinions in favour and against the closure of RTP2 is concerned, although there was greater balance between the two positions in the newspapers – perhaps as a result of editorial policies offering the same opportunities to the two sides in the conflict – an overwhelming majority of the online posts were against the closure (76.30%).

Table 9.5 – Central line of argument in articles and e-mails on the issue of RTP2

	Newspapers	E-mails
Promoting protest actions	-	3.90%
The need to restructure RTP	1.80%	9.40% (3)
Criticism of government proceeding from the RTP context	11.40% (4)	9.40% (3)
Criticism of government without analyzing RTP	-	5.10%
Spoke of the *End* of RTP	1.20%	18.70% (1)
Debate on 1 or 2 channels	2.40%	8.30% (4)
Discussed public service indicating personal definition	25.3% (2)	10.90% (2)
Focused on the idea of using RTP to pay costs of the private stations	1.80%	3.30%
Against high salaries of RTP professionals	-	5.50%
Solidarity with RTP workers	-	6.30%
Support for government decision	14.50% (3)	2.20%
Argument that RTP is a victim of the political power	1.2%	2.40%
RTP as a guarantee of democracy and identity	-	2.70%
Merely analyzed the events without taking a position for or against	28.90%(1)	-
Other views	7.20% (4)	9.40%(3)

Source: Analysis of the list of posts on the RTP site published between 10 and 22 May 2002.

When we look at the central lines of argument we also find substantial differences between the two fields. A first example is that the opinions expressed through the Internet also featured elements of protest organization, which were totally lacking in the newspapers opinions. Also, when one posts on the Internet one is much more direct in terms of the position one adopts. For example, the number of persons in newspaper opinion articles who merely analyzed the events without expressing agreement or disagreement is abnormally high (28.9%), while that line of argument was non-existent in the online opinions expressed.

The direct definition of what public television service is was more common in the newspaper articles, but, as we have seen, the definition made online was a negative one – i.e. what public service is not.

In the online field there was apparently greater diversity of opinions and more freedom to explore possibilities than when writing newspaper opinion articles, as demonstrated by the hypotheses of discussion of the "End of RTP" or the restructuring of RTP or the debate on one or two channels, which were all either less present or non-existent in the lines of argument presented in the newspapers.

Table 9.6 – Type of expression used in formulating opinions on the issue of RTP2

	Newspapers	E-mails
Questioned something or someone	1.70%	7.50%
Took a position	-	57.30%
Argued and defended a position	98.3%	29.90%
Insulted something or someone	-	3.50%

Source: Analysis of the list of posts on the RTP site published between 10 and 22 May 2002.

Another analysis dimension is the type of expression used. This is an important dimension, for the somewhat careless style or bad logical organization of ideas expressed online are often the object of criticism. One should make it clear here that both forms are valid writing formulas and are comparable, provided that we bear in mind that just as academic writing differs from journalistic writing, the writing used in the expression of opinions online is different to that used in newspaper opinion articles, but it is not of less value because of that.

The main difference between the two models is that the online field is less given to the argumentative exposition and defence of a position through comparison with the opposing opinions. In other words, online writing lives much more from the expression of an adopted position, even if the reasons for the choice are given. However, online opinions do pay less attention to justifying a certain option between two positions.

Online writing lives much more from the manifestation of opinion and the valuation of the option taken without a direct comparison with the other option.

Considering the attention given here to opinions expressed on the Internet, it is also worthwhile making a little incursion into the world of the blogs, or blogosphere, with a view to registering some considerations on what makes the expression of opinions there different to the opinions we referred to in the context of the protest against the *End of RTP*.

Although it is true that in more advance informational societies, such as the United States, blogs may function as alternative or reference media for newspapers and radio and television stations, in the transitional societies, such as Portugal, the situation seems to be somewhat different. Portuguese blogs can be seen essentially as an "extension of opinion columns" in the newspapers, even though their scope is clearly a different one. They do not seek to make profit through sales (although many of them have been published in book form) and normally the writing in them is a hybrid between the forum post style and the newspaper opinion column style.

Figure 9.4 – Pages from two blogs managed by Portuguese politicians/political commentators

In her analysis of the *blogosphere* phenomenon in Portugal, Baptista (2004) points out that approximately 60% of the creators of blogs surveyed responded that they had created their blog because of the need to express opinions or with a view to sharing information found on the Internet or outside it (32%) or also just for the sheer pleasure of writing. The blogosphere is a space that lives off the events taking place in the *world* surrounding the bloggers, be it an institution, a country, etc. Blogs also thrive on the reading of other blogs and the criticism of what is found there.

As Baptista (2004) points out, more than 90% of the respondents in her study state that the read other blogs, with a preference for those written by personalities from the world of politics or with prior journalistic experience.

Profile-wise, blog users are typically teachers (at all schooling levels), journalists and students, though there is also a strong presence of managers, lawyers and architects. They are concentrated in the 25 to 39 years age groups and, like the newspaper opinion articles, they majority of them are male (Baptista, 2004).

Obviously, the reasons for using blogs can be as varied as those expressed in Baptista (2004). However, the fact that a blog is run by a personality from the spheres of journalism and politics functions as a way of said blog gaining a position of prominence as an alternative source of information to the mass media themselves.

Hence, in addition to the pleasure of writing and the recognition amongst peers, blogs are, for their authors, one more instrument for the management of influence in the political and media agenda. Blogs are thus not an alternative to the mass media. They are a complement to them.

The objective of the majority of blogs is not protest or the proposal of alternative agendas. If they have any objective at all, it is the influencing of agenda according to the same rules and themes already present in the gatekeeping models of the generalist reference press.

However, more so than in the field of traditional journalism, the blogs seem to offer different formulas of appropriation for different cultures.

When we look at the US reality, we see that the role of blogs, though still to a limited extent, has other characteristics of networking with the more traditional media, such as radio, television and the print media.

According to a study carried out by the Pew Internet and American Life Project in 2005, some 27% of Internet users in the US read blogs, which represented a growth of 10% over the previous year. The blogosphere, like the Internet, is thus a reality in mutation. Nevertheless, only 7% of Americans have ever created their own blog and, as in Portugal, the readers (and, perhaps, producers) are mostly young people with very high education levels.

The great advantage of blogs, in the complementarity logic referred to above, is that they present stories that are normally outside the central and traditional circuit of journalistic reporting. Examples of that complementarity and anticipation are well known: such as the Clinton/Lewinsky affair or the situation on President Bush's National Guard service. However, the blogs are normally more echo chambers and channels for commentaries and opinions than generalized alternative news sources.

Blogs undoubtedly have advantages, but they also raise new questions because of their very own characteristics. Given the ease with which one can create blogs, they more easily become online diaries instead of newspapers. Not all attract an audience. However, the most successful can compete with many newspapers – both their online and printed versions.

Moreover, the blogs represent a new parallel culture that makes life both more difficult and more interesting for journalists. A central characteristic of blogs is their penchant for keeping a story alive much beyond the traditional short-term news cycle. Given their technological characteristics, they likewise offer the possibility of almost immediately testing the success of a certain topic.

Despite the possible biases mentioned above, opinions expressed in Internet forums, such as that on the *End of RTP,* offer a more democratic basis in the sense that they expand the number of citizens that can express their opinion beyond those traditionally published in the newspapers or in blogs. All the more so because the newspaper or blog opinion article is normally associated not only with those who have an "opinion" on a certain topic but also those who master the symbolic codes so as to be able to produce a relatively well elaborated writing model.

Given the analysis presented here, the "End of RTP" case can be typified as an opinion protest, i.e. a protest with the objective of changing the position of the government on a specific matter, making use of the publication of the opinion as if it were a self-poll. Obviously, this is a form of protest that is only possible in a democratic context. The participants in the protest had contradicting opinions as to what the future of RTP should be, although the majority of them were for RTP and against the government. Watching the television news and reading the news and opinion articles in the newspapers led them to understand that, more than a dispute between political forces with its number of members of parliament or parliamentary committees, what was taking place was a war of opinions protagonized by various ministers, members of parliament, journalists and columnists. Hence the best form of participating was perceived as being the protest through the expression of opinion, making use of petitions, but also online opinion forums.

The fact that the journalists temporarily gave up news reporting and instead produced reports that had the journalistic format of news reports, but the contents of opinions, also facilitated the general adoption of the opinion as a form of protest and seeking to influence the final position of the government.

Although this protest cannot be typified as a social movement, in a way it did fulfil its objectives, given that the government, despite having carried out a profound restructuring of RTP, did not close it down or visibly alter the broadcaster's list of objects, which outlines what the role of the public television service should be.

What the participants in this opinion protest achieved was a reinforcement of the public service, for they put across the message that the audiences want a public service, even if they do not watch it so regularly, and that they think it has an important role to play in the audiovisual landscape. In the end, they were given an RTP that was closer to the practice of public service than the RTP as it was in 2002.

The Pro-East Timor Movement: Human Rights, Mass Media and the Internet

When it gets its nationhood, as it surely will, East-Timor will be the first country to have been created in the Internet age, in part by the Internet age.

Ellis, Time Asia, 1999

This section will examine and analyze the *Movement for East Timor* in Portugal and at the global level in September 1999 and the role of the mass media and the Internet and other information and communication technologies in its creation.

Before the events of September 1999, the political participation of Portuguese civil society – in the form of social movements – had focused above all on national and local questions.

One had already witnessed an incorporation of the media by social movements – namely, trade unions and ecological organizations – but that incorporation had taken place essentially in the traditional media of television and the press. Furthermore, until September 1999, the use of the Internet in the social activism context had been very marginal only, with the exception of the Accessibility Campaign (Cheta, 2004) and the Terràvista protest in 1998.

The *Movement for East Timor* thus represented a turning point in terms of civic participation in Portugal for several reasons: it introduced a new set of questions, namely the defence of human rights; it developed around the need for global reach, projecting the collective action from the national to the global level; new social actors took political positions, from individual citizens to national companies; and the traditional media (MacQuail, 1998) and new media (Silverstone, 1999) took on a central role in the protests, with the journalists playing an active role in mobilizing the citizens and in coordinating the movement.

As one can infer from this analysis, we will argue that the Movement for East Timor is of great importance both for the study of the social movements and for the development of those movements in the context of the late modern age (Giddens, 1998).

On the following pages we will discuss how this protest should be regarded as a *networked social movement*, centred on cultural values, working from a local base with the aim of exercising influence on the global scale and incorporating the Internet as a new tool for the success of the protests (Castells, 2003).

However, with a view to contributing to the characterization of social movements, we would likewise argue that *for a social movement to be considered a networked one, it must make use of combined strategies involving different technologies.* Without the combined use of the Internet and television, radio and the press, the successful constitution of a network and the achievement of the objectives set by the social movement would be very difficult.

Manuel Castells (2004) points out that the contemporary social movements are tending towards assimilating the Internet as an instrument of action and organization.

However, although the Internet has gradually moved into the centre of the movements' global actions, we cannot ignore the integration of the traditional media by the movements and the role played by journalists and other social actors – such as new economy corporations – in the process. It is for this reason precisely that one argues that the capacity of these movements to manage the combination of the different media, around nodes for the allocation of specific mobilization and protest tasks to different media, may have become a common trait in the organization and functioning of social movements from the beginning of the new millennium.

To understand the Movement for East Timor it is first necessary to understand the social structure in which it developed – both at the national and international levels. In this perspective, in order to understand not only the emergence of the social movements but also their characteristics, we cannot look at the collective action independently of the social structure in which it takes place, but must take into consideration the historical context, such as the transformations in progress in the economic, social and cultural fields, particularly the decomposition of the classist social structures and the crisis in the traditional political representation of the citizens (Crook, Pakulski, Waters, 1992). The relative economic and military stability of the Western nations has allowed for the development of various institutions, which have, to a certain extent, been able to meet the citizens' basic needs.[165] However, stability, achieved through the development and expansion of the markets, also has a reverse side: the action of the State is frequently limited, which has often led to the group of civil society action as a form of making up for the loss of the State regulating power (Garner, 1996).

If the social movements define their identity and the scope of their action on the basis of a certain set of possibilities and opportunities we must pay attention to the particular cultural traits of each society (Cohen, Rai, 2000). Portugal, a recent arrival to the world of democratic states and only a member of the European Union since 1986, is currently in a process of transition from a proto-industrial society to an informational society. We must therefore take into account that, only in recent years, has more general concern developed for some of the social goals already present in the collective action of other modern societies: that was precisely the case in the Movement for East Timor.

Social movements should be understood in accordance with their own terms. In other words, *they are what they say they are.* There practices (and of these, above all their discourse practices) are their self-definition (Castells, 2004). Although it took on various forms, the Movement for East Timor was a vehicle for a common objective: putting an end to the suffering of the Maubere people or ending the abuses that were going on, namely the indiscriminate killing of the Timorese, the lack of freedom of expression and religion and the sexual abuse of women. In this sense, analytically, we must regard the Movement for East Timor as a human rights movement (Garner, 1996: 149).

A second question that must be analyzed is whether or not one can consider a human rights movement to be a social movement. According to Cohen and Rai, movements that seek to put an end to genocide or ethnocide, torture, imprisonment without trial, capital punishment and the detention

---

[165] Veen and Inglehart establish a cause and effect relationship between this context and the change we observe in the values upheld in developed societies, which has more to do with consumption and cultural expression than the production sphere (cited in Crook, Pakulski, Waters, 1992: 145/146 and Neveu, 1996: 69).

for religious beliefs or specific individual behaviour have not been duly included in the analysis of social movements, particularly in the established literature on the new social movements (Garner 1996; Cohen, Rai 2000). However, this is because the very emergence of the question of human rights is inconceivable outside the dynamics of the new social movement that the social construction of pain and the way in which it becomes a mobilizer for social practices should be integrated into the social movements theory (Baxi, 2000).

By reinterpreting the categorization proposed by Touraine (1982), Castells (2004) argues that the definition of a social movement is based on three principles: its Identity (its self-definition and the definition of the social actors it represents); its Adversary; and its Societal Goal (the social order the collective action is aimed at achieving).

In the case of the Movement for East Timor, the adversary was the set of political and social agents directly responsible for the abuses of the Maubere people, or to which the abuses could be indirectly imputed for reasons of negligence of failure to act. The movement's goal was the end of the violence and the presence of an international peacekeeping force in the territory. As for its identity, it aimed at representing all East Timorese people who could not make themselves heard outside their country and it was the result of an informal coalition of citizens (mostly Portuguese but also from other countries around the world) , Timorese associations and refugees, non-governmental organizations, civic associations, private companies and members of the State apparatus.

Given that all these elements are identifiable as participants in the protest for East Timor, it makes sense to consider it a social movement. However, the Movement for East Timor also has distinctive traits of a social movement of the Information Age (Castells, 2004).

Similar to what happened in the protests against the World Trade Organization in December 1999 (Castells, 2004a), although here the focus was on human rights, the movement acted locally but with the aim of exercising global influence – namely reaching the decision-making spheres within the United Nations – instrumentalizing the mass media and the Internet to achieve its objectives.

Following an initial process for the establishment of independence from Portugal after the revolution of April 1974, East Timor – which is situated to the north of Australia and has terrestrial borders with the Republic of Indonesia – was invaded by Indonesia in September 1975. For twenty-four years the East Timorese territory was illegally occupied and a long war was raged with the Maubere people, with FALINTIL (the East Timorese Liberation Army) and its leader, Xanana Gusmão.

On 30 August 1999, a referendum was held under the auspices of the United Nations in the former Portuguese colony. The great majority (78.5%) of the four hundred thousand voters in the referendum rejected the proposal of autonomy within Indonesia, thus opening the way for the territory's independence. Shortly after the results of the referendum were made known, a wave of widespread violence broke out that saw the death of thousands of people in East Timor.

While these events were developing in East Timor, citizens in Portugal who were acting in defence of the Maubere people developed an unparalleled social movement that was comparable only with what happened in the country in the years following the 1974 revolution, with the re-establishment of democracy.

The period between 4 and 20 September 1999, which was one of intense diplomatic activity on the part of the Portuguese Government, also saw a wave of actions of solidarity and the defence of human rights in East Timor as part of a vast social movement of nation and worldwide proportions.

Anyone who visited Portugal during those sixteen days would have witnessed signs of civic participation in the streets, which were the scenes of extremely creative forms of protest. From mural paintings to daily demonstrations outside the embassies of member states of the UN and the Security Council in Lisbon, and to the white clothes day and cars bearing white flags and written support messages – the movement's actions occupied the everyday life of Portuguese citizens. In one of many initiatives, the whole country downed tools, directly or indirectly, for three minutes and flowers were also thrown into the rivers.

These and other protest actions carried out during the month of September were given a decisive high visibility by the traditional mass media – radio, television and the press – which thus made a significant contribution to the achievement of the movement's goals.

The virtual protests, though less visible, also played an important role: more than one hundred thousand E-mails against the actions of Indonesia were sent to the United Nations; dozens of websites were created so as to provide a public forum for discussion and the fax lines of the five permanent members of the Security Council at the United Nations were literally blocked by the high number of incoming messages.

These developments would seem to confirm to a large extent the idea that the greater part of events in our lives takes place in contexts decisively influenced by information (Melucci, 1995). The role of the mass media and the Internet is of particular interest for understanding the specificities of the Movement for East Timor, for it is in them that one will find the organizational structure, many of the individual initiatives and their diffusion.

The traditional media – such as radio and the press and, to a certain extent, television – together with the Internet played a decisive role in the emergence, organization and development of the movement. On the one hand, their instrumentalization gave the participants in the movement tools that facilitated their action at the national and international levels, on the other, it was thanks to the action of the mass media in particular that the window of cultural and political opportunity was used for the emergence of the protest.

The historical contextualization of the events of September 1999 gives us a better understanding of the power of the media's role over this period in the struggle of the Timorese people.

It was thanks to the work of two freelance journalists that the Portuguese population in general became aware of the drama the Maubere people were experiencing (ETAN, 2002).

On 12 November 1991 the massacre in the Santa Cruz cemetery in Dili was taped on video, thus allowing the incident to be shown to the whole world. Although the massacre had a significant impact at the international political level, in Portugal the effect was tremendous, above all because prayers being said in Portuguese could be heard on the video during the shootings. These images and sounds were responsible for something that the political parties and non-governmental organizations had not been able to achieve since the invasion of East Timor in 1975: the establishment of a cultural link between the suffering of the Maubere people and the Portuguese people through their shared language and religion. These common identity traits were rediscovered by some and discovered by others through television.

Given that each of the various social identities of an individual is socially constructed and considering the fact that collective action is one of the forms by which the individual identity is synthetized, it makes sense to consider that each social movement will endeavour to attract the support of the citizens by being the vehicle for a certain interpretative matrix. Given that that matrix derives from the specificity of each context, the mediators representing the movement tend to personalize it in a process that is known as "matrix alignment" – a common denominator between the culture of the population whose support one is seeking and the movement's values and goals (Garner, 1996).

However, even though consensus on a given question may be achievable, only the mobilization of that consensus orients the individuals towards actions, not only because of the echo it produces in the individual identity of each one but also because of the connection of the consensus to practices and not just ideas (Tarrow, 1998; Garner, 1996). This is why visual symbolism is so important, above all in the mass media, which performs a decisive role in synthesizing the collective identities and in projecting the appropriate image to potential supporters and adversaries (Tarrow, 1998). This was the case with the Santa Cruz massacre. The visual symbolism transmitted by the images effectively worked as a catalyst for a collective identity amongst the Portuguese, creating the conditions for the emergence of collective action in September 1999.

The traditional mass media constitute the medium through which the majority of citizens make contact with the political sphere. Not only are certain societal problems often the result of assimilation and interpretation by the media of certain situations, but the media also given them visibility or, if we prefer, they mediatize certain facts, including those on the political agenda, creating new discourse modes and alerting the very political field (Neveu, 1996; Crook et al., 1992; Gibbins et al., 1999).

If it is true that the media have become an instrument the social movements cannot do without for reaching their potential supporters, the use of the media also brings with it specific problems. Firstly, the movement's discursive matrix is conditioned if it aims to attract media coverage (Garner, 1996). Secondly, given the range of topics favoured by the media and the high level of competition for mediatization in a limited space, the action of the movements frequently takes on the character of emotional performances (Neveu, 1996; Tarrow, 1998; Touraine, 1981).

For the social movements have to manage information strategies with a view to attracting the mediatization they need for mobilizing the support and the interaction with the public and political powers. It is in this field that the Movement for East Timor revealed characteristics that were atypical in social movements, namely the way in which it managed to capture the attention of the press, television and radio. In this case the strategies were created and vehicled by the media themselves and frequently idealized by journalists.

For a better understanding of the real importance of the media in this whole process, we must once again look at the structural specificities and the context of national political opportunity in which the movement emerged.

Portugal, even though it is a member of the European Union, is a country with average diplomatic influence in the international scene. It was not possible for it to send troops to East Timor due to various institutional limitations – and this knowledge had already been in the public domain for a long time, given the media coverage of the human rights abuses in Timor.

Hence, the question that hovered over the Portuguese could be summarized as follows: given the relative impotence of the politico-military sphere to carry out unilateral action, what contributions can the citizens make to solving the problem?

The answer was given by the media themselves in the way they decided to amplify the protests until they could be heard in international political decision-making spheres

In his study on the role of radio in the Movement for East Timor, Proença argues that during its period on uninterrupted broadcasting – the first 100 hours without commercial breaks from 7.00 a.m. on 5 September to 11.00 p.m. on 9 September – the TSF radio station acted not only as a news service but also as a radio station for social activism (Proença, 2000).

If the aim of the TSF news editor-in-chief was to create, in the streets, an effect capable of attracting the attention of the international media as a form of reaching audiences the world over, and particularly in those countries with voting rights on the UN Security Council, he could only do so by promoting initiatives with a strong emotional character that were suitable for televized broadcasting (Proença, 2000). Of the initiatives promoted by TSF, which were later embraced by the national television channels and press, the most effective in terms of individual mobilization were the "white clothes day", the "flowers in the rivers" action and the nationwide work stoppage for three minutes, which was supported by the national trade union federations.

In his analysis, Proença describes the way in which the choice of these initiatives was based on their symbolism and the degree of mediatization they could achieve (Proença L. 2000; Mazzoleni, 2002). The aim of the "white clothes day" was to establish an element common to all the protests in the world: as it is easily interpreted by different cultures, the colour white (meaning purity in the West, joy and happiness in the Orient and respect to the Muslim community) allowed the message to be amplified internationally. White was thus adopted as the protest colour – from the television news anchormen in white to the citizens using white clothing or hanging white flags from their windows or on their cars.

The second initiative was a form of mourning for all those who perished in East Timor. As one did not have bodies to mourn, the suggestion was that the citizens throw flowers into the rivers as a way of uniting both countries in the symbol and in the pain. To make the action more attractive to the media, the citizens were also invited to gather outside the US embassy in Lisbon. The final initiative, again coordinated by the various media and this time embraced by the trade unions, aimed at stopping the whole country for three minutes. This event was given widespread coverage by the international media, given that many Portuguese citizens stopped their cars in the streets and on the roads and downed tools or left their offices to go out onto the streets, where they gathered at the agreed hour.

These forms of protests had essentially two goals: on the one hand, uniting the whole protest; and, on the other, creating the necessary synergies so that the disrespect for human rights in East Timor entered the international public domain.

The radio newsroom editors and journalists played a decisive role in the mobilization process in the East Timor protest and provided the citizens with a medium through which they could express their solidarity by participating in the actions. This role was amplified when the print media and television joined the process.

During the month of September 1999, the two reference daily newspapers in Portugal, Público and Diário de Notícias, published 399 and 350 articles on the East Timor question respectively, while the weekly Expresso published 176 articles in the same period.

Only on four occasions did the headlines of the Portuguese newspapers not include references to East Timor, with the Portuguese news agency, Lusa, issuing a daily average 100 news reports on the matter.

To the definition of this information agenda one must add the daily mediatization of diverse small-scale initiatives carried out by normal citizens or by schoolchildren/students, the publication of the names of companies selling Indonesian products for the purpose of boycotting them, or the publication of bank account numbers for making donations for humanitarian aid.

An analysis of the empirical data available on the production of news during the month of September shows that journalists made a decision to abandon the impartiality that normally characterizes their editorial line

– which, as a general rule, promotes the agendas of the political parties and the pressure groups (Gibbins and Reimer, 1999) – giving priority to the defence of cultural values, such as human rights.

This decision proved to be decisive, given that their knowledge of how the media functioned, as a catalyst for the sharing of a feeling of East Timorese identity, made it possible for civil society to express it sentiments collectively and directed at the media. As the news director at TSF, Carlos Andrade, explained in an interview (Andrade, 1999), as far as the relationship between Portugal and East Timor from 1975 up to the protests of 1999 was concerned, one had to take into consideration three aspects of analysis: the politicians, who experienced the situation without much hope for a solution; the media, which understood the essence of the problem very early on; and the citizens, who kept East Timor close to their hearts.

Many of the actions promoted and editorials published during the period in question seem to fit in with what Shah terms *development journalism,* a form of journalism dedicated to the social, cultural and political aspects of development, in addition to the strictly economic aspects. It is a more democratic type of journalism that places the emphasis on bottom-up communication. A pragmatic type of journalism that is unconventional in its approach to the questions it deals with, incentivates action and the creation and maintenance of a mobilization space (Shah, 1999).

Shah (1999) also considers the attitude of the journalists as a possible substitute for the action of intellectual elites, under whose orientation a predisposition for collective action is habitually created. In that sense, we can consider that the journalists, similar to the intellectuals (Garner, 1996) in other past social protests contexts, can perform an essential role in the contextualization and synthesis of collective identities with a view to mobilizing a support basis for the movement, whereby this role was constructed dialectically simultaneously with the emergence of the movement. The identity of these journalists and the identity of the movement to which they helped to give rise are thus created interactively (Shah, 1999).

Up to this point we can establish that the media – i.e. the newspapers and radio and television stations – played a fundamental role in the Movement for East Timor, similar to what has happened in other social movements (Van Aelst et al., 2001; Downing, 2000).

Despite this situation, the social movements seem to regularly seek other communication platforms for obtaining support for their cause (Garner, 1996: 175), also innovating in the use of the information and communication technologies, whenever these technologies are of use for achieving their goals. Even the most influential social movements require the legitimacy and support that are given to them locally. However, they also need to act on the global level, given that the diffuse political power also acts on various levels simultaneously (Castells, 2004)

In the East Timor case, many of the protest movement supporters were geographically distant for each other, preventing face-to-face interaction (Smelser, 1988). Hence, the movement was forced to carry out actions simultaneously in four continents. In Asia (where East Timor and Indonesia are), Oceania (where the military intervention forces closes to the theatre of operations were located and where the ASEAN summit was being held at the time), North America (where the largest of Indonesia's allies, the US, is, and where the UN Security Council meets) and Europe.

From the moment onwards in which, vehicled by the Timorese resistance organizations and the Portuguese diplomacy, a central goal to be achieved by the protest was established – the sending of a UN peacekeeping force to East Timor – the use of the Internet was very much encouraged and promoted by the mass media themselves, by private companies in the telecommunications sector and by anonymous citizens.

The Guide to Online Activism Site (Silva, 2000), a protest directory, contained, on 3 February 2000, a total of 60 protest actions for East Timor. Although many of these actions did not have a visit counter, it is probable that approximately 190,000 people used the sites to send E-mails to, amongst others, US President Bill Clinton, Indonesian President Habibie and the Secretary General of the UN, Kofi Annan.

The first actions that used the Internet as an instrument, mainly for the sending of E-mails and faxes, began on 5 September at the initiative of Rádio TSF. An Internet user had offered his services to the station, compiling a list of the fax numbers and E-mail addresses of the individuals listed above for mass divulgation. Similar to what was happening at TSF, other media and commercial sites initiated protest actions, allowing for the contact list to circulate freely and informally and publicizing standard texts to be forwarded to the United Nations and the White House.

It is difficult to quantify exactly the volume of E-mail messages and faxes sent between 5 and 15 September. However, what we do know is that initiative led to the blockage of several telephone lines in the UN building and that the White House servers began to reject electronic mail from the .pt domain from 7 September onwards (Viegas, 1999).

The portals of the ISPs in Portugal and the telecommunications companies played a leading role in this process: more than half of the E-mails sent passed through SAPO – the portal of the leading Portuguese telecommunications company, Portugal Telecom – and the latter also created an exclusive fax line and free fax numbers, through which the citizens could send faxes directly to the White House and to the UN free of charge (Portugal Telecom, 1999).

Table 9.7 – Petitions and signature collections for E-mail actions supporting the East Timor cause

Solidarity with East Timor	Situation	Supporters	Duration
"Militia: Terror Still in Refugee Camps" Campaign	In progress	458	Since 6/11/99
"Against the Disarmament of FALINTIL II" Petition	In progress	278	Since 14/10/99
"Against the Disarmament of FALINTIL I" Petition	In progress	276	Since 16/10/99
"Science with East Timor" Petition	Concluded	349	From 11 to 15/9/99
"Online global human chain for Timor" Campaign	In progress	425	Since 12/9/99
"Human Chain for Timor on the Internet " (GUIA) Campaign	In progress	323	Since 10/9/99
"SOS East Timor" (Portugal Telecom) Campaign	Concluded	3,382	From 9 to 15/9/99
"An E-mail for East Timor" (Sapo) Campaign	Concluded	100,627	From 6 to15/9/98
"Against the Massacre in East Timor I" (TSF) Petition	Concluded	42,865	From 5 to 15/9/99
"UN in East Timor II" (SOS Timor) Petition	Concluded	9,600	From 5 to 6/9/99
"UN in East Timor I" (Lusitânia Expresso) Petition	Concluded	32,163	From 22/4 to 15/9/99

Source: Analysis http://members.tripod.com/~Protesto_MC/timor.html   Note: situation as at 3 February 2000.

The participation of commercial companies – whose operations, on principle, are aimed at making profit – is one of the most interesting aspects of this movement. It is possible that, in a context of general discontent amongst the people with Indonesia and support of the East Timor cause, this action taken by the companies could be construed as opportunism in terms of public relations or that, in certain events, the national identity can be a decisive element in the business strategies of private companies.

But the explanation for the behaviour can also be found in the specific Internet culture (Castells, 2004). The companies that supported the protest, be it on the technological or financial levels, are part of the New Economy (Castells, 2004), a sector in which the Internet culture is more widespread and in which the belief in human progress through technology is more consensual.

As these companies are holders of the technology – both in the form of portals and fax lines – necessary for achieving the movement's goals, we can consider that the social movements of the Information Age can include in their ranks not only citizens and non-governmental organizations but also New Economy enterprises.

Another example of protests carried out through the Internet were the forums organized by global mass media, particularly CNN and the BBC. The forums organized by the BBC constitute one of the most interesting empirical elements in this analysis, given that only one half of the messages and responses published in it came from Portugal, a fact that demonstrates the development of the movement from a local to a global one.

Table 9.8 – Online surveys of support for East Timor

Online Forum	Situation	Supporters	Duration
Send Portuguese soldiers to East-Timor? (Virtual Azores)	Concluded	84% Yes	From 12 to 15/9/99
Send US troops to East Timor? (MOJO Wire)	Concluded	64% Yes	From 10 to 15/9/99
Send UN troops to East Timor? (TIME)	Concluded	65% Yes	From 8 to 14/9/99
International force in East Timor? (Jakarta Post)	Concluded	94% Yes	From 9 to 10/9/99
United Nations in Timor ? (El Mundo)	Concluded	98% Yes	From 9 to 14/9/99
UN peacekeepers to East Timor? (CNN)	Concluded	95% Yes	From 7 to 10/9/99
Portuguese Military in East Timor? I (D. Digital)	Concluded	94% Yes	From 8 to 15/9/99
Exceptional Tax for East Timor? (Público)	**In progress**	54% No	Since 8/9/99
East Timor: Time to Intervene? (BBC)	Concluded	96% Yes	From 7 to 9//9/99
Indonesia and East Timor (CNN)	Concluded	52% Yes	07/09/1999

Source: Analysis http://members.tripod.com/~Protesto_MC/timor.html
Note: situation as at 3 February 2000.

On the BBC website one could find messages from British and US citizens expressing their support and underlining the similarities between the Timor and Kosovo situations and the need for the international community to find common criteria for violations of human rights (Viegas, Gomes, 1999).

Another indication of the protest's global extension is the number of sites still available today on East Timor and the number of languages they are written in. A similar analysis can also be made of the origin and quantity of messages sent to newsgroups during the month of September 1999.

The emphasis in the Information Age should not be on the information, but on the access to information. The technology did not make information a new recourse, as it always was that. What it has done is it has transformed the way we access information and the ICTs, by transforming that access, have redefined the ways in which we contact other citizens, services and technologies (Dutton 2000). The capacity to access and process information more rapidly and to establish connections between people around the world in real time enabled the movement to achieve its goals.

Table 9.9 – Messages sent in newsgroups relating to East Timor (September 1999)

Internet researches on East Timor in February 2002		Messages sent that Included the term "East Timor"	
Sites in...	Quantity	Newsgroups in	Messages sent
English	600,000	English	27,400
Portuguese	38,800	Portuguese	3,390
Spanish	35,900	Indonesian	982
French	24,900	Italian	786
German	20,000	Dutch	784
Indonesian	19,300	French	534
Italian	18,200	Spanish	429
Dutch	7,410	German	208
Total web pages	1,140,000	**Total messages sent**	190,000

Source: Google and Dejanews analysis 1/9/1999 to 30/9/1999.

So far we have looked at the *mediation* strategies in the context of the social movements, concentrating essentially on location, i.e. how, from the given country as a base, emergence, mobilization, organization, coordination and protest are structured through the mass media, Internet and other information technologies such as the fax.

However, if we wish to understand how the mobilization, organization and action are structured on the basis of Internet usage at the global scale, we must deepen our analysis somewhat and look at, for example, how a mailing list functions during a mobilization period – in this case the ETAN (East Timorese Action Network) mailing list.

The same can be said for the mass media, i.e. expanding our horizons as to the role of the media in the construction of autonomy must also take into account that one and the same matter – in this case the "situation in East Timor" – can be seen by the media in Portugal, elsewhere in Europe, the US, Oceania and the Far East through different lenses of journalistic objectivity in action.

By enabling the consultation of different online media, the Internet can give us a more diversified and, perhaps, more corrective perspective by providing different approaches to one and the same topic.

Nevertheless, for the Internet to be able to boost our communicative autonomy like that, it is first necessary that perception of the differences between the media of different countries on the same topics be part of our literacy bases on the media.

The analysis that follows is largely based on a collection of articles published in September 1999 in the two reference Portuguese daily newspapers (Diário de Notícias and Público) and on the an analysis of their content together with the 1,672 E-mails exchanged in the twenty day-period of 10 September to 30 September on the East Timor list.

The East Timor list was set up to serve as a support for a newsgroup called *reg.easttimor*, which, in turn, had originated in the Association for Progressive Communications (APC) and its member networks (PeaceNet, GreenNet, etc.).

Figure 9.5 – IGC Page

The core activity of the East Timor list, which is still active today, is the distribution of news from diverse sources, including groups originating in East Timor, ETAN/US, TAPOL and other support groups. Reports on and translations of news services and from the Indonesian, Portuguese, Australian, British and US press are also a regular part of the content, as well as official documentation and communiqués from the UN, governments and other sources.

Given that a large part of the information exchanged on the East Timor mailing list also refers to activist groups from Indonesia and other Asian countries, as well as their national media, a brief contextualization on Asia is called for before we proceed with our comparative analysis.

The connections between the media and democracy have long been a topic of debate and discussion. As key institutions in the public sphere, the media play a central role in public and political information, participation and the dissemination of information on political processes, making them indispensable for the practice of democracy.

Only when the citizens have access to information on political processes, parties, candidates and programmes can they make rational choices and effectively participate in the choices that impact their lives. The media also give us a sphere for debate and discussion and constitute the most efficient channels for airing public opinion and feedback.

In Asia, the media are considered central tools for creating national unity and identity. Governments in Asia tend to control the media using two mechanisms. The first is the use of the law and regulations restricting the practices of many media, including, for example the non-dissemination of politically sensitive material. The State thus keeps a tight control over publishing licences and the possibility of vetoing contents.

The second mechanism is that, in addition to the direct control of the public media sector, the State also has a policy of acquiring shareholdings in the private media (Banerjee, 2003).

The emergence of the Internet brought with it new hopes for Asia. However, the experiences of many countries have shown that socio-political, technological and economic factors have lessened the potential Internet both in the political discourse and practice (Banerjee, 2003). In addition to the political dimension, disparity between countries in terms of Internet access is, indeed, much greater in Asia than, for example, Europe.

Whereas, Singapore, South Korea, Hong Kong, Taiwan and Japan have Internet penetration figures equal to, or even higher than, the European averages, the remaining Asian countries have very low rates. In Indonesia, for example, less than 2% of the population, or approximately 4.5 million inhabitants, have Internet access. In the Asian geographic and political context there are clear barriers to the correct functioning of the media in place (Katz, 1980), such as selectivity (i.e., the selective exposure, perception and retention of information) and interpersonal relations (group membership and other group influence processes) (Banerjee, 2003).

Singapore is a good example of the systematic use of censorship and regulation of the Internet. The Singapore government has defined the Internet as a broadcasting medium, so that the regulations that apply to television can also be used in relation to the Internet. In 2001 the registration of political sites became compulsory and the ISPs were made responsible for the contents they make available. They must also register political contents hosted by them. Also, election campaigning via the Internet was prohibited, as was the use of SMS for campaign purposes (Banerjee, 2003).

Table 9.10 – Internet use in Asia, selected countries (%)

Country	Date	Number of users	Percentage of population	Source
China	July 2002	45.8 million	3.58%	CNNIC
Hong Kong	April 2002	4.35 million	59.58%	Nielsen NetRatings
India	2002	4.47 million	0.45%	IDC India
Indonesia	January 2002	4.4 million	1.93%	KOMITEL
South Korea	July 2002	25.6 million	53.8%	Ministry of Information and Communication
Japan	June 2002	56 million	44.1%	Ministry of Post and Telecommunications
Thailand	2001	3.53 million	5.4%	NECTEC
Malaysia	December 2001	5.7 million	25.15%	ITU
Philippines	September 2002	4.5 million	7.77%	The Philippines Star
Singapore	April 2002	2.31 million	51.84%	Nielsen NetRatings
Taiwan	July 2001	11.6 million	51.85%	Nielsen NetRatings
Vietnam	December 2001	400,000	0.49%	ITU
Cambodia	December 2001	10,000	0.08%	ITU
Sri Lanka	December 2000	121,000	0.63%	ITU
Laos	December 2001	10,000	0.17%	ITU

Source: Adapted from Indrajit Banerjee, Internet and Democracy in Asia, a critical overview and discussion, a paper presented on 28 January 2003 at the University of Copenhagen.

If we take another example, China, the control of sites there is systematic. Contents are banned and censored regularly, and the same legal instruments as in Singapore are also applied.

In Malaysia there are similar – though, perhaps, less common – situations of restrictions of expression, such as, the closure of the online newspaper Malysiakia in 2003, as it was considered too anti-government.

The examples of this dubious relationship with the State are multifarious and can likewise be found in India. In 2002, after having exposed a corruption scheme within the Indian government, tehelka.com was subjected to unprecedented investigations from the tax authorities and secret services that seriously disrupted the site's operations (Banerjee, 2003).

In the case of Indonesia, the changes in nature and degree of control over information played a crucial role in the political changes that took place in the late 1990s and, in particular, in the transition to democracy in 1998 and 1999. The explosion in the coverage of Indonesia in the international media and the role of the Internet were to crucial factors in the political transformation of the country (Winters, 2002).

The fact that the international media coverage was highly critical of the status quo in Indonesia – showing the country to be a military dictatorship, while the remaining ASEAN partners were seen as being in successful transition to democracy – constituted a factor of social instability between the Indonesian elites and those in power. The international coverage by the mass media and the Internet was aimed first and foremost at the Indonesian elites, and the latter then acted as mediators to the population in general and the domestic media (Winters, 2002). This process gave rise to a wave of social destabilization that heightened the effects of the already weak economic situation the country was experiencing (Castells, 2004).

According to the Lexis-Nexis 31 December 1999 (cited in Winters, 2002), the international media coverage of Indonesia increased from some 20,000 articles in 1992 to more than 160,000 in 1998. The two highest peaks in the international coverage took place in May 1998, when four university students were killed by the military, giving rise to mass protests that led to the fall of President Suharto on 21 April 1998, and in September 1999, when the Indonesian regime launched a "scorched earth" campaign on East Timor. This media attention on Indonesia had various effects. One was the much increased involvement of the international community with the reality in Indonesia. Many people who, up to then, had never heard anything about Indonesia were influenced by the negativity of the reports on the situation in the country. The second impact was making it possible for the Indonesians themselves, through CNN, CNBC and Star TV, to see what the world thought of the Indonesian situation.

While television provided this possibility of seeing how *the others* see the *other*, a role in which it is extremely effective (Silverstone, 1999), the Internet served not only as a source of information but also as a tool for activism and coordination amongst the opposition. According to Winters (2002), the Internet constituted one of the media through which the Suharto regime was questioned and the turning towards democracy was consubstantiated in Indonesia.

Amongst the largest contributors with daily posts to the East Timor list in September 1999 was the Joyo News Service: *"(...) during the months of struggle for independence for East Timor there was a feeling of permanent focus on the place"* (Joyo cited in Winters, 2002).

The Joyo News Service, which publishes in English only, was founded in the summer of 1996 by a roughly 30 year-old individual with contacts with Indonesia (Winters, 2002). The development of Joyo determined that the list came to serve dozens of Indonesian and global NGOs, Indonesian students and activists, practically all international journalists in Indonesia and dozens of Indonesian media editors, institutions such as the IMF, World Bank and the Asian Development Bank, academics and students around the world, embassies in Djakarta, the Indonesian elites, the Pentagon, CIA and US Department of State, etc.

In a brief exchange of E-mail, Joyo provided some complementary information on the operations without ever identifying himself/herself. The Joyo service began as an individual effort to show what was going on in Indonesia. The articles from the Internet were chose on the basis of criteria of their perspective and whether or not they were unique contributions. They were initially shared with a restricted number of friends and colleagues.

During the crisis of September 1999, the many daily E-mails sent to the East Timor list contained news and commentaries on Indonesia taken from the world press, radio and television. As Ellis (1999) points out in his article on Joyo, occasionally there also emerged *"(...) a World Bank report or an IMF memorandum obtained through a leak of information that contained embarrassing data for Djakarta or details of conversations between Megawati Sukarnoputri and President B. J. Habibie"*.

The importance of the Joyo News Service during the East Timor crisis exceeded that of a mere source of information for activists interested in the cause, for when Australian correspondents were trapped in the UNAMET in Dili on the days following the referendum in East Timor, they consulted Joyo News via satellite and were thus able to find out what was going on only metres away from the place they were surrounded in, what the world was doing about it and how Djakarta was reacting (Winters, 2002).

A detailed analysis of the East Timor list enables us to typify to a certain extent, though without generalizing, modes of operation and appropriation of lists as a form mobilization, information and actions. The main use of the East Timor list during the period from immediately following the referendum to the arrival of the UN peacekeeping force in the territory was essentially the sharing of information, which in most cases was news stories (71.7%) originating in multiple parts of the world or information on protest actions (21.4%).

Table 9.11– Contents of posts on the ETAN list

Type of usage	%
Invitation or information on protest actions	21.4%
Forwarding briefings or press releases	4.2%
Forwarding reports	2.3%
Forwarding news stories	71.7%
Others	0.5%

Source: analysis of the ETAN list.

The geographical sources on the East Timor list were certainly very diverse but they also illustrate a power typology. In other words, the entities most referenced are those that inform the countries with the greatest influence in solving the conflict or the most influential news agencies at the global level. This power typology of the information available traces an imaginary line linking the US, Australia, the UK, China (Hong Kong) and France.

Table 9.12 – Entities referenced as information source in ETAN posts

Entity	%
Associated France Press (France)	18.8%
NGOs	11.3%
Personal E-mails from activists	7.9%
Australian Broadcasting Corporation (Australia)	7.3%
Djakarta Post (Indonesia)	5.6%
Sydney Morning Herald (Australia)	4.7%
United Nations	3.4%
Other political bodies	3.2%
Associated Press (US)	2.8%
South China Morning Post (Hong Kong)	2.7%
New York Times (US)	2.3%
The Guardian (UK)	2.2%
Washington Post (US)	2.1%

Source: ETAN list.

Of the different bodies involved, if we do not take into account the sending of news stories that mostly came from organization such as Joyo, we see that the NGOs account for more than 10% of the messages sent, followed by activists acting on their own behalf (5.22%), illustrating that these were not only spaces for organizations, but that there were many individuals acting as freelancers. Timorese political organizations occupy on the third place (1.55%). This exemplifies that a large part of the success of a national protest, such as that of East Timor, has to do with raising support at the global level.

The common aggregating factor for the members of the lists is not the existence of common action agenda, for often each member is responsible for their own actions and for the way in which they are carried out, but rather the sharing of a common objective. In his case, the common objective was securing independence for East Timor and the withdrawal of the Indonesian occupying forces.

Table 9.13 – Use of the ETAN mailing list by organizations

Organization types	(%)
International NGO – human rights	2.82
NGO in support of East Timor	8.89
Governments supporting self-determination	0.99
Indonesian government	0.14
Religious body	0.28
Political party	0.71
Activist identified as such	5.22
Organization in defence of journalists and freedom of information	1.13
Religious organization providing support to the population	0.28
Other organizations	0.85
Print media	75.18
Television	0.99
United Nations organization	0.85
International trade union organization	0.14
East Timorese political organization	1.55

Source: East Timor List, ETAN.

One the interesting findings from the analysis or the practices on the ETAN list is that were was a division of the work amongst the various players – a kind of international work division according to the type of entity involved. Hence, the NGOs, religious associations providing direct support or religious hierarchy organizations and the East Timorese political organizations used the list mostly for invitations to protest actions sending information on actions carried out.

The freelance activists used the list more precisely for the collection of news and updating information on the development of events, while members of governments supporting self-determination combined information on institutional political actions in support of the East Timorese cause with briefings and press releases on the situation in Timor and their countries' official positions.

Another of the aspects of interest in characterizing how the ETAN list functioned is the comparison between the geographic origin of the newspaper providing the news and the geographic area to which the news related, i.e. what the content of the news report was. Although the list was about East Timor, most of the international attention was not on the territory of East Timor itself but on Indonesia, Australia and the US. More than 65% of the news articles analyzed relate to these three countries. Obviously, as communications with East Timor were cut off, news on the territory could not be so abundant, but what a reading of the list seems to emphasize is the fact that here, as in many other protest actions at the global level, final success in a given point on the globe (in this case, East Timor) depends on the successes accumulated in many other points – namely in those places that constitute the central nodes of the political, economic and military power networks.

Table 9.14 – Typologies of use of ETAN mailing list by organizations (%)

	Action/ information	Briefing/ press release	Article/ report	News
International NGO – human rights	100.00%	-	-	-
NGO in support of East Timor	90.48%	-	-	9.52%
Governments supporting self-determination	42.86%	57.14%	-	-
Indonesian government	-	100.00%	-	-
Religious body	100.00%	-	-	-
Political party	100.00%	-	-	-
Activist identified as such	2.70%	-	2.70%	94.59%
Organization in defence of journalists and freedom of information	75.00%	-	12.50%	12.50%
Religious organization providing support to the population	100.00%	-	-	-
Other organizations	50.00%	-	50.00%	-
Print media	-	1.69%	4.32%	94.00%
Television	-	-	-	100.00%
United Nations organization	33.33%	66.67%	-	-
International trade union organization	100.00%	-	-	-
East Timorese political organization	100.00%	-	-	-

Source: ETAN list.

One hypothesis that can be analyzed in this context of protests carried out locally with global objectives is the question whether a social agent that only has access to information, or rather news, available in the national space can construct a sufficiently detailed and unbiased analysis so as to be able to form an opinion and clearly take a stance on a certain event?

In quantitative terms, as the following figure shows (Figure 9.6), a comparison between the news published in the leading Portuguese newspapers and the news referenced in the ETAN list shows a high level of coincidence.

In qualitative terms, the answer to the question asked above seems to send us in another direction. Between the news stories most referenced in the print media in Portugal (i.e. in *Público* and *Diário de Notícias*) and those divulged in the ETAN list there are only two thematic coincidences: the military operations of the INTERFET force in the territory and the situation of the refugees and humanitarian aid. However, in value terms, not even in these two situations is there coincidence of editorial options between Portugal and the press of the remaining countries in the list. The INTERFET operations, which is the topic most referred to in Portugal, is only the fifth most common topic when one analyzes the ETAN list. The humanitarian question, which is in sixth place in the Portuguese news reporting ranking, is the third most common topic in the list.

Table 9.15 – Origin and geographic scope on the ETAN list

Geographic origin of the medium producing the news item on the ETAN list		Geographic scope of the news published on the ETAN list	
French	0.24%	France	1.21%
East Timorese	1.12%	Indonesia	40.08% (1)
English	10.75% (4)	Hawaii	0.20%
International agency	31.36% (1)	East Timor	5.67% (4)
Hong Kong	3.61%	Australia	16.60% (2)
Australian	20.77% (2)	Others	2.63%
Irish	1.44%	US	13.36% (3)
US	14.19% (3)	UN	1.01%
Indonesian	8.10% (5)	International agency	0.20%
Brazilian	0.08%	Thailand	0.40%
Singaporean	1.44%	New Zealand	3.64% (5)
Scottish	0.08%	Switzerland	1.01%
Canadian	1.36%	UK	2.83% (6)
Spanish	0.16%	Netherlands	0.20%
Portuguese	0.40%	Finland	0.20%
New Zealand	0.16%	Canada	2.23%
Malaysian	0.08%	Indonesia	0.40%
United Nations	4.49% (6)	Italy	1.01%
Philippine	0.08%	Hong Kong	1.42%
German	0.08%	China	0.61%
-	-	Japan	0.20%
-	-	Portugal	0.81%
-	-	New Caledonia	0.20%
-	-	Sweden	0.40%
-	-	Germany	0.20%
-	-	Singapore	0.81%
-	-	Vatican	0.20%
-	-	Philippines	0.40%
-	-	Belgium	0.40%
-	-	Spain	0.40%
-	-	Macao	1.01%

Source: ETAN list.

The major differences between the Portuguese press and the international press cited on the ETAN list mostly have to do with the Portuguese diplomacy and the internal situation in Portugal (which are totally non-existent topics for the international activists), and also in terms of the high level of personalization of the news stories in the Portuguese newspapers studies. Hence, news stories referring to Xanana Gusmão and Bishop Ximenes Belo dominate the Portuguese press, with approximately 6% more attention than on the ETAN list.

Figure 9.6 – Trends in news stories published in newspapers in Portugal and in newspapers in the ETAN list (% of total news stories)

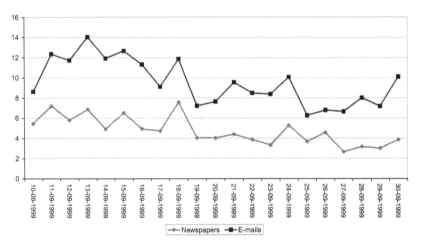

Note: Total of news stories in the Público and Diário de Notícias newspapers, 568; total news stories transcribed for ETAN list: 1199. [166]

---

[166] A brief chronology of the events leading up to and during the period under analysis in newspapers published in Portugal and posts to the ETAN list:

[*4 September* – The Timorese people vote for independence in the referendum]; [*5 September* – many parts of Dili in flames]; [*7 September* – Indonesia declares martial law in East Timor]; [*8 September* – 3 minutes' silence in Portugal and 300,000 people form human chain in Lisbon; massacres continue in Dili]; [*9 September* – Tony Blair and Bill Clinton reach an agreement on sending a peacekeeping force.]; [*10 September* – Ximenes Belo arrives in Lisbon; his route from the airport to the Salesian church (by car) is flanked by thousands of people. Kofi Annan says the UN cannot stand by indefinitely while Indonesia attempts to control the militias who are disseminating death and destruction in East Timor];[*20 September* – INTERFET troops arrive in Dili]; [*27 September* – Indonesian army begins to abandon Timor]; [*30 September* – Xanana Gusmão arrives in Lisbon]. Source: Proença (2000).

Another difference is in the higher valuation of the human rights viola-tion question, which features strongly in the mailing list (the second most common topic), and the incidence of news on the reconstruction of East Timor, a topic that is much more present in the Portuguese newspapers than in the mailing list.

As far as the last two topics are concerned, one can suggest that part of the differences between the Portuguese press and the international press on the ETAN list are due to the fact that, whereas for the international activists in the East Timor questions the violation of human rights was the central motivating factor, for Portugal the violation of human rights was a consequence of the earlier incapacity to resolve the situation of connection between an ex-Portuguese colony and Portugal.

There are media events that have commemorative functions, refer-ring to what should be remembered, while others have a restorative func-tion following social traumas (Dayan and Katz, 1992). In the case of East Timor and the media coverage of the month of September 1999, as Rocha (2003) suggests, the reconciliation of nostalgic impulses derived from an empire at the end of the line (terminated with the handing over of Macao in December 1999) with the appropriation of a new social conception on the defence of the right of intervention for reasons of human rights (as debated about Kosovo), together with a catharsis phenomenon in relation to a guilt complex resulting from the notion of an ill-accomplished decolonization process, goes some way to explaining both the topics chosen and the way in which the media chose to participate in the protest and how the citizens in Portugal adhered to the protest actions in masses.

Table 9.16 – News topics on East Timor and importance attributed to them, selected countries (%)

	News – ETAN list	News – newspapers PT
Portugal: protests and mobilization	-	4.42%
Rest of the world: protests and mobilization	0.17%	0.52%
US: protests and mobilization	0.17%	-
Indonesia: protests and mobilization	0.08%	-
Australia: protests and mobilization	0.25%	-
UNAMET abandons Dili	1.25%	1.82%
Portuguese diplomacy	0.08%	6.49% (3)
Diplomacy of other countries	0.50%	0.26%
Australian diplomacy	1.33%	0.26%
US diplomacy	3.42%	2.08%
UN diplomacy	2.17%	2.08%
EU diplomacy	0.25%	3.12%
Indonesian diplomacy and bilateral relations	1.75%	0.52%
Brazilian diplomacy	0.08%	-
UK diplomacy	0.75%	-
Other economic diplomacy	1.42%	-
Position of the Catholic Church	0.58%	1.30%
CNRT and FALINTIL	1.58%	2.60%
Reconstruction and independence of East Timor	2.92%	6.75% (2)
Position of the East Timorese Catholic Church	0.08%	0.26%
Situation of East Timorese refugees and humanitarian aid	8.34% (3)	5.19% (6)
Human rights violations in East Timor	11.76% (2)	4.94%
War crimes and subsequent trials	5.34% (6)	3.12%
Xanana Gusmão	1.92%	6.23% (5)
Bishop Ximenes Belo	0.67%	1.56%
INTERFET, mobilization	3.59%	3.90%
INTERFET, action in the territory	5.75% (5)	10.91% (1)
INTERFET, Portuguese military participation	-	2.34%
INTERFET, Australian military participation	4.50%	1.04%
INTERFET, military participation of other countries	1.00%	0.26%
INTERFET, French military participation	0.08%	-
INTERFEF, US military participation	1.67%	-
Internal situation in Indonesia	18.52% (1)	5.19% (6)
Militias, operations in East Timor and Kupang	5.84% (4)	3.12%
Journalists and freedom of the press	4.34%(7)	-
Other news	7.84%	15.06%
Internal Portuguese politics	-	4.68% (7)

Source: ETAN and Público and Diário de Notícias newspapers, 10/09/1999 to 30/09/1999.

However, Portugal is not the only country with a bias in terms of journalistic objectivity in covering the East Timor crisis. As the following table shows, the topics most dealt with in each country rarely coincide and in some cases are imbued with direct interest in the event, as in the case of Australia, where the fact that the INTERFET military force was made up largely of Australians constituted an added factor of interest that justified it being the second most frequent topic. The same can be said for the UK's military contribution.

Table 9.17 – News topics and importance attributed to them, selected countries (%)

	Internal situation in East Timor	INTERFET	Internal situation in Indonesia
England	34.8%	20.5%	-
Hong Kong	34.1%	-	27.3%
Australia	42.2%	20.3%	-
Ireland	35.3%	-	-
US	32.2%	-	28.4%
Indonesia	-	-	55.4%
Singapore	-	16.7%	44.4%
Portugal	60.0%	-	-

Source: ETAN list.

Furthermore, most of the press in Asian countries and the US focuses attention on the internal situation in Indonesia and East Timor. Also, amongst the topics dealt with by the media, we can find similar practices as far as the international news agencies are concerned. Although they operate at the international level, different business cultures, editorial policies and even the national context of which they are a part can explain some of the differences found in the topics chosen by the international news agencies.

Table 9.18 – ETAN and news agencies in the coverage of the Timor crisis [167]

	Associated Press (US)	Reuters (UK)	Agence France Press (France)
Protests and mobilization	2.20%	0.00%	1.00%
Diplomacy	15.60%	38.70% (1)	18.40% (3)
Internal situation, East Timor	26.70% (2)	9.70%	35.20% (1)
INTERFET	24.40% (3)	19.40% (3)	17.70%
Internal situation, Indonesia	28.90% (1)	22.60% (2)	20.60% (2)
Media and journalism	2.20%	0.00%	5.50%
Other news	0.00%	9.70%	1.60%

Source: ETAN list.

Hence, Associated Press (AP) focused more on Indonesia than Reuters and Associated France Press (AFP). AFP gave more coverage to the internal situation in East Timor and Reuters chose to analyze the diplomatic dimension of the conflict.

If we analyze the different topics in the light of a chronological assessment of the topics most present on a given day on the ETAN list and in the Portuguese newspapers, we see that there were also different tendencies.

On one and the same day, the topics on the list and in the Portuguese press were normally different or had a different focus of attention. Only in relation to an analysis of the internal situation in East Timor were there coincidences of topic and quantity.

The conclusion one can draw from this analysis of how one and the same topic, East Timor, is treated by different media in different geographic and cultural contexts in an environment of global protest is that the more media (newspapers, radio and television stations, activist lists, etc.) we have access to, the greater the probability of there being in-depth and correct knowledge of the situation and the greater the possibility of a protest firmly based on symbolic mediation achieving its objectives.

Given that the information provided by the media is diversified – sometimes due to an intentional bias, at other times simply because of editorial

---

[167] At this point it is worthwhile introducing some background information on the origin of the different news agencies referred to herein. Associated Press was founded in 1848, a year of revolution in Europe and therefore one of great news interest for the United States, from whence it hails. Today it distributes news stories, photos, and audio and video reports read by more than one billion people daily. Reuters, based in London, first began operating in the field of business in 1851. It became a public company in 1984. Agence France Press was founded in 1835 and still has its head office in Paris, with global operations that include regional centres in Washington, Hong Kong, Nicosia and Montevideo.

decisions (for a number of different reason) – and that the media also do not have the capacity to understand all the realities or physical or temporal capacity to look into everything that takes place, the Internet constitutes an essential tool for organizing, mobilizing, taking action and divulging information in the Information Age.

During the month of September the Movement for East Timor gradually lost momentum as the events reflected the objectives it had set. Curiously enough, the attention of the international media only became widespread after the dissemination of the first images of protests on the streets of Lisbon and after an increase in the number of support E-mails circulating on the Internet. The online forums and the global participation that they attracted are examples of how the reach the Movement for East Timor had was finally getting to the international public opinion.

The Movement's struggle for media coverage reached its high point when the images of the blockade of the United Nations premises in Dili were divulged in the whole world and it became clear that the information blockade imposed by Indonesia only served to confirm what was already circulating on the Internet: that mass violations of human rights were taking place in East Timor.

Table 9.19 – Time frame comparison of the two most featured East Timor-related topics in the written press, selected countries (%)

	Diplomacy		Internal situation in East Timor		INTERFET		Internal situation in Indonesia	
	ETAN	Newspapers PT	ETAN	Newspapers PT	ETAN	Newspapers PT	ETAN	Newspapers PT
10-09-1999	31.00%	52.38% (+)	35.70% (+)	14.29%	-	-	-	-
11-09-1999	36.50%	45.45% (+)	34.60% (+)	31.58%	-	-	-	-
12-09-1999	30.60% (+)	26.32%	-	-	-	-	24.20% (+)	21.05%
13-09-1999	-	20.00%	23.80%	40.00% (+)	23.80%	-	31.00%	-
14-09-1999	-	28.57%	27.30%	28.57% <>	-	-	33.00%	-
15-09-1999	-	26.09%	-	21.74%	27.00%	-	25.70%	-
16-09-1999	-	37.50%	31.40%	-	-	31.25%	30.00%	-
17-09-1999	-	23.53%	25.00% (+)	23.53%	-	-	27.30%	-
18-09-1999	-	-	25.90% (+)	13.79%	-	37.93%	29.60%	-
19-09-1999	-	-	24.30%	33.33% (+)	-	6.25%	21.60%	-
20-09-1999	-	-	25.90%	37.50%	-	31.25%	24.30%	-
21-09-1999	-	12.00%	32.80%	48.00% (+)	-	-	27.60%	-
22-09-1999	-	9.52%	32.20%	42.86% (+)	-	-	23.70%	-
23-09-1999	-	-	28.10%	37.50% (+)	-	31.25%	24.60%	-
24-09-1999	-	8.33%	41.80% (+)	37.50%	-	-	21.80%	-
25-09-1999	-	-	47.10%	46.15% <>	-	38.46%	20.60%	-
26-09-1999	-	-	47.10% (+)	16.67%	-	16.67%	29.40%	-
27-09-1999	-	-	47.40%	50.00% (+)	15.80%	25.00%	-	-
28-09-1999	-	-	52.70% (+)	35.71%	16.40%	28.57%	-	-
29-09-1999	-	-	37.70%	50.00% (+)	-	28.57%	15.10%	-
30-09-1999	18.40%	-	40.80% (+)	19.05%	-	7.14%	18.40%	-

Source: ETAN and Newspapers Público and Diário de Notícias de 10/09/1999 a 30/09/1999. Note: Total news published in Portugal and accounted for: 568; Total news transcripts in emails at East Timor mailing list: 1199. (+) refers to the news theme with the highest frequency for the day; <> stands for similar values for both media.

On 9 September 1999 British Prime Minister, Tony Blair, and US President, Bill Clinton, agreed on the need to send a multinational peacekeeping force to the territory under the auspices of the United Nations.

On 12 September Indonesia made a formal request to the UN Secretary General for sending of the multinational force and four days later, on 16 September, the UN Security Council approved Resolution 1264, giving the Secretary General a mandate to send troops and to establish an interim administration for the territory. The multinational force, led by Australia, arrived in Dili on 20 September 1999.

The Movement for East Timor therefore need eleven days of concerted actions, together with the instrumentalization of the traditional mass media and the Internet and the diplomatic action of the Portuguese State, to get the attention it desired from the international community and the governments represented on the Security Council.

Instrumentalization of the Networked Symbolic Mediation

In his analysis of the social and political conflicts emerging in the Information Age, Castells (2004) argues that the distinction between old and new movements is to a large extent illusory. While the new movements defend specific cultural values, the more traditional ones – such as the trade unions – have likewise developed in the direction of the defence or promotion of lifestyles and meanings (Castells, 2004). This view is shared by Cohen and Rai (2000), who argue that the human rights movements diminish the distinction between the new and old movements, given that they simultaneously seek transformations of a political and social nature.

If that is the case, what was new in the protests we have analyzed in this chapter – *Terràvista,* the *End of RTP2* and the *Movement for East Timor?* One possible answer is precisely the combined use of the Internet and the mass media in general for the mobilization, protests and action.

The Internet is identified by many authors as potentially the first real public sphere (Downing, 2000), in which political participation by the citizens is really possible, not only because it allows for the sharing of more non-censored knowledge (Ford and Gil, 2000) but also because it balances out the quasi-monopoly radio and television have given to the older instances of representation, such as the political parties and pressure groups (Gibbins and Reimer, 1999).

However, we must ask the question whether the Internet plays a purely instrumental role in the development of citizenship and political expression or whether, in addition to that role, it also transforms the political game rules for the simple reason that it takes part in it (Castells, 2004).

Not all analysts are optimistic on this question, particularly taking into account that access to the technology is not universal, and nor will it be so soon, and that even those who have the technology do not necessarily possess the literacy necessary for making optimal use of it. Taking these questions into account, the empirical analysis of the data available on the three case studies presented herein seems to confirm Touraine's idea that the contemporary social movements are decentralized, fluid, networked, technologically sophisticated and simultaneously local and global (Garner, 1996: 385).In agreement with both Castells and Touraine, we can argue that the novelty in the contemporary social movements is their networked character. However, if the network is the prevailing organizational form, resulting from the instrumentalization of the Internet, the movements only seem to be able to achieve their objectives when there are strategies that provide the networking of different media.

For this reason we would argue that *one can only consider a social movement as networked when it achieves the strategic and concerted use of the traditional and new media in the organization and implementation of actions.* In other words, when it is able to join in the interpersonal and mass communications dimensions into a new network communication strategy and agency.

The following table (Table 9.20) summarizes a proposal for the reading of the networking of different media for achieving the set objectives of protest movements, regardless of whether they can be characterized as social movements or not.

Table 9.20 – *Mediation* strategies in the context of social movements

	Emergence	Mobilization	Organization and coordination	Protest	Scope
Fax	-	-	-	Yes	National/Local
Television	Yes	Yes	-	Yes	International/ National/Local
Radio	Yes	Yes	Yes	-	National/ International/Local
Press	-	Yes	-	-	National/ International/Local
World Wide Web	-	Yes	Yes	Yes	International/ National/Local
E-mail	-	Yes	Yes	Yes	International/ National/Local
Chat	-	Yes	Yes	-	International/ National/Local
Mobile Phones	-	Yes	Yes	-	National/Local

As we have shown above, the concerted effort of the traditional media and the Internet was indispensable for the Movement for East Timor in achieving its goals, particularly in the way it managed to internationalize the protest so as to force the Security Council to act. [168] On the other hand, for the protest over the closure of Terràvista, the instrumentalization of the traditional media (television and the press) through the creation of news online, was the reason for the protest's success.

In the case of the protest against the End of RTP2, all the media were transformed into a vast network, vehicling opinions with the aim of giving visibility to individual opinions and, consequently, achieving the status of majority public opinion on the question at hand. In the sense the physical encounters or demonstrations played a residual role, this was a purely symbolic protest based on freedom of opinion and the idea that the use of the

---

[168]The case of the creation of a human chain for East Timor is an example of that relationship. At the beginning, on 5th September, the group organizing the human chain for East Timor contacted the CNRT, which appointed the Commission for the Rights of the Timor people as the interlocutor for dynamizing the event [João Coutinho Ferreira and Pedro Dionísio 2003] and radio as a permanent mobilizing factor and means of access at home, in the car, at work, etc.; television as a disseminator of the images to the international channels, such as CNN; the Internet, to create solidarity chains; the press, through the sports newspapers, for reaching other audiences. The final goal of the human chain East Timor was to be a media event that was innovative and had enough impact to create in Portugal and event broadcast on television that thus impacted the public opinion in the UN Security Council member states and, in turn, their governments. Coutinho, João and Dionísio, Pedro (2003).

media for voicing opinions can, in specific circumstances, particularly in a democratic state, be something similar to an opinion poll.

As Van Aelst and Walgrave (2001) point out, the mobilizers in collective actions are, in most cases, organizations. It is the organizations that endeavour to assert their positions on a certain topic to the public (*mobilization by consensus*) and seek to motivate the public to take action (*mobilization to action*). If the organizations are not physically present, informal communication networks can assume the role of mobilizers to action.

The modern mass media have taken on central importance in the life and death of the social movements, particularly for the way in which the later are able to manage the news through the creation of events for the media (Van Aelst, 2001). Normally, the mass media are merely filters, facilitators for, or at times even barriers, to collective action and not central actors with their own strategy and proactive role.

The mobilization theory suggests that the mass media are possible channels for mobilization by consensus and are privileged providers of information and reference matrixes. The same line of argument suggests that media such as radio, television and the press are less important for persuasive communication (mobilization to action) but play a central role in creating favourable climates for mobilization (mobilization by consensus) (Van Aelst, 2001).

While the case of the white marches against paedophilia in Belgium demonstrated how the media, in specific situations where there is a lack of organizations leading the processes to start with, can take on a pole of mobilization to action (Van Aelst, 2001), the analysis of the Movement for East Timor shows that, even when there are already organizations committed to a cause, the media can decide to cooperate with them both in the mobilization by consensus and the mobilization to action.

As the Movement for East Timor has shown, the media can play an active role even when there is no clear and manifest discontent amongst the people and the elites. A scandal that would give rise to a general lack of confidence is not necessary to bring about this active participation. Nevertheless, the active role of the media is limited to strictly symbolic and emotional questions that create atmospheres of consensus and sharing and in which the matter in question is relatively simple, i.e. in which the narrative allows for easy and direct labelling of those involved as "good" or "bad", and is politically impartial (Van Aelst, 2001).

It is likewise important that the environment in which the media operate is commercial and characterized by depoliticization and clear freedom of action in relation to economic and cultural interests.

One can, therefore, argue that the social movements, with a view to influencing the agendas of the decision-making powers, must adopt strategies of seduction of the traditional media (radio, television and the press) and simultaneously instrumentalize the new media, such as the Internet, thus allowing them to overcome distance and time restrictions and to take their protest to where it can really make a difference.

The reading of the case studies in this chapter therefore suggests that *the social and civic movements today are also a product of the network society of which they are a part.*

They use symbolic mobilization and have flexible resources, easier access to certain media, more rapid and cheaper mobility both in geographic and cultural interaction terms and can also rely on the cooperation of diverse types of other networked organization for the simplified organization of themed campaigns.

In the Network Society the development of a new communicational model has been taking shape. A communicational model characterized by the fusion of interpersonal communication and mass communication, connecting audiences and broadcasters under a hypertextual matrix linking several media devices (from newspapers to videogames). Hypertextual in the sense that several devices, analogical or digital, connect to each other and also in the sense that we attribute to different media different linking combinations and relationships, due to our own appropriations and representations.

In the same way, that new communicational mode, promotes articulation between the more classic concepts of text, flow and interpersonal communication, in what we can call "Networked Communication".

Networked Communication is able to join the interpersonal and mass communications dimension into a new network communication of strategy and agency.

Networked communication refers, then, to a media system where interactivity gives shape to it's organizational model, that offers two central nodes, one centred on low interactivity, where television rules, and another where the centre is the internet offering high interactivity.

Those different media nodes are connected mainly through interpersonal media (although they can appropriated to act as mass media) such as: mobile phones; email; iPods; etc.

Given the above, the social appropriation of communication by citizens and social movements in general should, in their development of communication and agency strategies, take notice of:

How the current meta-system of information is currently organized (with television and internet acting as the central and emerging players).

How the current entertainment meta-system is still mainly populated by television and cinema but that multimedia games have growing importance.

The *Networked Communication* model is the informational societies communication model. A model that must be understood also in it's needed literacies in order to have a broader choice on how to build our media diets, media matrix and internet gatekeeping, in order to achieve emergence, mobilization, and organize protests towards common social objectives.

Conclusion:
Browsing, News, Filters and Citizenship

Education should consist of teaching people to discern, a very difficult art. But when he opens a book at the first page, an average reader knows if it is an erotic novel or a book of philosophy and then decides. He chooses what he wants. That means that a minimum of literacy at least teaches one to understand immediately what one has in one's hand when one is in a book shop, if not more. Attaining the same level of knowledge in this telematic jungle is quite a problem. But it is something that will be taught in school in the future.

Umberto Eco, *The nomenclature and electronic democracy* (own translation)

In our informational societies, which are organized on the basis of a network paradigm and culture, the media and our practices in relation to them, are organized in networks of media diets, media matrixes and media biographies (Castells, 2002-2004; Miranda, 2002; Colombo, 2003-2004). In today's societies, and predictably in the near future as well, we are experiencing an unparalleled condition in our history that has created a new paradigm for the participation of individuals in society. That new paradigm is the fact that, for the first time, the conditions that make a citizen economically more valuable in the work sphere and those that enable full civic participation are the same. The collection, processing and sharing of information constitute the main conditions for the generation of wealth and economic success and also provide the necessary conditions for the full exercise of citizenship. In both dimensions, success depends on the informational literacy of the individuals. By this I mean the possession of the literacies necessary for creating the different autonomies that constitute our life trajectories, i.e. the capacity to generate our own individual or collective projects. Literacies, which, in a world in which we are living more and more through and with the media, transcend the space of writing and reading to take over the spaces of the image and sound as well.

In a culture of real virtuality (Castells, 2002), literacy is the same as mastering mediation – in the sense of understanding the information, entertainment and communication production models. Literacy thus means more than just the knowledge of how something is produced, but also the reading of written, sound and visual texts through computers, television, radios, newspapers, books, multimedia games and in mediation spaces as varied as telephone networks, television networks and networks of networks such as the Internet.

Literacy, in the network society, means the capacity to manipulate and assimilate information with the end purpose of the production of knowledge in a preponderantly mediated universe (Silverstone, 2004).

In an informational society organized in networks, of all the different forms of autonomy there is one that constitutes the basis for the others: communicative autonomy.

Communicative autonomy does not depend on access to information, entertainment and communication alone, for fruition thereof can have little capacity for individual empowerment if the necessary literacy is not given or is not used in the selection and filtering processes. So that one cannot remind often enough that access is not the same as knowledge (Oliveira, 1994).

The introduction to this book referred to a number of hypotheses with the aim of better understanding how the media in the network society are organized, function and are appropriated by us for the most diverse purposes and, in particular, for the exercise of citizenship.

In the network society, integration between different media, and not technological convergence (i.e. the sum of the various media in one single technological interface) is the scenario of the future. Not for technological reasons, but because that is the model that best responds to the cultural practices and the new models of public perception. The dominant paradigm is that of the autonomy of interfaces that inter-relate in a network logic, using for that connectivity between interfaces any technologies that facilitate the networking, such as the Internet or mobile phone SMS. The common denominator between technologies is network connectivity and not digitalisation. The latter is a necessary condition but, on its own, it does not influence the way in which the different media, be they personal or mass media, are evolving.

Clearly there are successful cases of technological convergence of interfaces, namely the hybridisation of radios, mp3 players and mobile phones and, to a lesser degree, multimedia game consoles and mobile phones. But these successes perhaps owe less to technological affinities between the interfaces and more to the fact that they respond to complex social functions that characterise lifestyles in advanced contemporary societies.

Lifestyles that promote the use of technologies that enable one to manage the boundary between the private and publics spheres. In other words, technologies that allow for networked connections. Technologies that, as a final consequence of the connectivity, enable one to respond to the identity and participation demands. Technologies that enable one to create and manage communication networks. Technologies that enable one to represent effectively the communication interface between the public and private spheres, allowing for personal privacy management and adapting to the personality of the user at the same time as giving them mobility.

In a world of niches and different tribes, people see in the media a form of help in recognizing the identity they have chosen and, at the same time, the possibility of expressing that identity, of cultivating their individual or community identities (Castells, 2003) in a logic of adherence and recognition.

Our representations in relation to the media, or media matrixes (Ortoleva, 2002), which orientate our media diets (Colombo, 2003) thus seek to configure more and more an *elective space* (Menduni, 2002), in which a *networked synthetic communication model* is developed. [169]

---

[169] *Elective space* applied to the media means a space that configures a world made up of different cultures, languages, objectives, lifestyles and cultural uses. When we individually chose one of the media, be it a personal or mass medium, we are giving it communicative maturity for that space (Menduni, 2002).

Browsing, News, Filters and Citizenship

Our participation practices and the way we use the different media configure a citizenship that can be described as *citizenship between browsers, filters and news.*

In a society in which mediation plays a central role, the management of citizenship not only has to do with the concretisation of a given action or taking a certain position. Most of the time our use of the mediation space has nothing to do with specific, pre-defined objectives. What we essentially do is to combine looking, listening, reading and observing, adding information in order to process it and transform it into knowledge. Our television and Internet practices have more in common with "window shopping" than "going shopping". Just as we mostly surf the Internet without concrete objectives, our television viewing is also more the result of discovering "what's on" than the concrete desire to see a programme or series that we follow, thus giving rise to phenomena such as zapping.

Civic participation in the informational societies implies, in addition to our non-mediated social relationships, extensive knowledge of the mediated reality. It is that knowledge – the sum of many segmented interests (which differ from subject to subject) – that constitutes the foundation for the management of citizenship. Only through that free – and not previously guided – experimentation with reading newspapers, watching television, surfing the Internet, listening to radio, experimenting mobile phone SMS functions, does one obtain the conditions necessary for the development of the informational literacy required by each person to be able to assert themselves in the different spheres of citizenship and achieve their autonomy objectives. Citizenship in the Information Age is also a product of the different windows that we browse on the Internet because only if we are aware of the diversity they contain can we make the right choices.

Traditionally, filters have always been a part of our experience, providing a basis for classification. That is true for book and magazine publishing companies, record companies and film and game production companies, the television and radio programme directors, but it is also true of journalists, editors, churches, scientific institutions, etc. – entities and persons that have the function of filtering and reorganizing knowledge and information. In the relationship between the filter and user, there is a restriction of intellectual liberty, but access of the user and the community to the essential information is guaranteed. It is thus that the filters influence the management of citizenship.

With the development of the Internet, the matrix of the relationship between filters and user has also changed and, consequently, the conditions for the management of citizenship as well. On the one hand, the Internet has reduced institutional filters, because it is possible to select information without going through the institutions and it allows one to compare the filtering carried out by states, churches, teachers, librarians, doctors, opinion leaders and entrepreneurs. On the other hand, it repeats online the filtering already carried out by newspapers, radio and television. In other words, the Internet, when looked at through the search engines, shows us a filtered reality that continues to give an out-of-proportion voice – considering the number of media online – to the newspapers, radio and television stations. The Internet has thus introduced new classification agents for the experience, such as the search engines and portals, giving rise to a new selection and classification phenomenon – Internet gatekeeping – and thus also altering the conditions of management of citizenship.

It would be difficult for us to imagine a world where we would no longer find the news at the newsagents, where we would not hear the news every half hour when we turn on the car radio, where we would not surf the Internet in search of a sports page when we arrive at work, where we would not (occasionally) be tempted to go check the website of a newspaper to see if anything new has happened, or where, when we get home, there would not be one of those faces on the television screen that we have become so accustomed to watching at dinner time reading the news to us.

News is part of our everyday life, so we do pay a certain amount of attention to it, even without such emotionally strong catastrophes such as the 9/11 disaster or the tsunami in South-east Asia in 2005. Because news is a mirror of reality, it informs our value constructions and helps us to define how the political, economic, military, social and cultural power relations are structured. Accordingly, when changes are made to its form and content, its editorial organisational models, its business management, its distribution model, the way in which we use it or in the time we give to it, we are also altering the conditions in which we exercise management of our citizenship. There is an intimate link between news and citizenship.

The news we see, read or hear today has changed because the formulation of the media system and the information meta-system has changed, though, in general, the continuity is greater than the change. The news remains *today*, as it was *yesterday*, the most common form of information on public events transmitted by the most diverse media, and its basic characteristics are update, relevance and reliability.

The change in the field of the news results, primarily, from many of the newspapers and radio and television stations going online. The fact that they have established an Internet presence has also brought about new strategies. In the case of television, this has given rise to a *networked television model*; for the newspapers, it has resulted in a repositioning in relation to television; and in the case of radio it has led to a consolidation of this communicative intimacy. But if the Internet has brought alterations with it, it is also true that the changes in the news field came before the massification of the Internet. The newspapers had already began to occupy themselves with an increasing number of social events, customs, varieties and rumours, thus altering the criteria for defining what was and what was not news. That logic contaminated television, first at the entertainment level and then the field of information, through the news, turning television programmes and presenters themselves into news stories.

A further transformation that news has undergone resulted from the extension of its personalisation practices, traditionally confined to political party leaders, to promote the anonymous individuals. Celebration in the news became a possibility for many who were not politicians, athletes or actors, thus producing a condition of ephemeral stardom, taking the form, in the news, of reports on someone's illness, a village feast and who organized it or injustices suffered at the hands of the State or an insurance company. This second change in the news dimension can be characterized as the application of the reality show narrative logic to information.

The fact that the massification of the Internet took place at the same time as the institutionalisation of populist journalism was also reflected in the content model offered by the portals, in which quality of content is defined as being that which keeps the users on the site and, only collaterally, the fact that is fulfils socially shared objectives and has intellectual or artistic merit. In the model practiced in portals, the editorial integrity of the information provided is not the central dimension of the act of informing, nor does it necessarily have to be a product of the creative and analytical capacities in relation to information on the part of the journalists. The information content can be anything and does not necessarily have to be the product of a specialist accredited as a journalist.

News has changed, though perhaps not radically, for the portals have given rise to the coexistence of news and information contents and, in the mass media, to the option between populist and serious journalism. Various types of information coexist, produced in accordance with different criteria with different objectives and also serving our interests and tastes in a different way.

The practical result of that change for the management of citizenship in its relationship with the news was the rise of a new classification environment for experience and a new mirror of reality, introducing new notions of update, relevance and reliability.

However, if these are the new conditions of citizenship management, it is also true that a new paradox has emerged in our societies.

Today, a few of us, making use of the symbolic mediation space offered by the mass media and interpersonal communication media, can confront the stronger and realize their objectives. But, at the same time, those that have that combination of literacies are also, today, proportionally less in number than those that, in previous periods of our history, successfully became involved in other non mediated mass movements, struggles and civic protests.

In this condition, formal education and the informal experimentation of the media play a fundamental role in our society, for only they can guarantee expansion of the number of those who will exercise full citizenship in all its multiple dimensions, from the civic to the economic dimension, and, consequently, the social and economic development of their societies.

Because citizenship, regardless of the era we are living in, is an expression of the will to improve our lives and our world, I will finish with the words of Hugo Pratt:

Hope.
The desire for a better life.
A few masochists apart, everyone focuses on that, at all latitudes.
To live better is the wish of all, but the paths we chose to try and get there are multiple and they vary just as the personality of each person varies.
The only paths I would consider condemnable are those that do wrong to others: I am for civility – but the civility of the strong, not that of weakness.

Hugo Pratt, *Le Désir D'être Inutile* (own translation)

Bibliography

ABERCROMBIE, Nicholas (1996): Television and Society. Cambridge: Polity Press, p. 197

ABRAMSON, Jeffrey B., ARTERTON, F. Christopher, ORREN, Gary R.. (1988) The Electronic Commonwealth: the Impact of New *Media* Technologies on Democratic Politics. NY: Basic Books, Inc.

ABRAMSON, Jeffrey, 'The Internet and Community', in the Emerging Internet, Queenstown, Institute for Information Studies, 1998.

AHOKAS, Ira e Kaivo-oja, Jari, Benchmarking European Information Society Developments, Foresight 5, 1, 2003, pp.44-54.

ALA, American Library Association, Available *Online* HTTP: http://www.acrl.org/ala/acrl/acrlissues/acrlinfolit/infolitoverview/infolitglossary/infolitglossary.htm .

ALGER, D. (1998); "Os Mega*media*, a Situação do Jornalismo e a Democracia", Harvard internacional Journal of Press/Politics, vol. 3, n°1, 1998, pp.126-133.

ALTMAN, David (2002) , Prospects for E-Government in Latin America: International Review of Public Administration, 2002, Vol. 7, No. 2.

ANACOM, Estatísticas do Serviço de Transmissão de Dados / Serviço de Acesso à Internet – 2° trimestre de 2004, Available *Online* HTTP :http://www.icp.pt/template12.jsp?categoryId=135882 .

ANDRADE, C. (1999) Tragédia obrigou a tomar partido, Diário de Notícias, 29 September.

AQUINO, Ruth, BIERHOFF, Jan, ORCHARD, Tim, STONE, Martha (2002), The European Multi*media* News Landscape, MUDIA, International Institute of Infonomics.

AROLDI, Piermarco, COLOMBO, Fausto (2002), The Impact of Internet on *Mass media* TV Audience and Internet Users: a Report on Four Generations of Italians, Paper Presented at the COST A20 Conference at the University of Tromsoe, Norway

AROLDI, Piermarco, COLOMBO, Fausto (2003), Le Età della Tv, Milano,VP Università.

ARTERTON, C.F. (1987) Teledemocracy, Can Technology Protect Democracy? Newbury Park/Beverly Hills/London/New Delhi: Sage.

BABERJEE, Indrajit (2003) Internet and Democracy in Asia: A Critical Overview and Discussion, Conference on "Democratic Governance and ICT", Department of Political Science, University of Copenhagen, Denmark.

BANERJEE, I. (2003), Internet and Democracy in Asia: A Critical Exploratory Journey, in Banerjee, I. (ed), Rhetoric and Reality: The Internet Challenge for Democracy in Asia,Singapore: Eastern Universities Press.

BAPTISTA, Joana (2004), O Fenómeno dos Blogues em Portugal, Tese de Licenciatura em Comunicação Social, no Instituto Superior de Ciências Sociais e Políticas. Available HTTP: http://seminarioinvestigacao.blogspot.com/ .

BARBER, Benjamin (1984) Strong democracy: participatory politics for a new age. Berkeley: University of California Press.

BARBER, Benjamin (1996) "Three challenges to reinventing democracy" in HIRST, P., KHILNANI, S. (1996) (eds.) Reinventing Democracy. Cambridge: The Political Quarterly.

BARBER, Benjamin (1999) "Three scenarios for the future of technology and strong democracy". Political Science Quarterly. 113: 573-590.

BASILI, C. (Ed.) (2003) Information Literacy in Europe: a first insight into the state of the art of Information Literacy in the European Union. Rome: Consiglio Nazionale delle Ricerche.

BASTOS, Alexandre Miguel (2002), Que lugar para a Música Portuguesa na Rádio, Projecto de Tese para o Mestrado de Comunicação, Cultura e Tecnologias de Informação, Lisboa, ISCTE.

BASTOS, Helder, "A Internet no Jornalismo", Observatório-Revista do Observatório da Comunicação, n°1, May 2000.

BASTOS, VIDAL, Alexandre Miguel (2003) Que Lugar para a Música Portuguesa na Rádio, Projecto de Tese no Mestrado de Comunicação, Cultura e Tecnologias de Informação, Departamento de Sociologia, Lisboa, ISCTE.

BAUDRILLARD, Jean, (1991), "Simulacros e simulação", Lisboa, Relógio D'Água.

BAXI, U. (2000), Human Rights – suffering between movements and markets, Cohen, R., Rai, S. (eds), Global Social Movements, Athlone Press

BEBIANO, Rui, Um Clamor Digital, Vida Mundial, 1 October 1999.

BECK, Ulrich (1992/1986) Risk Society. Towards a new modernity. London/New Delhi: Sage.

BECK, Ulrich (1997) The Reinvention of Politics. Rethinking Modernity in the Global Social Order. Cambridge: Polity Press.

BECK, Ulrich, GIDDENS, Anthony, LASH, Scott (2000/1994) Modernização Reflexiva: política, tradição e estética no mundo moderno. Oeiras: Celta.

BENAVENTE, Ana (1996) – A Literacia Em Portugal : Resultados de Uma Pesquisa Extensiva e Monográfica / Coord. Ana Benavente ; Alexandre Rosa, António Firmino Da Costa E Patrícia Avila.- Lisboa, Fundação Calouste Gulbenkian.

BENNET L., ENTMAN, Robert (2001), "Communication in the Future of Democracy: a conclusion" in BENNET L., ENTMAN, Robert, Medidated Politics, Cambridge, Cambridge University Press.

BENNET, Lance W. (2003), Coming to Europe? Why *Media* Market Deregulation is Good for Business but Bad for Public Information, in VIDAL BENEYTO, José, La Ventana Global, Madrid , Taurus.

BENNET, Lance, (2004), Communicating Global Activism," in Win van de Donk, Brian Loader, Paul Nixon, and Dieter Rucht, eds., Cyberprotest: New *Media*, Citizens, and Social Movements , London, Routledge,.

BENNETT, W. Lance, ENTMAN, Robert M. (2001) "*Media*ted Politics: An Introduction" in BENNETT, W. Lance, ENTMAN, Robert

M. (2001) *Media*ted Politics – Communication in the Future of Democracy. Cambridge: Cambridge University Press.

BRESCHT, Berthold, "Der Rundfunk als Kommunikationsapparat" in *Bjitter des Hessischen Landestheaters Darmstadt*, No. 16, July 1932, Available *Online* HTTP: http://telematic.walkerart.org/telereal/bit_brecht.html

BIMBER, Bruce (1998) "The Internet and Political Transformation: Populism, Community and Accelerated Pluralism". Polity XXXI (1): 133-160.

BITTANTI, Mateo, L'era dei videogiochi simbolici (1958-1984), Gruppo Editoriale Futura, 1999.

BOCZKOWSKI, Pablo J. (2002) "The Development and Use of *Online* Newspapers: What Research Tells Us and What We Might Want to Know", in LIEVROUW, Leah A., LIVINGSTONE, Sonia, Handbook of New *Media*: Social Shaping and Consequences of ICTs, London; SAGE.

BORGES, Jorge Luis (2004) La biblioteca total, Available *Online* HTTP : http://www.ciudadseva.com/textos/cuentos/esp/borges/bibliote. htm

BORGES, Jorge Luís, 'A Biblioteca de Babel' em Ficções, Lisboa, Teorema, 1998.

BORN, Georgina (2003), Strategy, Positioning and Projection in Digital Television, *Media*, Culture & Society vol.25 (2003): 773-799.

BOSSI, Vitorio, CORNERO, Loredana (1999), Dalla Parte Dello Spettatore, Roma, RAI-ERI.

BOUGNOUX, Daniel "Face à l'ogre audiovisuel", in PIERRE BOURDIEU L'intellectuel dominant, Magazine littéraire n°369, October 1998, Available Online HTTP : http://www.magazinelitteraire. com/dossiers/dos_bour.htm .

BOURDIEU, Pierre (1979) La Distinction: Critique Sociale du Jugement. Paris: Minuit.

BOURDIEU, Pierre (1989) O Poder Simbólico. Lisboa: Difel.

BOURDIEU, Pierre (2000), "A Televisão Precisa de um Contrapoder" <http://www.espacoacademico.com.br/010/10bourdieu.htm> (January 2001).

BOURDIEU, Pierre (2000), Sobre a Televisão, Oeiras; Celta.

BRANDT, D. (2002), PageRank: Google's Original Sin, Available *Online* HTTP: http://www.google-watch.org/pagerank.html .

BRAUDEL, Fernand, (2000), Escritos Sobre A História, Lisboa, Editorial Presença.

BROWN, Allan (2004), "Sweden Case Study", in Allan Brown and Robert G. Picard (eds.), Digital Television in Europe, NJ, Lawrence Erlbaum.

BUDGE, I. (1996) The New Challenge of Direct Democracy.Oxford: Polity Press.

BUSTAMANTE, E. (2002), Nuevas Fronteras Del ServiciPúblico, En Vidal Beneyto, J., La Ventana Global, Ed. Taurus, Madrid.

BUSTAMANTE, E.; Telefonica o la historia de España; in Comunicação & Política Vol.VII, n°1

BUSTAMANTE, Enrique (2003), Hacia un Nuevo Sistema Mundial de Comunicación. Las Industrias Culturales en la Era Digital, Barcelona, Gedisa Editorial.

CABRAL, Manuel Villaverde (1997) Cidadania política e equidade social em Portugal. Oeiras: Celta.

CABRAL, Manuel Villaverde (2000) "O exercício da cidadania política em Portugal" in Análise Social, n° 154-155 (July-September 2000).

CÁDIMA, Francisco Rui (1999) Desafios dos Novos Media: a nova ordem política e comunicacional. Lisboa: Editorial Notícias.

CÁDIMA, Francisco Rui (2000) "Miragens digitais", Presidência da República, Os Cidadãos e a Sociedade de Informação. Conferência promovida pelo Presidente da República, 9 e 10 December 1999, Lisboa, INCM.

CÁDIMA, Francisco Rui, "Televisão, Serviço Público e Qualidade", Observatório, OBERCOM, n°6, November 2002, 9-18.

CÀDIMA, RUI (2000), "A Televisão Digital e as Políticas do Audiovisual no Contexto da Sociedade de Informação", Observatório-Revista do Observatório da Comunicação, n°1, May 2000.

CALHOUN, Craig (1992) (ed.) Habermas and the Public Sphere. Cambridge, Mass: MIT Press.

CAMMAERSTS, Bart, VAN AUDENHOVE, Leo (2003), ICT-Usage Among Transnational Social Movements in the Networked Society: to organise, to mediate & to Influence, The European Media and Technology in Everyday Life Network, 2000-2003, Available Online HTTP: http://www.lse.ac.uk/collections/EMTEL/main1.html .

CAPELO, Fernanda de Mendonça (s.d.), A Educação em Portugal: breve historial, Available *Online* HTTP: http://www.batina.com/nanda/educa1.htm (June 2004).

CAPUCHA (2004), Desafios da Pobreza, Lisboa, ISCTE (Tese de Doutoramento).

CARAÇA, João (2001), Ciência, Lisboa, Quimera.

CARDOSO et al., (2005), Os deputados portugueses e a política informacional, Oeiras, Celta Editores.

CARDOSO, G.e Santos, S. (2003), Análise comparada das televisões portuguesas – 11, 12 e 15 Março 2003. ISCTE.

CARDOSO, Gustavo (1998) Para uma Sociologia do Ciberespaço: comunidades virtuais em português. Oeiras: Celta Editora.

CARDOSO, Gustavo (1999) "As causas das questões ou o Estado à beira da Sociedade de Informação" in Sociologia – Problemas e Práticas, n° 30 (June 1999). Lisboa: Celta Editora.

CARDOSO, Gustavo (2003), Internet, Lisboa, Quimera.

CARDOSO, Gustavo, LORGA, Catarina (2000). Os Portais como Novos *Media*dores de Informação na Internet, Paper Apresentado no IV Congresso de Sociologia da APS.

CARDOSO, Gustavo (2000), 'Prefácio' em A Segunda Era dos *Media*, Oeiras, Celta Editora, pp. i-iv.

CARDOSO, Gustavo (2000), "Os Jogos Multimédia como Meta-Sistema de Entretenimento", Observatório-Revista do Observatório da Comunicação, n°1, May 2000.

CARDOSO, Gustavo, CARRILHO, Maria, ESPANHA, Rita (2002), Novos Média, Novas Políticas? Debater a Sociedade de Informação, Oeiras, Celta.

CARDOSO, Gustavo, NASCIMENTO, Susana (2002) "*Online/Offline*: can you tell the difference? Portuguese views on Internet *Media*ted Communication" in Comunicazioni sociali – Rivista di *media*, spettacolo e studi culturali, Anno XXIV Nuova serie, n.1 Gennaio-Aprile 2002, Departamento de Comunicação da Università Cattolica Del Sacro Cuore, Milão.

CARDOSO, G. e Telo, D. (2003) Análise dos Telejornais da RTP1 em Silveira, Joel, Estudo para a AACS, não publicado.

CARDOSO, Gustavo, (2004), Trends and contradictions in the broadcasting System, From Interactive to Networked Television em Fausto Colombo (ed), Tv and Interactivity in Europe. Mythologies, theoretical perspectives, real experiences, Vita e Pensiero, Milano.

CARDOSO, Gustavo, FIRMINO DA COSTA, António (2004), A Sociedade Rede em Portugal, Lisboa, CIES/ISCTE.

CARDOSO, Gustavo, NETO, Pedro (2003b), "O Movimento por Timor, *Mass media* e Prostestos *Online*" in REBELO, José, Novas Formas de Mobilização Popular, Porto, Campo das Letras.

CAROLA, Sílvia (2002) BIG BROTHER – A Vigilância Vista de Dentro, Dissertação de Licenciatura, Departamento de Sociologia, Lisboa, ISCTE.

CARPINI, Michael X. Delli WILLIAMS, Bruce A. (2001) "Let Us Infotain You: Politics in the New *Media*" in BENNETT, W. Lance, ENTMAN, Robert M. (2001) *Media*ted Politics – Communication in the Future of Democracy. Cambridge: Cambridge University Press.

CASETI, Francesco, ODIN, Roger, «De la paléo à la néo-télévision», Communications, n° 51, Paris,1990, Seuil.

CASTANHEIRA, José Pedro (2003) Jornalismo *Online*: Problemas Técnicos e Metodológicos (estudo de um caso: os comentários dos leitores às notícias sobre a Fundação Jorge Álvares no Expresso *Online*, em 2000) , Dissertação da Pós-Graduação em Jornalismo do ISCTE/ESCS, Lisboa, ISCTE.

CASTELLS, Manuel (1997), "Manuel Castells on the Global Economy And the Technology Elite ",Available *Online* HTTP: http://www.transformaties.org/castells/bibliotheek/interviewupside.htm .

CASTELLS, Manuel (1998), "Information Technology, Globalization and Social Development", Conference Paper for the UNRISD Conference on Information Technologies and Social Development, Geneva, 22-24 June 1998, Available *online* HTTP: http://www.unrisd.org/infotech/conferen/castelp1.htm .

CASTELLS, M., (2000), Internet y la Sociedad Red, Available *Online* HTTP: <http://www.uoc.es/web/esp/articles/castells/castellsmain.html > (28 Feb 2002).

CASTELLS, Manuel (2000a) "Grassrooting the space of flows" in WHEELER, James, Aoyama, Yuko, Warf, Barney (eds.) Cities in the Telecommunications Age – The Fracturing of Geographies. London and New York: Routledge.

CASTELLS, Manuel, (January 2000b), Revolt Against Violence, UNESCO Courier.

CASTELLS, Manuel (2001)"Conversación con Manuel Castells", Quaderns n° 11, El pluralismo informativo en los medios audiovisuales, Available *Online* HTTP: < http://www.audiovisualcat.net/publicaciones/Q11castmc.pdf > (January 2004).

CASTELLS, Manuel (2002), A Sociedade em Rede. A Era da Informação. Economia, Sociedade e Cultura, Volume I, Lisboa, Fundação Calouste Gulbenkian.

CASTELLS, Manuel (2003b), La Societat Xarxa a Catalunya, Barcelona, Editorial UOC.

CASTELLS, Manuel (2003), O Poder da Identidade. A Era da Informação. Economia, Sociedade e Cultura, Volume II, Lisboa, Fundação Calouste Gulbenkian.

CASTELLS, Manuel (2004), O Fim de Milénio. A Era da Informação. Economia, Sociedade e Cultura, Volume III, Lisboa, Fundação Calouste Gulbenkian.

CASTELLS, Manuel (2004b), A Galáxia Internet, Lisboa Fundação Calouste Gulbenkian.

CASTELLS, Manuel e Ince, Martin (2004c) Conversas com Manuel Castells, Porto, Campo das Letras.

CATOLFI, Antonio (2002), "Funzioni Sociali del Giornale Radio" in MENDUNI, Enrico (2002), La Radio. Percorsi e Territori di un Medium Mobile e Interattivo, Bologna, Baskerville.

CENTER FOR PRISON STUDIES KINGS COLLEDGE, Available *Online* HTTP: http://www.kcl.ac.uk/depsta/rel/icps/worldbrief/highest_to_lowest_rates.php

CHADWICK, Andrew (2001) "The Electronic Face of Government in the Internet Age – Borrowing from Murray Edelman" in Information, Communication & Society 4:3, pp. 435-457. Available *Online* HTTP: <http://www.rhul.ac.uk/sociopolitical-science/About-Us/chadwick_electronic_face_of_government.pdf> (May 2002).

CHAMPAGNE, Patrick (1996), L'influence de la communication visuelle dans le travail de l'information écrite, et la construction télévisuelle de l'opinion. Available *Online* HTTP: http://www.homme-moderne.org/societe/socio/champagn/influen.html .

CHAMPAGNE, Patrick (2000), "Os Média, as Sondagens de Opinião e a Democracia" in Os Cidadãos e a Sociedade de Informação, Lisboa, Imprensa Nacional Casa da Moeda.

CHANDLER, Daniel (1998) "Imagining Futures, Dramatizing Fears: the Portrayal of Technology in Literature and Film", Available *Online* HTTP: < http://www.aber.ac.uk/~dgc/sf.html > (July 1999).

CHEONG Angus (2004) A Comparison of Survey results of 2001 and 2003 in Macao WORLD INTERNET PROJECT SURVEY (2004), Available *Online* HTTP: http://www.soc.toyo.ac.jp/~mikami/wip/wip_meeting/day2day3.html

CHETA, Rita (2004), Disembodied Citizenship? Re-@ccessing Disabled People's Voices in Portugal in Win van de Donk, Brian Loader, Paul Nixon, and Dieter Rucht, eds., Cyberprotest: New *Media*, Citizens, and Social Movements, London, Routledge.

CHEUNG, Charles. "A Home on the Web: Presentations of Self on Personal Homepages." Ch.4, Pgs.43-51. In David Gauntlett's, Web. Studies: Rewiring *Media* Studies for the Digital Age. Published by Arnold, in Great Britian in 2000.

CHYI, Hsiang Iris, LASORSA, Dominic L. (2002), An Explorative Study on the Market Relation Between *Online* and Print Newspapers, The Journal of *Media* Economics, 15 (2), 91-106.

CINEMA, TV AND RADIO IN THE EU STATISTICS ON AUDIOVISUAL SERVICES (Data 1980-2002) Luxembourg: Office for Official Publications of the European Communities, 2003.

CINTRA TORRES, Eduardo (2002), Reality Shows, Ritos de Passagem da Sociedade do Espectáculo, Coimbra, Minerva.

CINTRA TORRES, Eduardo (1998), Ler Televisão, Oeiras, Celta.

COCOA, César, DÍEZHANDINO, M.ª Pilar (1990), Periodismo Económico, Editorial Paraninfo, Madrid.

COHEN, R., RAI, S. (eds) (2000), Global Social Movements, Athlone Press

COLOMBO, Fausto (1993) Le nuove tecnologie della comunicazione. Milano: Bompiani.

COLOMBO, Fausto (1995), "Dentro l'ordine vive l'anarchia", Telèma nº 1 – Politica, Telematica, Democrazia, Available *Online* HTTP:<http://baldo.fub.it/telema/TELEMA1/Colomb1.html> (4 June 1999).

COLOMBO, Fausto (1995), "Il Videogioco come Mezzo di Comunicazione", Available *Online* HTTP:<http://www.telecomitalia.
it/cstudi/chieric6.htm > (May 1999).

COLOMBO, Fausto (1996), "La Forma Visiva del Testo", Available *Online*
HTTP:<http://www.*media*mente.rai.it/home/bibliote/intervis/c/
colo_f02.htm > (May 1999).

COLOMBO, Fausto (1996a), "Le Molteplici Dimensioni del Mondo delle
Reti", Available *Online* HTTP:<http://www.*media*mente.rai.it/
home/bibliote/intervis/c/colomb_f.htm > (May 1999).

COLOMBO, Fausto (1997), "The Evolution of the *Media* World", Available *Online* HTTP :< http://www.*media*mente.rai.it/home/bibli-
ote/intervis/c/colo_f03.htm

COLOMBO, Fausto (1999), "I *Media* alla Svolta del Duemila", Available
Online HTTP:<http://labcom.soc.uniroma1.it/forumrai/colom-
bo.htm >, (May 1999).

COLOMBO, Fausto (2000), "A Internet é um Meta*media*", Jornal Público,
30 January 2000.

COLOMBO, Fausto (2000a), "Alcune Questioni di Teoria Dell' Industria
Culturale", Available *Online* HTTP:<http://cepad.unicatt.it/for-
mazione/comsoc1/Cap1/1_06.asp >, (October 2000).

COLOMBO, Fausto (2000b), "Le Nuove Tecnologie Digitali e l'impacto
Culturale: Un Modello Descrittivo", Paper apresentado no
Mestrado de Comunicação, Cultura e Tecnologias de Infor-
mação, Departamento de Sociologia, Lisboa, ISCTE.

COLOMBO, Fausto (2000c), "Uma Memória Para a Tecnologia", Sociologia Problemas e Práticas, n°32, Lisboa, CIES/ISCTE, 2000.

COLOMBO Fausto, Farinotti Luisella, Pasquali Francesca (2001), I mar-
gini della cultura. *Media* e innovazione Milano: Franco Angeli.

COLOMBO, Fausto (2002),"La Radio Fuori dalla Radio", in MENDUNI,
Enrico (2002), La Radio. Percorsi e Territori di un Medium Mobile e Interattivo, Bologna, Baskerville.

COLOMBO, Fausto (2003), Introduzione Allo Studio Dei *Media*, Roma,
Carocci.

COLOMBO, Fausto (2003a), Users Practices of Web Navigation (or does
a Web Generation Really Exists?), Paper Presented at the "Towards New *Media* Paradigms: Content, Producers, Organisations and Audiences Conference" of the COST A20 Programme,
University of Navarra, Pamplona; Sapin,27-28 June 2003.

COLOMBO, Fausto, "La Comunicazione Sintetica", in COLOMBO, Fausto, BETTETINI, Gianfranco (1994), Le Nuove Tecnologie Della Comunicazione, Milano, Bompiani.

COLOMBO, Fausto, BELLAVITA, Andrea (2002a), "The Digital Satellite Broadcasting System in Italy: Between Mix and Hybridism.", The Public Vol.9 (2002), 4, 75-82.

COOKE, Lynne, "A Visual Convergence of Print, Television and the Internet", New Media & Society, vol7 (1): pp. 22-46, 2005.

COMISSÃO DE REFLEXÃO SOBRE O FUTURO DA TELEVISÃO EM PORTUGAL, Relatório final da comissão de reflexão sobre o futuro da televisão em Portugal, Presidência do Conselho de Ministros, Lisboa, October 1996.

CONNERTON, Paul (1993), Como as Sociedades Recordam, Oeiras, Celta Editora.

CORCORAN, Farrel (2004), Strong and Weak versions of interactive Television in Fausto Colombo (Ed), TV and Interactivity in Europe. Mythologies, theoretical perspectives, real experiences, Vita e Pensiero, Milano.

CORREIA, F.; The Portuguese media landscape, Available Online HTTP : http://www.ejc.nl/jr/emland/portugal.html

CORREIA, Fernando, "Concentração à Portuguesa", Le Monde Diplomatique, Edição Portuguesa, November 1999.

CORREIA, Fernando, "Novos Desafios, Problemas Novos", JJ-Jornalismo e Jornalistas, n°3, July/September 2000.

COUTINHO, João e Dipnísio, Pedro (2003) Cordão Humano por Timor, in Rebelo, José, (2003) Novas Formas de Mobilização Popular, Porto, Campo das Letra

CRISELL, A. 1994: Understanding Radio. London and New York: Routledge.

CROOK, S., PAKULSKI, J., WATERS, M. (1992), Postmodernization – change in advanced societies, London, Sage Publications

CUNHA, Carlos, MARTÍN, Irene, NEWELL, Jim, RAMIRO, Luis (2002) "Slow Adaptation and the Digital Divide: South European Party Systems and New ICTs", in GIBSON, Rachel, NIXON, Paul, WARD, Stephen (eds.) Net Gain? Political Parties and the Impact of New Information Communication Technologies. London: Routledge (forthcoming).

DAHL, Robert (1986) Dilemmas of Pluralist Democracy. New Haven: Yale University Press.

DAHL, Robert (1991) Democracy and Its Critics. New Haven: Yale University Press.

DAHL, Robert (1998) On Democracy. New Haven: Yale University Press.

DAHLBERG, Lincoln (2001) "Computer-*Mediated* Communication and the Public Sphere: A Critical Analysis", Journal of Computer-*Mediated* Communication <http://www.ascusc.org/jcmc/vol7/issue1/dahlberg.html> (December 2002)

DAHLBERG, Lincoln (2002), "Democracy via Cyberspace ",New *Media* & Society, Volume 3, n°2 pp. 157-179, 2002.

DAHLGREN, P., La Democracia Electrónica, Internet Y La Evolución Del Periodismo. Cómo Utilizar El Espacio Disponible, 2002, En Vidal Beneyto, J., La Ventana Global, Ed. Taurus, Madrid.

DAHLGREN, Peter (1995) Television and the Public Sphere: Citizenship, Democracy and the *Media*. London: Sage.

DAHLGREN, Peter (2001) "The Public Sphere and the Net: Structure, Space, and Communication" in BENNETT, W. Lance, ENTMAN, Robert M. (2001) *Mediated* Politics – Communication in the Future of Democracy. Cambridge: Cambridge University Press.

DAHLGREN, Peter, SPARKS, Colin (1992) (eds.) Journalism and Popular Culture. London: Sage.

DAHLGREN, Peter, SPARKS, Colin (1993) (eds.) Communication and Citizenship: Journalism and the Public Sphere. London: Routledge.

DAYAN, Daniel and Katz, Elihu (1992), *Media* Events. The Live Broadcasting of History, Harvard University Press.

DEBORD, Guy. La societé du spectacle. Paris: Éd. Gérard Lebovici, 1989.

DEUZE, M. (2004), A Internet e os diferentes tipos de jornalismo *Online*: Teoria, Pesquisa e Estratégias de Produção *Online* de Notícias, in Paquete de Oliveira, J.M.; Cardoso, Gustavo, et al. Comunicação, Cultura e Tecnologias de Informação, Lisboa Quimera.

DEUZE, M., (2001), Understanding the Impact of the Internet: On New *Media* Professionalism, Mindsets and Buzzwords, <http://www.ejournalism.au.com/ejournalist/deuze.pdf> , (January 2002).

DEUZE, Mark, (2003), «*Online* Journalism: Modelling the First Generation of News *Media* on the World Wide Web», in First Monday, volume 6, number 10, Available Online HTTP : www.firstmonday.dk/issues/issue6_10/deuze/, (8 December 2003).

DIÁRIO DE NOTÍCIAS (2004), Envio de emails para o Estado, 5 February 2004 .

DIÁRIO DE NOTÍCIAS, Pais pouco informados sobre Internet, Diário de Notícias, 12 April 2004.

DICK, Philip K :Blade Runner–Do Androids Dream of Electric Sheep–Perigo Iminente Portugal: Publicações Europa America, 1982.

DIEZ, Fatima Garcia (2004), El futuro de la tecnologia electoral en América Latina: soluciones técnicas y problemas políticos, apresentação pública no ISCTE.

DJIK, Jan Van (1999), The Network Society", London, Sage.

DJIK, Jan Van, "The One Dimensional Network Society of Manuel Castells, New *Media* & Society, Vol (1):127-138.

DIJK, Jan (eds.) (2000) Digital Democracy. Issues of Theory and Practice. London: Sage.

DOWNING, J. D.(ed.) (2000), Radical *Media* – rebellious communication and social movements, Sage Publications

DRUCKER, Peter F. (1999), Sociedade pós-capitalista. São Paulo, Pioneira, Publifolha.

DUBE, J.; Writing news *online*, citado em Resende, I.; Jornalismo económico: formato digital vs formato tradicional; Dissertação de Pós-Graduação

DUCOURANT, Hélène (1999), L'approche Bourdieusienne des Médias et ses Limites, Paper apresentado na Licenciatura de Sociologia do ISCTE, Lisboa.

DUTTON, William H. (2000) "Os cidadãos em rede e a democracia electrónica", Presidência da República, Os Cidadãos e a Sociedade de Informação. Conferência promovida pelo Presidente da República, 9 and 10 December 1999, Lisboa, INCM.

ECO, Umberto (1977), O signo. Lisboa: Presença.

ECO, Umberto (1985) La guerre du faux, Paris, Grasset.

ECO, Umberto (1990), Os limites da Interpretação, Lisboa, Difel,.

ECO, Umberto (1991), Apocalípticos e Integrados, Lisboa, Difel.

ECO, Umberto (1991a), Semiótica e Filosofia da linguagem, Lisboa, Difel.

ECO, Umberto (1995), "El Mundo Según ECO", Available *Online* HTTP:<http://www.telecable.es/personales/deleon/finisa/mundoeco.htm > (April 2000).

ECO, Umberto (1995a), "L'Informazione sugli specchi", Available *Online* HTTP: <http://www.nettuno.it/fiera/ifg/document/p14a.htm > (October 1999).

ECO, Umberto (1995b), "The Nomenclature and Electronic Democracy", Available *Online* HTTP: <http://www.*media*mente.rai.it/*media*mentetv/learning/ed_multi*media*le/english/bibliote/intervis/e/eco.htm > (April 1999).

ECO, Umberto (1996), " Da Internet a Gutemberg", Available *Online* HTTP:<http://www.hf.ntnu.no/anv/Finnbo/tekster/Eco/Internet.htm >,(April 2000).

ECO, Umberto (1996b), "Can Communication Be Taught?" Available *Online* HTTP:<http://www.tinet.ch/nuovacritica/unicommunications/oxford/e-eco1.htm > (October 2000).

ECO, Umberto (1996c), "Le Notizie Sonno Troppe Imparate a Decimarle, Subito.", Available *Online* HTTP: <http://baldo.fub.it/telema/TELEMA4/Eco4.html >(May 1999).

ECO, Umberto (1997), "Afterword", Available *Online* HTTP:<http://www.stanford.edu/dept/HPS/HistoryWired/Eco/EcoAfterword.html > (April 2000).

ECO, Umberto (1997a), "University and *Mass media*", Available *Online* HTTP: < http://www.uni-weimar.de/medien/archiv/ws9899/eco/text3.html > (January 2004).

ECO, Umberto (1997b), *Sobre a Imprensa*, Cinco Escritos Morais, Algés, Difel.

ECO, Umberto (2000), "Internet, una Rete Piena di Buchi", <http://quotidiano.monrif.net/art/2000/04/18/836575 > (August 2001).

ECO, Umberto (2000a), Quale Privacy, Paper Apresentado na Conferência Internacional sobre Privacidade em Veneza, 28 September de 2000.

ECO, Umberto (2000b), "Afterword" <http://www.stanford.edu/dept/HPS/HistoryWired/Eco/EcoAfterword.html > (February 1999).

ECO, Umberto (2000c), "L'ipnosi Radiofonica. O dell'Incerto Avvenire di un Mezzo Magico" < http://www.espressoedit.ktaweb.it/cgi-bin/spd-gettext.sh?ft_cid=44556 >

ECO, Umberto (2001), "Il Medium Precede Il Messaggio" <http://www.espresso*online*.kataweb.it/ESW_articolo/0,2393,12424,00.html > (August 2001).

ECO, Umberto (2003), Vegetal and Mineral Memory: the Future of Books, Al-Ahram Weekly, Issue nº665, 20-26 November 2003, Available *Online* HTTP: <http://weekly.ahram.org.eg/2003/665/bo3. htm

ECO, Umberto (2004), La Misteriosa Fiamma della Regina Loana, Milão, Bompiani.

ECO, Umberto (2004b), Il pubblico fa male alla televisione?, Available *Online* HTTP: http://www.espress*online*.it/eol/free/jsp/detail. jsp?m1s=o&m2s=null&idContent=479137&idCategory=4789

ECONOMIA PURA, Março 2004, nº63, Lisboa, pp.28.

EFF-ELECTRONIC FRONTIER FOUNDATION (2004), Internet Censorship Legislation & Regulation Available *Online* HTTP: http:// www.eff.org/Censorship/Internet_censorship_bills/ .

ELLIS, ERIC (1999), A 'Matt Drudge' You Can Respect TIME ASIA, September 7, 1999.

ESS SURVEY (2003), Available *Online* HTTP: http://ess.nsd.uib.no/

ENTMAN, Robert M., BENNETT, W. Lance (2001) "Communication in the Future of Democracy: A Conclusion" in BENNETT, W. Lance, ENTMAN, Robert M. (2001) *Media*ted Politics – Communication in the Future of Democracy. Cambridge: Cambridge University Press.

ETAN, Santa Cruz Massacre, Available *Online*. HTTP: http://etan.org/ timor/SntaCRUZ.htm (28 Feb 2002).

EUROBAROMETER 60, Public Opinion in the European Union, October- November 2003.

EUROBAROMETER 55.2 (2001), Available *Online* HTTP : http://europa. eu.int/comm/public_opinion/archives/eb/eb55/eb55_en.pdf

EUROBAROMETER 56 (2001) La participation des européens aux activités culturelles, Available *Online* HTTP :http://europa.eu.int/ comm/public_opinion/archives/ebs/ebs_158_complet_fr.pdf

EUROBAROMETER 50.1 (1998), Como se Vêem a Si Próprios — Um espelho da realidade, Sondagens de opinião, Available *Online* HTTP : http://europa.eu.int/comm/publications/booklets/eu_documentation/05/txt_pt.pdf .

EUROPEAN UNION (2000), European Report On The Quality Of School Education – Sixteen Quality Indicators, Available *Online* HTTP : http://europa.eu.int/comm/education/policies/educ/indic/rapinen. pdf .

FAIR (2004) "NY Times Responds to FAIR on Fallujah Killings" http:// www.fair.org/activism/times-fallujah-update.html

FAIR (1999) "Alert: Networks Need to be Sceptical of Both Sides" <http://www.fair.org/activism/korisa.html > (May 1999).

FENTRESS, James e Wickham Chris (1994), Memória Social: Novas Perspectivas Sobre O Passado. Lisboa. Editorial Teorema.

FERGUSON, M. (1990) "Electronic *media* and the redefining of time and space" in FERGUSON, M. (ed.) Public Communication, The New Imperatives. London/Newbury Park: Sage.

FITZMAIER et al. 2004, The Austrian Parliament and the use of ICT's in Hoff, Coleman, Fitzmaier e Cardoso, Use of ICT's by Members of Parliament, Information Polity, Special Issue, Volume 9, Numbers 1,2, 2004, The Netherlands, IOS Press.

FLEISCHNER, Edoardo, SOMALVICO, Bruno (2002), La TV Diventa Digitale. Scenari per una Difficile Transizione, Milano, FrancoAngeli.

FONDELLI, Barbara (2002), "I Siti Radiofonici:Indagine sulla Presenza Ondine della Radiofonia Italiana" in MENDUNI, Enrico (2002), La Radio. Percorsi e Territori di un medium mobile e interattivo, Bologna, Baskerville.

FORD, T., Gil, G. (2000), "Radical Internet use", DOWNING, J. D.(ed.) (2000), Radical *Media* – rebellious communication and social movements, London, Sage Publications.

FRAIN, Maritheresa (1997) "The Right in Portugal: the PSD and CDS/PP" in BRUNEAU, Thomas (ed.) (1997) Political Parties and Democracy in Portugal: Organizations, Elections and Public Opinion. Boulder, CO: Westview Press, pp. 77-111.

FREIRE, André (2001a) (coord.) Recrutamento Parlamentar – Os Deputados Portugueses da Constituinte à VIII Legislatura, STAPE.

FREIRE, André (2001b) Mudança eleitoral em Portugal: clivagens, economia e voto em eleições legislativas, 1983-1999. Oeiras: Celta.

FREIRE, André (2001c) Modelos do comportamento eleitoral: uma breve introdução crítica. Oeiras: Celta.

FREIRE, André et al (2002) O parlamento português: uma reforma necessária. Lisboa: Imprensa de Ciências Sociais (ICS).

FREIRE, André, BAUM, Michael (2002) "Clivagens, economia e voto em Portugal, 1999: uma análise das eleições parlamentares com dados agregados" in Sociologia Problemas e Prácticas, nº 37, pp. 115-140.

FREIRE, André, LOPES, Fernando Farelo (2002), Partidos políticos e sistemas eleitorais: uma introdução. Oeiras: Celta.

FREIRE, André, MAGALHÃES, Pedro (2002) A Abstenção Eleitoral em Portugal. Lisboa: Instituto de Ciências Sociais (ICS).

FRITH, Simon, Andrew Goodwin & Lawrence Grossberg: (1993), Sound & Vision. The music-video reader, London, Routledge.

FULLER, Steve (1999), Confronting the Social Character of Computers: the Challenges for Social Scientists in MILLSOM, Henry, IT in the Social Sciences, Oxford, Blackwell Publishers.

GALIMBERTI, Umberto, 1999 – Psiche e techne. L'uomo nell'età della tecnica, Feltrinelli, Milano.

GALLAND, Blaise, CHAPPELET, Jean-Loup (2001) "E-Parlement – L'appropriation de l'Internet par les parlementaires fédéraux", Cahier de l' Institute de Hautes Études en Administration Publique (IDHEAP).

GALPERIN, Hernan (2004) New Television, Old Politics: The Transition to Digital TV in the United States and Britain, Cambridge, Cambridge University Press.

GARNER, R. (1996), Contemporary movements and ideologies, New York, McGraw-Hill

GARNHAM, Nicholas (1998), "What are the Remaining Limitations of the Great Information Network?", Available *Online* HTTP: <http://www.*media*mente.rai.it/home/bibliote/biografi/g/garnham.htm > (April 1999).

GARNHAM, Nicholas (1999), "Barriers to Convergence", in DUTTON, William H., Society on the Line, Oxford, Oxford University Press.

GIBBINS, J., Reimer, B. (1999), The politics of Postmodernity, London, Sage Publications

GIBBINS, J., Reimer, B. (1999), The politics of Postmodernity, London, Sage Publications

GIBSON, R., NEWELL, J., WARD, S. (2000) "New Parties, New *Media*: Italian Party Politics and the Internet", South European Society and Politics, Vol. 5, no. 1, (Summer 2000), pp.123-42.

GIBSON, Rachel e Ward, Stephen J. (2003), The Internet and Representative Democracy. London: Routledge.

GIBSON, Rachel, WARD, Stephen (2000) "Perfect Information, Perfect Democracy, Perfect Competition: Politics and the Impact of New ICTs" in GIBSON, Rachel, WARD, Stephen (eds.) (2000)

Reinvigorating Democracy? British Politics and the Internet. Ashgate: Aldershot.

GIBSON, William (1996), I don't even have a modem, Available *Online* HTTP: http://www.josefsson.net/gibson/

GIDDENS, Anthony (1997), Modernidade e Identidade Pessoal, Celta Editores, Oeiras.

GIDDENS, Anthony (1997a), "Beyond Left and Right" Available *Online* HTTP: <http://www.heise.de/tp/english/special/eco/6205/1.html > (December 1998).

GIDDENS, Anthony (1998), As Consequências da Modernidade, Oeiras, Celta.

GIDDENS, Anthony (1999), "DNW Interview met Anthony Giddens", Available *Online* HTTP: <http://www.vpro.nl/programma/dnw/download/Interview_Giddens.shtml > (January 2002).

GIDDENS, Anthony, HUTTON, Will (2000) On the edge: living with global capitalism. London: Vintage.

GIDDENS, Anthony, Modernidade e identidade social, Lisboa, Celta, 1997.

GLOBAL REACH, Portuguese *Online*, Available *Online* HTTP: http://glreach.com/gbc/pt/portuguese.php3.

GNASSO, Stefano (2003) in Fausto Colombo, Piermarco Aroldi (a cura di) Le età della Tv Indagine su quattro generazioni di spettatori italiani. Milano, Vita e Pensiero.

GODOY Sergio (2004) WIP Chile 2004: Main Results WORLD INTERNET PROJECT SURVEY (2004), Available *Online* HTTP: http://www.soc.toyo.ac.jp/~mikami/wip/wip_meeting/day2day3.html

GOMES, Carmo (2003) "Literexclusão na Vida Quotidiana", Sociologia, Problemas e Práticas, n°41, 2003, pp.63-92.

GOMES, Carmo Maria do, ÁVILA, Patrícia, SEBASTIÃO, João, FIRMINO DA COSTA, António

(2001), Novas Análises dos Níveis de Literacia em Portugal: Comparações Diacrónicas e Internacionais, Actas do IV Congresso de Sociologia, APS.

GOMEZ, Ricardo (2000) "The Hall of Mirrors: The Internet in Latin America", Current History, February 2000, Vol. 99, No. 634.

GONÇALVES, Maria Eduarda (2000) "Democracia e Cidadania na Sociedade da Informação", Presidência da República, Os Cidadãos e a Sociedade de Informação. Conferência promovida pelo Presidente da República, 9 and 10 December 1999, Lisboa, INCM.

GRAÇA, Susana da Nóbrega (2002) BIG BROTHER – Audiências e Recepção, Projecto de Tese no Mestrado de Comunicação, Cultura e Tecnologias de Informação, Departamento de Sociologia, Lisboa, ISCTE.

GRAHAM, Andrew (1996), Public Policy and the Information Superhighway: The Case of the UK, in Kahin, B., Wilson, E., National Information Infrastructure Initiatives: Vision and Policy Design (Publication of the Harvard Information Infrastructure Project), Cambridge MA, MIT Press.

GRANADO, A. (2002); Os *media* portugueses na Internet, Available *Online* HTTP :http://ciberjornalismo.com/*media*portugueses.htm .

GRANADO, ANTÓNIO (2003), "Um Fenómeno com Seis Anos", Jornal Público 23 June 2003.

GRUPO DE TRABALHO SOBRE O SERVIÇO PÙBLICO DE TELEVISÃO (2002), Relatório sobre o ServiçPúblico de Televisão, PCM, Portugal.

HABERMAS, Jurgen (1984) Mudança estrutural da esfera pública: investigações quanto a uma categoria da sociedade burguesa. Rio de Janeiro: Tempo Brasileiro.

HABERMAS, Jurgen (1986), The Theory of Communicative Action: Reason and the Rationalization of Society Vol 1, Londres, Polity Press.

HACKER, Kenneth L., VAN DIJK, Jan (eds.) (2000) Digital Democracy. Issues of Theory and Practice. London: Sage.

HAGEN, Martin (1997), "A Typology of Electronic Democracy", Available *Online* <http://www.uni-giessen.de/fb03/vinci/labore/netz/hag_en.htm#1> (June 2002)

HAGEN, Martin (2000) "Digital Democracy and Political Systems" in HACKER, Kenneth L., VAN

HAGUE, Barry N., LOADER, Brian D. (1999) "Digital Democracy: an introduction" in HAGUE, Barry N., LOADER, Brian D. (eds.) (1999) Digital Democracy: Discourse and Decision Making in the Information Age. London and New York: Routledge.

HALL, Stuart, Representation: Cultural representations and signifying practices Sage Publications 1997

HAMELINK, Cees J. (1999), ICT's and Social Development. The Global Policy Context, UNRISD, Geneva, Suíça.

HAMELINK, Cees J. (2001), The Ethics of Cyberspace, London, Sage.

HAMELINK, Cees J. (2004), in Comunicação, Cultura e Tecnologias da Informação, Lisboa, Quimera.

HARTLEY, John (2004), Comunicação, Estudos Culturais e Media – conceitos-chave, Lisboa, Quimera.

HARTMANN, Maren (2003), The Web Generation? The (De)construction of Users, Morals and Consumption, The European Media and Technology in Everyday Life Network, 2000-2003.

hEilidhe, Sorcha Ni (2000), Political Economy of the Search Engine, Available Online HTTP: http://www.nua.ie/surveys/analysis/ weekly_editorial/archives/1999/issue1no67.html .

HEINONEN, Ari (1999), Journalism in the Age of the Net. Changing Society, Changing Profession, Acta Universitatis Tamperensis 685, Tampere, Tampere University Press.

HELD, David (1987) Models of Democracy. Cambridge: Polity Press.

HELD, David, McGREW, Anthony (eds.) (2000) The global transformations reader: an introduction to the globalization debate. Cambridge: Polity Press.

HILL, Kevin A., HUGHES, John E. (1998) Cyberpolitics: Citizen Activism in the Age of the Internet. Lanham, MD: Rowman & Littlefield.

HIMANEN, Pekka, Castells Manuel (2001a), The Information Society and the Welfare State: the Finnish Model, Oxford, Oxford University Press

HIMANEN, Pekka, CASTELLS, Manuel, TORNVALDS, Linus (2001b), The Hacker Ethic and the Spirit of the Information Age, London, Secker and Warburg.

HOCK, Randolph (2001), Web Search Engines, New Jersey, Cyberage Books.

HOFF, Coleman, Fitzmaier e Cardoso, Use of ICT's by Members of Parliament, Information Polity, Special Issue, Volume 9, Numbers 1,2, 2004, The Netherlands, IOS Press.

HOFF, Jens (2003), "MPs in the Network Society: agenda-setters or puppets on a string?" i Ari Salminen (red.): Governing Networks. EGPA Yearbook. IOS Press: Amsterdam , 2003, p. 227-239.

HOFF, Jens, HORROCKS, Ivan, TOPS, Pieter (2000) "Introduction: New technology and the 'crisis' of democracy" in HOFF, Jens, HORROCKS, Ivan, TOPS, Pieter (2000) (eds.) Democratic Governance and New Technology – Technologically *media*ted innovations in political practice in Western Europe. London and New York: Routledge/ ECPR Studies in European Political Science.

HOFF, Jens, HORROCKS, Ivan, TOPS, Pieter (2000) "Reflections on the models of democracy: cyberdemocracy?" in HOFF, Jens, HORROCKS, Ivan, TOPS, Pieter (2000) (eds.) Democratic Governance and New Technology – Technologically *media*ted innovations in political practice in Western Europe. London and New York: Routledge/ ECPR Studies in European Political Science.

HORTA, Ana Maria (2001), «Imaginário e imagens mediáticas: o caso de Macau», Comunicação apresentação no congresso da SOP-COM.

HORTON, Donald and R. Richard Wohl (1956): 'Mass Communication and Para-social Interaction: Observations on Intimacy at a Distance', Psychiatry 19: 215-29, Available *Online* HTTP: http://www.aber.ac.uk/*media*/Modules/TF33120/horton_and_wohl_1956.html.

HORVATH, John (1999), « Internet Ban in Yugoslavia ? », Telepolis, Available *Online* HTTP: <http://www.heise.de/tp/english/inhalt/co/2809/1.html > (May 1999).

IDATE (2004), Jeux Vídeo, Available *Online* HTTP: http://www.idate.fr/fr/multi/jvi/jeux_video.pdf .

IDC (2003), Worldwide Videogame Hardware and Software Forecast and Analysis, 2003-2007: Midlife Changes, November 26, 2003.

INGLEHART, Ronald e Catterberg Gabriela (2001), Trends in Political Action: The Developmental Trend and the Post-Honeymoon Decline, Available *Online* HTTP: http://www.worldvaluessurvey.org/Upload/5_Partapsa.pdf

INE (2004), População estrangeira em Portugal modera crescimento, Available *Online* HTTP: http://alea-estp.ine.pt/html/actual/html/act39.html

INTERNET SYSTEMS CONSORTIUM, Inc. (ISC) Available *Online* HTTP: http://www.isc.org/ds/WWW-200101/index.html

IP NETWORK GmbH, European TV Key Facts, January 2004.

IRVINE, Martin (1999), Technology, Ideology, and Social History, Available *Online* HTTP:http://cct.georgetown.edu/curriculum/505-98/techideology.html

IRVINE, Martin, (1999) "Technoculture from Frankenstein to Cyberpunk" Available *Online* HTTP:<http://www.georgetown.edu/irvinemj/ technoculture/ > (July 1999).

ITU (2003), Mobile cellular, subscribers per 100 people, International Telecommunications Union 2003, Available *Online* HTTP: http://www.itu.int/ITU-D/ict/statistics/at_glance/cellular03. pdf .

JAMESON, Frederic (1991), Postmodernism, or, The Cultural Logic of Late Capitalism, Durham, NC: Duke University Press.

KAITATZI-WHITLOCK, Sophia (2004), Banking on Interactivity em Fausto Colombo (ed), Tv and Interactivity in Europe. Mythologies, theoretical perspectives, real experiences, Vita e Pensiero, Milano.

KAMERER, D., Bressers, B. (1998); *Online* newspapers: a trend study of news content and technical features, AEJMC December, Available *Online* HTTP :http://list.msu.edu/cgi-bin/wa?A2=ind9812a &L=aejmc&F=&S=&P=6630 .

KARVONEN, Erkki (2001), "Are we living in the Information Society or in the Knowledge Society?" in Karvonnen, Erkki, Informational Societies, Tampere, Tampere University Press.

KASVIO, Anti (2001), "The emergence of "Information Society" as a Major Social Scientific Research Programme", in Karvonnen, Erkki, Informational Societies, Tampere, Tampere University Press.

KATZ, Elihu, "On Conceptualizing *Media* Effects," Studies in Communications 1: 1980.

KECK, E. (2000), The impact of the Internet on journalism: the newspaper metaphor, Available *Online* HTTP : http://uts.cc.utexas. edu/~keckem/research.html .

KELLNER, Douglas (1998), "Mapping the Present from the Future. From Braudillard to Cyberpunk" in *Media* and Culture, London, Routledge.

KELLNER, Douglas (2002), "New *Media* and New Literacies: Reconstructing Education for the New Millenium", in LIVINGSTONE, Sonia and LIEVROUW, Leah, The Handbook of New *Media*, London, Sage.

KELLNER, Douglas (2003), Contemporary Youth and the Postmodern Adventure, Available *Online* HTTP: http://utminers.utep.edu/ best/papers/phiecosoc/postmodernyouth.htm

KELLNER, Douglas Mackay (1989), Critical theory and society : a reader, New York : Routledge.

KELLNER, Douglas, (1995) *Media* Culture, Mapping the Present from the Future, Routledge, London.

KESHVANI, Nisar (2000) " Straits Times Interactive and the Age *Online*: Trends in the *Online* Newsroom", Paper Presented at the Australian and New Zealand Communication Association Conference 2000.

KIM, Pyungho, SAWHNEY, Harmeet, A Machine-Like New Medium –Theoretical Examination of Interactive TV, *Media*, Culture & Society vol.24 (2002): 217-233.

KIEFL, Barry (2003) International TV Programming and Audience Trends 1996-2001, A report prepared for the CRTC, ; Available *Online* HTTP : http://www.crtc.gc.ca/publications/reports

KLEISTEUBER et al.2004, German Bundestag and the use of ICT's in Hoff, Coleman, Fitzmaier e Cardoso, Use of ICT's by Members of Parliament, Information Polity, Special Issue, Volume 9, Numbers 1,2, 2004, The Netherlands, IOS Press.

KLEISTEUBER, Hans J. (1998), "The Digital Future" in SIUNE, Karen, McQuail Denis, *Media* Policy, London, Sage.

KLEISTEUBER, Hans J. (2003), "El Surgimento del Cyberespacio: la Palabra y la Realidad" in Beneyto, José Vidal (2003), La Ventana Global, Madrid, Taurus.

KUBICEK, Herbert (1996), "Multi*media*: Germany's Third Attempt to Move to an Information Society" in Kahin, B., Wilson, E., National Information Infrastructure Initiatives: Vision and Policy Design (Publication of the Harvard Information Infrastructure Project), Cambridge MA, MIT Press.

KUBICEK, Herbert, DUTTON, Willliam H., WILLIAMS, Robin (1997) (eds.) The social shaping of information superhighways. Frankfurt: Campus Verlag.

KUNG, Lucy (2002), Redefining public service broadcasting for the Internet Age, Paper Presented at the "Cost A20 Network Conference", Norway, Tromso, June 2002.

LAUDON, K.L. (1977) Communications Technology and Democratic Participation. New York: Praeger.

LAWRENCE e GILES, "Acessibility of information on the web", Nature, Vol 40, 1999.

Le GOFF, J., (1990), A Nova História, Coimbra, Almedina.

LE GUINOU, Brigitte, Patou, C. (2004), "ATTAC(K)ING Expertise: Does the Internet really democratize knowledge" in W. van de Donk, B. Loader, P. Nixon, D. Rucht (eds.), Cyberprotest: New *Media*, Citizens and Social Movements, London, Routledge.

LEE, Alice, "Info*media* Literacy. A Educational Basic for Young People in the New Information Age", IC&S, 2:2 1999, 134-155.

LÉONARD, Y. (1998) "Portugal" in HERMET, G., HOTTINGER, J.T., SEILER, D.L. (orgs) (1998) Les Partis Politiques en Europe de l'Ouest. Paris: Economica.

LEVY, Pierre (2000), Cibercultura, Lisboa, Instituto Piaget.

LIANG, Guo (2004) The Internet Growth in China: Drivers and Divides, WORLD INTERNET PROJECT

SURVEY (2004), Available *Online* HTTP: http://www.soc.toyo.ac.jp/ ~mikami/wip/wip_meeting/day2day3.html

LIPPMAN, Walter (1997), Public Opinion, Available *Online* HTTP:http:// xroads.virginia.edu/~Hyper2/CDFinal/Lippman/contents.html .

LIVINGSTONE, Sonia, LUNT, Peter (1994) Talk on television: audience participation and public debate. London: Routledge.

LIVINGSTONE, Sonia,"New *media*, new audiences?", New *Media* & Society, , London, Sage, n°1, 1999.

LOADER, Brian D. (1997) (ed.) The Governance of Cyberspace: Politics, Technology and Global Restructuring. London: Routledge.

LOADER, Brian D. (2000) "Reflexões sobre a Democracia Civil na Era da Informação: um estudo de caso do Nordeste de Inglaterra", Presidência da República, Os Cidadãos e a Sociedade de Informação. Conferência promovida pelo Presidente da República, 9 and 10 December 1999, Lisboa, INCM.

LOPES, Felisbela (1999), O Telejornal e o Serviço Público, Coimbra, Minerva.

LOSITO, Gianni, "La Ricerca Sociale e la Radio. Breve Storia di incomprensioni, negligenze e omissioni", in MENDUNI, Enrico (2002), La Radio. Percorsi e Territori di un Medium Mobile e Interattivo, Bologna, Baskerville.

LUHMANN, N. (1992), A improbabilidade da Comunicação, Lisboa, Vega-Passagens.

LUTFI, M. (2002), Elevating the standards of journalism: the impact of "*online media* watchdogs"and a case study of Medyakronik;

George Washington University, Available *Online* HTTP: http://cct.georgetown.edu/academics_thesis.cfm

LYON, David (1992) A sociedade da informação. Oeiras: Celta.

LYON, David (1995), "The Roots of the Information Society Idea" in HEAP, N., Thomas, R. et al., Information Technology and Society. A Reader. London Sage.

LYON, David (1999), "From Big Brother to Electronic Panopticon" in LYON, David, The Rise of the Surveillance Society, Minneapolis, University of Minnesota Press.

LYON, David, 'The world-wide-web of surveillance: the Internet and off-world power flows' Information, Communication and Society, 1:1 1998.

LYRA RESEARCH, INC. (2004) , DTV View Survey of Digital Vídeo Recorder Users, Available *Online* HTTP http://www.lyra.com/

FIRMINO da COSTA, António MACHADO, F., (1998), "Processos de uma Modernidade Inacabada" in VIEGAS, José Manuel e FIRMINO da COSTA, António, Portugal, que Modernidade?, Oeiras, Celta.

MAFFESOLI, M. (1998), Entretien avec M. Maffesoli sur le livre de P. Bourdieu, Available *Online* HTTP:http://www.mit.edu/~fca/papers/television.pdf .

MAGONE, José M. (1997) European Portugal: the Difficult Road to Sustainable Democracy. New York: St. Martins Press.

MAHEU, L. (1993), « Postmodernité et mouvements sociaux », AUDET, M., BOUCHIKHI, H. (eds), Structuration du social et modernité avancée – autour des travaux d'Anthony Giddens, Saint-Foy, Les Presses de l'Université Laval.

MAHEU, L. (ed.) (1995), Social movements and social classes – the future of collective action, London, Sage Publications.

MANDELLI, Andrea (1999), "È il Momento dei Portali. Dureranno?", Problemi dell'Informazione, XXIV, 1 December, 1999, pp.441-453.

MANSELL, Robin (1998), FAIR, Socio-Economic Impacts of Advanced Communications, "A Case of Electronic Commerce. The *Online* Music Industry", Available *Online* HTTP :<http://www.analysis.co.uk/acts/fair/ > (March 1998).

MANSELL, Robin (2001), New *Media* and the Power of Networks, First Dixons Public Lecture and Inaugural Professional Lecture, Dixons Chair in New *Media* and the Internet, London School of Economics and Political Science.

MARGOLIS, M., RESNICK, D, CHIN-CHANG, Tu. (1997) "Campaigning on the Internet: Parties and Candidates on the World Wide Web in the 1996 Primary Season", Harvard International Journal of Press/Politics, vol. 2 (1), pp. 59-78.

MARGOLIS, M., RESNICK, D, WOLVE, J. (1999) "Party Competition on the Internet: Minor Versus Major Parties in the UK and US", Harvard International Journal of Press/Politics, vol. 4 (4), pp. 24-47.

MARGOLIS, Michael e Resnick, David (2000), Politics as Usual: The "Cyberspace Revolution", Thousand Oaks CA, Sage.

MARSHALL, T.H. (1964), Citizenship and Social Class, Chicago: University of Chicago Press.

MARTINS, Jorge Manuel (2000) Jornalismo Digital/Ciberjornalismo. Estudo de casos:Diário Digital e TSF *Online*, Dissertação da Pós-Graduação em Jornalismo do ISCTE/ESCS, Lisboa, ISCTE.

MARTURANO, Marco, VILLA, Marina, VITTADINI, Nicoletta (1998), Cittadini, Giudici e Giocatore, Roma, VQPT-RAI-ERI.

MATHESON, Donald (2002) "News Weblogs:An Invitation to Abandon the Craft?" Available *Online* HTTP: <http://www.cf.ac.uk/jomec/contact/full%20paper.html > (December 2003).

MATHIAS, Paul (1997), La cité Internet, Paris, Presses de Sciences Politiques.

MATTELART, Armand (2003), "Premissas y Contenidos Ideológicos de la Sociedad de la Información", in BENEYTO, José Vidal (2003), La Ventana Global, Madrid, Taurus.

MATTELART, Armand, MATTELART, Michèle (1998), Theories of Communication, London, Sage.

MAYNARD, N. (2000); Digitization and the news; in Nieman Reports Vol. 54, n°4

MAZZEI, Giuseppe (2002), Verso il Tigitale, Roma, RAI-ERI.

MAZZOLENI, Giampero, BONI, Federico (2002), "La Radio Come Mezzo di Controinformazione e Mobilitazione Sociale"in MENDUNI, Enrico (2002), La Radio. Percorsi e Territori di un Medium Mobile e Interattivo, Bologna, Baskerville.

McCOURT, Tom, BURKART, Patrick (2003), "When Creators, Corporations and Consumers Collide: Napster and the Development of

Online Music Distribution", *Media*, Culture & Society, 2003, Vol.25: 333-350.

MCLUHAN, Marshall Understanding *Media* – The Extensions of Man, London, Routledge, 1997.

MCNAIR, B. (1998), The Sociology of Journalism. London: Arnold.

McQUAIL, Denis (1998), "Commercialization and Beyond"in McQUAIL, Denis, SIUNE, Karen, *Media* Policy, London, Sage.

McQUAIL, Denis, Mass Communication Theory – 4th Edition, London, Sage, 2000.

McQUAIL, Dennis (2003), McQuail's Reader in Mass Communication Theory, London, Sage.

MEDIA MONITOR (2003), e-telenews 2002. Um ano de Notícias, Grupo Markteste.

MEIER, Henk Erik (2003), " Beyond Convergence. Understanding Programming Strategies of Public Broadcasters in Competitive Environments", European Journal of Communication 2003, Vol 18 (3): 337-365.

MELUCCI Alberto (1995) Individualisation et globalisation : au-delà de la modernité ?,in Dubet, François e Wieviorka, Michel, Penser le sujet Autour d'Alain Touraine, Paris, Editions Fayard.

MELUCCI, A. (1995), "The new social movements revisited: reflections on a sociological misunderstanding", MAHEU, L. (ed.), Social movements and social classes – the future of collective action, London, Sage Publications

MENDES, Cristina (2003), A Infografia *Online* e o seu Contributo para a criação da identidade de um site de Informação de um Canal de Televisão, Projecto de Tese no Mestrado de Comunicação, Cultura e Tecnologias de Informação, Departamento de Sociologia, Lisboa, ISCTE.

MENDONÇA, Sandro, Cardoso Gustavo, Caraça João et al. (2004) , The Strategic Strength of Weak Signal Analysis, By sub-group Swgnals of working group 1,COST Action 22 Working Paper.

MENDUNI, Enrico (2002), La Radio. Percorsi e Territori di un Medium Mobile e Interattivo, Bologna, Baskerville.

MENEZES, João Paulo, (2003), Tudo o que se passa na TSF – para um livro de estilo, Lisboa, Jornal de Notícias.

MENSING, D. (1998), The economics on *online* newspapers, AEJMC , Reynolds School of Journalism, University of Nevada, Available

Online HTTP : http://list.msu.edu/cgi-bin/wa?A2=ind9812a&L =aejmc&F=&S=&P=7409.

MESQUITA, Mário (1998), O Jornalismo em Análise, Colecção Comunicação, Minerva, Coimbra.

MEYER, Thomas, HINCHMAN, Lew (2002) *Media* Democracy – How the *Media* Colonize Politics. Cambridge: Polity Press.

MEYROVITZ, Joshua (1993), Oltre il senso di Luogo, Bologna, Baskerville.

MIÈGE, Bernard (1997), La Société Conquise par la Communication, Grenoble, PUG.

MIGUEL, L. (1998); Mídia e manipulação política no Brasil – a Rede Globo e as eleições presidenciais de 1989 a 1998; in Comunicação & Política Vol.VI, nº2/3.

MIRANDA, José Bragança de (2002), "A Cultura das Redes", Revista de Comunicação e Linguagens, June 2002, Número Extra.

MIKAMI Shunji (2004) WIP Japan: Trends in Internet Use WORLD INTERNET PROJECT SURVEY (2004), Available *Online* HTTP: http://www.soc.toyo.ac.jp/~mikami/wip/wip_meeting/day-2day3.html

MÓNICA, Maria Filomena (1978), Educação e Sociedade no Portugal de Salazar, Lisboa, Editorial Presença.

MORIN, Edgar (1976), l'Esprit du temps, Paris, Grasset.

MORIN, Edgar (2003), An Interview with Edgar Morin, Available *Online* HTTP: <http://www.france.diplomatie.fr/label_france/ENGLISH/ IDEES/MORIN/morin.html > (July 2003).

MOTA, Helena Isabel (2002) A Neotelevisão: o Reino dos Reality Shows, Projecto de Tese no Mestrado de Comunicação, Cultura e Tecnologias de Informação, Departamento de Sociologia, Lisboa, ISCTE.

MONTIS, Ivan (2000), La tv ondine: strategie, formati, modelli in TETTAMANZI, Laura (2000), Spetatori nella Rete, Roma, VQPT-RAI_ERI.

MURDOCK, Graham (1992), Citizens, consumers, and public culture. p. 21. In: *Media* Cultures. Reappraising Transnational *Media*. (Ed.) Michael Skovmand and Kim Christian Schroder.

MURDOCK, Graham (1993), "Communications and the constitution of modernity", in *Media*, Culture and Society, Vol. 15, n.° 4, pp. 521-539.

NASCIMENTO, S., Cardoso G. (2003), Análise comparativa dos parlamentares Europeus, COST-A14, Cardoso, Gustavo (PT); Hoff,

Jens (DK), Kleisteuber Hans (G); Snellen, Ignace (NL); Smith, Colin (Sc); Elvebaek, Beate (NR); Filzmaier, Peter (A)

NEGROPONTE, Nicholas (1996) Being Digital. New York: Alfred A. Knopf.

NETO, Pedro (2002),A Presidência da República e as Tecnologias de Comunicação e Informação: dinâmicas de exercício de cidadania virtual, Casa Civil da Presidência da República Portuguesa.

NEVEU, E. (1996), Sociologie des mouvements sociaux, Paris, Éditions La Découverte.

NEVEU, Érik (2002), Sociologie du Journalism, Paris, Repéres.

NIELSEN//NETRATINGS, (2004), Available *Online* HTTP: http://www.nielsen-netratings.com/

NORA, P., (1990), "Memória Coletiva": In: Le Goff, J., A nova história, Coimbra, Almedina.

NORBERG, Eric G. (1996), Radio Programming. Tactics and Strategy, Boston, Focal Press.

NORDENSTRENG, Kaarle (2001), So What? Reflections on the Study of Information Society, in Karvonnen, Erkki, Informational Societies, Tampere, Tampere University Press.

NORRIS, Pippa (2000) "Democratic Divide? The Impact of the Internet on Parliaments Worldwide", Paper for presentation at the Political Communications Panel 38.10 '*Media* Virtue and Disdain', at the American Political Association annual meeting, Washington D.C., 31 August 2000, Available *Online* HTTP: <http://ksghome.harvard.edu/~.pnorris.shorenstein.ksg/acrobat/apsa2000demdiv.pdf> (May 2002).

NORRIS, Pippa (2001) 'Internet and Democracy.' Plenary session, IDEA International Forum on the Internet and Democracy, Stockholm 27-29 June 2001. Available *Online* HTTP: http://www.pippanorris.com

NORRIS, Pippa (2004) The Internet and Politics: Emerging Perspectives, in Doris A. Graber, Bruce Bimber, W. Lance Bennett, Richard Davis and Pippa Norris, Academy & the Internet. Eds. Helen Nissenbaum and Monroe E. Price. New York: Peter Lang.

NORTON, Philip (1998) (ed.) Parliaments and Governments in Western Europe. London: Frank Cass.

PÚBLICO E-mail Gratuito para Todos, Público, 15 February 1999.

PÚBLICO (2003), Petições ao Parlamento 25 January 2004.

PÚBLICO, suplemento Computadores, 15 November 2004.

PÚBLICO, Resultados dos Testes PISA, 7 December 2004.

O'SULLIVAN, John (2003), Same Old News? Properties of Print and Web News *Media* in Ireland, Paper Presented at the COST A20 Conference held in 2003 in Pamplona, Espanha.

OBERCOM (2002), Que Futuro Para os *Media* em Portugal, Observatório da Comunicação, Lisboa.

OBERCOM (2003), Anuário da Comunicação 2002-2003, Lisboa, Observatório da Comunicação.

OBERCOM (2003), O Audiovisual Português e a Migração para o Digital, Lisboa, Observatório da Comunicação.

OCDE (2001) , Share of Public Employment to Total Employment (1985-1999), Paris, OCDE.

OCDE (2001), Literacy in the Information Age, Final Report of International Adult Literacy Survey, Paris, OECD.

OCDE (2003), The e-government imperative, Paris, OCDE.

OCDE (2003), Education Outlook, Paris, OCDE.

OCDE (2004) Education Outlook, Paris, OCDE.

OCDE (2004), OECD PISA review Available *Online* HTTP: http://www. pisa.oecd.org/

OCDE (2004), Patent Database, September 2004, Paris, OCDE.

OCT, "Estatísticas da Sociedade de Informação, Portugal 1996-2001", March 2002.

OE, Kenzaburo (Dez. 1998), "Internet et moi", Le Monde Diplomatique, p. 27, Available *Online* HTTP: <http://www.monde-diplomatique. fr/1998/12/OE/11473.html> (4 Jan. 1999).

OFFICE FOR OFFICIAL PUBLICATIONS OF THE EUROPEAN COMMUNITIES (2003),Cinema, TV and radio in the EU Statistics on audiovisual services (Data 1980–2002) Luxembourg.

ORTOLEVA, P. (1991), La Societa' dell'Informazione, Roma, Anicia.

ORTOLEVA, Peppino (1997), « Modern Society and Technology », Available *Online* HTTP: <http://www.sanmarcoinlamis.net/archivio/ html/ortoleva.htm > (April 1999).

ORTOLEVA, Peppino (1997), *Media*storia. Comunicazione e Cambiamento Sociale nel Mondo Contemporaneo, Milano, Nuova Pratiche Editrice.

ORTOLEVA, Peppino (2002),"Un Mondo di Suoni. La Radio e il Resto" in MENDUNI, Enrico (2002), La Radio. Percorsi e Territori di un Medium Mobile e Interattivo, Bologna, Baskerville.

ORTOLEVA, Peppino (2003), Televisão, Trajectos, N°1, Lisboa, Editorial Notícias.

ORTOLEVA, Peppino (2004), O Novo Sistema dos *Media*, in Paquete de Oliveira, J.M.; Cardoso, G. e Barreiros, J. (2004), Comunicação, Cultura e Tecnologias de Informação, Lisboa, Quimera.

PADOVANI, Cinzia, TRACEY, Michael (2003), "Report on the Conditions of Public Service Broadcasting", Television & New *Media*, Vol.4 N°2, May 2003, 131-153.

PAKULSKI, J. (1995), "Social movements and class: the decline of the marxist paradigm", MAHEU, L. (ed.), Social movements and social classes – the future of collective action, London, Sage Publications.

PANTIC, Drazen (1998) "Internet Against Censorship", CyberSociology Magazine <http://wwww.socio.demon.co.uk/magazine/5/5_b_ 92.html > (April 1999).

PAPATHANASSOPOULOS, Stylanos (2002), European Television in the Digital Age, Cambridge, Polity Press.

PAQUETE DE OLIVEIRA, José Manuel, "A informação vai devorar a comunicação?", in Cultura e economia (Actas do Colóquio Lisboa Capital Europeia da Cultura, 1994), Lisboa, ICS, 1995, pp. 233-240.

PAQUETE DE OLIVEIRA, José Manuel, (1989), "Formas de `Censura Oculta' na Imprensa Escrita em Portugal no Pós-25 de Abril (1974-1987)", Tese de Doutoramento, Departamento de Sociologia, ISCTE, Lisboa.

PAQUETE DE OLIVEIRA, José Manuel, "A Integração Europeia e os Meios de Comunicação Social", Análise Social, 118-119, (1992) quarta série vol.XXVII, 995-1024.

PAQUETE DE OLIVEIRA, José Manuel, BARREIROS, José (coords.) (2000) Ciberfaces – A Sociedade de Informação em Análise: Internet, Interfaces do Social, Programa Praxis XXI, Fundação para a Ciência e Tecnologia/ Ministério da Ciência e da Tecnologia, ISCTE. Available *Online* HTTP: http://ciberfaces.iscte.pt

PAQUETE DE OLIVEIRA, José Manuel, CARDOSO, Gustavo, BARREIROS, José, Internet como Instrumento para la Participation

Ciudadana, in BENEYTO, José Vidal (2003), La Ventana Global, Madrid, Taurus.

PAULUSSEN, Steve, COPPENS, Tomas (2003), elections@psb.org. How Public Broadcasters Use their Websites in Times of Elections, Paper Presented at the "Towards New *Media* Paradigms: Content, Producers, Organisations and Audiences Conference" of the COST A20 Programme, University of Navarra, Pamplona; Sapin,27-28 June 2003.

PAVLIK, J.; The future of *online* journalism, citado em Kamerer, D., Bressers, B. (1998); *Online* newspapers: a trend study of news content and technical features; AEJMC December; Available *Online* HTTP : http://list.msu.edu/cgi-bin/wa?A2=ind9812a&L=aejmc &F=&S=&P=6630

PAVLIK, John V. (1995) New *Media* Technology and the Information Superhighway: Cultural and Commercial Perspectives, Prentice Hall.

PCM (2002), Novas Opções para o Audiovisual, Presidência do Conselho de Ministros de Portugal.

PENA PIRES, Rui (2003), Migrações e Integração Teoria e aplicações à sociedade portuguesa, Oeiras, Celta Editora.

PERRETTI, Fabrizio (2000), "La Grande Impresa Multi*media*le", Problemi dell'Informazione, XXV, 1 Março, 2000, pp.74-82.

PHILO, Greg ed., A Sociology of *media* power: key issues in audience reception research, Message Received, col. Glasgow *Media* Group, Longman, 1999.

PICARD, Robert G. (2003), Economics and Content of Web Portals: A Case Study of Yahoo!, Paper Presented at the "Towards New *Media* Paradigms: Content, Producers, Organisations and Audiences Conference" of the COST A20 Programme, University of Navarra, Pamplona; Sapin,27-28 June 2003.

PIMENTEL K., K. Teixeira (1992). Virtual reality: through the new looking glass, Mc Graw-Hill, New York.

PLATON, Sara, DEUZE, Mark, "Indy*media* Journalism", Journalism 2003, Vol.4(3): 336-355.

POOLE, I. (2001); Changing the color of digital ink – the quest to bring newspaper Internet operations out of the red and into the black; 497d *media* Industries. Available *Online* HTTP: http://www.personal.psu. edu/users/i/j/ijp105/497d%20From%20Red%20to%20Black. pdf.

PORTUGAL TELECOM (1999), Timor: para que os portugueses façam ouvir a sua voz, Available *Online*. HTTP: http://www.telecom.pt/ quemsomos/noticias/artigo.asp?id_artigo=476 (28 Fev 2002).

POSTER, Mark (1995) "Cyberdemocracy: Internet and the Public Sphere". MS, University of California,http://www.hnet.uci.edu/mposter/ writings/democ.html (May 2002).

POSTER, Mark (2000), A Segunda Era dos *Media*, Oeiras, Celta.

PRATT, Hugo (1991), Le Désir d'être inutile, Paris, Editions Robert Laffont.

PRESIDÊNCIA DO CONSELHO DE MINISTROS (2002), Novas Opções Para o Audiovisual, Lisboa, PCM.

PRESS FREEDOM SURVEY (2003), Available *Online* HTTP: http:// www.freedomhouse.org/

PRICE WATWEHOUSE AND COOPERS (2004), Global Entertainment and Media Outlook: 2004-2008.

PROENÇA, Luís Miguel (2000) A Rádio Porta Estandarte. A TSF e o Referendo em Timor Leste, Dissertação da Pós-Graduação em Jornalismo do ISCTE/ESCS, Lisboa, ISCTE.

PUTNAM, Robert , (1993), Making Democracy Work, Princeton, N.J.: Princeton University Press.

PUTNAM, Robert D. (1995) "The Strange Disappearance of Civic America", Available *Online* HTTP :http://www.prospect.org/print/V7/24/ putnam-r.html (June 2002)

PUTNAM, Robert D. (2000), Bowling Alone: The Collapse and Revival of American Community, New York, Simon & Schuster.

PUTNAM, Robert D. "The Prosperous Community – Social Capital and Public Life", Available *Online* HTTP : http://www.prospect.org/ print/V4/13/putnam-r.html (June 2002)

QUINN, G., Trench, B. (2002); MUDIA: Multi*media* content in the digital age; Available *Online* HTTP : http://www.mudia.org .

QUINN, Gary, TRENCH, Brian (2002), Prognostic Study of *Media* Content Usage, Centre for Society, Technology and *Media* at DCU, Dublin.

RABOY, Marc (2001), Public Service Broadcasting in Transition: A Documentary Reader (with Monroe E. Price). Report prepared for the European Institute for the *Media*.

RABOY, Marc(2001), National, Transnational and Global Approaches to Public *Media*, paper presented at "Rethinking Public *Media* in a

Transnational Era", Center for *Media*, Culture and History, New York University.

RAFAELI, S. (1988), «Interactivity: From New *Media* to Communication», in Robert P. Hawkins et al (Eds.), Advancing Communication Science: Merging Mass and Interpersonal Processes, Newbury, Calif.: SAGE, pp.110-134.

RAINIE, L. (2000); Why the Internet is (mostly) good for news; in Nieman Reports Vol. 54, n°4

RAMONET, Ignacio (1999), A Tirania da Comunicação, Porto, Campo das Letras.

REBELO, José (2002), O Discurso do Jornal, 2° Edição, Lisboa, Editorial Notícias.

REBELO, José (2003), "O ServiçPúblico de Televisão em Portugal" in A Comunicação, Temas e Argumentos, Coimbra, Minerva.

REGAN, T. (2000); Technology is changing journalism; in Nieman Reports Vol. 54, n°4.

REICH, Robert (1993), O Trabalho das Nações, Lisboa, Quetzal.

REIS, Filipe (2002) Algumas Observações sobre o localismo, Anuário da Comunicação 2001-2002, Lisboa, Observatório da Comunicação.

RELATÓRIO DE RECEBIMENTO DE CORRESPONDÊNCIA (2000-2004), Centro de documentação da Secretaria-geral da Presidência da República Portuguesa.

RESENDE, Isabel (2002), Jornalismo Económico: Formato Digital versus Formato Tradicional, Dissertação da Pós-Graduação em Jornalismo do ISCTE/ESCS, Lisboa, ISCTE.

RHEINGOLD, Howard (2000), The Virtual Community: Homesteading on the Electronic Frontier. Revised Edition. Cambridge: MIT Press.

RICHERI, Giuseppe (1996), "Condizioni di Base per l'affermazione dei Nuovi *Media*", <http:// http://www.*media*mente.rai.it/home/ bibliote/intervis/r/richer02.htm > (May 2000).

RICHERI, Giuseppe (1996), "La Storia dei *Media*", Available *Online* HTTP: <http://http://www.*media*mente.rai.it/home/bibliote/intervis/r/richer04.htm > (May 2000).

RICHERI, Giuseppe (2002), As Plataformas Digitais e a Evolução da Indústria Audiovisual, Observatório, n°2 (November 2002), Lisboa, OBERCOM.

RICHERI, Giuseppe (2004), A Indústria Discográfica e o Desafio da Rede, in Paquete de Oliveira, J.M.; Cardoso, G. e Barreiros, J. (2004), Comunicação, Cultura e Tecnologias de Informação, Lisboa, Quimera.

RIIS, Annemarie Munk (1996) The Information Welfare Society: Assessment of Danish Government Initiatives Preparing for the "Information Age" in Kahin, B., Wilson, E., National Information Infrastructure Initiatives: Vision and Policy Design (Publication of the Harvard Information Infrastructure Project), Cambridge MA, MIT Press.

ROCHA, Manuel João (2003), Quando os Jornais Vestem a Camisola – Leituras e Reflexões Sobre o Posicionamento do Diário de Notícias e Público no Pós-Referendo em Timor, Projecto de Tese no Mestrado de Comunicação, Cultura e Tecnologias de Informação, Departamento de Sociologia, Lisboa, ISCTE.

ROBINS, Kevin, Webster, Frank (1999), *Times of the Technoculture*, London, Routledge.

RODOTÀ, Stefano (1997), Tecnopolitica. La Democrazia e le Nuove Tecnologie della Comunicazione, Roma, Editori Laterza.

RODOTÀ, Stefano (2000) "Para uma cidadania electrónica: a democracia e as novas tecnologias da comunicação", Presidência da República, Os Cidadãos e a Sociedade de Informação. Conferência promovida pelo Presidente da República, 9 and 10 December 1999, Lisboa, INCM.

RÖMMELE, Andrea, 2003. "Political Parties, Party Communication and New Information and Communication Technologies", Party Politics, 9:1, p. 10.

ROSAS, Fernando (ed.) (1999), Portugal e a Transição para a Democracia (1974-76), Lisboa: Edições Colibri.

ROSCOE, Thimoty (1999), "The Construction of the World Wide Web Audience", *Media*, Culture and Society, Sage Publications, London, Vol.21: 673-684.

RUGGIERO, Thomas E. (2000) "Uses and Gratifications Theory in the 21st Century", Mass Communication & Society, 2000, Vol. 3, No. 1: Pages 3-37.

RUKAVISHNIKOV, Vladimir (2002), THE RUSSIAN PERCEPTION OF THE AMERICAN "WAR ON TERROR", Copenhagen Peace Research Institute, Working Paper, No. 27.

SABLOSKY, Juliet Antunes (1997) "The Portuguese Socialist Party" in BRUNEAU, Thomas (ed.) Political Parties and Democracy in Portugal: Organizations, Elections and Public Opinion. Boulder, CO: Westview Press, pp. 55-76.

SALAVERRIA, Ramón (2002), An Immature Medium. Strenghs and Weaknesses of the *Online* Newspapers on September 11, Paper Presented at the "Impact of the Internet on *Mass media*" Conference of COST A20, Tromso, Norway, June 2002.

SANABRIA, F. Información audiovisual. Teoría y técnica de la información radiofónica y televisiva. Barcelona, Bosch Comunicación, 1994.

SANTIAGO, Daniela (2003) O Reconforto da Televisão. Um Estudo da Tragédia de Entre-os-Rios, Dissertação do Mestrado de Comunicação, Cultura e Tecnologias de Informação, Departamento de Sociologia, Lisboa, ISCTE.

SANTO AGOSTINHO, O palácio da memória, Confissões, Livro X.

SANTOS, Rogério (2002), "Dez Anos de História da SIC (1992-2002)", OBERCOM, nº6, November 2002, 93-105.

SARAIVA, António Crónica Jogos de in Exame Informática March 2000.

SARAMAGO, José (1998), "On Communication", Available *Online* HTTP:http://mondediplo.com/1998/12/12saramago .

SARAMAGO, José (2000), "Folha de S. Paulo entrevista José Saramago,", Available *Online* HTTP: http://www2.folha.uol.com.br/biblioteca/1/04/2000111101.html.

SASSI, Sinikka (2000) "The Controversies of the Internet and the Revitalization of Local Political Life in In Hacker K. & Dijk J., *Digital Democracy: Issues of theory and practice.* London, Sage.

SAUTER, M. (2000); On the Web, it's survival of the biggest; in Nieman Reports (2000) Vol. 54, nº4

SCANNELL, P. (1996), Radio,Television and Modern Life, Oxford, Blackwell.

SCANNELL, Paddy (1997), "Public Service Broadcasting: the History of a Concept", in GOODWIN, Andrew, WHANNEL, Gary (1997), Understanding Television, London, Routledge.

SCHILLER, Herbert (1997), "Information Inequality", Available *Online* HTTP: <http://www.heise.de/tp/english/special/pol/8018/1.html > (August 1998).

SCHILLER, Herbert I. (1996), Information Inequalities, London, Routledge.

SCIFO, Barbara, PASQUALI, Francesca (1998), "I Giornali *Online*", Problemi dell'Informazione, XXIII, 1 March, 1998, pp.109-123.

SCOTT, A. & Street, J.: (2001) 'From *media* politics to e-protest? The use of popular culture and new *media* in parties and social movements', in: F. Webster: (ed) 'Culture and Politics in the Information Age, A New Politics?', London: Routledge.

SEIBEL, M.; Is including e-mail addresses in reporters' bylines a good idea?; in Nieman Reports (2000) Vol. 54, n°4

SERVAES, Jan, "The European Information Society: Much Ado About Nothing?",Gazette: the International Journal for Communication Studies 2002, Vol (64) (5): 433-447.

SEMANÁRIO, Mercado dos VídeoJogos reduzido a três empresas: Negócio em Portugal vale 5 milhões de contos, Semanário, Economia, 29 October 1999.

SHAH, H. (1999), Emancipation from modernization: development journalism and new social movements, in VINCENT, R., NORDENSTRENG, K., and TRABER, M. (eds), Towards equity in global communication – MacBride update, New Jersey, Hampton Press.

SHAIN, Jamal, BIERHOFF, Jan (2002), Connecting the *Media* and Research Worlds, MUDIA, International Institute of Infonomics.

SHERMAN, Chris, PRICE, Gary (2001), The Invisible Web, New Jersey, Cyberage Books.

SHOWDOWN, Available *Online* HTTP: http://www.searchengineshowdown.com/

SHOEMAKER, Pamela and REESE, Stephen. *Mediating the Message. Theories of Influences on Mass Media Content.* White Plains, N. Y.: Longman, 1996.

SHOEMAKER, Pamela J. (2005), News Around the World: Content, Practitioners, and the Public, Routledge, London.

SILVA, Ricardo (2000), "Guia do Activismo *Online*", Available *Online* HTTP: < http://members.tripod.com/~Protesto_MC/timor.html >(28 Feb 2002).

SILVERSTONE, R (1994) Television And Everyday Life, London: Routledge,

SILVERSTONE, Roger (1999), "What's new about new *media*", New *Media* & Society, pp. 10-12, 1999.

SILVERSTONE, Roger (2002), Regulation, *Media* Literacy and *Media* Civic, in Amy Mahan, Robin Mansell and Rohan Samarajiva (eds.) (2002), Networking Knowledge for Information Societies: Institutions & Interventions, Delft: Delft University Press.

SILVERSTONE, Roger (2003), "*Media*tion and Communication" in CALHOUN, Craig, ROJEK, Chris, TURNER, Bryan S., The International Handbook of Sociology, London, Sage.

SILVERSTONE, Roger, (2002), Porquê estudar os *media*?:O 11 de Setembro e a ética da distância, Comunicação, Cultura e Tecnologias de Informação, Lisboa, Quimera.

SILVERSTONE, Roger. (1999) Why Study the *Media*?, London, Sage.

SIMONELLI, Giorgio (2001), "Il Telegiornale: Storia, Modelli, Funzione", in Speciale TG, Forme e Contenuti Del Telegiornale, Novara, Interlinea.

SLEVIN, James (2002), Internet e Sociedade, Lisboa, Temas e Debates,

SLEVIN, James (2000), The Internet and Society, Oxford, Polity Press.

SMELSER, N. (ed.) (1988.1989), Handbook of Sociology, Newbury Park, Sage Publications.

SMITH, Anthony (1998), Television an International History, Oxford, Oxford University Press.

SMITH, Colin (2000) "British political parties: continuity and change in the information age" in HOFF, Jens, HORROCKS, Ivan, TOPS, Pieter (2000) (eds.) Democratic Governance and New Technology – Technologically *media*ted innovations in political practice in Western Europe. London and New York: Routledge/ ECPR Studies in European Political Science.

SMITH, Colin, WEBSTER, William (2003) Internet Based Technologies and Members of the Scottish Parliament, Conference on "Democratic Governance and ICT", Department of Political Science, University of Copenhagen, Denmark.

SNELLEN, I., VAN DEN DONK, W. (1998) (eds.) Handbook in the Information Age. Amsterdam: IOS Press.

SOBRAL, José (1999), Trajectos: o Presente e o Passado na Vida de uma Freguesia da Beira, Lisboa, Imprensa de Ciências Sociais.

SORENSEN, K (1994) 'Technology in Use: Two Essays in the Domestication of Artefacts,' Trondheim: senter for teknologi og Samfunn.

SOUSA, Vanda (2004), Príncipes encantados e heroínas melodramáticas no Big Brother I, Trabalho apresentado no seminário de indústrias culturais em Portugal do Mestrado em Comunicação e Indústrias Culturais da Universidade Católica Portuguesa.

SPARKS, Colin (2001) "The Internet and the Global Public Sphere" in BENNETT, W. Lance,

ENTMAN, Robert M. (2001) *Media*ted Politics – Communication in the Future of Democracy. Cambridge: Cambridge University Press.

SPARKS, Colin (2002) The Impact of the Internet on the Existing *Media*, Proceedings of Seminar Held at Intercollege, Nicosia, Cyprus.

SPARKS, Colin, (2002), "The Internet and the *Mass media* – The Development of *Online* Newspapers", <http://cost-a20.iscte.pt/Development_*Online*_Newspapers.ppt> (June 2002).

SPARKS, Colin, La Influencia de Internet en los Medios de Comunicacion Convencionales (2003), in BENEYTO, José Vidal (2003), La Ventana Global, Madrid, Taurus.

STALDER, Felix, "The Logic of Networks – Social Landscapes vis-a-vis the Space of Flows", Ctheory, Available *online* HTTP: http://www.ctheory.com/r46.html

STATE OF THE NEWS MEDIA (2005) Project for Excellence in Journalism, Available *online* HTTP: http://www.stateofthenewsmedia.org/2005/

STATISTICS ON AUDIOVISUAL SERVICES, data 1980-2000, Comissão Europeia Eurostat, Theme 4, Industry, Trade and Services, EC, 2002.

STEFIK, Mark J., Internet Dreams : Archetypes, Myths, and Metaphors, Cambridge, Mass.,The MIT Press, 1996.

STURKEN, Marita (1997), Tangled Memories: The Vietnam War, the AIDS Epidemic, and the Politics of Remembering. Berkeley, University of California Press.

SYVERTSEN, Trine (2003), " Challenges to Public Television in the Era of Convergence and Commercialization" Television & New *Media*, Vol.4 Nº2, May 2003, 155-175.

TABORDA, Maria João, "O EspaçPúblico da Telefonia Sem Fios,. A Rádio de Brecht à Internet.", Observatório-Revista do Observatório da Comunicação, nº1, May 2000.

TADAYONI, Reza (2004), Interactive Tv in convergence perspective, em Fausto Colombo (ed), Tv and Interactivity in Europe. Mythologies, theoretical perspectives, real experiences, Vita e Pensiero, Milano.

TADAYONI, Reza, HENTEN, Anders, (2002) Articulation of Traditional and Internet TV, Paper Presented at the COST A20 Conference, Tromso, Noruega.

TAPSCOTT, Don (1997), Growing Up Digital: Rise of the Net Generation, New York, McGraw-Hill Education.

TARROW, S. (1998), Power in movement – social movements and contentious politics, Cambridge, University Press

TAYLOR, Philip M. (1992) War and the *Media*: Propaganda and Persuasion in the Gulf War, Manchester, Manchester University Press.

TEHRANIAN, Majid (1999), Global Communication and World Politics, London, RIENNER ISEAS.

TETTAMANZI, Laura (2000), Spetatori nella Rete, Roma, VQPT-RAI_ERI.

TEVES, Vasco Hogan (1998), História da televisão em Portugal, Lisboa, TV Guia Editora.

THE GLOBAL COMPETITIVENESS REPORT 2004, World Economic Forum.

THE E-READINESS REPORT 2004, The Economist.

THOMPSON, John B. (1995) The *Media* and Modernity. Cambridge: Polity Press.

TOFFLER, Alvin (1984). A terceira vaga. Lisboa: Edição Livros do Brasil.

TOFFLER, Alvin (1991) Os novos poderes. Lisboa: Edições Livros do Brasil.

TOURAINE, A. (1981), O Pós-Socialismo, trans. António M. Rollo Lucas, Porto, Edições Afrontamento.

TRACEY, Michael (1998), The Decline and Fall of Public Service Broadcasting, Oxford, Oxford University Press.

TRAQUINA, Nelson (2003), Jornalismo, Lisboa, Quimera.

TRECHSEL, Alexander, KIES, Raphael, MENDEZ, Fernando, SCHMITTER, Philippe (2003), Evaluation of Use of New Technologies in Order to Facilitate Democracy in Europe. E-Democratizing the Parliaments and Parties in Europe, European University Institute, Florence, Italy.

TSAGAROUSIANOU, R., TAMBINI, D., BRYAN, C. (1998) (eds.) Cyberdemocracy – Technology, Cities and Civic Networks. London: Routledge.

TSAGAROUSSIANOU, Roza (1998), Electronic Democracy And The Public Sphere: Opportunities And Challenges' In Tzagaroussianou, Roza, Damian, Tambini, Bryan, Cathy (1998) Cyber-democracy – Technology, Cities And Civic Networks. London: Routledge.

TURNER, Bryan S. (1994) " Postmodern Culture/Modern Citizens" in STEENBERGEN, Bart Van (1994) The Condition of Citizenship, London, SAGE.

TURNER, Bryan S. (1993), *Contemporary Problems in the Theory of Citizenship* in TURNER, Bryan S. (1993), Citizenship and Social Theory, London,Sage.

TURKLE, Sherry (1997), A vida no ecrã- a identidade na era da Internet,. Relógio d'Água, Lisboa.

UMIC, 2004, Avaliação do Projecto-piloto de Voto Electrónico em Portugal, 2004.

UNCTAD (2000), "Building Confidence-Electronic Commerce and Development", Available *Online* <http://www.unctad.org/en/docs/posdtem11.en.pdf>, (December 2003).

UNDP (2001), Human Development Report 2001, Available *Online* HTTP:<http://www.undp.org/hdr2001/ >.

UNDP (2003), Human Development Report 2003, Available *Online* HTTP:<http://www.undp.org/hdr2003/ >.

VAN AELST, Peter e Walgrave Stefaan (2004), Gobal-protesters:Virtual or real? The role of the Internet in shaping the anti-globalisation movement, in Win van de Donk, Brian Loader, Paul Nixon, and Dieter Rucht, eds., Cyberprotest: New *Media*, Citizens, and Social Movements, Routledge.

VAN DER WURFF, Richard, LAUF, Edmund, LANCEE (2003) Bram, *Online* News Services in the Netherlands, Paper Presented at the COST A20 Conference, Towards New *Media* Paradigms: Content, Producers, Organisations and Audiences, Pamplona, Espanha.

VAN DIJK, Ian (1999), The Network Society. Social Aspects of New *Media*, London: SAGE.

VAN DIJK, Jan (2000) "Models of Democracy and Concepts of Communication" in HACKER, Kenneth L.,VAN DIJK, Jan (eds.) (2000) Digital Democracy: issues of theory and practice. London: Sage.

VEDEL, Thierry (1996), "The French Policy for Information Superhighways: The End of High-Tech Colbertism?" in Kahin, B., Wilson,

E., National Information Infrastructure Initiatives: Vision and Policy Design (Publication of the Harvard Information Infrastructure Project), Cambridge MA, MIT Press.

VEDEL, Thierry, CATINAT, Michel (2000) "Public Policies for Digital Democracy in HACKER, Kenneth L., VAN DIJK, Jan (eds.) (2000) Digital Democracy. Issues of Theory and Practice. London: Sage.

VIEGAS H., GOMES S. (1999) "BBC: duas mil mensagens", Público, 9 September.

VIEGAS H., GOMES S. (1999) "Pressionar os Grandes através da Internet", Público, 7 September.

VITTADINI, Nicoleta (2002), "Radioline. Rielaborazione Discursiva dei Contenuti Mediali nelle Community Radiofoniche", in MENDUNI, Enrico (2002), La Radio. Percorsi e Territori di un Medium Mobile e Interattivo, Bologna, Baskerville.

VITTADINI, Nicoleta, VILLA, Marina, MARTURANO, Marco (1998), Cittadini, Giudici e Giocatori. Le Forme di Partecipazione del Pubblico nella Neotelevisione, Roma, VQPT-RAI-ERI.

WALGRAVE, S., MANSSENS J. (2000) The Making of the White March. The Mass media as a mobilization alternative for movement organizations, in: Mobilisation, 5:2(2000), p. 217-239.

WALGRAVE, S., VAN AELST, P., "New Media, New Movements? The Role of the Internet in Shaping the 'Anti-Globalization' Movement, IC&S, 5:4 2002, 465-493.

WALLERSTEIN, Immanuel, (2002), "The Eagle Has Crash Landed", Available Online HTTP: <http://www.foreignpolicy.com/issue_julyaug_2002/wallerstein.html>

WARD, Katie (2003) An Ethnographic Study of Internet Consumption in Ireland: Between Domesticity and the Public Participation, The European Media and Technology in Everyday Life Network, 2000-2003 Available Online HTTP: http://www.lse.ac.uk/collections/EMTEL/

WEBALIZER, Servidor Internet da Presidência da República Portuguesa.

WEBSTER, Frank (1995), Theories of the Information Society, London, Routledge.

WEBSTER, Frank (1997), What Information Society? ,Available Online HTTP: http://www.dodccrp.org/publications/pdf/Alberts_Anthology_I.pdf

WEBSTER, Frank (2002), Desafios globais e respostas nacionais na era da informação, in Paquete de Oliveira, J.M.; Cardoso, Gustavo, et al. Comunicação, Cultura e Tecnologias de Informação, Lisboa Quimera.

WEBSTER, Frank, (2003), Culture and Politics in the Information Age, London, Routledge.

WEIR, D.; Web journalism crosses many traditional lines; in Nieman Reports (2000) Vol. 54, nº4.

WELLMAN, Barry (2004), "The Three Ages of Internet Studies: Ten, Five and Zero Years Ago", New *Media* & Society 2004, Vol6(1):123-129.

WIEVIORKA, Michel (2003), "Os Movimentos Anti-Mundialização" in REBELO, José, Novas Formas de Mobilização Popular, Porto, Campo das Letras.

WILLIAMS, Bruce A., CARPINI, Michael, "Unchained Reaction" in Journalism, 1, pp. 61-86, 2000.

WILLIAMS, Raymond (1999), The Technology and the Society in Mackay, Hugh e O'Sullivan,Tim (1999), The *Media* Reader: Continuity and Transformation, London, The Open University.

WINSTON, Brian (1999), *Media* Technology and Society. A History from the Telegraph to the Internet, London, Routledge.

WINTERS, Jeffery A.(2002), The Political Impact of New Information Sources and Technologies in Indonesia, Gazette: The International Journal for Communication Studies 2002, Vol (64) (2): 501-511.

WOLF, Mauro (2001), Teorias da Comunicação, Lisboa, Editorial Presença.

WOLTON, Dominique (1999), Pensar a comunicação, Lisboa, Difel.

WOLTON, Dominique (2000), E Depois da Internet?, Algés, Difel.

WORLD BANK REPORT, Available *Online* HTTP: http://www.worldbank.org/poverty/wdrpoverty/

WORLD DEVELOPMENT REPORT ON POVERTY, Available *Online* HTTP: http://www.worldbank.org/poverty/wdrpoverty/

WORLD INDICATORS, ITU, Available *Online* HTTP: http://www.itu.int/itunews/issue/2002/04/table4.html

WORLD INTERNET PROJECT SURVEY (2004), Available *Online* HTTP: http://www.digitalcenter.org/

WOUTERS, Paul, Iina Hellsten, and Loet Leydesdorff (2004), Internet time and the reliability of search engines by, First Monday, volume 9, number 10 (October 2004), Available *Online* HTTP:http://www. firstmonday.org/issues/issue9_10/wouters/ .

YTREBERG, Espen e Gunn, Enly (2004), SMS-based TV: The impact of convergence on TV production, Department of *Media* and Communication, University of Oslo.

ZAMARIA, Charles (2004) Canadian Internet Project WORLD INTERNET PROJECT SURVEY (2004), Available *Online* HTTP: http://www.soc.toyo.ac.jp/~mikami/wip/wip_meeting/day-2day3.html

ZITTEL, Thomas (2001) "Electronic Democracy and Electronic Parliaments – A Comparison between the US House, the Swedish Riksdagen, and the German Bundestag", Paper presented to the Joint Sessions of Workshops of the European Consortium of Political Research, Workshop 3: Electronic Democracy: Mobilization, Organization and Participation, Grenoble, 6-11 April 2001, Available *Online*: http://www.essex.ac.uk/ecpr/jointsessions/grenoble/papers/ws3/ zittel.pdf

www.ingramcontent.com/pod-product-compliance
Lightning Source LLC
LaVergne TN
LVHW042330060326
832902LV00006B/90